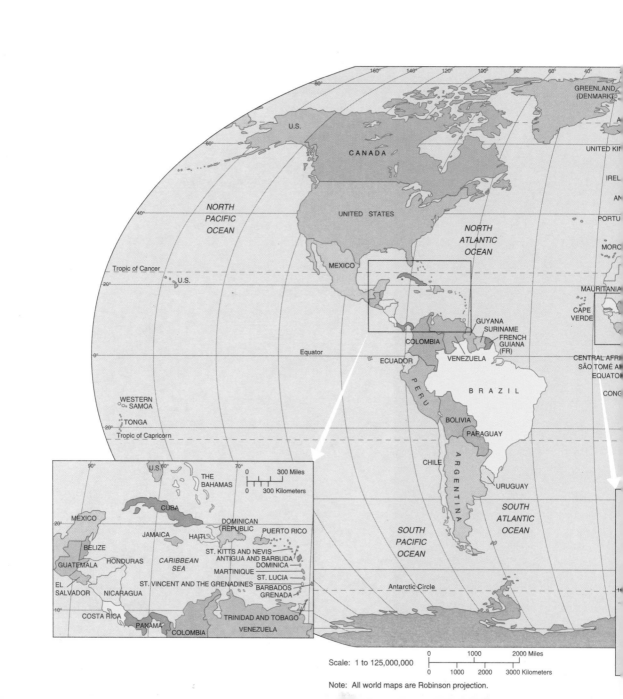

Scale: 1 to 125,000,000

Note: All world maps are Robinson projection.

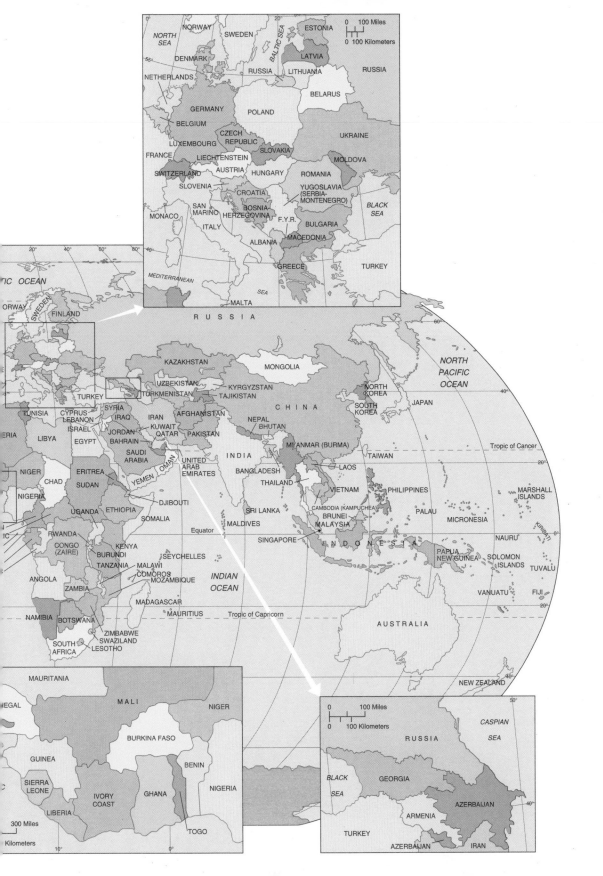

International Management

Text and Cases

Fifth Edition

Paul W. Beamish
Ivey Business School
The University of Western Ontario

Allen J. Morrison
Ivey Business School
The University of Western Ontario

Andrew C. Inkpen
Thunderbird, The American Graduate School of International Management

Philip M. Rosenzweig
IMD

Boston Burr Ridge, IL Dubuque, IA Madison, WI New York San Francisco St. Louis
Bangkok Bogotá Caracas Kuala Lumpur Lisbon London Madrid Mexico City
Milan Montreal New Delhi Santiago Seoul Singapore Sydney Taipei Toronto

The McGraw·Hill Companies

INTERNATIONAL MANAGEMENT: TEXT AND CASES
International Edition 2003

Exclusive rights by McGraw-Hill Education (Asia), for manufacture and export. This book cannot be re-exported from the country to which it is sold by McGraw-Hill. The International Edition is not available in North America.

Published by McGraw-Hill/Irwin, a business unit of The McGraw-Hill Companies, Inc., 1221 Avenue of the Americas, New York, NY 10020. Copyright © 2003, 2000, 1997, 1994, 1991 by The McGraw-Hill Companies, Inc. All rights reserved. No part of this publication may be reproduced or distributed in any form or by any means, or stored in a database or retrieval system, without the prior written consent of The McGraw-Hill Companies, Inc., including, but not limited to, in any network or other electronic storage or transmission, or broadcast for distance learning.
Some ancillaries, including electronic and print components, may not be available to customers outside the United States.

10 09 08 07 06 05 04 03
20 09 08 07 06 05 04
CTF BJE

Coventry University

Library of Congress Cataloging-in-Publication Data
International management : text and cases / Paul Beamish . . . [et al.].—5th ed.
    p.   cm.—(McGraw-Hill advanced topics in global management)
    Includes bibliographical references and index.
    ISBN 0-07-248581-7
    1.   International business enterprises—Management. 2. International business enterprises—Management—Case studies. I. Beamish, Paul W., 1953-II. Series.
HD62.4.B4 2003
658'.049—dc21   2002035256

When ordering this title, use ISBN 0-07-115140-0

Printed in Singapore

www.mhhe.com

to our children

Katie, Christine, Alexander & Daniel
Beamish

Robert, Andrew, Rachel & William
Morrison

Anne & Carly Inkpen

Thomas & Caroline Rosenzweig

Preface

International Management is an *international,* international-management book. The previous four editions were used in over 200 universities and colleges in over 20 countries. The fifth edition, we hope, will have even wider usage. Why our optimism? In brief, it is because the book focuses on issues of international management common and important to businesspeople everywhere.

International Management is about how firms become and remain international in scope. It focuses on the experiences of firms of all sizes, from many countries, as they come to grips with an increasingly competitive global environment. A central theme is the practice of management when a home-market perspective is no longer enough to achieve and sustain success. Through carefully selected comprehensive case studies and integrated text material, this book bridges both the internationalization process and multinational management.

Many texts focus on ongoing management issues in the world's larger MNEs—the lower right-hand cell in the following matrix. This is an important area, but one that presupposes a long history of experience and acquired skills. Our text takes a broader view, examining small and medium sized firms as well as large MNEs, and the process of internationalization as well as the challenges of ongoing management in multinationals.

	Internationalization	*Ongoing Multinational Management*
Small/Medium-Sized Firms	Smaller domestic firms moving abroad	Global niche competitors
Larger MNEs	Larger firms moving into more markets	Large, full-scale global competitors

The first half of *International Management* helps to demystify international business so a meaningful study of multinational management can occur. We focus on *internationalization*—developing an awareness of the impact of international forces on the firm's future and establishing and conducting transactions with firms internationally. We provide an understanding about the basic modes of involvement and deciding when each is most appropriate. For each mode, both inward- and outward-looking perspectives are considered: licensing (as licensor and licensee), trade (exporting and importing), joint ventures (with foreign companies abroad and at home), and subsidiaries (establishing foreign affiliates and as part of a foreign-controlled affiliate). As the left-hand cells in the matrix suggest, these issues are relevant for firms of all sizes.

In the second half of the book, we focus on how to establish a balance between the sometimes conflicting demands of the multinational headquarters, the multinational subsidiary, and the governments of all the countries in which the MNE operates. The cases are not limited to the experiences of the world's largest MNEs—they are also about smaller companies that must be global to survive and about the management of small subsidiaries. Nor are the cases solely focussed on the experience of MNEs from one country. In 1970, two-thirds of the world's largest companies were from the United States. Now only about one-fourth are U.S.-headquartered.

International Management is intended for use in international business and international management courses at the undergraduate, graduate, and executive levels. It can serve as the basis for an overarching course that deals with internationalization and multinational management, or for courses in each topic area. The chapters of text material can (and should) be supplemented with readings of the instructor's choice. Many of the suggested supplementary readings are from the *Journal of International Business Studies* which provides blanket permission to photocopy articles for classroom use at no charge.

This edition contains more cases (32 versus 31) and more chapters of text (15 versus 13) than the fourth edition. Of the 32 cases, 18 are new to the fifth edition; others have been significantly revised and updated. The new cases were selected on the basis of managerial relevance, overall fit with suggested themes, availability, and their effectiveness in the classroom. In regard to text material, there are entirely new chapters on Ethics, Managing the Global Workforce, and Strengthening International Government Relations, while all other chapters have been revised and updated. All but one of the chapters were (co)authored by us or one of our current or past colleagues. This has allowed us the opportunity to shape the body of text material into an integrated whole.

The cases in *International Management* have been extensively classroom-tested by us and colleagues around the world in executive, MBA, and undergraduate programs. Many are bestsellers. Another measure of their quality is that a number of them have been translated—into Japanese, French, Chinese, Spanish, Russian, and Indonesian. As well, several have won awards, including "The Global Branding of Stella Artois."

ACKNOWLEDGMENTS

The individual we most wish to acknowledge is Harold Crookell, a coauthor on the first edition. He passed away suddenly in 1991 and is sorely missed by all who knew him. His spirit of intellectual curiosity and dedication to the improvement of international management permeate this volume.

The authors are deeply indebted to a number of colleagues and institutions for the intellectual and financial support we have received:

Faculty Contributors of Cases/Chapters

Kersi Antia
Ivey Business School

Nicholas Athanassiou
Northeastern University

Tima Bansal
Ivey Business School

Stewart Black
*Center for Global Assignments
and University of Michigan*

Joseph DiStefano
IMD

Peter Killing
IMD

Masaaki (Mike) Kotabe
Temple University

Henry W. Lane
Northeastern University

Donald Lecraw
Ivey Business School

Isiaih Litvak
York University

Michael Moffett
Thunderbird

Roy Nelson
Thunderbird

Arvind Phatak
Temple University

Thomas A. Poynter, Principal
The Transitions Group, Inc.

David Sharp
Ivey Business School

Research Associates or Assistants

John Adamson, Simon Algar, Azimah Ainuddin, Cyril Bouquet, Harry Cheung, Chang Choi, Ken Cole, Donna Everatt, Anthony Goerzen, Ruihua Jiang, Katherine Johnston, Lambros Karavis, Vipon Kumar, Jeanne McNett, Meredith Martin, Janet Shaner, S. M. Steele, Chee Wee Tan, David Wesley.

Institutional Contributors

Richard Ivey School of Business, The University of Western Ontario, London, Canada
IMD—International Institute for Management Development, Lausanne, Switzerland
Thunderbird, The American Graduate School of International Management, Arizona, U.S.A.
The World Bank, Washington, D.C.

The following persons provided detailed reviews on this or an earlier edition:

Lance Brouthers, Ellen Cook, F. Derakhshan, George Gore, David Hopkins, Carol Howard, Stephen Jenner, Robert Moran, Cynthia Pavett, John Stanbury, Kenneth R. Tillery, Robert Vidal, Leland Wooton.

Input on the cases contained in the various editions has been received from:

Rafiq Ahmen, A. Ali, Joe Anderson, William J. Arthur, John Banks, Edgar Barrett, James Bowey, Brad Brown, Marie Burkhead, Jafor Chowdhury, Susan Crockett, Jafor Chowdhury, Andrew Delios, Chris Demchak, Charles Dhanaraj, John Dutton, L. R. Edleson, Nick Fry, Sanjay Goel, Robert Grosse, Ruth Gunn, S. D. Guzell, Steven H. Hanks, Louis Hébert, Mary Howes, S. Kumar Jain, Dale Kling, R. Kustin, Neng Liang, Clair McRostie, Shigefumi Makino, Alan Murray, Behnam Nakhai, Kent Neupert, R. F. O'Neil, Y. S. Paik, Less Palich, S. Porth, Rich Pouder, Mohammad Pourheydarian, Krishnan Ramaya, Kathy Rehbein, Lawrence Rhyne, Kendall Roth, Carol Sanchez, Bill Scheela, Jason Schweizer, Hendrick Seturie, Trudy Somers, William C. Sproull, John Stanbury, Phil Van Auken, Tom Voight, William A. Ward, Marion White, Georgie Willcox, Patrick Woodcock, and George Yates. Research assistance was received from Changwha Chung and Jaechul Jung.

We are grateful to all of these individuals and have tried to be as responsive as possible to their suggestions.

Finally, we wish to express our appreciation to our colleagues at Ivey. Richard Ivey School of Business is the second-largest producer of management case studies in the world. Eighteen of the 32 cases in this edition originated at Ivey. Any ongoing undertaking of this magnitude requires a great deal of financial and intellectual support.

Paul W. Beamish

Allen J. Morrison

Andrew C. Inkpen

Philip M. Rosenzweig

Contents

viii

About the Authors

PAUL W. BEAMISH is Associate Dean—Research and Professor in International Business at the Richard Ivey School of Business, The University of Western Ontario, London, Canada. From 1993 to 1997 he served as editor-in-chief of the *Journal of International Business Studies* (JIBS). He is the author or coauthor of over 100 publications in the international strategy area and series editor of over 40 volumes of cases for China. He has consulted and managed training activities in the public and private sectors, and he regularly acts as a joint venture facilitator for firms contemplating an alliance. His work has received awards from the Academy of Management, Academy of International Business, European Foundation for Management Development, and the Administrative Sciences Association of Canada. Before joining Ivey's faculty in 1987, he worked for Procter & Gamble Company of Canada and Wilfrid Laurier University.

ALLEN J. MORRISON is Professor of International Management at the Richard Ivey School of Business, The University of Western Ontario. Dr. Morrison has also been a Visiting Professor at the Anderson School at UCLA, and Professor of International Mangement at Thunderbird, The American Graduate School of International Management. Dr. Morrison's research and teaching interests center on multinational strategy and global leadership. He has authored or coauthored numerous articles and case studies, and seven books including *Global Explorers: The Next Generation of Leaders*. His views have been cited in such publications as *USA Today, Newsweek, Fortune,* and *The Wall Street Journal*. Dr. Morrison holds an M.B.A. degree from Ivey and a Ph.D. from the University of South Carolina.

ANDREW C. INKPEN is Professor of Management at Thunderbird, The American Graduate School of International Management in Glendale, Arizona. He holds a Ph.D. in Business from Ivey. He has also been on the faculties of Temple University, the National University of Singapore, and Nanyang Technological University. His research and teaching deal with the management of multinational firms, with a particular focus on strategic alliances, knowledge management, and organizational learning. He is the author or coauthor of more than 30 articles in journals such as *Academy of Management Review, California Management Review, Strategic Management Journal, Journal of International Business Studies,* and *Organization Science*. He is actively involved in international executive education and consulting. Before entering academe, he worked in public accounting and qualified as a Chartered Accountant in Canada.

PHILIP M. ROSENZWEIG is a professor at IMD in Lausanne, Switzerland. Before that, he was on the faculty of the Harvard Business School (1990 to 1996). His research has explored a number of aspects of international management, including organization design, human resource management, cross-cultural management, and ethical issues in foreign investment. He has published many case studies and articles that have appeared in *Academy of Management Review, Management Science, Journal of International Business Studies, California Management Review,* and *European Management Journal.* He is also active in international executive education, having taught in Japan, France, the Netherlands, Hungary, Peru, and the United Arab Emirates. He completed his Ph.D. at the Wharton School of the University of Pennsylvania, and has an M.B.A. from UCLA. He was employed by Hewlett-Packard Co. from 1980 to 1986.

Part One

Text

Chapter One

The Internationalization Process

Firms become international in scope for a variety of reasons: a desire for continued growth, an unsolicited foreign order, domestic market saturation, the potential to exploit a new technological advantage, and so forth. The dominant reason, however, relates to performance. There is clear evidence that among the largest multinational enterprises (MNEs), a strong correlation exists between improved performance and degree of internationalization (see Exhibit 1.1). Geographic scope is positively associated with firm profitability, even when controlling for the competing effect of the possession of proprietary assets. There is intrinsic value in internationalization itself.

Internationalization is the process by which firms increase their awareness of the influence of international activities on their future, and establish and conduct transactions with firms from other countries. International transactions can influence a firm's future in both direct and indirect ways. Business decisions made in one country, regarding such things as foreign investments and partnership arrangements, can have significant impact on a firm in a different country—and vice versa. The impact of such decisions may not be immediately and directly evident. The development of an awareness and appreciation for the role of foreign competition becomes an integral—and sometimes overlooked—part of the internationalization process.

Internationalization has both inward-looking and outward-looking dimensions. The outward-looking perspective incorporates an awareness of the nature of competition in foreign markets, and includes the following modes of activities:

a. Exporting.

b. Acting as licensor to a foreign company.

This chapter was prepared by Paul W. Beamish.

EXHIBIT 1.1
**MNE Performance
and Degree of
Internationalization***

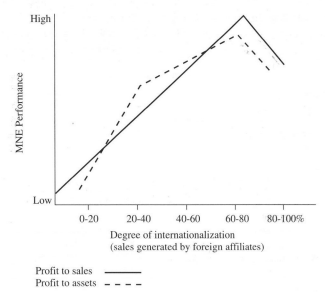

Profit to sales   ———————
Profit to assets   – – – –

* Data are based on the 100 largest U.S. MNEs and the 100 largest European MNEs.

c. Establishing joint ventures outside the home country with foreign companies.

d. Establishing or acquiring wholly owned businesses outside the home country.

These outward-oriented elements are similar to those in the stages model of international expansion. The stages model is an outward-looking perspective developed to reflect the commonly observed pattern of increased commitment to international business. In the stages model,[1] a firm might progress from (a) indirect/ad hoc exporting—perhaps from unsolicited export orders—to (b) active exporting and/or licensing to (c) active exporting, licensing, and joint equity investment in foreign manufacture to (d) full-scale multinational marketing and production.

These are, of course, broad-based stages. In practice, there are many more subcategories. Within exporting, for example, firms may start with order-filling only. Soon after, however, they may be confronted with questions of whether to use exporting middlemen who take ownership (distributors) or those who are commissioned agents; and whether to export directly (either through the firm's own sales force, an export department, or a foreign sales company) or indirectly (through brokers or export agents). From a service sector perspective, comparable issues exist, such as whether to use management contracts or to develop in-house capability.

Similarly, if an investment is to be made, there are questions regarding scale of investment (sales office, warehouse, packaging and assembly, or full-scale production), level of ownership (wholly, majority equity, equal, minority equity), and type of partner. As Exhibit 1.2 illustrates, there are numerous variations on the types of foreign direct investment possible.

EXHIBIT 1.2   **The Foreign Direct Investment of MNEs**

Choosing the Scale of Investment, Type of Partner, and Ownership Arrangement

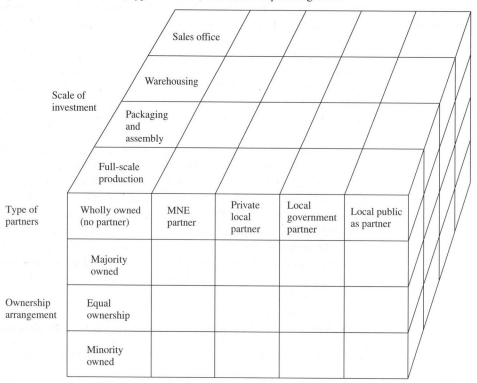

Another way of considering the various forms of foreign investment (and there are over 300,000 subsidiaries around the world) is illustrated in Exhibit 1.3. Each of these four forms has merit, although generally greenfield and joint venture tend to be superior performers versus acquisitions (because here there is a tendency to pay too much and/or to have integration problems.)

The sequential approach in the stages model is intuitively appealing in that it suggests that as firms develop experience and confidence with international busi-

EXHIBIT 1.3   **Forms of Foreign Investment**

	Partially Owned	Wholly Owned
Existing Business	Capital Participation	Acquisition
New Business	Joint Venture	Greenfield

ness, they will be willing to increase the scale of their investment and commitment in some sort of predictable fashion. The stages model also implies that over time, the firm's international operations will evolve toward modes such as wholly owned subsidiaries that promise greater risk (due to the required scale of investment) with the offsetting ability to exert greater control.

Not all firms follow such a path. Some start and stay with a particular mode or some skip stages, while others even change modes to a direction opposite to that suggested by the stages model. So while the stages model provides a useful way to organize our discussion, it is by no means reflective of, or appropriate for, all firms' approaches to international business. It is a descriptive model. It reflects what firms often do, not what they must or ought to do.

We also observe the formation of firms that, by necessity or design, are international at, or soon after, inception. These so-called "born globals" can take many forms, depending on the number of countries involved and the number of value chain activities that must be coordinated. (See Exhibit 1.4). Firms that are international from inception are often led by entrepreneurs who are able to overcome not just the liabilities of newness and size, but the liability of being foreign. Many firms do not originate with both international business competency and confidence. These firms, which are often SMEs (small and medium sized enterprises), thus have added challenges as they engage in the internationalization process from an entrepreneurial base.

Internationalization affects firms in equally important ways from an inward perspective, which incorporates an awareness of the impact of global competitors on the ability of domestically oriented firms to compete. The related modes of activites include:

a. Importing/sourcing.

b. Acting as licensee from a foreign company.

c. Establishing joint ventures (JVs) inside the home country with foreign companies.

d. Managing as the wholly owned subsidiary of a foreign firm.

EXHIBIT 1.4
Types of International New Ventures

Source: B. M. Oviatt and P. McDougall, "Toward a Theory of International New Ventures," *Journal of International Business Studies,* Vol. 25, No. 1, 1994, p. 59.

All of these modes and influences are relevant to the internationalization process and all are often overlooked. There are numerous reasons for considering importing rather than purchasing domestically, for considering foreign licensors or joint venture partners rather than strictly local ones, or if selling an entire business, considering foreign purchasers as an alternative to becoming the subsidiary of a domestic firm. Drawing upon resources and alternatives that are present elsewhere can help the firm see new opportunities, improve its bargaining power with local firms, make more informed decisions, and compete better at home.

Many firms have an appreciation for the nature and degree of competition in one or more foreign markets. Yet often they will not aggressively seek out markets that differ in language, geographic proximity, cultural similarity, and so forth. Some have suggested that for certain products, the world is a single market. The so-called Triad market (Japan, North America, and western Europe) is made up of over 630 million buyers with similar tastes.[2] This view raises a number of issues to be explored in later chapters. Which products/services would fall into this cat-

EXHIBIT 1.5   Some Variables Influencing the Location of Value Added Activities by MNEs in the 1970s and 1990s

Type of FDI	In the 1970s	In the 1990s
A. Resource Seeking	1. Availability, price, and quality of natural resources. 2. Infrastructure to enable resources to be exploited, and products arising from them to be exported. 3. Government restrictions on FDI and/or on capital and dividend remissions. 4. Investment incentives, e.g., tax holidays.	1. As in the 1970s, but local opportunities for upgrading quality of resources and the processing and transportation of their output are a more important locational incentive. 2. Availability of local partners to jointly promote knowledge and/or capital-intensive resource exploitation.
B. Market Seeking	1. Mainly domestic, and occasionally (e.g., in Europe) adjacent regional markets. 2. Real wage costs; material costs. 3. Transport costs; tariff and nontariff trade barriers. 4. As A.3 above, but also (where relevant) privileged access to import licenses.	1. Mostly large and growing domestic markets, and adjacent regional markets (e.g., NAFTA, EU, etc.). 2. Availability and price of skilled and professional labor. 3. Presence and competitiveness of related firms, e.g., leading industrial suppliers. 4. Quality of national and local infrastructure, and institutional competence. 5. Less spatially related market distortions, but increased role of agglomerative spatial economies and local service support facilities. 6. Macroeconomic and macro-organizational policies as pursued by host governments. 7. Increased need for presence close to users in knowledge-intensive sectors. 8. Growing importance of promotional activities by regional or local development agencies.

(continued)

egory? How would a firm know that it may have a globally competitive product/ service? If it did, how could it take the product/service effectively to numerous distant markets? To complicate this even further, we must consider how the answers to these and other questions change over time. For example, many of the reasons for making a foreign investment decades ago are different today (see Exhibit 1.5). The nonstatic nature of the environment is simultaneously one of the greatest attractions and frustrations for the international manager.

In terms of the new entrant to international business, how do managers make the decision to get involved internationally using any mode? Individual managers and groups of managers often possess distinct attitudes toward international business. These can range from being home-country oriented (ethnocentric),[3] to host-country oriented (polycentric), to world oriented (geocentric). There are two major risks associated with an ethnocentric, or home-country, focus. The first of these is a lack of awareness and appreciation for opportunities that exist external to the domestic market. The counterpoint to these potential opportunities is the

EXHIBIT 1.5   *(concluded)*

Type of FDI	In the 1970s	In the 1990s
C. Efficiency Seeking	1. Mainly production cost related (e.g., labor, materials, machinery, etc.). 2. Freedom to engage in trade in intermediate and final products. 3. Presence of agglomerative economies, e.g., export processing zones. 4. Investment incentives, e.g., tax breaks, accelerated depreciation, grants, subsidized land.	1. As in the 1970s, but more emphasis placed on B2, 3, 4, 5 and 7 above, especially for knowledge-intensive and integrated MNE activities, e.g., R&D and some office functions. 2. Increased role of governments in removing obstacles to restructuring economic activity, and facilitating the upgrading of human resources by appropriate educational and training programs. 3. Availability of specialized spatial clusters, e.g., science and industrial parks, service support systems etc.; and of specialized factor inputs. Opportunities for new initiatives by investing firms; an entrepreneurial environment, and one which encourages competitiveness enhancing cooperation within and between firms.
D. Strategic Asset Seeking	1. Availability of knowledge-related assets and markets necessary to protect or enhance ownership-specific advantages of investing firms—and at the right price. 2. Institutional and other variables influencing ease or difficulty at which such assets can be acquired by foreign firms.	1. As in the 1970s, but growing geographical dispersion of knowledge-based assets, and need of firms to harness such assets from foreign locations, makes this a more important motive for FDI. 2. The price and availability of "synergistic" assets to foreign investors. 3. Opportunities offered (often by particular subnational spatial units) for exchange of localized tacit knowledge, ideas and interactive learning. 4. Access to different cultures, institutions and systems; and different consumer demands and preferences.

Source: John H. Dunning. "Location and the Multinational Enterprise: A Neglected Factor?" *Journal of International Business Studies,* Vol. 29, No. 1, p. 53, 1998.

potential threat of foreign competition in the home market. Numerous businesses have been hurt as a result of the naive view that if a product or service is NIH (not-invented-here), it won't be effective.

Relevant to all of the various perspectives and modes of involvement is the firm's need for methods of coming to grips with various international cultures. Firms do not typically have the resources available to develop a detailed understanding of numerous cultures. Yet to compete internationally, some degree of understanding is required. But how much? And which cultures does it make more sense to try to learn about?

There are still business people who persist in believing that international competition cannot affect them because they are too small, or because they are solely focused on the local market. Foreign competition affects every sector of every economy. Education is an important consideration at each stage of the internationalization process.

In the balance of this chapter, some of the issues we will deal with in the subsequent chapters and cases will be briefly considered.

THE GLOBAL BUSINESS ENVIRONMENT

A key element of the internationalization process concerns where an organization chooses to do business outside its country. Many firms conduct an incomplete analysis of potential markets. This is due, in part, to a lack of awareness regarding global demographics.

Many criteria are available for assessing market compatibility. Chapter 2 provides some introductory material on population, gross national product, country growth rates, and so forth. Basic statistics on countries are included. This material is particularly useful when the firm is looking at opportunities on a worldwide (see Cameron case), regional (see MTN: Investing in Africa case), national (see Samsung China case) or even city (see Global Branding of Stella Artois case) basis.

THE WORLD OF INTERNATIONAL TRADE

Chapter 3 presents an overview of the international trade environment, with particular emphasis on the need to appreciate the role of foreign competition in both the home market and foreign markets. A great deal of emphasis is placed on demystifying the nature of international business, in part through an overview of the trade framework.

The trade framework considers social, technological, economic, and political (STEP) environments, which make any country more or less attractive for international investment and trade. As part of this analysis, the distinctions between comparative and competitive advantage, theories of international trade, and the nature of exchange rates are reviewed.

MANAGING EXPORT OPERATIONS

Exporting can often be the basis for all or part of an entire course on international marketing. This is so because, as both the Chinese Fireworks Industry case and the Selkirk case demonstrate, the export decision process is complex, requiring resolution of a number of fundamental questions. Firms of any size are faced with the same questions of where to expand (at home or abroad); if exporting, to which markets; the best way to enter these markets (i.e., what distribution arrangement, method of pricing, level of promotion, whether to adapt the product, and so forth); and the ongoing management of their foreign export operations. These questions are considered in detail in Chapter 4.

GLOBAL SOURCING STRATEGY

The decision to import a good or service must be made in the context of whether it would be better to purchase locally or to produce the product oneself. A firm with a home-country orientation may not even consider the possibility of importing. Not surprising, larger firms tend to have an advantage over smaller ones because they possess more resources with which to assess the importing alternative.

An excellent set of production and sourcing decisions that firms confront would include:[4]

1. From where should the firm supply the target market?

2. To what extent should the firm itself undertake production (degree of integration)?

3. To the extent that it does not, what and where should it buy from others?

4. To the extent that a firm opts to do at least some manufacturing, how should it acquire facilities?

5. Should the firm produce in one plant or many, related or autonomous?

6. What sort of production equipment (technology) should it use?

7. What site is best?

8. Where should research and development be located?

Importing should be a significant area of investigation, yet even purchasing texts frequently devote only limited space to international considerations. Of all the parts in the internationalization process, either from an outward or inward perspective, importing may well be the most underresearched. Although there has been recent progress[5] much work remains. Chapter 5 deals with global sourcing strategy. It emphasizes logistical management of the interface of R&D, manufacturing, and marketing activities on a global basis. Cases such as Intel Site Selection in Latin America and Looks.com—A Gray Issue provide comprehensive vehicles for sourcing discussion.

LICENSING

Our knowledge of international licensing is incomplete but growing. There are unresolved issues regarding the types of firms that license-out; the predominant industries that are involved; the revenues generated; the extent to which they consider alternative modes; the countries they license to; whether they tend to consider it a stage in an internationalization process (or an end in itself); the costs of negotiating, administering, and policing license agreements; the frequency with which they lose proprietary advantages after licensing out; the most common terms in their license agreements; the areas in which there is the most disagreement; and so forth. Despite these limitations, we do know that firms license out their technology, trademarks, or other proprietary advantages in order to generate additional profits. Further, we know that licensing involves billions of dollars annually.

For the licensor, licensing is a chance to exploit its technology in markets that are too small to justify larger investments or in markets that restrict imports or FDI, or as a means of testing and developing a market. Firms are far more willing to license their peripheral technologies than their core technologies: no one wants to create a future competitor.

For the licensee, there are two principal advantages of licensing. The first is that it permits the acquisition of technology more cheaply than by internal development. Second, it allows the firm to acquire a technology that, when combined with other skills already present, permits it to diversify. It is important for technology buyers to (a) develop a minimum level of technical competence, (b) know their needs, and (c) consider alternative modes such as JVs.[6] This latter point is particularly relevant in the Cameron case.

While there are typically lower levels of commitment associated with a licensing strategy, there are nonetheless risks for both parties. For the licensor there are the risks of losing a technological advantage, reputation, and potential profits (see the Time Warner and the ORC Patents case). For the licensee, there are the risks that the technology will not work as expected or will cost more to implement than anticipated. Chapter 6 provides an introduction to the whole area of licensing.

THE DESIGN AND MANAGEMENT OF INTERNATIONAL JOINT VENTURES

International joint ventures are alliances formed by organizations from two or more countries. They are formed for a variety of reasons: to mesh complementary skills from different organizations, to assure or speed market access, to leapfrog a technological gap, to strategically respond to more intense competition, and so forth.

Joint ventures do not have to be physically located outside your home country to be "international." For an American, for example, an auto plant in the United States co-owned by American and Japanese partners is an international joint venture. In fact, given differences in language, culture, and management practices, such a joint venture would have greater international complexity than, for example, an American-Canadian joint venture physically located in Canada.

Joint ventures are one of many forms of cooperation, each of which has unique characteristics in terms of (a) whether it is equity-based, (b) the length of the agreement, (c) whether a whole range of resources and rights is transferred, (d) the method of resource transfer, and (e) the typical compensation method (see Exhibit 1.6). As the cases note, many firms often overlook the potential use of alternative cooperative approaches.

Chapter 7 considers why companies create joint ventures as well as providing some guidelines for their successful design and management. This serves as a useful basis for the internationalization case study Nora-Sakari, which looks at a proposed alliance. While this and other cases such as GM and AvtoVAZ deal with proposals, they differ significantly in terms of country, scale, alliance type, motives for formation, and partner choice. Other cases such as Euro Air consider the challenges of managing within a nonequity alliance.

Before any investment occurs—joint venture or otherwise—there is of course a need to be clear why the investment is occurring, why the particular market is

EXHIBIT 1.6 **A Typology of International Industrial Cooperation Modes***

Form of Cooperation	Equity or Nonequity	Length of Agreement	Transfer of Resources and Rights	Method of Transfer	Typical Compensation Method[†]
1. Wholly owned foreign subsidiaries	Equity	Unlimited	Whole range?	Internal to firm	Profits
2. Joint ventures	Equity	Unlimited	Whole range?	Internal to firm	Fraction of shares/dividends
3. Foreign minority holdings	Equity	Unlimited	Whole range?	Internal to firm	Fraction of shares/ dividends
4. "Fade-out" agreements	Equity	Limited	Whole range? (for limited period)	Internal to firm changing to market	Fraction of shares/ dividends
5. Licensing	Nonequity	Limited by contract	Limited range	Mixed**	Royalty as percent of sales
6. Franchising	Nonequity	Limited by contract	Limited + support	Market	Royalty as percent of sales and markups on components
7. Management contracts	Nonequity	Limited by contract	Limited	Market	Lump sum. Royalty.
8. Technical training	Nonequity	Limited	Small	Market	Lump sum
9. Turnkey ventures	Nonequity	Limited	Limited in time	Market	Lump sum
10. Contractual joint ventures	Nonequity	Limited	Specified by contract	Mixed	Function of the change in the costs and revenues of the venture, firm, or dominant partner
11. International subcontracting**	Nonequity	Limited	Small	Market	Markups
12. Strategic buyer– supplier coalitions**	Nonequity	Limited by contract but long-term	Limited + support	Mixed	Markups. Respective decreased costs/increased revenues.

*Adapted from Peter J. Buckley and Mark Casson, *The Economic Theory of the Multinational Enterprise* (New York: St. Martin's Press, 1985), except where noted with double asterisk (**).

[†]Derived primarily from F. Contractor and P. Lorange, *Cooperative Strategies in International Business* (Lexington, MA: D. C. Heath, 1988).

EXHIBIT 1.7   But Before the Alliance . . .

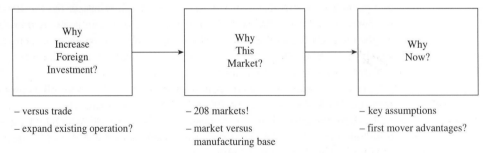

| Why Increase Foreign Investment? | → | Why This Market? | → | Why Now? |

– versus trade

– expand existing operation?

– 208 markets!

– market versus manufacturing base

– key assumptions

– first mover advantages?

being chosen, and whether now is the appropriate time (Exhibit 1.7). With these and the mode question resolved, we can consider the issues which more typically characterize the management of multinational enterprises.

INTERNATIONAL STRATEGY FORMULATION

Chapter 8 looks at how international firms formulate product-market strategy to maximize the international competitiveness of the firm. The chapter and cases examine the pressures that exist for the multinational firm both to achieve global efficiencies and to be locally responsive. These pressures are easy to understand but difficult to deal with simultaneously.

At the same time as managers identify the incentives to become more international, they begin to run up against the sovereign interests of the various countries they may wish to do business in. The local governments will often use regulations to further their own interests in such things as employment, where production occurs, development of local businesses, foreign exchange controls, and so forth. This orientation must be balanced against the multinational's interest in operating efficiently and coordinating its global activities.

If this were not enough, there are also pressures to adapt products to local conditions, perhaps organize to reflect a unique environment, and be generally responsive to the variety of differences that can exist between regions, countries, and cultures. Not surprisingly, subsidiary managers will often have very different ideas about how a subsidiary can best be managed. These in turn must be reconciled with the headquarters perspective and sovereignty concerns. All of the cases dealing with multinational management can be reviewed from these three perspectives. As you would expect, substantial overlap often exists.

THE IMPACT OF GLOBALIZATION ON THE ORGANIZATION OF ACTIVITIES

A major reason for the rise of multinational enterprises is their demonstrated ability to organize business activities on a multicountry basis. Organization involves both geographic configuration and international coordination and integration.

Chapter 9 introduces the organization structures through which international companies carry out their activities. The structures considered include the international division, area division, global product division, and the transnational option. Each structure represents a compromise—an attempt to balance the inherent strengths and weaknesses of the form chosen. Each structure must reconcile ease of administration with customer responsiveness, and parent company versus subsidiary perspectives. All of this must be done in the context of the sovereign concerns of different national governments, and sometimes widely different cultures.

Some of the cases which allow for a more detailed consideration of organization issues include Quest Foods Asia Pacific and the CRM Initiative, Blue Ridge Spain, and Meridian Magnesium.

THE EVOLVING MULTINATIONAL

Most multinationals undertake a series of foreign market entries over the course of years. Not surprisingly, they evolve in very different ways in order to reflect market complexity and the need to differentiate various subsidiaries.

The focus of Chapter 10 is on the evolving multinational enterprise. This evolving nature is considered along three dimensions: geographic, a line of business, and function. Insights are offered regarding factors that facilitate or impede evolution.

Emphasis then shifts to the ways in which evolution along these dimensions can be integrated. Of particular emphasis here is the way in which knowledge can be leveraged (see for example the Honeywell Inc. and Global R & D case).

THE GLOBAL MANAGER

Chapter 11 identifies and describes the skill set of the global manager. Effective global executives require the ability to develop and use global strategic skills, manage change and transition, manage cultural diversity, design and function in flexible organization structures, work with others and in teams, communicate, and learn and transfer knowledge in an organization. This list can be viewed as a daunting challenge—or a lifelong opportunity.

The process of developing managers with these abilities involves human resource management policies and the managing of international assignments. This in turn is linked to selection, training, and repatriation. A number of the cases which follow consider the required skills for the effective global manager. See for example Bristol Compressors, Larson in Nigeria, and HCM Beverage.

STRENGTHENING INTERNATIONAL GOVERNMENT RELATIONS

Chapter 12 looks at selective ways of strengthening international government relations. Major sources of trade regulation that affect both the exporter and foreign investor are considered. While this suggests impediments, in fact many opportunities exist to work with governments in a positive fashion, depending on the

MNEs approach to government. Various approaches are reviewed. Then several specific examples, (such as via privatization initiatives) are reviewed as ways of creating and deepening international government relations.

THE GLOBAL LEADER

Finding people to lead (versus administer) the operations of multinational enterprises is the key challenge for international success. Most senior executives in the larger MNEs feel that there are both insufficient numbers of global leaders and too many leaders who do not possess the needed capabilities! This chapter explores some of the strategies that can be used to develop global leaders, including the importance of travel, teams, training, and transfers.

ETHICAL CHALLENGES OF INTERNATIONAL MANAGEMENT

One of the most difficult yet critical issues for international managers is the effective management of ethics. While all managers face ethical issues, global managers arguably confront them more frequently and must resolve dilemmas that often are complicated by a cultural overlay. Culture impacts ethical norms because culture is inherently value-laden.

Chapter 14 reviews the types of actions involved in ethical decisions, codes of international conduct, and three basic philosophical perspectives as applied to international ethical challenges. A number of cases in the book, including Steve Parker, Sicom and CD Piracy, and DSL de Mexico, provide the opportunity for a deeper investigation and application.

MANAGING THE GLOBAL WORKFORCE

A challenge facing many multinational enterprises is to forge consistency in output and behavior in its global workforce while also fostering diversity. Here diversity means more than numerical composition, also involving better individual performance through inclusion and better group performance through knowledge exchange. The Rentsch in Poland and Mabuchi Motor Co. (in China) cases explore in detail some of the challenges of developing and managing a global workforce that are introduced in this final chapter.

Conclusion   The chapters and cases that follow deal with issues of both internationalization and ongoing multinational management. They are intended to help build an understanding of the impact of global competition; an appreciation for the various modes of involvement; and a sensitivity to, and experience with, international management.

Supplementary Reading

Anderson, O. "On the Internationalization Process of Firms: A Critical Analysis," *Journal of International Business Studies,* Vol. 24, No. 2, 1993.

Beamish, Paul W. "The Role of Alliances in International Entrepreneurship" in R. Wright (ed) *Research in Global Strategic Management.* Greenwich CT. JAI Press, (in press).

Calof, Jonathan, and Paul W. Beamish. "Adapting to Foreign Markets: Explaining Internationalization," *International Business Review,* Vol. 4, No. 2, 1995, pp. 115–131.

Delios, Andrew, and Paul W. Beamish. "Geographic Scope, Product Diversification and the Corporate Performance of Japanese Firms," *Strategic Management Journal,* Vol. 20, No. 8, 1999. pp. 711–727.

Eriksson, Kent, Jan Johanson, Anders Majkgård, and D. Deo Sharma. "Experiential Knowledge and Cost in the Internationalization Process," *Journal of International Business Studies,* Vol. 28, No. 2, 1997.

Forsgren, M. *Managing the Internationalization Process.* London: Routledge, 1989.

Hadjikhani, Amjad, and Jan Johanson (eds). Special Issue on the Internationalization Process of the Firm, *International Business Review,* Vol. 11, No. 3, 2002.

Johanson, Jan, and Jan-Erik Vahlne. "The Internationalization Process of the Firm—A Model of Knowledge Development and Increasing Foreign Market Commitments," *Journal of International Business Studies,* Spring-Summer 1977.

Kogut, B., and H. Singh. "The Effect of National Culture on the Choice of Entry Mode," *Journal of International Business Studies,* Fall 1988.

Leenders, M., and D. Blenkhorn. *Reverse Marketing.* New York: The Free Press, 1988.

Lu, Jane W., and Paul W. Beamish, "The Internationalization and Performance of SMEs," *Strategic Management Journal,* Vol. 22, No. 6/7, 2001, pp. 565–586.

Ohmae, Kenichi. *Beyond National Borders.* Homewood, Ill.: Dow Jones-Irwin, 1987.

Pauwels, Pieter, and Paul Matthyssens. "A Strategy Process Perspective on Export Withdrawal," *Journal of International Marketing,* Vol. 7, No. 3. 1999, pp. 10–37.

Reuber, A. R., and E. Fischer. "The Influence of the Management Team's International Experience on the Internationalisation Behavior of SMEs," *Journal of International Business Studies,* Vol. 28, No. 4, 1997, pp. 807–825.

Robinson, Richard D. *Internationalization of Business.* Chicago: The Dryden Press, 1984.

Root, Franklin R. Entry Strategies for International Markets. Lexington, Mass.: Lexington Books, 1987.

Rosenzweig, Philip M., and Janet L. Shaner. "Internationalization Reconsidered: New Imperatives for Successful Growth," in *Reassessing the Internationalization of the Firm,* Vol. 11, 2001, pp. 159–177. Elsevier, New York.

Sullivan, Daniel. "Measuring the Degree of Internationalization of a Firm," *Journal of International Business Studies,* Vol. 25, No. 2, 1994, pp. 325–342.

Welch, L. S., and R. Luostarinen. "Internationalization: Evolution of a Concept," *Journal of General Management,* Winter 1988, Vol. 14, No. 2, pp. 34–35.

Zahra, Shaker A., R. Duane Ireland, and Michael A. Hitt. "International Expansion by New Venture Firms: International Diversity, Mode of Market Entry, Technological Learning, and Performance," *Academy of Management Journal,* Vol. 43, No. 5, 2000, pp. 925–950.

Endnotes

1. See Franklin R. Root, *Entry Strategies for International Markets* (Lexington, Mass: Lexington Books, 1987), p. 19.
2. See Kenichi Ohmae, *Beyond National Borders* (Homewood, Ill.: Dow Jones-Irwin, 1987).
3. See H. V. Perlmutter, "The Tortuous Evolution of the Multinational Corporation," *Columbia Journal of World Business,* January/February 1969, pp. 9–18; H. V. Perlmutter & D. A. Heenan, "How Multinational Should Your Top Managers Be?" *Harvard Business Review,* Vol. 6, 1974, pp. 121–132; S. J. Kobrin, "Is There a Relationship between a Geocentric Mind-Set and Multinational Strategy?" *Journal of International Business Studies,* Vol. 3, 1994, pp. 493–511; and J. Calof and P. Beamish, "The Right Attitude for International Success," *Business Quarterly,* Vol. 59, No. 1, 1994, pp. 105–110.
4. See R. D. Robinson, *Internationalization of Business* (Chicago: The Dryden Press, 1984).
5. See M. Leenders and D. Blenkhorn, *Reverse Marketing* (New York: The Free Press, 1988).
6. See J. Peter Killing, "Technology Acquisition: License Agreement or Joint Venture?" *Columbia Journal of World Business,* Autumn 1980, pp. 38–46.

Chapter Two

The Global Business Environment

Effective international management starts with a knowledge of key variables in the global economic environment. In any industry in any country, managers must have an overall knowledge of the wheres, whats, whys, and hows of the countries and regions of the world. This knowledge starts with the size and growth rates of country markets; their populations; their trade volumes, compositions, and growth rates; their natural resource bases and labor costs; and their financial positions. This knowledge can be used as an initial way to identify the threats and opportunities that might arise in their international operations. It can assist them to identify countries and regions to which they might export, from which they might import, and in which they might invest in production operations.

Although we live in an information age, often we are ignorant of these basic facts: Which countries have the highest gross national income (GNI) per person? Which are the 10 most populous countries in the world? Which countries grew the fastest over the past 10 years? Which countries have the largest markets? Which countries have the largest volumes of international trade? Which countries have had the highest growth rates in their trade volumes over the past decade? Which countries are among the top 10 as sources for foreign direct investment? As host countries?

The purpose of this chapter is to present data—population, GNI, purchasing power parity, and international trade statistics—to respond to some of these questions. It also highlights the problems and limitations of the data and shows how the data can be used by international managers to begin to address some of the basic decisions of international management. In subsequent chapters additional data on trade and foreign investment will be presented. It should be emphasized, however,

This chapter was prepared by Paul W. Beamish.

that these publicly available data are only a start. Once the relevant publicly available data have been gathered, additional data often must be gathered, sometimes by first-hand research. Eventually all the data must be interpreted, and decisions reached using these data as inputs. There is the story of a salesperson who went to one country to investigate the market for shoes. The summary of the trip report was: "No market here; no one wears shoes." Several years later another salesperson went to the same country. The summary of this trip was: "Huge market here; no one wears shoes."

POPULATION

From a year 2000 base of six billion people, earth's population is expected to grow to 8.5 billion by the year 2025. These people are unevenly distributed, with over half the world's population in Asia Pacific countries and only 5 percent in North America. About 900 million people (less than one in six) are currently located in the 36 high-income countries where per capita GNI is $9,266 or more (Exhibit 2.1). This portion will drop in the decades ahead. These population trends have enormous implications for global employment. For example, the current movement of high-volume, semi-skilled manufacturing jobs from high-income to low-income countries can only increase. Real wages in low-income countries with large and/or fast-growing populations, such as India, the Philippines, Indonesia, Bangladesh, Kenya, Syria, and Nicaragua, will likely not rise dramatically. They will be low-wage countries into the foreseeable future. Exports of low-cost, labor-intensive products from these countries will continue to exert pressure on producers of competing products in high-income countries.

High population growth rates also have implications for the types of products that are and will be in demand. Globally, 30 percent of the world's population is under the age of 15. Yet in 55 countries, 40 percent or more of the population is under the age of 15. Examples here include Pakistan and many countries in Africa. At the other end of the age spectrum, less than 7 percent of the world's population is over 65 years old. Here again the age profile is heavily skewed. Industrialized countries such as Japan, Italy and Sweden average 17 percent of their populace at a "senior citizen" (65+) level.

Substantial variability exists among countries with respect to the concentration of the population within the country. In many African countries, over 90 percent of the population is in rural areas. In other countries—such as Singapore, England, Australia, the Netherlands, Venezuela, Uruguay, and Germany—over 85 percent of the population lives in urban areas. Urban concentrations provide an opportunity for international managers to focus their efforts on geographically concentrated consumers and access the country's labor force. Nowhere is this truer than in the metropolitan areas where the population exceeds 10 million: Mexico City, Tokyo-Yokohama, Sao Paulo, New York, Calcutta, Shanghai, Mumbai (Bombay), Jakarta, Manila, Buenos Aires, Seoul, Rio de Janeiro, Los Angeles, and London. Beyond the concentration of the population in urban centers are the growth rates

EXHIBIT 2.1   Statistics on 208 Countries

Economy	Population (Thousands)	Gross National Income (GNI) $	GNI per Capita $[a]	Purchasing Power Parity (International Dollars)
Afghanistan	26,550	—	—	—
Albania	3,411	3,833	1,120	3,600
Algeria	30,399	47,897	1,580	5,040
American Samoa	—	—	—	—
Andorra	67	—	—	—
Angola	13,134	3,847	290	1,180
Antigua and Barbuda	68	642	9,440	10,000
Argentina	37,032	276,228	7,460	12,050
Armenia	3,803	1,991	520	2,580
Aruba	101	—	—	—
Australia	19,182	388,252	20,240	24,970
Austria	8,110	204,525	25,220	26,330
Azerbaijan	8,049	4,851	600	2,740
Bahamas, The	303	4,533	14,960	16,400
Bahrain	691	6,247	9,370	14,410
Bangladesh	131,050	47,864	370	1,590
Barbados	267	2,469	9,250	15,020
Belarus	10,005	28,735	2,870	7,550
Belgium	10,252	251,583	24,540	27,470
Belize	240	746	3,110	5,240
Benin	6,272	2,345	370	980
Bermuda	63	—	—	—
Bhutan	805	479	590	1,440
Bolivia	8,329	8,206	990	2,360
Bosnia and Herzegovina	3,977	4,899	1,230	—
Botswana	1,602	5,280	3,300	7,170
Brazil	170,406	610,058	3,580	7,300
Brunei	338	7,754	24,100	24,910
Bulgaria	8,167	12,391	1,520	5,560
Burkina Faso	11,274	2,422	210	970
Burundi	6,807	732	110	580
Cambodia	12,021	3,150	260	1,440
Cameroon	14,876	8,644	580	1,590
Canada	30,750	649,829	21,130	27,170
Cape Verde	441	588	1,330	4,760
Cayman Islands	35	—	—	—
Central African Republic	3,717	1,031	280	1,160
Chad	7,694	1,541	200	870
Channel Islands	149	—	—	—
Chile	15,211	69,850	4,590	9,100
China	1,262,460	1,062,919	840	3,920
Colombia	42,299	85,279	2,020	6,060
Comoros	558	212	380	1,590
Congo, Dem. Rep.	50,948	5,024	100	680
Congo, Rep.	3,018	1,735	570	570
Costa Rica	3,811	14,510	3,810	7,980
Cote d'Ivoire	16,013	9,591	600	1,500

(continued)

EXHIBIT 2.1 *(continued)*

Economy	Population (Thousands)	Gross National Income (GNI) $	GNI per Capita $[a]	Purchasing Power Parity (International Dollars)
Croatia	4,380	20,240	4,620	7,960
Cuba	11,188	—	—	—
Cyprus	757	9,361	12,370	20,780
Czech Republic	10,273	53,925	5,250	13,780
Denmark	5,336	172,238	32,280	27,250
Djibouti	632	553	880	—
Dominica	73	—	—	—
Dominican Republic	8,373	17,847	2,130	5,710
Ecuador	12,646	15,256	1,210	2,910
Egypt, Arab Rep.	63,976	95,380	1,490	3,670
El Salvador	6,276	12,569	2,000	4,410
Equatorial Guinea	457	363	800	5,600
Eritrea	4,097	696	170	960
Estonia	1,369	4,894	3,580	9,340
Ethiopia	64,298	6,737	100	660
Faeroe Islands	45	—	—	—
Fiji	812	1,480	1,820	4,480
Finland	5,177	130,106	25,130	24,570
France[b]	58,892	1,438,293	24,090	24,420
French Polynesia	235	4,064	17,290	23,340
Gabon	1,230	3,928	3,190	5,360
Gambia, The	1,303	440	340	1,620
Georgia	5,024	3,183	630	2,680
Germany	82,150	2,063,734	25,120	24,920
Ghana	19,306	6,594	340	1,910
Greece	10,560	126,269	11,960	16,860
Greenland	56	—	—	—
Grenada	98	370	3,770	6,960
Guam	155	—	—	—
Guatemala	11,385	19,164	1,680	3,770
Guinea	7,415	3,303	450	1,930
Guinea-Bissau	1,199	217	180	710
Guyana	761	652	860	3,670
Haiti	7,959	4,059	510	1,470
Honduras	6,417	5,517	860	2,400
Hong Kong, China	6,797	176,157	25,920	25,590
Hungary	10,022	47,249	4,710	11,990
Iceland	281	8,540	30,390	28,710
India	1,015,923	454,800	450	2,340
Indonesia	210,421	119,871	570	2,830
Iran, Islamic Rep.	63,664	106,707	1,680	5,910
Iraq	23,264	—	—	—
Ireland	3,794	85,979	22,660	25,520
Isle of Man	75	—	—	—
Israel	6,233	104,128	16,710	19,330
Italy	57,690	1,163,211	20,160	23,470
Jamaica	2,633	6,883	2,610	3,440

EXHIBIT 2.1   *(continued)*

Economy	Population (Thousands)	Gross National Income (GNI) $	GNI per Capita $[a]	Purchasing Power Parity (International Dollars)
Japan	126,870	4,519,067	35,620	27,080
Jordan	4,887	8,360	1,710	3,950
Kazakhstan	14,869	18,773	1,260	5,490
Kenya	30,092	10,610	350	1,010
Kiribati	91	86	950	—
Korea, Dem. Rep.	22,268	—	—	—
Korea, Rep.	47,275	421,069	8,910	17,300
Kuwait	1,984	35,771	18,030	18,690
Kyrgyz Republic	4,915	1,345	270	2,540
Lao PDR	5,279	1,519	290	1,540
Latvia	2,372	6,925	2,920	7,070
Lebanon	4,328	17,355	4,010	4,550
Lesotho	2,035	1,181	580	2,590
Liberia	3,130	—	—	—
Libya	5,290	—	—	—
Liechtenstein	32	—	—	—
Lithuania	3,695	10,809	2,930	6,980
Luxembourg	438	18,439	42,060	45,470
Macao, China	438	6,835	14,580	18,190
Macedonia, FYR	2,031	3,696	1,820	5,020
Madagascar	15,523	3,869	250	820
Malawi	10,311	1,744	170	600
Malaysia	23,270	78,727	3,380	8,330
Maldives	276	541	1,960	4,240
Mali	10,840	2,548	240	780
Malta	390	3,559	9,120	16,530
Marshall Islands	52	102	1,970	—
Mauritania	2,665	978	370	1,630
Mauritius	1,186	4,449	3,750	9,940
Mayotte	145	—	—	—
Mexico	97,966	497,025	5,070	8,790
Micronesia, Fed. Sts.	118	250	2,110	—
Moldova	4,282	1,428	400	2,230
Monaco	32	—	—	—
Mongolia	2,398	947	390	1,760
Morocco	28,705	33,940	1,180	3,450
Mozambique	17,691	3,746	210	800
Myanmar	47,749	—	210	—
Namibia	1,757	3,569	2,030	6,410
Nepal	23,043	5,584	240	1,370
Netherlands	15,919	397,544	24,970	25,850
Netherlands, Antilles	215	—	—	—
New Caledonia	213	3,203	15,060	21,820
New Zealand	3,831	49,750	12,990	18,530
Nicaragua	5,071	2,053	400	2,080
Niger	10,832	1,939	180	740
Nigeria	126,910	32,705	260	800

(continued)

EXHIBIT 2.1   *(continued)*

Economy	Population (Thousands)	Gross National Income (GNI) $	GNI per Capita $[a]	Purchasing Power Parity (International Dollars)
Northern Mariana Islands	72	—	—	—
Norway	4,491	155,064	34,530	29,630
Oman	2,395	—	—	—
Pakistan	138,080	61,022	440	1,860
Palau	19	—	—	—
Panama	2,856	9,308	3,260	5,680
Papua New Guinea	5,130	3,607	700	2,180
Paraguay	5,496	7,933	1,440	4,450
Peru	25,661	53,392	2,080	4,660
Philippines	75,580	78,778	1,040	4,220
Poland	38,650	161,832	4,190	9,000
Portugal	10,008	111,291	11,120	16,990
Puerto Rico	3,920	—	—	—
Qatar	585	—	—	—
Romania	22,435	37,380	1,670	6,360
Russian Federation	145,555	241,027	1,660	8,010
Rwanda	8,508	1,988	230	930
Samoa	170	246	1,450	5,050
San Marino	27	—	—	—
Sao Tome and Principe	148	43	290	—
Saudi Arabia	20,723	149,932	7,230	11,390
Senegal	9,530	4,714	490	1,480
Seychelles	81	573	7,050	—
Sierra Leone	5,031	647	130	480
Singapore	4,018	99,404	24,740	24,910
Slovak Republic	5,402	19,969	3,700	11,040
Slovenia	1,988	19,979	10,050	17,310
Solomon Islands	447	278	620	1,710
Somalia	8,778	—	—	—
South Africa	42,801	129,171	3,020	9,160
Spain	39,465	595,255	15,080	19,260
Sri Lanka	19,359	16,408	850	3,460
St. Kitts and Nevis	41	269	6,570	10,960
St. Lucia	156	642	4,120	5400
St. Vincent and the Grenadines	115	313	2,720	5,210
Sudan	31,095	9,599	310	1,520
Suriname	417	788	1,890	3,480
Swaziland	1,045	1,451	1,390	4,600
Sweden	8,869	240,707	27,140	23,970
Switzerland	7,180	273,829	38,140	30,450
Syrian Arab Republic	16,189	15,146	940	3,340
Taiwan[c]	22,400	270,485	12,075	17,400
Tajikistan	6,170	1,109	180	1,090
Tanzania	33,696	9,013	270	520
Thailand	60,728	121,602	2,000	6,320

EXHIBIT 2.1   *(concluded)*

Economy	Population (Thousands)	Gross National Income (GNI) $	GNI per Capita $[a]	Purchasing Power Parity (International Dollars)
Togo	4,527	1,318	290	1,410
Tonga	100	166	1,660	—
Trinidad and Tobago	1,301	6,415	4,930	8,220
Tunisia	9,564	20,057	2,100	6,070
Turkey	65,293	202,131	3,100	7,030
Turkmenistan	5,199	3,886	750	3,800
Uganda	22,210	6,699	300	1,210
Ukraine	49,501	34,565	700	3,700
United Arab Emirates	2,905	49,205	18,060	19,410
United Kingdom	59,739	1,459,500	24,430	23,550
United States	281,550	9,601,505	34,100	34,100
Uruguay	3,337	20,010	6,000	8,880
Uzbekistan	24,752	8,843	360	2,360
Vanuatu	197	226	1,150	2,960
Venezuela	24,170	104,065	4,310	5,740
Vietnam	78,523	30,439	390	2,000
Virgin Islands (U.S.)	121	—	—	—
West Bank and Gaza	2,966	4,892	1,660	—
Yemen, Rep.	17,507	6,554	370	770
Yugoslavia, Fed. Rep.	10,637	10,028	940	—
Zambia	10,089	3,026	300	750
Zimbabwe	12,627	5,851	460	2,550

[a]Calculated using the World Bank Atlas method.
[b]Figures for France include French Guiana, Guadaloupe, Martinique, Reunion.
[c]Taiwan figures from Taipei Economic and Cultural Office.

of these and other centers. These high growth rates have implications for growth in demand for products and services to support the infrastructure, such as equipment and services to provide electricity, housing, roads, transportation, telecommunications, and all types of environmental cleanup. On the other hand, they have implications for the availability of urban labor.

One of the trends of the last few decades is the increasing number of people who go abroad to find jobs and to increase incomes. Over 80 million people work outside their home country. International migration of this magnitude has a major impact on overall trade and balance of payments when the funds that workers remit to their home countries are considered. For example, the World Bank has estimated that Filipino workers abroad remit $8 billion per year, compared to exports of about $13.5 billion.

COUNTRIES

The 1991 World Bank Atlas provided statistics on 185 countries and territories. The 2002 World Bank Atlas provided statistics on 207 countries and territories. Country proliferation is relevant not just to mapmakers and statisticians. It has obvious and immediate implications for multinational enterprises and international traders and their need to coordinate with national governments, to define territorial scope of operations, to analyze foreign exchange rates, and so forth.

Country proliferation seems likely to continue. In 1993, Czechoslovakia was split into the Czech Republic and Slovakia. Yugoslavia now comprises a variety of countries. Separatist elements exist in many of the countries of Africa and Asia, such as Indonesia, the Philippines, and India. Whether due to differences in culture, ethnic origin, language, or religion, this trend complicates the life of the international manager.

Beyond the proliferation in the number of countries, many countries are also highly diverse in terms of religion, ethnic groups, language, and income level. This diversity has implications for effective management practices in all the functional areas as well as general management in many countries. The department of geodesy and cartography of the state geological committee of the Russian Academy of Sciences has devised an "Ethnic and Linguistic Homogeneity Index" of most of the countries of the world. The index ranges from 100 for North and South Korea to 7 for Tanzania. This index gives some idea of the diversity facing international managers within each country.[1]

ECONOMIC DEVELOPMENT

Global economic activity continues to be dominated by a small number of countries. Yet the ranks of the traditional G7 nations (the United States, Japan, Germany, France, Italy, United Kingdom, Canada), the countries with the largest economies as measured by GNI, are under challenge. As of 2000, when measured using purchasing power parity, China, India, Mexico, Russia and Brazil have economies that are larger than that of Canada, and China would be the second largest economy worldwide.

The economic figures for many countries can serve as a useful approximation of reality, while for others they are notoriously inaccurate. Some countries intentionally understate their GNI to attract development aid. Others simply have poor tracking mechanisms. As well, wars and insurrections can dramatically reduce—or increase—economic activity.

The data on GNI are designed to capture the volume of goods and services produced and consumed in a country. Hence, GNI is a first rough measure of market size. In 2000, the GNI of countries ranged from $9.6 trillion for the United States to $4.5 trillion for Japan, $2.1 trillion for Germany, down to $43 million for São Tomé and Principe.

Beyond the size of an economy, its growth rate is also important, since it signals the speed at which markets are growing. Many of the fastest-growing economies continue to be concentrated on the Asia-Pacific Rim. The "Asian flu" of the late 1990s did not uniformly affect every country in the region. And many of the slowest-growing economies continue to be concentrated on the African continent. Many of the economies that have experienced negative growth have been concentrated in central and eastern Europe. Within the geographical regions, however, growth is far from uniform.

GNI per capita figures can give an indication of the income levels of countries. Income levels in turn can indicate the types of products that may be in demand and wage levels. These figures must be interpreted with care, however. They have three major faults. GNI is a measure of the goods and services that are produced by the economy and sold via the market as recorded by the government. For developing countries, many goods and services are produced for self-consumption or bartered. Government reporting systems often do not record these transactions or the transactions of small producers. The so-called subculture economies (SCEs) often include indigenous peoples, people who do not participate in the official economy, people who produce mostly for themselves and their families, and those working under ill-structured manufacturing environments (for example, producers of handicrafts, cultural products, handmade clothing, and so on). In some countries, 20 to 30 percent of the population works in the SCE. A similar problem exists to a lesser extent in many high-income countries.

In addition to the SCE, the production and consumption of illegal goods and services are not reported to the government, and, hence, do not appear in GNI statistics. Neither does production and consumption of goods and services that are not reported to the government in order to avoid sales and income taxes. Studies of several countries estimate that this "underground economy" may equal as much as 20 to 30 percent of reported GNI.

A second problem arises when GNI is compared among countries. The GNI of the United States is expressed in dollars, that of Japan in yen, Germany in deutsche marks, and so on. Comparisons need to be made using a common measure. Most often a country's GNI in domestic currency is converted into U.S. dollars at the prevailing exchange rate (or using an average of the past several years). But unless the exchange rate is maintained at its long-run equilibrium value, this conversion can give misleading results. For example, from 1990 to 1994 the Philippine peso rose from 28 per dollar to 24.5 per dollar and the Philippine GNI in pesos rose from 1,077 billion to 1,694 billion. These numbers led to a rise in GNI (expressed in dollars) from $38 billion to $66.4 billion, a 75 percent increase in GNI and a 60 percent increase in GNI per capita in just four years. If U.S. inflation over this period of a total of about 15 percent is subtracted to give real growth expressed in dollars, these numbers are reduced to 60 percent and 45 percent. Yet real growth in the Philippine GNI and GNI per capita totalled 10.4 percent and 1.4 percent, respectively, over this period. The problem here and in other intercountry comparisons is that the real exchange rate of the Philippines appreciated by about 50 percent over the period.[2]

The final problem is that prices for the same product may not be the same among countries when expressed in a common currency. If a cup of coffee costs 5 cents in India and 3 dollars in Japan, one cup of coffee produced in India would add 5 cents to GNI, but the same cup of coffee produced in Japan would add 3 dollars to Japan's GNI. This effect lowers the GNI (and, hence, the GNI per capita) figures for countries with low prices relative to ones with high prices. This problem can be addressed by restating GNI figures of each country with the same prices for all goods and services. This method is called the purchasing power parity (PPP). If PPP is applied to relatively expensive high-income countries, it usually leads to a fall in reported GNI per capita. Using 2000 data, the GNI per capita of Switzerland on a PPP basis was $30,450 compared with $38,140 using the standard method. This implies that goods and services in Switzerland were on average 12 percent more expensive than in the United States.[3] When the price differences are removed, Switzerland's GNI falls by 25 percent. Using the PPP, in 2000, U.S. GNI per capita of $34,100 was the highest in the world among countries with populations over one million, followed by Switzerland, Norway, Belgium, Denmark and Canada—and ahead of Japan, Germany, France, UK and Italy. Conversely, the GNI per capita levels of low-income countries are raised under the PPP method, in some cases by as much as much as a factor of six.

The PPP method also addresses the problem of changing exchange rates, since it uses common prices in all countries. GNI measured at PPP gives a more realistic measure of the size of a country's markets and its income levels. Notice that it leads to a compression of the range of GNI per capita figures, i.e., the income gap between the richest and the poorest countries is reduced, as is the gap between the incomes of high income countries.

A word of caution is necessary here. The PPP method uses cost comparisons for average consumers. It is not an appropriate measure to use when considering overseas operations or the living expenses of expatriate managers. For example, China's GNI per capita in 2000 as reported by the World Bank was $840 and its PPP GNI per capita was $3,920. This implies a price differential of nearly five times. Yet, for an expatriate manager living in Beijing compared with costs in Boise, Idaho, housing, car, food, and education expenses are all substantially higher, with only a few items being markedly less expensive.

Beyond the average level of income, the distribution of income around this level also has important implications for international management. China's reported GNI per capita was $840 in 2000. Even adjusting for purchasing power parity to $3,920, China still appears to have a low level of income and, hence, little demand for luxury products. Yet Shanghai traffic is chronically jammed, and in the jam are a high proportion of luxury automobiles.

Growth in GNI and GNI per capita reflects rising demand and rising income levels and, hence, market opportunities. These growth figures are usually more accurate than the data on the levels themselves. Increasing demand not only makes a country more attractive as a trade destination or investment site, it may also facilitate entry. Existing suppliers may face capacity constraints. Sales by a new competitor, although reducing the market shares of existing firms, may not reduce their absolute sales volumes. Hence, competitive reaction may be muted.

Some firms have been more astute than others at responding to the changing income levels in certain countries. Phillips has the major share of the electric lamps sold in Indonesia. As electricity is extended into the countryside, it has introduced 15-watt bulbs priced at less than half the price of its 100-watt bulbs (even though the delivered cost is almost the same) to fit the income levels, demand characteristics, and voltage levels in these areas. Over time, it introduces higher-priced, higher wattage bulbs as income levels rise and as the people become accustomed to using (Phillips) electric lighting.

To this point, the analysis has been based on the past performance of the economy. This analysis is useful for many purposes, such as market size, income distribution, and wage rates. But as with many areas of business management and strategy, some indications of future performance are also useful. Forecasting growth has proven to be difficult at best for economists. Two organizations, the World Economic Forum and the Institute for Management Development, each construct a "World Competitiveness Report," which rank countries based on hundreds of factors that are thought to contribute to future growth. The overall rankings for each are in Exhibit 2.2. There are some significant differences between the two sets of rankings: the UK is ranked fourth by one method, twelfth in the other; Canada is third in one ranking, ninth in another; Taiwan is seventh in one ranking, eighteenth in the other. But there is a rough correspondence between the two rankings. Beyond these overall rankings, the two reports also rank countries based on natural resource availability, labor costs and quality, political stability, tax rates, and so on. These reports can provide a wealth of data on current and future economic conditions in many countries in the world.

Overall economic development has improved dramatically in the past 25 years—including the standard of living in the developing countries. Per capita incomes have grown nearly one and a half percent per year for the five billion people in the developing countries. This has brought real progress in the quality of life: infant mortality has dropped, life expectancy has risen, primary school enrollments and adult literacy have improved, food production growth has exceeded population growth, and so forth.

None of this is to suggest that there is not still substantial need for further economic development. Arguably the world's greatest scandal is that over a billion people in the developing world live in extreme poverty—subsisting on less than $1.00 a day. Since "a rising tide does float all boats," the effective international manager can have a positive impact on this situation.

TRADE, NATURAL RESOURCES, AND FOREIGN INVESTMENT

An analysis of the trade volumes, growth rates, composition, and destinations and sources can provide useful insights into emerging sources of supply, shifting comparative and competitive advantage, and new markets. Trade as a percentage of GNI is

EXHIBIT 2.2 World Competitiveness Rankings

Economy	World Economic Forum	IMD Ranking	Economy	World Economic Forum	IMD Ranking
Finland	1	3	Thailand	33	38
United States	2	1	South Africa	34	42
Canada	3	9	Costa Rica	35	—
Singapore	4	2	Greece	36	30
Australia	5	11	Czech Republic	37	35
Norway	6	20	Trinidad Tobago	38	—
Taiwan	7	18	China	39	33
Netherlands	8	5	Slovak Republic	40	37
Sweden	9	8	Poland	41	47
New Zealand	10	21	Mexico	42	36
Ireland	11	7	Lithuania	43	—
United Kingdom	12	19	Brazil	44	31
Hong Kong	13	—	Jordan	45	—
Denmark	14	15	Uruguay	46	—
Switzerland	15	10	Latvia	47	—
Iceland	16	13	Philippines	48	40
Germany	17	12	Argentina	49	43
Austria	18	14	Dominican Republic	50	—
Belgium	19	17	Egypt	51	—
France	20	25	Jamaica	52	—
Japan	21	26	Panama	53	—
Spain	22	23	Turkey	54	44
Korea	23	28	Peru	55	—
Israel	24	16	Romania	56	—
Portugal	25	34	India	57	41
Italy	26	32	El Salvador	58	—
Chile	27	24	Bulgaria	59	—
Hungary	28	27	Vietnam	60	—
Estonia	29	22	Sri Lanka	61	—
Malaysia	30	29	Venezuela	62	48
Slovenia	31	39	Russia	63	45
Mauritius	32	—	Indonesia	64	49
			Colombia	65	46

Source: The World Economic Forum, The Global Competitiveness Report 2001. IMD, The World Competitiveness Yearbook 2001.

very important to some countries, such as Hong Kong, Ireland, the Netherlands, and Taiwan.[4] For other countries—particularly those with large domestic markets such as the United States, Japan, and Brazil—trade as a percentage of GNI is much lower. Over the past decade, growth in trade has been highest in many of the countries of the Asia-Pacific Rim and has stagnated in many of the countries of Africa (see Exhibit 2.3).

By the year 2000, the United States still accounted for the largest share of world merchandise trade, with approximately 12.3 percent of world exports and a whopping 18.9 percent of world imports, followed by Germany and Japan (Exhibit 2.3).

EXHIBIT 2.3 Leading Exporters and Importers in World Merchandise Trade, 2000
($ billions and percentage)

Rank				2000		Rank				2000	
1998	1999	2000	Exporters	Value	Share%	1998	1999	2000	Importers	Value	Share%
1	1	1	United States	781.1	12.3%	1	1	1	United States	1,257.6	18.9%
2	2	2	Germany	551.5	8.7	2	2	2	Germany	502.8	7.5
3	3	3	Japan	479.2	7.5	5	4	3	Japan	379.5	5.7
4	4	4	France	298.1	4.7	3	3	4	United Kingdom	337.0	5.1
5	5	5	United Kingdom	284.1	4.5	4	5	5	France	305.4	4.6
7	6	6	Canada	276.6	4.3	7	7	6	Canada	244.8	3.7
9	9	7	China	249.3	3.9	6	6	7	Italy	236.5	3.5
6	7	8	Italy	237.8	3.7	11	10	8	China	225.1	3.4
8	8	9	Netherlands	212.5	3.3	9	9	9	Hong Kong, China	214.2	3.2
11	11	10	Hong Kong, China	202.4	3.2	8	8	10	Netherlands	198.0	3.0
10	10	11	Belgium	186.1	2.9	13	12	11	Mexico	182.6	2.7
12	12	12	Korea, Rep. of	172.3	2.7	10	11	12	Belgium	173.0	2.6
13	13	13	Mexico	166.4	2.6	16	14	13	Korea, Rep. of	160.5	2.4
14	14	14	Taipei, Chinese	148.3	2.3	12	13	14	Spain	153.5	2.3
15	15	15	Singapore	137.9	2.2	14	16	15	Taipei, Chinese	140.0	2.1
16	16	16	Spain	113.7	1.8	15	15	16	Singapore	134.5	2.0
19	20	17	Russian Fed.	105.2	1.7	17	17	17	Switzerland	83.6	1.3
20	18	18	Malaysia	98.2	1.5	23	21	18	Malaysia	82.2	1.2
17	17	19	Sweden	86.9	1.4	18	20	19	Sweden	72.8	1.1
30	25	20	Saudi Arabia	84.1	1.3	20	19	20	Australia	71.5	1.1
18	19	21	Switzerland	81.5	1.3	19	18	21	Austria	68.6	1.0
21	21	22	Ireland	79.9	1.3	29	23	22	Thailand	61.9	0.9
24	23	23	Thailand	69.1	1.1	21	22	23	Brazil	58.5	0.9
22	22	24	Austria	63.9	1.0	26	29	24	Turkey	53.5	0.8
23	24	25	Australia	63.9	1.0	27	24	25	Iceland	50.9	0.8
26	27	26	Indonesia	62.1	1.0	28	26	26	India	50.5	0.8
29	29	27	Norway	60.0	0.9	24	25	27	Poland	48.9	0.7
25	28	28	Brazil	55.1	0.9	22	28	28	Russian Fed.	45.5	0.7
27	26	29	Denmark	49.6	0.8	25	27	29	Denmark	44.3	0.7
28	30	30	Finland	45.6	0.7	30	30	30	Portugal	38.2	0.6
31	32	31	India	42.3	0.7	37	32	31	Israel	38.1	0.6
35	33	32	United Arab Emirates	39.9	0.6	31	31	32	Norway	34.4	0.5
32	31	33	Philippines	39.8	0.6	32	34	33	Finland	33.9	0.5
42	42	34	Venezuela	31.8	0.5	33	33	34	Philippines	33.8	0.5
33	34	35	Poland	31.7	0.5	41	42	35	Indonesia	33.5	0.5
41	38	36	Israel	31.3	0.5	40	36	36	Czech Rep.	32.2	0.5
44	43	37	Iran, Islamic Rep. of	30.0	0.5	42	38	37	Hungary	32.1	0.5
37	35	38	South Africa	30.0	0.5	39	35	38	United Arab Emirates	31.9	0.5
38	37	39	Czech Rep.	29.0	0.5	36	37	39	Saudi Arabia	30.3	0.5
40	39	40	Hungary	28.1	0.4	38	39	40	South Africa	29.7	0.4
			Total	5,836.5	91.7%				Total	6,006.0	90.1%
			World	6,364.0	100.0%				World	6,669.0	100.0%

Source: WTO, International Trade Statistics 2001.

The United States also had by far the largest share of world trade in commercial services (Exhibit 2.4). Over the past two decades, the trade exposure of the United States, defined as exports plus imports as a percentage of GDI, has increased. But by the year 2000, the trade exposure of the United States was still below that of most major countries.

Over the past decades, there have been three trends in the trade of manufactured products. The volume of trade in manufactured products has risen dramatically. The number of source countries has risen as well. And the composition of the trade of many countries has changed. These trends have been driven by the spread of product and process technology, the fall of transportation costs relative to production costs, and the reduction of tariff and nontariff barriers to trade (until the past five years). Rising real wages in some high-income countries and in the NICs (newly industrializing countries) have led to labor-intensive products being produced in lower-income countries. Nontariff barriers to trade, such as quotas, have also provided incentives for firms to move production to countries that have not had quotas imposed on them. For example, one U.S. importer of jeans compared a list of all the countries on which the United States imposed quotas on jeans and a list of all low-wage countries. He then went to several countries in southern Africa (which did not face quotas) to find firms with supply capabilities. He now imports jeans from Botswana.

Another influence on the volume, patterns, and composition of trade has been the change in the trade strategies of many developing countries—most notably China, Brazil, and Mexico, and more recently India and Indonesia—toward export promotion. The large populations of these countries and the rapid growth of their labor forces imply that real wages will continue to be low for many years into the future. Hence, unlike the NICs, they should remain low-cost producers of labor-intensive products for many years to come.

Trade in services has increased as a percentage of international trade and there is every likelihood that this trend will continue in the future. The United States leads the world in exports of services: financial services, visual and audio media, shipping, insurance, advertising, and so on. In the coming decades, tourism is likely to be the highest growth sector in trade. Already trade in tourism is the major export of many countries (Exhibit 2.4).

Over the past few decades, the relative value of unprocessed natural resources in international trade has declined. But, over the past decade, a combination of technology transfer and relatively low labor and, in some instances, land costs has led to a rapid increase in the number of countries that have begun to export fresh and processed agricultural and fishery products. These products have often been sold as "off brands" or "house brands" to price-sensitive consumers in high-income countries. Examples are: canned sardines, tuna fish, and pineapple (Thailand and Indonesia), orange juice (Brazil), apple juice (many countries), and fresh flowers (several countries in South America, and Africa). In the years to come, it is likely that this trend will continue and that greater volumes of an increased variety of agricultural products will be exported from a wider number of countries. The other factor in trade in agricultural products over the past 15 years

EXHIBIT 2.4 **Leading Exporters and Importers in World Trade in Commercial Services, 2000**
($ billions and percentage)

Rank 1998	Rank 1999	Rank 2000	Exporters	2000 Value	2000 Share%	Rank 1998	Rank 1999	Rank 2000	Importers	2000 Value	2000 Share%
21	21	21	Ireland	79.9	1.3	29	23	22	Thailand	61.9	0.9%
1	1	1	United States	274.6	19.1%	1	1	1	United States	198.9	13.8%
2	2	2	United Kingdom	99.9	7.0	2	2	2	Germany	132.3	9.2
3	3	3	France	81.2	5.7	3	3	3	Japan	115.7	8.1
4	4	4	Germany	80.0	5.6	4	4	4	United Kingdom	82.1	5.7
6	6	5	Japan	68.3	4.8	5	5	5	France	61.5	4.3
5	5	6	Italy	56.7	4.0	6	6	6	Italy	55.7	3.9
8	7	7	Spain	53.0	3.7	7	7	7	Netherlands	51.1	3.6
7	8	8	Netherlands	52.3	3.6	8	8	8	Canada	41.9	2.9
10	10	9	Hong Kong, China	42.1	2.9	9	9	9	Belgium-Luxembourg	38.3	2.7
9	9	10	Belgium-Luxembourg	42.0	2.9	13	10	10	China	35.9	2.5
11	11	11	Canada	37.2	2.6	14	13	11	Korea, Rep. of	33.4	2.3
15	14	12	China	30.1	2.1	12	11	12	Spain	30.8	2.1
12	12	13	Austria	30.0	2.1	11	12	13	Austria	29.1	2.0
14	15	14	Korea, Rep. of	29.2	2.0	10	14	14	Ireland	28.7	2.0
17	16	15	Singapore	26.6	1.9	15	15	15	Hong Kong, China	26.2	1.8
13	13	16	Switzerland	26.4	1.8	16	16	16	Taipei, Chinese	25.7	1.8
22	20	17	Denmark	20.6	1.4	17	17	17	Sweden	23.4	1.6
19	18	18	Taipei, Chinese	20.2	1.4	18	18	18	Singapore	21.3	1.5
18	17	19	Sweden	20.0	1.4	24	20	19	India	19.9	1.4
16	21	20	Turkey	19.2	1.3	21	22	20	Denmark	18.3	1.3
21	19	21	Australia	17.8	1.2	19	19	21	Australia	17.7	1.2
28	24	22	India	17.6	1.2	20	27	22	Russian Fed.	17.4	1.2
20	22	23	Ireland	16.6	1.2	27	25	23	Mexico	16.8	1.2
23	25	24	Norway	15.0	1.0	26	23	24	Malaysia	16.6	1.2
31	28	25	Israel	14.3	1.0	22	28	25	Brazil	15.9	1.1
37	26	26	Malaysia	13.6	0.9	23	21	26	Switzerland	15.5	1.1
26	27	27	Mexico	13.6	0.9	28	26	27	Thailand	14.7	1.0
24	23	28	Thailand	12.8	0.9	25	24	28	Norway	14.5	1.0
33	29	29	Egypt	9.7	0.7	32	30	29	Israel	12.1	0.8
25	30	30	Russian Fed.	9.6	0.7	34	31	30	Saudi Arabia	10.9	0.8
29	32	31	Poland	9.5	0.7	33	33	31	Argentina	8.6	0.6
36	33	32	Brazil	8.8	0.6	35	34	32	Finland	8.2	0.6
32	31	33	Portugal	8.3	0.6	31	32	33	Turkey	7.6	0.5
35	34	34	Czech Rep.	7.1	0.5	37	36	34	Poland	7.4	0.5
38	36	35	Hungary	6.2	0.4	38	38	35	Egypt	7.2	0.5
37	35	36	Finland	6.0	0.4	36	37	36	Portugal	6.4	0.4
39	38	37	South Africa	4.9	0.3	30	35	37	Philippines	6.1	0.4
40	37	38	Saudi Arabia	4.8	0.3	39	39	38	Czech Rep.	5.8	0.4
41	41	39	Argentina	4.4	0.3	40	40	39	South Africa	5.4	0.4
46	42	40	New Zealand	4.2	0.3	43	41		New Zealand	4.5	0.3
			Total	1,314.5	91.6%				Total	1,289.4	89.7%
			World	1,435.4	100.0%				World	1,436.9	100.0%

Source: WTO, International Trade Statistics 2001.

has been the transformation of the EU (European Union) as a whole from the largest importer to the largest exporter of agricultural products. (This development was the root cause of one of the major points of friction in the Uruguay round of the GATT negotiations. See Chapter 4.)

Foreign direct investment has become one of the major means by which companies operate internationally and by which countries are linked. Foreign direct investment (FDI) influences not only the flow of capital but also the flows of product and process technology and trade patterns and volumes. Foreign investment often flows in response to market opportunities, factor costs (such as wages), natural resource availability and cost, the political and economic stability of countries, and the international debt position of the host country. Inflows of FDI not only affect the flows of imports into a country but often, at a later time, affect its exports. Hence, monitoring the volumes and industry composition of FDI is often an early warning signal concerning future exports.

Several other features of FDI flows are of note. They are highly concentrated among a relatively few countries. About three-fourths of the flows of FDI are among the high-income countries, especially within the Triad of Europe, Japan, and North America. Of the FDI that flows to lower-income countries, about two-thirds is concentrated among 10 countries. FDI flows tend to be more volatile over time, both in aggregate and at the country level, than are GDI, domestic investment, and trade. Starting in 1986, FDI boomed, growing at 28.3 percent annually through 1990, compared with growth rates of 13 percent for merchandise exports and 12 percent for nominal GDI. This increase was largely fueled by substantial increases in outward investment from Japan. According to UNCTAD (United Nations Conference on Trade and Development), in 2000, estimated global sales generated by foreign subsidiaries of multinational enterprises (MNEs) totaled $15.7 trillion. This compared with world exports of goods and services (excluding factor payments) of $6.4 trillion. About a third of international trade is estimated to be intrafirm, i.e., between subsidiaries of MNEs in different countries.

Another feature of FDI is that the number of firms that have become multinational enterprises (MNEs) has increased steadily over the decades, and the number of home countries in which MNEs are based has increased as well. These trends have increased the complexity of the world competitive environment. In the second half of the 1980s, Japan became the largest source country for FDI, overtaking the United States and Britain. In the mid-1990s, the United States regained first place among outward investing countries. The United States also became the largest host country for inward FDI (Exhibit 2.5). Among Developing Countries, China has the largest stock of inward FDI.

Finally, it is worth asking which firms are making the actual investments. The UNCTC estimates there are over 60,000 transnational corporations with over 800,000 affiliates abroad. Exhibits 2.6 and 2.7 provide respectively some detail on the world's 25 largest TNCs overall, plus the 10 largest from developing countries. The sales and employment levels of some of these firms are much larger than the gross national income and populations of many of the world's countries.

EXHIBIT 2.5   FDI Statistics

	France	Germany	Japan	United Kingdom	United States	Developing Economies
Outflows of FDI (1997-2000, $ billions)	377	289	106	639	509	261
Shares of FDI outflows (1991-1996, percent)	9%	9%	8%	12%	24%	13%
Shares of FDI outflows (1997-2000, percent)	11%	9%	3%	19%	15%	8%
Inward stock of FDI (2000, $ billions)	267	461	54	483	1239	1979
Percentage of world total, inward FDI stock (2000)	4%	7%	1%	8%	20%	31%
Outward stock of FDI (2000, $ billions)	497	443	282	902	1245	710
Percentage of world total, outward FDI stock (2000)	8%	7%	5%	15%	21%	12%

THE ENVIRONMENT

The days of uncontrolled international economic growth with little consideration for the environment are over. For example, in 1993, progress on signing a North American Free Trade Agreement was in jeopardy due to U.S. concerns over whether Mexico would legislate (and enforce) environmental protection.

For the multinational enterprise and its managers, the task of doing business internationally has become more complicated as everyone becomes aware of the impact of economic development on the environment. Waste creation (and disposal), water supply and use, air quality, overfishing and overlogging, acid rain, and so forth variously affect businesses no matter where they are located. As an example, in the Philippines some Japanese companies have complained that new environmental standards for new investments are more stringent than they are in Japan—and that even if they were willing to bear the costs of meeting them, the government does not have the equipment to test for compliance to these standards. In addition, the number of constituencies that multinational firms are potentially answerable to has increased dramatically with the heightened awareness of our interconnectedness. This has raised both ethical and legal problems for MNEs. As but one of many examples, some countries have relatively loose standards for water discharge from rayon plants to encourage investment, employment, and output in this industry and allow supplying its downstream textile industry at low cost. What are the legal and ethical responsibilities of MNEs when choosing their technology in undertaking such an investment? Both MNEs and national governments are increasingly trying to balance economic growth and environmental management.

EXHIBIT 2.6 The World's 25 Largest TNCs, Ranked by Foreign Assets, 1999 (Billions of dollars and number of employees)

Corporation	Country	Industry[b]	Assets		Sales		Employment		TNI[a] Percent
			Foreign	Total	Foreign	Total	Foreign	Total	
General Electric	United States	Electronics	141.1	405.2	32.7	111.6	143000	310000	36.7
Exxon Mobil Corporation	United States	Petroleum expl/ref/distr	99.4	144.5	115.5	160.9	68000	107000	68.0
Royal Dutch/Shell Group[c]	The Netherlands/ United Kingdom	Petroleum expl/ref/distr	68.7	113.9	53.5	105.4	57367	99310	56.3
General Motors	United States	Motor Vehicles	68.5	274.7	46.5	176.6	162300	398000	30.7
Ford Motor Company	United States	Motor Vehicles	—	273.4	50.1	162.6	191486	364550	36.1
Toyota Motor Corporation	Japan	Motor Vehicles	56.3	154.9	60.0	119.7	13500	214631	30.9
Daimler Chrysler AG	Germany	Motor Vehicles	55.7	175.9	122.4	151.0	225705	466938	53.7
TotalFina SA	France	Petroleum expl/ref/distr	44.7	77.6	31.6	39.6	50538	74437	70.3
IBM	United States	Computers	44.7	87.5	50.4	87.6	161612	307401	53.7
BP	United Kingdom	Petroleum expl/ref/distr	39.3	52.6	57.7	83.5	62150	80400	73.7
Nestle SA	Switzerland	Food/beverages	33.1	36.8	45.9	46.7	224554	230929	95.2
Volkswagen Group	Germany	Motor Vehicles	—	64.3	47.8	70.6	147959	306275	55.7
Nippon Mitsubishi Oil Corp. (Nippon Oil Co. Ltd)	Japan	Petroleum expl/ref/distr	31.5	35.5	28.4	33.9	11900	15964	82.4
Siemens AG	Germany	Electronics	30.2	76.6	53.2	72.2	251000	443000	56.8
Wal-Mart Stores	United States	Retailing	30.2	50.0	19.4	137.6	—	1140000	25.8
Repsol-YPF SA	Spain	Petroleum expl/ref/distr	29.6	42.1	9.1	26.3	59852	29262	51.6
Diageo Plc	United Kingdom	Beverages	28.0	40.4	16.4	19.0	58694	72479	79.4
Mannesmann AG	Germany	Telecom/engineering	—	57.7	11.8	21.8	150000	130860	48.9
Suez Lyonnaise des Eaux	France	Diversified/utility	—	71.6	9.7	23.5	46104	220000	49.1
BMW AG	Germany	Motor Vehicles	27.1	39.2	26.8	36.7	155427	114952	60.9
ABB	Switzerland	Electrical Equipment	27.0	30.6	23.8	24.4	115717	161430	94.1
Sony Corporation	Japan	Electronics	—	64.2	43.1	63.1	222614	189700	56.7
Seagram Corporation	Canada	Beverages/media	25.6	35.0	12.3	11.8	—	—	88.6
Unilever	United Kingdom/ The Netherlands	Food/beverages	25.3	28.0	38.4	44.0	222614	246033	89.3
Aventis	France	Pharmaceuticals/ chemicals	—	39.0	4.7	19.2	—	92446	54.0

Source: UNCTAD, World Investment Report 2001: Promoting Linkages, table iii, p. 90.

[a]TNI is the abbreviation for "transnationality index." The transnationality index is calculated as the average of three ratios: foreign assets to total assets, foreign sales to total sales and foreign employment to total employment.

[b]Industry classification for companies follows the United States Standard Industrial Classification as used by the United States Securities and Exchange Commission (SEC).

[c]Foreign assets, sales and employment are outside Europe.

.. Data on foreign assets, foreign sales and foreign employment were not made available for the purpose of this study. In case of non-availability, they are estimated using secondary sources of information or on the basis of the ratios of foreign to total assets, foreign to total sales and foreign to total employment.

Note: the list includes nonfinancial TNCs only. In some companies, foreign investors may hold a minority share of more than 10 percent.

EXHIBIT 2.7   **The Largest 10 TNS from Developing Economics, Ranked by Foreign Assets, 1999
(Millions of dollars, number of employees)**

Corporation	Country	Industry[b]	Assets		Sales		Employment		TNI[a] Percent
			Foreign	Total	Foreign	Total	Foreign	Total	
Hutchison Whampoa Ltd.	Hong Kong, China	Diversified	—	48157	2096	7108	—	42510	38.0
Petróleos de Venezuela	Venezuela	Petroleum expl/ ref/distr	8009	47250	13332	32600	15000	47760	29.8
Cemex SA	Mexico	Construction	6973	11896	2504	4841	—	20902	54.6
Petrons-Petroliam Nasional Berhad	Malaysia	Petroleum expl/ /ref/distr	—	31992	—	15957	—	18578	19.8
Samsung Corporation	Korea, Rep. Of	Diversified/Trade	5127	21581	6339	37180	1911	4600	27.4
Daewoo Corporation	Korea, Rep. Of	Diversified/Trade	—	16460	—	18618	—	12021	49.4
Lg Electronics Inc.	Korea, Rep. Of	Electronics/ electrical equip	4215	17273	6383	15590	27000	50000	39.8
Sunkyong Group	Korea, Rep. Of	Energy/Trading/ Chemicals	4214	34542	10762	43457	2273	26296	15.2
New World Development Co., Ltd.	Hong Kong, China	Construction	4097	14789	368	2259	788	22945	15.8
Samsung Electronics Co., Ltd.	Korea, Rep. Of	Electronics/ electrical equip	3907	25487	5214	28024	6039	39350	16.4

Source: UNCTAD, World Investment Report 2001: Promoting Linkages, table III.9, p. 105.

Summary

These are only a few of the facts that are useful and relevant for international managers. They can provide but a start for an understanding of the international environment in which international managers must operate. Beyond these basics, an international manager needs more product-specific information. For example, if the manager works for a garment producer, information on the top exporters and importers and the growth rates of these imports and exports of textiles and garments is needed. Which country had the largest increase in garment exports over the past 10 years? Which country's exports are most highly concentrated in garments? Which countries are gaining comparative advantage in textiles and garments and which ones are losing it? How are markets and production of textiles segmented worldwide? And so on.

Also, as described in more detail in the next chapters, increasing international trade and investment are no longer undertaken on a country-by-country basis, but rather are undertaken on a regional, even global basis. This complicates the analysis manyfold.

An incredible amount and variety of data are available to managers. Knowledge of appropriate international data and the skills to interpret these data are an important start in reaching effective international management decisions.

Supplementary Reading

CIA. *The CIA World Factbook* (Washington, D.C.: CIA, annual editions; also available on CD-ROM and at http://www.odci.gov/cia).

Dreifus, Shirley B., and Michael Moynihan. *The World Market Atlas.* New York: Business International Corporation, annual editions.

IMD. *The World Competitiveness Yearbook 2001.* Lausanne: IMD, 2001; a summary is also available at http://www.imd.ch/wcy.html.

Kidron, Michael, and Ronald Segal. *The State of the World Atlas.* 5th ed. New York: Penguin Books, 1995.

Kurian, George. *The New Book of World Rankings.* 3rd ed. New York: Facts on File, 1991.

Tsai, Terence. *The Fight to Be Green: The Struggle for Corporate Environmentalism in China and Taiwan.* London: Macmillan Press, 1999.

The World Bank. *The World Bank Atlas.* Washington, The World Bank, annual editions. www.worldbank.org/data/

World Economic Forum. *Global Competitiveness Report 2001.* Geneva: World Economic Forum, 2001.

Endnotes

1. See *The New Book of World Rankings and The CIA World Factbook* (referenced at the end of this chapter) for these and other interesting statistics.
2. See Chapter 3 for a description of the real exchange rate. This has particularly important implications in periods of rapid fluctuations. For example, in early 1999 the Philippine peso had declined to 38 per dollar.
3. The news magazine *The Economist* regularly publishes its "Big Mac Index," which compares prices of a Big Mac hamburger from McDonald's restaurants among a number of countries as a measure of relative prices. Switzerland regularly has the highest-priced Big Macs, when converted to dollars, suggesting it is the most overvalued currency.
4. Again there is a problem with these figures. International trade takes place in international currencies. Hence there is not a problem with understating it or overstating it based on differing prices, the PPP problem described above. GDP and GNP figures, however, are over- and understated because of differing prices. This tends to overstate the trade exposure of low-cost, usually developing, countries and understate the trade exposure of high-cost countries such as Switzerland and Japan.

Chapter Three

The World of International Trade

International trade has been carried on between countries and geographical regions for thousands of years. Over the centuries, international trade, although periodically interrupted by wars and natural disasters, has gradually expanded, usually at a faster pace than the expansion of world output. The impetus for the existence and expansion of international trade is the same as that for any commercial transaction: value creation. International trade creates value for both producers and consumers. International trade increases demand for exportable products, thereby raising prices and volumes. It increases the supply of importable products, thereby reducing prices and increasing product availability and variety for consumers. International trade increases the efficiency of resource allocation worldwide, reduces production costs through economies of scale, and lowers input costs.

International trade can also lead to increased exposure for both firms and countries to the forces in the international economy: changes in prices and demand in export markets, changes in prices and supply of imported products, and changes in exchange rates. The increased openness to the international economic environment can increase the variability of a firm's profits and of a nation's GNP growth rate and hence increase the risks of a firm's operations and reduce the stability of a country's economy. International trade can also lead to disruption and restructuring as domestic firms are forced to compete with less expensive or higher quality imported products. On the other hand, international trade can allow firms to diversify away from dependence on demand in one country and can allow a country to diversify its economy through exports.

Every major firm is affected by international trade in one way or another: as an exporter; as an importer; as a competitor with imports; or as a financial institution

This chapter was prepared by Andrew Inkpen.

involved in trade finance, foreign exchange markets, and international debt management. Similarly, the economies and firms in every country are affected by international trade flows—and there is every likelihood that these effects will increase into the foreseeable future.

A knowledge of international trade—the forces behind it and the means by which it is carried out—is essential to all business managers, not just to those directly engaged in international business operations. International trade, exporting and importing, is often the first form of international operations for firms in the manufacturing, natural resource, energy, and agricultural sectors. In 2000, world merchandise trade exceeded $6.4 trillion, up from less than $5 trillion in 1995. The dollar value of world commercial services exports was $1.4 trillion in 2000.

International trade is inextricably linked with foreign direct investment, international technology transfer, and international finance: international trade often leads to foreign direct investment which in turn often changes trade flows and patterns. Trade also leads to international financial flows and in turn trade is affected by foreign exchange availability and exchange rate movements. Technology transfer is often accomplished through international trade in capital goods and, in turn, technology transfer leads to trade in raw materials and semifinished and final products.

THE INTERNATIONAL TRADE ENVIRONMENT

The real value (the volume) of world exports expanded nearly threefold (10.2 percent per year on average) between 1970 and 1980 (from $700 billion to $2 trillion in constant 1980 dollars). This expansion was fostered by falling tariff and non-tariff barriers to trade in most countries, decreased transportation and communication costs, and by the export-oriented growth strategies of many countries during this period. During the global recession in the early 1980s, world trade declined in real terms by a greater amount than did world GDP. The decline in world trade worsened the recession in many countries. From 1990 to 2000, however, the average annual increase in world merchandise export *volume* was 7 percent. The *volume* of world merchandise exports grew by 12 percent in 2000, the highest rate recorded in more than two decades (See Exhibit 3.1 for the growth rates in international trade and world GDP).

Measured in terms of combined merchandise imports and exports, the United States is the largest trading nation in the world, with 12.3 percent of world exports and 18.9 percent of world imports in 2000. The relative trading power of the United States, which had fallen over the past several decades, improved in the 1990s. The positions of Italy, Canada, the Netherlands, and Belgium also have improved, while those of Russia, Saudi Arabia, and Sweden have fallen. The most dramatic changes have come from export-oriented newly industrializing countries (NICs), and in particular, Asian countries such as South Korea, Malaysia, Singapore, Taiwan, and Thailand. Although the Asian financial crisis in 1997 resulted in declining imports for Indonesia, South Korea, and Thailand, the end of the decade

EXHIBIT 3.1   Growth in the Volume of World Merchandise Exports and GDP 1989–2000
(Annual percentage change)

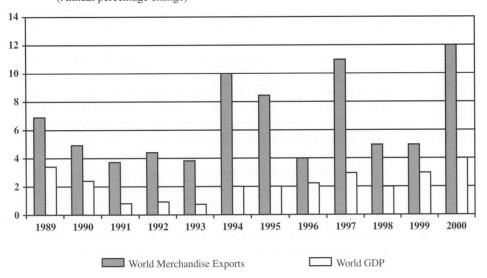

showed that imports were again on the rise. In 2000, Indonesia's imports increased 40 percent, Korea's 34 percent, Thailand's 23 percent, and Malaysia's 27 percent.

The fall of the US dollar[1] from 1985 to 1988 led to a strong recovery of U.S. exports and a reduction in the growth rate of imports. Export volume increased by 68 percent from 1985 to 1991, while import volume increased by 20 percent. This situation led to increased trade deficits as import growth exceeded export growth. The rise in the value of the dollar in the mid-1990s contributed to further trade deficits. By 2000, the merchandise trade deficit of the U.S. had increased to $476 billion.

Until the early 1980s, the U.S. current account was roughly in balance. Since 1982, however, its trade deficits have led to substantial current account deficits totaling $1,260 billion over the 1982 to 1995 period. In 1999 alone, the U.S. current account deficit was $450 billion. Current account deficits translate roughly into surpluses on the capital account. Hence, the United States went from being a net creditor with the rest of the world of about $400 billion to a net debtor of about $900 billion in 1994. If the United States is to stop going further and further into debt with the rest of the world, its trade balance will have to improve in the next decade following its deterioration in the 1990s. The trade deficit will have to become a trade surplus to compensate for the interest and dividends on its accumulated international debt and net inward foreign direct investment. The longer this reversal from a trade deficit to a trade surplus is delayed, the greater the eventual surplus will have to be—otherwise U.S. international indebtedness will continue to rise.

As the trade deficit in the United States declined starting in the late 1980s through the early 1990s, its trading partners had to absorb about a $90 billion annual turnaround on their trade accounts through increased import growth rates and decreased export growth rates. This had a depressing effect on their economies, while at the same time it spurred U.S. economic growth. The deterioration of the U.S. trade account throughout the 1990s reduced U.S. economic growth and increased growth for its trading partners. If the U.S. trade deficit is to become a trade surplus, the trade accounts of its partners will have to accommodate this through substantial increases in import growth rates and a slowing of export growth rates. Most developing countries are not in a position to increase imports or decrease exports; they have debt problems of their own. If anything, their goals are to accelerate export growth. The oil exporters will not absorb it; oil prices will be stable at best, and U.S. imports of oil will continue to rise.

That leaves Japan, some European countries, Canada, and Asian countries such as Taiwan, South Korea, Singapore, and Hong Kong to make the adjustment. However, with continued economic malaise in Japan, a reduction of Asian exports is unlikely. And no country wants to reduce exports or increase import growth rates for fear of reducing its own economic growth rate. One reaction to the U.S. trade and international debt problems has been a rise in protectionism, as each country has tried to shift the adjustment costs onto someone else. From 1980 to 1988, the percentage of U.S. imports under some form of nontariff restraint rose from 8 to 24 percent. These trade restraints cost U.S. consumers tens (some say hundreds) of billions of dollars per year. The United States has also enacted trade legislation that requires the government each year to assemble a "hit list" of countries that are not dealing fairly with American exports, investments or intellectual property (patents and trademarks). This list is then used as a basis of negotiations with these countries, and in the event the outcomes of these negotiations are not satisfactory, to impose trade sanctions. The rancor of the trade disputes between the United States and Japan, China and even Canada was in part due to the United States' mounting trade deficits.

Major political leaders may also have significant implications for the world trade environment. The Uruguay round of GATT negotiations resulted in the establishment of the World Trade Organization (WTO) and produced some of the most basic changes to the GATT since it was implemented in 1947. In North and South America, the Free Trade Area of the Americas (FTAA) is under negotiation among 34 nations in the American hemisphere for completion in 2005. Yet in the political campaign of 1996, NAFTA itself came under attack by some U.S. politicians as being detrimental to U.S. interests.

The gains from the negotiation and implementation of trading agreements such as GATT, NAFTA, and FTAA can be great. The conclusion of the Uruguay round of negotiations is expected to result in global income gains of $230 billion per year by the year 2005 (in 1992 dollars). More than half of this income gain is expected to go to developed countries, and one-third of the gain will accrue to developing countries. Most of the reductions in protection were in the manufacturing sector. Services received almost no liberalization, while agriculture received some limited reduction in protection.

Liberalization in the agriculture sector would affect the European Community to a large degree. Prior to the conclusion of the Uruguay round, trade distorting policies in the European Union under the Common Agricultural Policy (CAP) turned the EU from the largest net importer of food products to the largest net food exporter in less than two decades. The CAP cost the EU about $40 billion per year in direct subsidies. The CAP cost consumers in the EU countries roughly an equal amount in higher prices and added 4 percent to the unemployment rate in Europe. In the late 1980s, it precipitated the largest trade war in 40 years, as the United States and Canada responded to agricultural subsidies in Europe with massive increases in the subsidies to their own farmers.[2]

The Uruguay round of the GATT resulted in some reductions in agriculture protection. Nontariff barriers to trade in agriculture were converted to tariff equivalents, which were scheduled for reduction in the future. The extension of GATT over trade in agricultural products was important in placing agricultural trade under firmer international regulations, and for setting the stage for future gains over time and in later negotiations. The establishment of the WTO also helps to alleviate fears of the development of a "fortress Europe" for exporters from Japan and North America. In 2001, China and Taiwan gained formal approval for entry into the WTO.

Prior to the Uruguay round, North America's other large trading partner, Japan, had reduced its explicit tariff and nontariff barriers to trade on most products to levels below those in most other countries and had ceased its policy of undervaluing its exchange rate (to increase exports and reduce imports). In the first half of the 1990s, the yen continued its appreciation against major currencies in the world, and especially against the U.S. dollar. Japan's real exchange rate appreciated by over 60 percent from 1985 to 1994. By the end of 1995, 100 yen could purchase $1 U.S., a marked change from the 240 yen required for $1 U.S. in 1985. Over the next few years the yen fluctuated in value against the U.S. dollar, dropping as low as 147 yen to the dollar in 1998 and rising to 101 in January 2001. In early 2002 the exchange rate was about 130 yen to the dollar. Over this period, Japan continued to run large merchandise trade surpluses. In 2000 Japan's merchandise trade surplus was $100 billion. These mounting trade surpluses have often brought Japan's trading policies under the scrutiny of its major trading partners, although in 2002 there was less concern than in previous years. The reason is that world trade patterns have changed dramatically over the past few decades and head-to-head competition between Japanese companies and U.S. companies has declined. As well, Japanese manufacturers are increasingly shifting their operations to China. Toshiba, for example, stated in 2002 that it planned to produce 80 percent of its copiers sold worldwide in China.

Historically, Japan's domestic market structure and its international trade was dominated by large trading houses and industrial groups. Its distribution channels for manufactured products have proven difficult at best for Western exporters to penetrate. The Japanese government has followed a mercantilist trade strategy toward high-technology trade products in emerging industries, such as telecommunications and computers, through a combination of direct subsidies, market protection, and government purchasing regulations. Under duress, Japan has agreed to replace quantitative restrictions on rice imports with tariffs, but the replacement process has been slow and the initial tariffs were on the order of 700 percent.

One view of Japan's future trade and economic strategies has been graphically expressed by the late Mr. Morita (former chairman of the board of Sony) and Mr. Ishihara (an elected official) in *The Japan That Can Say "No."* They wrote about a Japan that is largely independent of U.S. economic and political pressures and has reoriented itself toward leading a trading bloc of the countries of the Asia-Pacific Rim, including China. Although there have been proposals for the formation of a formal East Asian trading bloc with Japan as a major player, as yet these have not come to fruition. The Asian financial crisis resulted in many new questions about Asian integration and trade. As well, Japan in 2002 remained mired in a deflationary recession that showed no signs of ending. However, Japan's foreign direct investment and trade activities in Southeast and East Asia are contributing to the economic integration of the national economies of this region.

Among developing countries, there are also major pressures on the trade system. In general throughout the 1980s and the 1990s, the governments of most developing countries moved toward a more liberal position in international trade, both to expand exports and to open their economies to imports. Developing countries have often faced export markets made difficult to penetrate by tight regulations, and this difficulty has contributed to pressure and discontent with the international trade system on the part of developing countries, particularly as it applies to trade in labor intensive products such as textiles, clothing, and footwear.

The conditions of trade established during the Uruguay round help to alleviate some of the pressure and discontent with international trade. Developing countries such as Indonesia, Malaysia, the Republic of Korea, and Thailand stand to benefit most from the new trading agreements. These countries, which are highly competitive exporters of textiles and clothing, have been committed to the liberalization of trade in agriculture and manufacturing. The elimination of the Multifibre Arrangement (a voluntary export restraint agreement), for example, enables these countries to expand their production of low-cost, labor-intensive products. Countries in South Asia (India, Nepal, Pakistan, and Bangladesh) are similarly expected to benefit from the Uruguay round. China and Taiwan, now WTO members, should also benefit.

In 2001 the 141 members of the World Trade Organization met in Doha, Qatar and agreed to launch a new round of multilateral trade liberalizing negotiations. The objective was to get a trade agreement by 2005 that would dramatically expand free trade in areas such as agriculture and services. However, unilateral actions by the United States not long after the Doha meeting gave rise to new fears about an escalation of global trade disputes. In 2002 the United States government imposed 30 percent tariffs on foreign steel and followed this action with a farm bill that extended or re-introduced subsidies for a wide range of farm products. Both actions by the United States unleashed a firestorm of protest from U.S. trading partners around the world.

There are other areas of uncertainty—both opportunity and risk—for firms engaged in international trade: the drive for modernization and deregulation in the economies of China and India; continued economic and political reforms in the eastern European countries; financial turmoil in Argentina and other South American nations; political issues associated with the relationship between the West and the Arab nations; the inability of Japan to correct its economic problems. Yet, it is within this environment that firms must compete in world trade markets if they are to survive, much less prosper.

In short, the pressures on the international trading system in the new millennium are enormous. This is the world of international trade.

A FRAMEWORK FOR INTERNATIONAL TRADE

The international trading environment is complex and ever changing. To manage international trade operations within this environment, a framework of analysis is useful. A framework can be used to disentangle the many factors that drive international flows of goods and services. This section presents one possible framework for analyzing a firm's international trade environment.

To simplify the exposition of this framework, the initial viewpoint will be of a firm with production operations in a single country as it analyzes trade operations with another country. Although this viewpoint is obviously unrealistic in a world of global competition with complex trading arrangements and in which some 33 percent of international trade is carried out by multinational enterprises (MNEs) at the intrafirm level, it can serve as a reasonable starting point for our analysis. Further on, this simple framework is expanded to include multicountry and multifirm trade. Subsequent chapters will describe global sourcing and the complex trade and investment relationships that exist within and between multinational enterprises.

An Overview of the Trade Framework

A Framework for Trade Analysis

1. The Social, Technological, Economic, and Political (STEP) system and how this system affects the firm's comparative and competitive advantage.

2. Countries abroad as markets for exports and sources of imports.

3. Tariff and nontariff barriers to trade and government incentives to promote trade.

4. Linking producers and buyers through trade intermediaries.

The Step System and Comparative and Competitive Advantage

Each firm operates within the social, technological, economic, and political (STEP) environment of the country in which it produces. The STEP environment has a strong influence on the firm: the cost, quality, and range of products it produces, domestic demand for its products, the product and process technology it uses, its efficiency and scale of operations, the cost and availability of natural resources and factor inputs, such as capital and labor, the range of support industries, and how and where it markets its products. The firm's STEP environment influences the *comparative* advantage of the products it produces relative to products produced by other firms abroad. The firm's STEP environment may also influence its *competitive* advantage in the national market and abroad. Trends in this STEP environment relative to the trends in the STEP environment of other countries have a strong influence on a firm's ability to enter or to continue international trading operations.[3]

For example, Singapore's rapid economic development over the past 20 years has led to a substantial rise in real wages relative to those in most other countries. In response to this change in Singapore's comparative advantage in labor-intensive products, firms in the export-oriented, labor-intensive garment industry became less and less competitive on world markets, that is, they lost their comparative advantage arising from Singapore's past relatively low labor costs and high worker efficiency. In response to this change, some firms have changed their *comparative* advantage in the production of low-cost, low-quality, standardized garments to a *comparative* advantage in high-quality designer garments (based on Singapore's relatively low-wage skilled workers). More likely, Singapore-based garment firms have invested abroad. To do this, they have utilized their competitive advantage in managing a low-wage labor force and in their channels of distribution from Singapore to other lower-wage countries onto export markets. Firms that could not respond to these changes in Singapore's comparative advantage with changes in their competitive advantage have gone out of business. Changes in all the elements of the STEP system in which the firm operates can have similar effects on its ability to export or to compete with imports. In other countries, social pressures have led to implementation of strict environmental protection measures. These measures have changed the comparative advantage of heavy, pollution-intensive industries in these countries, such as steel, chemicals, and pulp and paper. Government policies and economic forces can influence the location of technology generation and its diffusion within the country and worldwide by subsidizing these industries in a number of ways. These policies have changed the comparative advantage of some countries in technology-intensive industries.

The STEP system in which a firm operates—and how it responds to and influences comparative and competitive advantage—forms the first block in the analytical framework. This emphasis on the effects of a firm's external environment on its ability to trade is not meant to be deterministic, however. A firm can develop a competitive advantage that enables it to export even though the STEP system in its home country places it at a comparative disadvantage. Kaufman Shoes in Canada exports work boots and after-ski boots worldwide. Kaufman has developed a competitive advantage based on quality, style, and design that has allowed it to compete internationally even though the shoe industry as a whole in Canada is at a comparative disadvantage in international trade. Similarly, in the mid-1980s, Proton component televisions were developed in Taiwan by contracting for state of the art, U.S. design technology. By this means it developed a competitive advantage at the very top end of the line in televisions, despite Taiwan's comparative disadvantage in state-of-the-art technology generation (as opposed to technology transfer and adaptation). For both these firms, however, the STEP systems in which they operate do not foster their competitive advantage, rather they detract from it. Kaufman must constantly strive to maintain its competitive advantage in quality, design, and style over firms in lower-wage countries whose skills on these dimensions are increasing year by year. Similarly, when Proton failed to continue to upgrade its technology by further purchases from abroad, firms in Japan, the United States, and Europe with in-house technology generation capabilities (which Proton lacked) matched its quality at a lower price.

A competitive advantage based on government subsidies (when the country does not have and cannot develop a comparative advantage in the firm's products) is always at risk if funding for these programs is reduced or they are terminated. The budget constraints under which many countries are operating in the 1990s have placed, and will continue to place, pressure on subsidies that come out of the government budgets. As an extreme example, Indonesia fostered the development of a mainframe aircraft producer, IPTN, through heavy direct government subsidies and a monopoly on the captive market in Indonesia. When these subsidies were terminated and the domestic market dried up, IPTN faced extreme difficulties. A similar conclusion would hold for agribusiness firms in Europe and Japan, for example, which rely on heavy government protection and subsidies.

Conversely, a country may have a comparative advantage in a product, but producers in the country may not be able to turn it into competitive advantage either in export markets or in their domestic market. This situation often results when the governments in other countries are heavily subsidizing or protecting their own producers. Exports of palm-oil-based products in Southeast Asia are impeded by subsidies and barriers to trade in the United States and Europe designed to protect domestic producers of vegetable oils; sugar producers in the Philippines have often faced world prices below their production costs, even though the Philippines has a comparative advantage in sugar; U.S. exports of computers, telecommunications equipment, and aircraft are impeded by national programs in Europe, Brazil, Japan, and elsewhere.

Market Identification

For a firm with both a comparative and competitive advantage that gives it the potential to undertake ongoing exports, the next step in the analysis is to identify markets abroad to which it can export its product. This step entails analysis of trends in demand arising from changes in population, income levels, and consumer preferences in potential export markets. If there is a demand for the firm's products in a market, the supply capabilities of domestic firms and other exporters worldwide to meet this demand at lower prices or higher quality must be assessed. For example, paper consumption in Japan has risen rapidly with the rise in Japan's GNP and consumer incomes. Concerns with environmental pollution have placed restrictions on the ability of its pulp manufacturers to increase output to meet this demand. This trend toward an imbalance between demand and supply has created the potential for increased exports to Japan for both pulp and paper products. Japanese pulp and paper firms have also responded to this trend by locating production facilities abroad to produce pulp for their downstream paper production facilities. For a pulp and paper producer in North America, the analysis would then revolve around the issue of whether these developments present an opportunity to increase exports to Japan. The analysis of export markets forms the second block in the framework.

Impediments to Trade

The third block of analysis concerns the impediments to trade flows, both natural ones, such as transportation costs, and measures governments have taken to impede or to facilitate the linking of producers and buyers through international trade. Government policies to restrict and to promote trade can have a decisive influence on (1) trade flows, (2) the competitive position of firms in export markets, (3) the availability and price of imports, and (4) the ability of firms to compete with imports. Hence, an analysis of the level and trends in tariff and nontariff barriers to trade is an essential component of the international trade framework. Governments can also facilitate exports directly by such measures as concessional export financing, export subsidies, differential taxation of export earnings, and financing for export market development.

Trade Intermediaries

If the firm has a competitive advantage *and* if there is demand for its product in an export market *and* if government intervention in the international trade system (or through movements in real exchange rates) does not prevent the producer from accessing buyers in the export market, the final area of analysis concerns the linkages of producers in one country to buyers in the export market. A competitive product and a receptive market are not enough; the product must somehow be transported from the factory to the point of shipment (port or airport) to export market, be received in the export market, clear customs, move through distribution channels to the point of sale, be sold to the customer, and be serviced after sale. International channels of distribution are often long, multilayered, complex, difficult to analyze and understand, and expensive to access or to develop. Channel costs may represent three times the production cost of a product.

Marketing in a country with which a producer is not familiar can present substantial problems as well. The success or failure of a firm's export initiative may stand or fall on the pricing, promotion, advertising, and distribution policies it follows in export markets. These subjects are examined in more detail in the next chapter.

The framework presented above may seem quite complicated at first, but it represents the bare bones of the international trading system in which exporters and importers must manage their trade operations. Each block in this analytical framework is examined in more detail in the next sections of this chapter and in the following chapter.

COMPARATIVE AND COMPETITIVE ADVANTAGE

It is important for managers of firms engaged in international trade to understand the driving forces behind the international flow of goods and services. As with any form of voluntary exchange between independent, value-maximizing agents, international trade takes place when value is created for the participants in the transaction above the value they can receive through alternative uses of their resources. Put more bluntly, trade must be profitable for both the seller and the buyer or it will not continue—at least over the long run.

For the exporter, the value of international trade comes from some combination of higher prices, increased volume, decreased costs (through economies of scale and learning by doing), and the effects of international trade on product quality and design. For the importer, value may be created through lower prices, greater variety, increased quality, and diversification of sources of supply. International trade operations may also affect the risks faced by importers and exporters alike: risks may be decreased by diversifying sales among several markets and sources among several producers; risks may be increased through greater exposure to the effects of trade restrictions, exchange rate movements, and demand, supply, and price fluctuations in foreign markets. Managers of international trade operations must balance the effects of international trade on both profits and risks in order to maximize the value of the firm through its international trade operations.

Managers must bear in mind that the goal of international trade operations is to increase the value of the firm; exports for exports' sake (except in the short run to gain market share) are not the goal. Similarly, for countries, the goal of international trade is not to increase exports (and to decrease imports), but rather to increase national income through international trade. Exports in general and of a specific product are *not* "good" in and of themselves, and imports in general or of specific products are *not* "bad." Yet this view often seems to be the presumption behind the policies of governments around the world as they try to promote exports and to impede imports in general and of specific products.

In fact, exports might be considered "bad." A nation's resources—labor, capital, technology, natural resources—are used to produce exports, but consumers abroad receive the benefits of consuming them and they reduce the supply of goods available for domestic consumption. Imports could be considered "good." They are produced using the resources of other countries, but are consumed domestically, and they increase the goods and services available for domestic use. Exports are only "good" to the extent that the receipts from export sales allow a country to finance imports or to service its accumulated international debt. Similarly, accumulating foreign exchange reserves is beneficial only to the extent that these reserves may allow a country to smooth out the effects of short-term fluctuations in export receipts and import payments and to import products in the future. These facts are difficult for individuals and governments to accept.

This view of value creation as the driving force behind international trade raises the question of what factors lead a firm (or a country) to produce a product for export or to import a product from abroad. How and why is value created when some products are exported and others imported? To understand the answer to this most fundamental question of international trade requires a (short) digression into the theory of international trade. Understanding this theory is important to managers. International trade theory can be thought of as the fundamental tides beneath the turbulent waves of day-to-day international trade activity. Understanding both the tides and the waves of international trade is important for managers engaged in international trade operations.

Absolute and Comparative Advantage

Consider the two countries, *A* and *B*, which produce two products, *X* and *Y*, with labor as the only input to the production process. Before trade, country *A* produces and consumes 16 units of product *X*, using 8 hours of labor and produces and consumes 4 units of product *Y* using 4 hours of labor. Country *B* produces and consumes 4 units of *X* using 4 hours of labour and produces and consumes 4 units of *Y* using 2 hours of labor (Exhibit 3.2). In country *A*, the price of *Y* relative to *X* would be 2 (since it takes twice as long to produce a unit of *Y* as it does to produce a unit of *X*); in country *B* the price ratio is 1/2 (since it takes half as long to produce a unit of *Y* as it does to produce a unit of *X*). Country *A* has an *absolute* advantage in product *X*; country *B* has an absolute advantage in product *Y*. If the two countries are opened to trade, country *A* will tend to specialize in product *X* and country *B* will tend to specialize in product *Y*. If there is total specialization, country *A* could produce 24 units of *X* (12 hours times 2 units per hour) and country *B* could produce 12 units of *Y* (6 hours times 2 units per hour), compared to total production of 20 units of *X* and 8 units of *Y* with no trade. With international trade, both more *X* and more *Y* are produced and consumed and both countries are better off. Under trade, the price of *Y* relative to *X* will fall somewhere between 2 and 1/2.

The gains from trade may not be shared equally, however. For country *A*, producers and workers in the *Y* industry and heavy consumers of product *X* have lost; the *Y* producers have gone out of business, the Y workers have had to shift to the production of *X*, and *X* consumers are facing higher prices for *X*. Producers and workers in the *X* industry and heavy consumers of *Y* have won. The same applies to country *B*; producers and workers in the *X* industry and heavy consumers of *X* have won. Overall, however, both countries have gained, since there is more output to be consumed in both countries. The distribution of the gains among the two countries is also uncertain. In general, the smaller the country and the greater its absolute advantage in one product relative to the absolute advantage of the other

EXHIBIT 3.2
Absolute Advantage

	Output		Output/Hour		
	X	*Y*	*X*	*Y*	*Labor Hours*
Country *A*	16	4	2	1	12
Country *B*	4	4	1	2	6
Total output (no trade)	20	8			
Total output (trade)	24	12			

country, the greater its share of the gains. A small, natural-resource-intensive country like New Zealand has more to gain from trade than a large country with a more balanced economy such as the United States.

Now consider two other countries, *C* and *D,* producing *X* and *Y* (Exhibit 3.3). Country *C* produces 12 units of *X* in 3 hours and 4 units of *Y* in 2 hours; country *D* produces 7 units of *X* in 7 hours and 7 units of *Y* in 7 hours. Notice that country *D* is less efficient in producing *both* products. But trade is still possible and yields gains. With trade, country *C* will specialize in *X,* while country *D* will specialize in *Y,* since the ratio of *C*'s efficiency in *X* relative to *Y* is higher than that in *D.* If there is total specialization, then country *C* could produce 20 units of *X* and country *D* could produce 14 units of *Y.* Before trade, total production was just 19 units of *X* and 11 units of *Y.* The important point here is: even if one country is more efficient in *both* products, there are still gains for each country through trade. In this example, since country *D* is less efficient than country *C* in both products, with trade, although both countries have gained, incomes will still be higher in *D* than in *C.* To be more concrete, even if both steel producers and garment producers in the United States were more productive than steel and garment producers in India, there would still be gains for both countries if the United States produced steel and India produced garments. This is the theory of *comparative* advantage.

For managers, there are two lessons to be learned from this analysis. It is important to understand what factors contribute to the comparative advantage of both country *C* in product *X* and country *D* in product *Y.* The reason is *not* that producers in country *C* are more or less efficient than those in country *D.* The important factor is the *ratio* of the efficiency in the two industries in country C *compared* with their *ratio* in country *D.* If, through technology generation or transfer, education programs, and so on, producers of product *X* in country *D* improve their efficiency to above 2 units per hour (and assuming that all other producers do not increase their efficiencies), then country *D* would become a net exporter of *X, even though* there had been no changes in the relative efficiency of producers in country *C and* even through producers of *X* in country *C* were still more efficient than those in country *D.* Such a situation has occurred in such products as orange and apple juices, canned pineapples, tomatoes, and cut flowers. Producers in developing countries have increased their efficiencies through transfer of agricultural technology and reduced transportation costs over the past decade to the point where they have a comparative advantage in these products. In analyzing the effects of trade on an industry, the important factor is the comparison of these two ratios among trading partners and how they change over time.

EXHIBIT 3.3
Comparative
Advantage

	Output		Output/Hour			
	X	Y	X	Y	*Labor Hours*	*Py/Px*
Country *C*	12	4	4	2	5	2
Country *D*	7	7	1	1	14	1
Total output (no trade)	19	11				
Total output (trade)	20	14				

Pineapple producers and canners in Hawaii are the most efficient in the world. Yet over time, the efficiency of producers in other countries has increased rapidly, and first Taiwan, then Thailand, and more recently Indonesia have displaced Hawaiian produceers from the market and forced them to close. A similar situation has occurred for garment producers in North America. They are highly efficient and their efficiency has increased over time relative to many other manufacturing industries. Yet the efficiency of garment manufacturers in low-wage countries has increased even more rapidly compared with the efficiency of other producers in these countries. The result has been the gradual decline of garment manufacturers in North America and the rise of exports from first Japan, then from Korea, Taiwan, and Hong Kong, and more recently from Thailand, India, China, Turkey, and Indonesia.

Although the theories of absolute and comparative advantage as presented above involve only two countries producing two products and using one factor of production with a constant return-to-scale production function, they can be generalized to many countries, many products, many factors inputs, and diminishing returns to scale. The conclusions of this more complicated analysis generally are the same as those for the simple analysis presented above: trade enhances the welfare of both countries, but the distribution of these gains among participants within each country and among the countries is not uniform. The more complicated theories also show that:

1. Trade improves the relative welfare of the factors of production that are used intensively in the exported product. For example, if a country exports steel (a capital-intensive product), the welfare of those who have capital will be improved relative to those who supply labor.

2. If labor and capital are immobile among sectors, then the returns to the factors of production (labor and capital) in the exporting industry will improve relative to those in the importing sector.

3. The welfare of consumers of the export products will decline relative to consumers of imported products (since prices of the exported product will rise relative to the imported product). For example, if a country exports food and imports consumer durables, the welfare of the poor, whose budgets contain a relatively high proportion for food, will decline relative to the rich, who can afford consumer durables.

4. Countries will tend to export products that use their relatively inexpensive and abundant factors of production intensively. For example, a country in which labor is relatively inexpensive compared with capital will export labor-intensive products and import capital- intensive ones.

5. Trade brings about an equalization of the returns to factors of production; that is, trade tends to equalize capital costs and wage rates among countries over time.

The overriding conclusion of this analysis is that a country will *always* have a comparative advantage in some product groups. The product groups may change over time, however. A situation will never arise in which a country will lose comparative advantage in almost all product groups and not gain it in others. High wages do not make a country noncompetitive on export markets. They make it uncompetitive in labor intensive products. A deteriorating trade deficit is *not* a sign of a loss of comparative advantage. As discussed below, it is a sign that the country's real exchange rate has risen to an inappropriate level. The U.S. trade deficit that grew in the 1980s, and is still present in 2002, is *not* due to the loss of its comparative advantage. The United States still has a comparative advantage in some products (although the products in which it had a comparative advantage might have changed). The origin of the U.S. trade problems are an appreciation of its real exchange rate over the 1977–85 period. Over this period the real exchange rate of the U.S. dollar rose by almost 50 percent against the currencies of its trading partners. The exchange-rate appreciation had the effect of pricing products in which the United States had a comparative advantage out of world markets.

NEW THEORIES OF INTERNATIONAL TRADE

The theories of absolute and comparative advantage are most easily used to explain *inter*industry trade, that is, trade in which one country exports a product of industry X and imports a product of industry Y. But much of international trade is composed of *intra*industry trade, that is, trade among countries in products in the same industry. France both exports and imports garments; the United States both exports and imports steel; England both exports and imports consumer electronics, and so on. In fact, a majority of the trade in manufactured products among high- income countries is comprised of intraindustry trade.[4]

There are basically two explanations for intraindustry trade. The first is well within the framework of comparative advantage as presented above. France exports high-quality, high- fashion garments and imports low-quality, standard ones; the United States imports standard steels and exports specialized steels; England imports mass-market consumer electronics and exports state-of-the-art ones, and so on. Each country, then, is exporting the products that make intensive use of its relatively abundant factors of production (fashion designers, steel technologists, and sound engineers).

This is only part of the explanation, however. In industries in which there are economies of scale in production, R&D, distribution, advertising, and sales operations, a firm may be able to establish a *competitive* advantage in the domestic and international market. Duralex glasses, Bally shoes, YKK zippers, and Heineken beer are examples of products that have successfully established a sustainable competitive advantage based on cost and product differentiation.

Once a firm has achieved a competitive advantage based on cost or product differentiation (through branding, R&D, design, or service), it may be able to use its current competitive position to erect barriers to entry for other, later entrants. One way to do this is to signal implicit or explicit threats to potential competitors that the firm will lower prices or increase volumes if entry does occur. If incumbent firms were to follow through with these threats of retaliation, new entrants might find themselves in an untenable position. To gain market share they would have to price below established producers (due to brand loyalty), yet, initially, their costs would be high due to their initial small market share (and hence production volumes) and their limited experience. Barriers to entry are especially high in industries in which there are large economies of scale (implying high up-front capital investments), large initial R&D expenditures, and high cost to establishing a brand name. In such industries, if incumbent firms are far down on the learning curve, operating at efficient scale, or have a considerable degree of brand loyalty, these threats may be sufficiently "credible" to dissuade potential entrants from starting production.

Clusters of Interconnected Companies

There is another set of conditions that some groups of firms and whole industries in some countries have been able to develop which has allowed them to achieve and sustain a competitive advantage in world trade. Rarely is a firm a free-standing entity that can produce all the necessary inputs for production, perform all the design and R&D for product development, and provide all the marketing and after-sales services by itself. Firms most often rely on a wide variety of suppliers for inputs, outside design and R&D firms for design and product development, and a wide range of sales and after-sales support firms. In some regions and some countries, industry clusters have developed over time. Ideas are exchanged among personnel of these firms. A trade infrastructure is built up to support them, with elements internal to the firms, in separate support firms, and in transportation and communications systems. The demand by this cluster of firms for specific job skills is met in part by in-house training and in part by government programs that set up an education system to provide workers with those skills. This view of how international competitive advantage can be created and sustained has been most forcefully presented by Michael Porter in *The Competitive Advantage of Nations.* In the first chapter of this book a list of 100 industry clusters is presented for 10 countries. To pick a few examples: food additives and furniture in Denmark; cutlery and printing presses in Germany; ceramic tiles, footwear, and wool fabrics in Italy; air-conditioning machinery, musical instruments, and forklift trucks in Japan; pianos, travel goods, and wigs in Korea; ship repair in Singapore; mining equipment, environment control equipment, and refrigerated shipping in Sweden; dyestuffs, heating controls, and survey equipment in Switzerland; confectionery, auctioneering, and electrical generation equipment in the United Kingdom; and detergents, agricultural chemicals, and motion pictures in the United States. In Canada (not covered in Porter's book), a similar situation exists for packaging equipment. Often these industries are clustered geographically as well as nationally.

Probably the most extensively studied industrial cluster is Silicon Valley. In the *The Silicon Valley Edge,* Stephen Cohen and Gary Fields contrast Silicon Valley with traditional clusters such as Italian tile firms or the Detroit automotive district. According to the authors, Silicon Valley is a world of strangers with no deep history, little sense of civic engagement, few familial ties, and little structured community. Silicon Valley's strength as a cluster is based on its social capital created through collaborative partnerships that drive technological dynamism. Trust based on performance provides the foundation, which means that newcomers and outsiders can enter the network as long as they deliver on their promises.

Porter concludes that among the firms and supporting infrastructure in these clusters there are substantial economies of scale, positive spillover effects (externalities), and interlinkages that promote both competition and cooperation. Rivals compete intensely to win and retain customers. Without vigorous competition, a cluster will fail. Porter argues that clusters affect competition in three broad ways: first, by increasing the productivity of companies in the area; second, by driving the direction and pace of innovation, which drives future productivity growth; and three, by stimulating the formation of new businesses, which expands and strengthens the cluster itself.

Porter argues in his later work that in the new economics of competition, what matters most in all industries is not inputs and scale but productivity. Based on this argument, there is no such thing as a low-tech industry. There are only low-tech companies that fail to use world-class technology to enhance productivity and innovation. An important implication for global competition is that locational factors such as low wages and taxes lose their importance in the absence of efficient infrastructure, sophisticated suppliers, and other cluster benefits that can offset savings from low input costs. As global competition changes the nature of traditional comparative advantages, a growing number of multinationals are moving their headquarters to more vibrant clusters. For example, when the two pharmaceutical firms, Pharmacia of Sweden and Upjohn of the United States, merged in 1995, a decision was made to locate the head office in London. A few years later the firm relocated to New Jersey, the most competitive location for the pharmaceutical industry.

The unique competitive conditions created by clusters cannot be replicated in another country or region unless a similar cluster is developed. Such development can be extremely difficult, since the whole of the cluster is greater than the sum of its parts. Hence, substantial parts of the cluster must exist before the individual firms can compete internationally. Porter also concludes that it is possible for countries to foster the upgrading of clusters through government action to influence demand patterns, education and training programs, industry protection, and trade promotion. For example, at one time the United States, the United Kingdom, and Sweden had clusters in shipbuilding. But first Japan and more recently Korea have been able to develop clusters in these industries and out-compete them internationally. Similar shifts in the location of clusters have occurred in cars, semiconductors, apparel, and footwear.

It is unlikely that government policy can successfully create new clusters and instead, should focus on strengthening productivity in existing clusters. There are various examples of concerted attempts to develop clusters that have not been successful. For example, the apparel industry in Japan tried to develop a sustainable competitive advantage in high-fashion clothing. The design schools of Europe were flooded with students from Japan, and Japanese high-fashion houses were developed. Despite the success of some firms, such as Hanae Mori and Isye Myake, the clothing industry in Japan has continued to decline. Porter also acknowledges that the concentration of Japanese industry in the Tokyo and Osaka region, and the consequent inefficiencies due to congestion, is the result of a powerful and intrusive central government.

"First-mover advantages" and the presence of industry clusters can be overcome by new entrants with sufficient resources to bear the initial losses entry entails.[5] Such strategic moves by individual firms can be assisted by government policy, which can give a firm a "deep pocket" to finance its initial losses on entry or that can give it a protected domestic market for initial sales. This situation may have occurred for firms in Japan and some of the newly industrializing countries. This view of the driving force behind international trade in these types of products gives credence, at least in theory, to government intervention in international trade both to protect existing national firms in such industries from attack by new entrants and to assist new national firms as they break into the market.

Two trends have reinforced the ability of firms and industrial clusters to establish a sustainable competitive advantage based on economies of scale and product differentiation, and two trends have lessened their ability. National incomes per capita, wages, and capital costs among countries in the upper third of the world income distribution have tended to become more homogeneous over time, and the importance of endowments of many natural resources has declined. Among these countries, competitive advantage has become based less on relative factor endowments and costs and more on firm-specific ownership advantages—such as economies of scale, management, technology, brand names—as well as on highly developed support industries, education, worker skills, and trade infrastructure. As incomes have risen, buyers have become more discriminating in their purchases as to style, quality, fashion, design, and performance. Consumers have also come to value a wider range of products with a wider range of product attributes. These trends have increased the ability of producers to differentiate their products entering international trade. In the United States, shoes made by Bally (produced in Italy and Switzerland) compete with shoes from Gucci (Italy), Church (England), and Alden (United States) at the top end of the market in the $200 plus range. But shoes from Indonesia, Taiwan, China, and South Korea are demanded in the $10 to $20 price range.

The increasingly rapid pace of technology transfer and diffusion has led to a growing number of firms (in a growing number of countries) possessing or having access to more or less the same product and process technology. In industries in which technological ability (including design and quality control) has become more widely diffused, competition may once again become based on relative factor costs. Falling transportation costs and trade barriers have also accentuated the force behind comparative advantage. Many firms have become multinational enterprises. These firms, to the extent that relative factor costs are still important, can rationalize production and sales on a global basis. Increasingly, however, knowledge intensive products, in which manufacturing labor and materials account for a limited amount of product cost, are becoming more important. As a result, in industries such as software and entertainment and even automobiles, the idea of moving production to a low cost location makes little sense.

The Benefits of Trade

The overwhelming conclusion of all the theories of international trade is that trade creates value for *all* the participants. The more open a country is to trade, the better off it will be in the long run. In the short run, there may be adjustment problems for some sectors and some firms within these sectors, but, overall, all countries win. In Chapter 2, "world competitiveness rankings" were given for a number of countries. This should *not* be interpreted to mean that, as in a sports contest, some countries will win and others lose in international competition through trade and foreign investment. Individual companies may win or lose, but at the national level, countries all win by opening up to trade (and foreign investment). A more apt comparison is with dancing, rather than a sports contest. The closer we dance together, the greater the benefits will be for both partners (although there may be some stumbling and hurt toes as we learn to dance together).

These newer theories of the driving forces behind international trade have several implications for managers. It is necessary to analyze which of the forces will predominate in the industry in which the firm operates. That is, can the firm establish a sustainable competitive advantage based on some proprietary ownership advantage that will allow it to operate internationally, or will the forces of comparative advantage predominate? Governments may intervene in the market to assist firms in some industries to "create" their own comparative and competitive advantage. In theory, governments can increase national welfare by protecting firms in this type of industry from trade competition while they are still struggling to gain scale efficiency, undertake R&D, differentiate their products, and promote exports. Many governments around the world have "targeted" manufacturers of products such as computers, biotechnology, aircraft, telecommunications, robotics, ceramics, and fiber optics, for protection and incentives during their developmental stages. For firms in these industries, government policies at home and in competing countries may be the key to competitive success in export as well as in domestic markets.

A word of warning is needed, however. Often, management and governments have focused their attention on the "hot" industries on the cutting edge of technology when they have tried to identify the "winners of tomorrow" in export markets. For many, even most, of the industries in which firms have achieved a sustainable competitive advantage, technology of the bubbling test tube and whizzing computer variety is *not* the norm. German firms export knives and garden equipment; English firms export razors, combs, cookies, and candy; Swiss firms export shoes, textiles, and cereals; American firms export software, clothing, and processed food products; Canadian firms export packaging machinery, feed mixers, dental drills, and garbage cans; Japanese firms export zippers, disposable lighters, and books; Swedish firms export saws and scissors; and Taiwanese firms exports semiconductors and laptop computers. These firms have all achieved a sustainable competitive advantage in export markets, based not on "high" technology but on design, quality, and marketing expertise.[6]

Firms that enter the hot industries based on government incentives may find themselves caught in a worldwide subsidy war in which competitive advantage is based more on which governments are willing to subsidize the most and which governments ultimately flinch from the mounting costs of these subsidies. If several governments continue to subsidize their "national champions," worldwide overcapacity may exist in the long run, prices will remain below costs, and the ultimate winners will be consumers in importing countries.

REAL EXCHANGE RATES

Beyond comparative and competitive advantage, there are two important factors that influence trade flows: the real exchange rate and demand conditions over the business cycle. The concept of the "real exchange rate" is a difficult one to master and to use. But the influence of real exchange rates on trade flows is so great that it should be mastered. Everyone is familiar with exchange rates in general. If we travel abroad we change our domestic currencies into the currencies of the countries that we visit at the prevailing exchange rate. For example, in early-2002, one U.S. dollar could be changed into 130 yen or into 1.57 Canadian dollars. This is the *nominal* exchange rate. The nominal exchange rate is important for international business. A Canadian importer receives a shipment from the United States with payment in dollars. Canadian dollars must then be converted into U.S. dollars at the prevailing exchange rate and sent to the United States. This is a straightforward transaction and easy to understand. If the nominal exchange rate between the U.S. dollar and the Canadian dollar falls to $1.60, the importer will have to pay $1.60 Canadian to buy one U.S. dollar. Such a fall of the Canadian dollar can have important implications for the prices the importer must charge when the product is sold or on its profit margins if prices cannot be changed.

The "real" exchange rate is more difficult to understand, but it is of even greater importance in many instances. The concept of the real exchange rate can be illustrated with a stylized example. In year one, assume that U.S. and Japanese producers of machine tools are making normal economic profits; the landed, duty-paid price of a U.S. machine tool in Japan is $100,000; the nominal exchange rate is 100 yen = $1; and the price of comparable machine tools *in yen* is 10,000,000. The U.S.-produced machine tool is then competitive in Japan (since $100,000 = 10,000,000 yen and exports take place). Over the next year, inflation in the United States is 10 percent and in Japan it is only 3 percent, *and* the *nominal* exchange rate remains at 100 yen = $1. What has happened to the ability of the U.S. producer to export to Japan? If the total costs of the U.S. producer (including a normal profit) have risen by the average rate of U.S. inflation, its costs would be $100,000 × 1.10 = $110,000 = 11,000,000 yen. The price of Japanese competitors *in yen* has risen by the Japanese rate of inflation to 10,000,000 × 1.03 = 10,300,000. Hence, the U.S. producer must either cut prices in dollars to $103,000 and severely reduce its profit margins or the Japanese importer will not be able to sell the product in competition with Japanese- made products.

In this example, although the *nominal* exchange rate has remained constant, the ability of the U.S. producer to export to Japan has declined due to differing inflation rates between Japan and the United States. The real exchange rate is a measure of this loss of competitive ability due to differing inflation rates (and hence changing relative costs). In this example, the *real* exchange rate has *risen* by about 7 percent. The real exchange rate can be thought of as an index number. In the example, if it were 100 in year one, it would have risen to 106.8 ($1.10/1.03 \times 100$) in year two. (For small percentage inflation rates, the calculation can be simplified to: the real exchange rate in year two = 100 + U.S. inflation − Japanese inflation rate = 100 + 10 − 3 = 107.) In order for the U.S. producer to remain competitive, the *nominal* exchange rate in this example would have had to fall by 6.36 percent to 93.6 ($1.03/1.10 − 1 = 0.0636$), more or less the inflation rate differential. If this had occurred, then the *real* exchange rate would have remained constant.

Just as a rise in the real exchange rate reduces the competitive ability in export markets of national producers, it also increases the competitive ability of producers abroad to export to the domestic market. Hence, all else equal, a rise in the real exchange rate leads to reduced export growth rates and increased import growth rates. Conversely, a fall in the real exchange rate leads to increased export growth rates and reduced import growth rates. Notice that this effect is *independent* of either comparative or competitive advantage of the nation or of its firms.

For managers engaged in international trade operations, an analysis of movements of the real exchange rates is crucial for determining success in export markets and success in competing with imports. For example, the United States once had a comparative advantage in sophisticated machine tools. As U.S. currency increased in value, U.S. producers found themselves priced out of export markets on the one hand and under threat of import competition on the other.

Estimates of the real exchange rate of major trading countries are available on a monthly basis from many sources, most notably the *International Financial Statistics Yearbook* (published by the International Monetary Fund).[7] For example, over the 1978 to 1996 period (with 1990 indexed as 100), the real exchange rate of the U.S. dollar rose from 108.8 in 1978 to as high as 156.5, fell to 91.9 in 1995, rose to 96.9 in 1996, and rose to 113 in 2000. The effects of these movements in the U.S. real exchange rate on U.S. exporters and firms that compete with imports were dramatic–and completely swamped out any effects of relative competitive ability due to "Japanese management," technological superiority, product quality differentials, or national trade strategies, factors which have figured prominently in the press as causes of the U.S. trade deficit.

Exhibit 3.4 displays the real exchange rate of the U.S. dollar from 1975 to 2000 and the U.S. trade balance *lagged by two years* (i.e., from 1977 to 1998). The lag was included since imports and exports respond to changes in the real exchange rate with a lag. Firms take time to switch among sources of supply on the international market and to fill export and import orders. With the fall of the dollar in 1985, U.S. exports began to expand rapidly and import growth was reduced. From 1985 to 1991, U.S. export volume increased by 68 percent and import volume increased by 26 percent. Over the same period, export and import volumes in Japan increased 65 and 17 percent, respectively; for Germany the figures were 24 and 61 percent.[8] This dramatic reversal of the fortunes of U.S., Japanese, and German exporters was largely the result of the changes in the real exchange rates of these countries.[9]

EXHIBIT 3.4   **U.S. Real Exchange Rates, 1975–98, and Balance of Trade, 1977–2000**

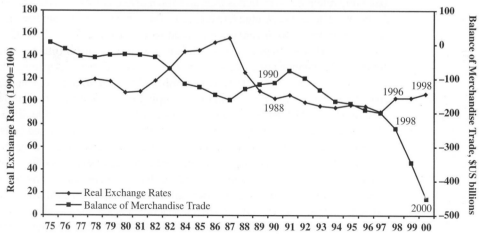

In Japan, the situation was roughly the reverse of that in the United States. From an index of 82.8 in 1985, its real exchange rate rose to 116.6 in 1988, declined to 100 in 1990, rose continuously to a high of 166.7 in mid-1995, fell dramatically to 124 in mid-1996, and was 152 in mid-2000. These real exchange rate movements have had a significant effect on Japanese firms and the economy as a whole. Major Japanese firms have had to downsize and lay off workers, relocate production abroad, and increase productivity substantially. This restructuring and redeployment of resources was one of the major factors that contributed to the slow growth of the Japanese economy in the 1990s.

As part of this block of the analysis, the key role of the level and potential movements of the real exchange rate between the two countries must be assessed. The IMF publishes real exchange rates for many countries in the *International Financial Statistics Yearbook.* For those countries for which data are not available, a rough approximation of the movement of the real exchange rate can easily be made. Essentially, if the inflation rate in one country exceeds that of another, in order for its real exchange rate to remain constant, its nominal exchange rate must devalue by the inflation rate differential. In the example above, the U.S. inflation rate was 7 percent higher than that in Japan. So, for the real exchange rate to remain constant, the yen would have to appreciate against the dollar by about 7 percent. If it did not, but rather appreciated by only 2 percent, then the real value of the dollar would have risen by about 5 percent.

An increase in a country's real exchange rate has many of the same effects as a reduction in its tariff rate: it makes market access easier as the prices of imports relative to domestic production fall. A fall in the real exchange rate has the opposite effect. It is difficult to overemphasize the importance of movements of the real exchange rate of the home country and potential destination countries for international trade flows and for the success of import and export operations.

The importance of the real exchange rate holds for large and small countries and for high-income and developing countries alike.[10] In the early 1990s, foreign investors perceived that the Philippines had a relatively stable government. Foreign direct and portfolio investment began to pour into the Philippines. At the same time, transfers from abroad (largely by Filipino overseas workers) accelerated. The consequent 25 percent rise in the real exchange rate of the Philippines from 1991 to 1995 led to a reduction in export growth, an increase in import growth, and a reduction in manufacturing employment of 16 percent, despite a surge of foreign investment.

Real exchange rates may change for several reasons. If there is a gap between investment demand and domestic savings, real interest rates will rise and capital will flow in from abroad, thereby driving up the real exchange rate. The inevitable imbalances that this appreciation of the real exchange rate will cause will lead to mounting external debt and eventually to an unwillingness of investors abroad to hold more debt. Capital inflows will decline and the real exchange rate will fall. For the United States, high investment demand (due to an expanding economy) and a low savings rate (due to low personal savings and large government deficits) led to high real interest rates, capital inflows, a rise in the real exchange rate, and a deterioration of U.S. trade accounts from 1977 to 1985. Over the 1985 to 1988 period, private investors outside the United States became increasingly reluctant to hold more U.S. dollar-denominated debt, capital inflows from these sources declined, and the real exchange rate declined.

Similarly, short-term government macroeconomic policy (to reduce inflation, for example) may lead to relatively high interest rates and an appreciation of the real exchange rate. Over the 1986 to 1991 period, Canada's real exchange rate rose by 27 percent in response to a government policy of halting inflation by setting high interest rates. The policies worked, but at the expense of the trade sector. Once inflation was reduced and the government relaxed its monetary policies in 1991, the real exchange rate fell significantly, dropping from 100 in 1990 to 83 in 1996.

Real exchange rates may also increase (decrease) if a country's terms of trade (the ratio of unit export prices to unit import prices) move in its favor (against it). If this change is permanent, then the real exchange rate will remain at this higher level. For example, if the decline in oil prices over the 1981–88 period were permanent, the real exchange rates of oil-exporting countries would have to fall permanently in order for them to maintain their trade accounts at a sustainable level. In fact, the real exchange rates of oil exporters, such as Saudi Arabia and Bahrain, did fall from 40 to 50 percent with the decline in oil prices in the mid-1980s through the early 1990s.

A country's real exchange rate can also appreciate if some valuable natural resource is discovered within the country. For example, when natural gas was discovered in Holland's offshore waters, its real exchange rate rose as this gas was exported. The rise in Holland's real exchange rate caused manufacturers in Holland to be priced out of export markets for manufacturing products and led to a decline in its manufacturing sector, the so-called Dutch disease. If a country's productivity increases relative to that of its trading partners, its real exchange rate will rise, unless the government acts to hold it down by accumulating foreign exchange reserves and investing abroad. In this case, the country will generate ever increasing trade surpluses until the time when it lets its exchange rate rise to an appropriate level. This phenomenon occurred in such countries as Japan, South Korea, and Taiwan over the 1985 to 1988 period. Singapore is an interesting example of a country that has resisted this pressure to revalue its currency. From 1985 to 1996, it maintained the real exchange rate of the Singapore dollar while at the same time accumulating $71 billion in foreign exchange reserves by 1997 ($23,000 per capita, by far the largest per capita foreign exchange reserves in the world outside the oil-exporting countries). In the future, despite the unwillingness of the Singapore government to revalue its currency, its real value will have to rise.

The examples given above should not lead to a conclusion that real exchange rates are highly volatile. The real exchange rates of Switzerland and Austria have not changed by more than 15 percent over the past decade. Real exchange rates move dramatically only in response to strong economic forces, such as the financial crisis in Asia in the late-1990s. It is, however, important to identify those times when real exchange rates move away from their long-run equilibrium position and to make appropriate decisions regarding trade and investment.

The theory and evidence from international finance shows that over the short run the foreign exchange market is "perfect," i.e., that investors on average cannot make economic profits in speculating in foreign exchange. Over the longer term, however, it is possible to forecast movements in the real exchange rate (and hence the nominal exchange rate) when the real exchange rate is significantly above or below its long-run equilibrium value. The long run is the appropriate time frame for those engaged in international trade (a long-term investment in export markets) and foreign direct investment. Although it is impossible to "beat" the foreign exchange market consistently over the short term, from time to time it is both possible and necessary to predict the direction of real and nominal exchange rate movements accurately over the longer term. This task is part of an international manager's job.

For managers, there are several implications of this analysis of the effects of movements in real exchange rates on the competitive advantage of their firms. First, they must try to determine if changes in real exchange rates are short- or long-term. The effects of short-term movements in real exchange rates on their competitive ability should be taken into account when making such decisions as whether to change the volume and prices of their exports in response to exchange-rate movements or to absorb the impact of these changes on the profitability of export operations.

In the early 1980s, with the rise of the real value of the U.S. dollar, Japanese car producers increased their market penetration by pricing aggressively in dollars (while still maintaining their profit levels in yen). When the combination of increased imports and the recession led to layoffs and losses in the U.S. car industry, the U.S. government was induced to negotiate restraint agreements on cars from Japan. Japanese car manufacturers responded to volume restrictions by raising prices on existing models and by introducing new models at even higher prices (to clear the market) and made enormous profits in the U.S. market. With the fall of the dollar in 1985, the Japanese were faced with a dilemma: either raise U.S. prices dramatically and lose market share or have profit levels decline. A similar dilemma was faced by Japanese consumer electronics firms. Both groups of firms did raise prices, but not to the extent of the decline of the dollar against the yen. The result was that by the early 1990s most Japanese car and consumer electronics firms were running operating losses (partially offset by nonoperating profits on their portfolio investments of their previous profits). Over the longer term, when the Japanese saw that the real value of the yen would remain high, they upgraded product quality, increased efficiency, laid off workers, and invested heavily abroad.

The second implication for managers is that identification of times when their home country's real exchange rate is above its long-run equilibrium level and when a destination country's real exchange rate is below this level can assist in identifying export market opportunities, since, unless the change in permanent, ultimately overvalued and undervalued exchange rates will move back to their equilibrium levels. Third, identification of short- and long-run movements of real exchange rates in the future can assist in identification of threats and opportunities arising from international markets.

Another implication of real exchange-rate movements goes beyond international trade into both portfolio and direct investment management. As mentioned above, the rise of the U.S. dollar through 1985 was largely fueled by huge inflows of investment in U.S. financial instruments: short- and long-term bonds and stock purchases. These investors used their relatively cheap foreign currencies to buy relatively expensive dollars to make these investments. When the dollar fell, the value of these investments in terms of foreign currencies fell as well. For these investors, the good news was that they earned relatively high returns (interest and stock appreciation and dividends) in dollars; the bad news was that they lost substantial capital when they converted their depreciated U.S. dollars into their national currencies. Japanese financial institutions were reported to have lost upward of $40 billion (in terms of yen).

For direct investors in plant and equipment, the situation was somewhat different. They too converted relatively cheap foreign currencies to buy relatively expensive dollars. And they were hurt when the dollar declined. On the other hand, as the dollar fell, the cost competitiveness of their investments increased (just as it did for U.S. manufacturers) and hence profits rose above projections. However, these profits were in dollars.

For all these reasons, a close watch should be kept on movements of real exchange rates. Further, forecasts of real exchange-rate movements should be made. Although this forecasting exercise is difficult, it can be extremely useful. And not to forecast is to miss opportunities and to court trouble. All else equal, for real exchange rates, what goes up must come down, and vice versa.

One of the problems in this analysis, however, is to decide whether a rise in the real exchange rate is a movement back toward equilibrium or away from equilibrium. A good starting point can be found by determining a time period when the country's trade is roughly balanced, then counting back two years (to account for lag effects) and defining this level as 100. Movements away from 100 in the real exchange rate will tend to be movements away from equilibrium, which eventually will be reversed. Other indications of an *overvalued* real exchange rate are persistent and worsening trade deficits, high real interest rates, unusual capital inflows, and chronic international debt problems. For countries with a high concentration of exports in a particular natural resource product, such as oil or natural gas, a long-term shift (up or down) will put pressure on the real exchange rate (up or down). Conversely, for countries with persistent trade surpluses, mounting foreign exchange reserves, and burgeoning international investments, there will be pressures for the real exchange rate to rise.

DEMAND

The final factors influencing international trade (both imports and exports) are demand conditions over the business cycles in the domestic market and in export markets, and source countries for imports. If the domestic economy is expanding relative to the economies of other countries, exporters will tend to divert production to the domestic market, where demand and prices are rising. Producers abroad, faced with slack demand at home, will tend to try to push excess production onto export markets. For example, the large Japanese trade surplus in 1998 was in part due to the *fall* of the yen over the past few years. But it was also influenced by the deceleration of the growth rate of the Japanese economy and import demand there and the increase in import demand in the United States as the U.S. economy expanded.

Summary

The *first* step in a firm's analysis of its international trade position is to analyze the forces in the national economy that give rise to some form of comparative advantage or disadvantage. The exporter must also analyze what competitive advantage the firm has or can develop, based either on the country's comparative advantage, or on "ownership advantages"—such as economies of scale, marketing, management, and R&D—which cannot easily be duplicated by other competitors worldwide. In general, the more closely a firm's competitive advantage is aligned with the country's comparative advantage, the more easily it can develop, maintain, and increase its competitive advantage. In Thailand there is a saying, "It's easier to help an elephant get up when it's getting up than it is to hold it up when it wants to lie down." Our youth culture phrases this as "Go with the flow." These sayings apply to international trade.

Supplementary Reading

Cline, William R. *American Trade Adjustment: The Global Impact.* Policy Analysis in International Economics Series No. 26. Washington, D.C.: Institute for International Economics, 1989.

Cohen, Stephen and Gary Fields. Social Capital And Capital Gains: An Examination Of Social Capital In Silicon Valley. In *Understanding Silicon Valley: The Anatomy of an Entrepreneurial Region* (ed, Martin Kenney). Stanford, CA: Stanford University Press, 2000, pp. 190–217.

The Global Competiveness Report 2001–2002. New York: Oxford University Press, 2002.

Jackson, John. *The World Trading System: Law and Policy of International Economic Relations,* 2nd ed. Cambridge, MA: MIT Press, 1997.

Krugman, Paul R., and Maurice Obstfeld. *International Economics: Theory and Practice,* 5th ed. Reading, MA: Addison-Wesley, 2000.

Porter, Michael E. "Clusters and the New Economics of Competition." *Harvard Business Review,* November–December, pp. 77–90, 1998.

Porter, Michael E. *The Competitive Advantage of Nations.* New York: Free Press, 1990.

Thurow, Lester. *Head to Head: The Coming Economic Battle Among Japan, Europe, and America.* New York: William Morrow and Company, 1992.

The World Competitiveness Yearbook 2000. Lausanne, Switzerland: IMD, 2000.

World Trade Organization, *www.wto.org.* Geneva, Switzerland: 2002.

Yergin, Daniel. *The Commanding Heights: The Battle Between Government and the Marketplace That Is Remaking the Modern World.* New York: Simon & Schuster, 1998.

Endnotes

1. The concept of the "real value" of a currency is treated further on in this chapter. In short, the real value of a country's currency (its real exchange rate) increases (decreases) if changes in its nominal exchange rate are greater (less) than the differential inflation rates between it and its trading partners (when exchange rates are expressed in terms of the amount of foreign currency that can be purchased with one unit of domestic currency).

2. Prior to reform in 1992, direct agricultural subsidies took up to two-thirds of the European Union budget. Direct agricultural subsidies *per farmer* in 1989 were about $10,000 in the EU, $16,000 in Canada and Japan, $21,000 in the United States, and $30,000 in Sweden. (As quoted in Clayton Yeuter, "Back 40 Blues," *The World in 1990* (London, Economist Publications, 1990). Even after EU reform, half the EU budget in 1998 went to subsidising farming, an industry employing only about 5 percent of the EU's working population.

3. See Paul Beamish, "European Foreign Investment: Why go to Canada," *European Management Journal,* Vol. 14, No. 1, 1996 for an application of the STEP analysis.

4. The percentage of intraindustry trade in international trade depends on the definition used for "industry": the broader the definition, the greater the percentage. For example, the percentage of intraindustry trade in "textiles and garments" is higher than it would be for "men's T-shirts."

5. This may have been the case of Great Giant Pineapple (GGP), a subsidiary of Genung Sewu, a large conglomerate in Indonesia. Initially GGP priced 15 percent below the producer in Thailand with the worst reputation for quality *and* graded all its pineapple rings as "Grade C" to ensure that, in delivering at least the quality described in the contract (and usually higher quality), it could keep its name among buyers as living up to its contract. By 1989, with its reputation established and with 8 percent of the world market, GGP was pricing above the Thai producer with the best reputation *and* was selling grades A and B slices. By 1996, GGP had 15 percent of the world market for canned pineapple.

6. See Porter, *The Competitive Advantage of Nations,* Chapter 1, Table 1.2, pp. 27–28, for a complete list of the 100 industries that he and his co-authors studied. In particular note that many of the firms and the industries that have been able to establish a competitive advantage are not particularly high-tech. Rather, their competitive advantage is based on quality, design, innovation, and so on.

7. See the technical notes in the IMF publication for a description of how the various measures of real exchange rates have been calculated.

8. These figures are for the overall exchange rates, not the bilateral ones between the United States and Japan or Germany. The fluctuations of these rates were higher still. Similarly, the trade statistics are for total, not bilateral, trade. If the bilateral trade figures had been given, both the change in real exchange rates and the change in export growth rates would have been substantially greater.

9. Demand conditions also influence international trade and are an important factor in explaining post-1991 changes in the U.S. balance of trade. This point is discussed at the end of this chapter.

10. The exception to this generalization is when a country counteracts movements in its real exchange rate by additional offsetting export promotional measures and import impeding measures. Korea is one example of a country which through 1985 was able to follow such a policy.

Chapter Four

Managing Export Operations

In Chapter 3, the STEP framework was introduced. This framework can be used by managers to analyze a firm's comparative and competitive advantage in export markets. A firm's competitive advantage can be moderated by movements in the real exchange rate and in demand conditions abroad. The second block of analysis centers on the analysis of export markets to assess their potential demand for the firm's products. The firm may have a product with a competitive advantage, but it also needs to identify a market in which users value its product above the products that are currently available in the market from domestic producers and exporters from other countries. One procedure for accomplishing this analysis involves three steps. Initially, the analysis will focus on single-country markets, but later on in the chapter regional and global markets will be brought into the analysis.

Step 1: Segment World Markets

Market segmentation lies at the heart of marketing for many products, especially the differentiated products that have become increasingly important in international trade. This chapter, however, is not the place for an elaborate description of market segmentation techniques; this can be found in introductory marketing textbooks.

In segmenting markets in countries abroad, several fundamental questions must be addressed: Is there a market segment in the potential export market that will value the product characteristics of the exporter's product? Is this segment large enough to justify the costs of exporting? Is this segment adequately served by existing domestic producers or other exporters? Can it be accessed by the exporter?

Markets can be segmented in a number of ways. The two most important are product quality and product features. Both of these two segmentation techniques have implications for product price. Typically, the higher the quality and the greater the number of distinctive product features, the higher the costs of production and marketing and the higher the price. One of the characteristics of international

This chapter was prepared by Paul W. Beamish.

markets is the wide range of quality and product characteristics that are in demand by some groups of potential buyers. As examples, sweaters sell for $8 at a discount store, while across town at a fashionable store sweaters are sold for over $500; name-brand ballpoint pens, such as Cross or Mount Blanc, sell for $70 to $200, while Bic pens are sold for 50 cents—sometimes in the same store.

Initially, in the 1960s, Japanese automobile firms entered the U.S. market by following a niche strategy aimed at the low end of the market. They targeted buyers with low incomes, buyers who wanted a second car, and buyers who were more interested in basic transportation than in quality or features. Over time, these Japanese producers have upgraded their products to compete in ever higher priced segments of the market. On the other hand, in the 1980s, when Honda entered the U.S. market for products using small, gas-powered engines—such as lawn mowers, outboard motors, and generators—it chose the very high end of the market to cater to high-income consumers who wanted dependability, quality, unique design, and high performance and had the money to pay for these features. When Samsung entered China with color televisions, a key issue was which segment to target.

Market segments often differ between countries in the number, size, and characteristics by which they are segmented. In the United States, markets may be segmented regionally, whereas in Japan there may be few regional differences. Markets in a populous country, such as the United States, may have more segments (with enough demand in each segment to make the segmentation effort pay off) than in less populous countries. The proportion of the market in each segment often differs among countries. For consumer products, differences in the age distribution of the population, income level and growth, and the distribution of income may affect segment size and relative importance.

If, for example, the exporter's product is of high quality or has unique design features, one starting point would be to segment countries by Gross National Income (GNI) per capita (as a proxy for personal disposable income) and then to focus on countries with high GNI per capita. This crude segmentation could be refined, however, by examining the income distributions of both the initial target group and lower-income countries (that had been left out of the group) to identify countries with a disproportionately high percentage of high-income or high-wealth residents, such as many of the countries in South America and some of the countries in the Asia-Pacific region. If the exporter's product were most appropriate for one age group, trends in these countries in the age distribution of the population could then be examined. For products appropriate for older people, Japan and some European countries would stand out; for the youth market, certain South American countries; for infants, certain African countries, Canada, and the United States.

Consumer tastes also influence segment size. Consumers in Japan, for example, place considerable value on product quality and design features and often prefer to buy a limited number of high-quality, high-priced products, rather than a large number of low-quality, low-priced products. Countries could also be grouped by weather conditions—average temperature and range, and amount of rainfall—for products whose performance and appropriateness are dependent on these conditions. For tropical countries, both packaging and product may have to be changed to be more resistant to humidity and high temperatures. As an example, Tetra packs for juices and milk are more prevalent in tropical countries, particularly lower-income ones where refrigeration is not widespread.

For industrial machinery and inputs, the level and dispersion of wages and technical skills and the composition of industrial output affect the size and importance of market segments. Very high technology, highly automated, but flexible machinery might be targeted at northern Europe, Japan, and Canada; somewhat more standardized, mass-production machinery might be directed at the newly industrializing countries; and older, standardized machinery targeted at the developing countries. For example, Husky Injection Moulding has been able to extend the life of its product line by selling its highest-priced, most-advanced, high-speed equipment to the United States, Europe, and Japan, while at the same time selling its older, much cheaper, slower equipment to countries in which demand is lower. Similarly, countries could be segmented according to their natural resource and agricultural bases by exporters of production equipment for mining and agriculture or for processing of these products.

Fast growth often leads to strains on infrastructure. In some emerging markets, for example, the demand for electricity has grown 8 to 10 percent a year for the last decade, leading to a huge demand for electrical generating equipment and services. Similar demand growth can be found in fast-growing countries for construction and earth-moving equipment, water distribution and treatment facilities, telecommunications equipment, sewage treatment equipment, pollution control equipment, and garbage handling and processing equipment. In many developing countries, privatization of many basic infrastructure operations has led to a burgeoning demand for investment in these services.

Once the potential export destinations have been placed in groups with higher and lower priority, the market potential in each country needs to be examined in more detail. Part of this analysis has already been accomplished in the analysis of the previous block, when the firm's sustainable competitive advantage was identified. The consumers and industrial buyers that value the firm's product in the home country and give it a competitive advantage there are often similar to the ones that will value it in export markets. The consumer segment that values a firm's high-quality pots and pans in the home market may be the same as the consumer segment in export markets. As well, in many cases firms with export potential will have received (and sometimes filled) unsolicited orders from customers or importers abroad. The problem, then, is to discover if there is sufficient demand in these export markets to justify a more concerted export marketing effort. After payment of transportation costs, agents' fees, and tariffs, the price the firm must charge to be profitable in an export market may have risen several-fold above the price that its normal target segment is willing to pay. Then the problem is to determine if there are sufficient potential purchasers in the segment who can and are willing to buy in this price range and if the firm's product will have a competitive advantage in this segment. For example, a pots and pans manufacturer in the United States may have a competitive advantage in the large middle segment of the U.S. market, but in Japan it will have to aim at the top end of the market, a smaller segment. Yogurt sells for 50 cents a container in Australia, but yogurt exported from Australia to Indonesia sells there for $2 a container while Häagen-Dazs ice cream sells for $10 a pint.

Three conditions may be particularly important in this type of analysis: (1) emerging demand met by innovations in product technology in one country that are mirrored in other countries, (2) the deregulation and restructuring of markets, and (3) government policies and programs. As examples, changing energy prices have led to emerging demand for vehicles powered by natural gas in many countries. Compressed natural gas units to power vehicles developed in response to demand conditions in one country may face the same demand conditions in other countries. The restructuring of markets in Japan in response to rising incomes and efforts by the Japanese government to open up the country to international trade has presented opportunities for many exporters to penetrate channels of distribution (such as door-to-door sales, large discount stores, and catalog sales), and to increase sales of heavily branded luxury products.

Identification of emerging product and segment demand is a prime tool of export marketing. It is often easier to penetrate a rapidly growing market or segment of the market than to penetrate markets and segments in which demand is stagnant. In these more dynamic markets and segments, existing suppliers may be experiencing problems with expanding capacity, or they may have grown complacent as their sales have boomed. At least part of the success of the Airbus during the 1980s stemmed from the capacity problems experienced by Boeing in the face of escalating demand for civilian aircraft. In buoyant markets and segments, existing suppliers may be less prone to retaliate against a new exporter. Although existing suppliers may lose market share to the newcomer, their sales levels will continue to increase. In emerging markets and segments, the distribution system may also be in a state of flux, and traditional buyer-seller relationships may be weaker than in slower-growing markets and segments.

Step 2: Select an Entry Strategy to Promote Sustainable Competitive Advantage

Once a viable segment of the market has been selected, the next step is to determine the best strategy by which to penetrate this segment. Strategy formulation does not end with matching product characteristics to market segments. It should include channels of distribution, sales and advertising techniques, service before and after sales, and so on. Some producers give substantial support to wholesalers and retailers. They provide fast delivery, inventory support, and technical assistance and training before the sale and repair and maintenance support after the sale. On the other hand, some firms have been successful in export markets by providing a lower level of these services to their distribution networks and to consumers and, instead, competing more on the basis of price.

Having a different strategy than the major competitors in the market also has advantages. Large entrenched producers with strong brand images may find it difficult to respond to exporters following a strategy that differs from their own. A similar situation exists in many markets for entrants at the bottom end of the market. The branded major producers may not be able to respond without damaging their brand images.

The final, and arguably the most important, decision in a firm's export strategy is whether to sell a standardized product worldwide or whether to tailor products and the entire marketing mix to meet individual country requirements. There is no one right or wrong answer to this problem. The correct answer depends on a host of considerations, such as the ability and capacity of the firm to modify products, the R&D and design costs of modifications, and the effects on production, inventory, and distribution costs of producing and marketing a more diverse set of products.

In the past, exporters in different countries tended to follow one of three different strategies. In general, firms in Japan tended to export one standardized product to all markets; firms in the United States tended to follow a product life-cycle strategy by first introducing a new product in the U.S. market and later exporting it as demand by other countries became more similar to U.S. demand; and firms in Europe tended to be more responsive to local market conditions and to view each market as a separate entity. These generic strategies tended to converge and overlap during the 1980s, as firms tried to incorporate all the strengths of flexibility to respond to individual market needs, global marketing to gain economies of scale, and international learning to access and supply worldwide product and process innovations. As examples, Toyota, after initially selling the same car in Canada as it did worldwide, now tailors its cars sold in Canada to better withstand diverse weather conditions: extremes of heat and cold and prolonged exposure to salt. Kodak introduced a new line of film first in Japan, then in Europe, and only a year later in the United States.

Export strategies can be changed over time in response to changing exchange rates and consumer preferences. Initially, Japanese car firms exported inexpensive standard cars that competed on price, not quality, design, or features. Over time, they broadened their product line to access consumers with different preferences to increase market share.

In general, most exporters would prefer to follow a standard product and marketing-mix strategy worldwide. Such a strategy reduces production, logistics, and inventory costs, complexity, market and product research and development, and managerial time. Such a strategy is obviously more appropriate for some products than for others. If demand characteristics are similar in many potential export markets, then a standardized product approach is often most appropriate, and vice versa. The same Pringles potato chips are exported all over the world. On the other hand, U.S. cookie, ketchup, and cereal manufacturers have had to modify the sugar content of their product for export to Europe. The key question to be addressed is the extent to which demand will be increased through product and marketing-mix changes (at constant prices) and to what extent differentiation will lead to higher costs, higher prices, and decreased demand. Usually, tailoring a product for individual markets through product modification will increase market share. Unless the full costs of this tailoring can be recouped in higher prices or increased demand, however, following this strategy will not be successful, where success is defined in terms of profits on export markets.[1] Even for the same product, different companies can successfully follow different strategies. In personal health care products, for example, Ponds sells the same face cream worldwide, while other producers tailor their products to individual markets, based on such characteristics as skin color, texture, and weather conditions. P&G sells Tide laundry detergent in bars in many developing countries, where most washing is done by hand. But it also sells its standard powdered detergent. Philips sells the same lighting products worldwide. But firms from Taiwan sell lower-quality lighting products at lower prices to developing countries.[2]

A company may follow a combination of both strategies for one product. It can sell a standard product in markets of one group of countries and tailor its product for another group of countries. Similarly, a company may follow a standard product strategy for one product and a tailored product strategy for another. Coca-Cola, for example, follows a standard product strategy for Coke, but a tailored product strategy for Fanta by which it sells a wide range of flavors in some countries.

Step 3: Take a Long-Run Perspective

Export markets are not built overnight. Building and maintaining a sustainable competitive advantage in any one export market, let alone worldwide, is an investment (although for accounting purposes it must unfortunately be treated as a current cost). The initial R&D, channel development, and advertising (all necessary to launch a product) are best viewed as investments, not current costs. So, too, should the costs of entering export markets be viewed as investments. They are investments whose payoffs come only over time. A firm must invest the time and the money in export markets. It must gain expertise in export operations and in identifying export markets; identify, select, and manage channels of distribution into those markets; gain the technical expertise to modify products for export markets; and develop on-the-ground experience in an export market. As well, often initial losses are incurred to penetrate markets through low prices. All these costs are investments in export markets, not expenses.

Firms that make a commitment to support exports through the formation of a separate export unit within their organization, significantly outperform firms that treat exports as just a part of their domestic business. Further, firms that structure exports around subsequent stages of internationalization achieve progressively higher overall export revenues.

This characterization of the initial stages of export marketing as an investment strengthens the value of the systematic approach to export operations outlined in this framework. The costs of undertaking the research involved in using this framework to analyze export opportunities are low, compared with the costs of investment in product and process R&D, channels of distribution, and market development that often follow a decision to enter an export market.

FACTORS THAT IMPEDE AND FACILITATE TRADE

If a firm's product has a competitive advantage in export markets, and if there is a country market or a segment within that market that values the product sufficiently above the products of competing suppliers to offset the costs of exporting, attention can be turned to the factors that may impede or facilitate access to this demand. These factors can be divided into natural and government-imposed ones. The latter are discussed in Chapter 12 in greater detail. Natural factors include transportation costs and the cost of doing business in a different country. Government-imposed factors include impediments such as tariff and nontariff barriers to trade and undervalued exchange rates. On the other hand, governments of the exporting country can also facilitate trade through export incentives, concessional financing for exports, information services, sponsored trade fairs, and export missions.

Over the decades, transportation, communications, and travel costs have fallen, thereby reducing some of the natural impediments to trade and world competition. National differences have also decreased due to the convergence of income levels in many countries, mass media, and travel (and arguably the spread of English as the language of international business). National differences in language, culture, social values, and political systems, however, can still represent major barriers to trade, especially for a new exporter. Many Canadian firms have experienced difficulty in operating in the United States even though the two countries seem to be quite similar. The Japanese language is a major barrier to exporting to and operating in Japan. People differ among countries in how they relate to each other and in how they do business. These differences act as impediments to trade. Lack of knowledge and expertise in doing business abroad in general and in specific export markets is a key barrier to trade. It is a key impediment for firms in their efforts to realize the potential competitive advantage of their products. Conversely, having this knowledge and expertise is a key competitive strength, but one that can be developed only at considerable cost. The manager of a large Japanese trading company in Singapore has stated that the company is not much interested in its operations in Singapore. The Singapore economy and government regulations are too open, transparent, and straightforward. This company largely left Singapore to new, smaller firms who competed fiercely with each other and made small profits. The manager preferred operations in Indonesia, where markets and government regulation were complex and filled with "anomalies," which, once understood, led to substantial profits.

CHANNELS OF DISTRIBUTION AND EXPORT MARKETING

The last block of analysis involves identifying the means by which the product can be moved from the producer to the ultimate buyer.

Four characteristics of the channels of distribution that link producers in one country with buyers in another are especially important:

1. International channels of distribution are usually more complex and have more layers than do channels in the national market. A typical channel for the domestic market would be: producer–wholesaler–retailer. For export it might be: producer–export agent–import agent–major wholesaler–small wholesaler–retailer.

2. The costs of international channels are usually higher than those of domestic channels, so a higher percentage of the final price to the buyer comes from the costs of building, accessing, and operating through international channels of distribution.

3. An exporter may have to operate through different types of channels of distribution on export markets than it uses in its domestic market. For example, in the domestic market, its scale of operations or the value of close customer contact may argue for an in-house distribution and sales system all the way to the ultimate purchaser. To set up such a system in an export market might be prohibitively expensive, given planned export volumes. Conditions in export markets might be such that expertise in local marketing techniques (which the firm does not possess) may be more important than product knowledge. Regulations in the export market may hinder or even prohibit a firm from entering into distribution and sales operations. Conversely, in a firm's domestic market, there may be a well-developed system of independent distributors for the firm's product, whereas in the export market such a distribution system may not exist or company personnel may not have the skills required to distribute and sell the firm's product effectively.

4. International channels of distribution are often also the source of information to the firm about conditions in its export markets, and how and why its product is succeeding or failing in these markets. In such a situation, a firm must either integrate forward into distribution and sales, place some of its personnel in the export market, or develop close ties and good information flows between itself and its distributors abroad.

For these four reasons, a firm's strategy toward, and management of, its international channels of distribution are usually relatively more important, more costly, and more difficult for export marketing than are its channels for marketing in the domestic market. A firm can have a competitive product, but if it chooses the wrong channel of distribution or mismanages its relationships with the channel, its export performance will be reduced below potential. As well, exporters, particularly new exporters, have less expertise with international channels of distribution than they have with the channels in their national markets.

Firms entering export operations are often caught in a bind when they select their channels of distribution. The more closely the channel matches the one they use in their domestic market, the greater their expertise at managing the channel, and the higher the probability of success. On the other hand, the more appropriate the channel is for the export market, the higher the probability of export success. The implications of these two generalizations on the factors influencing export success for channel selection may differ, however. A firm may use an in-house wholesale and retail system in the domestic economy, but access to a similar system in an export market may not be available, purchasing one may be too expensive, or the firm may not want to risk investing so much capital outside its home country. In this situation, it must turn to independent agents or distributors to gain access to the export market. Similarly, a firm may use direct selling in the domestic market, but such an approach may be inappropriate in the export market.

There is a wide variety of possible channels of distribution from which an exporter may choose: brokers, factors, manufacturer's representatives, export agents, wholesalers, retailers, import jobbers, trading houses, and so on. These trade intermediaries can be characterized in two dimensions. The first dimension is ownership of the goods: agents who act on the firm's behalf for a fee versus distributors who pay for, take title to, and sell the goods on their own behalf. The second dimension is channel control: a direct approach (in which the firm owns and operates the channels) versus an indirect approach (in which the channels are independent of the firm).

Selection among these four basic alternative combinations (and the many different types of organizations within each type) is a difficult but important task. The decision will rest on such criteria as the size, capabilities, and resources of the exporter; its strategy in the export market; the degree of risk it is willing to undertake; the extent of its current and future export sales; the importance of coverage, penetration, control, and information feedback; and the differences between the export market and the domestic market.

Conflicts can easily arise between exporters and independent (indirect) channels over many issues. Often importers desire sole import rights for the product in the country. Exporters want sole product rights—that is, for the importer to carry no competing products. There can be conflicts over pricing, cost sharing for advertising and service, margins, new product introduction, and so on. The benefits of using indirect channels are that typically resource costs are lower and the independent channels may have superior firsthand knowledge of, and access to, customers in the export market. The major costs are in loss of control, less ability to push goods through the channels by discounts, promotions, and direct selling or to pull goods through the channels through control of advertising. Use of indirect channels usually reduces information flows and reduces knowledge acquisition of market information when compared with direct channels. The costs and benefits of using direct (company-owned) channels tend to be the reverse of the costs and benefits of indirect channels: initially less firsthand knowledge of, and expertise in, the market; less access to customers, greater up-front costs on the one hand, but fewer conflicts, increased control, and greater information flows on the other.

Often an exporter's success with using indirect (independent) channels of distribution rests on whether its bargaining power is greater or less than that of its independent agent/distributor. Superior bargaining power can rest with either side and largely depends on which side provides the most value, which side faces the greatest range of alternatives, and which side needs the other the most. The importance of channels of distribution and the difficulty in accessing them often tip the balance of bargaining power in favor of independent agents and distributors in the local market. Yet foreign firms have been able to access these channels or to develop their own through direct selling and in-house distribution and sales networks. Whatever channels are chosen and whatever the relative bargaining power, the complexity and the length of international channels of distribution add to their cost.

PRICING IN EXPORT MARKETS

Product pricing is an important and difficult decision in any market. Four pricing strategies can be identified that are unique to export markets: (1) requiring prices in export markets that yield higher returns than are available in domestic markets; (2) pricing to yield similar returns in domestic and export markets; (3) pricing to yield lower returns, or even losses, in export markets—at least in the short run; (4) and pricing to sell production in excess of the needs of the domestic market so long as these sales make a contribution to fixed overhead and profit.

The first pricing strategy is often based on the belief that export operations are riskier relative to domestic sales, and they often entail hidden costs that are not picked up by standard accounting systems. Under this viewpoint, the prices and profits recorded on export sales must be higher than those for domestic markets if exports are to be undertaken. This sort of rigid, cost-plus approach may result in uncompetitive prices.

The second strategy is based on the viewpoint that export markets do not necessarily differ from domestic markets. This strategy is often taken by experienced exporters, for whom there is little differentiation between export and domestic sales. It is also taken by new and inexperienced exporters, who take an "if they order it, we'll ship it" attitude toward export markets. While exporters here do not assume that export prices will differ much from domestic levels, they nonetheless retain the flexibility to adapt prices somewhat to local conditions.

The third strategy reflects an approach that views export markets as the potential growth markets of the future. These are the markets in which the firm must operate if it is to survive in the long run. These aggressive exporters are willing to take short-term losses to buy market share, to develop products that are appropriate for export markets, and to achieve economies of scale. They believe that in the long run, once their position in export markets has been established, their costs will be lowered and they will be able to earn satisfactory returns. This strategy, however, may make the firm vulnerable to antidumping action by domestic competitors in the export market.

The final strategy reflects a view of export markets as a dumping ground for production in times of excess capacity. Although this type of export does make a contribution to profits, firms that view export markets in this way cannot be regarded as true export marketers. Further, such firms are very vulnerable to antidumping duties.

Whatever pricing strategy is chosen, the relatively high fixed costs per unit that are typical of international distribution channels have a significant effect on the ability of the firm to use price as a competitive weapon. To take an extreme case, often the costs of international distribution are a fixed amount per unit (due to transportation costs based on weight or volume, tariffs levied on a per unit basis, and channel costs/fees on a per unit basis). They do not vary with cost or price. Then a change of 10 percent at the producer price level may only change the price faced by the buyer by 2 percent. Yet a 10 percent reduction in price may reduce the producer's margins over direct costs by 50 percent. Buyer response to such a price cut would have to be enormous for this price cut to be worthwhile.

At least some of the costs of distribution are indeed set with respect to the producer's selling price, such as inventory costs, some agents' fees, and some components of tariff charges. Sales taxes are usually based on the landed, duty-paid price of the product. They vary with price. But there is also a fixed component due to the fixed transportation costs per unit. Most of the fees charged by independent agents are usually based on producer prices, as are the markups taken through the channels of distribution. Despite these portions of the price paid by purchasers that varies with the producer prices, in export marketing there is usually a higher component in final prices that varies with the number of units sold than for domestic marketing. This characteristic of export marketing must be taken into consideration by firms in their export marketing pricing strategies.

STAGES OF EXPORT MARKET INVOLVEMENT

For firms operating solely in the domestic market, starting a new business or introducing a new product are major strategic moves and are undertaken only after careful research, analysis, and consideration. The decision to enter export operations at all or in a particular export market is more often quite haphazard and made by chance, or the decision itself may go unnoticed. Most frequently, a firm will enter export operations based on an unsolicited order from abroad, or an offer from an agent or importer abroad to represent the firm or sell its products. Other unplanned entries into export marketing may come from internal factors, such as overproduction, declining domestic sales, and excess capacity. Such external events as competitive pressures, "follow the leader" behavior, government-sponsored trade fairs, and funded export missions may also lead to unplanned entry into export markets.

Most firms initially develop, produce, and market products for their domestic markets without regard for export markets. They may even turn down orders from abroad. If a firm continues to receive unsolicited orders, it may move toward filling orders as they are received, despite the problems of documentation and payment that may arise. Gradually, the firm may develop management expertise in the basic mechanics of exporting, and these orders begin to become a significant part of sales. In this situation, a firm may begin to explore why these orders have been received. It may try to determine if there is a potential to increase sales to the firms that have already placed orders and to other firms in the same export market.

In the next stage of export involvement, the firm begins to evaluate the impact of export sales on its performance in a more systematic way. If it finds this impact to be positive, it may begin to change its export operations to increase their effectiveness. It is at this stage when a systematic analysis of exporting, as described in these chapters, can be of value. In the final stage, exports become a major, even the deciding, factor in the firm's strategy and operations. For firms at this stage, products are often developed and introduced in relationship to export markets as well as the domestic market.

This process of internationalization may be short-circuited at any stage if the results of export operations are not seen as favorable. Such a decision may be incorrect if the firm has not really given export operations the same attention that it has given domestic markets. Conversely, a firm may have no choice but to start at some more advanced stage. The domestic market may be too small to support any operations at all, much less a scale-efficient one. Increasingly, however, the evolution of the international trading environment has forced more and more firms at a faster and faster pace through these stages of internationalization to become full-fledged export marketers. Exhibit 4.1 summarizes many of the key conceptual issues for each of the major export stages according to various features.

EXHIBIT 4.1   **Conceptual Issues Emerging from Export Development Models**

	Export Stages		
Model Features	**Pre-Engagement**	**Initial**	**Advanced**
(i) Facilitators and Inhibitors:			
Managerial characteristics	A number of objective and subjective managerial parameters might act as inhibitors in the firm's export engagement.	Certain managerial characteristics, such as cosmopolitan, multilingual and educated management, might facilitate the involvement of firms in export activities.	Management quality and dynamism is an important facilitator in advanced export operations.
Management style	The firm's management style applies only to the domestic business situation, and it is rather institutionalized and structured.	The decisionmaker approaches export marketing in a rather informal, disjointed, and unplanned manner.	With the establishment of appropriate systems and processes relating to foreign business, decision-making styles tend to become more formalized, continuous, and structured.
Organizational determinants	Certain organizational determinants might prevent the engagement of the firm in foreign operations.	Some organizational factors, particularly those relating to the firm's competitive advantages, might facilitate the engagement of the firm in international operations.	The firm capitalizes on differential advantages, such as possession of unique products, competitive prices, and technological intensiveness, to gain a foothold in foreign markets.
Organizational resources	There is typically a limited number of corporate resources that are used exclusively for domestic operations.	The firm gradually commits small amounts of financial, human, and allied resources to international operations, due to the high uncertainty prevailing in foreign markets.	An increasing amount of organizational resources is released to export operations, but their allocation is based upon real market conditions and strategic preferences.
(ii) Information needs and acquisition:			
Information requirements	There is limited or no knowledge about export operations: firms actively seeking to export want information about foreign market possibilities.	The firm has limited experience and knowledge about exporting and, therefore, seeks information of a more experiential and general nature.	As the firm gains more experience and exposure to export activities, it searches for more objective and specific information.

EXHIBIT 4.1   *(continued)*

Model Features	Export Stages		
	Pre-Engagement	Initial	Advanced
Information acquisition	Lack of information about exporting results in high levels of uncertainty in international markets compared to the domestic market.	The availability of information about export business and foreign marketing practices is still limited, thus creating considerable uncertainty.	The firm gradually obtains more export-related information, particularly of an experiential nature, leading to reduced levels of uncertainty regarding overseas markets.
(iii) Stimuli and barriers:			
Stimulating forces	The nonexporting firm is not responsive to various export stimuli to which it is exposed due to managerial, organizational, or environmental constraints.	The firm is more likely to be motivated in international business by reactive and external factors, exemplifying passive and tactical thinking toward exporting.	The export stimulation of the firm is more likely to occur due to proactive and internal factors, indicating an aggressive and strategic approach to international business.
Barrier factors	The would-be exporter is exposed to a number of export barriers, the most important being its inability to locate/analyze foreign markets.	The firm experiences obstacles that are related mainly to difficulties in understanding the mechanics and day-to-day activities of exporting.	Export obstacles are associated mainly with strategic marketing issues and external constraints in foreign markets.
(iv) Market selection, entry/expansion:			
Market selection	The firm deals exclusively with the domestic market from where it might choose to serve specific segments.	The firm selects few countries that are more psychologically close to its home business and, therefore, easier and less costly to penetrate.	The firm gradually expands its foreign operations to a greater number of host countries that are psychologically more distant.
Entry mode	The firm uses only domestic distribution methods since its goods are sold exclusively in the home market.	The firm enters foreign markets via indirect export methods, such as export merchants, trading companies, resident buyers, and export agents.	The firm distributes its products to overseas markets using direct export methods, such as agents, distributors, and sales branches.
Market expansion	The firm is likely to undergo an extraregional expansion, that is, expansion within regions of its own country base.	Limited corporate resources, fear of the unknown, and other barriers are responsible for the firm adopting a concentrated foreign market focus.	As the firm acquires more resources, seeks to exploit more foreign opportunities, and gains expertise in handling export problems, it spreads to a large number of markets.
(v) Marketing strategy:			
Marketing control	The firm maintains full or partial control over the elements of the marketing mix, because it deals exclusively with the domestic market.	The firm is highly dependent on overseas buyers' guidelines and actions with regard to product, pricing, distribution, and promotional requirements in foreign markets.	The firm gradually internalizes and ultimately gains full control of the elements of the export marketing mix strategy.
Marketing adaptations	The firm's marketing strategy is relatively standardized as it deals exclusively with local customers.	The firm is more likely to adopt more standardized export marketing strategies.	Considerable adaptations in the elements of the marketing mix are likely to take place, particularly as regards to products and promotion.

Source: L. C. Leonidou and C. S. Katsikeas, "The Export Development Process: An Integrative Review of Empirical Models," *Journal of International Business Studies,* Vol. 27, No. 3, 1996, pp. 532–33.

TRADE INTERMEDIARIES

Import Traders

The topic of importing has received relatively little attention in books on international marketing or international business. Yet for every export, there is an import. And arm's-length importing still represents the majority of imports. This section focuses on "pure" importers, i.e., importers who purchase products abroad for resale. The important topic of sourcing imports for use as inputs in the production process is the subject of the next chapter.

This section is quite brief, since much of the basic framework of analysis has already been presented. However from the perspective of the importer, the export framework presented earlier cannot simply be turned inside out. As Exhibit 4.2 points out, the assumed importer behaviors associated with the relevant export decisions are not identical with actual importer behavior. An importer assesses the

EXHIBIT 4.2   Understanding Importer Behavior

Relevant Export Decisions	Assumed Importer Behavior	Actual Importer Behavior
Export initiation	• Exporters export to importers. • Importers lured into importing when exporters offer better deals.	• "Global" importers recruit, select, train exporters. • Buyers forced into importing when existing vendors failed to meet task-requirement and nontask expectations.
Export targeting	• Importers search the world for best exporters. • Best vendors included in choice set via screening analysis. • Best importers always available, "out there"; no deadline in targeting.	• Importers search heuristically to minimize cognitive effort and risk. • Choice set limited by accessibility in bilateral search and discovery. • Search terminated when "good enough" vendor found.
Export entry	• Vendor evaluation is transaction-based, process objective, and analytical. • Vendor evaluation compensatory, all relevant factors considered. • Best vendor chosen on the merits of export proposal (bid). • Export strategy based on 4Ps.	• Vendor evaluation is relationship-based, previous association important. • Vendor evaluation judgmental based on available info. and cognitive heuristics. • Qualified vendor chosen for non-task-related benefits. • More than 4Ps at work.
Export management	• Exporters are the prime movers of international trade. • Importers implement export strategy formulated/supported by exporters. • Export marketing decision controlled by exporters.	• World markets are increasingly "buyer's markets"; much international exchange is buyer-coordinated importing rather than producer-initiated exporting. • Importers have strategies of their own. • Importers may take control of export marketing decisions in importer-led international exchange.

Source: N. Liang and A. Parkhe, "Importer Behavior: The Neglected Counterpart of International Exchange," *Journal of International Business Studies,* Vol. 28, No. 3, 1997, p. 523.

comparative and competitive advantages of producers outside the home market; assesses the evolving demand and supply characteristics of the home market to look for gaps in markets or segments of markets that these producers' products could fill; assesses the impediments to connecting producers abroad with buyers in the home market and the factors that might facilitate this linkage; and assesses the channels of distribution that might be used to link producers abroad with buyers in the home market. An importer could either have the objective to resell the imported products (an import marketer) to other buyers or to use these products as raw or semifinished materials, or as components in its own final products (an import purchasing manager).

Pure importers usually have an "ownership advantage" related to the domestic market in which they operate, such as knowledge of the domestic market, ownership of or access to the channels of distribution, or expertise in evaluating government regulation of imports, or business practices in the domestic market. Importers typically possess one of two other ownership advantages: knowledge and expertise in operations in one or more foreign countries or knowledge and expertise in the production capabilities of some product or range of products worldwide. The knowledge of domestic conditions allows importers to create value for producers abroad relative to the value they could access by exporting directly to buyers in the domestic economy. Knowledge of production capabilities worldwide allows them to create value for domestic producers (for imported inputs) and domestic retailers relative to the value they would receive if they tried to search out these products for themselves.

Pure importers are market connectors; they create value through linking producers abroad to buyers in the domestic market. If they do not continue to create value after the initial link has been made, producers abroad may begin to sell directly to the buyers in the domestic market. Similarly, purchasers in their domestic market will make direct connections with producers abroad.

Export Traders

In the section on export operations, the viewpoint of an export producer, rather than a pure export trader, was taken. This was done since in most respects the analysis of the international trade environment is the same from both perspectives. The major difference between the producer-exporter and the export trader is that the latter has the opportunity to buy products from (or act as an agent for) different producers in the same or different industries. In this respect, an export trader shares many of the same characteristics as an import trader. The "ownership advantages" of export traders typically lie in knowledge of markets in particular countries or in knowledge of worldwide markets for particular products. They are also market connectors and face the same problems as pure importers once they have linked domestic producers with buyers in export markets.

Trading Houses

In some cases, pure import operations and pure export operations may be joined together within the same firm: the trading house. Typically, however, a trading house will specialize in either exports or imports. The exception to this generalization is found in the large trading houses in Japan, Hong Kong, and Korea and to some extent in Europe and in firms that specialize in trading such commodities as energy products, minerals, and agricultural products.

Import and export operations also exist together in some export producers. These firms may need to source inputs for their production operations and to fill out their product lines from abroad and to export their output as well. As discussed below, some export sales are contingent on reciprocal imports under various forms of countertrade. These operations can be handled by this type of department as well.

In summary, managers of export operations or those about to engage in export operations need to address five questions:

1. Does our product and firm have a sustainable competitive advantage in export markets and, if so, why?

2. What are the export markets and the segments of those markets that will value our product sufficiently (relative to other competing products) to offset our costs of production and distribution?

3. Should the firm export a standard product with a standard marketing mix worldwide or should it tailor its products and marketing mix to individual export markets?

4. What natural and government-imposed trade barriers impede linking production in one country to purchase in another, and what factors might facilitate this linkage?

5. What are the most appropriate channels of distribution for our product to achieve our goals in export markets?

GLOBAL TRADE AND INVESTMENT

So far, the viewpoint of exporting has been one of a producer-exporter or importer or a trade intermediary exporting products to one country market. This viewpoint, although useful to present the basics of international trade, is highly simplistic and may give a false impression of international trade. This basic model can be extended to encompass a more realistic view of world trade. The model of international trade presented so far can be extended to make it more realistic in three ways.

First, as tariff and nontariff barriers to trade have fallen globally and as free trade areas have developed, firms often now analyze trade opportunities on a regional, even global, basis. For example, exports to a small market such as Belgium may be of limited interest, but exports to Belgium as a gateway to Europe make a much more interesting proposition.

Second, exports are often not sent directly from one home production site to an export market abroad. Rather, inputs are sourced in a number of countries and assembled in other countries, and the final product is sold in yet other countries. Japanese car producers manufacture parts in Japan and ship them for assembly in

Europe, in North America, and in developing countries. In turn they source some parts in these countries for use in Japan and in their assembly operations abroad.

Third, trade has become intricately linked with foreign investment, joint ventures, licensing, franchising, contract production, and component sourcing. These topics are described in later chapters. In particular there is a strong link between trade and foreign investment. A large component of international trade is carried out by multinational enterprises (MNEs). About a third of all world trade in manufactured products is through MNEs. Most U.S. merchandise exports were undertaken by U.S. MNEs or affiliates of foreign-owned MNEs operating in the United States. A similar situation prevailed in the United Kingdom. Japanese MNEs accounted for over 40 percent of exports from and 60 percent of imports to Japan. A considerable proportion of the trade conducted by MNEs is within the firm (i.e., between units of the MNE located in different countries).

Is the analytical framework developed so far useful for analyzing trade by MNEs? What then are the differences between trade via or within MNEs and arm's-length trade? The answer to the first question is yes, but with some modifications. By definition, an MNE has investments and (usually) production operations in more than one country. At the headquarters level of the MNE, basic decisions are made about where different activities along the value-added chain are located geographically. For example, one U.S. manufacturer of scientific instruments performs R&D and product design in the United States and produces the key high-quality, low-tolerance components there. It exports raw materials to its subsidiary in Puerto Rico for production of lower-tolerance, labor-intensive standard components. Components from its U.S. and Puerto Rican facilities are exported to Malaysia for assembly. The finished instruments are then exported to Singapore for inspection and then to Ireland for final testing. The final products are then re-exported all over the world at the direction of the head office. Managers in the head office then balance production costs and capabilities with transportation costs in an effort to minimize the costs of production, transportation, and inventories. They also search out markets for the firm's products worldwide. At the conceptual level, their analysis and activities are similar to the ones described in the framework for export operations, but on a larger and more complex scale. For managers at the subsidiary level, however, trade is performed at the direction of the head office staff. At the subsidiary level, although managers are engaged in export and import operations, the volume, type, and destination of the subsidiary's exports are controlled from the head office.

As international business has evolved over the decades, the forms of international involvements have increased in number and complexity. Besides exports, a firm utilizes its core skills to service markets abroad via investment in production facilities in another country, by licensing its product or process technology, or by contract production. In the early 1990s, IKEA, the Swedish household products company, decided to move some of its product sourcing to Southeast Asia. To accomplish this move, it tried to avoid equity participation in production facilities. Rather, it formed long-term relationships with producers who it determined had the basic production and management capabilities to produce to its design and quality specifications. It now distributes and sells these products worldwide. IKEA, however, engages in extensive training with its suppliers. It also will supply equipment and train producers in its use. In exchange, it receives price concessions on its future purchases. IKEA supplies these producers with the designs and needed imported inputs. Although IKEA's contract suppliers both import inputs and export their output, for all intents and purposes they are not engaged in international trade.

Countertrade

A special form of exporting is countertrade, the linked exchange of goods for goods in international trade. From the mid-1970s to the mid-1980s, countertrade expanded rapidly. In the 1990s, however, the growth of countertrade slowed with the changes in the former "second world." Nonetheless, countertrade still remains an important feature of international trade, particularly in certain industries and countries. Further, it is a way of dealing with currency volatility.

The term countertrade covers eight types of trade operation:

1. Barter: The simultaneous exchange of goods without money.

2. Counterpurchase: The assumption by the exporter, through a separate but linked contract, of an obligation to import some percentage of the price of the goods exported in the form of goods purchased in the importing country.

3. Compensation or buyback: The agreement by an exporter of plant and equipment to buy back some portion of output of the goods produced by the equipment it exports from the importing firms.

4. Production sharing: Similar to buyback, but used in mining and energy projects, where the developer is paid out of a share of the production of the mine or well.

5. Industrial offsets: An obligation undertaken by the exporter to produce or assemble part of the product and source parts in the importing country. Exporting from the importing country may also be undertaken as part of an industrial offset arrangement.

6. Switches: An undertaking by the exporter to import goods from a third country with which the importing country has developed a trade surplus in its "clearing account" under a bilateral trade agreement.

7. Unblocking funds: The use of suppliers' credits that cannot be repatriated due to foreign exchange controls (blocked funds) in the importing country to purchase goods there for export.

8. Debt for equity swaps: The conversion of international debts owed by the importing country to equity in some operation there.

Countertrade contracts can be very complicated and costly to negotiate and to execute. They are filled with pitfalls for the unwary exporter. Only 1 in 10 countertrade arrangements is ever finalized. For an inexperienced exporter or an exporter who is not familiar with countertrade, the best course of action is to seek the advice and support of an experienced countertrader. Many exporters have been caught unaware when countertrade demands are introduced in the negotiation process of a trade arrangement.

Countertrade contracts have nine important characteristics:

1. The timing of the flow of goods (will the export precede, be simultaneous with, or follow the countertraded import?).

2. The duration of the contracts (within what time period must the matching import be made?).

3. The countertrade percent (what percent of the export price must be taken back in countertraded products?).

4. Voluntary or mandatory countertrade.

5. The penalties for noncompliance with the countertrade contract.

6. The product requirements for the linked imports (is the exporter free to choose any goods to fulfill the countertrade obligation or must the exporter source from an approved list?).

7. Whether the countertraded goods must be incremental to the exporter's previous purchases in the importing country.

8. Country destination of the linked imports (can they be sold to any country or must their final destination be the exporter's home country?).

9. Whether the exporting firm itself must fulfill the countertrade obligation or whether it can transfer it to another party.

Each of these provisions is subject to negotiations between the exporter and the importer or the importing country's government. As can be appreciated from the preceding description of countertrade operations, they require exporters to develop a new set of skills—often at great cost in terms of management time, risks, and failed and unprofitable countertrade arrangements. Essentially, countertrade requires a "double coincidence of needs": the importer needs the exporter's product, and the exporter either needs products from the importer or the importing country or can identify buyers who do. In general, countertrade is an inefficient form of trade. It creates costs and risks for both importers and exporters and reduces the value created by international trade. In general, using money to facilitate trade is much more efficient than countertrade.

Major Project Development

The importance of major project development in international trade and investment increased during the 1990s, and there is every prospect that it will continue to increase into the future. These projects are often for infrastructure development such as electricity generation, telecommunications, water and sewage treatment facilities, and even roads and ports. These major projects are of three types: turnkey projects; build, operate, and transfer projects; and build, operate, and own projects.

In a turnkey project, the project manager undertakes to construct a major project, such as a smelter or electrical generating plant, and then turn it over to its owners when it is in full operation. Turnkey projects offer exporters a means of increasing their exports dramatically by one sale. Turnkey projects differ on two dimensions: self-engineered versus construction to specification; fixed price versus cost plus. In the self-engineered project, the exporter undertakes to meet certain performance requirements set by the importer, but the actual equipment and plant design is left up to the exporter. For example, the exporter might undertake to construct a pipeline with the capacity to pump a specified quantity of natural gas per day from one location to another. The size and thickness of the pipe and the power and number of the pumping stations are left to the discretion of the exporter; the exporter bears the risk of not meeting the performance requirements. In construction to specification, the exporter undertakes to construct the project to the importer's specifications. As long as these are met, the risk of performance failure rests with the importer.

Both self-engineered and construction to specification contracts can be undertaken on a fixed-price or a cost-plus basis. On a cost-plus contract, the risk of cost overruns lies with the purchaser. With a fixed-price contract, the risk lies with the exporter. Usually the purchaser specifies in the bid documents the types of contract to be undertaken. An inexperienced, risk-averse purchaser may choose a fixed-price, self-engineered contract to shift the risk to the exporter. This type of contract usually leads to a higher bid price, since the exporter must be compensated for the increased risk it undertakes.

For turnkey projects, bids are usually submitted by a small number of exporters or groups of exporters. The importer typically screens the bidders prior to the actual bid to eliminate bidders who lack the required technical skills to undertake the contract. In this situation, with only a few bidders, the higher an exporter bids, the greater the expected profits, but the lower the probability of winning the bid. Assessing the trade-off between higher profits and decreased probability of winning the bid is one of the key factors in turnkey operations. Often, after the bids have been opened, the importer will go back to the exporters and try to negotiate with those with the lowest bids to get them to reduce their bids by playing one against the other.

Build, operate, and transfer (BOT) and build, operate, and own (BOO) projects have many of the same features as turnkey projects. Firms bid for the right to construct the project. BOT and BOO projects of course differ from turnkey projects in that the winning firm also operates the facility after it is completed, hence there is an element of foreign direct investment in these types of projects. For BOT projects, ownership is limited to a certain time period, at which time the project is to be transferred to another organization, usually the host country government. For both BOT and BOO projects, output prices and volume over time are often specified.

Exports, Imports, and International Finance

Three important aspects of international finance need to be understood by every exporter and importer: the effect of the real exchange rate on competitive advantage, the effect of variations in the nominal exchange rate on export and import profitability, and the effect of trade on financing needs and sources.

Movements in the nominal exchange rate can have a dramatic impact on the profitability of international trading operations. Take the case of an importer in Canada sourcing from the United States. The importer buys a machine worth $100,000 for sale to a Canadian company with a 10 percent markup over landed cost with delivery six months later. If, over this six-month period, the U.S. dollar appreciates against the Canadian dollar by 2 percent, the importer's gross profit margin is reduced by 20 percent.

An importer has several options through which to handle this risk. It can insist that the U.S. exporter price the machine in Canadian dollars and set its markup based on this price. This alternative simply shifts the exchange rate risk back onto the U.S. exporter and may result in a higher purchase price. The importer may decide to bear the risk and hope that the Canadian dollar does not fall, or even that it may rise. In this case, the importer may try to shift the cost of this risk onto the ultimate customer by increasing its selling price. This action, however, may result in the loss of the sale.

Alternatively, the importer may use some type of currency hedge to eliminate the exchange-rate risk. At the time of the sale, the importer can exchange the Canadian dollar equivalent of $100,000 U.S. (minus the six-month interest rate) into U.S. dollars and place them in a six-month financial asset. When the machine is shipped, the importer can then cash in the U.S. dollar-denominated financial asset and pay for the purchase. Alternatively, the importer could also enter the foreign exchange market and buy $100,000 U.S. six months forward at the six-month forward rate prevailing at the time. When the machine is shipped in six months, it can exercise its forward contract for U.S. dollars at the exchange rate that was set six months before. The forward market for currencies (in this example, U.S. and Canadian dollars) is exactly the same as the spot market for foreign exchange. The rate is set by the supply and demand for U.S. and Canadian dollars six months forward. Buying dollars forward obligates the purchaser to exercise the contract in six months at the rate set at the time of the purchase in the forward market for foreign exchange.

By either of these two methods, the importer can be certain of the Canadian dollar cost of the U.S. import. The importer can then price to the ultimate purchaser in terms of this Canadian dollar price. A Canadian producer that sources inputs in the United States could follow the same procedure before making a purchase in order to be able to compare the Canadian dollar price of the import with the prices of other inputs in the Canadian market.

There is another aspect of international trade that has important implications for corporate finance: the effect of international trade on working capital requirements. For international trade, in most cases there is a longer time period between when a product is produced and the time the ultimate purchaser receives it. Someone must finance the capital requirements and pay the capital costs of these larger inventories of final products: the producer, the exporter, the importer, or some financial intermediary. Who finances these inventory costs depends on the financial strength of the importer and the exporter. For example, the exporter can demand payment when the goods are shipped through an irrevocable letter of credit that is discharged when the goods are loaded on the international carrier. In this case, the importer must arrange the financing for the period from the time the goods are exported until they are sold and the importer receives payment. Similarly, the importer could demand that payment be made only when the goods arrive in the destination country. Whichever party finally agrees to finance this inventory, arranging the financing often proves to be difficult and costly.

The problem lies with the valuation and security of the goods from the viewpoint of whoever is going to finance them. If, for example, the importer rejects the goods when they arrive as being not to specification or damaged, what is their value and how can it be recovered? As an extreme example, an American producer of customized vehicles received an order from Libya for ambulances that were to be specially modified for desert conditions. The size of the order was several times the net worth of the company. Who would finance such a specialized product by such a country? The sale fell through for lack of financing.

An alternative approach is to require that the importer open an irrevocable letter of credit for the amount of the purchase. The exporter is then paid via this letter when the goods are shipped. This shifts the financing costs onto the importer. It also shifts other problems onto the importer, since the importer has already paid for the products. The products may be of unacceptable quality, or not to specification, or the order may not be complete, or the product may be damaged during shipping. These problems can be addressed through the use of inspection and certification firms that act on behalf of the importer and through buying insurance.

The importance of export financing as an export tool has grown over the years as more and more importers and importing countries have experienced problems in accessing foreign exchange to pay for imports. The debt situation in many countries has further increased the importance of export financing in export marketing. A firm may have a competitive product, there may be demand for the product in an export market, but trade may be blocked unless some means is found to finance the sale.

The governments of most European countries and the United States, Japan, and Canada have set up government-owned and funded institutions to provide export financing. The interest rates and the terms and conditions on the loans provided by these institutions are designed to promote exports from their countries. When firms from different countries bid on an export contract, there is a tendency for these government-backed banks to make the terms of the loans more and more favorable in order to win the contract for the exporter they are supporting. Interest rate wars can easily break out. To prevent this situation from occurring, an informal agreement has been reached among them that they will not provide funds at rates below their own cost of capital. This agreement has proven impossible to enforce, however. The cost of capital of these banks is difficult to calculate and varies over time and among countries. Exporters often exert pressure through the government for these banks to make their terms more favorable so that they can win the export contract. Governments themselves often have an interest in promoting exports of certain products or exports to certain countries.

Summary

In the previous chapter, a framework was developed to analyze international trade operations. In that chapter, the factors that influence comparative and competitive advantage and the effect of real exchange rates on export performance were described. This chapter started off where the previous chapter ended. It described how to analyze export markets and various strategies for entering those markets. As the final block in the analysis, it described how the producer itself might enter export markets and use various pricing strategies in export markets. Beyond direct exports by the firm, there are also several types of trade intermediaries through which a firm can export, such as importers and exporters and trading houses. The basic model was then extended to the more complex forms of trade that are currently prevalent: the linkages between trade, joint ventures, foreign direct investment, licensing, and contract production. The model was also extended to regional trade and trade, investment, production, and sales in several countries along the value-added chain.

The last section of the chapter dealt with several special topics, such as countertrade, turnkey, BOT, and BOO projects, and trade finance. These two chapters cover the basics of international trade operations.

In the future, there is every prospect that a higher and higher percentage of world output will be traded internationally. For firms in many industries, the question is not, "Should we trade internationally?" They have no choice if they are to maintain and enhance their competitive position. Rather, the question is, "How can we trade more effectively?" Expertise in international trade will become an increasingly important skill for managers to acquire.

Supplementary Reading

Beamish, Paul W., Karavis, L., Goerzen, A., and C. Lane. "The Relationship Between Organizational Structure and Export Performance," *Management International Review,* Vol. 39, No. 1, 1999 pp. 37–54.

Czinkota, Michael R., and Ilkka A. Ronkainen. *International Marketing.* 5th ed. Fort Worth, TX.: Dryden Press, 1998.

Dhanaraj, Charles and Paul W. Beamish. "A Resource Based Approach to the Study of Export Performance," *Journal of Small Business Management,* (Forthcoming).

Harper, Timothy. *Cracking the New European Markets.* New York: John Wiley & Sons, 1990.

JETRO. *Selling in Japan. The World's Second Largest Market.* Tokyo: JETRO, 1985.

Peng, Mike, W., and Anne S. York, "Behind Intermediary Performance in Export Trade: Transactions, Agents, and Resources," *Journal of International Business Studies,* Vol. 32, No. 2, 2001, pp. 327–346.

Peng, Mike W., and Anne Ilinitch. "Export Intermediary Firms: A Note on Export Development Research," *Journal of International Business Studies,* Vol. 29, No. 3, 1998 pp. 609–620.

Preeg, Ernest. *Traders in a Brave New World: The Uruguay Round and the Future of the International Trading System.* Chicago: University of Chicago Press, 1995.

Quelch, John A., and Christopher A. Bartlett. *Global Marketing Management.* 4th ed. Reading, MA: Addison-Wesley Publishing Company, Inc., 1999.

Raymond, Mary Anne, Tanner Jr., John F., and Jonghoon Kim. "Cost Complexity of Pricing Decisions for Exporters in Developing and Emerging Markets." *Journal of International Marketing,* Vol. 9, No. 3, 2001, pp. 19–40.

Renner, Sandra L., and W. Gary Winget. *Fast-Track Exporting.* New York: AMACOM, 1991.

Ricks, David. *Blunders in International Business.* Cambridge, MA: Basil Blackwell, 1993.

Schaffer, Matt. *Winning the Countertrade War: New Export Strategies for America.* New York: John Wiley & Sons, 1989.

Stottinger, Barbara. "Strategic Export Pricing: A Long and Winding Road," *Journal of International Marketing,* Vol. 9, No. 1, 2001.

Thorelli, Hans B., and S. Tamer Cavusgil, eds. *International Marketing Strategy.* 3rd ed. Elmsford, NY: Pergamon Press, 1995.

Triller, Lawrence W. Going Global: *New Opportunities for Growing Companies to Compete in World Markets.* Homewood. IL: Business One Irwin, 1991.

Weiss, Kenneth D. *Building an Export/Import Business.* New York: John Wiley & Sons, 1991.

Endnotes

1. See Adrian Ryans, "Strategic Market Entry Factors and Market Share Achievement in Japan," Journal of International Business Studies, Fall 1988.
2. Ironically, Philips' expensive, but long-life, energy-efficient "new lighting" fluorescent lamps (which it developed for high-income markets) face severe problems in some developing countries. The problem is not competition with lower-price products; the problem is that to achieve energy efficiency and long life, the voltage tolerances on these products make them inappropriate for countries with problems in voltage swings and low voltage.

Chapter Five

Global Sourcing Strategy: R&D, Manufacturing, and Marketing Interfaces

Global competition suggests a drastically shortened life cycle for most products, and no longer permits companies a polycentric, country-by-country approach to international business. If companies that have developed a new product do follow a country-by-country approach to foreign market entry over time, a globally oriented competitor will likely overcome their initial competitive advantages by blanketing the world markets with similar products in a shorter period of time.

A frequently used framework to describe cross-national business practices is the international product cycle theory. The theory has provided a compelling description of dynamic patterns of international trade of manufactured products and direct investment as a product advances through its life cycle. According to the theory, changes in inputs and product characteristics toward standardization over time determine an optimal production location at any particular phase of the product's life cycle.

However, three major limitations of the international product cycle theory have to be borne in mind:

1. Increased pace of new product introduction and reduction in innovational lead time, which deprive companies of the age-old polycentric approach to global markets.

This chapter was prepared by Masaaki Kotabe of Temple University.

2. Predictable sourcing development during the product cycle, which permits a shrewd company to outmaneuver competition.

3. More active management of locational and corporate resources on a global basis, which gives a company a preemptive first-mover advantage over competition.

Today, quick technological diffusion has virtually become a matter of fact. Without established sourcing plans, distribution, and service networks, it is extremely difficult to exploit both emerging technology and potential markets around the world simultaneously. General Electric's swift global reach could not have been possible without its ability to procure crucial components internally and on a global basis. As a result, the increased pace of new product introduction and reduction in innovational lead time calls for more proactive management of locational and corporate resources on a global basis. In this chapter, we emphasize logistical management of the interfaces of R&D, manufacturing, and marketing activities on a global basis—which we call global sourcing strategy—and also the importance of the ability to procure major components of the product in-house such that companies can proactively standardize either components or products. Global sourcing strategy requires a close coordination among R&D, manufacturing, and marketing activities across national boundaries.[1]

There always exist conflicts in the tug-of-war of differing objectives among R&D, manufacturing, and marketing. Excessive product modification and proliferation for the sake of satisfying the ever-changing customer needs will forsake manufacturing efficiency and have negative cost consequences, barring a perfectly flexible computer-aided design (CAD) and computer-aided manufacturing (CAM) facility. CAD/CAM technology has improved tremendously in recent years, but the full benefit of flexible manufacturing is still many years away.[2] Contrarily, excessive product standardization for the sake of lowering manufacturing costs will also be likely to result in unsatisfied or undersatisfied customers. Similarly, innovative product designs and features as desired by customers may indeed be a technological feat but might not be conducive to manufacturing. Therefore, topics such as product design for manufacturability and components/product standardization have become increasingly important strategic issues today. It has become imperative for many companies to develop a sound sourcing strategy in order to exploit most efficiently R&D, manufacturing, and marketing on a global basis.

EXTENT AND COMPLEXITY OF GLOBAL SOURCING STRATEGY

Managers should understand and appreciate the important roles that product designers, engineers, and production managers, and purchasing managers, among others, play in corporate strategy development. Strategy decisions cannot be made in the absence of these people. The overriding theme throughout the chapter is that successful management of the interfaces of R&D, manufacturing, and marketing activities determines a company's competitive strengths and, consequently, its market performance. Now we will look at logistical implications of this interface management.

Toyota's global operations illustrate one such world-class case. The Japanese carmaker is equipping its operations in the United States, Europe, and Southeast Asia with integrated capabilities for creating and marketing automobiles. The company gives the managers at those operations ample authority to accommodate local circumstances and values without diluting the benefit of integrated global operations. Thus, in the United States, a Toyota subsidiary in California, designs the bodies and interiors of new Toyota models, including Lexus and Solara, a sporty new coupe. Toyota has technical centers in the United States and in Brussels to adapt engine and vehicle specifications to local needs. Toyota operations in Southeast Asia supply each other with key components to foster increased economies of scale and standardization in those components—gasoline engines in Indonesia, steering components in Malaysia, transmissions in the Philippines, and diesel engines in Thailand.

Undoubtedly, those multinational companies, including Toyota, not only facilitate the flow of capital among various countries through direct investment abroad but also significantly contribute to the world trade flow of goods and services as well. Multinational companies combine this production and distribution to supply those local markets hosting their foreign subsidiaries, and then export what remains to other foreign markets or back to their parents' home market.

Let us revisit the significance of multinational companies' role in international trade. The most recent United Nations official report shows that in 1999, 34 percent of world trade is intrafirm trade between multinational companies and their foreign affiliates and between those affiliates, and that an additional 33.3 percent of world trade is exports by those multinational companies and their affiliates. In other words, two-thirds of world trade is managed one way or another by multinational companies.[3] These trade ratios have been fairly stable over time.[4]

As a result, the total volume of international trade among the core Triad regions (i.e., USA, Europe, and Japan) alone increased to over $700 billion in 2000 from $44.4 billion in 1970, or by four times in real terms. This phenomenal increase in international trade is attributed largely to foreign production and trade managed by multinational companies.

Two notable changes have occurred in international trade. First, the last 25 years have observed a decline in the proportion of trade between Europe and the United States in the Triad regions, and conversely an increase in trade between the United States and Japan, and in particular, between Europe and Japan. It strongly indicates that European countries and Japan have found each other increasingly important markets above and beyond their traditional markets of the United States. Second, newly industrialized countries (NICs) in Asia, (South Korea, Taiwan, Hong Kong, and Singapore), have dramatically increased their trading position vis-à-vis the rest of the world. Not only have these NICs become prosperous marketplaces, but more significantly they have become important manufacturing and sourcing locations for many multinational companies.

From the sourcing perspective, U.S. companies were procuring a less expensive supply of components and finished products in NICs for sale in the United States. As a result, U.S. bilateral trade with NICs has increased to $165 billion in 2001 from $1.8 billion in 1970. Trade statistics, however, do not reveal anything other than the amount of bilateral trade flows between countries. It is false to assume that trade is always a business transaction between independent buyers and sellers across national boundaries. It is equally false to assume that a country's trade deficit in a certain industry equates with the decline in the competitiveness of companies in that industry. As evidenced above, an increasing segment of international trade of components and finished products is strongly influenced by multinational companies' foreign direct investment activities.

TRENDS IN GLOBAL SOURCING STRATEGY

Over the last 20 years or so, gradual yet significant changes have taken place in global sourcing strategy. The cost-saving justification for international procurement in the 1970s and 1980s was gradually supplanted by quality and reliability concerns in the 1990s. However, most of the changes have been in the way business executives think of the scope of global sourcing for their companies and exploit various opportunities available from it as a source of competitive advantage. Peter Drucker, a famed management guru and business historian, once said that sourcing and logistics would remain the darkest continent of business—the least exploited area of business for competitive advantage. Naturally, many companies, regardless of their nationality, that have a limited scope of global sourcing are at a disadvantage over those that exploit it to the fullest extent in a globally competitive marketplace.

Trend 1: The Decline of the Exchange Rate Determinism of Sourcing

Since the mid-1970s, exchange rates have fluctuated rather erratically over time. If a country's currency appreciates, its companies would find it easy to procure components and products from abroad. Contrarily, if one's currency depreciates, its companies would find it increasingly difficult to depend on foreign supplies as they have to pay higher prices for every item sourced from abroad. In these scenarios, companies consider the exchange rate determining the extent to which they can engage in foreign sourcing.

However, this exchange rate determinism of sourcing is strictly based on price factor alone. Indeed, exchange rate fluctuations arguably have little impact on the nature of sourcing strategy for crucial components.[5] Foreign sourcing also occurs for noncost reasons such as quality, technology, and so on. First of all, since it takes time to develop overseas suppliers for noncost purposes, purchasing managers cannot easily drop a foreign supplier even when exchange rate changes have an adverse effect on the cost of imported components and products. Second, domestic suppliers are known to increase prices to match rising import prices following exchange rate changes. As a result, switching to a domestic supplier may not ensure cost advantages. Third, many companies are developing long-term relationships with international suppliers—whether those suppliers are their subsidiaries or independent contractors. In a long-term supply relationship, exchange rate fluctuations may be viewed as a temporary problem by the parties involved. Finally, some companies with global operations are able to shift supply locations from one country to another to overcome the adverse effects of exchange rate fluctuations. Obviously, these factors other than cost have kept many companies from reducing their dependence on foreign supplies of components and finished products.[6]

Trend 2: New Competitive Environment Caused by Excess Worldwide Capacity

The worldwide growth in the number of manufacturers has added excess production capacity in most industries. The proliferation of manufacturers around the world in less sophisticated, less capital-intensive manufactured products is much greater than in more complex, knowledge-intensive products such as computers. Thus, there has been a tremendous downward pressure on prices of many components and products around the world. Although the ability to deliver a high volume of products of satisfactory quality at a reasonable price was once the hallmark of many successful companies, an increasing number of global suppliers have eventually rendered the delivery of volume in an acceptable time no longer a competitive weapon. There has since occurred a strategic shift from price and quantity to quality and reliability of products as a determinant of competitive strength.[7] Better product and component quality, lower price, unavailability of item domestically, and more advanced technology abroad are among the most important reasons for increased sourcing from abroad (See Exhibit 5.1).[8]

EXHIBIT 5.1 **Key Factors for Sourcing from Abroad**

Factor
Very Important
1. Better quality
2. Lower price
3. Unavailability of items in the U.S.
Important
4. More advanced technology abroad
5. Willingness to solve problems
6. More on-time delivery
7. Negotiability
8. Association with foreign subsidiary
Neutral
9. Geographical location
10. Countertrade requirements
11. Government assistance

Source: Adapted from Hokey Min and William P. Galle, "International Purchasing Strategies of Multinational U.S. Firms," *International Journal of Purchasing and Materials Management,* Summer 1991, p. 14.

Trend 3: Innovations in and Restructuring of International Trade Infrastructure

Advances in structural elements of international trade have made it easier for companies to employ sourcing for strategic purposes. The innovations and structural changes that have important influences on sourcing strategy are (1) the increased number of purchasing managers experienced in sourcing, (2) improvements made in transportation and communication (e.g., fax), (3) new financing options, including countertrade (see Chapter 4), offering new incentives and opportunities for exports from countries without hard currency, (4) manufacturing facilities diffused throughout the world by globally minded companies, and (5) neighboring country sourcing opportunities. For example, maquiladora plants on the Mexican side of the U.S. border provide a unique form of sourcing option to manufacturers operating in the United States. Similarly Hong Kong–based companies may source out of nearby Shenzhen.

Trend 4: Enhanced Role of Purchasing Managers

During the last 15 years, manufacturers were under pressure to compete on the basis of improved cost and quality as just-in-time (JIT) production was adopted by a growing number of companies. JIT production requires close working relationships with component suppliers and places an enormous amount of responsibility on purchasing managers. Furthermore, sourcing directly from foreign suppliers requires greater purchasing know-how and is riskier than other alternatives that use locally based wholesalers and representatives. Locally based representatives are subject to local laws and assume some of the currency risk associated with importing. However, now that purchasing managers are increasingly making long-term commitments to foreign suppliers, direct dealings with suppliers is justified. According to one major survey, the dominant form of purchasing from abroad was to buy directly from foreign sources.[9] The finding suggests that purchasing managers are confident about their international know-how and that they may be seeking long-term sourcing arrangements.

Trend 5: Trend toward Global Manufacturing

During the 1980s, while U.S. companies continued to locate their operations in various parts of the world, companies from other countries such as Japan, Germany, and Britain expanded the magnitude of their foreign manufacturing operations at a much faster pace. Foreign share of manufacturing in the United States increased from 5.2 percent in 1977 to over 15 percent recently. As a global company adds another international plant to its network of existing plants, it creates the need for sourcing of components and other semiprocessed goods to and from the new plant to existing plants. Global manufacturing adds enormously to global sourcing activities either within the same company across national boundaries or between independent suppliers and new plants.

Mature companies are increasingly assigning independent design and other R&D responsibilities to satellite foreign units so as to design a regional or world product. As a result, foreign affiliates have also developed more independent R&D activities to manufacture products for the U.S. markets in addition to expanding local sales.[10]

POTENTIAL PITFALLS IN GLOBAL SOURCING

Global sourcing strategy requires close coordination of R&D, manufacturing, and marketing activities, among others, on a global basis. However, while national boundaries have begun losing their significance both as a psychological and as a physical barrier to international business, the diversity of local environments still plays an important role not as a facilitator, but rather as an inhibitor, of optimal global strategy development. Now the question is to what extent successful multinational companies can circumvent the impact of local environmental diversity.

Indeed, we still debate the very issue raised more than 30 years ago: counteracting forces of "unification versus fragmentation" in developing operational strategies. As early as 1969, Fayerweather[11] wrote emphatically:

> What fundamental effects does [the existence of many national borders] have on the strategy of the multinational firm? Although many effects can be itemized, one central theme recurs, that is, their tendency to push the firm toward adaptation to the diversity of local environments which leads toward fragmentation of operations. But there is a natural tendency in a single firm toward integration and uniformity which is basically at odds with fragmentation. Thus the central issue...is the conflict between unification and fragmentation—a close-knit operational strategy with similar foreign units versus a loosely related, highly variegated family of activities.

The same counteracting forces have since been revisited in such terms as "standardization versus adaptation" (1960s), "globalization versus localization" (1970s), "global integration versus local responsiveness" (1980s), and, most recently, "scale versus sensitivity" (1990s). Terms have changed, but the quintessence of the strategic dilemma that multinational companies face today has not changed and will probably remain unchanged for many years to come.

One thing that has changed, however, is the ability and willingness of these companies to integrate various activities on a global basis in an attempt either to circumvent or to nullify the impact of differences in local markets to the extent possible. It may be more correct to say that these companies have been increasingly compelled to take a global view of their businesses, due primarily to increased competition, particularly among the Triad regions of the world: namely, North America, western Europe, and Japan. Remember "If you don't do it, somebody else will at your expense." This contemporary view of competitive urgency is shared by an increasing number of executives of multinational companies, irrespective of nationality.

The lack of competitive urgency can indeed be a problem. In his Business Not As Usual, for instance, Mitroff[12] was very critical of the lack of this competitive urgency in the U.S. automobile industry in the 1970s and 1980s. He argued that the automobile industry minimized the need for constant innovation and its adoption into the working design of cars until it was forced on it by foreign competition. Not surprisingly, the result was an extreme isolation from the rest of the world—"a tunnel vision of the worst kind" (p. 84). This is not an isolated incident, however. Mitroff's indictment arguably applies to other industries, such as machine tool and electronics, in the United States.

In contrast, the last 25 years have seen a tremendous growth and expansion of European and Japanese multinational companies encroaching on the competitive strengths of U.S. multinational companies in almost all the markets around the world. While U.S. multinational companies have subsidiaries all over the world, they have been somewhat reluctant to develop an integrated and well-coordinated global strategy that successful European and Japanese multinational companies have managed to establish. At the core of an integrated global strategy lies the companies' ability to coordinate manufacturing activities with R&D, engineering, and marketing on a global basis. Indeed, European and Japanese multinational companies have heavily invested in, and improved upon, their strengths in manufacturing that many U.S. multinational companies have ignored. As a result, U.S. companies tend to have ill-coordinated manufacturing strategy that results in a poor match between their manufacturing system capability and markets. This functional mismatch has been traced to U.S. management's strategic emphasis having drifted away from manufacturing to marketing and to finance over the years.

As a result, manufacturing management gradually lost its influence in the business organization. Production managers' decision-making authority was reduced such that R&D personnel prepared specifications with which production complied and marketing imposed its own delivery, inventory, and quality conditions, but not productivity considerations. In a sense, production managers gradually took on the role of outside suppliers within their own companies. Production managers' reduced influence in the organization led to a belief that manufacturing functions could be transferred easily to independent operators and subcontractors, depending upon the cost differential between in-house and contracted-out production. Thus, in order to lower production costs under competitive pressure, U.S. multinational companies turned increasingly to outsourcing of components and finished products from newly industrializing countries such as South Korea, Taiwan, Singapore, Hong Kong, Brazil, and Mexico, among others. Akio Morita, a co-founder of Sony, a highly innovative Japanese electronics company, chided such U.S. multinational companies as "hollow corporations" which simply put their well-known brand names on foreign-made products and sell them as if the products were their own.[13]

However, we should not rush to a hasty conclusion that outsourcing certain components and/or finished products from foreign countries will diminish a company's competitiveness. Many multinational companies with plants in various parts of the world are exploiting not only their own competitive advantages (e.g., R&D, manufacturing, and marketing skills) but also the locational advantages (e.g., inexpensive labor cost, certain skills, mineral resources, government subsidy, and tax advantages) of various countries. Thus, it is also plausible to argue that these multinational companies are in a more advantageous competitive position than are domestic-bound companies.

Then, isn't the "hollowing-out" phenomenon indicative of a superior management of both corporate and locational resources on a global basis? What is wrong, if anything, with Caterpillar Tractor Company procuring more than 15 percent of components for its tractors from foreign suppliers? How about Honeywell marketing in the United States the products manufactured in its European plants? Answers to these questions hinge on a company's ability and willingness to integrate and coordinate various activities.

VALUE CHAIN AND FUNCTIONAL INTERFACES

The design of global sourcing strategy is based on the interplay between a company's competitive advantages and the comparative advantages of various countries. Competitive advantage influences the decision on what activities and technologies a company should concentrate its investment and managerial resources in, relative to its competitors in the industry. Comparative advantage affects the company's decision on where to source and market, based on the lower cost of labor and other resources in one country relative to another. As shown in Exhibit 5.2, the value chain concept offers a general framework for understanding what it takes to manage the interrelated value-adding activities of a company on a global basis.[14] A company is essentially made up of a collection of activities that are performed to design, manufacture, market, deliver, and support its product. This set

EXHIBIT 5.2   **R&D, Manufacturing, and Market Interfaces**

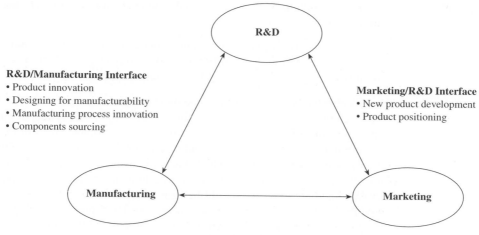

of interrelated corporate activities is called the value chain. Therefore, to gain competitive advantage over its rivals in the marketplace, a company must perform these activities either at a lower cost or in such a way as to offer differentiated products and services, or accomplish both.

The value chain can be divided into two major activities performed by a company: (1) primary activities consisting of inbound logistics (procurement of raw materials and components), manufacturing operations, outbound logistics (distribution), sales, and after-sale service, and (2) support activities consisting of human resource management, technology development, and other activities that help promote primary activities. Competing companies constantly strive to create value across various activities in the value chain. Of course, the value that a company creates is measured ultimately by the price buyers are willing to pay for its products. Therefore, the value chain is a useful concept that provides an assessment of the activities that a company performs to design, manufacture, market, deliver, and support its products in the marketplace.

Five continuous and interactive steps are involved in developing such a global sourcing strategy along the value chain.[15]

1. Identify the separable links (R&D, manufacturing, and marketing) in the company's value chain.

2. In the context of those links, determine the location of the company's competitive advantages, considering both economies of scale and scope.

3. Ascertain the level of transaction costs (e.g., cost of negotiation, cost of monitoring activities, and uncertainty resulting from contracts) between links in the value chain, both internal and external, and selecting the lowest cost mode.

4. Determine the comparative advantages of countries (including the company's home country) relative to each link in the value chain and to the relevant transaction costs.

5. Develop adequate flexibility in corporate decision making and organizational design so as to permit the company to respond to changes in both its competitive advantages and the comparative advantages of countries.

In this chapter, we focus on the three most important interrelated activities in the value chain: namely, R&D (i.e., technology development, product design, and engineering), manufacturing, and marketing activities. Management of the interfaces, or linkages, among these value-adding activities is a crucial determinant of a company's competitive advantage. A basic framework of management of R&D, manufacturing, and marketing interfaces is outlined in Exhibit 5.2. Undoubtedly, these value-adding activities should be examined as holistically as possible, by linking the boundaries of these primary activities. Thus, global sourcing strategy encompasses management of (1) the interfaces among R&D, manufacturing, and marketing on a global basis and (2) logistics identifying which production units will serve which particular markets and how components will be supplied for production.

R&D/Manufacturing Interface

Technology is broadly defined as know-how composed of product technology (the set of ideas embodied in the product) and process technology (the set of ideas involved in the manufacture of the product or the steps necessary to combine new materials to produce a finished product). However, executives tend to focus solely on product-related technology as the driving force of the company's competitiveness. Product technology alone may not provide the company a long-term competitive edge over competition unless it is matched with sufficient manufacturing capabilities.[16] The British discovered and developed penicillin, but it was a small U.S. company, Pfizer, which improved on the fermentation (i.e., manufacturing) process and, as a result, became the world's foremost manufacturer of penicillin.

Ignoring manufacturing as a strategic weapon, many companies have historically placed emphasis on product innovations (i.e., product proliferation and modifications). However, as technological leads over foreign competition have evaporated, there will be fewer products that companies can export simply because no one else has the technology to manufacture the products. Stressing the historical linkage of imitation and product innovations, it is contended that imitation (manufacturing process learning), followed by more innovative adaptation, leading to pioneering product design and innovation, forms the natural sequence of industrial development. In other words, product innovation and manufacturing activities are intertwined so that continual improvement in manufacturing processes can enable the company not only to maintain product innovation-based competitiveness but also to improve its product innovative abilities in the future.

Manufacturing processes should also be innovative. To facilitate the transferability of new product innovations to manufacturing, a team of product designers and engineers should strive to design components so that they are conducive to manufacturing without undue retooling required and that components may be used interchangeably for different models of the product. Low levels of retooling requirements and interchangeability of components are necessary conditions for efficient sourcing strategy on a global scale. If different equipment and components are used in various manufacturing plants, it is extremely difficult to establish a highly coordinated sourcing plan on a global basis.

Manufacturing/Marketing Interface

There exists a continual conflict between manufacturing and marketing divisions. It is to the manufacturing division's advantage if all the products and components are standardized to facilitate standardized, low-cost production. The marketing division, however, is more interested in satisfying the diverse needs of consumers, requiring broad product lines and frequent product modifications adding cost to manufacturing. How have successful companies coped with this dilemma?

Recently, there has been an increasing amount of interest in the strategic linkages between product policy and manufacturing long ignored in traditional considerations of global strategy development. With aggressive competition from multinational companies emphasizing corporate product policy and concomitant manufacturing, many companies have realized that product innovations alone cannot sustain their long-term competitive position without an effective product policy linking product and manufacturing process innovations.

Four different ways of developing a global product policy are generally considered an effective means to streamline manufacturing, thus lowering manufacturing cost, without sacrificing marketing flexibility: (1) core components standardization, (2) product design families, (3) universal product with all features, and (4) universal product with different positioning.[17]

Core Components Standardization. Successful global product policy mandates the development of universal products or products that require no more than a cosmetic change for adaptation to differing local needs and use conditions. A few examples illustrate the point. Seiko, a Japanese watchmaker, offers a wide range of designs and models, but based only on a handful of different operating mechanisms. Similarly, the best-performing German machine tool making companies have a narrower range of products, use up to 50 percent fewer parts than their less successful rivals, and make continual, incremental product and design improvements, with new developments passed rapidly on to customers.

Product Design Families. This is a variant of core component standardization. For companies marketing an extremely wide range of products due to cultural differences in product-use patterns around the world, it is also possible to reap economies of scale benefits. For example, Toyota offers several car models based on a similar family design concept, ranging from Lexus models to Toyota Avalons, Camrys, and Corollas. Many of the Lexus features well received by customers have been adopted into the Toyota lines with just a few minor modifications (mostly downsizing). In the process, Toyota has been able to cut product development costs and meet the needs of different market segments. Similarly, Electrolux, a Swedish appliance manufacturer, has adopted the concept of "design families," offering different products under four different brand names but using the same basic designs. A key to such product design standardization lies in standardization of components, including motors, pumps, and compressors. Thus, Electrolux North America and Zanussi in Italy, Electrolux's subsidiaries, have the main responsibility for components production within the group for worldwide application.

Universal Product with All Features. As noted above, competitive advantage can result from standardization of core components and/or product design families. One variant of components and product standardization is to develop a universal product with all the features demanded anywhere in the world. Japan's Canon has done so successfully with its AE–1 cameras and newer models. After extensive market analyses around the world, Canon identified a set of common features customers wanted in a camera, including good picture quality, ease of operation with automatic features, technical sophistication, professional looks, and reasonable price. To develop such cameras, the company introduced a few breakthroughs in camera design and manufacturing, such as use of an electronic integrated circuitry brain to control camera operations, modularized production, and standardization and reduction of parts.

Universal Product with Different Positioning. Alternatively, a universal product can be developed with different market segments in mind. Thus, a universal product may be positioned differently in different markets. This is where marketing promotion plays a major role to accomplish such a feat. Product and/or components standardization, however, does not necessarily imply either production standardization or a narrow product line. For example, Japanese automobile manufacturers have gradually stretched out their product line offerings, while marketing them with little adaptation in many parts of the world. This strategy requires manufacturing flexibility. The crux of global product or component standardization rather calls for proactive identification of homogeneous segments around the world, and is different from the concept of marketing abroad a product originally developed for the home market. A proactive approach to product policy has gained momentum in recent years as it is made possible by intermarket segmentation. In addition to clustering of countries and identification of homogeneous segments in different countries, targeting different segments in different countries with the same products is another way to maintain a product policy of standardization. For example, Honda has marketed almost identical Accord cars around the world by positioning them differently from country to country.

Marketing/R&D Interface

Both R&D and manufacturing activities are technically outside marketing managers' responsibility. However, marketing managers' knowledge of the consumers' needs is indispensable in product development. Without a good understanding of the consumers' needs, product designers and engineers are prone to impose their technical specifications on the product rather than fitting them to what consumers want. After all, consumers, not product designers or engineers, have the final say in deciding whether or not to buy the product.

Japanese companies, in particular, excel in management of the marketing/R&D interface. Indeed, their source of competitive advantage often lies in marketing and R&D divisions' willingness to coordinate their respective activities concurrently. In a traditional product development, either a new product was developed and pushed down from the R&D division to the manufacturing and to the marketing division for sales or a new product idea was pushed up from the marketing division to the R&D division for development. This top-down or bottom-up new product development takes too much time in an era of global competition in which a short product development cycle is crucial to meet constant competitive pressure from new products introduced by rival companies around the world.

R&D and marketing divisions of Japanese companies are always on the lookout for use of emerging technologies initially in existing products to satisfy customer needs better than their existing products and their competitors'. This affords them an opportunity to gain experience, debug technological glitches, reduce costs, boost performance, and adapt designs for worldwide customer use. As a result, they have been able to increase the speed of new product introductions, meet the competitive demands of a rapidly changing marketplace and capture market share.

In other words, the marketplace becomes a virtual R&D laboratory for Japanese companies to gain production and marketing experience as well as to perfect technology. This requires close contact with customers, whose inputs help Japanese companies improve upon their products on an ongoing basis.

In the process, they introduce new products one after another. Year after year, Japanese companies unveil not-entirely-new products that keep getting better in design, more reliable, and less expensive. For example, Philips marketed the first practical VCR in 1972, three years before Japanese competitors entered the market. However, Philips took seven years to replace the first generation VCR with the all-new V2000, while the late-coming Japanese manufacturers launched an onslaught of no fewer than three generations of improved VCRs in this five-year period.

The continual introduction of newer and better designed products also brings a greater likelihood of market success. Ideal products often require a giant leap in technology and product development, and naturally are subject to a much higher risk of consumer rejection. Not only does the Japanese approach of incrementalism allow for continual improvement and a stream of new products, but it also permits quicker consumer adoption. Consumers are likely to accept improved products more quickly than very different products, since the former are more compatible with the existing patterns of product use and lifestyles.

LOGISTICS OF SOURCING STRATEGY

Sourcing strategy includes a number of basic choices companies make in deciding how to serve foreign markets. One choice relates to the use of imports, assembly, or production within the country to serve a foreign market. Another decision involves the use of internal or external supplies of components or finished goods. Therefore, the term "sourcing" is used to describe management by multinational companies of the flow of components and finished products in serving foreign markets.

Sourcing decision making is multifaceted and entails both contractual and locational implications. From a contractual point of view, the sourcing of major components and products by multinational companies takes place in two ways: (1) from the parents or their foreign subsidiaries on an "intrafirm" basis and (2) from independent suppliers on a "contractual" basis. The first type of sourcing is known as intrafirm sourcing. The second type of sourcing is referred to commonly as outsourcing. Similarly, from a locational point of view, multinational companies can procure components and products either (1) domestically (i.e., domestic sourcing) or (2) from abroad (i.e., offshore sourcing). Therefore, as shown in Exhibit 5.3, four possible types of sourcing strategy can be identified.

In developing viable sourcing strategies on a global scale, companies must consider not only manufacturing costs, the costs of various resources, and exchange rate fluctuations, but also availability of infrastructure (including transportation, communications, and energy), industrial and cultural environments, the ease of working with foreign host governments, and so on. Furthermore, the complex nature of sourcing strategy on a global scale spawns many barriers to its successful execution. In particular, logistics, inventory management, distance, nationalism,

EXHIBIT 5.3   **Types of Sourcing Strategy**

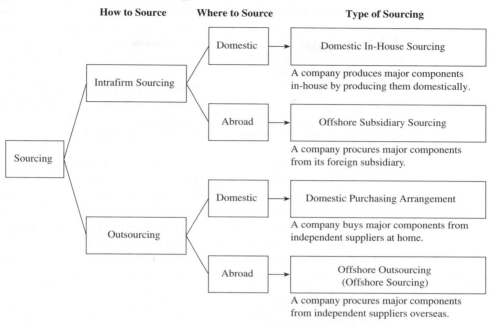

| How to Source | Where to Source | Type of Sourcing |

Domestic → **Domestic In-House Sourcing**

A company produces major components in-house by producing them domestically.

Abroad → **Offshore Subsidiary Sourcing**

A company procures major components from its foreign subsidiary.

Domestic → **Domestic Purchasing Arrangement**

A company buys major components from independent suppliers at home.

Abroad → **Offshore Outsourcing (Offshore Sourcing)**

A company procures major components from independent suppliers overseas.

and lack of working knowledge about foreign business practices, among others, are major operational problems identified by multinational companies engaging in international sourcing. For a detailed examination, see the case "Intel's Site Selection Decision in Latin America".

Many studies have shown, however, that despite, or maybe, as a result of, those operational problems, where to source major components seems much less important than how to source them. Thus, when examining the relationship between sourcing and competitiveness of multinational companies, it is crucial to distinguish between sourcing on a "contractual" basis and sourcing on an "intrafirm" basis, for these two types of sourcing will have a different impact on their long-run competitiveness.

Intrafirm Sourcing.   Multinational companies can procure their components in-house within their corporate system around the world. They produce major components at their respective home base and/or at their affiliates overseas to be incorporated in their products marketed in various parts of the world. Thus, trade does take place between a parent company and its subsidiaries abroad, and also between foreign subsidiaries across national boundaries. This is often referred to as intrafirm sourcing. If such in-house component procurement takes place at home, it is essentially domestic in-house sourcing. If it takes place at a company's foreign subsidiary, it is called offshore subsidiary sourcing. Intrafirm sourcing makes trade statistics more complex to interpret, since part of the international flow of products and components is taking place between affiliated companies within the same multinational corporate system, which transcends national boundaries. As stated earlier, in 1999, about one-third of world trade was intrafirm trade between multinational companies and their foreign affiliates and between those affiliates.

An issue which is prevalent in some industries and in some parts of the world is parallel importing. Here the identical product is sourced wholesale from unauthorized distributors (usually in neighbouring countries) through the "gray" market. The Looks.com case provides a detailed examination.

Outsourcing. In the 1970s, foreign competitors gradually caught up in a productivity race with U.S. companies. This coincided with U.S. corporate strategic emphasis drifting from manufacturing to finance and marketing. As a result, manufacturing management gradually lost its organizational influence. Production managers' decision-making authority was reduced when R&D personnel prepared specifications with which production complied and marketing imposed delivery, inventory, and quality conditions. Productivity considerations were ignored. In a sense, production managers gradually took on the role of outside suppliers within their own companies.

This led to an erroneous belief that manufacturing functions could, and should, be transferred easily to independent operators and subcontractors, depending upon the cost differential between in-house and contracted-out production. A company's reliance on domestic suppliers for major components is basically a domestic purchase arrangement. Furthermore, in order to lower production costs under competitive pressure, U.S. companies turned increasingly to outsourcing of components and finished products from abroad, particularly from newly industrialized countries including Singapore, South Korea, Taiwan, Hong Kong, Brazil, and Mexico. Initially, subsidiaries were set up for production purposes (i.e., offshore subsidiary sourcing), but gradually, independent foreign suppliers took over component production for U.S. companies. This latter phenomenon is usually called offshore outsourcing (or offshore sourcing, for short).

Component procurement from overseas (i.e., offshore subsidiary sourcing and offshore outsourcing) has been a serious social and economic issue, as it affects domestic employment and economic structure. Companies using such strategy have been described pejoratively as hollow corporations. It is occasionally argued that U.S. companies are increasingly adopting a "designer role" in global competition—offering innovations in product design without investing in manufacturing process technology.

This widespread international sourcing practice could have a deleterious impact on the ability of any company to maintain an initial competitive advantage based on product innovations. Indeed, keeping abreast of emerging technology through continual improvement in R&D and manufacturing is the sine qua non for the company's continued competitiveness.

LONG-TERM CONSEQUENCES

There are two opposing views of the long-term implications of offshore sourcing. One school of thought argues that many successful companies have developed a dynamic organizational network through increased use of joint ventures, subcontracting, and licensing activities across international borders. This flexible network system is broadly called strategic alliances. Strategic alliances allow each participant to pursue its particular competence. Therefore, each network participant can be seen as complementing rather than competing with the other participants for the common goals. Strategic alliances may even be formed by competing companies in the same industry in pursuit of complementary abilities (new technologies or skills) from each other. The other school of thought argues, however, that while the above argument may be true in the short run, there could also be negative long-term consequences resulting from a company's dependence on independent suppliers and subsequently the inherent difficulty for the company to keep abreast of constantly evolving design and engineering technologies without engaging in those developmental activities. These two opposing arguments will be elaborated below.

Strategic Alliances

The advantage of forming a strategic alliance is claimed to be its structural flexibility. Strategic alliances can accommodate a vast amount of complexity while maximizing the specialized competence of each member, and provide much more effective use of human resources that would otherwise have to be accumulated, allocated, and maintained by a single organization. In other words, a company can concentrate on performing the task at which it is most efficient. This approach is increasingly applied on a global basis with countries participating in a dynamic network as multinational companies configure and coordinate product development, manufacturing, and sourcing activities around the world.

First, due to the need for fast internationalization and related diversification, strategic alliances provide a relatively easy option to access the world markets and to combine complementary technologies. Thus, AT&T needed Olivetti's established European network to enter the European market for telephone switchboard equipment. Similarly, Toyota established a joint venture with General Motors so that the Japanese car maker could learn to work with UAW union members while General Motors could learn just-in-time inventory management from Toyota.

Second and more relevant to sourcing issues, an increasing number of companies have funneled out manufacturing functions to independent partners. The risk of course is that the "partner" may eventually enter the business on their own!

Dependence

Companies that rely on independent external sources of supply of major components tend to forsake part of the most important value-creating activities to, and also become dependent on, independent operators for assurance of component quality. Furthermore, those multinational companies tend to promote competition among independent suppliers, ensure continuing availability of materials in the future, and exploit full benefits of changing market conditions. However, individual suppliers are forced to operate in an uncertain business environment that inherently necessitates a shorter planning horizon. The uncertainty about the potential loss of orders to competitors often forces individual suppliers to make operating decisions that will likely increase their own long-term production and materials costs. In the process, this uncertain business environment tends to adversely affect the multinational companies sourcing components and/or finished products from independent suppliers. The rapid decline of IBM offers a vivid example of the problems caused by its dependence on independent suppliers for crucial components in the personal computer market.

Gradual Loss of Design and Manufacturing Abilities

Those multinational companies that depend heavily on independent suppliers also tend in the long run to lose sight of emerging technologies and expertise, which could be incorporated into the development of new manufacturing processes as well as new products. Thus, continual sourcing from independent suppliers is likely to forebode companies' long-term loss of the ability to manufacture at competitive cost and, as a result, loss of their global competitiveness. However, if technology and expertise developed by a multinational company are exploited within its multinational corporate system (i.e., by its foreign affiliates and by the parent company itself), the company can retain its technological base to itself without unduly disseminating them to competitors. The benefit of such internalization is likely to be great, particularly when technology is highly idiosyncratic or specific with limited alternative uses, or when it is novel in the marketplace. For such a technology, the market price mechanism is known to break down as a seller and potential buyers of the technology tend to see its value very differently. Potential buyers, who do not have perfect knowledge of how useful the technology will be, tend to undervalue its true market value. As a result, the seller of the technology is not likely to get a full economic benefit of the technology by selling it in the open market.

In addition, by getting involved in design and production on its own, the multinational company can keep abreast of emerging technologies and innovations originating anywhere in the world for potential use in the future. Furthermore, management of the quality of major components is required to retain the goodwill and confidence of consumers in the products. As a result, "intrafirm" sourcing of major components and finished products between the parent company and its affiliates abroad and between its foreign affiliates themselves would more likely enable the company to retain a long-term competitive edge in the world market.

OUTSOURCING OF SERVICE ACTIVITIES

In 2000, the United States was ranked the largest exporter and importer of services, providing $274.6 billion of services to the rest of the world and receiving $198.9 billion worth of services. Furthermore, according to a recent U.S. government estimate, approximately 16 percent of the total value of U.S. exports and imports of services were conducted across national boundaries on an intrafirm basis (i.e., between parent companies and their subsidiaries). Increasingly, U.S. companies have expanded their service procurement activities on a global basis in the same way they procure components and finished products.

The ability and opportunity for firms to procure components/finished goods that have proprietary technology on a global basis also applies equally to service activities. The technological revolution in data processing and telecommunications (trans-border data flow, telematics, etc.) either makes the global tradability of some services possible or facilitates the transactions economically. Furthermore, because the production and consumption of some services do not need to take place at the same location or at the same time, global sourcing may be a viable strategy.

Thanks to the development of the Internet and e-commerce, certain service activities are increasingly outsourced from independent service suppliers. The Internet also accelerates growth in the number of e-workers. This net-savvy and highly flexible corps is able to perform much or all of their work at home, or in small groups close to home, irrespective of their locations. International e-workers can also operate in locations far from corporate headquarters. They will be part of the growth in *intellectual outsourcing.* Already such e-workers can write software in India for a phone company in Finland, provide architectural services in Ireland for a building in Spain, and do accounting work in Hong Kong for an insurance company in Vancouver. Globalization of services through the Internet is likely to expand considerably in the future.[18]

Particularly, Bangalore, India should be noted. The region is described as the Silicon Valley of that country. Bangalore has rapidly evolved to become the center of offshore programming activities. Many U.S. companies have begun to outsource an increasing portion of software development from companies in Bangalore. For example, Aztec Software & Technology Services Ltd., an Indian company, has worked with Microsoft Corp.'s SQL Server group for more than 18 months on the SQL Server 7.0 release and even developed a few tools for the technology. The company also collaborated with programmers at IBM's Almaden Research Center, San Jose, to develop the Datalinks linking technology for databases. BFL Software Ltd., employing more than 400 technical people in two factories, is another Indian software company with close U.S. ties. Its client roster includes Compaq Computer Corp. and Federal Express Corp. Alternatively, those U.S. companies could set up their own support operations in Bangalore, if they needed to have a closer control of their local operations.[19]

Outsourcing of service activities has been widely quoted in the popular press as a means to reduce costs and improve the corporate focus; that is concentrating on the core activities of the firm. However, outsourcing may also serve other purposes, including (a) as a means of reducing time to implement internal processes, (b) as a means of sharing risk in an increasingly uncertain business environment, (c) to improve customer service, (d) to get access to better expertise not available in-house, (e) for headcount reduction, and (f) as a means to instill a sense of competition, especially when departments within firms develop a perceptible level of inertia.[20]

In the case of service companies, the distinction between core and supplementary services is necessary in strategy development. **Core services** are the necessary outputs of an organization that consumers are looking for, while **supplementary services** are either indispensable for the execution of the core service or are available only to improve the overall quality of the core service bundle. Using an example of the healthcare industry, the core service is providing patients with good-quality medical care. The supplementary services may include filing insurance claims, arranging accommodation for family members (especially for overseas patients), handling off-hour emergency calls, and so on.

Core services may gradually partake of a "commodity" and lose their differential advantage vis-à-vis competitors as competition intensifies. Subsequently, a service provider may increase its reliance on supplementary services to maintain and/or enhance competitive advantage. "After all, if a firm cannot do a decent job on the core elements, it is eventually going to go out of business."[21] In other words, the reason why a service firm exists is to provide good-quality core services to its customers; however, in some instances, it simply cannot rely solely on core services to stay competitive. We can expect that core services are usually performed by the service firm itself, regardless of the characteristics of the core service. On the other hand, although supplementary services are provided to augment the core service for competitive advantage, the unique characteristics of supplementary services may influence "how" and "where" they are sourced.[22]

Summary

The scope of global sourcing has expanded over time. Whether or not to procure components or products from abroad was once determined strictly on price and thus strongly influenced by the fluctuating exchange rate. Thus the appreciation of its currency prompted companies to increase offshore sourcing, while the depreciation of its currency encouraged domestic sourcing. Today many companies consider not simply price but also quality, reliability, and technology of components and products to be procured. These companies design their sourcing decision on the basis of the interplay between their competitive advantages and the comparative advantages of various sourcing locations for long-term gains.

Trade and foreign production managed by multinational companies are very complex. In growing global competition, sourcing of components and finished products around the world within the multinational company has increased. The development of global sourcing and marketing strategies across different foreign markets has become a central issue for many multinational companies. Traditionally, a polycentric approach to organizing operations on a country-by-country basis allowed each country manager to tailor marketing strategy to the peculiarities of local markets. As such, product adaptations were considered a necessary strategy to better cater to the different needs and wants of customers in various countries. Product adaptation tends to be a reactive, rather than a proactive, strategic response to the market. A high level of product adaptation may make it difficult for multinational companies to reap economies of scale in production and marketing and to coordinate their networks of activities on a global scale.

Global sourcing strategy requires close coordination of R&D, manufacturing, and marketing activities on a global basis. Managing geographically separated R&D, manufacturing, and marketing activities, those companies face difficult coordination problems of integrating their operations and adapting them to different legal, political, and cultural environments in different countries. Furthermore, separation of manufacturing activities involves an inherent risk that manufacturing in the value chain will gradually become neglected. Such a neglect can be costly as continued involvement in manufacturing leads to pioneering product design and innovation over time. An effective global sourcing strategy calls for continual efforts to streamline manufacturing without sacrificing marketing flexibility. To accomplish this, a conscious effort to develop either core components in-house or develop product design families or universal products is called for.

A caveat should also be noted. While a company's ability to develop core components and products and market them in the world markets on its own is preferred, the enormousness of such a task should be examined in light of rapid changes in both technology and customer needs around the world. Those changes make the product life cycle extremely short, sometimes too short for many multinational companies to pursue product development, manufacturing, and marketing on a global basis without strategic alliance partners. Benefits of maintaining an independent proprietary position should always be weighed against the time cost of delayed market entry.

Although most of our knowledge about sourcing strategy comes from manufacturing industries, a similar logic applies to sourcing of service activities. As a result of the explosive growth of the Internet and e-commerce, supplementary service activities—a type of services that help improve the delivery of the company's core businesses—are increasingly outsourced from independent suppliers around the world.

Supplementary Reading

Cavusgil, S. Tamer, Attila Yaprak, and Poe-lin Yeoh. "A Decision-Making Framework for Global Sourcing," *International Business Review,* Vol. 2, 1993, pp. 143–56.

Cohen, Stephen S., and John Zysman. "Why Manufacturing Matters: The Myth of the Post-Industrial Economy," *California Management Review,* Vol. 29, Spring 1987, pp. 9–26

Kotabe, Masaaki. "Efficiency vs. Effectiveness Orientation of Global Sourcing Strategy: A Comparison of U.S. and Japanese Multinational Companies," *Academy of Management Executive,* Vol. 12, November 1998, pp. 107–19.

_____. Global Sourcing Strategy: R&D, Manufacturing, and Marketing Interfaces. New York: Quorum Books, 1992.

Markides, Constantinos, and Norman Berg. "Manufacturing Offshore Is Bad Business," *Harvard Business Review,* Vol. 66, September–October 1988, pp. 113–20.

Monczka, Robert M., and Robert J. Trent. "Global Sourcing: A Development Approach," *International Journal of Purchasing and Materials Management,* Vol. 27, Spring 1991, pp. 2–8.

Murray, Janet Y., Masaaki Kotabe, and Albert R. Wildt. "Strategic and Financial Performance Implications of Global Sourcing Strategy: A Contingency Analysis," *Journal of International Business Studies,* Vol. 26, First Quarter 1995, pp. 181–202.

Porter, Michael E., ed. Competition in Global Industries. Cambridge, MA: Harvard Business School Press, 1986.

Endnotes

1. Masaaki Kotabe, R&D, *Manufacturing, and Marketing Interfaces* (New York: Quorum Books, 1992).
2. "A Survey of Manufacturing Technology," *The Economist,* March 5, 1994, pp. 3–18.
3. Khalil Hamdani, The Role of Foreign Direct Investment in Export Strategy," presented at 1999 Executive Forum on National Export Strategies, International Trade Centre, the United Nations, September 26-28, 1999.
4. United Nations Centre on Transnational Corporations, Transnational Corporations in World Development: Trends and Perspectives, New York: United Nations, 1988; Organization for Economic Cooperation and Development, Intra-Firm Trade, Paris, OECD, 1993; Stefan H. Robock, "U.S. Multinationals: Intra-Firm Trade, Overseas Sourcing and the U.S. Trade Balance," a paper presented at the 1999 Academy of International Business-Southeast Conference, June 4-5, 1999.
5. Janet Y. Murray, "A Currency Exchange Rate-Driven vs. Strategy-Driven Analysis of Global Sourcing," *Multinational Business Review,* Vol. 4, No. 1, Spring 1996, pp. 40–51.
6. "Guess Who Isn't Buying American: For Many U.S. Companies, Imported Goods Are Cheaper and Better-Made," *Business Week,* November 2, 1992, pp. 26–27.
7. Martin K. Starr and John E. Ullman, "The Myth of Industrial Supremacy," in Martin K. Starr, ed., *Global Competitiveness* (New York: W.W. Norton and Co., 1988).
8. Hokey Min and William P. Galle, "International Purchasing Strategies of Multinational U.S. Firms," *International Journal of Purchasing and Materials Management,* Summer 1991, pp. 9–18.
9. Somerby Dowst, "International Buying: The Facts and Foolishness," *Purchasing,* June 25, 1987.
10. Masaaki Kotabe and K. Scott Swan, "Offshore Sourcing: Reaction, Maturation, and Consolidation of U.S. Multinationals," *Journal of International Business Studies,* Vol. 25, First Quarter, 1994, pp. 115–40.
11. John Fayerweather, *International Business Management: Conceptual Framework* (New York: McGraw-Hill, 1969), pp. 133–4.

12. Ian I. Mitroff, *Business Not As Usual: Rethinking Our Individual, Corporate, and Industrial Strategies for Global Competition* (San Francisco, CA: Jossey-Bass, Inc, 1987).

13. "Special Report: The Hollow Corporation," *Business Week,* March 3, 1986, pp. 56–59.

14. Michael E. Porter, ed., *Competition in Global Industries* (Cambridge, MA: Harvard Business School Press, 1986).

15. Richard D. Robinson, ed., *Direct Foreign Investment: Costs and Benefits* (New York: Praeger Publishers, 1987).

16. Bruce R. Guile and Harvey Brooks, *Technology and Global Industry: Companies and Nations in the World Economy* (Washington, DC: National Academy Press, 1987).

17. Hirotaka Takeuchi and Michael E. Porter, "Three Roles of International Marketing in Global Strategy," in Michael E. Porter, ed., *Competition in Global Industries* (Boston, MA: Harvard Business School Press, 1986, pp. 111–46).

18. Robert D. Hormats, "High Velocity," *Harvard Business Review,* 21 (Summer 1999), pp. 36–41.

19. Tim Scannell, "U.S. Skills Shortage Prompts Integrators to Search Offshore," *Computer Reseller News,* March 15, 1999, pp. 1–2.

20. Maneesh Chandra, "Global Sourcing of Services: A Theory Development and Empirical Investigation," Ph.D. dissertation, The University of Texas at Austin, 1999.

21. C.H. Lovelock, "Adding Value to Core Products with Supplementary Services," in C.H. Lovelock, ed., *Services Marketing,* 3rd ed., Englewood Cliffs, NJ: Prentice-Hall, 1996.

22. Terry Clark, Daniel Rajaratnam, and Timothy Smith, "Toward a Theory of International Services: Marketing Intangibles in a World of Nations," *Journal of International Marketing,* 4(2), 1996, pp. 9–28; and Janet Y. Murray and Masaaki Kotabe, "Sourcing Strategies of U.S. Service Companies: A Modified Transaction-Cost Analysis," *Strategic Management Journal,* 20 (September 1999), pp. 791–809.

Chapter Six

Licensing

Licensing is a contractual arrangement whereby the licensor (selling firm) allows its technology, patents, trademarks, designs, processes, know-how, intellectual property, or other proprietary advantages to be used for a fee by the licensee (buying firm). Licensing is a strategy for technology transfer. It is also an approach to internationalization that requires less time or depth of involvement in foreign markets, compared with export strategies, joint ventures, and foreign direct investment (FDI).

A closely related contractual arrangement to licensing is franchising. Franchising is an organizational form where the franchisor (parent company/owner) of a service, trademarked product, or brand name allows the franchisee to use the same in return for a lump-sum payment and/or royalty, while conforming to required standards of quality, service, and so forth. (See the Blue Ridge Spain case for an illustration.)

Most international licensing agreements are between firms from industrialized countries. As well, licensing occurs most frequently in technology-intensive industries. It is not surprising, then, that the overall use of licensing varies greatly from country to country. For example, licensing of foreign technology by Korean firms exceeded $4 billion in 1995, with 75 percent of that going to U.S. or Japanese licensors.

A great deal of international licensing also occurs in industries that are not technology-intensive. These industries range from food to sports teams to publishing. Retail sales of licensed merchandise, exceeds $100 billion. The popular press is replete with announcements regarding international licensing (see the box on page 116 for examples).

From a global perspective, nearly 800 franchisors have sold franchises abroad, accounting for tens of thousands of overseas locations. For example, in 2001 over half of KFC's more than 10,000 locations were outside the USA, and of these, the majority were via franchise.

Much of the licensing discussion that follows assumes a technology transfer. This would generally constitute a more complex form of licensing than that involving trademarks, for example.

The term "licensing" is also frequently used internationally in reference to national governments, which provide licenses for foreign banks or insurance

This chapter was prepared by Paul Beamish.

companies to operate in their market, for resource companies to undertake exploration, and so forth. This is a different form of permission than the focus of this chapter.

When Is Licensing Employed?

The strategic advantages to be gained by licensing depend on the technology, firm size, product maturity, and extent of the firm's experience. A number of internal and external circumstances may lead a firm to employ a licensing strategy. From the perspective of the licensor these would variously include:

1. A firm lacks the capital, managerial resources, or knowledge of foreign markets required for exporting or FDI, but it wants to earn additional profits with minimal commitment.

2. Licensing is a way of testing and proactively developing a market that can later be exploited by direct investment.

3. The technology involved is not central to the licensor's core business. Not surprisingly, single—or dominant—product firms are very reluctant to license their core technology, whereas diversified firms are much more willing to license peripheral technologies.

4. Prospects of "technology feedback" are high (i.e., the licensor has been contractually ensured of access to new developments generated by the licensee and based on licensed knowledge).

5. The licensor wishes to exploit its technology in secondary markets that may be too small to justify larger investments; the required economies of scale may not be attainable.

6. Host-country governments restrict imports or FDI, or both; or the risk of nationalization or foreign control is too great.

7. The licensee is unlikely to become a future competitor.

8. The pace of technological change is sufficiently rapid that the licensor can remain technologically superior and ahead of the licensee, who is a potential competitor. As well, if the technology may become obsolete quickly, there is pressure to exploit it fully while the opportunity exists.

From the perspective of the licensee, the main advantage of licensing is that the licensee's existing products or technology can be acquired more cheaply, faster, and with less risk from third parties (licensors) than by internal R&D. Another advantage is that the licensee can gain product designs for a desired diversification, to complement other assets it possesses such as production or marketing capability.

Risks Associated with Licensing

The most important risk associated with licensing (or franchising) is that the licensor risks the dissipation of its proprietary advantage, since the licensee acquires at least a portion of the advantage via licensing. Thus, any licensor should try to ensure that its licensee will not be a future competitor or act opportunistically. Not surprisingly, many license agreements are made between firms from different countries so as to reduce the likelihood of creating a competitor in the domestic market. Other approaches include limiting the licensee's market and insisting on technology feedback or flowback clauses.

Licensed trademarks remain the licensor's property in perpetuity, whereas licenses normally have a finite lifetime. A licensor may retain considerable bargaining power in proportion to the perishability of the licensed technology and the licensor's ability to provide a continuing supply of new technology in the future.

A second risk with licensing is that the licensor jeopardizes its worldwide reputation if the licensee cannot maintain the desired product standards and quality or if it engages in questionable practices. Because the licensor will typically become aware of licensee questionable practices only after the fact, this suggests the need to devote more time during the original negotiations to understanding the character of the licensee.

Another consideration with licensing is that profits to the licensor may not be maximized. This is because (a) their involvement in the licensed markets is indirect, (b) exchange rates change, (c) some countries limit the amount of outward payments for licenses, and so forth.

Some of the standard elements of a license agreement are more difficult than others for the licensor to enforce. These would include (a) guaranteeing flowback of actual improvements, (b) sublicensing, (c) diligence that the terms are being honored, and (d) quality control. As a result, sometimes licensing may not provide even the minimum expected benefits.

Intellectual Property Rights

In many countries intellectual property legislation either does not exist or is not enforced. Not surprisingly, a major issue for many companies is infringement of their intellectual property rights as the Sicom and CD Piracy case illustrates. With billions of dollars at stake, this issue has also become a key element in trade negotiations.

Some companies have deemed it necessary to enter into license agreements as a means of offsetting trademark piracy. The logic behind such "reluctant licensing" is that by licensing a local firm the local firm will, in turn, take the necessary steps to stop unlicensed domestic competitors from using the intellectual property.

There are numerous implications with such a scenario. For example, many organizations are feeling pressure to internationalize their operations sooner than they were expecting. As a consequence, they view licensing as a defensive solution, rather than an opportunity.

Costs of Licensing

Licensing is sometimes incorrectly viewed as a one-time transaction involving little in the way of costs for the licensor. In reality, there are costs associated with (a) the protection of industrial property, (b) establishing the license agreement, and (c) maintaining the license agreement.

Protection costs are not solely the costs of registering one's patents or trademark. They also potentially entail defending one's intellectual property in a court of law, as the Time Warner and ORC Patents case illustrates.

Establishment costs would include expenses for searching for suitable licensees, communication, training, equipment testing, and so forth. Some products/technologies lend themselves to licensing, while others do not. The greater the cost and complexity of modifying the underlying intellectual property, the more difficult it is to effectively employ a licensing strategy.

Maintenance costs might include backup services for licensees, audit, ongoing market research, and so forth. These are nontrivial expenses. For example, Seattle-based consultants from Starbucks Coffee visit each foreign store (licensee) at least once a month. Monitoring costs will directly and significantly affect the willingness of companies to license or franchise internationally.

To all of these out-of-pocket expenses must be added opportunity costs. Opportunity costs are made up of the loss of current or prospective revenues from exports or other sources.

Unattractive Markets for Licensing

A number of conditions directly impact "real" licensing returns and make a particular country an unattractive market for licensing. The first of these conditions occurs where there is a regulatory scheme governing licensing. In some countries—such as France, Ireland, and Spain—licenses are not valid until government approval or registration is completed.

A second condition occurs when licenses granting exclusive rights to certain products or territories are not allowed. In some cases, governments may prohibit them because competition will be substantially lessened. Also, some countries place limits on the allowable duration of agreements.

Another condition occurs when there are foreign exchange controls or other restrictions on royalty payments (license fees). Frequently, a withholding tax on royalty payments to nonresident licensors may be applied. In Europe, the combined withholding tax and VAT (value-added tax) can range up to about 50 percent.

Finally, some countries impose royalty and fee limits. Some use a 10 percent limit, while others employ a more stringent 3 percent limit. Any of these government-set rates can, and frequently do, change over time.

Overall, licensing tends to be more attractive when agreements formed in the country enjoy the benefit of freedom of contract. Here the parties may, for the most part, create their own legal framework by the manner in which the contract is written.

Major Elements of the License Agreement

The license agreement is the essential commercial contract between licensee and licensor, which specifies the rights to be granted, the consideration payable, and the duration of the terms. The licensed rights usually take the form of patents, registered trademarks, registered industrial designs, unpatented technology, trade secrets, know-how, or copyrights. The license agreement should make explicit reference to the product as well as to the underlying "intangible" or "intellectual" property rights.

Recent International Licensing Announcements

Licensed properties account for nearly half of the $4 billion in home decorating retail sales sold for the Halloween season, including 70 percent of costumes sales, 50 percent of decorations and greeting cards, and 10 percent of candies.

Corning takes legal action against European and U.S. companies for infringing Corning's optical fiber patent.

New York, NY, January 20, 1999—The International Licensing Industry Merchandisers' Association announced a major initiative in conjunction with a consortium of marketing experts to develop the most significant study to date on the business of licensing.

Art licensing represents $5.2 billion of the licensing industry and is growing steadily. The boom in art licensing is a direct result of the need for manufacturers to provide product offerings to the growing needs of their discriminating consumers. Cause-related licensing, catalog, business premiums, consumer premiums, and Internet marketing are emerging niche channels for art licensed images.

Starbucks, the U.S. coffee chain, hopes to have 500 branches in Asia by 2003. Though Starbucks prefers the control which joint ventures offer, it is not willing to pay for half of each branch it opens. Although franchising could get around this problem, Starbucks is not comfortable having a franchise partner select subfranchisers, as is usually the case. Licensing agreements allow Starbucks to maintain control over its expansion while limiting its financial exposure. The licensee funds the capital costs of expansion—and bears the risks of a downturn. Detailed licensing agreements give the local companies exclusive rights to develop and operate Starbucks retail stores. However, they also stipulate that Starbucks remains involved in every aspect of planning, operations, design, and training.

On June 26, 2001, hundreds of independent record companies in Britain and Europe signed a licensing agreement with Napster to immediately make thousands of tracks available to computer-users worldwide.

Palm made new licensing deals with major chip makers, Intel, Motorola, and Texas Instruments, to expand the Palm operating system into all kinds of mobile devices from handhelds to cell phones and perhaps even wristwatches.

Apple Computer became the first nonaffiliated company to license Amazon.com's controversial patented technology that lets repeat customers purchase items with one click of the mouse.

Warner Brothers Korea, the copyright holder of the Harry Potter franchise within the country, signed licensing agreements with 17 companies including Coca-Cola Korea and Lego Korea. Lego Korea, which introduced Harry Potter toys in October 2001, has made $2.3 million in sales of the character products.

Ericsson, the world's leading supplier of communications equipment, is signing a licensing deal with Samsung Electronics to offer its cable- free wireless technology.

Home Depot Inc. and media giant Walt Disney Co. have signed a licensing agreement that will allow Home Depot to develop a line of Disney-branded children's paints.

California-based InterTrust Technologies announced a $28.5 million patent licensing deal with Sony Corp. Sony is paying for a license to uses its Digital Rights Management (DRM) software, which is used to deter music piracy.

Cambridge Antibody Technology (CAT), a UK-based biotech company, has announced a licensing deal with Human Genome Sciences (HGS). This deal gives HGS the right to develop an antibody against the TRAIL receptor 2. That receptor can cause the death of tumour cells, and CAT discovered the antibody that can activate the receptor.

Although no definitive standard form exists for license agreements, certain points are typically covered. In many cases, licensors will have developed standard forms for these contracts, based on their past experiences in licensing. Typically, a license agreement will include the following:

1. A clear and correct description of the parties to the agreement, identifying the corporate names of each party, its incorporating jurisdiction, and its principal place of business.

2. A preamble or recitals describing the parties, their reasons for entering into the arrangement, and their respective roles.

3. A list of defined terms for the purposes of the particular contract to simplify this complex document and to eliminate ambiguity or vagueness (e.g., definitions of the terms licensed, product, net profit, territory, and so forth).

4. A set of schedules, in an exhibit or appendix, where necessary, to segregate lengthy detailed descriptions of any kind.

5. The grant that is fundamental to the agreement and explicitly describes the nature of the rights being granted to the licensee. This grant may be based on promotion methods, trade secrets, list of customers, drawings and photographs, models, tools, and parts; or know-how. Know-how, in turn, may be based on invention records, laboratory records, research reports, development reports, engineering reports, pilot plant design, production plant design, production specifications, raw material specifications, quality controls, economic surveys, market surveys, etc.

6. A description of any geographical limitations to be imposed on the licensee's manufacturing, selling, or sublicensing activities.

7. A description of any exclusive rights to manufacture and sell that may be granted.

8. A discussion of any rights to sublicense.

9. The terms relating to the duration of the agreement, including the initial term and any necessary provisions for the automatic extension or review of the agreement.

10. Provisions for the granting of rights to downstream refinements or improvements made by the licensor in the future.

11. Provisions for "technological flowback" agreements where some benefit of improvements made by the licensee reverts to the licensor. The rights to the future improvements by either the licensor or licensee are often used as leverage in negotiations.

12. Details regarding the royalties or periodic payments based on the use of licensed rights. The percentage rate of the royalty may be fixed or variable (based on time, production level, sales level, and so forth), but the "royalty base" for this rate must be explicitly defined. Some methods of calculating royalties include percentage of sales, royalties based on production, percentage of net profit, lump-sum payments, or payment-free licenses in cross-licensing arrangements. Aulakh et al. found that "Licensor's monitoring of the licensee and interfirm interaction are significantly higher in a royalties-based agreement, and that licensor firms prefer lump-sum fee agreements when faced with uncertainties related to intellectual property protection and ability to repatriate earnings from foreign markets." (p. 417)

There are no hard-and-fast rules for establishing royalty rates. One arbitrary rule (see Contractor in Supplementary Reading) is the "25 percent rule of thumb," which suggests that the licensor aim for a 25 percent share of the licensee's related profits and then convert this profit level to a certain royalty rate. Others suggest that licensors will often specify a minimum or target absolute compensation. This can be derived from technology transfer cost considerations or a judgment of how much it may cost the prospective licensee to acquire the technology by other means or from an "industry norm." Royalty escalation clauses and the currency of payment should also be specified.

It is often quite difficult for the licensor to accurately estimate the market potential for its property. As a consequence, the licensee, with its greater knowledge of local conditions, is often in a stronger position when the royalty rate terms are being negotiated.

13. Specification of minimum performance requirements (e.g., minimum royalty payments, unit sales volumes, employment of personnel, minimum promotion expenditures, and so forth) to ensure the "best efforts" of the licensee so that the license potential is fully exploited. For example, most license agreements that confer exclusive selling rights in a given area to the licensee also require either a sizable down payment or a minimum annual royalty payment. Otherwise, the licensee may "sit on" the license and block the licensor from entering the market in question.

14. Other clauses common to most license agreements include those to protect the licensed rights against licensees and third parties and those regarding title retention by the licensor, confidentiality of know-how, quality control, most-favored-licensee status, the applicable language of the contract, and any provisions with respect to the assignability of rights by the licensee.

The above list of elements common to most license agreements is by no means exhaustive. For a more detailed checklist for license agreements, see Stitt and Baker in Supplementary Reading. Any potential license agreement should be reviewed by company counsel. It must be noted that every license agreement is unique in some way and, therefore, great care should be taken in its negotiation and formal documentation.

Supplementary Reading

Licensing

Arora, A. and A. Fosfuri. "Wholly Owned Subsidiary Versus Technology Licensing in the Worldwide Chemical Industry," *Journal of International Business Studies,* Vol. 31, No. 4, 2000, pp. 555–572.

Atuahene-Gima, Kwaku. "International Licensing of Technology: An Empirical Study of the Differences between Licensee and Non-Licensee Firms," *Journal of International Marketing,* Vol. 1, No. 2, 1993, pp. 71–87.

Aulakh, Preet S., S. Tamer Cavusgil, and M.B. Sarkar. "Compensation in International Licensing Agreements," *Journal of International Business Studies,* Vol. 29, No. 2, 1998, pp. 409–20.

Buckley, Peter J. "New Forms of International Industrial Co-operation." In *The Economic Theory of the Multinational Enterprise.* Ed. P. J. Buckley and M. Casson. London: Macmillan, 1985.

Business International Corporation. International Licensing Management. New York: Business International Corporation, 1988.

Caves, Richard E. *Multinational Enterprise and Economic Analysis,* 2nd ed. Cambridge, MA: Cambridge University Press, 1996.

Clegg, Jeremy. "The Determinants of Aggregate International Licensing Behavior: Evidence from Five Countries." *Management International Review,* Vol. 30, No. 3, 1990, pp. 231–51.

Contractor, Farok J. "A Generalized Theorem for Joint-Venture and Licensing Negotiations," *Journal of International Business Studies,* Summer 1985, pp. 25–47.

Ehrbar, Thomas J. *Business International's Guide to International Licensing: Building a Licensing Strategy for 14 Key Markets around the World.* New York: McGraw-Hill, 1993.

Hill, Charles W. L. "Strategies for Exploiting Technological Innovations: When and When Not to License," *Organization Science,* Vol. 3, No. 3, 1992, pp. 428–41.

Horstmann, Ignatius, and James R. Markusen. "Licensing versus Direct Investment: A Model of Internalization by the Multinational Enterprise," *Canadian Journal of Economics,* Vol. 20, No. 3, 1987, pp. 464–81.

Mottner, Sandra and James P. Johnson. "Motivations and Risks in International Licensing: A Review and Implications for Licensing to Transitional and Emerging Economies," *Journal of World Business,* Vol. 35, No. 2, 2000. pp. 171–188.

Root, Franklin, R. *Entry Strategies for International Markets.* Lexington, MA: Lexington Books, 1987.

Stitt, Hubert J., and Samuel R. Baker. *The Licensing and Joint Venture Guide,* 3rd ed. Toronto: Ontario Ministry of Industry, Trade, and Technology, 1985.

Teece, D. J., P. Grindley and E. Sherry, *Understanding the Licensing Option.* New York, 2000. Oxford University Press.

Franchising

Alon, I., *The Internationalization of U.S. Franchising Systems.* New York, New York, 1999. Garland Publishing Inc.

Fladmoe-Lindquist, Karin, and Laurent L. Jacque. "Control Modes in International Service Operations: The Propensity to Franchise," *Management Science,* Vol. 41, No. 7, 1995, pp. 1238–49.

Fladmoe-Lindquist, Karin. "International Franchising: A Network Approach to FDI." Y. Aharoni and L. Nachum (Eds.), 2000. *Globalization of Services,* New York, Routledge.

Shane, Scott A. "Why Franchise Companies Expand Overseas." *Journal of Business Venturing,* Vol. 11, 1996, pp. 73–88.

Chapter Seven

The Design and Management of International Joint Ventures

An international joint venture is a company that is owned by two or more firms of different nationality. International joint ventures may be formed from a starting (or greenfield) basis or may be the result of several established companies deciding to merge existing divisions. However they are formed, the purpose of most international joint ventures is to allow partners to pool resources and coordinate their efforts to achieve results that neither could obtain acting alone.

International joint ventures and other forms of corporate alliances have become increasingly popular. For example, in the airline sector, virtually every major carrier has links with foreign carriers. These may be equity- or nonequity (i.e., code share, frequent flyer programs, etc.)-based and are culminating in truly global network arrangements such as Star Alliance and One World.

As Exhibit 7.1 illustrates, a broad range of strategic alliances exists. They vary widely in terms of the level of interaction and type. Most of the comments in this chapter focus on equity joint venture—the alliance form usually requiring the greatest level of interaction, cooperation, and investment. However, some but not all the issues are applicable to other forms of alliances. For example, IKEA, the giant Swedish furniture retailer, operates a series of nonequity buyer–supplier alliances around the world. IKEA provides component suppliers with product design, technical assistance, leased equipment, and even loans. IKEA's suppliers get new skills, direct access to a large and growing retailer, and steadier sales. This not

This chapter was prepared by Paul W. Beamish.

EXHIBIT 7.1   **Range of Strategic Alliances**

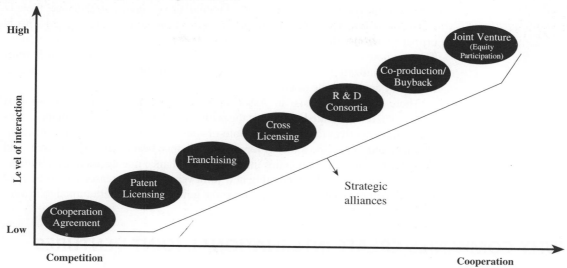

only generates for IKEA low-cost and high-quality supply but a sense of partnership with, and loyalty to/from, suppliers.

Joint ventures have moved from being a way to enter foreign markets of peripheral interest to become a part of the mainstream of corporate activity. Virtually all MNEs are using international joint ventures, many as a key element of their corporate strategies. Merck, for example, has joint ventures with Johnson & Johnson (2001 JV sales of $.4 billion), Aventis Pasteur (2001 JV sales of $.5 billion), Rhône-Poulenc (2001 JV sales of $1.7 billion), and so forth. Even firms that have traditionally operated independently around the world are increasingly turning to joint ventures.

The popularity and use of international joint ventures and cooperative alliances remained strong through the 1990s. The rate of joint venture use does not change much from year to year. In general, joint ventures are the mode of choice about 35 percent of the time by U.S. multinationals and in 40 to 45 percent of foreign subsidiaries formed by Japanese multinationals.

The popularity of alliances has continued despite their reputation for being difficult to manage. Failures exist and are usually widely publicized. Dow Chemical, for example, reportedly lost more than $100 million after a dispute with its Korean joint venture partners caused the firm to sell its 50 percent interest in its Korean venture at a loss, and to sell below cost its nearby wholly owned chemical plant. Also, after Lucent's joint venture in wireless handsets with Philips Electronics ended, Lucent took a $100 million charge at the time on selling its consumer phone equipment business. Similarly, HealthMatics, a joint venture between Glaxo Smith Kline and Physician Computer Network Inc. shut down after losing more than $50 million.

While early surveys suggested that as many as half the companies with international joint ventures were dissatisfied with their ventures' performance, there is reason to believe that some of the earlier concern can now be ameliorated. This is primarily because there is far greater alliance experience and insight to draw from. There is now widespread appreciation that joint ventures are not necessarily transitional organization forms, shorter-lived, or less profitable. For many organizations they are the mode of choice.

There now also exists an Association of Strategic Alliance Professionals (A.S.A.P.). It was created to support the professional development of alliance managers and executives to advance the state-of-the-art of alliance formation and management and to provide a forum for sharing alliance best practices, resources and opportunities to help companies improve their alliance management capabilities.

Why do managers keep creating new joint ventures? The reasons are presented in the remainder of this chapter, as are some guidelines for international joint venture success.

WHY COMPANIES CREATE INTERNATIONAL JOINT VENTURES

International joint ventures can be used to achieve one of four basic purposes. As shown in Exhibit 7.2, these are: to strengthen the firm's existing business, to take the firm's existing products into new markets, to obtain new products that can be sold in the firm's existing markets, and to diversify into a new business.

Companies using joint ventures for each of these purposes will have different concerns and will be looking for partners with different characteristics. Firms wanting to strengthen their existing business, for example, will most likely be looking for partners among their current competitors, while those wanting to enter

EXHIBIT 7.2
Motives for International Joint Venture Formation

	Existing Products	New Products
New Markets	To take existing products to foreign markets	To diversify into a new business
Existing Markets	To strengthen the existing business	To bring foreign products to local markets

new geographic markets will be looking for overseas firms in related businesses with good local market knowledge. Although often treated as a single category of business activity, international joint ventures are remarkably diverse, as the following descriptions indicate.

STRENGTHENING THE EXISTING BUSINESS

International joint ventures are used in a variety of ways by firms wishing to strengthen or protect their existing businesses. Among the most important are joint ventures formed to achieve economies of scale, joint ventures that allow the firm to acquire needed technology and know-how, and ventures that reduce the financial risk of major projects. Joint ventures formed for the latter two reasons may have the added benefit of eliminating a potential competitor from a particular product or market area.

Achieving Economies of Scale   Firms often use joint ventures to attempt to match the economies of scale achieved by their larger competitors. Joint ventures have been used to give their parents economies of scale in raw material and component supply, in research and development, and in marketing and distribution. Joint ventures have also been used as a vehicle for carrying out divisional mergers, which yield economies across the full spectrum of business activity.

Very small, entrepreneurial firms are more likely to participate in a network than an equity joint venture in order to strengthen their business through economies of scale. Small firms may form a network to reduce the costs, and increase the potential, of foreign market entry, or to meet some other focused objective. Most of these networks tend to have a relatively low ease of entry and exit and a loose structure and require a limited investment (primarily time, as they might be self-financing through fees). International equity joint ventures by very small firms are unusual because such firms must typically overcome some combination of liabilities of size, newness, foreignness, and relational orientation (often the small firms were initially successful because of their single-minded, do-it-themselves orientation).

Raw Material and Component Supply   In many industries the smaller firms create joint ventures to obtain raw materials or jointly manufacture components. Automakers, for instance, may develop a jointly owned engine plant to supply certain low-volume engines to each company. Producing engines for the parents provides economies of scale, with each company receiving engines at a lower cost than it could obtain if it were to produce them itself.

The managers involved in such ventures are quick to point out that these financial savings do not come without a cost. Design changes in jointly produced engines, for example, tend to be slow because all partners have to agree on them. In fact, one joint venture that produced computer printers fell seriously behind the state of the art in printer design because the parents could not agree on the features they wanted in the jointly designed printer. Because all of the venture's output was sold to the parents, the joint venture personnel had no direct contact with end customers and could not resolve the dispute.

Transfer pricing is another issue that arises in joint ventures that supply their parents. A low transfer price on products shipped from the venture to the parents, for instance, means that whichever parent buys the most product obtains the most benefit. Many higher-volume-taking parents claim that this is fair, as it is their volume that plays an important role in making the joint venture viable. On the other hand, some parents argue for a higher transfer price, which means that the economic benefits are captured in the venture and will flow, most likely via dividends, to the parents in proportion to their share holdings in the venture. As the share holdings generally reflect the original asset contributions to the venture and not the volumes taken out every year, this means that different parents will do well under this arrangement. Clearly, the potential for transfer price disputes is significant.

Research and Development   Shared research and development efforts are increasingly common. The rationale for such programs is that participating firms can save both time and money by collaborating and may, by combining the efforts of the participating companies' scientists, come up with results that would otherwise have been impossible.

The choice facing firms wishing to carry out collaborative research is whether to simply coordinate their efforts and share costs or to actually set up a jointly owned company. Hundreds of multicompany research programs are not joint ventures. Typically, scientists from the participating companies agree on the research objectives and the most likely avenues of exploration to achieve those objectives. If there are, say, four promising ways to attack a particular problem, each of four participating companies would be assigned one route and told to pursue it. Meetings would be held, perhaps quarterly, to share results and approaches taken and when (hopefully) one route proved to be successful, all firms would be fully informed on the new techniques and technology.

The alternative way to carry out collaborative research is to establish a jointly owned company and to provide it with staff, budget, and a physical location. Yet even here, problems may occur. In the United States, the president of a joint research company established by a dozen U.S. computer firms discovered that the participating companies were not sending their best people to the new company. He ended up hiring more than 200 of the firm's 330 scientists from the outside.

A sensitive issue for firms engaging in collaborative research, whether through joint ventures or not, is how far the collaboration should extend. Because the partners are usually competitors, the often expressed ideal is that the joint effort will focus only on "precompetitive" basic research and not, for example, on product development work. This is often a difficult line to draw.

Marketing and Distribution   Many international joint ventures involve shared research, development, and production but stop short of joint marketing. The vehicles coming out of the widely publicized joint venture between Toyota and General Motors in California, for instance, are clearly branded as GM or Toyota products and are sold competitively through each parent's distribution network. Antitrust plays a role in the decision to keep marketing activities separate, but so does the partners' intrinsic desire to maintain separate brand identities and increase their own market share. These cooperating firms have not forgotten that they are competitors.

There are, nevertheless, some ventures formed for the express purpose of achieving economies in marketing and distribution. Here, each firm is hoping for wider market coverage at a lower cost. The trade-off is a loss of direct control over the sales force, potentially slower decision making, and a possible loss of direct contact with the customer.

Somewhat similar in intent are cooperative marketing agreements, which are not joint ventures but agreements by two firms with related product lines to sell one another's products. Here companies end up with a more complete line to sell, without the managerial complications of a joint venture. Sometimes the cooperative marketing agreement can in fact entail joint branding.

Divisional Mergers   Multinational companies with subsidiaries that they have concluded are too small to be economic have sometimes chosen to create a joint venture by combining their "too small" operations with those of a competitor. Fiat and Peugeot, for example, merged their automobile operations in Argentina, where both companies were doing poorly. The new joint venture started life with a market share of 35 percent and a chance for greatly improved economies in design, production, and marketing. Faced with similar pressures, Ford and Volkswagen have done the same thing in Brazil, creating a jointly owned company called Auto Latina.

A divisional merger can also allow a firm a graceful exit from a business in which it is no longer interested. Honeywell gave up trying to continue alone in the computer industry when it folded its business into a venture with Machines Bull of France and NEC of Japan. Honeywell held a 40 percent stake in the resulting joint venture.

Acquiring Technology in the Core Business

Firms that have wanted to acquire technology in their core business area have traditionally done so through license agreements or by developing the technology themselves. Increasingly, however, companies are turning to joint ventures for this purpose, because developing technology in-house is seen as taking too long, and license agreements, while giving the firm access to patent rights and engineers' ideas, may not provide much in the way of shop floor know-how. The power of a joint venture is that a firm may be able to have its employees working shoulder to shoulder with those of its partner, trying to solve the same problems. For example, the General Motors joint venture with Toyota provided an opportunity for GM to obtain a source of low-cost small cars and to watch firsthand how Toyota managers, who were in operational control of the venture, were able to produce high-quality automobiles at low cost. Most observers have concluded that the opportunity for General Motors to learn new production techniques was more significant than the supply of cars coming from the venture.

Reducing Financial Risk

Some projects are too big or too risky for firms to tackle alone. This is why oil companies use joint ventures to split the costs of searching for new oil fields, and why the aircraft industry is increasingly using joint ventures and "risk-sharing subcontractors" to put up some of the funds required to develop new aircraft and engines.

Do such joint ventures make sense? For the oil companies the answer is a clear yes. In these ventures, one partner takes a lead role and manages the venture on a day-to-day basis. Management complexity, a major potential drawback of joint ventures, is kept to a minimum. If the venture finds oil, transfer prices are not a problem—the rewards of the venture are easy to divide between the partners. In situations like this, forming a joint venture is an efficient and sensible way of sharing risk.

It is not as obvious that some other industry ventures are a good idea, at least not for industry leaders. Their partners are not entering these ventures simply in the hopes of earning an attractive return on their investment. They are gearing up to produce, sooner or later, their own product. Why would a company be willing to train potential competitors? For many firms, it is the realization that their partner is going to hook up with someone anyway, so better to have a portion of a smaller future pie than none at all, even if it means you may be eventually competing against yourself.

TAKING PRODUCTS TO FOREIGN MARKETS

Firms with domestic products that they believe will be successful in foreign markets face a choice. As discussed in Chapter 1, they can produce the product at home and export it, license the technology to local firms around the world, establish wholly owned subsidiaries in foreign countries, or form joint ventures with local partners. Many firms conclude that exporting is unlikely to lead to significant market penetration, building wholly owned subsidiaries is too slow and requires too many resources, and licensing does not offer an adequate financial return. The result is that an international joint venture, while seldom seen as an ideal choice, is often the most attractive compromise.

Moving into foreign markets entails a degree of risk, and most firms that decide to form a joint venture with a local firm are doing so to reduce the risk associated with their new market entry. Very often, they look for a partner that deals with a related product line and, thus, has a good feel for the local market. As a further risk-reducing measure, the joint venture may begin life as simply a sales and marketing operation, until the product begins to sell well and volumes rise. Then a "screwdriver" assembly plant may be set up to assemble components shipped from the foreign parent. Eventually, the venture may modify or redesign the product to better suit the local market and may establish complete local manufacturing, sourcing raw material and components locally. The objective is to withhold major investment until the market uncertainty is reduced.

Following Customers to Foreign Markets   Another way to reduce the risk of a foreign market entry is to follow firms that are already customers at home. Thus, many Japanese automobile suppliers have followed Honda, Toyota, and Nissan as they set up new plants in North America and Europe. Very often these suppliers, uncertain of their ability to operate in a foreign environment, decide to form a joint venture with a local partner. There are, for example, a great many automobile supplier joint ventures in the United States originally formed between Japanese and American auto suppliers to supply the Japanese "transplant" automobile manufacturers. For the Americans, such ventures provide a way to learn Japanese manufacturing techniques and to tap into a growing market.

Investing in "Markets of the Future"   Some of the riskiest joint ventures are those established by firms taking an early position in what they see as emerging markets. These areas offer very large untapped markets, as well as a possible source of low-cost raw materials and labor. The major problems faced by Western firms in penetrating such markets are their unfamiliarity with the local culture, establishing Western attitudes toward quality, and, in some areas, repatriating earnings in hard currency. The solution (sometimes imposed by local government) has often been the creation of joint ventures with local partners who "know the ropes" and can deal with the local bureaucracy.

Even a local partner, however, is no guarantee of success, as the rules of the game can change overnight in such regions. This can be due to a new government coming to power, a revision of existing practice in response to a financial crisis, pressure from international funding agencies, and so forth.

BRINGING FOREIGN PRODUCTS TO LOCAL MARKETS

For every firm that uses an international joint venture to take its product to a foreign market, a local company sees the joint venture as an attractive way to bring a foreign product to its existing market. It is, of course, this complementarity of interest that makes the joint venture possible.

Local partners enter joint ventures to get better utilization of existing plants or distribution channels, to protect themselves against threatening new technology, or simply as an impetus for new growth. Typically, the financial rewards that the local partner receives from a venture are different from those accruing to the foreign partner. For example:

- Many foreign partners make a profit shipping finished products and components to their joint ventures. These profits are particularly attractive because they are in hard currency, which may not be true of the venture's profits, and because the foreign partner captures 100 percent of them, not just a share.

- Many foreign partners receive a technology fee, which is a fixed percentage of the sales volume of the joint venture. The local partner may or may not receive a management fee of like amount.

- Foreign partners typically pay a withholding tax on dividends remitted to them from the venture. Local firms do not.

As a result of these differences, the local partner is often far more concerned with the venture's bottom line earnings and dividend payout than the foreign partner.

This means the foreign partner is likely to be happier to keep the venture as simply a marketing or assembly operation, as previously described, than to develop it to the point where it buys less imported material.

Although this logic is understandable, such thinking is shortsighted. The best example of the benefits that can come back to a parent from a powerful joint venture is Fuji Xerox, a venture begun in Japan in 1962 between Xerox and Fuji Photo. This is among the best known American–Japanese joint ventures in Japan.

For the first 10 years of its life, Fuji Xerox was strictly a marketing organization. It did its best to sell Xerox copiers in the Japanese market, even though the U.S. company had done nothing to adapt the machine to the Japanese market. For example, to reach the print button on one model, Japanese secretaries had to stand on a box. After 10 years of operation, Fuji Xerox began to manufacture its own machines, and by 1975 it was redesigning U.S. equipment for the Japanese market. Soon thereafter, with the encouragement of Fuji Photo, and in spite of the resistance of Xerox engineers in the United States, the firm began to design its own copier equipment. Its goal was to design and build a copier in half the time and at half the cost of previous machines. When this was accomplished, the firm set its sights on winning the Deming award, a highly coveted Japanese prize for excellence in total quality control. Fuji Xerox won the award in 1980.

It was also in 1980 that Xerox, reeling under the impact of intense competition from Japanese copier companies, finally began to pay attention to the lessons that it could learn from Fuji Xerox. Adopting the Japanese joint venture's manufacturing techniques and quality programs, the parent company fought its way back to health in the mid-1980s. By 1991, Xerox International Partners was established as a joint venture between Fuji Xerox and Xerox Corporation to sell low-end printers in North America and Europe. In 1998, exports to the United States grew substantially with digital color copiers and OEM printer engines. By 2002, Fuji Xerox Co. Ltd. had about $8 billion in revenues, was responsible for the design and manufacture of many digital color copiers and printers for Xerox worldwide, and was an active partner in research and development. Both the lessons learned from Fuji Xerox and the contributions they have made to Xerox have inevitably helped Xerox prosper as an independent company.

USING JOINT VENTURES FOR DIVERSIFICATION

As the previous examples illustrate, many joint ventures take products that one parent knows well into a market that the other knows well. However, some break new ground and move one or both parents into products and markets that are new to them.

Arrangements to acquire the skills necessary to compete in a new business is a long-term proposition, but one that some firms are willing to undertake. Given the fact that most acquisitions of unrelated businesses do not succeed, and that trying to enter a new business without help is extremely difficult, choosing partners who will help you learn the business may not be a bad strategy if you are already familiar with the partner. However, to enter a new market, with a new product, and a new partner—even when the probability of success for each is 80 percent—leaves one with an overall probability of success of $(.8 \times .8 \times .8)$ about 50 percent!

In recent years, there has been some discussion about whether joint ventures can be viewed as vehicles for learning. Here the modes of learning go beyond knowledge transfer (i.e., existing know-how) to include transformation and harvesting. In practice, most IJV partners engage in the transfer of existing knowledge, but stop short of knowledge transformation or harvesting. Although many multinational enterprises have very large numbers of international equity joint ventures and alliances, only a small percentage dedicate resources explicitly to learning about the alliance process. Few organizations go to the trouble of inventorying/cataloguing the corporate experience with joint ventures, let alone how the accumulated knowledge might be transferred within or between divisions. This oversight will be increasingly costly for firms, especially as some of the bilateral alliances become part of multilateral networks.

REQUIREMENTS FOR INTERNATIONAL JOINT VENTURE SUCCESS

The checklist in Exhibit 7.3 presents many of the items that a manager should consider when establishing an international joint venture. Each of these is discussed in the following sections.

EXHIBIT 7.3
Joint Venture Checklist

1. Test the strategic logic.
   - Do you really need a partner? For how long? Does your partner?
   - How big is the payoff for both parties? How likely is success?
   - Is a joint venture the best option?
   - Do congruent performance measures exist?
2. Partnership and fit.
   - Does the partner share your objectives for the venture?
   - Does the partner have the necessary skills and resources? Will you get access to them?
   - Will you be compatible?
   - Can you arrange an "engagement period"?
   - Is there a comfort versus competence trade-off?
3. Shape and design.
   - Define the venture's scope of activity and its strategic freedom vis-à-vis its parents.
   - Lay out each parent's duties and payoffs to create a win-win situation. Ensure that there are comparable contributions over time.
   - Establish the managerial role of each partner.
4. Doing the deal.
   - How much paperwork is enough? Trust versus legal considerations?
   - Agree on an endgame.
5. Making the venture work.
   - Give the venture continuing top management attention.
   - Manage cultural differences.
   - Watch out for inequities.
   - Be flexible.

Testing the Strategic Logic

The decision to enter a joint venture should not be taken lightly. As mentioned earlier, joint ventures require a great deal of management attention, and, in spite of the care and attention they receive, many prove unsatisfactory to their parents.

Firms considering entering a joint venture should satisfy themselves that there is not a simpler way, such as a nonequity alliance of the type referred to in Chapter 1, to get what they need. They should also carefully consider the time period for which they are likely to need help. Joint ventures have been labeled "permanent solutions to temporary problems" by firms that entered a venture to get help on some aspect of their business; then, when they no longer needed the help, they were still stuck with the joint venture.

The same tough questions a firm may ask itself before forming a joint venture need to be asked of its partner. How long will the partner need it? Is the added potential payoff high enough to both partners to compensate for the increased coordination/communications costs which go with the formation of a joint venture?

A major issue in the discussion of strategic logic is to determine whether congruent measures of performance exist. As Exhibit 7.4 suggests, in many joint ventures, incongruity exists. In this example the foreign partner was looking for a joint venture that would generate 20 percent return on sales in a 1–2 year period and require a limited amount of senior management time. The local partner in turn was seeking a JV that would be quickly profitable and be able to justify some high-paying salaried positions (for the local partner and several family members/friends). While each partner's performance objectives seem defensible, this venture would need to resolve several major problem areas in order to succeed. First, each partner did not make explicit all their primary performance objectives. Implicit measures (those below the dotted line in Exhibit 7.4), are a source of latent disagreement/misunderstanding. Second, the explicit versus implicit measures of each partner were internally inconsistent. The foreign partner wanted high

EXHIBIT 7.4   **Measuring JV Performance: The Search for Congruity**

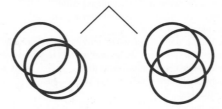

Foreign Partner

1. Profitability — 20% ROS
   (within 12–24 months).

2. Require limited senior
   management time.

- -

3. Maximize local sales.

4. Exploit peripheral or
   mature technology.

Local Partner

1. Profitability
   (within 9–12 months).

2. High-paying salaried
   positions.

- -

3. Opportunity to export.

4. Obtain newest
   technology.

profitability while using little senior management time and old technology. The local partner wanted quick profits but high-paying local salaries.

Partnership and Fit

Joint ventures are sometimes formed to satisfy complementary needs. But when one partner acquires (learns) another's capabilities, the joint venture becomes unstable. The acquisition of a partner's capabilities means that the partner is no longer needed. If capabilities are only accessed, the joint venture is more stable. It is not easy, before a venture begins, to determine many of the things a manager would most like to know about a potential partner, like the true extent of its capabilities, what its objectives are in forming the venture, and whether it will be easy to work with. A hasty answer to such questions may lead a firm into a bad relationship or cause it to pass up a good opportunity.

For these reasons, it is often best if companies begin a relationship in a small way, with a simple agreement that is important but not a matter of life and death to either parent. As confidence between the firms grows, the scope of the business activities can broaden.

A good example is provided by Corning Glass, which in 1970 made a major breakthrough in the development of optical fibers that could be used for telecommunication applications, replacing traditional copper wire or coaxial cable. The most likely customers of this fiber outside the United States were the European national telecoms, which were well known to be very nationalistic purchasers. To gain access to these customers, Corning set up development agreements with companies in England, France, Germany, and Italy that were already suppliers to the telecoms. These agreements called for the European firms to develop the technology necessary to combine the fibers into cables, while Corning itself continued to develop the optical fibers. Soon the partners began to import fiber from Corning and cable it locally. Then, when the partners were comfortable with each other and each market was ready, Corning and the partners set up joint ventures to produce optical fiber locally. These ventures have worked extremely well, and their continuing success became particularly important in the late 1980s, as growth in the U.S. market leveled off. Corning is widely acknowledged as one of the world's most successful users of joint ventures.

When assessing issues around partnership and fit, it is useful to consider whether the partner not only shares the same objectives for the venture but also has a similar appetite for risk. In practice this often results in joint ventures having parents of roughly comparable size. It is difficult for parent firms of very different size to establish sustainable joint ventures because of varying resource sets, payback period requirements, and corporate cultures.

Corporate culture similarity—or compatibility—can be a make-or-break issue in many joint ventures. It is not enough to find a partner with the necessary skills, you need to be able to get access to them and to be compatible. Managers are constantly told that they should choose a joint venture partner they trust. As these examples suggest, however, trust between partners is something that can only be developed over time as a result of shared experiences. You can't start with trust.

Shape and Design

In the excitement of setting up a new operation in a foreign country, or getting access to technology provided by an overseas partner, it is important not to lose sight of the basic strategic requirements that must be met if a joint venture is to be successful. The questions that must be addressed are the same when any new business is proposed: Is the market attractive? How strong is the competition? How will the new company compete? Will it have the required resources? And so on.

In addition to these concerns, three others are particularly relevant to joint venture design. One is the question of strategic freedom, which has to do with the relationship between the venture and its parents. How much freedom will the venture be given to do as it wishes with respect to choosing suppliers, a product line, and customers? In the Dow Chemical venture referred to earlier, the dispute between the partners centered on the requirement that the venture buy materials, at what the Koreans believed to be an inflated price, from Dow's new wholly owned Korean plant. Clearly the American and Korean vision of the amount of strategic freedom open to the venture was rather different.

The second issue of importance is that the joint venture be a win-win situation. This means that the payoff to each parent if the venture is successful should be a big one, because this will keep both parents working for the success of the venture when times are tough. If the strategic analysis suggests that the return to either parent over time will be marginal, the venture should be restructured or abandoned.

Finally, it is critical to decide on the management roles that each parent company will play. The venture will be easier to manage if one parent plays a dominant role and has a lot of influence over both the strategic and the day-to-day operations of the venture, or if one parent plays a lead role in the day-to-day operation of the joint venture. More difficult to manage are shared management ventures, in which both parents have a significant input into both strategic decisions and the everyday operations of the venture. A middle ground is split management decisions, where each partner has primary influence over those functional areas where it is most qualified. This is the most common and arguably most effective form.

In some ventures, the partners place too much emphasis on competing with each other about which one will have management control. They lose sight of the fact that the intent of the joint venture is to capture benefits from two partners that will allow the venture (not one of the partners) to compete in the market better than would have been possible by going it alone.

The objective of most joint ventures is superior performance. Thus the fact that dominant-parent ventures are easier to manage than shared-management ventures does not mean they are the appropriate type of venture to establish. Dominant parent ventures are most likely to be effective when one partner has the knowledge and skill to make the venture a success and the other party is contributing simply money, a trademark, or perhaps a one-time transfer of technology. Such a venture, however, begs the question "What are the unique continuing contributions of the partner?" Shared-management ventures are necessary when the venture needs active consultation between members of each parent company, as when deciding how to modify a product supplied by one parent for the local market that is well known by the other, or to modify a production process designed by one parent to be suitable for a workforce and working conditions well known by the other.

A joint venture is headed for trouble when a parent tries to take a larger role in its management than makes sense. An American company with a joint venture in Japan, for instance, insisted that one of its people be the executive vice president of the venture. This was not reasonable, because the man had nothing to bring to the management of the venture. He simply served as a constant reminder to the Japanese that the American partner did not trust them. The Americans were pushing for a shared-management venture when it was more logical to allow the Japanese, who certainly had all the necessary skills, to be the dominant or at least the leading firm. The major American contribution to the venture was to allow it to use its world-famous trademarks and brand names.

A second example, also in Japan, involved a French firm. This company was bringing complex technology to the venture that needed to be modified for the Japanese market. It was clear that the French firm required a significant say in the management of the venture. On the other hand, the French had no knowledge of the Japanese market and, thus, the Japanese also needed a significant role in the venture. The logical solution would have been a shared-management venture and equal influence in decisions made at the board level. Unfortunately, both companies wanted to play a dominant role, and the venture collapsed in a decision-making stalemate.

Doing the Deal

Experienced managers argue that it is the relationship between the partners that is of key importance in a joint venture, not the legal agreement that binds them together. Nevertheless, most are careful to ensure that they have a good agreement in place—one that they understand and are comfortable with.

The principal elements of a joint venture agreement are listed in Exhibit 7.5. Most of these are straightforward and relate to topics discussed in this chapter. One item on the list that has not been discussed is the termination of the venture.

Although some managers balk at discussing divorce during the prenuptial period, it is important to work out a method of terminating the venture in the event of a serious disagreement, and to do this at a time when heads are cool and goodwill abounds. The usual technique is to use a shotgun clause, which allows either party to name a price at which it will buy the other's shares in the venture. However, once this provision is activated and the first company has named a price, the second firm has the option of selling at this price or buying the first company's shares at the same price. This ensures that only fair offers are made, at least as long as both parents are large enough to be capable of buying each other out.

Making the Venture Work

Joint ventures need close and continuing attention, particularly in their early months. In addition to establishing a healthy working relationship between the parents and the venture general manager, managers should be on the lookout for the

EXHIBIT 7.5
Principal Elements of a Joint Venture Agreement

- Definitions
- Scope of operations
- Management:
  1. Shareholders and supervisory roles regarding board
  2. Executive board
  3. Arrangements in the event of deadlock
  4. Operating management
- Arbitration
- Representations and warranties of each partner
- Organization and capitalization
- Financial arrangements
- Contractual links with parents
- Rights and obligations and intellectual property
- Termination agreements
- Force majeure
- Covenants

[handwritten: ⟹ Recommendation Clear in the agreement]

[handwritten: in limitation]

Source: "Teaming Up for the Nineties—Can You Survive without a Partner?" Deloitte, Haskins & Sells International, undated.

impact that cultural differences may be having on the venture and for the emergence of unforeseen inequities.

International joint ventures, like any type of international activity, require that managers of different national cultures work together. This requires the selection of capable people in key roles. Unless managers have been sensitized to the characteristics of the culture that they are dealing with, this can lead to misunderstandings and serious problems. Many Western managers, for instance, are frustrated by the slow, consensus-oriented decision-making style of the Japanese. Equally, the Japanese find American individualistic decision making to be surprising, as the decisions are made so quickly, but the implementation is often so slow. Firms that are sophisticated in the use of international joint ventures are well aware of such problems and have taken action to minimize them. Ford, for example, has put more than 1,500 managers through courses to improve their ability to work with Japanese and Korean managers.

It is important to remember that cultural differences do not just arise from differences in nationality. For example:

- Small firms working with large partners are often surprised and dismayed by the fact that it can take months, rather than days, to get approval of a new project. In some cases the cultural differences appear to be greater between small and large firms of the same nationality than, say, between multinationals of different nationality, particularly if the multinationals are in the same industry.

- Firms working with two partners from the same country have been surprised to find how different the companies are in cultural habits. A Japanese automobile firm headquartered in rural Japan may be a very different company from one run from Tokyo.

- Cultural differences between managers working in different functional areas may be greater than those between managers in the same function in different firms. European engineers, for example, discovered when discussing a potential joint venture with an American partner that they had more in common with the American engineers than with the marketing people in their own company.

A very common joint venture problem is that the objectives of the parents, which coincided when the venture was formed, diverge over time. Such divergences can be brought on by changes in the fortunes of the partners. This was the case in the breakup of the General Motors–Daewoo joint venture in Korea. Relations between the partners were already strained due to GM's unwillingness to put further equity into the venture, in spite of a debt to equity ratio of more than 8 to 1, when, faced with rapidly declining market share, the Korean parent decided that the venture should go for growth and maximize market share. In contrast General Motors, itself in a poor financial position at the time, insisted that the emphasis be on current profitability. When Daewoo, without telling General Motors, introduced a concessionary financing program for the joint venture's customers, the relationship was damaged, never to recover.

A final note concerns the unintended inequities that may arise during the life of a venture. Due to an unforeseen circumstance, one parent may be winning from the venture while the other is losing. A venture established in the late 1990s between Indonesian and American parents, for instance, was buying components from the American parent at prices based in dollars. As the rupiah declined in value, the Indonesian partner could afford fewer components in each shipment. The advice of many experienced venture managers is that, in such a situation, a change in the original agreement should be made, so the hardship is shared between the parents. That was done in this case, and the venture is surviving, although it is not as profitable as originally anticipated.

In reviewing any checklist of the things to be considered when forming a joint venture, it is important to recognize that such a list will vary somewhat depending on where the international joint venture is established. Exhibit 7.6 summarizes 12 characteristics of joint ventures according to whether they are established in developed versus developing countries.

Most of the descriptions of the characteristics considered are self-explanatory. Yet, more fine-grained analyses are always possible. For example, the discussion in this chapter has generally assumed a traditional equity joint venture, one focused between two firms from two different countries. Yet other types of equity joint ventures exist (see Exhibit 7.7), including those between firms from two different countries that set up in a third country (i.e., trinational), those formed between subsidiaries of the same MNE (i.e., intrafirm) and those formed with companies of the same nationality but located in a different country (i.e., crossnational domestic joint ventures). Further, many joint ventures have more than two partners. Interestingly, the traditional JVs (formed by Japanese MNEs) tend to simultaneously be more profitable and to have a higher termination rate than the alternative structures available.

EXHIBIT 7.6   **Summary of Differences of Joint-Venture Characteristics**

| Characteristics | Developed Country | Developing Country | |
	Market Economy	Market Economy	Planned Economy (China)
Major reason for creating venture	Skill required	Government pressure	Government pressure
Frequency of association with government partners	Low	Moderate	Very High
Overall use of JVs versus other modes of foreign involvement	Significant (20-40%)	High (but contingent on country, industry, and technology level)	Very high (regardless of country, industry, or technology level) but declining
Usual origin of foreign partner	Other developed countries	Developed countries	Ethnic Related Locales (i.e., Hong Kong, Taiwan)
Proportion of intended JVs actually implemented	High	Relatively high	Low (under 50%)
Use of JVs with a predetermined duration	Low (except in certain industries)	Low	Previously high, but declining
Most common level of ownership for foreign MNE	Equal	Minority	Minority
Number of autonomously managed ventures	Small	Negligible	Negligible
Ownership-control relationship	Direct (dominant control with majority ownership; shared control with equal ownership)	Difficult to discern because most MNEs have a minority ownership position	Indirect
Control-performance relationship in successful JVs	Inconclusive	Shared or split	Split control
Instability rate	30%	45%	Low
MNE managerial assessment of dissatisfaction with performance	37%	61%	High

Sources: Paul W. Beamish, "The Characteristics of Joint Ventures in Developed and Developing Countries," *Columbia Journal of World Business,* Fall 1985, pp. 12–19; and Paul W. Beamish "The Characteristics of Joint Ventures in The People's Republic of China," *Journal of International Marketing,* Vol. 1, No. 2, pp. 29–48.

Summary

For the reasons outlined in this chapter, international joint ventures are an increasingly important part of the strategy of many firms. They are, however, sometimes difficult to design and manage well, in part because some organizations do not treat them as "true" alliances (see Exhibit 7.8). The fact that some ventures are performing below their management's expectations should not be an excuse for firms to avoid such ventures. In many industries, the winners are going to be the companies that most quickly learn to manage international ventures effectively. The losers will be the managers who throw up their hands and say that joint ventures are too difficult, so we had better go it alone.

EXHIBIT 7.7   Japanese JV Ownership Structure, Performance, and Termination Rate

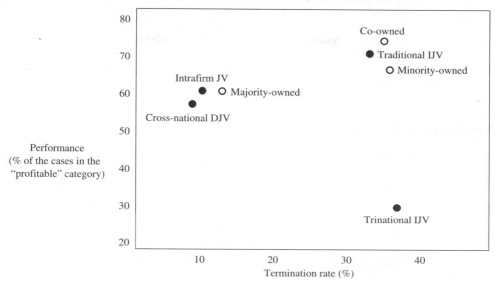

EXHIBIT 7.8   The True Alliance versus the Pseudo Alliance

	The True Alliance	**The Pseudo Alliance**
Planned level of parent input and involvement	Continuing	One-time
Distribution of risks/rewards	Roughly even	Uneven
Parent attitude toward the JV	A unique organization with unique needs	One more subsidiary
The formal JV agreement	Flexible guideline	Frequently referenced rulebook
Performance objectives	Clearly specified and congruent	Partially overlapping/ ambiguous

In the future, will we see more or fewer international joint ventures? Certainly the reduction in investment regulations in many countries, coupled with increased international experience by many firms, suggests there may be fewer joint ventures. Yet other countervailing pressures exist. With shortening product life cycles, it is increasingly difficult to go it alone. And with the increase in the number of MNEs from emerging markets, both the supply and demand of potential partners will likely escalate.

Supplementary Reading

Beamish, Paul W., and J. Peter Killing, eds. *Cooperative Strategies: European Perspectives, Cooperative Strategies: North American Perspectives,* and *Cooperative Strategies: Asian Perspectives.* San Francisco: The New Lexington Press, 1997. (Three volumes.)

_____ . Special Issue on Cooperative Strategies, *Journal of International Business Studies,* Vol. 27, No.5, 1996.

Datta, Deepak K. "International Joint Ventures: A Framework for Analysis," *Journal of General Management,* Vol. 14, No. 2, Winter 1988.

Delios, Andrew and Paul W. Beamish, "Joint Venture Instability Revisited: Japanese Foreign Subsidiary Survival," *Management International Review,* 2002. (Forthcoming).

Doz, Yves L., and Gary Hamel. *Alliance Advantage.* Cambridge, MA: Harvard Business School Press, 1999.

Fey, Carl, and Paul W. Beamish. "Organizational Climate Similarity and Performance: International Joint Ventures in Russia," *Organization Studies,* 22 (5): 2001. pp. 853–882.

Hamel, Gary, Yves Doz, and C. K. Prahalad. "Collaborate with Your Competitors—and Win," *Harvard Business Review,* January-February 1989.

Inkpen, Andrew C., and Paul W. Beamish. "Knowledge, Bargaining Power and International Joint Venture Stability." *Academy of Management Review,* Vol. 22, No. 1, 1997.

Inkpen, Andrew C. "A Note on the Dynamics of Learning Alliances: Competition, Cooperation and Relative Scope," *Strategic Management Journal,* Vol. 21, No. 7, 2000. pp. 775–779.

Killing, Peter. "How to Make a Global Joint Venture Work." *Harvard Business Review,* May–June 1982, pp. 120–127.

Lane, Henry W., and Paul W. Beamish. "Cross-Cultural Cooperative Behavior in Joint Ventures in LDCs." *Management International Review,* Special Issue 1990, pp. 87–102.

Makino, Shige and Kent E. Neupert. "National Culture, Transaction Costs, and the Choice Between JV and Wholly Owned Subsidiary," *Journal of International Business Studies,* 31(4), 2001. pp. 705–713.

Schaan, Jean-Louis. "How to Control a Joint Venture Even as a Minority Partner," *Journal of General Management,* Vol. 14, No. 1, Autumn 1988.

Schaan, Jean-Louis, and Paul W. Beamish. "Joint Venture General Managers in Developing Countries," In *Cooperative Strategies in International Business.* Ed. F. Contractor and P. Lorange. Lexington, MA: Lexington Books, 1988, pp. 279–99.

Chapter Eight

International Strategy Formulation

This chapter focuses on international strategy formulation. Implicit in the discussion is the notion that international strategy evolves with changes in the competitive environment. As barriers to market penetration have been dismantled and as technologies have emerged that facilitate international communication and organizational control, businesses have worked hard to expand their scope to include new international markets. Globalization, a term used somewhat loosely to describe an interdependent, borderless world, has now become a common objective for businesses of all sizes. Since the mid-1990s, Internet technologies have contributed to globalization by increasing the ability of smaller companies to tap global markets and by giving larger companies new tools to expand their reach. As a result of a broad movement toward global competition, businesses have increasingly abandoned traditional approaches to international competition in favor of new, more innovative strategies.

Despite the global transformation of many businesses, two new trends threaten to slow the process. The first is the rising tide of antiglobalization. Fuelled by the increasing homogenization of cultures and the huge success of some global companies, antiglobalization demonstrations have become much more aggressive. The antiglobalization movement has encouraged some companies to rethink where and how they compete. The second trend of note is the emergence of the Internet. While the Internet can help big companies improve operating efficiencies and expand their reach, the Internet can also draw power away from large companies. The ability of the Internet to "make markets" means that the ownership advantages enjoyed by large MNCs are at risk of being diminished.

In this chapter we first review how changes in the competitive environment have facilitated globalization. We then discuss the forces that encourage companies to focus more attention on local issues. The chapter then discusses how the

This chapter was prepared by Allen Morrison.

combination of global and local forces impact international strategy formulation. We also review the limitations of analytical frameworks and discuss how substantial benefits can result from the use of nonanalytical tools in formulating international strategies. Finally, the chapter concludes with specific recommendations to managers struggling to formulate effective international strategies.

UNDERSTANDING INDUSTRY PRESSURES

As the millennium unfolds, MNCs are confronted with a bewildering array of strategy options. Most MNCs conceptualize strategy as a hierarchy that includes corporate-level strategies and business unit or divisional initiatives. Corporate strategies typically focus on two things: (1) determining the industries in which the MNC will compete, and (2) determining how the various businesses within the MNC will coordinate activities. Business unit or divisional strategies focus on market share battles through competitive and international positioning. In many companies, business unit managers rather than corporate executives are the primary drivers of international strategy.

Because most MNCs have multiple business units they invariably have multiple international strategies. Each international strategy is driven by a business unit striving to match its unique skills with market opportunities. For example, IBM designs and manufactures microprocessors, a globally demanded product. Competing in this industry requires IBM to construct world-scale fabrication facilities that produce globally standardized semiconductor products. IBM also competes in service industries where customers require enormous care and localized attention. A strategy based on maximizing local responsiveness seems most appropriate for much of IBM's service activities. To maximize its overall competitiveness, IBM encourages each business to approach international markets in ways that are most consistent with industry pressures. As a result, a starting point for understanding MNC strategy is the industry in which the business unit or division competes.

Every industry—whether high-tech or low-tech, service or manufacturing—is confronted by two different types of pressures: pressures to be globally integrated, and pressures to be locally responsive. These pressures drive business strategy and cannot be overlooked in formulating an appropriate international strategy.

PRESSURES TOWARD GLOBALIZATION

Pressures that encourage businesses to adopt global integration strategies include both broad facilitating factors and industry-specific imperatives. Four of the most important facilitating factors include:

- Freer trade.

- Global financial services and capital markets.

- Advances in communications technology.

- The Internet.

Together, these facilitating factors have made global competition possible but not necessarily desirable for all businesses. To determine whether global integration is advisable, businesses are encouraged to lower the microscope to examine pressures that are specific to their particular industry. These industry-specific imperatives include:

- Universal customer needs.

- Global customers.

- Global competitors.

- High investment intensity.

- Pressures for cost reduction.

Broad Facilitating Factors

Freer Trade   Since the end of World War II, declining tariffs and the emergence of regional trading blocs have had an enormous impact on world trade and investment. Successive rounds of General Agreement on Tariffs and Trade (GATT) agreements, plus multilateral cooperation under the World Trade Organization have resulted in the adoption of new commercial liberalization policies by numerous governments. In 2000, the value of world merchandise exports topped $6.2 trillion, up 12.5 percent and triple the growth rate in 1999; service exports reached $1.6 trillion in value, up 6 percent over the previous year. In 2000, U.S. exports of merchandise reached $781 billion; the U.S. export of services surpassed $274 billion and U.S. imports of goods and services were $1.46 trillion. By 2000, the WTO estimated that 22 million jobs in the United States were dependent on trade.[1]

Regional trading blocs have strengthened business ties in North America, Europe, Southeast Asia, Africa, and Latin America. The removal of tariffs and nontariff barriers signals a weakening of the economic role of nation states and an invitation to companies to "think globally." On February 28, 2002, 12 members of the European Union completed a multiyear process of phasing out their national currencies in favor of the Euro currency unit as the basis of trade and commerce. The following countries are participating: Belgium, Germany, Greece, Spain, France, Ireland, Italy, Luxembourg, The Netherlands, Austria, Portugal, and Finland. Companies and consumers in these countries have found it much easier to comparison shop and otherwise carry out business across a broad geographic base.

It should be pointed out that the objectives of the European Union, and the free trade agreements established by ASEAN and Mercosur countries, as well as Canada, the United States and Mexico are quite different instruments. The European Union is designed to limit national sovereignty by creating supranational political and administrative bodies. In contrast, free trade agreements attempt to achieve the economic benefits of tariff removal without so much loss of national sovereignty. While Europe is harmonizing its regulatory affairs, most of the rest of the world is not.

Developing countries are also benefiting from trade liberalization. The world's 49 least-developed countries as a group saw their gross domestic products and trade expand faster than global averages in 2000. In 2000, the value of merchandise exports grew by an astonishing 28 percent for this group. That same year, the growth in merchandise exports for all developed countries was 15 percent, three times higher than average GDP growth rates.[2]

Global Financial Services and Capital Markets   The globalization of financial services and capital markets has facilitated the efforts of many businesses to globally integrate their activities. Capital can now be sourced through transnational banks (for example, Citibank or HSBC), overseas venture capitalists (for example, Investcorp, a Saudi-owned firm) and other sources via the Internet. Recent trends in financial technology allow the trading of financial instruments 24 hours per day, 365 days per year, irrespective of national location. In addition, the ability of MNCs to manage interest rate risk and currency exchange rates through hedging and computerized market trading have reduced the importance of placing investment capital under one national umbrella.

One sign of the growth in international financial services is the growth in foreign direct investment (FDI). Estimates are that FDI flows for 2001 topped $760 billion, fuelled by mega cross-border mergers. Examples of these deals include Deutsche Telkom's $24.6 billion acquisition of U.S.-based VoiceStream Wireless, and Citigroup's $12.5 billion purchase of Mexico's Banamex. In 2000, 56 percent of all cross-border mergers were financed through shares.[3] The globalization of financial services companies and the increasing accessibility of international securities and debt markets has no doubt contributed to the growth in FDI and cross-boarder mergers and acquisitions.

Advances in Communications Technology   Managing a far-flung international business requires extensive communication in order to maintain organizational control. Advances in computer and fax technology have made such communication easier and less costly. The availability of huge, online data bases, in-house email systems, and the Internet have greatly increased the ability of companies to manage international operations. Direct electronic links, for example, have enabled Boeing and a consortium of Japanese partners to design aircraft together. Advances in information technology have also made it possible for the financial services industry in New York to export thousands of back-room data processing jobs to lower cost Ireland. They have also allowed Singapore Airlines to perform essentially all of its software development work in Madras, India.

The Growth of the Internet   The pervasive growth of the Internet has had a huge and incalculable impact on globalization. While Internet usage varies across countries, it is rapidly growing essentially everywhere in the world. US business-to-business sales are predicted to reach $3 trillion by 2004.[4] Between 1999 and 2001, Internet usage in China doubled every six months. By mid-2001, the number of

Internet users in China exceeded that of Australia and by the end of 2002, it is anticipated that the number of Internet users in China will exceed that of Japan giving China the top spot in Asia.[5]

At one level, the Internet facilitates communication within and across countries. Through sophisticated customer relationship management (CRM) systems and electronic data interchange systems (EDI), customers can now access the worldwide R&D, production, marketing, and distribution systems of many suppliers and buyers. Internet exchanges can also now link buyers and sellers of all sizes around the world, making markets where none previously existed. For small suppliers in developing countries, the ability to list and sell products around the world is now a distinct possibility.

At another level, the Internet has had a substantial impact on company productivity with resulting increases in income levels. Estimates from UNCTAD are that if the Internet led to a simple 1 percent improvement in productivity, the world's developing economies would see a $118 billion increase in service growth.[6] This in turn would result in market growth for local as well as international companies.

Industry-Specific Pressures

Universal Customer Needs   While advances in telecommunications have enabled companies to better control global activities, television, movies, radio, the print media, and telephones have dramatically increased the information available to consumers around the world. By seeing what other people have or enjoy doing, consumers put enormous pressure on businesses to globalize. Successful world products like watches, cameras, fast food, blue jeans, luxury writing instruments, personal computers, and cellular telephones are welcomed in more and more countries around the world. Many sports have also become globalized. The popularity of U.S. sports, for example, has led to sell-out crowds for American football and basketball games in Europe and Japan and a surging public interest in sports celebrities whose names are used to sell everything from perfume to pizza. Depending on the industry, people increasingly want the same products and services irrespective of their country of origin.

Global Customers   Many MNCs do not sell directly to consumers but focus instead on other MNCs as customers. When customers are global, they demand standardized inputs around the world. Case in point: PriceWaterhouseCoopers. In 2000, Nortel Networks contracted with PriceWaterhouseCoopers to take over all of its traditional human resource back office functions. The contract has global implications for PriceWaterHouseCoopers which must deliver standard HR systems around the world.

Prince, a Michigan-based manufacturer of dashboard components and interior paneling for the automotive industry, is another example of a company that has been encouraged to globalize by key customers. One of Prince's biggest customers is GM. General Motors has made major progress in globalizing its purchasing activities. To GM this means that it now searches the world for the best products at the lowest prices. An automotive components company like Prince must be able to meet GM's *global* standards for quality, features and pricing. As GM moves into new markets, these suppliers are expected to respond. In order to streamline design, keep costs low and maximize production efficiencies, Prince and GM have developed a very close working relationship. As GM expands its presence in Latin America, it has encouraged Prince to establish a major production facility near its manufacturing complex in Brazil. Prince must respond in a positive way or risk jeopardizing its core North American partnership with GM.

Global Competitors   No pressure is quite so strong as an international competitor taking your market share. Some industries are dominated by global businesses that establish competitive norms. Once competitive norms have been set in an industry, businesses can chose either to follow the pack and adhere to the norms or pursue much narrower niche strategies.

High Investment Intensity   Investment intensity includes costs for developing products and gearing up for production. In general, the higher the investment intensity, the greater the pressure on businesses to globally standardize output. Boeing, for example, spent just under $6 billion bringing the B-777 aircraft to market. The strategy for Boeing is now to maximize the number of planes sold in order to cut the R&D costs allocated to each plane. In another example, Gillette launched its new MACH3 razor on April 14, 1998. The company spent six years and $750 million to bring the three-bladed razor to market versus only $200 million launching the simpler Sensor brand razor in 1989. In order to recoup the enormous investment costs, Gillette spent an estimated $300 million marketing the razor; of this amount, $100 million was directed at U.S. sales and $200 million was budgeted for international sales. By the beginning of 2000, MACH3 was sold in 100 countries, a feat that took Sensor five years to achieve. Other industries, from computer software, telecommunications equipment, and automobiles, face similar pressures to amortize development costs through rapid globalization.

Pressures for Cost Reduction   In industries where price is the key purchase criterion, producers have a great incentive to find new ways to lower costs to maintain profits. Depending on industry conditions, economies of scale and learning can both have enormous impacts on operational efficiency. The greater the potential impact of learning and economies of scale, the greater the incentive for companies to maximize output. From a global strategy perspective, a key determination is the volume level at which minimum per unit costs can be achieved. If minimum per unit costs can be achieved at an output of 200,000 units per year and if domestic demand is only 50,000 units per year, businesses have an incentive to standardize output and get into the export business for the remaining 75 percent of output. Of course, whether the business actually exports or not will depend in part on the importance the customer places on price. In the petroleum industry price is critical and so producers push production volumes out as far as possible. In the newspaper industry, local content and responsiveness are more important than production efficiencies.

PRESSURES TOWARD LOCALIZATION

Although over the past decade the pendulum has swung decisively in the direction of globalization, this is not true for all industries. The transition to globalization has not been universal and may yet pass many industries by. Localization pressures include both country-specific factors and MNC-specific factors. Country-specific factors include five primary pressures:

- Trade barriers.
- Cultural differences.
- Nationalism.
- The Internet.
- Antiglobalization activists.

MNC-specific factors include four principal pressures that either limit an MNC's ability to respond to globalization pressures or facilitate its ability to be locally responsiveness:

- Organizational resistance to change.
- Transportation limitations.
- New production technologies.
- Just-in-time manufacturing.

Country-Specific Pressures

Trade Barriers Tariff barriers encourage businesses to compete internationally through FDI rather than trade. Servicing a local market through a dedicated manufacturing facility enables businesses to maximize local responsiveness which is typically an objective of government imposed barriers. With tariffs in place, competitors are encouraged to establish autonomous operations in a host country thereby preserving national culture and sovereignty. When tariffs decline, the international competitiveness of a country's industries becomes more vital. Serious loss of market share to imports often triggers nontariff barriers in nations concerned over the short-term loss of jobs. Subsidies directed at domestic producers represent a common nontariff barrier.

Every country is guilty of subsidizing domestic production in some industries. Countries in the EU have restrictions on foreign ownership of a wide range of industries, including broadcasting, airlines, defense, and energy transmission. And both direct and indirect subsidies continue to abound. The WTO estimates that in 2002, rich countries were paying $1 billion per day in agricultural subsidies alone.[7] They further estimated that if all countries were to cut tariffs and subsidies by one-third, the impact on economic development would be substantial: India would see its GDP increase by 1.6 percent; Thailand would see its GDP grow by a whopping 4.2 percent!

One of the better-known examples of government subsidies and protection can be found in the steel industry. Government assistance to the EU steel industry is estimated to have totaled nearly 2.5 billion euros between 1995-1999. This figure excludes indirect subsidies for such things as employment, training, R&D, and environmental protection. The domestic customers of EU steel producers also receive substantial subsidies. Between 1995 and 1999, for example, the EU subsidized the transport sector approximately 170 billion euros; ship builders and automobile manufacturers received 7.4 billion euros and 1.9 billion euros respectively. It has been estimated that total EU subsidies to companies in all sectors, paid out of community and national budgets, reached nearly 1 trillion euros during the last half of the 1990s alone.[8] Government subsidies combined with the collapse of steel markets in the former USSR and sagging international demand for steel, led to a veritable flood of cheap steel products into the United States in the late 1990s and early 2000. In response, in March 2002, U.S. President George W. Bush imposed steep tariffs and quotas on a wide range of steel imports from the European Union, Japan, and South Korea. The European Union immediately announced an appeal to the WTO and threatened to retaliate against U.S. exporters in other industries.

Voluntary export restrictions represent another common nontariff barrier to trade. In the early 1980s, Japanese automobile manufacturers agreed to limit exports of automobiles to the United States. One study found that as a result of the export restrictions, Japanese automobile manufacturers began shifting production to the United States creating an estimated 55,000 jobs by the middle of the decade.[9] However, the study also found that both U.S. and Japanese automobile manufacturers raised prices substantially as a result of the export restrictions. It was estimated that Japanese manufacturers captured an additional $2.2 billion in cash flow by using increases in prices to limit volume; U.S. producers captured an additional $2.6 billion by matching Japanese price increases. In all, the study estimated that the same reduction in Japanese automobile exports could have been achieved with an imposition of an 11 percent tariff. In the final analysis, export restrictions may have helped Japanese manufacturers more than they hurt.

Technical standards represent another barrier to trade. The DVD player and recording industries provide an excellent example of the power of standards to either encourage or retard trade. In early 2002, 10 of the largest Japanese, European and South Korean electronics companies were in talks to establish a common technology standard for next-generation recordable optical discs. Three main standards competed for the attention of often-bewildered consumers: DVD-RAM, supported by Matsushita and Toshiba; DVD-RW, developed by Pioneer and Sharp; and DVD+RW, promoted by Sony and Philips. Competing standards acted as a brake to the globalization of the DVD recording industry. As an example, Japan's shipments of DVD *players,* for which there is a single technical standard, reached 1.57 million units in 2001. That same year, Japanese shipments of DVD *recorders,* which used the three different technical standards, totaled just 131,000 units. At issue in the industry meetings was whether the 10 firms would agree to jointly developing a common standard for large-capacity optical discs that relied on blue semiconductor lasers that would significantly boost the capacity of DVD recorders.[10]

Cultural Differences   While satellite television and the international media are shrinking the world and homogenizing consumer tastes, national culture continues to pull in the opposite direction. Traditions and religious beliefs run deep and often conflict with international media messages. Although individuals may display an initial interest in a product because it is "foreign," they may also shun the same product over time because of the changes in lifestyles it promotes. For example, McDonald's opened its first store in India in late October 1996 in the city of Delhi. In a country that venerates the cow, McDonald's substituted the Big Mac with the Maharaja Mac made with mutton, and offered vegetarian rice-patties flavoured with vegetables and spice. Despite these moves, McDonalds' has weathered a number of nationwide protests aimed at stopping the company from using beef products in other countries. To the extent different cultures lead to divergent consumer preferences, global product strategies can miss the mark, or can require major adaptation from market to market.

Another example of the power of cultural differences involved the Kellogg Company in the United Arab Emirates (UAE). In April 2002, the General Secretariat of Municipalities ordered the withdrawal of a number of Kellogg products from the UAE following consumer complaints that some contained pork derivatives. UAE is a predominantly Muslim country and the Islamic religion outlaws the consumption of pork products. Following the ordered withdrawal, the General Secretariat ordered each municipality in the UAE to conduct extensive laboratory testing for pork derivatives in Kellogg's Frosties Cherry, Frosties Strawberry, Brown Sugar, and Cinnamon Pop Tarts. At the time, Kellogg imported products into the UAE from the United States, Germany, and Switzerland and the ban affected only products exported from the United States. The move followed similar action taken against Wrigley's chewing gums. In March 2002, after thorough investigation, it was determined that Wrigley's gums were free from any pork derivatives.

Many products with global appeal are simply unaffordable to huge numbers of people. Either people are unfamiliar with high-end Western brands, or if they are, they simply lack the money to purchase them. Understanding demand patterns can be complex because even if the demand for certain kinds of products is there, it may be next to impossible for companies to tap. Take computer software as an example. One report released in June 2002 reported computer software piracy rates of 94 percent in Vietnam; 92 percent in China and 87 percent in Russia.[11] While software users in these country want current software, the combination of weak enforcement of piracy laws, easy access to pirated software, and low income levels have essentially shut major software companies like Microsoft and SAP out of these markets. Even when markets are open, huge income disparities within countries can limit the overall size and appeal of certain countries. The Samsung China case study is an ideal vehicle for exploring the challenges of selling the "right" mix of color televisions—arguably one of the most global of products—in China.

Nationalism   From the republics of former Yugoslavia, to post-September 11 United States, to the Basque region of Spain and the Canadian province of Quebec, nationalism remains a powerful force in the lives of many people. Nationalism is almost always powerfully emotional. By representing common values and attitudes, nationalism provides the basis for social cohesion and can be used to justify obstructions in the international movement of goods and services. In countries where national institutions and power systems have been fractured, tribalism has seen a renaissance. Tribal loyalties, often born of common language and history, are fast replacing national allegiances in countries torn by civil war or economic strife. By focusing attention inwardly, both nationalism and tribalism foster values that deter globalization.

Political uncertainty in many countries is also encouraging people to focus inwardly on local events and issues. Countries as diverse as the United States, Colombia, Afghanistan, Pakistan, India, Ireland, Zimbabwe, Russia, and Israel have all struggled with huge domestic security problems that have distracted policy makers and business executives. In Japan and Korea, ongoing and seemingly intractable economic problems have hit national psyches hard and have diminished the global aspirations of many companies. Political and economic uncertainties have pushed many MNCs to re-examine their exposure to international markets.

The Internet   Just as the Internet is a powerful force for globalization, it is also a force that contributes to localization. Case in point: Intuit. Inuit produces tax, accounting, and personal finance software products, and does a thriving business in the United States. When the company decided to go global, it reasoned that since tax and finance packages needed to be designed for local market laws and practices, product development should be done at the local level.

To serve Europe, Intuit replicated its product development and service system on a smaller scale in France, Germany, and the U.K. Despite seemingly smart plans, within two years Intuit was losing large sums abroad because of the costs of running those local operations and of maintaining communication and oversight. In response Intuit first moved most European operations to Munich, keeping only skeleton customer service groups in the other countries. As losses continued, Intuit pulled all European software development back to North America and turned over the sales and servicing of those products to European alliance partners. The key for Intuit has been its ability to use the Internet as a substitute for bricks and mortar assets in far-flung locations. And still Intuit controls 60 to 80 percent of the market in the major European countries.

The arrival of the Internet has occurred just as many businesses have begun to shift the focus of their strategies. In the past, many companies conceived of strategy as "competitive positioning" or determining how to beat the competition in the battle for customers. Throughout the 1990s, a different trend emerged: strategy based not on competitive positioning but core competencies. Instead of taking an "outward-in" approach to strategy (competitive positioning), a growing number of companies have pursued an "in-ward" out approach by focusing on what they do best (core competencies).

Companies that build strategy on core competencies have found a friend in the Internet. This is because the Internet allows them to focus on developing and maintaining world-class competencies—"sticky tape" for 3M, "software" for Microsoft—while using local companies to bring the company's products and services to overseas markets. Local companies become the key to penetrating markets and the Internet becomes the ideal control and communications channel.

Anti-Globalization Activists   Activists, while in many ways consistent with nationalists, are a distinct force that gnaws away at globalization. Activists are often driven by zeal uncommon in the general public. While partisan and often very well organized, some also act outside established legal systems. Most have websites and sophisticated fund-raising capacities. One such organization, "Stop the FTAA," boasts organizations in 110 cities throughout the Western hemisphere.

Beginning in Seattle in 1999, the world has been racked with seemingly endless street demonstrations *against* globalization. In some cases—most notably in Genoa, Quebec City, and Seattle—these demonstrations have turned violent as waves of protesters clash with police with a zeal not seen since the anti-American riots of the 1960s. To these people, successful globalization is limited globalization—or better yet, no globalization at all. Protesters now pop up at essentially every major meeting of the WTO or G8 leaders. Security risks have encouraged the World Economic Forum to move its annual meeting from Davos, Switzerland, to a more secure location. Companies are also often the targets of antiglobalization efforts. Royal Dutch Shell, General Motors, and McDonald's are but a few of the companies that have been targeted by antiglobalists.

An increasing number of companies are taking the antiglobalization movement seriously. Some are beefing up their public relations departments to ensure that their messages are being heard. Others are modifying behavior. And in some cases, big MNCs are finding customers in the very groups that mock their efforts. In early 2002, a violent new video game called "State of Emergency" was released by Scotland's Rockstar Games and VIS Entertainment. The video game caused a stir, not only for its gory depiction of globalization gone mad, but because it is designed for and marketed by Sony—one of the companies antiglobalists have been so critical of.

MNC-Specific Pressures

Organizational Resistance to Change   For MNCs, globalization means imposing central control on country managers who in many cases have been functioning with substantial autonomy. This imposition of corporate control often means the redesign of an affiliate's products to meet global specifications or the rationalization of operations for the good of the overall corporation. In either case, the "not invented here" syndrome may intervene. For MNCs with histories of autonomous affiliates—companies like General Motors, Siemens, IBM, Philips, and Nestlé—organizational resistance to global integration has become a major obstacle. A case in point is Warner Lambert's pharmaceutical operations in Europe. In 1970 Warner Lambert acquired Parke-Davis in an effort to expand its international position in pharmaceuticals. With decades of experience in Europe, Parke-Davis had established manufacturing operations in France, the U.K., Italy, Spain, Germany, Belgium, and Ireland. Affiliates in these countries were given considerable autonomy and developed substantial competencies. Beginning in the mid-1980s, Warner Lambert began a major initiative to reduce the number of pharmaceutical manufacturing units in Europe while concurrently specializing production in the units that remained. Fearful of losing power and convinced that the parent was overestimating the impact of globalization, affiliate managers fought back. Working together, the major affiliates were able to convince the parent to proceed much more cautiously than planned. Decisions that were expected to have been made in weeks or a few months ended up being moved to committees that took over three years to process. While the parent has now made a number of rationalization decisions, the major European affiliates have been successful in retaining much of their original powers.

Other companies have experienced similar resistance to change. In Europe, powerful unions have opposed Europeanwide re-engineering. At IBM, for example, French unions filed suit in 1994 to stop the company from cutting 1,300 jobs. In September 1994, IBM Europe's chairman, Hans-Olaf Henkel, resigned after IBM Chairman Lou Gerstner forced a reorganization of the European sales force that augmented the role of corporate head office decision makers over regional chiefs.[12]

Management Shortcomings   Despite interests in expanding overseas, companies continue to report a shortage of global leaders. One study of *Fortune 500* companies found that less than 15 percent reported having enough competent global leaders.[13] Quality leaders who can manage cross-culturally are in short supply in many companies. Furthermore, managers with the requisite skills risk burn-out in careers that for many involves nonstop travel and months away from home. Travelling hundreds of thousands of miles per year, spending 200-plus days a year on the road, and suffering incessant jet-lag are some of the prices of running far-flung operations. Some managers are simply saying no to globalization: not for business reasons, but for personal and family reasons.

Transportation Difficulties   Businesses with products that are highly susceptible to spoilage or which have a high weight to value ratios are not typically good candidates for globalization. The dairy and bread industries, for example, tend to be some of the most locally responsive in part because of short shelf-lives. Other industries such as fresh seafood and cut flowers have largely overcome spoilage problems by developing special packaging and efficient transportation procedures. However, long distance shipping adds substantial costs to the consumer and are only justifiable to the degree premium prices can be passed on. In industries with high weight to value products, transportation costs may outweigh any benefits of global integration. Sand, gravel, coal, potted plants, diapers, and paint are examples of products whose high weight to value ratio discourage global integration.

New Production Technologies   New computer assisted design and manufacturing technologies have allowed an increasing number of industries to maximize efficiencies at relatively small production volumes. Multiple products in a single factory are more practical because machine change-over time has been reduced dramatically. New technologies have also made it possible to introduce new products in record time, making speed a new source of competitive advantage. Whistler, one of the largest manufacturers of radar detectors in the United States, introduced leading edge technology in product design and manufacturing configuration and raised its pass rate on its assembly line from 75 percent to over 99 percent. In doing so, it cut production delays and reduced overall costs, saving hundreds of U.S.-based jobs that were slated for transfer to South Korea. Digitization has contributed to many of these changes. In the publishing industry, for example, digitization now makes it economically viable to produce books with much smaller production runs than would have been commercially viable even five years ago.

Mass customization is sweeping many industries. It is based on the objective of fulfilling the needs of *individual* customers. New production and communications systems allow companies like Levi Strauss & Co. to create Personal Pair™ pants for finicky customers. For a $10 premium, personal measurements can be taken in four distinct areas: waist, hips, rise, and inseam. These measurements are then sent to a specially designed Levi's plant in Tennessee, the pants are cut and sewn, and then shipped to the awaiting customer, all within a two-week period of time.[14] The era of "one-size fits all" appears to be coming to an end—at least in some industries.

Just-in-Time Manufacturing   Heavy equipment manufacturers and automotive assemblers have led the way in pursuing just-in-time manufacturing strategies. In many cases suppliers to these industries are required to ship an agreed upon quantity of components so that they arrive at the customer's plant within hours of assembly. By adopting just-in-time manufacturing, the assemblers are able to pass inventory costs as well as other risks on to suppliers. In many cases these savings more than offset the potential production economies that may result from global component manufacturing. Businesses that supply inputs to just-in-time customers face serious limitations insofar as globalization is concerned.

GLOBALIZATION IMPACTS INDUSTRIES

Globalization and localization pressures vary from industry to industry. While a reduction in trade barriers may have a dramatic impact on the computer industry, it may be of little consequence to the cement industry. Similarly, while advances in telecommunications may make it easier to develop standardized advertising programs, global advertisements may be inappropriate in industries whose products remain deeply imbedded in local cultures. Not only do the direction of globalization and localization pressures vary, but the intensity of the pressures can differ substantially as well. Relatively few industries emphasize all globalization or localization pressures to the maximum degree. For example, while many segments of the food processing industry could theoretically achieve considerable cost savings through global production, the industry's globalization potential is limited by spoilage problems and low value-to-weight which makes shipping prohibitively expensive.

Before further exploring MNC strategies, it is useful to determine which industries or products require local adaptation and therefore strong local responsiveness strategies and which face strong globalization pressures (i.e., major scale economies in production, R&D or marketing) and therefore strong central control. The following two-by-two matrix attempts to do this by contrasting the pressures toward globalization with the pressures toward localization (Exhibit 8.1).

In the two right quadrants, local adaptation is important. In the two top quadrants, the pressures toward globalization are significant. The top left quadrant identifies industries where local differences are minor and the benefits to global integration are significant. The bottom right quadrant represents the opposite extreme where local differences are significant and there are few advantages to globalization. The bottom left quadrant represents industries where local differences are minor but globalization is limited by other factors (e.g., transportation in the case of cement). The types of organization strategy best suited to the key quadrants are shown in the diagram and are discussed below. It is important to repeat, however, that when we talk of globalization pressures increasing, what we mean is that more and more products and industries are moving up from the bottom quadrants to the top quadrants.

EXHIBIT 8.1
Mapping Industries

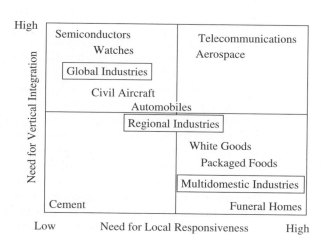

GLOBALIZATION IMPACTS BUSINESS STRATEGY

In determining an appropriate international strategy, a complete and comprehensive assessment needs to be made of the industry pressures confronting the business. The objective is to pattern business strategy after the opportunities and threats in the industry.

Multidomestic Strategies

The establishment of stand-alone overseas affiliates is consistent with the adoption of multidomestic strategies. Businesses pursuing multidomestic strategies first develop products for their home markets and then offer them for sale or adaptation to their overseas affiliates. The role of each affiliate is to absorb the parent company's technology and adapt the resulting products to suit local conditions and tastes. If specialization is at the heart of global strategies, duplication and autonomy are at the heart of multidomestic strategies. In the pure multidomestic model, it is technology and skills that cross national boundaries, not products.

During the high-tariff decades after World War II, multidomestic strategies were prevalent. However, with the first emergence of globalization pressures in the 1970s, multidomestic strategies have become less desirable in many industries. Without becoming more global, companies risk seeing their sources of competitive advantage erode over time.

Regional Strategies

Regional strategies are increasingly appropriate in a wide range of industries. While regional pressures come from a variety of sources, the most important developments are in the formalization of trading blocks. Companies in the NAFTA region, European Union, Asean, and Mercosur often find it advantageous to adopt regional strategies. Regional strategies make the most sense when market demand is homogenous within the region and when barriers to intraregional trade and investment are low.

Separately, regional strategies can also be appealing as a stepping-stone to full-blown global competition. The advantage of regional strategies is that they can produce many of the same efficiencies as global strategies without the costs and complexity. Regional production facilities have been often found to be as scale efficient as global facilities while being more forgiving of the need to tailor key product features for local markets. Regional plants also avoid many of the very real staffing, communication and motivational problems of huge global facilities. By shifting operations and decision making to the region, the company may also be better able to maintain an insider advantage.

Under regional strategies, companies extend home country loyalties to the entire region. Local markets are intentionally linked within the region. Market share battles are predominantly regional, and competitive positioning varies from region-to-region. It is within the region that top managers determine investment locations, product mix, competitive positioning, and performance appraisals. Managers are given the opportunity to solve regional challenges regionally.

Examples of companies with regional strategies include General Motors in the automobile industry, Safeway in grocery retailing, Whirlpool in white goods (large home appliances like washers and dryers) and Thomson in consumer electronics. Each of these companies views regional markets as largely homogenous, but markets across regions as quite unique. Strategy is based on maximizing economies of scale at the regional level. Separate regional headquarters are set up with largely autonomous decision makers from one country to the next. In the case of Thomson, for example, North American and European operations are run separately. In North America, Thomson has established a network of suppliers and subassemblers—largely in Mexico—to maintain the regional integrity of its operations.

Global Strategies

Under a global strategy, businesses focus on maximizing international efficiency by locating activities in low-cost countries, producing standardized products from world-scale facilities, globally integrating operations, and subsidizing intercountry market share battles. Global businesses conceive and design products for world markets from the outset. Frequently, affiliates in key markets have input into product design, but once the parent organization launches a new product, the affiliate's role reverts to that of implementer.

Global products usually emphasize international similarities rather than cultural differences. Not surprisingly, marketing strategies are typically established in and by the parent organization. Products are manufactured wherever in the world the necessary quality standards can be achieved at the lowest cost including transportation to key markets. As a practical matter, large markets attract production because market share is often enhanced by the presence of a production facility. Also, host country governments sometimes induce local production through nontariff barriers to trade, but the classic global strategy is conceived without artificial impediments to the movement of goods.

MNCs pursuing globally integrated strategies often have considerable bargaining power vis-à-vis host governments as a result of their ability to control both how and where activities are geographically positioned and how they are coordinated. These abilities are manifest in two broad areas.[15] First, globally integrated MNCs can bias the financial results of affiliates and thereby shift profits from high to low tax rate countries. The manipulation of financial results can be achieved through transfer pricing and favorable remittance policies.

A second way globally integrated MNCs exert power over host governments is through their ability to control the direction and location of technology and skills. MNCs often have the capability to rapidly reconfigure value-adding activities. By focusing on shifting patterns of comparative advantage and cost differences across countries, MNCs can quickly move operations from one country to another. This mobility, combined with the ownership of technology, skills, and jobs and the ability of MNCs to generate tax revenues, results in countries often competing against each other for new investment as well as the retention of existing MNC activities.

Even subnational governments are getting into the bidding game. In Phoenix, Arizona, for example, the city council in 1995 voted to approve major tax breaks and infrastructure investments to encourage Sitix, a division of Japan giant Sumitomo Corporation, to invest almost $500 million in a silicon wafer manufacturing plant. The Phoenix area was already home to major microprocessor fabrication plants by Intel, Motorola, and SGS-Thomson and was concerned about maintaining its global position as a center of high-tech excellence. Whether it is Phoenix, Paris, Bangkok, or Dubai, tax breaks and infrastructure support are commonly used by municipal governments to lure business investors. And generally, the bigger the potential investment, the greater the incentives offered.

KEY CONSIDERATIONS IN ADOPTING AN INTERNATIONAL STRATEGY

Although global strategy has been viewed as ideal in global industries, not all businesses compete in global industries nor are all businesses capable of pursuing a global strategy. Resource constraints, bureaucratic obstacles and histories of affiliate autonomy have forced a large number of businesses to pursue a variety of non-global options. In determining an appropriate international strategy—whether multidomestic, regional or global—the following steps should be considered.

1. Invest Heavily in Data Collection

In the final analysis, decisions to adopt a particular international strategy are made by people. There is an important human dimension to globalization that goes beyond rational analysis. Peoples' *perspectives* of the world—whether accurate or not—play important roles in decisions to pursue one strategy over another.

The challenge for managers is to accurately assess the opportunities and threats facing their company. Unfortunately, it is human nature to pay attention to what is most familiar, meaning that many managers and their companies are missing huge opportunities. Another concern is that people tend to look for cues from other companies. If everyone is setting up shop in China, for example, can they really all be wrong? Or if every other business in the industry is embracing regionalization, shouldn't regionalization be the way to go? In reality it takes an enormous amount of faith for a manager to act contrary to industry norms. It takes courage to stand apart from the crowd, to travel against the current of public opinion. This is particularly the case when the decision maker's experience is limited or if the company has little objective data to call its own. It ultimately comes down to the manager's confidence and faith in his or her company's ability to collect and interpret the "right" data quickly.

One of the problems with data collection is that the information—particularly in emerging countries—is often suspect. One simple example illustrates this point. In May 1998, the government of Hong Kong forecast annual economic growth of 3.5 percent for 1998. At the same time, Daiwa Institute of Research predicted a contraction in the economy of 0.7 percent; JP Morgan anticipated a decline of 0.6 percent. Interestingly, both the IMF and Bank of America predicted the Hong

Kong economy would grow by a full 3 percent in 1998, Goldman Sachs forecast economic growth at 2.5 percent, Morgan Stanley predicted growth at 2 percent, and the OECD anticipated growth at 0.9 percent.[16] While it could be argued that some of the data sources had greater vested interests in Hong Kong's recovery than others, all of these sources of information were generally accepted as credible.

In assessing market opportunities, companies are advised to use multiple data sources. They should tap external sources and develop their own internal sources. The importance of developing multiple points of data input cannot be overstated. At the end of the day, decision makers need considerable judgment in weighing what will often be conflicting data.

2. Determine the Potential for Critical Scale Economies

Some industries are particularly susceptible to economies of scale; others are not. In general, the capital intensity of an industry is an important determinant of the potential for economies of scales. In industries like microprocessors, companies are spending upwards of $2 billion on single fabrication plants. In order to pay down fixed costs, companies have a huge incentive to standardize output and push per unit costs down to a bare minimum. In other industries like shoe repair or high-end jewelry manufacturing, there are relatively few cost advantages that come from scale.

Reaping the benefits of economies of scale can be more difficult than the theory might suggest. Exhibit 8.2 presents the hypothetical example of a company with two affiliates. Under this example, the affiliate in country A produces only

EXHIBIT 8.2   **The Impact of Economies of Scale on Transfer Pricing**

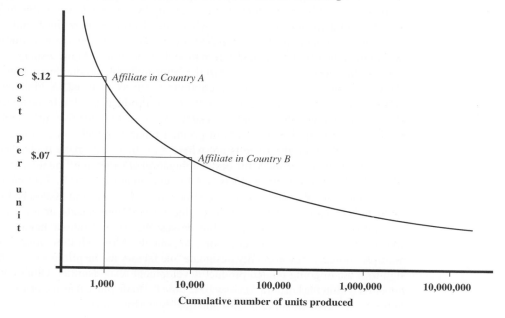

1,000 units of output per month at a unit cost of $0.12. The affiliate in country B produces 10,000 units per month at a per-unit cost of $0.07. If the affiliate in country A shuts down its factory and sources from country B its costs will go down to just below $0.07 per unit. However, if country A's marginal tax rate is higher than that of country B, the company may want to charge the affiliate in country A the old rate of $0.12 per unit. In this way, profits are shifted from country A to country B and taxes are minimized. The opportunities for economies of scale can be elusive in the absence of effective decision making and execution.

3. Weigh the Value of other Globalization Benefits

While scale economies are an important potential benefit of globalization, they are not the only benefit. Advertising and promotion can in some cases be globalized too. It is just as possible to advertise to global similarities as to national differences, but to do it successfully requires a lot of understanding of the mood and mind-set of different regions. There is an enormous difference between successful global advertising, and the view that what's good for Iowa or Ontario is good for India or Malaysia. The same is true for global product design.

Just as the globalization benefits are not the same for all industries, they differ significantly from product-to-product and from activity to activity. Key questions include: how homogeneous are customer needs from one country to another? What savings are possible from designing the product for global markets and manufacturing it to global capacity? What technology does large-scale specialized production make possible? Can the company benefit by adopting a common approach to marketing the product around the world? What problems might arise in particular countries or regions from such an approach? As questions like these are answered product-line by product-line and activity by activity, it is possible to identify where globalization fits best and where localization is more important.

Offshore production is often the first thought of North American or European firms threatened by heightened international competition. Many managers may feel that the perfect solution is to shift the labor-intensive production processes to low-wage countries and otherwise continue business as usual. A globalization strategy, however, implies much more than this. Products need to be designed for key world markets; furthermore, designs need to be sensitive to production processes and to global standards of product reliability, technology and quality. Under globalization, the issue is not where a business can make it cheaper, but where a business can achieve the best combination of technology, quality, and cost.

On this basis, different products end up being manufactured in different countries. Some factories concentrate on component parts; others on assembly. In both cases, factories are set up to serve the business's worldwide needs, or at least a major portion of them. Many large businesses are nervous about having single sources of supply of key products or components. Although they often develop multiple sources, they normally designate one factory as the prime source and assign to it the ongoing related product development responsibility. Other competing units within the corporation may over time try to displace it as the prime source of products based on superior cost and quality performance.

The potential of the Internet to transform the economics of globalizing activities must be fully weighed. Some activities can be e-enabled and ported to customers around the world; others cannot. The impact of the Internet to accelerate globalization can be enormous. But so can the Internet empower local companies with knowledge and resources that undermine traditional sources of competitive advantage enjoyed by big MNCs.

4. Rotate Country Managers More Frequently to Help Them Develop a Global Vision

Country managers with long-term appointments do not easily develop global perspectives, and it is difficult to globalize an organization successfully without those perspectives in place. One way to accelerate globalization is to move senior people from one international affiliate to another, or from the affiliate to head office and back. Of course, this means sending in nonnationals to run affiliates, but if the rotation is understood as global management training, resentment of the nonnational boss can be minimized. There are other benefits to rotation too. The corporation is able to utilize managers from all over the world in whatever positions they best fit. Furthermore, morale in the affiliates is sometimes higher because managers there see opportunities beyond their own borders.

A wide variety of corporations including Ford, Nortel Networks, 3M, ABB, Samsung, and Dow Chemical use management rotation regularly to build up a core of international managers. Not everyone likes to be moved around the world, however. Some managers like the opportunity when they are early in their careers, but not when they have to worry about their children's schooling and other family matters. It is also expensive. Expatriate managers usually get paid a premium for living abroad or get their living accommodation paid. Family trips back home and private schooling for dependent children are also often part of the package. Building a global management team leads to some expensive traditions in corporate culture. These benefits are also often very visible to host country nationals who often view them as excessive.

5. Reassess the Performance Measurement System and Reward System

Under traditional multidomestic strategies, country managers have broad strategic autonomy over activities in their country and should therefore reasonably be evaluated on the basis of country-specific results. Broad measures of growth and return on invested capital are commonly used criteria. However, to hold a manager responsible for results after his or her autonomy is reduced under globalization is more problematic. The company, of course, is more interested in its overall global results than in the results of any one affiliate, but if results are to be used to measure a manager's performance, they must somehow fit the manager's responsibility. While normal growth and return on investment criteria might apply to products made for the domestic market only, imported products may be better evaluated with a system that measures sales growth by market segment. And products made for world markets may require a system that evaluates cost of production only. On the other hand, if the affiliate has the marketing assignment for its global products, the measurement system might include growth of export sales.

Clearly, globalization leads to more complex measurement systems. That is because responsibility is divided in different ways. This is evidenced in Exhibit 8.2 where the affiliate manager in Country A may be responsible for perpetually subsidizing the profits of another affiliate. Being responsible to sell a product designed for the global market at a price set by the head office is quite different from selling a domestically designed product at a price set at home. Measurement systems have to reflect these changes in responsibility. They are complicated further by transfer prices on intercorporate trade, and intercorporate trade increases significantly under globalization.

6. Take a Balanced Approach

Thus far, the chapter has taken a strong analytical bent in recommending a clear process for strategy formulation. Huge benefits can result for companies that approach strategy formulation in a systematic manner. Data collection, industry analysis, and assessments of strengths and weaknesses are critical in developing strategic options and in making sound strategic decisions. However, an analytical approach to strategy does have several important limitations.[17]

Companies that take a strictly analytical approach have a hard time creating effective visions for the future. Visioning is dependent on moments of "illumination" during which great insights into possible future states of the company are formed. Visions are based on ideas and mental images of the future and involve stretch targets that do not emerge through normal analytical processes. Visioning is an inherently emotional process rooted as much in ambition and personality as an accurate assessment of current potential.

While good strategy is dependent on a thorough analysis of factors that are both external and internal to the company, they are given meaning and direction by the company's vision. Companies that are most successful globally invariably have a vision for themselves as global players. In most cases these visions are generated not so much by systematic planning processes as they are by leaders who have a unique sense of the business's long term potential in an uncertain future. The Dubai Aluminum case study provides a good vehicle for exploring not only how leaders impact company vision, but also how leaders struggle to make accurate assessments of the external pressures and internal realities facing the company.

The second important concern about strategy formulation based on analytics is that the approach does not work very well in emerging industries or in rapidly changing industries. Analytics would never have led Sony to introduce the Walkman or 3M to introduce Post-It Notes. In emerging industries, the best decisions are those that emerge through experimentation. In many cases, 10 new ideas are tried out and the one that succeeds in the market place becomes the focus of the company's strategy. In rapidly changing industries, strategy execution almost always trumps strategy formulation.

In industries that are rapidly changing—computer storage devices and Internet services as examples—competitive analysis is often a useless process. By the time you collect and analyze the data, the world has changed. In these cases, strategy focuses on the race to invent new products, often for markets that do not yet exist. In these industries, international strategy is rarely a priority because the companies that invent the technologies focus on the invention process and turn the production and globalization challenges over to others.[18]

The trend toward globalization is now unstoppable. Given the huge number of foreign affiliates as well as the growing number of domestic competitors in overseas markets, determining an appropriate international strategy is a complex, difficult job. Given the rate of change in the environment, even the best strategy rapidly diminishes in value. As a result, managers must be constantly on the alert for not only new market opportunities, but new competitors as well. While analytics are a critical component in the process, balance and judgment are required.

In the final analysis, no strategy is perfect. Good strategy is dependent on good leadership, good execution, and usually a bit of good luck! At the end of the day, decision makers need to balance a number of factors in determining an appropriate international strategy for their organization. The better strategies of tomorrow will no doubt accommodate the need for greater complexity and flexibility. This is the focus of Chapter 9.

Supplementary Reading

Bartlett, C., and Ghoshal, S. "Going Global: Lessons from Late Movers," *Harvard Business Review,"* March–April, 2000, pp. 132–142.

Beck, J., and Morrison, A. J. "Mudslides and Emerging Markets," *Organizational Dynamics,* Fall, 2000, pp. 19–92.

Friedman, T. *The Lexus and the Olive Tree.* New York: First Anchor Books, 2000.

Hamel, Gary and Prahalad, C. K., "Do You Really Have a Global Strategy?" *Harvard Business Review,* July–August, 1985, pp. 139–148.

Kim, W. Chan and Mauborgne, Renee, "Making Global Strategies Work," *Sloan Management Review,* Spring, 1993, pp. 11–27.

Morrison, Allen, *Strategies in Global Industries: How U.S. Businesses Compete.* Westport, CT: Quorum Books, 1990.

Morrison, Allen, and Kendall Roth, "A Taxonomy of Business-Level Strategies in Global Industries," *Strategic Management Journal,* Vol. 13, 1992, 399–417.

Ohmae, Kenichi, "Planting for a Global Harvest," *Harvard Business Review,* July–August, 1989.

O'Meara, P., Mehlinger, H., and Krain, M. (eds.). *Globalization and the Challenges of the New Century: A Reader.* Bloomington, IN: Indiana University Press, 2000.

Porter, Michael. "Changing Patterns of International Competition," *California Management Review,* Vol. 28, 1986, 9–40.

Prahalad, C. K. and Yves Doz. *The Multinational Mission: Balancing Local Demands and Global Vision.* New York: The Free Press, 1987.

Rodrik, D. *Has Globalization Gone Too Far?* Washington, DC: Institute for International Economics, 1997.

Schutte, Hellmut. "Strategy and Organization: Challenges for European MNCs in Asia." *European Management Journal,* 15 (4) 1997, 436-445.

Schwartz, P., and Gibb, B. *When Good Companies Do Bad Things: Responsibility and Risk in an Age of Globalization.* New York: Wiley, 1999.

Yip, George. *Total Global Strategy: Managing for Worldwide Competitive Advantage.* Englewood Cliffs, NJ: Prentice Hall, 1992.

Yip, George, Johansson, Johny, and Roos, Johan. "Effects of Nationality on Global Strategy," *Management International Review,* 37 (4) 1997, 365–385.

Endnotes

1. World Trade Organization, 2001.
2. World Trade Organization, 2001.
3. UNCTAD, World Investment Report, 2001.
4. UNCTAD, E-Commerce and Development Report, 2001.
5. China Internet Network Information Center, 2001.
6. UNCTAD, E-Commerce and Development Report, 2001.
7. Mike Moore, Director General of the World Trade Organization, "Globalization: The Impact of the Doha Development Agenda on the Free Market Process," February 2002.
8. "The Steel-State Nexus," *The Wall Street Journal,* February 27, 2002.
9. See, Hufbauer, G., Berliner, D., and Elliot, K. *Trade Protection in the United States: 31 Case Studies.* Washington, DC: Institute for International Economics, 1986.
10. "Firms In Talks On Common Standards For New Optical Discs," *The Wall Street Journal,* February 17, 2002.
11. International Planning and Research Corporation, "Seventh Annual Business Software Global Software Consulting Alliance Piracy Study," June 2002.
12. W. Echikson, "IBM's European Travail," *Fortune,* October 3, 1994, p. 88.
13. S. Black, A. Morrison, and H. Gregersen. 1999. *Global Explorers: The Next Generation of Leaders,* (New York: Routledge, 1999).
14. For more information on mass customization, see D. Anderson, J. B. Pine, and B. J. Pine. *Agile Product Development for Mass Customization: How to Develop and Deliver Products for Mass Customization, Niche Markets, JIT, Build-to-Order and Flexible Manufacturing.* (New York: McGraw Hill, 1996).

15. For a more complete discussion of the concerns of host countries regarding integrated MNCs, see Y. Doz, "Government Policies and Global Industries," in M. Porter (ed.), *Competition in Global Industries,* (Boston: Harvard Business School Press, 1986), pp. 225–266.

16. J. Lloyd-Smith and N. Reynolds. "SAR Seen Casualty of Regional Fallout," *South China Morning Post Business Post,* May 13, 1998, p. 1.

17. For an overview of these concerns, see H. Mintzberg and F. Westley. "Decision Making: It's Not What You Think." *Sloan Management Review,* Spring, 2001, pp. 89–93.

18. For more on the challenges of strategy formulation in rapidly changing industries, see R. D'Aveni. *Hypercompetion: Managing the Dynamics of Strategic Maneuvering,* (New York: Free Press, 1994); and C. Christensen, *The Innovator's Dilemma: When New Technologies Cause Great Firms to Fail,* (Boston: Harvard Business School Press, 1997).

Chapter Nine

The Impact of Globalization on the Organization of Activities

This chapter focuses on the organization of business activities in the face of rising globalization. How companies organize activities—research and development, production, marketing, and service, among others—often means the difference between failure and success. The best-designed strategies have to be implemented to work. As a result, getting the organization "right" is the key to effective strategy execution.

Organization decisions ultimately focus on how activities are *configured* and *coordinated*.[1] Configuration pertains to the geographic positioning of activities and is driven by a company's interest in accessing markets and sources of comparative advantage. Activities range from being "concentrated" (i.e., each activity is located in a single country from which the world is served), or "dispersed" (i.e., all critical activities are located in each overseas country). In contrast, coordination pertains to the integration or interdependence of activities and is driven by a company's interest in exploiting competitive advantages across countries. Coordination ranges from very low—where each activity of a business is performed independently—to very high, where the same activities are tightly coordinated or closely integrated across countries. How a company configures and coordinates its activities says a lot about its strategy but also about how its strategy is executed.

This chapter examines how rising globalization pressures have forced managers to re-examine every aspect of the configuration and coordination of their

This chapter was prepared by Allen Morrison.

company's activities. More particularly, it focuses on the organization of activities and the interplay between international strategy and structure. The chapter reviews the pros and cons of different structures and addresses how the Internet is creating new organizational options for multinational—and local—companies.

COMMON INTERNATIONAL ORGANIZATION STRUCTURES

International Division Structure

Much of the early work on international organization structures took the logical approach of relating it to the growth of a company's international activity. For example, a company might begin with an export department to handle the technical requirements of shipping products across national borders. With success in export markets would come a greater awareness of international opportunities, and the next organizational stage might be the establishment of an international division to look after both exports and foreign investments. The organization structure of a company with an international division might appear as shown in Exhibit 9.1.

Under an international division structure, all functional activities—with the possible exception of sales—are concentrated at home. When international sales and profits are a minor percentage of a division's overall activity, it is difficult to get a busy division manager to spend time cultivating overseas relationships and building international activity. Time tends to get spent where the big sales and profits are. Building and cultivating business are best done by a division devoted exclusively to that task—hence the international division.

One clear advantage of an international division structure is that it allows a company to give international sales much greater support and attention. As a result, the manager of the international division has to understand the product-market strategies of each product division and adapt them to international markets. Another advantage is that the company is much more able to share learning across product divisions. Rather than have every division spend time duplicating efforts to figure out the nuances of each foreign market, the international division has to do this just once. Also, by representing the entire company in a foreign market, the company can better use size to its advantage in negotiations with governments, suppliers, and distributors.

EXHIBIT 9.1
The International Division Structure

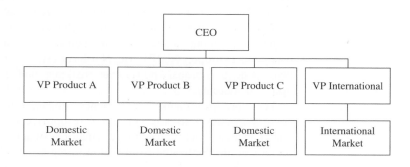

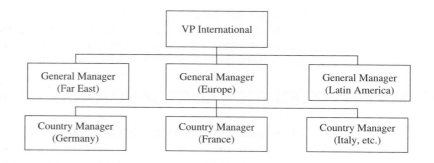

EXHIBIT 9.2
The Area Division Structure

Area Division Structure

As international sales grow as a percentage of total company sales, many successful companies evolve out of an international division structure and create an area division structure (Exhibit 9.2). While an area division will often continue to report to a corporate vice president international, strategic decision making is shifted to regional managers or country managers within the region. As a result, the position of vice president international is one of the few positions in a company where success can bring declining influence. Examples of companies with strong area or regional organizations include General Motors, IBM, Philips, Dow Chemical, and HSBC.

As discussed in Chapter 8, area or regional structures often capture the majority of efficiency advantages that result from globalization. Relatively few activities actually require global volumes to reach maximum levels of economic efficiency.[2] Furthermore, area organizations may be more efficient and effective than global structures because of increased local responsiveness, reduced bureaucracy, communication efficiencies, and improved employee morale. In many cases area structures can also facilitate faster delivery, enable greater customization, and allow the company to maintain smaller inventories than would be necessary under more complex organization forms.

Characteristics   Under an area division structure, regional managers have a high degree of autonomy in how they adapt the strategies of the home country product divisions to meet the particular circumstances of their regions and countries. The Kellogg Company of Battle Creek, Michigan, has made a major commitment to its area division structure. Kellogg has 12 of the world's 15 best-selling brands of ready-to-eat cereal. However, the company decides which brands to sell, manufacture, and market on an area basis. The company's four area presidents (Europe, Asia-Pacific, North America, and Latin America) have been given wide discretionary power over breakfast foods marketing, pricing, production, and sourcing.

The more local conditions influence consumer demand, the more autonomy country managers usually get. Local responsiveness is its main achievement. Under an area division structure, the majority of activities are "dispersed" across regions or are duplicated from region to region. At General Motors, for example, major assembly plants are located in each regional market of the world. Product development, purchasing, and marketing and sales activities are regionally coordinated.

Multidomestic Affiliates   In some companies, area headquarters maintain tight operating control within the region; in other companies, area headquarters play a more modest oversight role and leave the key operating decisions to country managers. This is appropriate when local customization, production, and customer service are critical. In multidomestic affiliates, local CEOs report to area presidents, manage a wide array of the parent company's product lines, but have considerable leeway in making production, marketing, and servicing decisions.

Host countries have long used the term *miniature replica* to describe the traditional multidomestic affiliate. The term arises because the affiliate is like a scaled-down version of the parent, in that it produces generally the same products but in lower volume for a smaller "domestic" market. In many cases, trade barriers keep international markets separated and permit the affiliate to operate profitably, even though its production costs are often higher than the parent company's because of the need to produce multiple products in relatively small volume. The diagram in Exhibit 9.3 captures the key features of a traditional multidomestic affiliate.

Multidomestic affiliates are typically evaluated by profit center criteria keyed to results rather than adherence to head office policies. Usually, local nationals are appointed as country managers and management turnover is relatively slow. The role of country manager is similar to the role of the parent CEO, except for the more limited geographical sphere of activity. Each affiliate takes on a character and personality of its own and formulates its own internal strategy.

From a head-office perspective, an area-centered structure is ideal as long as it is advantageous to disperse key activities and control them with local decision makers. An advantage of affiliate autonomy is that it reduces the pressure on head

EXHIBIT 9.3   Multidomestic Affiliate Structure

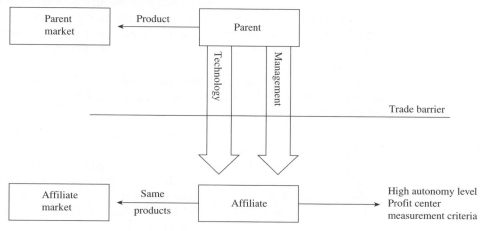

office managers to pay attention to far-flung operations. Attention is expensive, particularly when cultural, political, and market differences increases. Time spent thinking about foreign issues is time not spent on home country customers or core technologies. Furthermore, most managers do not have time to read newspapers from multiple continents, nor do they have the interest or stamina required to tolerate the constant travel required to keep abreast with foreign markets, customers, managers, and affiliate initiatives.

By adopting multidomestic affiliate structures, companies can avoid many of the costs associated with globalization. The people challenge is very real in global companies. Multidomestic affiliates do not need to make huge investments in elaborate global leadership development and retention programs. Companies like GE, Sony, and Daimler-Chrysler spend tens of millions of dollars every year on formal training programs designed to create globally competent managers. Many firms also use costly international assignments as mechanisms to develop global thinking. Because as many as one-quarter of repatriated managers leave their companies within a year of returning home, using foreign assignments as a tool to develop global thinking is another expense that can be avoided.

Given the high levels of affiliate autonomy and the results-oriented performance measurement systems, one might suppose that host governments would be relatively pleased with multidomestic structures. Complaints against multidomestic structures, however, have been numerous. One of the most frequent concerns has been that "miniature replica" affiliates do not do much R&D; they simply bring in parent technology and adapt it where necessary. Most studies confirm that this complaint is fairly accurate. Given the small size of many host country markets, affiliates often cannot afford to pay for their own R&D and still make a profit. They tend to manufacture many products in scale inefficient plants—a strategy that can only succeed with imported technology and tariff protection. Another complaint has been that "miniature replica" affiliates do not export, and as a result do not bring jobs and hard currency to developing countries. Again, this complaint has, with notable exceptions, proven fairly accurate. The reason for it has not been parent unwillingness as much as the affiliate's inability to export competitively. In many cases, that inability is due to the affiliates' lack of cost competitiveness—they are typically high-cost producers relative to their parents; and to the affiliate's lack of product differentiation—they typically use parent technology.

In addition to host country concerns about multidomestic affiliates, companies struggle with their own set of issues. In particular, high local autonomy tends to generate three problems:

1. Communications between home country product divisions and distant overseas affiliates are often more complex and risk breaking down. Corporate policies and standards may not be effectively communicated to or adopted by the affiliates. In many cases important product-market information also fails to reach the field abroad. We see an example of this challenge in the Black & Decker-Eastern Hemisphere and the ADP Initiative case study. In this example, Bill Lancaster, the President of Black & Decker Eastern Hemisphere, is left trying

to decide how and when to introduce a U.S.-designed management appraisal system in Asia.

2. Affiliate autonomy is not conducive to MNC learning. Excellent practices and products can typically be found in each affiliate. To maximize learning, every affiliate must promote its products and practices within the MNC as well as embrace appropriate new practices and products generated by other affiliates. The greater the affiliate autonomy, the lower the likelihood that excellent practices and products will either be communicated or adopted.

3. As affiliates develop self-sufficiency, the power of home country managers is challenged. For products that are viewed as strategically important, home country managers may try to disrupt moves by affiliates to achieve greater autonomy. This can lead to dysfunctional behaviors and morale problems.

There is a growing realization among developing countries that multidomestic affiliates cannot play an effective role in the emerging globalization of business. Hence, many countries are lowering tariffs in an effort to transform their industrial structures and make them more competitive. As barriers to trade are reduced, the costs of maintaining multidomestic affiliates becomes more apparent and an increasing number of companies are restructuring in favor of a more regional or global approach. But if host countries complained about foreign ownership under the miniature replica structure, they are likely to continue to do so under more global structures. The complaints, however, will have a different ring to them.

Global Product Divisions

As a general rule, the relative importance of product managers increases with the number of products being offered by a company. As the diversity of *foreign* products increases, many successful companies have adopted global product division structures. Du Pont became the first major U.S. company to adopt a modern divisionalized structure not long after the turn of the century. By 1970, as many as 90 percent of *Fortune 500* companies had adopted product divisional structures.

Divisions are usually organized to correspond to particular industries, or industry segments. Hong Kong-based Hutchison Whampoa Ltd., is one of the best examples of a diversified, multidivisional MNC. It has extensive interests including food processing, retailing, container ports, manufacturing, shipping, oil and gas, and real estate. Its real estate business includes commercial and residential development, landholding, and hotel operations. Hutchison Whampoa's shipping interests include container and other terminal facilities in Asia and Europe. Each of these businesses is organized as a separate company, responsible to group headquarters and Chairman Li Ka-shing. Other MNCs, including ICI, AOL Time Warner, Matsushita, GE, Philip Morris, and Siemens have highly diversified operations that lend themselves to distinct industry analyses and diverse business unit strategies.

Under a divisionalized structure, all functional activities (for example, R&D, production, marketing) are controlled by a product group. An example of a global product divisional structure is included in Exhibit 9.4.

EXHIBIT 9.4
Global Product
Division Structure

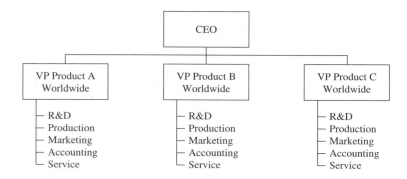

Characteristics   When global product divisions take over, they tend to achieve direct lines of communication into key markets and can therefore get their product and market know-how through to the field unimpeded. Because activities are tightly coordinated by divisional head office, country managers are often involved only in the local administrative, legal, and financial affairs of the company. Product decisions are made by head-office managers and input from overseas affiliates is often discouraged. Because products are globally standardized, head office managers typically have limited interest in the ideas that come from overseas affiliates. The role of affiliates is to implement strategy not formulate it. What is lost in terms of local responsiveness is gained in terms of global efficiencies.

Global product division structures represent a chain of vertically integrated activities that potentially span the globe. Product division managers can configure activities according to variances in costs or skills across countries. This makes product divisions ideal for global strategies. Under a global product division structure, some activities may be dispersed—for example, component manufacturing and assembly—while others may be centrally located—for example, research and development. The advantages of global structural flexibility is the ability to quickly shift production locations according to changes in labor costs, product quality, political risk, or exchange rates.

One of the reasons that many large companies have shifted to global product division structures is because it helps managers more easily focus on maximizing competitiveness. When a company's competitive domain is conceptualized along industry lines, competitors can be clearly identified and decisions focused on upgrading functional skills. The result is manufacturing facilities that are more focused on specific products, robotized in terms of technology, and diversified in terms of markets served.

GLOBAL AFFILIATES

Under a global product division structure, affiliates around the world do not operate with a great deal of autonomy. They become an integrated part of a global organization and often play no independent strategic role at all. If production does

EXHIBIT 9.5
Global Affiliate
Structure

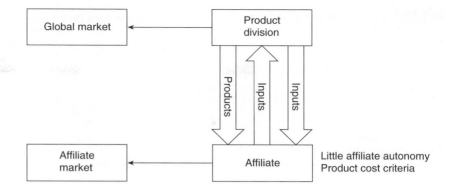

take place in a particular affiliate, it will often be specialized production of a single model or component for use throughout the corporation. Hence the design and specification of what is produced is seldom handled by the affiliate because it is not aimed primarily at the affiliate's market. In these conditions, coordination between parent and affiliates is critical, and is often achieved by sending parent executives to run affiliate operations for three to five year terms. Because specialization is at the heart of global company strategies, affiliates are expected to be obedient and are evaluated as cost centers. The profit center concept just does not fit the strategy.

Affiliates operating under a global product division structure are largely treated as a source of supply or as sales offices. Inputs—technology and components—are provided by either the parent or other affiliates within the vertically controlled structure. They are then further processed and re-exported back to the parent or sister affiliates within the division. Examples include Matsushita, which manufactures big-screen televisions for world markets in China, and Sharp, which makes washing machines for global customers in the Philippines. While affiliate exports may or may not return to the parent's home country, divisional managers control the product's look and feel, its market destination, and its sales price. Once final assembly has occurred, the parent generally supervises international marketing; while affiliates may employ their own marketing staff, they are typically accountable to divisional marketing managers. The diagram in Exhibit 9.5 captures the key features of a global affiliate structure.

Contrasting Area and Global Product Division Structures

Area and global product division structures can both be appropriate depending on a company's objectives. Area structures work best when international sales represent an important percentage of total sales and when the requirements for local responsiveness are high. Global product division structures work best when the number of products the company produces has proliferated and when globalization requirements are high. To establish the contrast more clearly, Exhibit 9.6 summarizes the essential differences between multidomestic area and global product division structures.

EXHIBIT 9.6 Contrasting Global Product and Multidomestic Area Structures

	Global Product Structure	Multidomestic Area Structure
Product line	Specialized	Duplicated
Market emphasis	International	National
Transfers	Product/Technology	Technology/Skills
Affiliate evaluation	Cost center	Profit center
Affiliate role	IMplement strategy	Develop & implement strategy
Affiliate autonomy	Low	High
Affiliate management	Foreign, short-term	Local, long-term

Under the global product division structure, efficient communication of product know-how is critically important. The country manager under a global structure plays administrative and legal roles rather than strategic ones. Not surprisingly, the global product structure works best in conditions where product knowledge is more vital than market knowledge. While outputs are tightly controlled, specific operations in any given country may not be well coordinated, and there may be some duplication of selling effort. However, each product line gets someone's maximum attention.

Under the area division structure, region and country managers are ultimately responsible for corporate strategy in their regions or countries. Their task is to adapt corporate strategy to local conditions. To do so, they have to become familiar with the products and markets of each division. Knowledge of local politics, markets, suppliers, and channels constitutes their distinctive competence within the company. They may not give each product the same degree of effort, but will seek out first their strongest competitive opportunities, that is, where market demand is highest or competition weakest.

The biggest weaknesses in the global product structure are the growing dependence of affiliates on the parent and the lack of substantive ideas or initiatives arising from affiliates. As a result, global product structures are notoriously inflexible. A case in point is Matsushita Electric Industrial, which first introduced a product division structure in 1933. Matsushita's tightly controlled structure was designed to build managerial talent, promote internal competition and maximize international growth by treating each product division as an independent small business. Overseas marketing affiliates were established, international sales soared, and profits were consolidated on a global basis. By the mid-1980s, Matsushita had emerged as the world's largest producer of consumer electronics. Despite this success, Matsushita faced serious challenges in the 1990s. Demand for its mainstream color television and VCR products flattened and profit margins slipped substantially. Many observers blame Matsushita's once successful product division structure for much of the company's woes. By locating most R&D activities in Japan, Matsushita has missed out on a stream of critical innovations taking place in the United States and Europe. The company has also faced growing demands by host governments for more local production and innovation. As technologies such as semiconductors, computers, and robots have blurred, Matsushita's reliance on strictly defined product divisions has only compounded the problems associated with product division inflexibility.

While global product structures have serious shortcomings, area structures may not be the perfect solution. The biggest weakness in the area structure is the difficulty the parent has imposing an overarching strategy on its autonomous affiliates and hence obtaining some of the benefits of specialization. As a result, area structures are notoriously inefficient. Rather than produce standardized products in world-scale production facilities, area structures rely on smaller plants that are less scale efficient. Because research and development, purchasing, marketing, and distribution are also duplicated across geographic territories, cumulative overhead costs can be much higher than with most product structures. In an increasingly competitive world, these added costs are often difficult to sustain. The Blue Ridge Spain case study highlights the often difficult trade-offs between global and area structures.

The weaknesses in both the area and global product structures are enhanced when a company adopts a structure inconsistent with its international strategy. In other words, if a company has a strategy that emphasizes affiliate input about local markets and yet adopts a global product structure, then lack of affiliate initiative becomes a serious impediment. On the other hand, if a company can increase its efficiency by rearranging its production and standardizing needless differences, but has adopted an area structure, then the autonomy of affiliate managers becomes a serious impediment.

Hybrid Structures

What should be clear by now is that both the global product and multidomestic area structures can have serious limitations. One gets you greater global efficiencies and the other gets you greater local responsiveness. Since perfect organizations never exist in real life, one is tempted to suggest simply picking the one closest to the company's product-market thrust and learning to live with the organizational deficiencies. That is sound advice for many companies. However, for a number of companies these deficiencies are too costly. Telecommunications is a good illustration. Telecommunication equipment companies face powerful pressures toward globalization from high R&D costs and available scale economies, and also powerful pressures toward localization from differences in the systems around the world and the politicization of the industry in many countries. Firms facing such challenges sometimes try to capture the benefits of both the global and the multidomestic structures by developing hybrid structures.

Transnational Structures

When companies ask, "Isn't there some way to have it all?" the transnational organization and the matrix system have been suggested by some as the proffered solution.[3] The key elements of transnational structures include a two-way flow of ideas and resources, frequent movement of people between units, extensive use of local boards of directors, and a global perspective on the part of both parent and affiliate. The affiliates of transnational corporations have a good deal more autonomy than those in global corporations, but still they are an integrated part of a global strategy. In the transnational corporation, initiatives arise in affiliates as well as parents, and interaffiliate linkages are encouraged. Rather than function as a hierarchy, transnational organizations function as a *network* of horizontal decision making. The trade-offs between globalization and localization are made in the field by managers committed to the corporation and its competitive objectives and aware of local market anomalies and differences. The organizational challenge is to ensure a continuous supply of such managers over time.

A transnational structure attempts to concurrently capture all of the advantages of area and global product division structures. In order to achieve these dual sets of benefits, the configuration and coordination of activities are mixed; affiliates play leadership roles for some activities and supporting roles for others. Decisions are based on maximizing the use of company skills and competencies, irrespective of activity location or affiliate nationality. To be both efficient and effective, linkages between the company's headquarters and affiliates as well as across affiliates are subject to rapid change.[4] As a result, a company with a transnational structure acts essentially as a network of activities with multiple headquarters spread across different countries. Affiliates are given complete control over local products, provide support roles for some global products, and control other global products. Affiliate roles shift over time and learning and sharing are emphasized. To work effectively, transnational structures emphasize extensive horizontal linkages, effective communication and extreme flexibility so that companies are able to develop competitive responses not only at head office but in the periphery as well.[5]

A good example of a company with a transnational organization structure is DaimlerChrysler, the world's third largest carmaker in terms of sales and fifth largest in terms of the number of cars sold. Formed in 1998 by the $40 billion acquisition of U.S.-based Chrysler by Germany's Daimler-Benz, the combined company employed 372,000 people and had sales of $134 billion in 2001. Chrysler's well-known brands included Dodge, Jeep, and Plymouth. Daimler-Benz was best known for making luxury sedans, but also commercial vehicles, sport utility vehicles, and aerospace products. With joint headquarters in Detroit and Stuttgart, the new company has provided Chrysler with new international channels of distribution for its Jeeps and minivans. It has also given Daimler-Benz significant benefits by tapping into Chrysler's market savvy in North America. In addition, the new company has the potential to achieve cost and revenue gains that come through sharing market information, combining purchasing and cross-utilizing some components and platforms. In short, DaimlerChrysler promises the type of huge scale efficiencies that come through global efficiencies combined with greater local responsiveness that comes through domestically focused operations.

The reason so many companies are experimenting with multihub network organizations of this kind is more than just the desire to have the coordination benefits. Other factors are at play. The rise of international alliances is more manage-able for firms with strong global affiliates. Also, the supply of global managers is not so dependent on head office. Good people join affiliates—because they have interesting enough mandates to attract good people—and end up in other parts of the corporation, including head office. Quality global managers are in short sup-ply and locating them only at head office contributes little to global leadership de-velopment elsewhere in the company.

Transnational Affiliates and the Development of Mandates Transnational or-ganizations are designed to concurrently maximize efficiency, local responsive-ness and organizational learning. Transnational affiliates may manufacture one or two products for world markets, but also handle worldwide responsibilities for other products. In other words, the affiliate functions like a domestic product di-vision in some areas while assuming global responsibilities in others. The diagram in Exhibit 9.7 tries to capture these features of a transnational structure.

What excites many affiliate managers under the transnational structure is that it allows for direct access to world markets. Access is achieved through the devel-opment of world product mandates in the affiliate's area of specialization. World product mandates represent global strategies controlled by the affiliate as opposed to the parent. The Quest Foods case study provides an excellent example of the process affiliates often go through in developing a global mandate. Exhibit 9.8 provides examples of affiliates that have developed global product mandates. In each of these examples, world product headquarters are located in key affiliate countries. Technically, the parent's home country is treated as a foreign market for these products.

Despite these high profile examples, most parent companies remain reluctant to give up control of R&D and product renewal for products that they themselves developed. Sometimes the key professionals involved do not want to be transferred to an overseas location and do not see any reason why they should be. As a result, many world product mandate arrangements that do exist come through affiliate initiative in companies whose cultures reward innovative effort. In other cases,

EXHIBIT 9.7 **Transnational Affiliate Structure**

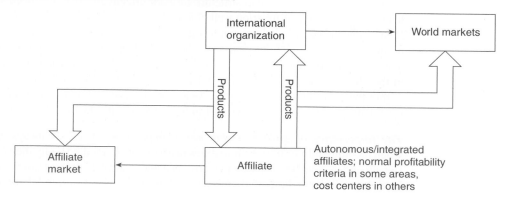

EXHIBIT 9.8   Examples of Affiliates with Global Product Responsibilities

Company	Home Country	Host Country	Product Mandate
Hyundai Electronics Industries	South Korea	United States	Microprocessors
Bombardier	Canada	Germany	Rail transport
Motorola	United States	Canada	Two-way radios
Siemens	Germany	United Kingdom	Air-traffic management
Du Pont	United States	Switzerland	Lycra business
Nestlé	Switzerland	United Kingdom	Confectionery
ExxonMobil	United States	United Kingdom	Aviation fuels
ICI	United Kingdom	The Netherlands	Flavors and fragrances
Akzo	Netherlands	Germany	Fibers
Invensys	United Kingdom	United States	Automation systems
Pechiney	France	United States	Beverage cans
Sony	Japan	United States	Motion pictures/television program
Nortel Networks	Canada	United States	Computer networking
Amcor	Australia	Canada	PET packaging

companies acquire overseas firms with global products and then turn these firms into affiliates. Canada-based Bombardier's acquisition of passenger rail car manufacturer Adtranz of Germany in 2000 is a good example of this.

Even in the case of hard-fought-after mandates, overseas affiliates are often disappointed at their limited control over the globalization of their products and services. Take Opel, for example. Executives at Opel, the German affiliate of General Motors, have become increasingly unhappy over the parent company's raids on the subsidiary's bank accounts and talent pool. Many of these assets and the best managers are being shipped off to such countries as Brazil, China, Poland, India, and the United States. They are also upset that the parent company frequently tells them that their German-designed Opel cars must be redesigned for U.S. markets. The problem for Opel is that it has been losing market share in Europe, and its executives would like to keep its money and talented managers and designers at home where they feel they are needed the most.[6]

In order for a transnational structure to work effectively, affiliates need strong leaders who are able to function well alongside parent company senior executives. If an affiliate becomes a sole or major source of supply and marketing of a specified product area worldwide, its managers soon find themselves operating in the top management committees of the parent organization. The parent must have confidence in the affiliate's ability to globally manage its product and to function effectively within the overall corporate system. As a rule, this means a network of affiliates interchanging sales forces and cross-linking R&D and production facilities.

The Importance of Affiliate Depth and Competence   There is always danger when recommending strategic initiatives to affiliates. If handled badly they can seriously undermine the affiliate's performance and can easily cause a quick exit for both the affiliate and the affiliate's general manager. For example, affiliates are

EXHIBIT 9.9   Affiliate Competence and Affliate Initiative

	Low Affiliate Capability	High Affiliate Capability
High localization pressures	Form alliances or Make acquisitions	Take strategic initiative
High globalization pressures	Follow parent instructions	Influences parent strategies

Source: This diagram is adapted from a diagram in Bartlett and Ghoshal's "Tap Your Affiliates for Global Reach."

unlikely to be successful making a major acquisition without its parent's approval. The reality is that in some areas of activity, affiliate initiative is more acceptable than in others. Every company is different, of course, but if an affiliate wants to understand when to take strategic initiatives and when to wait for direction, the diagram in Exhibit 9.9 may help.

What the diagram suggests is that affiliates should be careful about taking initiatives. First, they should assess their own capability in the area in question; then they should assess the parent's capability. As a rule, the parent's competence to act in the affiliate's market will depend on whether the affiliate's market is significantly different from what the parent is used to (i.e., high localization pressures). If it is, and if the affiliate has a good depth of knowledge in the area, it should provide strategic leadership. If neither the parent nor the affiliate has the necessary competence, the company should either get out of the segment or the affiliate should try to build capability, perhaps by alliance or acquisition. In product areas where globalization potential prevails, the affiliate will need to pay close attention to parent company expertise. When the affiliate's technological and market knowledge is low relative to the parent's—for example, in conditions of global rationalization—the affiliate should simply follow parent company direction. However, when the affiliate's competence is also high—that is, when they have a product mandate—the affiliate should try to influence parent strategy.

Affiliate managers, whether taking strategic initiative or following parent instructions, must be well-connected at headquarters. It is not a good idea to presume the competence level of the parent in a given product area. One has to know. At the same time, it is not a good idea to make an acquisition or take a strategic initiative without prior parent approval. Taking initiative is not the same as declaring independence. It is interdependence that is needed, and interdependence requires a measure of integration and working together. Taking the initiative in an interdependent relationship means bringing ideas and plans to the key management committees and championing them. Success is achieved through the quality of the ideas and through the competence with which they are expressed, but also through the preconditioning of other executives present. That is why it is essential for affiliate managers to be well plugged in at headquarters. They need to understand the mindset of the other executives, and they need opportunities to influence it.

Challenges with Developing Transnational Structures   Managing under multiple mandates is difficult. Most managers want more rather than less clarity and exactness in roles and measurements. For example, take the challenge of managing in the ABB Group. ABB was formed in 1988 with the merger of Asea and Brown Boveri. In 2001, the ABB Group had 156,000 employees, and sales of just under $24 billion split across Europe (54 percent), The Americas (25 percent), Asia (11 percent) and Middle East and Africa (10 percent). The company is divided into 7 core businesses and includes hundreds of companies and affiliates in more than one hundred countries. Each of ABB's business managers acts in many ways like air traffic controllers. They know where they want the businesses to go, they can set the flight plans, but the country managers ultimately act as pilots. Some may deviate from the plan; some may not be listening.

Running a transnational is not a job for the faint-hearted. To make ABB work, the company under the direction of then CEO Percy Barnavik adopted an elaborate computer system to track monthly reports from each of the operating units. This system, ABB Accounting and Communication System or ABACUS, was used to track almost 30 financial variables. Keeping the ABACUS system up-to-date was considered one of the most important management tasks in the firm. The reports generated by ABACUS were closely monitored at ABB's corporate headquarters in Zurich. Those who worked at head office used English as the official language although most were native Swedish speakers. By maintaining a small headquarters staff of only 170 people, ABB's CEO Percy Barnavik was able to assemble a group that shared the same world-view and that was absolutely loyal to him. Loyalty and operating proximity were critical to Barnevik who was eager to stay abreast of everything happening in the global organization. Barnevik is reported to have obsessed over the ABACUS reports. In an average year, he spent over 200 days on the road managing the far-flung empire. Everywhere he went, he constantly reviewed the ABACUS reports, bringing them with him wherever he went and pouring over them in spare moments. ABB's transnational strategy and structure worked so well because of the pivotal role of the CEO who seemingly filtered the entire company through his head. When Barnevik left ABB in 1996, his successor Goran Lindahl threw out the ABACUS system. He either was not able or prepared to play Barnevik's role as linch-pin in the organization. Since then, ABB's performance has been anything but impressive. Sales growth has stagnated and profits have disappeared.

The transition to a transnational organization is inherently bumpy and highly dependent on charismatic CEOs who act as the glue that holds the disparate organization together. Strong leadership is essential particularly because transnational structures ask employees to think first of the corporation. Transnational companies that concurrently pursue global efficiencies and local responsiveness risk crossing signals and doing neither well. Unless properly led, affiliates remain suspicious of each other and many product managers, despite pleas to think globally, continue to favor home country employees and markets.

The DaimlerChrysler example discussed earlier in the chapter also reveals how hard it is to actually run transnational organizations. Despite huge promise, the benefits of merging Daimler-Benz with Chrysler have proven elusive. Since the merger, the stock in the combined company has dropped almost 52 percent versus gains of 68 perent by Nissan and 12 percent by Honda over the same period. In early 2002, DaimlerChrysler's performance was ranked last in the Dow Jones Automobile Manufacturers Index. Problems managing across geographies and bridging company and country cultures have been greater than anticipated. Also, conflicts over control and roles have been problematic.

Because of the difficulties of effective implementation, the transnational structure is increasingly viewed as an idealized form instead of a widespread reality. The problem is ultimately one of definition. The transnational structure theoretically achieves the optimal blend of global efficiency and local responsiveness. But these descriptive statements do not constitute a definition of the transnational structure. How does a firm know when it has one? For some, the presence of a shared responsibility matrix structure is the best evidence. In such a structure, geographic areas and product divisions share responsibility for affiliate decisions. The idea is that by sharing the responsibility one forces a constructive dialogue through which the best decision emerges. In this sense, the best decision is one that balances the need for local adaptation with the need for global efficiency. Since the optimal balance is subjective and constantly shifting, it is difficult for a firm to know whether it has achieved it regardless of the structure it follows. Furthermore, people's egos sometimes get in the way, and the matrix structure often fails to achieve its purpose. It is entirely possible to have a transnational perspective without a matrix structure. One simply finds a way to put the matrix mentality into the heads of country managers, or of product division managers as the case may be. Figuring out how to make a transnational structure work may be one of the biggest managerial challenges of the early 21st century.

What is clear from these characteristics is that they are more about managerial attitude than about organization structure. That is why the transnational organization is an idealized form. However, what it stands for is important to companies anxious to hold on to good people throughout the world. Without good people, it is difficult for any organization to learn about critical commercial information elsewhere in the world and remain competitive. Without an interesting role or mandate for the affiliate, it is difficult to hold on to good talent there, and the company grows increasingly dependent on culturally bound head office management. When this occurs, the ability of the company to learn and adapt is impaired. In some industries this is a dangerous state of affairs given that technology generation has become a truly global phenomenon. The transnational approach is really about learning. It is about raising the awareness level of key executives worldwide about the corporate mission, and providing them an ongoing opportunity to influence it. It is much more about style, attitude and mind-set than it is about formal organization structure. The Meriden Magnesium case study provides a rich format to discuss the benefits of global technology transfers and the challenges in making it work effectively.

The Seamless Organization

A driving goal of an increasing number of companies is the development of a seamless organization. Seamlessness comes only through destroying barriers inside and outside the organization. In many ways formal organization structures are the antithesis of seamlessness because they promote barriers between affiliates and headquarters, between affiliates and affiliates, and between the company and suppliers and customers. These barriers prevent learning, produce inefficiencies, and blunt responsiveness. Increasingly, companies are struggling to tear down these barriers to maximize ultimate value for the customer while at the same time promoting an organizational context that engenders commitment and hard work among employees.[7]

The Importance of Teams   Teams are the primary unit of analysis in the seamless organization. Teams involve groups of individuals who are brought together to achieve a common objective. Teams can also involve outsiders such as buyers and suppliers. For example, Boeing spent several years working with a consortium of its largest airline customers in designing the B-777 aircraft. Airline personnel became fully involved in developing the final configuration of the aircraft. At one point, United Airlines had nearly 500 people working at Boeing on B-777 design issues. This involvement improved the overall quality of the final aircraft and engendered a much greater commitment of the airline companies to the B-777 specifically and Boeing more generally. Other companies have exerted enormous efforts on developing seamless interactions with customers and suppliers. In 2000, Nortel Networks contracted with PriceWaterhouseCoopers to take over all of its traditional human resource back office functions. In that same year, Varig Airlines spun off its cargo operations in order to focus on its core passenger service business. And in 2001, Lucent signed a five-year deal with Celestica worth an estimated $10 billion to take over several of its U.S. manufacturing facilities. Today, it is hard to find any medium or large companies that do not embrace seamless partnerships involving at least some traditionally critical activities.

Seamless organizations are also preoccupied with erasing boundaries inside the company. Much of the re-engineering and downsizing efforts of the 1990s have been devoted to delaying management, cutting bureaucracy and getting the people who need to talk to each other together. Teams have become a common mechanism used by companies to link people from different divisions, functions and geographies. As such, internal teams represent a type of organizational structure that may replace the more rigid boxes and lines in standard organization charts. In an era of globalization and accelerating technological change, teams can help speed organizational adaptation and improve the overall quality of decisions. Linking people with multiple backgrounds promotes an atmosphere where new ideas can emerge and where arrogance is reduced.

Technologies such as Lotus Notes, email, and video-conferencing enable global teams to keep in close contract. Teams may stay intact for weeks or years. Members may come and go and the team's objectives may evolve. While the fluidity and flexibility of teams may be a great strength in terms of responsiveness, they are also troubling to some individuals who crave structure and clarity. Seamless organizations draw heavily on personal relationships and the desire and ability of individuals to work effectively together. The human element of effective teamwork is discussed in greater detail in Chapter 10.

The Impact of the Internet on Organization Structures   The efficiencies of the Internet seriously challenge traditional approaches to organizing. At one level, companies are increasingly e-enabling activities like purchasing, sales, and service. E-enablement allows companies to interface directly with distant companies without substantial overseas assets. The Internet offers two powerful advantages over face-to-face transactions. The first is convenience. Sales information can be sent directly to customers' offices or homes, irrespective of worldwide location. Customers themselves can fill out product requests and transmit them electronically. The second advantage is lower cost. In the United States, a direct sales call by an industrial product sales person costs about $400 for time and travel. A customer visit to the company office might cost $40. A 15-minute customer call to order product at the call center is about $4. All those numbers increase by some order of magnitude in the international arena. But if the customer, domestic or foreign, places the order via the Internet, the cost is roughly 40 cents.

The growth of Internet exchanges now enables companies of all sizes to access global suppliers and buyers without necessarily having a global presence. It also brings market realities to parts of the world where they have been thin or nonexistent. The Internet is liberating markets of all kinds including financial, labor, raw materials, and intermediate goods. The result is that some of the advantages that big multinational companies have enjoyed through their ownership of overseas affiliates are disappearing.

Increasingly companies like Coca-Cola, McDonald's, and Wal-Mart are experimenting with hybrid structures that minimize the role of ownership in controlling overseas assets. Under these hybrid approaches, the role of the head office is more clearly focused on establishing and maintaining world-class processes. These processes or the know-how associated with running these processes is then essentially "sold" to overseas affiliates or alliance partners who pay the equivalent of a fee to the parent company, much like franchisees do with franchise models. The head-office then monitors and controls the affiliate through Internet linkages.

A good example of this is McDonald's in Indonesia, a country where 85 percent of the population is Muslim. Bambang Rachmadi, a local entrepreneur, owns a franchise chain of 85 McDonald's restaurants in Indonesia. His 8,000 employees are all local Indonesians. The menu, which stresses chicken and rice dishes over Big Macs, uses mostly home-grown food. Signs written in Arabic tell customers that each sandwich is "halal" certified, meaning it is prepared according to Muslim laws. Following September 11, 2001, a six-foot-high banner with the following inscription was draped outside a downtown Jakarta restaurant: "In the name of Allah, the merciful and the gracious, McDonald's Indonesia is owned by an indigenous Muslim."[8]

Despite its high degree of localization, McDonald's headquarters in Oak Brook, Illinois, plays an important role in the restaurant's success. First, it is the owner and guardian of the brand. And irrespective of the local food items on the menu, customers flock to McDonald's in Indonesia because of the power of the brand. Second, McDonald's plays a critical role in sourcing many of the nonlocal raw materials. For example, the beef comes mainly from company-approved suppliers in New Zealand and Australia. The Indonesian franchisee would have a very difficult time locating quality beef suppliers and negotiating favorable trading terms without corporate support. Third, McDonald's closely monitors the operations in far away Indonesia using the latest communications technologies. Monitoring is critical to protect the company's reputation for quality. Through the Internet, McDonald's headquarters tracks the temperature of all grills in their 24,500 restaurants in 116 countries—including Indonesia—worldwide. Without globally uniform systems, the brand would deteriorate, and the franchise model would collapse. Internet technologies make it all possible. And the good news for headquarters is that it cost them just pennies a day for the monitoring. For all of this, Mr. Bambang pays 5 percent of revenue (not profit) to McDonald's Corp.

Are there risks? The Internet along with related technologies is not yet established everywhere. Sixty percent of Americans have access to the Internet, and 70 percent of those have bought a product online in the last year. But only about 7 percent of Japanese are online, and in Europe, although many are "plugged in," only a small percentage are buying anything over the Internet. That difference, though, is likely to diminish. Internet penetration outside the United States is predicted to increase, with estimates for 2003 showing nearly 70 percent of Internet users living outside North America. As use of the Internet grows worldwide, e-commerce is expected to follow.

Summary

This chapter has focused on the challenges and opportunities associated with the international organization of activities. Given the preponderance of globalization pressures, the traditional area division structure with its high autonomy and multidomestic focus is not likely to endure unscathed. MNCs will increasingly abandon country-focused structures in favor of either the global product or transnational structures. The transition is not likely to be without pain. Moving to a more global product structure means imposing corporate will on hitherto autonomous affiliates. It means changing affiliate mandates and reducing strategic independence. There are going to be a lot of organizational wrecks on the shoals of globalization.

The reality is that almost every company customizes its structure in some way by using a combination of tools to organize and control activities. Few companies are identical to the structures described in this chapter. Most rely on mixed structures that are influenced by idiosyncratic histories and the personalities of key decision makers. Despite these differences, competitive advantage may well be achieved by those companies that can reinvent themselves by empowering those who need power and by rationalizing those who do not. Appropriate structures are ultimately determined by understanding the tasks that need to be done both today and tomorrow. As environmental change accelerates, speed and flexibility will undoubtedly be more valuable over the next decade than size and past successes.

Supplementary Reading

Bartlett, Christopher A. and Sumantra Ghoshal. "Organizing for Worldwide Effectiveness: The Transnational Solution," *California Management Review,* Fall 1988.

Bartlett, Christopher A. and Sumantra Ghoshal. "Tap Your Subsidiaries for Global Reach," *Harvard Business Review,* November–December 1986.

Bartlett, Christopher A. and Sumantra Ghoshal. *Managing Across Borders– The Transnational Solution.* Boston: Harvard Business School Press, 2001.

Birkinshaw, Julian and Neil Hood. "An Empirical Study of Development Processes in Foreign-Owned Subsidiaries in Canada and Scotland," *Management International Review,* Vol. 37 (4), 1997, pp. 339–364.

Birkinshaw, Julian and Nick Fry. "Subsidiary Initiatives to Develop New Markets," *Sloan Management Review,* 39 (3), pp. 51–61.

Crookell, Harold. "Managing Canadian Affiliates in a Free Trade Environment," *Sloan Management Review,* Fall 1987.

D'Aveni, Richard. *Hyper-Competition: Managing the Dynamics of Strategic Maneuvering.* New York: The Free Press, 1994.

Davenport, Tom and John Beck. *The Attention Economy.* Boston: Harvard Business School Press, 2001.

Egelhoff, William G. "Strategy and Structure in Multinational Corporations: A Revision of the Stopford and Wells Model." *Strategic Management Journal,* January–February 1988.

Hamel, Gary and Prahalad, C. K. *Competing for the Future.* Boston: Harvard Business School Press, 1994.

Hedlund, Gunnar. "The Hypermodern MNC—A Heterarchy?" *Human Resource Management,* Spring 1986, Vol. 25, No. 1.

Morrison, Allen, David Ricks and Kendall Roth. "Globalization Versus Regionalization: Which Way for the Multinational?" *Organizational Dynamics,* Winter 1991.

Paterson. S. L., and Brock, D. M. "The Development of Subsidiary-Management Research: Review and Theoretical Analysis." *International Business Review,* Vol. 11, pp. 139–163, 2002.

Porter, Michael. "Changing Patterns of International Competition." *California Management Review,* Vol. 28, pp. 9–40, 1986.

Porter, Michael. "Clusters and the New Economics of Competition." *Harvard Business Review,* November-December 1998, pp. 77–90.

Prahalad, C. K. and Yves Doz. *The Multinational Mission: Balancing Local Demands and Global Vision.* New York: The Free Press, 1987.

Roth, K. and A. J. Morrison. "Implementing Global Strategy: Global Affiliate Mandates." *Journal of International Business Studies,* Vol. 23, No. 4 1992.

Taggart, James. "Strategy Shifts in MNC Subsidiaries." *Strategic Management Journal,* 19 (7), 1998, pp. 663–681.

1997 World Investment Report: Transnational Corporations, Market Structure and Competition Policy. New York: United Nations.

Endnotes

1. For a more complete discussion of the concepts of configuration and coordination in international organizations, see M. Porter, "Changing Patterns of International Competition," *California Management Review,* 28, 1986, pp. 9–40.
2. For a more complete discussion of regional organizations, see Morrison, A. J., Ricks, D., Roth, K. "Globalization versus Regionalization: Which Way for the Multinational," *Organizational Dynamics,* Winter 1991, pp. 17–29.
3. For further information about transnational structures see Bartlett and Ghoshal, *Managing Across Borders—The Transnational Solution,* (Boston: Harvard Business School Press, 1989). The authors present the transnational structure as an idealized form rather than a reality in business. At the same time, they hold it out as a structure toward which many international businesses are moving because of the deficiencies of alternative approaches.
4. A discussion of "speed" advantages of transnationals is found in Bartlett, C. (1986), "Building and Managing the Transnational: The New Organizational Challenge." In M. Porter (Ed.), *Competition in Global Industries,* (Boston: Harvard Business School Press).
5. G. Hedlund. "The Hypermodern MNC: A Heterarchy?" *Human Resource Management,* 25 (1), 1986, pp. 9–35.
6. For more on Opel's concerns, see "Who Pays for the Ice Cream Soda?" *Forbes,* August 11, 1997, pp. 62–63.
7. The notion of ultimate value was championed by Richard D'Aveni, *Hyper-Competition: Managing the Dynamics of Strategic Maneuvering,* (New York: The Free Press, 1994).
8. J. Solomon, "Amid Anti-American Protests, Mr. Bambang Invokes Allah to Sell Big Macs in Indonesia," *The Wall Street Journal,* October 26, 2001, p. 1.

Chapter Ten

The Evolving Multinational

INTRODUCTION

A number of chapters in this book have discussed specific forms of foreign market entry, such as managing exports and imports, licensing, and joint ventures. Each of these might be the best way to enter a specific foreign market at a particular time. Yet it is important to recognize that most multinationals do not make just one foreign entry, but typically make a series of foreign entries over the course of years. While it is important to understand the advantages and challenges of any particular entry, we should also bear in mind the overall development of the multinational firm.

The previous chapter identified some challenges of organizing and managing the MNC. The transnational model was suggested as a way for MNCs to gain global integration as well as local responsiveness. This model argued that multinational firms should be thought of as multicentered organizational forms, with subsidiaries playing different roles within a larger network structure. By adopting an internally differentiated form, rather than insisting on identical roles for each foreign subsidiary, the MNC can tap the distinctive capabilities of each subsidiary and optimize its worldwide operations. Such MNCs are also better positioned to benefit from network flexibility, as they can shift production and sourcing among subsidiaries as various external conditions—competitive, financial, or regulatory—change.

Many management experts agree on the desirability of the transnational model, but there is much less agreement about how MNCs can achieve this differentiated form. After all, very few MNCs begin as complex, internally differentiated organizations. Most begin in a single country, and establish subsidiaries in foreign countries over many years. Once established, these foreign subsidiaries usually begin operation in just one or a few lines of business, and over time take on more lines of business. Furthermore, each line of business may begin by performing a restricted

This chapter was prepared by Philip M. Rosenzweig.

set of functions, such as sales or final assembly, and take on added responsibilities over time. It is by evolving along each of these three dimensions—a geographic dimension, a line of business dimension, and a functional dimension—that MNCs achieve a complex and internally differentiated form. The result is an MNC with subsidiaries in a number of foreign markets, each of which is active in a somewhat different mix of businesses, and each of which plays a somewhat different role, ranging from a minor one to a role of worldwide strategic leadership.

This chapter focuses on the evolution of MNCs. We take a broader look at the firm's trajectory, looking not only at entry into new geographic markets but also into new lines of business and functions performed by each line of business. The first part of the chapter examines evolution along these three dimensions, offering insights into some of the factors that facilitate or impede evolution. The second part discusses the ways in which evolution along these dimensions is integrated, with knowledge leveraged so that the MNC can evolve in an efficient manner, minimizing duplication and performing activities in an optimal manner. We take the view that the ability to leverage knowledge among MNC dimensions is central to their effective management.

DIMENSIONS OF EVOLUTION

Geographic Expansion

In recent years we have begun to see examples of firms that are "born multi-national"—that from their birth have productive operations in more than one country. But these firms are a distinct minority. The great majority of MNCs begin in a home country and expand abroad. The sequence by which firms expand from their home country into foreign markets is influenced by several factors, including geographic proximity, cultural similarity, and similarity in economic development.

Geographic Proximity   The first location for foreign direct investment is often a neighboring country. Entering a neighbor country is a natural first step, as the firm can more easily identify market opportunities and gather vital information about competitive reactions and government policies in a nearby country than in a distant one. Firms may also prefer to enter neighboring countries first, as the cost of communicating with the foreign subsidiary is lower. Once the firm has expanded into nearby countries, it may then move sequentially into countries that are farther away, minimizing the incremental distance of each move. Over time, through this process of entry based on geographic proximity, the firm can achieve a broad international position.

Cultural Similarity   The sequence of geographic expansion may also reflect cultural similarity between the MNC's home country and the host country. Success in a foreign country requires an understanding of local customs and consumer habits: effective communication with customers, suppliers, and employees; and good relations with governmental bodies. For all these reasons, firms often prefer to enter countries that are relatively similar in culture, that is, where the "psychic distance" is low. As they gain experience in countries that are relatively similar to their own, MNCs learn how to manage outside their home country and may subsequently enter countries that are progressively less similar. Eventually they may be able to enter countries that are at a considerable psychic distance from their country of origin.

Similarity in Economic Development   The level of host country economic development also affects the choice of which markets to enter. MNCs are often attracted to foreign markets where consumer buying habits and levels of disposable income are similar to those of home market consumers. In such markets, the MNC's product formulation and its marketing approach may require only modest adaptation. As the MNC learns how to compete effectively in foreign markets of similar economic standing, it develops capabilities that allow it to enter increasingly different foreign markets.

Although they are often studied separately, geographic proximity, cultural similarity, and similarity in economic development are all examples of organizational learning and capability development. In each instance, firms first expand into countries where the capabilities developed in their home market are most likely to be successful, but defer entry into countries where success is less likely. Accumulating experience in initial foreign markets enables the firm to develop new capabilities, which allow it to expand into countries that are more distant and less similar. MNC geographic expansion is not merely the sequential exploitation of existing capabilities in markets that are progressively farther from home, but the development of new capabilities as well.

An example of geographic expansion through capability development is provided by Colgate-Palmolive, the American consumer products firm, which was founded in the 19th century and slowly developed into a far-flung MNC. Colgate-Palmolive's first foreign market entry was to Canada, a neighboring country that was similar to the United States both culturally and in economic development. By the 1940s, Colgate-Palmolive had established subsidiaries in 20 countries, virtually all of which were either geographically close to the United States (Canada and Mexico), shared an Anglo-Saxon culture and English language (Canada, United Kingdom, Australia, and New Zealand), or were similar to the United States in economic development (Canada, several countries in western Europe, Scandinavia, Australia, and New Zealand). By restricting itself to these countries, Colgate-Palmolive needed to make only modest adaptations in product formulation and in its marketing approach; it refrained from entering countries where it would have faced sharp differences in culture and economic development.

Based on its experiences in these initial 20 countries, Colgate-Palmolive was later able to enter more-distant markets. In the 1950s and 1960s it expanded into Central America, which was geographically close to the United States but less similar in culture or economic development. More recently, the firm expanded to several Asian and African nations, as well as to newly opened markets in eastern Europe—countries that were far from the United States, culturally dissimilar, and often sharply different in economic development. By the mid-1990s, Colgate-Palmolive managed subsidiaries in 75 countries on six continents. Its broad geographic position had not been achieved in one or even a few steps, but was the result of a gradual process of geographic expansion.

Colgate-Palmolive's pattern of incremental geographic expansion is typical of older MNCs, which evolved over the course of many years. Today's younger MNCs, including firms such as Finland's Nokia and Germany's SAP, cannot afford to evolve over decades, but must establish a presence in multiple countries in a short period of time. Even so, the sequence of geographic expansion is similar: from closer and more similar to farther away and less similar. Of course, there has also been a shift in the relative importance of the three factors. As the challenge of managing across long distances has declined given the enormous improvements in communication and transportation, it has become less critical for firms to follow strictly a pattern of geographic proximity. Moreover, the need to minimize "psychic distance" may also be lower than in decades past, as business practices continue to converge and as more people around the world can communicate in a common business language—English. As a consequence, firms expanding abroad in the 1990s may be less concerned with minimizing geographic distance and "psychic distance," and may more readily enter foreign markets based on economic criteria such as similar levels of economic development.

Line of Business Diversification

Some MNCs are single-business firms, but most compete in multiple lines of business. Even so, their foreign subsidiaries often begin by competing in one or a few of the parent's lines of business, over time adding more lines of business, and eventually operating in many or all of the parent's businesses. For many MNCs, line of business diversification represents a second dimension of evolution. Interestingly, there has been relatively little research into line of business diversification within foreign subsidiaries. It has been more common to speak of "the country subsidiary" as if it were monolithic, yet it is clear that most MNCs ramp up their activities over time, rather than entering in all lines of business at once.

How do foreign subsidiaries add lines of business? A recent study of Japanese electronics firms in the United States from 1976 to 1989 showed a sequential pattern of entry, beginning with lines of business that enjoyed the greatest advantage over local firms. By choosing their strongest line of business, these firms offset the disadvantages due to lack of familiarity with the local market and its competitive environment. As the subsidiary gained experience in doing business locally, it added lines of business that offered it a lower competitive advantage. Finally, when it learned to compete effectively in the local environment, it could add lines of business that offered little or no competitive advantage, but that sought to learn from technologically superior U.S. firms. Several subsidiaries of Japanese electronics firms added lines of business in precisely this fashion, adding new lines of business only when confident of success. This sequence is illustrated in Exhibit 10.1.

EXHIBIT 10.1
Typical Pattern of
Line of Business
Diversification

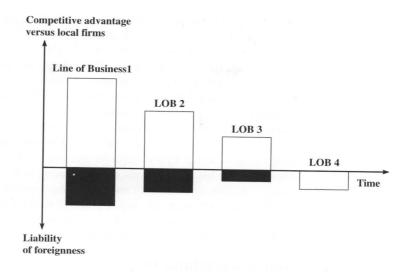

Liability of Foreignness   A good example of sequential line of business entry is provided by Sony Corporation. Sony first entered the United States in 1972 with a television assembly plant in San Diego, California. For Sony, televisions represented a core line of business, in which it enjoyed a strong competitive advantage over U.S. firms. Two years later it entered a second line of business, audio equipment, and shortly thereafter in a third, magnetic tape. In both of these, as well, Sony had a strong advantage over local firms. Sony's diversification resumed in the mid-1980s when a shift in the yen-dollar exchange rate stimulated further foreign investment. At that time, with a strong U.S. country organization and substantial experience, Sony entered lines of business with a different motivation. Rather than exploit its existing advantages, it now entered in businesses where it sought to tap U.S. technological leadership, such as data storage systems and personal telecommunications. Related to entry by line of business is the choice of entry mode, where once again Sony's experience was consistent with existing theory. At first Sony relied on small-scale greenfield investments as a way to ensure careful replication of its home country advantage; later, as it gained confidence in its ability to manage in the United States and as it sought to capture host country capabilities, it began to make acquisitions.

   This pattern of incremental evolution may appear typical of Japanese firms, which are often thought to take a gradual and long-term perspective. Recent evidence, however, has shown that an evolutionary approach to the addition of lines of business describes the behavior of many MNCs, not just Japanese MNCs. Data from European electronics firms entering the United States show largely the same pattern. Some European chemicals firms also exhibit a sequential approach to line of business entry, as exemplified by the French firm Rhône-Poulenc, which first entered the United States in areas of traditional strength such as agrochemicals and basic chemicals, and later acquired positions in surfactants and pharmaceuticals to tap local expertise and leverage it around the world.

Of course, line of business diversification does not happen automatically. It's driven by a process of evaluation, action, monitoring, and further action. At each step, the firm determines if the benefits of adding new lines of business are sufficient to offset disadvantages faced in the local market. Over time, as local expertise is accumulated and the subsidiary offers a strong infrastructure for country management, the firm may become increasingly confident of its ability to add new lines of business. With each successive entry the firm adds to its resources: it develops a reputation as a good employer and as a good customer for local suppliers, it learns about local regulations, and in general it accumulates capabilities that make it possible for the firm to enter additional lines of business. Entry into these later lines of business might only be possible because of a strong country organization, which can provide management support, financial infrastructure, and technical expertise to new lines of business.

Functional Migration

A third dimension of evolution, called functional migration, takes place within each line of business. Functional migration speaks to the development of activities performed by lines of business within a country. The seminal work on internationalization by Johanson and Vahlne showed that Swedish MNCs tended first to export to foreign markets, then to set up foreign sales subsidiaries to manage these imports, and eventually to establish wholly owned subsidiaries. Once established, lines of business continued to perform functions in their home country that lent themselves to economies of scale, such as R&D, product design, and strategic leadership. They performed in the host country only those functions that called for local knowledge, typically marketing and distribution. Over time, however, the subsidiary may take on additional functions, including assembly, local design, and procurement. In some instances, when the subsidiary develops worldwide expertise in the line of business, it might take on the role of business planning and even strategic leadership. In other instances, subsidiaries establish particular functions that serve as "centers of excellence" for the MNC. This common sequence of functional migration is depicted in Exhibit 10.2.

The process of functional migration is seen most clearly in greenfield investments, where subsidiaries begin with a limited number of functions and add new ones over time. Entry through acquisition quite naturally exhibits a different pattern. If the MNC acquires a local firm that is vertically integrated, it often gains all functions in a single step. Very often, however, MNCs enter a foreign market by acquiring a local company that performs some but not all functions. For example, some MNCs acquire local firms in order to gain an established distribution network through which they can sell imported products. Initial functions are acquired rather than set up from scratch, but subsequent functions—including assembly and product design—are added over time. The subsidiary still migrates from left to right in Exhibit 10.2, but begins somewhere along the continuum rather than at the extreme left. In other instances, firms enter a foreign market with

EXHIBIT 10.2
Typical Pattern of
Functional Migration

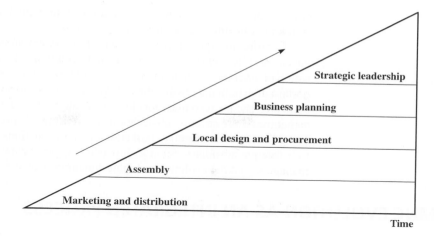

Strategic leadership

Business planning

Local design and procurement

Assembly

Marketing and distribution

Time

a greenfield investment, then add functions through the acquisition of local firms. Examples include the acquisition of manufacturing capacity (especially attractive when the industry has considerable excess capacity and building a new plant makes little sense) or the acquisition of a local R&D lab. Thus, acquisitions may differ from greenfield investments in that they accelerate functional migration, yet they typically do not alter the basic sequence.

As with line of business diversification, functional migration depends on an intrafirm decision process. To illustrate, consider the functional migration of Sony's television line of business in the United States. Until 1972, Sony wanted all manufacturing to take place in Japan; no functions were performed in the United States aside from sales and marketing. What triggered a change was the charge of dumping, which led Sony's CEO, Akio Morita, to consider direct investment in the United States. The combination of internal assessments and external forces led to the decision to invest in the United States initially at a low level of functionality, performing only final assembly. Technical knowledge, including both process know-how and product know-how, was transferred by expatriates from Sony's television division in Japan to San Diego, where an identical assembly process was built. In addition to receiving financial resources and technical and managerial know-how from its Japanese parent, the new subsidiary secured resources locally, leasing factory space, hiring local employees, and purchasing some inputs and equipment locally. By combining resources from its parent with resources secured locally, the San Diego plant began to perform its initial functions, assembling kits into working televisions. The plant was carefully monitored by managers in Japan, who wanted to know whether American workers could achieve satisfactory performance. Once Sony management was satisfied with the quality of final assembly in its U.S. plant, it began to add more functions. Soon CRT manufacturing was shifted to the United States in light of the expense and breakage associated with transpacific shipment of glass tubes. In time, additional functions were performed, including local sourcing of inputs, additional product design, and, finally, 25 years after first entry, strategic leadership for the television line of business in North America.

Migrating to higher levels of functionality is not an easy matter. In fact, the obstacles shift over time. At early steps of evolution, which usually means the location of assembly or manufacturing activities in the new subsidiary, the most important impediments involve the effective transfer of technical know-how and the ability to secure resources locally. Later stages encounter very different—and sometimes more severe—obstacles, as the objective is not merely to replicate existing functions in a foreign market, but to shift functions from the home country to a foreign subsidiary. Such a shift may trigger resistance from home country managers, making evolution to higher functions a very difficult matter.

MNC EVOLUTION AS AN INTEGRATED PROCESS

So far we've examined three separate dimensions of evolution. We described the progression of an MNC from a home-based firm to one that is active in multiple countries, in each country active in multiple lines of business, and within each line of business moving from limited functionality to higher levels of functionality.

Of course, the hallmark of an MNC is that its dimensions are not separate and unrelated, but interconnected. As noted by Doz and Prahalad, the ability to leverage knowledge across and among dimensions is precisely what gives MNCs their most compelling advantage. Evolution along one dimension is not independent of evolution along other dimensions, but both affects and is affected by activities elsewhere. In the following sections, we identify three different ways that MNC evolution is integrated across dimensions.

Accelerated Evolution

We noted above that the accumulation of knowledge allows MNCs to evolve along each of three dimensions. Learning about doing business in foreign countries helps further geographic expansion, learning about a given host country enables a sequential line of business addition in that country, and so forth. Of course, experience gained by a line of business in one country not only leads to greater knowledge of that country, it can also lead to greater knowledge of the line of business, which can be leveraged across countries to speed up the entry of that business in other countries. In this way, leveraging knowledge across dimensions results in evolution that is faster and more extensive at any point in time than it would otherwise have been.

Again Sony provides an example. As described above, Sony first set up a television assembly plant in the United States in 1972, then entered into additional lines of business over the next few years. In 1974, Sony set up a television assembly plant in Europe, and soon entered into audio equipment. Entry in Europe in audio equipment was facilitated by two kinds of knowledge accumulation: greater expertise about Europe gained through the initial entry to Europe in televisions, and also knowledge about audio products that was transferred from the U.S. operation to the new plant in Europe. By leveraging lines of business knowledge across countries, Sony more efficiently and more successfully added a new line of business in Europe.

Functional migration can also be accelerated by knowledge of particular functions accumulated across lines of business in the same country. For instance, it may be difficult for the first line of business in a country to undertake a new function, such as local parts procurement, product design, or strategic planning. Once the first line of business has successfully added that function, its experience can be leveraged to other lines of business in the same country, helping speed up their migration to the same level of functionality. Similarly, functional knowledge can be leveraged across countries to accelerate functional migration elsewhere in the world.

Punctuated Evolution

Leveraging knowledge among dimensions of an MNC can also lead to evolution that is discontinuous, or that skips steps. We call this punctuated evolution. Punctuated evolution can take place along each of the three dimensions. The notion is always the same: by identifying and taking advantage of economies of scale and scope, firms may be able to share capabilities across dimensions, obviating the need to perform every step. The result is a more efficient evolution, as the firm maximizes the salutary effects of scale and scope economies.

Assume that a line of business within a subsidiary performs a variety of functions. If a new line of business is added, that line of business may perform its own functions or it may make use of functions already performed by existing lines of business. For example, if the first line of business develops an effective procurement system, or establishes a strong treasury and legal department, and if these functions offer economies of scope, lines of businesses added subsequently may avail themselves of these functions and avoid having to perform them. These lines of business may still add functions in the sequence shown in Exhibit 10.2, but may be able to skip certain ones.

MNCs may also be able to share functions across countries within a single line of business. For instance, if one line of business performs manufacturing at a sufficient capacity to serve a neighboring country as well, the line of business in the neighboring country may not need to perform any manufacturing. Similarly, the presence of a strong R&D lab in one country may obviate the need for a subsidiary in another country to perform its own R&D. In each instance, scale economies associated with the function in one country may render unnecessary the performance of that function in another country. These latter lines of business may well exhibit a sequence of functional migration similar to that shown in Exhibit 10.2, but will skip functions where they are more efficiently performed elsewhere.

If all functions in a given line of business offer economies of scale, it might be unnecessary to perform any functions of that line of business in a second country. In that event, there would be no need to add that line of business in a second country, since the second country could be served by the first for that line of business. If we extend this logic one step further, it could be that all lines of business can serve a neighboring country, making it unnecessary to establish a subsidiary in that country at all. Examples of this kind are increasingly common in the European Union, where the establishment of a subsidiary in one EU country may enable a firm to operate in other EU countries without setting up separate subsidiaries. For instance, the Turkish bank, Finansbank, needed to enter only one EU country—the Netherlands—to be able to conduct banking in all EU countries. Other examples are found in Latin America or in Asia, where a mature subsidiary in one country is considered adequate to handle all or virtually all activities in an adjacent market.

By identifying and taking advantage of economies of scale and scope, MNCs may evolve in a discontinuous manner, skipping functions in given lines of business, skipping lines of business in some countries, or even deciding not to enter particular countries at all. MNCs that evolve in a punctuated manner will exhibit a pattern of development that is irregular and asymmetrical, but that achieves a minimum of duplication and therefore secures a greater level of efficiency.

Reverse Evolution

In recent years, as global competition has intensified due to a convergence of consumer demand, increasing opportunities for economies of scale and scope, and rising levels of industrialization around the world, many MNCs have begun to restructure their worldwide operations. In some instances they have consolidated existing functions and lines of business, and in other instances have shut down entire subsidiaries. The effect has been reverse evolution.

When might reverse evolution be most common? Firm factors and industry factors are both likely to be important. Regarding firm factors, the potential for efficiencies through global restructuring might be most common in MNCs that expanded many years ago. Because close coordination of foreign subsidiaries was relatively difficult, older MNCs were frequently organized on a country-by-country basis and pursued a multidomestic strategy. These MNCs often performed all functions in each line of business, resulting in a high level of duplication among countries. Recently, because of enhanced global communications and transportation, opportunities have arisen to capture greater scale and scope economies, leading to a consolidation of functions among lines of business, as well as a consolidation of lines of business among country subsidiaries. A prime example of this consolidation is Matsushita in Europe. Matsushita had evolved in Europe on a country-by-country basis, yet by the mid-1990s it found its organization to be inefficient; it needed to adopt a pan-regional approach. The pressure for restructuring is also likely to be greater in global industries, where competition on a global scale imposes an imperative for worldwide efficiency. As firms in an industry begin to manage their activities on a worldwide basis, other firms will face an imperative to do likewise.

Taking these points together, MNCs that are most likely to restructure their activities are those that expanded abroad long ago and now find themselves in highly global industries. As an example consider IBM, the computer giant that expanded abroad long ago. When IBM set up foreign subsidiaries in many South American countries, these subsidiaries performed a full set of functions. Recently, in response to intense pressures to improve efficiency and cut costs, IBM consolidated its South American activities into three regions—Brazil; the Andean region (Venezuela, Colombia, Ecuador, Peru, and Bolivia); and southern cone (Argentina, Paraguay, Uruguay, and Chile). In the latter two regions, where several country subsidiaries were consolidated into a single entity and managed jointly, a number of functions were located in a single country and discontinued in the others. In the Andean region, for instance, human resource management was centralized in Peru; the HR function in other Andean countries was eliminated. The subsidiaries in the other Andean nations, which had performed all functions, now experienced the elimination of several functions.

Reverse evolution is difficult, as there is natural resistance within the firm to restructuring and consolidation, yet the end result is similar to that of punctuated evolution: an asymmetrical mix of functions in each line of business, a varying set of lines of business in each country, and even an irregular set of subsidiaries around the world. The exact profile of an MNC's activities will, of course, be shaped by the most efficient use of scale and scope economies. Further, as with accelerated evolution and punctuated evolution, there are clear performance implications of reverse evolution: MNCs that can identify potential economies of scale and scope, and that can restructure their activities swiftly and efficiently, will be in a better position to compete on a global basis than those that evolved in a graduated fashion but now fail to undertake such restructuring.

Summary

Multinational firms are increasingly viewed as multicentered and internally differentiated firms, yet the process by which firms achieve this complex form has not received much attention. This chapter has viewed MNC evolution as consisting of three separate dimensions: geographic expansion, line-of-business diversification, and functional migration. Evolution along each dimension takes place through a process of knowledge development. We have also maintained that these three dimensions are not separate and independent, but can affect each other. In fact, it is by leveraging knowledge among dimensions that MNCs avoid unnecessary duplication and achieve a profile of internal differentiation and asymmetry. By identifying opportunities for scale and scope economies, and by actively leveraging knowledge across dimensions, MNCs can evolve toward an optimal configuration. While it is important to understand the nuances of particular approaches to market entry, it is also vital that we take a holistic perspective and seek to manage the entire worldwide network, sharing functions among some lines of business, or serving some national markets from adjacent countries.

The importance of these topics is likely to grow given the ongoing globalization of economic activity. Firms that expanded abroad early in the century could afford to evolve incrementally over several decades. Competitive pressures did not compel them to accelerate their evolution; rather, they could watch the progress of overseas subsidiaries and undertake further evolution when they were ready. By contrast, firms that expanded abroad in recent decades have had to move more aggressively to build a differentiated network, seeking the benefits of scale and global integration in years rather than decades. Today the pressure is greater than ever for firms to achieve a differentiated and mature global position in a short time. It has become important for firms to think clearly about the distinct dimensions of evolution, about the impediments faced on each dimension, and about ways to leverage learning across dimensions.

Supplementary Reading

Bartlett, Christopher A., and Sumantra Ghoshal. *Managing Across Borders: The Transnational Solution.* Boston: Harvard Business School Press, 1989.

Birkinshaw, Julian. "Approaching Heterarchy: A Review of the Literature on Multinational Strategy and Structure," *Advances in International Comparative Management,* Vol. 9, 1994, pp. 111–44.

Chang, Sea-Jin. "International Expansion Strategy of Japanese Firms: Capability Building Through Sequential Entry," *Academy of Management Journal,* 1995, pp. 383–407.

Chang, Sea-Jin, and Philip M. Rosenzweig. "Functional and Line of Business Evolution Processes in MNC Subsidiaries: Sony in the USA, 1972–1995." In *Multinational Corporate Evolution and Subsidiary Development,* Julian Birkinshaw and Neil Hood (eds). London, Great Britain: Macmillan Press Ltd., 1998.

Doz, Yves L., and C. K. Prahalad. "Managing DMNCs: A Search for a New Paradigm," *Strategic Management Journal,* Vol. 12, 1991, pp. 145–64.

Johanson, Jan, and Jan-Erik Vahlne. "The Internationalization Process of the Firm: A Model of Knowledge Development and Increasing Foreign Market Commitments," *Journal of International Business Studies,* Vol. 8, 1977, pp. 23–32.

Kogut, Bruce, and Sea-Jin Chang. "Technological Capabilities and Japanese Foreign Direct Investment in the United States." *Review of Economics and Statistics,* Vol. 73, 1991, pp. 401–13.

Kogut, Bruce, and Udo Zander. "Knowledge of the Firm and the Evolutionary Theory of the Multinational Corporation," *Journal of International Business Studies,* Vol. 24, No. 4, 1993, pp. 625–45.

Malnight, Thomas W. "Globalization of an Ethnocentric Finn: An Evolutionary Perspective." *Strategic Management Journal,* Vol. 16, 1995, pp. 119–41.

Nelson, Richard R., and Sidney G. Winter. *An Evolutionary Theory of Economic Change.* Cambridge, MA: The Belknap Press of Harvard University Press, 1982.

Chapter Eleven

The Global Manager

This book is about how firms become and remain international in scope and how they come to grips with an increasingly competitive global environment. Firms often fail abroad, however, not because their strategy or structures necessarily were wrong, but because the operating plan may have been incomplete, or executives were not well prepared for their assignments. Failure may come when executives are sent overseas and are not able to understand the new culture or to function in their new environment. Someone has to implement, or oversee the implementation of, a strategy or a plan. To do this means leaving headquarters and traveling to another country where it is necessary to work with people from another culture. In our experience, companies and managers often fail not because they had the wrong strategy, but because they were not capable of implementing it successfully. Preparation for these cross-cultural encounters is important, since the costs of failure can be high, either in terms of lost contracts and sales or in out-of-pocket costs like premature returns from long-term assignments.

International business and management are not impersonal, conceptual activities. People are required to put understanding into practice. For example, licensing agreements do not materialize from thin air and joint ventures do not spring into being unaided—managers make these arrangements happen. These agreements become reality because managers go to other countries to work out deals. The globalization phenomenon is not limited in impact to some impersonal entity called a corporation. It has an impact on managers—real people—in their daily lives. Expatriates employed in a foreign subsidiary will be working with host country nationals at many levels in the organization and, most likely, with people from government. Headquarters personnel will interact with local country managers and staff members from other cultures as headquarters and regional offices become more "international." They require new skills to cope with the demands globalization brings in order to be successful in their roles and careers.

This chapter was prepared by Henry W. Lane and Joseph J. DiStefano.

Some of the substantive issues facing managers in a diversified multinational corporation (DMNC) include:[1]

- Integrating large international acquisitions.

- Understanding the meaning of performance and accountability in a globally integrated system of product flows.

- Building and managing a worldwide logistics capability.

- Developing country-specific corporate strategies that take into account the political as well as economic imperatives.

- Forming and benefiting from collaborative arrangements around the world.

- Balancing the pressures for global integration and local demands.

Managers of the future will require knowledge of the type suggested but also an ability to take action. Although this was true in the past also, the knowledge base is now different and the skills required are dramatically different. What has changed? One of the most dramatic changes has been that now implementation takes place in many different cultures, often simultaneously. In these days of increased globalization even if one does not leave one's own country, it still will be highly likely that it will be necessary to work with someone from another culture.

The global manager will have to master more than concepts and theories; he or she will also have to command new skills. If one looks at the requirements for success in the global economy, it seems pretty clear that a global manager is going to have to have a repertoire comprising a comprehensive knowledge base and a well-developed set of relational and cross-cultural skills. It will include knowledge about business and technical matters, social, political and economic systems, and culture; an ability to define and solve problems in the face of uncertainty; implementation skills; and a keen sense of how and when previous experience is relevant in new cultural settings.

The purpose of this chapter is to identify and describe the skill set of the global manager. These include those skills necessary for possible international assignments. We realize that it is not possible to develop those skills by reading a chapter in a book, but we can challenge the readers to start thinking about where and how they will start acquiring these skills.

SKILLS OF THE GLOBAL MANAGER

What does the emergence of the term "global manager" really imply? In the broadest terms, it means reorganizing the way one thinks as a manager and as a student of management. As one executive put it, "To think globally really requires an alteration of our mind-set."[2] Thinking globally means extending concepts and models from one-to-one relationships (we to them) to holding multiple realities and relationships in one's head simultaneously, and acting skillfully on this more complex reality. The shift means that even if one has a regional responsibility, say, as

reorganization of resources, human networks, technology, and marketing and distribution systems. The shortening of product life cycles, driven by technological change in the products and how they are manufactured and delivered, contributes to the acceleration of change.

As difficult as these constant changes are to manage, the overall transition to global operations represents a formidable challenge in itself. Existing international operations, often marked by standardization of products and uniformity of procedures, may be a barrier to effective globalization. For example, a long history of mass-producing standard products may make it especially difficult to invest in and effectively operate flexible factories, one way that firms may offer differentiated products to different markets on a global scale.[8]

For a successful transition to global operations, it is also important that country managers are in agreement with the strategy. If poorly implemented, the move to globalization can pit headquarters managers against country or field managers. There is a tendency for autonomous units in a firm to protect their own turf. If global strategy is perceived as a move toward a centralization of responsibility, a local manager's role may become less strategic. Subsidiary managers who joined a company because of its commitment to local autonomy and adapting products to local environments may become disenchanted or even leave the organization.[9]

In terms of organization structure, effective global managers will need the skills to manage the transition from independence/dependence to interdependence, from control to coordination and cooperation, and from symmetry to differentiation.

Another method of making the transition to global operations is through the formation of a strategic alliance, or the formation of a network to reduce, for example, the high cost of R&D. As noted in Chapter 7, managing within international alliances or joint ventures is not the same as managing within a wholly owned subsidiary. Managing change within an alliance requires particular attention to the needs of the different partners, and an ability to enter into multiple trusting relationships.

Ability to Manage Cultural Diversity[10]

As one starts to function internationally, an understanding of culture and its impact on behavior, particularly management behavior and practices, becomes essential. Very often, people experience difficulties when they have to work in another culture because peoples' world views and mental programs are different in different cultures. Culture has been called "the collective programming of the mind which distinguishes one human group from another."[11] As a result of having different mental programs, people often see situations differently and have different approaches and solutions to problems. Each tends to believe that his or her way is the right way and makes the most sense. The result can be frustration, conflict, and an inability to successfully carry out strategy or plans. Understanding has two parts: cultural awareness or how another person's culture affects his or her behavior; and self-awareness or understanding how our own culture affects our behavior. It is not sufficient to understand how others differ, if we do not understand how we also differ.

The first imperative for effectively managing cultural diversity is cultural sensitivity. The marketers of Coca-Cola, the world's most recognized brand, attribute their success to the ability of their people to hold and to understand the following perspectives simultaneously:

- Their corporate culture.
- The culture of their brand.
- The culture of the people to whom they market the brand.[12]

Sometimes cultural sensitivity leads to marketing one's products to a particular market segment across cultural boundaries, basically finding common subcultures within otherwise diverse cultures. In a classic study of international marketing practices of several bed linen companies headquartered in the United Kingdom, findings stressed the ability to develop a high level of cultural awareness in order to:

- Obtain high product acceptance in light of the fact that culturally rooted differences have a significant impact on a product's success in a global market.
- Understand that the older the consumption pattern, the less likely a global product will be a success.
- Recognize universal themes by segmenting according to similarities instead of geographical differences.[13]

Lack of cultural awareness can be devastating to organizations competing globally. An organization not managed according to values felt by its members is likely to experience conflict. Hidden values and beliefs must be recognized and understood in order to manage effectively. In the 1970s, in the Republic of Panama, there were more than 20 serious disputes between MNCs and local labor that were related to popular culture. Also during that period, all six Central American republics imposed restrictions on expatriate managers that resulted in their replacement by nationals.[14]

Global managers must have the ability to recognize that cultural differences operate internally and externally. It is important to understand the influence of the home office's own cultural filters when dealing with foreign affiliates and to accept that the home office way of doing things will not be appropriate in all instances. In today's global environment, a firm's home culture must no longer dominate the entire organization's culture.[15] Instilling such an attitude, a global mind-set, is not as simple as sending a memo announcing the change. Attitudes are notoriously resistant to change.

There are four distinct attitude clusters that are useful in thinking about, and characterizing, corporate worldviews or mind-sets: ethnocentric, polycentric, regiocentric, and geocentric.[16] These attitudes may be reflected in a firm's structure; authority and decision-making processes; selection, development, evaluation, control, and reward systems; information flows; and geographical identification.[17] In short, these attitudes permeate the strategy and operations of a company and its managers. A brief description of these attitudes follows.

种族优越感,

Ethnocentrism (Home Country Orientation) This is a preference for using home country personnel in key positions around the world and rewarding them better than the locals. As with an ethnocentric attitude, there is also a belief in the inherent superiority of the home country personnel, systems, and ways of operating:

> . . . This group is more intelligent, more capable, or more reliable . . .
> ethnocentrism is often not attributable to prejudice as much as to inexperience or
> lack of knowledge about foreign persons and situations.[17] (p. 17)

Polycentrism (Host Country Orientation) This attitude sees and focuses on the differences among cultures and finds foreigners difficult to understand. It also tends to be a low-involvement attitude, since everything in the other country is believed to be so difficult to understand:

> In justifying a decision, headquarters executives of such a company might say:
> "Let the Romans do it their way. We really don't understand what's going on there,
> but we have to have confidence in them. As long as our foreign managers earn a
> profit, we want to remain in the background." Local nationals in polycentric
> organizations occupy virtually all the key positions in their respective local
> subsidiaries and appoint and develop their own people . . . Headquarters with its
> holding company attitude is manned by home-country nationals who try not to
> interfere in the territory of each local manager. This low profile approach of
> headquarters is justified on managerial and political grounds.[17] (p. 20)

Regiocentrism (Regional Orientation) Corporations with this attitude see

> . . . advantages in recruiting, developing, appraising and assigning managers on a
> regional basis. Such a personnel policy is viewed as supportive of functional
> rationalization . . . Such an approach has the merit of anticipating emerging
> politico-economic communities.[17] (p. 20)

Geocentrism (World Orientation) This attitude

> . . . is evidenced in the attempt to integrate diverse regions through a global
> systems approach to decision-making. Headquarters and subsidiaries see
> themselves as parts of an organic worldwide entity. Superiority is not equated with
> nationality. Executives convey in their key decisions the attitude that the distinctive
> competence of the truly multinational firm is its capacity to optimize resource
> allocation on a global basis. Good ideas come from any country and go to any
> country within the firm.[17] (pp. 20–21)

Recent research[18] has found support for a link between a firm's mind-set or orientation and its mode of international operations. In a study of small and medium-sized Canadian companies, it was found that ethnocentric firms favored less-risky and higher control modes such as exporting and sales subsidiaries; firms with the other sets of attitudes were more likely to use a wider range of modes (with their associated risks) up to, and including, local production. A relationship was also found between international performance and attitude. Geocentric firms had the highest level of performance; poly/regiocentric were in the middle; and ethnocentric firms had the lowest performance.

Even though there may be real economic benefits to expanding the world view of executives and corporations, developing recognition of the existence and benefits of diversity in global management does not come easily to North American executives, who often have less exposure to multicultural realities in their workplace than, for instance, their European counterparts. For example, Nestlé has a long history of having many nationalities among its top 100 executives (one count had it over 40), while, in one survey, IBM had the largest number among U.S. large companies—only 11! Although these types of anecdotal reports may be misleading, the limited language ability of many North American managers makes the same point another way. Language training, cross-cultural and expatriate experiences early in careers, membership on international task forces, and global content in all management training programs are among a few ways to counter the ethnocentricity of domestic managers, regardless of their country of origin. Using the case exercise presented later in this text entitled "Where Have You Been?" we have found a correlation between high mobility and exposure to other countries with a geocentric mind-set.

Learning to manage global cultural diversity effectively can start with the recognition of cultural diversity at home. The requirement to hire African Americans, Hispanics, and Native Americans in the United States is forcing many firms to come to grips with new mixes of employees. Demographic projections, which suggest that early in the next century, white males will represent only one in five of the workforce in the United States, also mean cultural diversity will be a domestic reality. There are large minorities of people newly arrived from India, Pakistan, Vietnam, Hong Kong, Central America, and eastern Europe. The opportunities to gain insight and experience in managing cultural diversity are local as well as global.

To manage diversity, domestically or globally, a modern human resource strategy requires some minimal orientations:

- An explicit recognition by headquarters that its own way of managing reflects the home culture values and assumptions.

- An explicit recognition by headquarters that foreign subsidiaries may have different ways of managing people, which may be more effective.

- A willingness to acknowledge cultural differences, and to take steps to make them discussible and, thus, usable.

- A commitment to the belief that more creative and effective ways of managing people can be developed as a result of cross-cultural learning.[19]

Ability to Design and to Function in Flexible Organizations

Given the complexities of the global economy and its attendant demands on managers, it is unlikely that any single organizational form will be adequate to the tasks. Global managers will surely need significantly increased creativity in organizational design, but limited organizational capability may represent the most critical constraint in responding to the new strategic demands.

As mentioned earlier, an individual manager cannot be expected to develop and use all the diverse skills required for successful global management. It is essential then that the organization support global managers. Global managers will, therefore, be called on to design and operate the very organizations that will help them to be more effective.

The best managers are already creating borderless organizations where the ability to learn, to be responsive, and to be efficient occurs within the firm's administrative heritage.[20] This suggests that a wide range of people in such firms must demonstrate the capacity for strategic thinking and action, assisted by open communication of plans, decentralization of strategic tasks, early opportunities for development of top management capabilities, and control systems measuring performance across many dimensions.[21] These new organizations will have multiple centers of influence and managers will move between jobs at these centers. This lateral movement between centers and jobs will be common and will displace hierarchy and promotion "up the ladder."

To ensure that the potential cultural diversity in such situations is taken advantage of, managers will need the ability to create an alignment of authority and responsibility between home office and field offices that moves decision making as close as possible to the customer. Balance is required though and, as noted earlier, the ability to coordinate manufacturing interdependencies to maximize economies of production will be a key task of the global manager.

To operate effectively in these radically different global organizations will take new skills and old skills honed to a new sharpness. Some of the abilities and characteristics needed by the global manager to function in flexible organizations will be:

- High tolerance for ambiguity.

- New levels of creativity and inventiveness in organizational design.

- The ability to learn, be responsive, and be efficient, all simultaneously.

- The ability to identify and implement diverse managerial behaviors and ideas for ongoing renewal of the organization.

- The ability to coordinate complicated financial, human resource, marketing, and manufacturing interdependencies, not only across functions, but also within each business activity.

- The ability to recognize different manufacturing, marketing, and organizational problems and priorities across different locations and to accommodate these with new structures and processes.[22]

The Larson in Nigeria case explores, in part, the profile of a subsidiary general manager who may not be right for the environment.

Ability to Work with Others and in Teams

Even before the advent of global companies, effective teamwork was becoming essential for managerial success. As specialization of people and differentiation in organizations increased (often driven by technological improvements, fragmentation of markets, explosions in product variations, etc.), there was a concomitant increased need for integration—for putting the specialized units back together in the service of the organization's objectives. Teams, committees, and task forces were among the devices used to accomplish the desired integration.

With the increased complexity of global operations, the ability to function in work teams—especially in culturally diverse groups—is even more important. A Conference Board Report on the experiences of 30 major MNCs in building teams to further their global interests showed the following:

- Teams used solely for communication or to provide advice and counsel still exist, but more and more firms are also using teams in different and more participative and powerful ways.

- Global teamwork can do more than provide improved market and technological intelligence. It can yield more flexible business planning, stronger commitment to achieving worldwide goals, and closer collaboration in carrying out strategic change.

- Teams that span internal organization boundaries or that span the company's outside boundary (joint venture partners, suppliers, customers) are often required.[23]

The need for transnational teamwork shows up in different ways in different functions. Consider the different assumptions about the nature and purpose of accounting and auditing in various parts of the world, for example. In one country financial statements are meant to reflect fundamental economic reality and the audit function is to ensure that this is so. In another country the audit is to check the accuracy of the statements vis-à-vis the economic records. In still another country it is only to make sure legal requirements have been met.[24] Imagine, then, the need for cross-cultural understanding and sensitivity in auditing an international subsidiary or the teamwork needed to develop international audit standards.[25]

Other functions pick up the teamwork theme differently. In operations management, the literature emphasizes the need to develop system-sensitive outlooks and processes that will develop personal relationships across subsidiaries.[26] The human resource literature emphasizes the need to develop capabilities for leading multinational teams in flexible and responsible ways. The global marketing literature discusses the ability to take advantage of a local execution strategy where "not invented here" becomes "now improved here."[27] Using this strategy, an international core team is formed to gather ideas and to pass them to local levels where the final marketing decisions are made and implemented.

The ability to work effectively with other people and in teams will be critical to the successful implementation of a global strategy. Participation in global teams should, therefore, occur early in the careers of managers in order to transform these developing people into globally effective managers.

Other elements in this ability to work with others include challenges faced by the subsidiary general manager within the host country to build management depth (See Bristol Compressors case) and achieve greater buy-in from local staff (see HCM Beverage case).

Ability to Communicate

It is obvious that in a global environment managers will need to be able to communicate with diverse groups of people. To do so effectively will require multilingual skills and high levels of cross-cultural awareness and sensitivity. In addition to the positive effects of good communication skills among colleagues and with customers, there is another advantage of particular importance to geographically dispersed and culturally diverse organizations. Sensitive communications will also build trust, and a common message can help build a strong corporate culture emphasizing shared, global value systems.

In addition to the skills necessary for effective interpersonal communication, managers will need to be able to take advantage of increasingly global communications systems resulting from broadcast deregulation and growth in global media firms such as Sky Channel and Pan European Press. Data gathered in 1987 indicate that the market for Pan European advertising campaigns has been growing at a rate of more than 25 percent per year, in spite of the many technological difficulties encountered by the new satellite technology. As always, the need to be sensitive to local requirements is evidenced by several lawsuits launched against the global media by local advertisers wishing to retain advertising revenue and by regulatory bodies seeking to retain control over advertising content.[28]

The advent of global communications exposes managers to new risks as well as new advantages. CNN aired on their European broadcasts, an interview with a U.S. senator from the steps of the Capitol in Washington. Apparently directing his comments to his constituents in his home state, the senator was engaging in Europe-bashing in defense of local industries. At the same time U.S. trade representatives were trying to negotiate sensitive issues with their European Community counterparts in Brussels. The senator was probably unaware that this interview would be aired the same day throughout Europe. Global communications provide as great an opportunity to offend as they do to please.

Ability to Learn and to Transfer Knowledge in an Organization

Given the diversity of market requirements and needs, the dispersion of manufacturing and sourcing, the rise of R&D leadership in Europe and Japan, and the importance of technological advances for product and process innovations, learning and transfer of knowledge are key to global success. Managers who are globally competent will be deeply curious; organizations that are successful will be able to coordinate, transfer, and use the knowledge gained by curious executives rapidly and effectively.

At the individual level, broad interests, an openness to a variety of experiences, and a willingness to experiment and to take risks are all ingredients of success. A visiting scholar from the People's Republic of China typified these characteristics for the authors. Soon after her arrival she knew more people than several others who had been at our institution for many months. Although her specialty was finance, she audited classes across all functions. She interviewed the "old-timers," secretaries, researchers, students, and seasoned teachers. Nor were her interactions confined to work. She learned humor; visited churches; traveled across the country by air, bus, train, and boat; went to country fairs; and even insisted on trying golf! By the end of her year, she understood the institution better than most who had been in it for several years; she understood the country almost as well as any native. Then, she transferred her knowledge to her colleagues in China and abroad through an extraordinary report[29] and through a series of lectures and seminars.

At an organizational level even more can be done. For example, at Citicorp, operating managers are encouraged to look for opportunities in one country that can be transferred elsewhere. These opportunities, or experiments, are the responsibility of national managers, while their transfer is the responsibility of corporate management.[30] The use of cross-national task forces for problems of corporate-level concern (or for problems that reoccur in various parts of the world) is also a feature of that company.

The transfer of technology is also important. Global MIS systems are now required and a manager must have the skills necessary to access and interpret worldwide information. One way to transfer technology is through the development of strong functional management to allow the building and transference of core competencies.

Yet there are indications that too often companies neglect the rich information made available to them by expatriates in other countries, especially when they return to their home country. These organizations not only lose out on a valuable opportunity to transfer some cross-cultural managerial knowledge, but also cause the expatriate to experience some potentially serious reentry difficulties.[31]

The ability of organizations to learn and to transfer knowledge will only increase in importance as markets continue to globalize. In a global environment, the ability of people to learn from diverse sources and to transfer knowledge within their organization is essential for success.

Summary Profile

This review might lead the reader to conclude that an effective global manager is superhuman. But keeping in mind the necessity of teamwork and the potential support to the managers through effective organizational design, systems, and processes, the prospect of developing global skills might be seen as an exciting challenge rather than an impossible task. To develop skills to the level necessary will be a lifelong process because the demands will likely expand along with the global economy. Each of us needs to continue to improve in the aforementioned areas as we move through the beginning of the new century.

DEVELOPING GLOBAL MANAGERS

American companies went through a period of reducing the number of expatriates they sent overseas for many reasons.[32] One major reason was the expense associated with relocating them and their families. Their salaries were usually higher than those of local managers, and they usually received benefits to make an overseas move attractive. Many of these benefits were not usually provided to local employees. Benefits often included items like housing or housing allowance, moving expenses, tax equalization, home leave, overseas premiums, cost of living allowances, and schooling for children. The incremental costs to the MNE of using expatriates can be shockingly high, particularly in some locales. A high-quality apartment rental accommodation for a senior manager posted to Hong Kong can run US$100,000/year. North American managers transferred to Switzerland claim that "everything" is more expensive than what they are accustomed to paying at home for a comparable material living standard.

In addition to lowering costs, having fewer expatriates has resulted in reduced conflict between employees and groups in the local environment. As well, it has increased the development of host country managerial and technical capabilities.

Although this trend could be seen as a positive step in the globalization process of American companies, there is a question about whether the real reason for the reduction was Americans' inability to function abroad successfully. Estimates of expatriate failure rate run between 20 percent and 50 percent, and the average cost per failure to the parent company ranges from $55,000 to $150,000.[33] There are studies claiming the failure rate is between 30 and 70 percent. The accurate identification of the actual rate of failure is less important than how high the range is. The fact that this range represents a large number of managers who cannot function successfully in other cultures is disturbing. The reduction in expatriate personnel also has ramifications for strategic management and control, such as less identification with, and knowledge about, the global operations and organization, and less control by headquarters over local subsidiaries. Thus:

> . . . There is increasing value to expatriate assignment as firms become global competitors . . . A means must be found to provide this experience to as many managers as possible. That would probably involve shorter-term expatriate assignments whose purpose is avowedly developmental—for both the individual and the organization.[34]

A more recent phenomenon affecting the mobility of many (especially North American and European) managers is the dual-career reality of their family unit. Dual careers have introduced new complexities for MNEs wishing to develop global managers.

Careful selection and preparation of expatriates—and their families—for their foreign assignments should be high-priority issues for multinationals. Unfortunately, this has not generally been the case. Now, corporations must reconsider their human resource management policies, including expatriation, in light of globalization. Cross-cultural understanding and experience are essential in today's business environment, and foreign assignments can be a critical part of a manager's development. However, experience in a job in another country does not automatically ensure a manager's increased sensitivity to cultural issues or an ability to transfer whatever has been learned to other managers. Cross-cultural training, even for experienced people, can add significantly to their understanding of their past experiences and to their skill in future assignments.

International experience is an important consideration in firms' recruiting and hiring practices. A study of 122 major Canadian corporations found a preference for hiring people with international experience for international positions.[35] The respondents to the survey also stated that expertise in international business was among the important skills that executives needed. Although corporations will have to spend more time, effort, and money in providing international experiences to their managers in order to help develop the global skills required for the future, individuals can take responsibility for their own development by seeking out international opportunities such as teaching language courses in other countries or working for agencies such as the U.S. Peace Corps or Canadian University Students Overseas (CUSO). In addition, acquiring fluency in a second or third language would be helpful.

MANAGING INTERNATIONAL ASSIGNMENTS

As was mentioned earlier, there are strategic implications to the use of expatriate personnel. MNCs must think about expatriation as a strategic tool that is used to develop managers with a global orientation, but also that is used to manage key organizational and country relationships.[36] Although organizational and management development are important, the emphasis should be:

> . . . on long-term commitment to learning about international markets. If high-potential individuals are carefully selected and trained for overseas positions, they will not only facilitate the maintenance of an international network of operations in the short term but should be allowed to continue providing informational support upon their return.[37]

Although it might sound pretty straightforward, the process of developing globally minded managers with the requisite skills is more difficult than it appears. The quote contains the conditions that most often are not met—if high-potential individuals are carefully selected and trained—and which are crucial to the successful use of expatriation for development and strategic purposes.

Selection   In 1973, published research[38] showed that people were selected for international assignments based on their proven performance in a similar job, usually domestically. The ability to work with foreign employees was at, or near, the bottom of the list of important qualifications. Unfortunately, 20 years later the situation has not changed dramatically for the better.[39] Very often technical expertise and knowledge are used as the most important selection criteria. Although these are important considerations, they should not be given undue weighting relative to a person's ability to adapt to, and function in, another culture. It does no good to send the most technically qualified engineer or finance manager to a foreign location if he or she cannot function there and has to be brought home prematurely. As noted earlier, the cost of bad selection decisions is high to the corporation as well as to the individual and to his or her family.

In a very useful model of overseas effectiveness, which focuses on adaptation, expertise, and interaction,[40] for a person to be effective, he or she:

> must adapt—both personally and with his/her family—to the overseas environment, have the expertise to carry out the assignment, and interact with the new culture and its people.[41]

Training   The training that a person undergoes before expatriation should be a function of the degree of cultural exposure to which he or she will be subjected.[42] Two dimensions of cultural exposure are the degree of integration and the duration of stay. The integration dimension represents the intensity of the exposure. A person could be sent to a foreign country on a short-term, technical, trouble-shooting matter and experience little significant contact with the local culture. On the other hand, a person could be in Japan for only a brief visit to negotiate a contract, but the cultural interaction could be very intense and may require a great deal of cultural fluency to be successful. Similarly, an expatriate assigned abroad for a period of years is likely to experience a high degree of interaction with the local culture from living there.

One set of guidelines[43] suggests that for short stays (less than a month) and a low level of integration, an "information-giving approach" would suffice. This includes area and cultural briefings, and survival-level language training, for example. For longer stays (2–12 months) and a moderate level of integration, language training, role-plays, critical incidents, case studies, and stress reduction training are suggested. For people who will be living abroad for one to three years and/or will have to experience a high level of integration into the culture, extensive language training, sensitivity training, field experiences, and simulations are the training techniques recommended.

Effective preparation would also stress the realities and difficulties of working in another culture and the importance of establishing good working relationships with the local people.

Repatriation   Selecting the right people, training them properly, and sending them and their families to their foreign posting is not the end of the exercise. Getting these people back and integrated into the company so that the company can continue to benefit from their experience and expertise has been shown to be a problem. Research suggests that the average repatriation failure rate—those people who return from an overseas assignment and then leave their companies within one year—is about 25 percent.[44] If companies want to retain their internationally experienced managers, they are going to have to do a better job managing the repatriation process.

The international assignment may be an important vehicle for developing global managers; achieving strategic management control; coordinating and integrating the global organization; and learning about international markets and competitors, as well as foreign social, political, and economic situations. However, this idealized goal of becoming a global, learning organization will be reached only if the right people are selected for foreign assignments, trained properly, repatriated with care, valued for their experience, and are used in a way that takes advantage of their unique background.

Supplementary Reading

Adler. *Nancy International Dimensions of Organization Behavior,* 2nd ed. Boston: PWS-Kent, 1991.

Beamish, Paul W., and Jonathan L. Calof. "International Business Education: A Corporate View," *Journal of International Business Studies,* Fall 1989.

Black, J. Stewart, and Hal B. Gregersen. "Serving Two Masters: Managing the Dual Allegiance of Expatriate Employees," *Sloan Management Review,* Summer 1992.

Black, J. Stewart, Hal B. Gregersen, and Mark E. Mendenhall. *Global Assignments: Successfully Expatriating and Repatriating International Managers.* San Francisco: Jossey-Bass, 1992.

Cascio, Wayne F., and Manuel G. Serapio, Jr. "Human Resources Systems in an International Alliance: The Undoing of a Done Deal," *Organizational Dynamics,* Winter 1991.

Dowling, Peter, and Randall Schuler. *International Dimensions of Human Resource Management,* Boston: PWS-Kent, 1990.

Javidan, Mansour, and Robert J. House, "Cultural Acumen for the Global Manager: Lessons from Project GLOBE," *Organizational Dynamics,* Spring 2001.

Kedia, Ben L., and Ananda Mukherji, "Global Managers: Developing a Mindset for Global Competitiveness," *Journal of World Business,* Fall 1999.

Lane, Henry W., Joseph J. DiStefano, and Martha Maznevski. *International Management Behavior,* 4th ed., Cambridge, MA: Blackwell Publishers, 2000.

Maisonrouge, Jacques G. "The Education of a Modern International Manager," *Journal of International Business Studies,* Spring/Summer 1983.

Mendenhall, Mark, and Gary Oddou. *Readings and Cases in International Human Resource Management,* Boston: PWS-Kent, 1991.

O'Grady, Shawna, and Henry W. Lane. "The Psychic Distance Paradox," *Journal of International Business Studies,* Vol. 27, No. 2, 1996.

Pucik, Vladimir, Noel M. Tichy, and Carole K. Barnett, eds., *Globalizing Management: Creating and Leading the Competitive Organization.* New York: John Wiley & Sons, 1992.

Rhinesmith, Stephen H. *A Manager's Guide to Globalization: Six Keys to Success in a Changing World.* Burr Ridge, IL: Business One Irwin, in cooperation with The American Society for Training and Development,1992.

Rosenzweig, Philip M., and Nitin Nohria. "Influences on Human Resource Management Practices in Multinational Corporations," *Journal of International Business Studies,* Vol. 25, No.2, 1994.

Endnotes

1. C. K. Prahalad, "Globalization: The Intellectual and Managerial Challenges," *Human Resource Management,* Spring 1990, Vol. 29, No. 1, p. 29.
2. Personal communication from Mr. Bernard Daniel, Secretary-General, Nestlé Vevey, Switzerland.
3. Patricia A. Galagan, "Executive Development in a Changing World," *Training and Development Journal,* June 1990, pp. 23–41.
4. Brenda McMillan, Joseph J. DiStefano, and James C. Rush, "Requisite Skills and Characteristics of Global Managers," Working Paper, National Centre for Management Research and Development, Western Business School, The University of Western Ontario, London, Canada N6A 3K7, 1991.
5. Subsequent to our literature review and the publication of an earlier version of this chapter in International Management Behavior, 2nd ed. (Boston: PWS-Kent, 1992), Stephen Rhinesmith published a book, *A Manager's Guide to Globalization,* in which the chapter headings closely parallel the set of skills we elaborate below, giving further credence to their emerging importance.
6. Stephen H. Rhinesmith, John N. Williamson, David M. Ehlen, and Denise S. Maxwell, "Developing Leaders for the Global Enterprise," *Training and Development Journal,* April 1989, pp. 25–34.
7. Masaaki Kotabe, *Global Sourcing Strtategy: R&D, Manufacturing, and Marketing Interfaces,* (New York: Quorum Books, 1992).
8. Sandra M. Huszagh, Richard J. Fox, and Ellen Day, "Global Marketing: An Empirical Investigation," *Columbia Journal of World Business,* Vol. 20, Issue 4, 1986, pp. 31–43.
9. John A. Quelch and Edward J. Hoff, "Customizing Global Marketing," *Harvard Business Review,* May–June 1986, pp. 59–68.
10. This is a skill set that shows the potential transfer of learning between domestic and international or global activities. The recent explosion of books on managing diversity in North America demonstrates this point. Books such as Sondra Thiederman's *Profiting in America's Multicultural Marketplace,* (Lexington: Lexington Books, 1991); Roosevelt Thomas's Beyond Race and Gender: *Unleashing the Power of Your Total Workforce by Managing Diversity,* (New York: AMACOM, 1991); John Fernandez's *Managing a Diverse Work Force: Regaining the Competitive Edge,* (Lexington: Lexington Books, 1991); and Ann Morrison's *The New Leaders: Guidelines on Leadership Diversity in America,* (San Francisco: Jossey-Bass, 1992) include concepts and approaches similar to those written about international activities.
11. Geert Hofstede, *Culture's Consequences: International Differences in Work-Related Values,* (Beverly Hills, CA: Sage Publications, 1980).

12. Harold F. Clarke, Jr., "Consumer and Corporate Values: Yet Another View on Global Marketing," *International Journal of Advertising,* Vol. 6, 1987, pp. 29–42.

13. Jeryl M. Whitelock, "Global Marketing and the Case for International Product Standardization," *European Journal of Marketing* (UK), Vol. 21, Issue 9, 1987, pp. 32–44.

14. Antonio Grimaldi, "Interpreting Popular Culture: The Missing Link Between Local Labor and International Management," *Columbia Journal of World Business,* Vol. 21, Issue 4, Winter 1986, pp. 67–72.

15. Nancy J. Adler and Fariborz Ghadar, "International Strategy from the Perspective of People and Culture: The North American Context," *Research in Global Business Management,* Vol. 1 (Greenwich, CT: JAI Press Inc., 1990).

16. Howard V. Perlmutter, "The Tortuous Evolution of the Multinational Corporation," *The Columbia Journal of World Business,* January 1969. pp. 9–18.

17. David A. Heenan and Howard V. Perlmutter, *Multinational Organizational Development: A Social Architectural Perspective,* (Reading, MA: Addison-Wesley, 1979).

18. Jonathan L. Calof, *The Internationalization Process: An Examination of Mode Change, Mode Choice, and Performance;* unpublished Ph.D. dissertation, The University of Western Ontario, London, Canada, 1991.

19. Andre Laurent, "The Cross-Cultural Puzzle of International Human Resource Management," *Human Resource Management,* Vol. 25, Issue 1, Spring 1986, pp. 91–102.

20. C. A. Bartlett and S. Ghoshal, *Managing Across Borders,* (Boston: Harvard Business School Press, 1989).

21. For an article describing these and other organizational innovations, see Gunnar Hedlund, "The Hyper-modern MNC—A Heterarchy?" Human Resource Management, Vol. 25, No. 1, Spring 1986, pp. 9–35.

22. K. Ferdows, J. G. Miller, J. Nakane, and T. E. Vollmann, "Evolving Global Manufacturing Strategies: Projections into the 1990s, *International Journal of Operations and Production Management,* Vol. 6, No. 4, 1986, pp. 6–16.

23. Ruth G. Shaeffer, "Building Global Teamwork for Growth and Survival," *The Conference Board Research Bulletin,* No. 228.

24. Leslie G. Campbell, *International Auditing.* (New York: St. Martin's Press, 1985), p. 141.

25. William S. Albrecht, Hugh L. Marsh Jr., and Frederick H. Bentzel Jr, "Auditing an International Subsidiary," *Internal Auditor,* Vol. 45, Issue 5, October 1988, pp. 22–26; Joseph Soeters and Hein Schreuder, "The Interactions Between National and Organizational Cultures in Accounting Firms," *Accounting, Organizations and Society,* Vol. 13, No. 1, 1988, pp. 75–85; and Nicholas M. Zacchea, "The Multinational Auditor: Overcoming Cultural Differences to Apply Audit Standards," *Internal Auditor,* Vol. 45, Issue 5, 1988, pp. 16–21.

26. Briance Mascarenhas, "The Coordination of Manufacturing Interdependencies in Multinational Companies," *Journal of International Business Studies,* Winter 1984, pp. 91–106.

27. Teresa J. Domzel and Lynette S. Unger, "Emerging Positioning Strategies in Global Marketing," *Journal of Consumer Marketing,* Vol. 4, Issue 4, Fall 1987, pp. 23–40.

28. Laurel Wentz, "Global Marketing and Media: TV Nationalism Clouds Sky Gains," *Advertising Age,* Vol. 58, Issue 53, December 14, 1987, p. 56.

29. Jiping Zhang, *The Building and Operation of a North American Business School* (in Chinese), (Beijing: Tsinghua University Press, 1990) (English version published March 1987 by the Western Business School, The University of Western Ontario, London, Ontario N6A 3K7.)

30. Alan J. Zakon, "Globalization Is More than Imports and Exports," *Management Review,* Vol. 77, Issue 7, July 1988, pp. 56–57.

31. Robert T. Moran, "Corporations Tragically Waste Overseas Experience," *International Management* (UK), Vol. 43, Issue 1, January 1988, p. 74.

32. Stephen J. Kobrin, "Expatriate Reduction and Strategic Control in American Multinational Corporations." *Human Resource Management,* Vol. 27, No. 1, 1988. See also Michael Harvey, "Empirical Evidence of Recurring International Compensation Problems," *Journal of International Business Studies,* Vol. 24, No. 4, 1993.

33. Ibid.

34. Ibid., p. 74.

35. Paul W. Beamish and Jonathan L. Calof, "International Business Education: A Corporate View," *Journal of International Business Studies,* Vol. 20, No. 3, 1989.

36. Nakiye A. Boyacigiller, "The International Assignment Reconsidered," in *International Human Resource Management,* Mark Mendenhall and Gary Oddou, eds., (Boston: PWS-Kent, 1991), p. 154.

37. Ibid.

38. E. L. Miller, "The International Selection Decision: A Study of Some Dimensions of Managerial Behavior in the Selection Decision Process," *Academy of Management Journal,* Vol. 16, No. 2, 1973, pp. 239–52.

39. Mark E. Mendenhall, Edward Dunbar, and Gary R. Oddou, "Expatriate Selection, Training and Career Pathing: A Review and Critique," *Human Resource Management,* Vol. 26, No. 3, 1987.

40. Daniel J. Kealey, *Cross-cultural Effectiveness: A Study of Canadian Technical Advisors Overseas,* (Ottawa: Canadian International Development Agency, 1990). This study was based on a sample of over 1,300 people, including technical advisors, their spouses, and host-country counterparts.

41. Ibid., p. 8.

42. Mendenhall et al., op. cit.

43. Ibid.

44. Meg G. Birdseye and John S. Hill, "Individual, Organizational/Work and Environmental Influences on Expatriate Turnover Tendencies: An Empirical Study," *Journal of International Business Studies,* Vol. 26, No. 4, 1995. J. Stewart Black and Hal R. Gregersen, "When Yankee Comes Home: Factors Related to Expatriate and Spouse Repatriation Adjustment," *Journal of International Business Studies,* Vol. 22, No. 4, 1991; J. Stewart Black, Hal R. Gregersen, and Mark E. Mendenhall, "Toward a Theoretical Framework of Repatriation Adjustment," *Journal of International Business Studies,* Vol. 23, No. 4, 1992.

Chapter Twelve

Strengthening International Government Relations

The purpose of this chapter is to look at selective ways of strengthening international government relations. The first section reviews some of the major sources of trade regulation that affect both the exporter and the foreign investor. This is essential context. The second part reviews the major opportunities and threats from government actions, and some political[1] strategy implications. The third part considers the role and impact of one of the major areas of international business–government interaction in recent years: the privatization of state owned enterprises. The final part focuses on the proactive management of government relations.

I. Trade Regulation

The GATT and the WTO   In the middle of the last century, three organizations were established to improve the performance of the world economy: the International Monetary Fund to regulate exchange rates and international capital movements, the World Bank to assist developing countries, and the General Agreement on Tariffs and Trade to deal with two aspects of international trade: tariffs and nontariff barriers to trade.

From the end of World War II through the early 1980s, trade negotiations under the auspices of the GATT succeeded in reducing barriers to trade, particularly tariff barriers, significantly. During the Tokyo round of trade negotiations in the mid-1970s, attention was turned toward reducing nontariff barriers to trade as

This chapter was prepared by Paul Beamish.

well. By 1979, only partial success had been achieved, in part, due to the number, the complexity, and the sensitivity of nontariff barriers. A study conducted by the GATT Secretariat identified over 600 nontariff barriers to trade. These ranged from quotas and antidumping and countervailing duty laws to labeling, product standards, customs inspection procedures, and government procurement regulations.

The relative lack of success was partly due to the subtle nature of the motivations for, and the administration of, many nontariff barriers to trade. For example, a country's health and safety standards could be formulated in response to legitimate concerns on these issues, or they could be designed to block trade. Requirements for periodic onsite plant inspections by nationals of the importing country could legitimately be a means of ensuring quality control to meet these standards. Alternatively, these inspections could be required to impose costs on potential exporters.

The Uruguay round of the GATT negotiations ran from 1986 to 1993. It addressed even more challenging problems. These problems were also addressed in an environment that was less hospitable to trade liberalization. A wide variety of issues were considered: standards, also known as technical barriers to trade; trade in agricultural products, a most politically charged issue; trade in services, such as banking and insurance, advertising, media, and tourism; intellectual property rights—protection of patents, trademarks, copyrights, and brand names; barriers to trade in technology, such as regulations on mandatory licensing or maximum licensing fees; and trade-related investment measures (TRIM) that link investment incentives to exports; the Multifiber Agreement (MFA), the safeguard measures (often called the escape clause) used to deal with import surges, and voluntary export restraints (VERs).

The number of countries involved in the negotiations had also expanded to 117 (with 113 contracting countries). These negotiations took place in a more difficult environment than was the case in previous rounds. The United States was running a large trade deficit. Europe was struggling with the integration of the former Eastern bloc countries into a more unified trading area. At the same time, economic growth in many European countries had stagnated, and unemployment was over 10 percent. The electorate in many countries was increasingly restive.

Many developing countries needed to achieve, maintain, and increase their trade surpluses if they were to have any chance of servicing their external debts. Expanding exports was one of the few alternatives open to them if they were to achieve even some modest economic growth. The political stability of many developing countries is directly linked to export expansion. These developing countries were not particularly interested in, and were often antagonistic to, the goals of high-income countries for liberalization of trade in services, agricultural products, protection of intellectual property rights, and technology transfer. They saw these initiatives as leading to domination by foreign financial and media firms; higher prices for imported food and loss of food self-sufficiency; higher prices for products with patents, brand names, and trademarks; and higher prices for and reduced volumes of technology transfer. Their interests lay in regaining the market access they had lost over the past decade to protectionist measures implemented by high-income countries and in enhancing access in the future. In particular, they wanted the removal of the MFA, which reduced their ability to increase exports of textiles and garments, and the "escape clause," which could be invoked to limit export growth in other products.

The Uruguay round came into full effect in 1995. By and large it was a success, although a qualified one. Many issues were agreed to in principle, but the crucial details were left for future negotiations. High-income countries agreed to reduce their tariffs over time from an average of 6.4 percent to 4.0 percent. Of special interest to developing countries, the proportion of imports from developing countries allowed duty-free access would increase from 20 percent to 43 percent, and tariffs on agricultural products from these countries would be reduced by 34 percent over time. The MFA will be phased out through the year 2005, and the use of VERs was further circumscribed.

High-income countries, especially the United States, also made substantial progress toward achieving their negotiating goals. Trade in services was brought within rules and disciplines of the organization with the creation of a General Agreement on Trade in Services. This agreement relates to trade in financial services, telecommunications, air transport, and the movement of labor. In agriculture, nontariff barriers to trade are to be replaced with their tariff equivalents and these tariffs reduced over time by 36 percent for high-income countries and 24 percent for developing countries. A number of export subsidy schemes were prohibited and others reduced. As well, intellectual property rights were placed within the MFN (Most Favored Nation) framework. This means that if two countries have MFN status in trade, they must also extend reciprocal protection of intellectual property rights.

Over the 12-year period from 1993 to 2005, the reduction of trade barriers under the Uruguay round is expected to lead to a 1 percent per year increase in the growth rate of trade volume (from 3 percent to 4 percent per year) such that trade will be $745 billion 1992 dollars higher in 2005. World income will be $230 billion higher in 2005 (in 1992 dollars), about 1 percent of world income. Of this amount, about $80 billion (about one-third) will accrue to developing countries, although the total of their GDPs is only about one-fifth world GDP.

Perhaps most important, a World Trade Organization was formed. The WTO includes the GATT, the GATS, a Dispute Settlement Board (DSB), a Trade Policy Review Board, and a Ministerial Conference, which meets every two years. The formation of the WTO represents a major achievement for advocates of freer trade. It represents a move toward the model of an International Trade Organization, proposed after World War II, with broad powers over all forms of trade. It can also serve as an ongoing forum for further trade negotiations and dispute settlement.

There remains much to do on the WTO's agenda for the future. First and foremost is to finalize the details of the issues that were left unresolved at the end of the Uruguay round. The issues of trade and the environment, and trade and labor standards—contentious issues of particular interest to high-income countries— need to be addressed. On the one hand, to do this will require formulation of worldwide environmental codes and labor codes. On the other, it will require formulation of rules under which countries can block trade in products that were not produced according to these codes. This will be a formidable task. Another important area to be included within the WTO is foreign investment. Trade and foreign investment are closely linked, with about one-third of world trade undertaken by MNEs. As yet, however, country-level investment regulations are not governed by any global agreements.

The U.S.–Canada Free Trade Agreement and NAFTA   In January 1988, the United States and Canada entered into a free trade agreement (FTA), thus creating the world's largest free trade area. The agreement culminated what had been an almost century-long process of formalizing and securing trade between Canada and the United States. Since the two nations enjoy the world's largest bilateral trade, with each country being the other's largest trading partner, the FTA was expected to be of considerable benefit to both nations. Of particular importance, the agreement did not set up a customs union or trading bloc. It is fully consistent with the letter and intent of the WTO; each country remains free to pursue independently its trade policy with other nations.

With a general liberalization of trade, involving reduced duties across almost every sector of the economy, the FTA is in the long-run interests of both nations. What is particularly significant, especially for the Canadians, is the dispute resolution mechanisms. In the past, whenever the United States passed a trade bill, Canadian lobbyists would have to pressure for Canadian exemption based on the "special relationship" between the United States and Canada. This moral suasion was not always successful and was understandably unreliable. The FTA established a panel of judges with an equal number of American and Canadian representatives. After a number of disputes on, among other things, forest and agricultural products, both nations appear to have been willing to abide by the panel's rulings, although individual companies and industries on both sides of the border are not happy with it.

Building on the momentum of the FTA, Canadian and American trade negotiators opened talks with Mexican representatives to establish a North American free trade agreement. NAFTA created the largest trading area in the world, surpassing the trade area created by the FTA. It was a logical extension of the FTA. Concerns about the agreement generally centered on differential labor rates and working conditions and environmental issues. The claim was that companies in Mexico, especially foreign multinational enterprises, would have access to a considerably cheaper labor pool and safety standards and would not be subject to the more rigorous and expensive environmental regulations in place in the United States and Canada.

The Association of Southeast Asian Nations (ASEAN)   In South Asia, similar efforts have been made for economic integration as in North America and Europe. In August 1967, the Association of Southeast Asian Nations (ASEAN) started with five members, Indonesia, Malaysia, Philippines, Singapore, and Thailand. Brunei Darussalam joined in 1984, Vietnam in 1995, Laos and Myanmar in 1997, and Cambodia in 1999.

The Fourth ASEAN Summit in 1992 included the launching of a scheme toward an ASEAN Free Trade Area or AFTA. The strategic objective of AFTA is to increase the ASEAN region's competitive advantage as a single production unit. The elimination of tariff and nontariff barriers among the member countries is expected to promote greater economic efficiency, productivity, and competitiveness.

Even though ASEAN has been regarded as a loose economic cooperation channel, compared with NAFTA, and EU, the status of ASEAN is expected to change. In November 2001, China agreed to establish a free trade agreement with ASEAN within the next 10 years.

Asia-Pacific Economic Corporation (APEC) Asia-Pacific Economic Corporation (APEC) was established in 1989 in response to the growing interdependence among Asia-Pacific economies. In 2002, there were 21 member economies, including USA, Canada, Japan, China, Australia, etc., comprising 2.5 billion people, a combined gross domestic product of over US$19.4 trillion in 2000 and over 49 percent of world trade. APEC has since become the primary regional vehicle for promoting open trade and practical economic cooperation. Its goal is to advance Asia-Pacific economic dynamism and sense of community. As yet, however, APEC has not reached an agreement to develop free trade.

ANDEAN and MERCOSUR The ANDEAN Community is a subregional organization endowed with an international legal status, which is made up of Bolivia, Colombia, Ecuador, Peru, and Venezuela and the bodies and institutions composing the Andean Integration System (AIS). Andean integration has passed through a series of different stages. Low economic growth rate, hyperinflation, soaring unemployment rate, and unstable political leadership have all hindered ANDEAN from evolving toward integrated free trade.

Composed of South American countries like ANDEAN, the Common Market of the South (MERCOSUR) is an economic integration project of Argentina, Brazil, Paraguay, and Uruguay with Chile and Bolivia as associate members. The objective of this Southern Cone Common Market is to create a customs union which would eliminate all tariffs on over 90 percent of trade, and set a common external tariff which would be applied to all nonmember exports.

The European Union The integration of Europe has been a slow and at times tortuous process. However, in the more than 40 years since efforts at increased European integration were begun, what is now the European Union has grown to include 15 nations. What is most distinctive about the EU is that it is founded on the principle of supranationality (i.e., the EU councils and commissions are intended to be paramount over national laws and legislatures). For trading purposes, this means that member nations cannot enter into any trade agreements that are inconsistent with EU regulations. Within EU itself, the elimination of tariffs was achieved in 1961, as the establishment of a common external commercial policy and a common agricultural policy. With the passing of the Single Market Act in 1985, all member nations committed themselves to realizing the single market by the end of 1992. This act removed all barriers to trade in goods and services; barriers to mobility for the citizens of EU member countries; and all national regulations that might discriminate against a product, business, or individual from a member country.

The net impact on trade and investment is still uncertain. Already it has induced multinational enterprises based in countries outside Europe to invest there to have free access to this huge market. What is less certain is whether the new economic system will turn these countries into "Fortress Europe" or whether it will promote multilateral freer trade. In trade negotiations, the EU must negotiate as a unified bloc with a uniform position. Individual countries within the EU can try to influence its position on various trade issues, but they cannot "go it alone" and maintain their own position.

For managers of international trade operations, the results of all these sets of negotiations are of prime importance. Expansion of international trade operations is often a long-term investment. To make the correct decision, and to implement it effectively, will require ever-increasing levels of knowledge, expertise, and sophistication in assessing the environment for international trade and in engaging in international trade operations.

II. Opportunities/Threats

Whether domestically or internationally, governments act in a wide variety of ways to create both opportunities and threats for business (see Exhibit 12.1). Among the most important government actions are (1) *regulation,* which can increase costs but also control competition or even give a competitive advantage (if firms have adapted to particularly stringent regulations in one location and are therefore better able to handle such regulations elsewhere); (2) *taxation,* which can reduce returns but also increase competitive advantage if a firm faces lower taxation than its competitors; (3) *expenditure,* which can create competitive disadvantage or advantage depending on whether government grants and subsidies received are larger than what competitors receive; (4) *privatization,* which can increase competition but also result in a more even treatment; (5) *consultation,* which can become an opportunity for business to influence government policy but also provides government an opportunity to manipulate (i.e., co-opt) business by using the consultative process to justify decisions already made.

EXHIBIT 12.1 **Opportunities and Threats from Government Actions**

Threats	Government Actions	Opportunities
Increase costs	⇐Regulation⇒	Control competition
Reduce ROI	⇐Taxation⇒	Competitive advantage
Competitive disadvantage	⇐Expenditure⇒	Subsidies, grants, customer
Increased competition	⇐Privatization⇒	Level playing field
Co-opt	⇐Consultation⇒	Influence policy

EXHIBIT 12.2
Political Strategy

Formulation

- Objective(s)
- Issue(s)
- Stakeholders (allies, opponents, targets)
- Position/Case ("public interest")

Implementation

- Timing
- Technique(s)—Direct (negotiate, litigate)
             —Indirect (advocacy advertising, political contributions)
- Vehicle(s) (e.g. coalition, Government Relations department, consultants)
- Style (e.g., confrontation or conciliation)

Political Strategy   Given the variety of threats and opportunities facing business because of government actions, it is essential that each firm formulate and implement a political strategy (see Exhibit 12.2) both in home and host countries. In formulating such a strategy, the following elements need to be considered: (1) objective(s) (e.g., obtain favorable legislation/interpretation of legislation); (2) issue(s) (e.g., current, emerging); (3) stakeholders to determine allies, opponents, targets; (4) position/case (in terms of "public interest").

In implementing a political strategy, the following elements need to be considered: (1) timing; (2) technique(s) (i.e., direct—e.g., negotiation, litigation— or indirect—e.g., advocacy advertising, political contributions); (3) vehicle(s) (e.g., trade association, government relations (GR) department, GR consultant, coalition); and (4) style (e.g., confrontation, conciliation). The development of political strategies is a nontrivial undertaking. The absence of it will result in a missed opportunity to strengthen international government relations.

III. Privatization

As noted in the previous section, expanding exports is one of only a limited number of alternatives open to national governments that want to achieve economic growth. Another alternative, one which has seen significant emphasis in the past decade is privatization/sale of government owned enterprises. Exhibit 12.3 summarizes many of the objectives and motivations that accrue to each of the three major stakeholders—MNEs, governments, and privatizing enterprises—when the arrangements are successful. An understanding of any government's objectives in privatization is critical to strengthening the relations with that government.

IV. Approaching Governments Proactively

Strategic Approach to Government   Rugman and Verbeke have provided a very useful overarching framework in regards to MNEs' strategic approach to government policy (see Exhibit 12.4). They distinguish between the MNE's original objective in business–government interactions (to achieve the benefits of integration

EXHIBIT 12.3
Objectives and Motivations of MNC-SOE Alliances and Acquisitions

Source: Dennis A. Rondinelli and Sylvia Sloan Black, Multinational Strategic Alliances and Acqusitions in Central and Eastern Europe: Partnerships in Privatization, Academy of Management Executive, Vol. 14, No. 4. 2000.

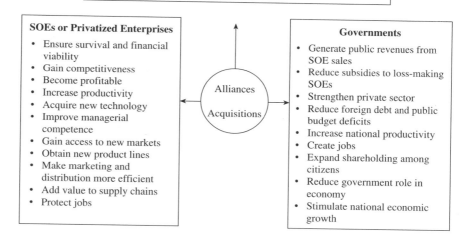

Multinational Corporations
- Increase profits
- Reduce political risks
- Achieve economies of scale and scope
- Control or preempt competition
- Expand market share
- Gain access to new markets
- Obtain lower-cost production or distribution facilities
- Develop or adapt technology jointly
- Expand domestic sales and services through overseas operations
- Obtain new labor or technology resources
- Achieve first mover advantages

SOEs or Privatized Enterprises
- Ensure survival and financial viability
- Gain competitiveness
- Become profitable
- Increase productivity
- Acquire new technology
- Improve managerial competence
- Gain access to new markets
- Obtain new product lines
- Make marketing and distribution more efficient
- Add value to supply chains
- Protect jobs

Alliances

Acquisitions

Governments
- Generate public revenues from SOE sales
- Reduce subsidies to loss-making SOEs
- Strengthen private sector
- Reduce foreign debt and public budget deficits
- Increase national productivity
- Create jobs
- Expand shareholding among citizens
- Reduce government role in economy
- Stimulate national economic growth

versus the benefits of national responsiveness) and the MNE's strategic perception of government policy (viewed as something which can versus cannot be potentially influenced by MNE managers). These distinctions are important because behavior follows from the underlying predisposition/assumption. While some firms may cover each of the four quadrants in Exhibit 12.4 depending on the area of regulation, the country and the particular subsidiary, most firms in fact are arguably inclined to take one, rather than a contingency, approach.

The position taken in this chapter is that government policy can potentially be influenced by MNE managers, to help achieve the benefits of national responsiveness. As such, we emphasize here some of the benefits of negotiating/bargaining/cooperating; in sum, taking a proactive approach.

Bargaining   A dominant characteristic of host government behavior is the way they discriminate. Some force certain subsidiaries into unwanted joint ventures, and impose taxes and limit prices, while allowing others 100 percent foreign ownership and financially supporting them. Even when legislation calls for the equal treatment of all foreign firms, discriminatory enforcement can occur. The basis of this discrimination lies in the differing characteristics of subsidiaries. A key

EXHIBIT 12.4
MNEs Approach to Government Policy

Source: Derived from Alan M. Rugman and Alain Verbeke, Multinational Enterprises and Public Policy, Journal of International Business Studies, Vol. 29, No. 1, 1998.

		MNE's Perception of Government Policy	
		Viewed as Outside the Influence of MNE Managers	Viewed as Potentially Influenced By MNE Managers
MNE's Objectives in Business-Government Interactions	**To Achieve Benefits of Integration**	1 "Government policy as lever for global competitiveness" approach Example: Porter's home base/cluster concept	3 Non-location-bound firm specific advantages in MNE government interaction Example: use of strategic trade policy arguments to obtain government favours.
	To Achieve Benefits of National Responsiveness	2 "Good corporate citizen" approach Government policy not viewed as a major determinant of international competitiveness	4 Location-bound firm specific advantages in MNE-government interaction Government policy viewed as something which can be influenced through lobbying, i.e., a proactive strategy

element is the bargaining power[2] associated with each subsidiary. In this context, bargaining power refers to the control the MNE parent has over those resources necessary to operate the subsidiary successfully.

The bargaining power of the host nation comes from two sources. One source directly counters the power of the MNE, namely the host nation's ability to replace the business resources normally supplied by the MNE. The nation's stock of managerial, technical, and similar resources is either internally generated or is obtained through consultants, license agreements, and the like. The capabilities of host nations are growing.

The second source of host nation bargaining power comes from its control over the subsidiary's access to the host nation's market, raw materials, labor, and capital.[3] As these factors grow in importance, more MNEs compete to locate there, thus maximizing the bargaining power of the host nation. Hence, the larger and more attractive the local market becomes, the more intervention the firm will experience, all things being equal.

A major source of bargaining power for MNEs stems from sourcing or vertical integration as discussed in Chapter 5. Obviously, there are strong disincentives for local business or government to intervene in a firm that, say, imports a proprietary one-third-completed product for further assembly, with sales locally and to other parts of the MNE. While obvious examples occur in the auto industry, manufacturers

EXHIBIT 12.5   **Specific Government Measures to Create and Deepen Linkages**

Information and Matchmaking	Technology Upgrading	Training	Finance
Provision of Information • Handouts and brochures • Constantly updated electronic databases • Linkage information seminars • Exhibitions and missions *Matchmaking* • Acting as honest broker in negotiations • Supporting supplier audits • Providing advice on subcontracting deals • Sponsoring fairs, exhibitions, missions, and conferences • Organizing meetings, visits to plants	• Technology transfer as a performance requirement • Partnership with foreign affiliates • Incentives for R&D cooperation • Home-country incentives	• Promoting supplier associations • Collaboration with the private sector for one-stop service • Support for private sector training programs • Collaboration with international agencies	• Legal protection against unfair contractual arrangements and other unfair business practices • Encouraging a shortening of payment delays through tax measures • Limiting payment delays through legislation • Guaranteeing the recovery of delayed payments • Indirect financing to suppliers channeled through their buyers • Tax credits or tax reductions and other fiscal benefits to firms providing long-term funds to suppliers • Co-financing development programs with the private sector • Director role in providing finance to local firms • Mandatory transfer of funds from foreign affiliates to local suppliers *Home country measures* • Two-step loans • Using ODA.

Source: UNCTAD, World Investment Report 2001: Promoting Linkages, table VI. 1, pg. 210.

of industrial tools, of some specialized chemicals, and of electronics, can implement this strategy as well. Japanese MNEs are frequent users of this strategy, using world-scale plants and trading houses. To guarantee effectiveness, multiple sourcing of the same components or products within the MNE system is necessary to ensure that the subsidiary will not be held hostage by a government taking advantage of its role as a sole supplier within the multinational system.

A problem that makes MNEs hesitate is that for much of their history most MNEs responded to government by having less to do with them.[4] They justified this response by referring to the highly unpredictable nature of government. In contrast, new strategies sometimes call for increased investment and involvement.

In the past decade, the vast majority of regulatory changes by the various governments of the world have been favorable to FDI. Governments have created a large number of measures to create and deepen linkages between potential investors and local firms (see Exhibit 12.5).

Summary

Any proposed strategy for working with governments affects the MNE's allocation of human, technical, and capital resources and introduces new managerial activities to the parent's organization. The new strategy must also be institutionalized, or integrated into the MNE's organization.

From our introductory chapters on the global environment and internationalization, through the entire process of multinational management, our constant emphasis has been on ways of understanding and improving the practice of international management. As this chapter has demonstrated, even government relations, viewed by so many as totally beyond the control of the MNE, can in part, be strengthened.

Supplementary Reading

Behrman, J. N. and R. E. Grosse. *International Business and Governments: Issues and Institutions.* Columbia, South Carolina, University of South Carolina, 1990.

Blumentritt, T. P. and D. Nigh. "The Integration of Subsidiary Political Activities in Multinational Corporations," *Journal of International Business Studies,* Vol. 33, No. 1, 2002, pp. 57–77.

Boddewyn, Jean J. "Political Aspects of MNE Theory," *Journal of International Business Studies,* Vol. 19, No. 3, 1988.

Brewer, Thomas L. "An Issue-Area Approach to the Analysis of MNE-Government Relations," *Journal of International Business Studies,* Vol. 23, No. 2, 1992.

Butler, Kirt C., and D. C. Joaquin. "A Note on Political Risk and the Required Return on Foreign Direct Investment," *Journal of International Business Studies,* Vol. 29, No. 3, 1998.

Caves, R. E. *Multinational Enterprise and Economic Analysis.* Second Edition, 1996, Cambridge, Cambridge University Press.

Doz, Y. L., and C. K. Prahalad, "How MNEs Cope with Host Government Intervention," *Harvard Business Review,* March-April 1980.

Harvey, Michael G. "A Survey of Corporate Programs for Managing Terrorist Threats," *Journal of International Business Studies,* Vol. 24, No. 3, 1993.

Hillman, A. J. and M. A. Hitt. "Corporate Political Strategy Formulation: A Model of Approach Participation, and Strategy Decisions," *Academy of Management Review.* Vol. 24, No. 4, 1999, pp. 825–842.

Loewendahl, H. B. *Bargaining with Multinationals: The Investment of Siemens and Nissan in North-East England.* Basingstoke, UK & New York, US: Palgrave. 2001.

Luo, Y. "Toward a Cooperative View of MNC-Host Government Relations: Building Blocks and Performance Implications," *Journal of International Business Studies,* Vol. 32 No. 3, 2001, pp. 401–419.

Makino, Shige, and Paul W. Beamish. "Local Ownership Restrictions, Entry Mode Choice, and FDI Performance: Japanese Overseas Subsidiaries in Asia," *Asia Pacific Journal of Management,* Vol. 15, 1998, pp. 119–36.

Miller. Kent D. "A Framework for Integrated Risk Management in International Business," *Journal of International Business Studies,* Vol. 23, No. 2, 1992.

Minor, Michael S. "The Demise of Expropriation as an Instrument of LDC Policy, 1980-92," *Journal of International Business Studies,* Vol. 25, No. 1, 1994, pp. 177–88.

Ramamurti, R. "The Obsolescing 'Bargaining Model'? MNC-Host Developing Country Relations Revisted," *Journal of International Business Studies,* Vol. 32, No. 1, 2001, pp. 23–39.

Rondinelli, D. A. and S. S. Black. "Multinational Strategic Alliances and Acquisitions in Central and Eastern Europe: Partnerships in Privatization," *Academy of Management Executive,* Vol 14, No. 4. 2000. pp. 85–98.

Rugman, A. M. and Verbeke, A. "Multinational Enterprises and Public Policy," *Journal of International Business Studies,* Vol. 29, No. 1, 1998. pp. 115–136.

Endnotes

1. See Theodore H. Moran, "International Political Risk Assessment, Corporate Planning and Strategies to Offset Political Risk," in *Managing International Political Risk: Strategies and Techniques,* eds. F. Ghadar, S. J. Kobrin, and T. H. Moran (Washington, D.C.: The Landegger Program in International Business Diplomacy, Georgetown University, 1983), pp. 158–66.

2. The concept of "bargaining power" finds its roots in the work of Raymond Vernon, *Sovereignty at Bay: The Multinational Spread of U.S. Enterprises,* (New York: Basic Books, 1971); T. H. Moran, *Multinational Corporations and the Politics of Dependence: Copper in Chile,* (Princeton, N.J.: Princeton University Press, 1974); T. A. Poynter, "Government Intervention in Less Developed Countries: The Experience of Multinational Companies," *Journal of International Business Studies,* Spring-Summer 1982; N. Fagre and L. T. Wells, Jr., "The Bargaining Power of Multinationals and Host Government," *Journal of International Business Studies,* Fall 1982; Donald J. Lecraw, "Bargaining Power, Ownership and Profitability of Subsidiaries of Transnational Corporations in Developing Countries," *Journal of International Business Studies,* Spring-Summer 1984, and more recently Ramamurti, 2001.

3. For a detailed discussion of sources of a nation's bargaining power see Ramamurti, 2001.

4. For a more general discussion of the organizational issues involved when MNEs deal with host governments, see Amir Mahini, *The Management of Government Relations in U.S. Multinationals,* D.B.A. dissertation, Harvard Business School, 1982.

Chapter Thirteen

Global Leadership

Without doubt, the global marketplace of today is a highly risky place. For managers, it is filled with new competitors, new cultures, complex markets, political uncertainty, and huge logistical problems. Despite these challenges, the global marketplace is also filled with enormous promise. International markets are always larger than domestic markets. The world's largest economy, the U.S. economy, represents less than one-quarter of the world's GNP. For U.S. companies, the importance of global markets is even more pronounced. Not only are international markets substantial, but often the best ideas, the best technologies, and the most dangerous competitors are found off-shore. As the new millennium unfolds, managers can no longer afford to ignore global markets.

While the focus of this book has been on international management, its ultimate impact is on the practice of *global leadership.* Global leaders ultimately determine the map that that will guide both themselves and their companies to new heights of international competitiveness. Leadership is all about influencing the actions and beliefs of others. Global leaders are able to do this across multiple countries and markets in ways that maximize profits for their companies. Required is a combination of both knowledge and skills that will enable managers to operate effectively as leaders everywhere in the world.

The need for global leaders has never been greater. This includes not only those on international assignments, but those who work on a day-to-day basis with global business issues within their companies, and those who work for domestic companies that have international competitors or global aspirations. One recent study, reported the results of a survey of 110 Fortune 500 companies.[1] The researchers asked senior executives at participating firms whether they had *enough* global leaders in their companies. The results, reported in Exhibit 13.1, indicate that for the sampled companies, only 15 percent had enough or more than enough global leaders. The same study also asked whether the existing cadre of managers had the requisite skills to be effective global leaders. These results are reported in Exhibit 13.2. Sixty-seven percent of companies indicated that their current managers either had no capability or less global leaderships capability than required.

This chapter was prepared by Allen Morrison.

EXHIBIT 13.1
The Quantity of
Global Leaders

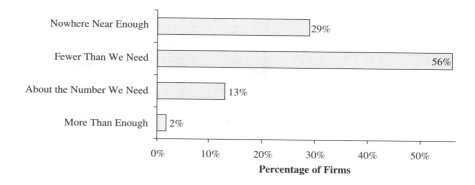

EXHIBIT 13.2
The Quality of
Global Leaders

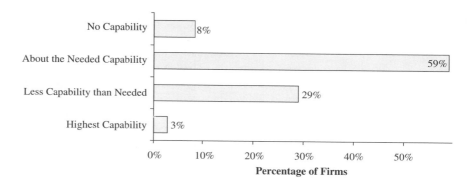

Clearly, most companies lack enough high quality global leaders. For the most part, they have unlimited market opportunities and adequate financial resources. But companies lack the kinds of leaders who have the ability to recognize the opportunities and who can mobilize the resources within the company to move forward.

In finding and nurturing effective global leaders, most observers also believe that leadership is not so much a function of position as it is a function of attitude and competencies. Positions in an organization chart do not identify the real leaders. Instead, leadership is rooted in an individual's ability to convince employees of the need to change and to move forward with them in new and challenging ways.

THE IMPORTANCE OF GLOBAL LEADERSHIP

During much of the post-World War II era, international business was a topic of interest to a limited number of business professionals. These individuals typically worked in specialized international departments in large companies. In most companies, international business was considered secondary to domestic operations, almost an after-thought. However, beginning in the 1970s, the world began to get a lot smaller. As trade and investment soared and as high profile Japanese MNCs began to make inroads in U.S. and European markets, an increasing number of managers awoke to the potential of the global marketplace.

Initially, most practitioners used *domestic* leadership models in "going global." In the United States, leadership models have generally been grounded on several beliefs about both roles and markets. One common belief is in the importance of hierarchical command and control structures. Many U.S. models emphasize strong, decisive decision making, delegation, and tight control. In these models, good leaders are those who quickly size up the situation, decide what to do, delegate, and hold people accountable. Action is emphasized over contemplation. And command and control are emphasized over persuasion and participation.

Another common belief in U.S. leadership models is that markets can be beat—at least in the short-term. Leaders are those who recognize and quickly move to take advantage of short-term market inefficiencies, both those that are internal and external to the firm. (External market inefficiencies primarily include opportunities in competitive markets, capital markets, and labor markets. Internal inefficiencies include matters of employee discrimination and operational redundancies.) As a result, good leaders are resolute in performing internal audits and conducting external market research. Not surprisingly, under the U.S. approach to leadership, knowledge becomes a key determinant of success. The more you know, the more opportunities you recognize and the more your input is valued.

In most cases, individuals tend to move into leadership positions when they exemplify dominant national leadership models. Americans have been fascinated with leaders like Jack Welch, Michael Dell, Lou Gerstner, and Michael Eisner. Books about their lives have sold millions and countless aspiring American executives have seemingly followed their every word. Why? Because their behaviors are consistent with a U.S.-centric model of leadership: they have powerful command and control skills, demonstrate strong analytical abilities, and know how to make lots of money for their shareholders. They are role models—for better or worse—in a world that craves role models. But interestingly, they are American role models for a largely American audience.

The U.S. leadership field has multiple foci and, without doubt, much can be learned about global leadership by studying U.S. models. Unfortunately, the majority of leadership models generated in the United States have had problems when applied outside the United States.[2] What works in one country often produces less desirable outcomes in other countries. An important reason for this is the difference in cultural norms and values between countries. In matters as diverse as gift giving, compensation, job security, and employee motivation, cultural norms vary widely.[3] As a result, leadership models that are effective in one part of the world often have problems being applied elsewhere.

European, Asian, and Latin American leadership models are often different from each other and from U.S. models. For example, in one study of 10 multinational corporations from 8 different countries, researchers found that while Australians believed leaders needed to be catalysts of cultural change, Japanese and Koreans did not think this was a critical characteristic of leaders.[4] The researchers also found that a disproportionate number of Koreans and Germans valued leaders who placed a high value on integrity and trust. Meanwhile, French employees wanted leaders who demonstrated skills at managing internal and external networks. Interestingly, Americans, Germans, Australians, Italians, Koreans, and British managers placed far less emphasis on these skills. Finally, Italians were shown to value leaders who were flexible and adaptive; Australians and Americans generally cared about these competencies much less.

A number of studies have shown that leadership models differ because of cultural differences on a range of variables including interpersonal relationships, profits, bureaucracy, ethics and risk taking.[5] A well-known expression in Japan, "the nail that stands up gets pounded back down," suggests that Japanese leaders should be good at both building consensus and "fitting in." In China, maintaining and developing relationships are valued much more than exploiting market inefficiencies. As a result, skills associated with conducting market research and strategic thinking are valued less in China than in the United States. Also educational achievement and having attended "elite" graduate schools are far less important to being *accepted* as a leader in China than in the United States. Rather, in China family connections and long-term relationships are viewed as more important.

National leadership models generally work best when leaders deal with people from their same culture. However, the leadership models that were so effective at home begin to create real problems as companies globalize. Not surprisingly, ethnocentric leadership models have a difficult time being globalized. In order for a company to operate most effectively overseas, its leaders must develop competencies that go beyond what is familiar in the home country.[6] In general, the best Japanese, German, Canadian, Chinese, or American leaders do not make the best global leaders.

Developing and keeping a team of effective global leaders is a huge challenge. Prior to his departure in 2001, Ford's president and CEO, Jacques Nasser, had assembled perhaps the most globally oriented leadership team of any large company. While Nasser had worked at Ford for over 30 years, only 6 of those years were actually spent in Detroit. Born in a mountain village in Lebanon and raised in Australia from the age of four, Nasser was the quintessential global leader. He has held key posts in Australia, Thailand, the Philippines, Venezuela, Mexico, Argentina, Brazil, and Europe, had a degree in international business, and spoke five languages. Other members of Ford's top management team included worldwide design chief J. Mays who came to Ford in late 1997 from Audi and Volkswagen. Another team member was Welshman Richard Parry-Jones, group vice president for product development and quality. Parry-Jones had also spent most of his career in Europe. A fourth team member was James Padilla, group vice president for manufacturing. Padilla ran Ford's South American operations and was instrumental in turning around quality and productivity problems at Jaguar in the United Kingdom. A fifth member of the management team Vaughn Koshkarian, vice president of public affairs, was most recently CEO of Ford Motor (China). The international composition of Ford's top management team ensured that global issues received considerable ongoing attention.

Irrespective of the composition of a leadership team, global leaders have perspectives that transcend national differences and embrace the most effective practices, wherever they are in the world. A global mindset is one that is not based on sequentially accessing markets; for example, methodologically looking at country A, then country B, then country C. On the contrary, global leaders have the ability to look at everything relevant to the company more or less simultaneously. They hold the whole world in their heads and have the capacity to recognize familiar, organized patterns of information that allow them to act rapidly in the best interests of the company.[7]

Global companies need more than simply a mixture of American, European, and Asian approaches to leadership. They require leadership models that can be applied everywhere in the world that they compete. Such a model would transcend and integrate national leadership schemes and become a powerful tool for hiring, training, and retaining the leaders of tomorrow.

THE CHARACTERISTICS OF EFFECTIVE GLOBAL LEADERS

Over the past decade, an extensive list of articles and books has been published specifically on the topic of global leadership. These publications range from prescriptive books,[8] which address the need for more and better global leaders, to comprehensive academic articles based on systematic, multimethod research efforts. Not surprisingly, the number of descriptive articles and books far outweighs the number of rigorous, systematic studies. Also, the quality of research and writings on global leadership varies widely.

One of the most comprehensive studies of global leadership was conducted over a three-year period in the late 1990s.[9] The authors interviewed more than 130 senior executives in more than 60 MNCs throughout North America, Europe, Australia, and Asia. These individuals were identified by their companies as role models or "archetypal" global leaders. One of the questions these leaders were asked was simply, "What are you good at?" Interestingly, the responses were quite similar.

The research concluded that about two-thirds of the competencies of effective global leader is actually generalizable. The other one-third of leadership competencies are idiosyncratic or specific to the MNC, its home country, the manager's position in the company, and the industry. For example, the leader of a French group of accountants at Renault needs a somewhat different competency base than the leader of a group of Japanese product developers at Hitachi. Because every situation is somewhat unique, global leaders need some competencies that reflect local conditions.

Despite the need for idiosyncratic competencies, the majority of global leadership competencies are highly generalizable. Every global leader needs a set of knowledge and skills that operate around the world. Three distinct sets of competencies or characteristics were identified in the research: *demonstrating savvy, exhibiting character,* and *maintaining perspective.* These are shown in Exhibit 13.3.

EXHIBIT 13.3
**The Characteristics
of Effective Global
Leaders**

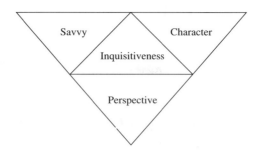

Demonstrating Savvy

Savvy is about knowing what needs to be done. Global leaders demonstrate two types of savvy: global *business* savvy and global *organizational* savvy. Global business savvy is ultimately based on the leader's ability to make money for the firm on a worldwide basis. As discussed in Chapter 3, making money globally comes through recognizing three different types of market opportunities:

- *Arbitrage opportunities,* which involve differences in the cost of inputs and quality differences across countries.

- *New market opportunities* for the company's goods and services.

- *Efficiency maximizing opportunities,* which can be generated through economies of scale and the elimination of redundancies.

Recognizing each of these global market opportunities requires considerable insight and sensitivity. Many of the background concepts associated with global business savvy are provided in Chapters 1 through 5 and Chapter 8 of this book. In addition, an education in and knowledge of such disparate topics as international finance, marketing, and accounting are very helpful.

Global leaders crave data and are fact-based in their decision making. Good data collection allows leaders to recognize possible gaps between the real strength of markets and wishful thinking. Understanding market potential is a huge challenge, particularly when the markets are unfamiliar and when companies follow their customers overseas. Many well-meaning companies have been badly burned by events beyond their control, but which could have been averted with more and better data. Recent examples include:

- In 1997, 56 of Thailand's 58 banks collapsed.

- In 1998, GNP in Indonesia fell by 15 percent.

- In 1998, the Russian government defaulted on $40 billion in bonds resulting in collapse in the economy and reports of hardships for many.

- Between 1990 and 1998, commercial property values in 6 Japanese cities fell by 75 percent.

- Between mid-1997 and year-end 1998, real estate prices fell by 50 percent in Hong Kong.

- In December 2001, the Argentinean government suspended payments on $141 billion in debt. Rioting erupted and the economy sank into depression.

In many cases, foreign business leaders were caught completely off-guard by these events. Global business savvy is about recognizing both opportunities and threats ahead of the competition and *before* they happen.

Global organizational savvy is required to secure the resources necessary to implement international strategies. Organizational savvy includes knowing the right people in the company, knowing where the skills and competencies are located, and knowing how things *really* work in the company. Many of the competencies associated with organizational savvy are described in Chapter 9. Some of the key knowledge areas include:

- Awareness of the product lines offered by key subsidiaries.

- Familiarity with the cost structures and overall competitiveness of key subsidiaries.

- Understanding how to attract resources and top management attention.

- Insights into where managerial and employee talent are located within the global organization.

Exhibiting Character

Exhibiting character is the second characteristic of effective global leaders. Character has two different dimensions. First, it includes the ability to *emotionally connect* with people. Second, it involves the ability to *demonstrate high personal integrity.* Both of these dimensions of character are essential in developing and retaining goodwill and trust in a globally diverse workforce. Without goodwill and trust, leadership is impossible.

Emotional connections involve the establishment of close personal relationships with people. The ability to work well with others and in teams is discussed at length in Chapter 11. Emotional connections are important for three main reasons: first, they help leaders better understand local market conditions; second, they help leaders better understand conditions within the company, including what is happening in the lives of employees; and third, they help leaders identify and mentor future leaders within the organization. All three of these benefits assist global leaders both in formulating and implementing current and future international strategies.

Connecting emotionally enables global leaders to overcome the very real communication barriers that divide people culturally and geographically. Beyond understanding the words, emotionally connecting with people requires the interchange of *feelings.* As explained in Chapters 6 and 7, close personal relationships can also play an important role in the formation and stability of alliances, including licensing and equity joint ventures. In many parts of the world, personal relationships instead of legal contracts hold alliances together.

Integrity is the second dimension of character. It plays a critical role in company morale, and significantly affects the credibility of the leader. As discussed in Chapter 14, integrity involves both the external and internal activities carried out by the leader. External activities are those where individuals represent the company. One example of an external activity is establishing and maintaining customer relationships; another is negotiating and managing of buyer/supplier contracts. Internal activities include such things as conducting performance appraisals, allocating resources, and giving direction to employees. Ample opportunities exist in both external and internal activities for leaders to abuse trust and act unethically. Perceived power differences between a leader and local employees or between global and local companies can exacerbate the tendencies of some people to act in ways that would be frowned upon—or perhaps even be illegal—at home.

The failure to embrace consistent ethical standards—whether involving external or internal activities—jeopardizes the ability of managers to lead globally. Rumors of activities undertaken in one part of the world almost always spread. Reputations are made and in some cases lost according to behaviors conducted in the far-flung reaches of the world. This applies to both companies and leaders. Lapses in ethical judgment, while not always fatal, are difficult to recover from and almost always undermine a leader's ability to engender the type of goodwill necessary to lead effectively.

Maintaining Perspective

Maintaining perspective is the third characteristic of effective global leaders. Perspective has two dimensions: the first is the *ability to manage uncertainty,* and the second is the ability to *balance globalization and localization pressures.* Maintaining perspective is one of the most difficult tasks for global leaders who are constantly bombarded by conflicting and often irreconcilable demands. The need for perspective is the central issue in the Global Enterprises case study. In this case study, the CEO is confronted by a group of direct reports whose self-interests are at odds with one another. Without perspective, the CEO risks making poor decisions and undermining corporate performance.

Uncertainty is an inescapable aspect of global business in general and leadership more specifically. Leaders ultimately arbitrate on matters involving the company's strategy, structure, systems, and people. The scale and scope of these issues is huge in global companies. While managers often pay substantial attention to initial investment or start-up decisions, it takes extraordinary effort to stay abreast of technological, political, competitive, and market developments, as they simultaneously take place around the world. It also takes considerable stamina to remain current in monitoring the competitiveness of a company's far-flung activities.

Because competitive norms, markets, values, and governments differ so widely, the level of uncertainty faced by global leaders is of an order of magnitude higher than that which is confronted by domestic leaders. This is particularly true when leaders deal with emerging markets. In emerging markets, the quality and quantity of available competitive, economic, social, and political data are often severely lacking or are of dubious quality. Global leaders routinely confront either a flood of data or a dearth of data. Deciding what is believable and what is not is a huge challenge.

Many Western managers are uncomfortable acting with little data or data that is of dubious quality. Their normal approach is to research issues until the risk of decision making is minimized to the lowest level possible. If data cannot be collected or if the data is unreliable, decisions are delayed. In contrast, global leaders are superb at deciding when to act and when to keep researching. This ability to get the timing of decision making right, while uncommon, is a critical characteristic of effective global leaders.

Balancing tensions between globalization and localization is the second dimension of perspective. As discussed in Chapter 9, notwithstanding the general movement toward globalization, many activities and company policies can and should remain local. Global–local tensions are common across a range of issues, including whether:

- Products should be globally standardized or locally designed.

- Employment policies should be set by corporate headquarters to apply worldwide or whether they should be determined on a country-by-country basis.

- Fund-raising should be centrally controlled or left to the discretion of affiliate managers.

- Affiliates have the right to export products and compete with other affiliates.

- Companies should rely on global websites for product information and sales or whether affiliates should be given a free-hand to develop their own sites.

- The company's brands should be globally maintained or revised and maintained by local affiliates.

Enormous judgment is required to effectively address these questions. Often the answers are not readily apparent. In many cases, a particular course of action creates winners and losers within the organization and with this, negative feelings for the decision maker. As a result, balancing tensions presents not only personal challenges but requires intellectual stretch as well. Global leaders do not just put up with these tensions, they actually enjoy the challenge of figuring out solutions to the very real conflicts they face.

Inquisitiveness

A fourth component of global leadership is *inquisitiveness*. Inquisitiveness acts as a kind of "glue" that holds global leadership competencies together and keeps leaders relevant. Inquisitiveness is not a competency, but rather a state of mind. Someone who is inquisitive is eager to learn and goes out of his or her way to stay current with a wide range of relevant issues. Without inquisitiveness, it is impossible to develop a clear understanding of global markets or organizational resources. Without inquisitiveness, a manager never learns about changing local conditions, local values, or gets close to employees and customers. And without inquisitiveness, effective and timely decision making about which activities to globalize and which activities to localize is impossible.

The reality is that as companies globalize, some managers pay a lot of attention to global issues while others essentially ignore them. Some managers seem to be genuinely interested in what is happening in far-flung parts of the world. They watch global competitors, keep track of political events around the world, assess customers in other countries, and actually think about the competitive positions of the distant activities over which they have responsibility. In contrast, other managers have little interest in events outside their home country and, even if they have responsibility for international activities, rarely spend time thinking about what is going on overseas. Despite the potential of global markets, they prefer the familiarity of domestic customers and the security of focusing on a limited number of competitors.

In many companies, managers acknowledge the benefits of going global—after all, everyone else is doing it—and may even support an initial decision to globalize a certain process or function. But after the decision to globalize is made, their attention wanes. Globalization *gets* their attention, but because of a lack of inquisitiveness, does not *keep* their attention. And lapses of attention can be devastating for companies; particularly those up against tough and aggressive global competitors.

In assessing your own level of global inquisitiveness, some of the following questions might be helpful:

- Do you pay the most attention to domestic competitors or do you pay equal attention to all competitors, irrespective of their home countries?

- When traveling to a new country, do you go out of your way to learn about the culture, political systems, and history of the country you are visiting?

- When traveling in a foreign city, do you spend most of your spare time in your hotel room or do you enjoy venturing out into the streets, museums, and markets?

- When traveling overseas, do you insist on using familiar hotel chains (Marriott, Hilton, Shangri-La, Kempinski, etc.)?

- Do you enjoy reading the latest books on business, history, culture, international relations, etc.? Or do you prefer to read books on sports or entertainment?

- Do you go out of your way to get to know the people you work with—their family situations, educational background, personal experiences?

- When faced with a troubling business issue involving a foreign affiliate, do you ask for input from people at head office or people who work in the affiliate?

- Do you spend a lot of time thinking about how your company's products and services could be better sold overseas?

Inquisitiveness and Personal Change

Inquisitiveness is a complex topic. It is ultimately tied to personal change and a commitment to continual self-improvement. Personal change is always a challenge. Smart and successful people are often the most threatened by change. In part, this stems from their lack of experience with failure. Years of personal success can lead to complacency and arrogance. Both are inconsistent with inquisitiveness and effectiveness as a global leader.

When faced with a new challenge, most people have a tendency to rely on what has worked well in the past. They work harder, they try more earnestly, perhaps they even try to think more intensely. But in the end, most people come back to doing what they have always done. Because of this, American leaders have a tendency to exaggerate their American features when faced with the challenges of globalizing. They want more hierarchy, more process controls, more market research, more short-term performance evaluations, and so on. They try to be better at doing what they know how to do. In their own ways, the Japanese act the same way; so do the British, the French, the Germans, and everyone else. We all tend to revert to existing mental maps or paradigms of how the world works.

Those who are highly inquisitive focus much more on doing the *right thing* than they do on *perfecting* what they are currently doing. This takes courage. It also takes great insights and enormous self-confidence to move outside familiar paradigms. For these reasons, there are far more followers of global leaders than there are global leaders themselves. Perhaps this is why the surveys indicate that companies want more and better global leaders. If becoming a global company means downplaying nationality, then becoming a global leader means the same thing. Downplaying nationality is never easy, particularly when it comes to changing individual interests.

THE PARADOX OF GLOBAL LEADERSHIP

The great paradox of global leadership is that despite the desire of companies for more and better global leaders, relatively few companies are doing much about it. In the earlier cited study of global leadership, only 8 percent of Fortune 500 companies reported having comprehensive systems in place to identify, develop, and retain global leaders.[10] Another 16 percent reported having some established global leadership development system in place, and 76 percent reported that they either had an ad hoc approach in place or that they were just starting to think about global leadership development. Seemingly, while the vast majority of companies want more and better global leaders, relatively few are doing much about it.

The implications for future global leaders are significant. First, because of the perceived shortage of effective global leaders, those who have the requisite competencies will be in very high demand. They can expect premium salaries and lots of career opportunities. Second, the global leaders of the future will take charge of their personal development today. Because the big majority of companies lack comprehensive global leadership development programs, every opportunity for self-development must be sought. Smart managers will assume that in the end their companies will actually do little to manage or channel their development. And third, those with global leadership aspirations will aggressively pursue a range of developmental opportunities. These activities should include overseas travel, participation in cross-cultural teams, involvement in formal training programs at universities and institutes, and international assignments. Each one of these developmental activities has advantages and disadvantages, depending on an individual's personal situation.

The developmental needs of every individual are different. Some lack global business acumen, others lack the ability to connect with people from other cultures, and still others have a difficult time dealing with the complexity of global business. This book plays an important role in assisting individuals as they strive to become more effective global leaders. Each of the case studies that follows centers on a decision maker as he or she struggles with a wide range of tough issues. Mastering these issues will provide an important contribution to the development of the global leaders of tomorrow.

Supplementary Reading

Adler, N., and Bartholomew, S. Managing Globally Competent People. *Academy of Management Executive,* 6 (3), 1992, pp. 52–65.

Bartlett, C., and Ghoshal, S. "What is a Global Manager?" *Harvard Business Review,* September-October 1992, pp. 124–132.

Black, S., Morrison, A., and Gregersen, H. *Global Explorers: The Next Generation of Leaders.* New York: Routledge, 1999.

Brake, T. *The Global Leader: Critical Factors for Creating the World Class Organization.* Chicago: Irwin Professional Publishing, 1997.

Caligiuri, P. and Di Santo, V. "Global Competence: What is it, and Can it be Developed Through Global Assignments?" *HR. Human Resource Planning,* 24 (3), 2001, pp. 27–35.

Cumings, B. "The American Ascendancy: Imposing a New World Order," *The Nation,* 270 (18), 2000, pp. 13–20.

Dorfman, P. International and Cross-Cultural Leadership, in B. J. Punnett and O. Shenkar, eds., *Handbook for International Management Research.* Cambridge, MA: Blackwell, 1996, pp. 267–349.

Govindarajan, V., and Gupta, A., "Building an Effective Global Business Team," *Sloan Management Review,* 42 (4), 2001, pp. 63–71.

Gregersen, H., Morrison, A., and Black, S. "Developing Leaders for the Global Frontier," *Sloan Management Review,* 40 (1), 1998, pp. 21–32.

Gupta, A., and Govindarajan, V. "Converting Global Presence into Global Competitive Advantage," *Academy of Management Executive,* 15 (2), 2001, pp. 45–58.

House, R. J., Hanges, P., Agar, M., and Ruiz-Quintanilla, A. *Conference on Global Leadership and Organizational Behavior (GLOBE).* Calgary, Canada, 1994.

House, R. J. "Understanding Cultures and Implicit Leadership Theories Around the Globe: An Introduction to Project GLOBE," *Journal of World Business,* 37 (1), 2002, pp. 3–10.

Jackofsky, E., Slocum, J., and McQuaid, S. "Cultural Values and the CEO: Alluring Companions," *Academy of Management Executive,* 2(1), 1998, pp. 39–49.

Jago, A., and Vroom, V. "Hierarchical Level and Leadership Style," *Organizational Behavior and Human Performance,* 18, 1977, pp. 131–145.

Kets de Vries, M., and Florent-Treacy, F. *The New Global Leaders: Richard Branson, Percy Barnevik, and David Simon.* New York: Jossey-Bass, 1999.

Laurent, A. "The Cultural Diversity of Western Conceptions of Management," *International Studies of Management and Organization,* 8 (2), 1983, pp. 75–96.

McCall, M., and Hollenbeck, G. *Developing Global Executives.* Boston: Harvard Business School Press, 2002.

Misumi, J. *The Behavioral Science of Leadership: An Interdisciplinary Japanese Research Program.* Ann Arbor, MI: University of Michigan Press, 1985.

Pfeffer, J. "Competitive Advantage Through People," *California Management Review,* Winter 1994, pp. 9–28.

Schriesheim, C. A., and Kerr, S. "Theories and Measures of Leadership: A Critical Appraisal," *Leadership: The Cutting Edge.* Carbondale, IL: Southern Illinois University Press, 1977, pp. 9–45.

Tung, R., and Miller, E. "Managing in the Twenty-first Century: The Need for Global Orientation," *Management International Review,* 30, 1990, pp. 5–18.

Yeung, A. and Ready, D. Developing Leadership Capabilities of Global Corporations: A Comparative Study in Eight Nations. *Human Resource Management* Vol. 34 (4), 1995, pp. 529–547.

Yukl, G. A., and Van Fleet, D. "Theory and Research on Leadership in Organizations," *Handbook of Industrial and Organizational Psychology.* Palo Alto, CA: Consulting Psychology Press, 1992, pp. 147–197.

Endnotes

1. H. Gregersen, A. J. Morrison, and S. Black. "Developing Leaders for the Global Frontier," *Sloan Management Review,* Fall 1998, 40 (1), pp. 21–32.
2. E. Jackofsky, J. Slocum, and S. McQuaid. "Cultural Values and the CEO: Alluring Companions," *Academy of Management Executive,* 2 (1), 1988, pp. 39–49.
3. M. Nyaw and I. Ng. "A Comparative Analysis of Ethical Beliefs: A Four Country Study," *Journal of Business Ethics,* 13, 1994, pp. 543–555.
4. A. Yeung and D. Ready. "Developing Leadership Capabilities of Global Corporations: A Comparative Study in Eight Nations." *Human Resource Management,* vol. 34 (4), Winter 1995, pp. 529–547.
5. See, for example, N. Boyacigiller and N. Adler. "The Parochial Dinosaur: Organizational Science in a Global Context," *Academy of Management Review,* 16 (2), 1991, pp. 262–290; G. Hofstede, *Culture's Consequences: International Differences in Work-Related Values,* (Beverly Hills: Sage Publications, 1980).
6. T. Yamaguchi. "The Challenge of Internationalization: Japan's Kokusaika," *Academy of Management Executive.* 2 (1), 1988, pp. 33–36.
7. For more on the importance of global "mindsets" see J. Beck and A. Morrison. "Mudslides and Emerging Markets," *Organizational Dynamics,* Fall 2000, pp. 19–32.
8. See for example, T. Brake. *The Global Leader: Critical Factors for Creating the World Class Organization,* (Chicago: Irwin Professional Publishing, 1997).
9. S. Black, A. Morrison, and H. Gregersen. *Global Explorers: The Next Generation of Leaders,* (New York: Routledge, 1999).
10. H. Gregersen, A. Morrison, S. Black. "Developing Leaders for the Global Frontier," *Sloan Management Review,* 40 (1), 1998, pp. 21–32.

Chapter Fourteen

Ethical Challenges of International Management

The effective management of ethics is one of the most difficult and yet critical aspects of effective global management. Making the "right" ethical decisions can be challenging in the best of circumstances; internationally, the difficulties seem to increase exponentially. While domestic managers inevitably address ethical issues, global managers confront them more frequently and deal with dilemmas that are often much more difficult to resolve.

Ethics focuses on the study of morals and moral choices and governs personal and company behaviors. Culture impacts ethical norms because culture is inherently value laden. Ethical behavior in one culture may be perceived as inappropriate in another. Cultures also change over time, and in some countries values are changing more rapidly than in others. In ancient times it took hundreds and in some cases thousands of years before practices such as human sacrifice and slavery to be viewed as "wrong" or "immoral." In modern times, the ethical issues are different and subject to more rapid change. Attitudes about such matters as tax evasion, employee rights, bribery, and environmental degradation vary widely within and across countries and can change dramatically in just a few years time. In many ways, ethics are a moving target. As such, they require a unique set of skills for global managers.

Negotiating through the minefield of international ethics is a gigantic challenge. Exposure to different ethical norms can be "eye opening" to managers who are new to international business. But even the most experienced international managers often struggle to understand the nuances of cultures and values that govern ethical behavior. Simple matters such as dress, deportment, and language intonation can have ethical connotations in certain cultures.

This chapter was prepared by Allen Morrison.

Integrity is tightly linked to the concept of ethics. Integrity is demonstrated when an individual or company behaves in a manner consistent with ethical norms. Individuals may be acting ethically by home country standards but unethically by another country's standards. Consequently, while the manager may "feel" he or she has acted appropriately, the actions may be interpreted very differently. What one feels to be right and what is perceived by others to be right are sometimes very different. This is important because integrity forms the bedrock of character and is essential in individual and company competitiveness. Without integrity, managers will engender neither the goodwill nor trust required to lead.

ETHICS INVOLVE TWO TYPES OF ACTIONS

Ultimately, ethics are demonstrated through actions. What managers actually do— their behaviors and decisions—reflects their integrity. Global managers show their integrity through two types of actions: actions that are external to the company and actions that are internal to the company.[1] Internal and external actions often have unforeseen ripple effects. Sometimes these effects cancel each other out; other times they amplify either the good or the bad.

Integrity in External Actions

External activities are those through which the company or leader is represented to the outside world. To outsiders, managers are often the "face" of the company. Whether in a formal or informal capacity and whether intended or not, managers can portray the company in either ethically positive or negative ways. Furthermore, what managers say and do often commits the company to actions that affect the external environment and create a reputation for the company as well. Even when these actions have no discernable impact on the external environment, observers often interpret them positively or negatively.

Demonstrating integrity in external activities has great consequences for companies and managers. One high-profile example is found in the actions of Arthur Andersen in its auditing of Enron's finances. The ethical judgments of key decision makers at Arthur Andersen over the shredding of Enron documents have caused fatal damage to the entire accounting firm. Other companies have been hit with their own ethical challenges. Few big companies can look back over the past without recognizing at least a few ethical missteps—both at home and abroad.

In a U.S. context, fear of an indictment is a powerful motivation for obeying the law. While ethics are not always captured in a country's legal codes, laws can assist managers and companies to draw the lines of appropriate and inappropriate behavior. In an international context, U.S. companies can draw some guidance from the provisions of the Foreign Corrupt Practices Act (FCPA). The FCPA prohibits U.S. companies or employees of U.S. companies from bribing (1) foreign government officials or (2) officers of political parties in foreign countries. While the FCPA does not technically apply to the overseas affiliates of U.S. companies,

companies can be held criminally liable if policies or money can be traced back to the U.S. parent. In addition to U.S. laws, the 29 member nations of the OECD established stringent rules banning bribery in November 1997. The rules went further than those covered by the FCPA to include bribery of executives at state-owned enterprises as well as all members of parliament.

Despite these government actions, crafty managers can find plenty of loopholes and gray areas not formally covered by the FCPA or the OECD regulations. One area left open to interpretation, for example, is the definition of a bribe. Where is the line drawn between a gift and a bribe? Is a $1 pen a gift but a $1,000 pen a bribe? Another concern—particularly for the FCPA—is how to draw the line between the government and private sector. In countries like China, Saudi Arabia, and Indonesia, it is often impossible to reach consensus on where the government sector ends and the private sector begins. Further, while the FCPA and OECD regulations apply to company agents in foreign countries, it is extremely difficult to control the behavior of agents. If agents are paid $1 million dollars to open doors for companies and then spend $750,000 on bribes, is the head office legally accountable? Also, observers have criticized the FCPA and OECD regulations as being weak on the activities of joint venture partners.

Normative versus Descriptive Ethics Managers need to be careful in differentiating between the dominant values and behaviors within a culture (i.e., *descriptive* ethics) from the leader's personal judgments of appropriate behaviors (i.e., *normative* ethics). One huge challenge is in understanding ethical norms in each part of the world where the company conducts business. What do people believe, why do they believe it, and how deep are their beliefs?

The breadth and depth of ethical norms can differ significantly from culture to culture. Several studies have shown a correlation between corrupt practices and national income levels.[2] In one noteworthy case in April 1996, Malaysia's Trade Minister, Rafidah Aziz, told a conference of visiting business executives that bribery and other forms of corruption were normal business practices in her country. While the candor of the Minister's statement surprised some conference participants, it reflected what had become common business norms in her country. Whether poverty breeds corruption or corruption leads to poverty, there is no doubt that corruption interferes with free markets and economic development. In 1997, the World Bank estimated that as much as 5 percent of exports to developing countries—$50 to 80 billion per year—was consumed as payments to corrupt officials.[3] Other studies have shown that in countries that lack comprehensive regulations for curtailing corruption, foreign direct investment inflows are negatively impacted.[4] The challenge of managing in an environment like this is found in the DSL de Mexico case study.

While corrupt practices are more prevalent in some developing economies, the relationship between poverty and corruption is far from perfect. In the late 1990s and early part of the new millennium, corruption scandals have toppled politicians and business leaders in the United States, Belgium, France, Japan, Germany, Italy, and Sweden, to name but a few wealthy countries. If anything, increasing economic development and greater education have emboldened people throughout the developing world and have led to important changes in the political and business climate. In Bulgaria, Zimbabwe, Pakistan, Indonesia, India, Venezuela, and Korea, angry crowds impatient with lethargic reforms have taken to the streets in protest.[5] While progress has been made, wholesale cultural change is difficult to predict.

Three Kinds of Choices When an individual's or a company's ethical standards are different in a negative way from the norms of behavior in a particular country, three kinds of decisions can be made. The first alternative is for the company simply to avoid doing business in the country in question. While this is not an infrequent occurrence, few companies publicly announce that they are pulling out of a country because of ethics or that they are blacklisting countries because of rampant corruption. To save face and keep the door open to revisit the decision later, "business reasons" are often cited as the reason for pulling out of a country.

A second alternative is to continue doing business in the country in question while strictly adhering to "higher" global standards. Out of concern that gifts and gratuities might unduly influence company policy or employee behavior, many companies target this area with their most stringent ethics policies. One high profile example of this is General Motors. In response to allegations of abuses, including the 1995 allegation that several managers in GM's Adam Opel unit participated in a kickback scheme, GM announced in June 1996 a comprehensive policy on gifts and gratuities. The policy essentially outlawed either the giving or receiving of gifts beyond a trivial value anywhere in the world. Wal-Mart's policy is even tougher: it bars employees from accepting or giving gifts of *any* monetary value anywhere in the world.

While concise and easy to interpret, stringent gifts and gratuities policies risk putting companies at a competitive disadvantage versus other companies that do not have such policies. Not only do they sometimes lose business, they risk offending locals with policies that might be interpreted as arrogant. For example, a manager's inability to pay for a customer's dinner or a round of golf is viewed with disdain in many parts of the world.

A final option is for the company and leader to adopt a "when in Rome, do as the Romans do" approach to ethics. Situational ethics is based on the notion that the only valid guide for ethics is the context of the decision. One country's standards, while different from another's, are neither higher nor lower. The argument is that there are no ethical absolutes, particularly in business. Consequently, what works in Country A should have no bearing on what works in Country B.

While it is in some ways logical, a checkerboard approach to ethics can be highly dangerous for companies and managers. Reputations are made and can be lost based on global conduct. Questionable behavior in one country can rarely be contained. Eventually the entire world finds out. Also, inconsistent behaviors not only confuse observers but raise questions about the company's (and its leader's) commitment to *any* principles. While business is business, the importance of trust cannot be overstated.

Integrity in Internal Actions

Integrity is also tested in interactions that are internal to the company. Internal actions involve policies and behaviors that either directly or indirectly impact employees within the company. Because the impact is internal, the external fallout may be minimal or nonexistent. As a consequence, individual managers may be under less pressure to act ethically on internal matters than they are on matters that capture the public's attention. Despite this, ethics are directly correlated with an individual's ability to lead. Unethical behavior can undermine a manager's authority, severely impact morale, and seriously damage a company's ability to execute its strategy.

As a company's operations are exposed to multiple ethical norms across countries, the possibility for ethical conflicts inside the organization mounts. National culture has a direct impact on how managers are *expected* to interact with their employees. The differences can be substantial and raise important ethical questions for global managers. One large study, for example, showed that men in Hong Kong and Taiwan were more likely than men in Canada and Japan to discriminate against women. The same study found that Canadians were less likely to show concern for the employment security of their employees than managers in Hong Kong and Taiwan.[6]

Employee Rights   In controlling for national differences, some researchers have advocated establishing standard employee "rights" around the world.[7] To be effective, these rights need to be embedded in company policies and over time become enmeshed in a company's culture. The objective is to create organizational norms of behavior that supercede national norms and cover all employees. Five areas are the focus of most attention:

- Worker safety.

- Equality in hiring.

- Equality of opportunity for assignments, development, and promotions.

- Comparable compensation.

- Freedom of expression.

However, while employees share a common interest in each of these five areas, the depth of concern and interpretations of meaning can vary significantly from country to country. Some managers play to the lowest standards; others raise standards to the highest levels. It takes a strong leader to impose global standards on employees who may not demand them. At ARCO China, for example, all offshore workers on its drilling platform in the South China Sea must wear safety goggles, even though this standard is not the norm in China nor is it demanded by most employees. While ARCO China could likely get away with lower safety standards in China, it chooses otherwise for ethical reasons. How can it reasonably assert that the safety of workers in the United States is more important than the safety of workers in China? Other companies have compensation, diversity, and family leave policies that are more generous than national norms in the majority of the countries in which they compete. They view their generous treatment of employees as not only a source of long-term competitive advantage but also the "right thing to do." After all, if employees at the head office are treated this way, why not all employees around the world?

Personal Interactions   In addition to influencing behaviors through policies and standards, managers also have *personal* interactions with employees on a regular basis. These interactions come through their direct contact with subordinates, peers, superiors, and, increasingly, contractors. They also socialize and interact with employees with whom they have no direct business connections. During these interactions, some managers have a tendency to differentiate according to country of origin, race, language, gender, and so on. This can be translated into overtly offensive behavior or more subtle differences in how employees are treated. Examples of these kinds of behaviors include

- Sexual harassment.

- Using condescending or belittling language when addressing employees.

- Demanding favors of employees, such as the running of personal errands.

- Physically abusing employees.

While domestic managers face unlimited opportunities for unethical behaviors, tendencies are often amplified when managers travel to or work in countries where perceived power differences between managers and employees are large and where employees feel powerless to speak out against the egregious behaviors of Western executives. One large U.S. company recently fired its country manager in India because of abusive behavior. In his exit interview the manager was confronted with evidence of his condescending behavior and belittling comments. The evidence was collected over a period of five years by visiting expatriate managers. Not a single local employee complained about the abuse, and, in fact, many low-level employees were highly complimentary of their boss because to them his abuse was expected and "normal."

The good news is that inappropriate behaviors can rarely be kept secret. Word of ethical lapses in one country is often rapidly communicated throughout the global organization. Soon everyone knows. In addition to suffering embarrassment and possible dismissal, managers who act unethically jeopardize their ability to lead. Once established, reputations are hard to change, meaning that the damage may take years to repair. To avoid conflicts and the giving of offense, mangers need to exercise care and judgment in making and applying decisions, particularly when they involve unfamiliar issues that cross cultural norms.

Codes of Conduct: Controlling External and Internal Behaviors

In an effort to control for inappropriate external and internal behaviors and to strengthen their reputations both at home and abroad, many companies have adopted stringent codes of conduct. One of the initial advocates of codes of conduct was

U.S. civil rights advocate Reverend Leon Sullivan. In 1977, Dr. Sullivan drafted wide- reaching guidelines designed to persuade American companies to treat employees in South Africa the same way they were treated in the United States. In the late 1990s, with apartheid officially over, Dr. Sullivan, working with U.N. Secretary General Kofi Annan, turned his attention to creating a set of ethical guidelines for all MNCs—U.S. and foreign alike. The guidelines covered a range of corporate responsibility initiatives including human rights, business ethics, the environment, and equal opportunity. By 2002, over 100 prominent companies had signed their support for what has become known as the *Global Sullivan Principles.*

Other companies have adopted custom-made codes of conduct. One of the first industries off the mark has been the apparel industry which employs millions of people around the world, often in low-wage countries. By the mid-1990s companies like Levi Strauss, Nike, and Liz Claiborne had come under heavy criticism for either using sweatshop factories or turning a blind eye to subcontractors who run harsh factories with questionable labor practices. In response, many of these companies have adopted stringent codes of conduct for both themselves and their suppliers and have hired outside auditors to monitor and report compliance. Nike has even started posting the results of its external audits on its website. In Nike's view, strict codes of conduct are simply good business. According to one Nike spokesperson, "If you work with factories to make them better places of employment, quality improves, productivity goes up, there's less waste and you retain workers longer."[8]

Other companies have taken different approaches in establishing codes of conduct. They limit codes of conduct to the actions of individual employees—stealing, bribing, paying kickbacks, sexual harassment, etc. But they do not believe it is appropriate to impose global standards on local factories where working conditions, compensation, and job opportunities are bound by very different norms and worker expectations. While better working conditions and higher paying jobs may benefit some, they can also lead to far few jobs for people desperate for any kind of work. So which is more ethical: good jobs for a few or bad jobs for many? It is often a tough call. And beyond the ethical issues, there are practical issues as well. Wal-Mart, for example, sources from more than 20,000 factories worldwide. Simply keeping track of working conditions, wage rates, employee morale, and so on, would be extremely difficult. And even if Wal-Mart or any other company could track these factories, how often should it audit operations and to whom should it talk when it conducts the audits? Finally, in the case of noncompliance, what time if any should it give subcontractors to improve performance? These are all tough issues that need to be addressed if a meaningful code of conduct is to be put in place.

PHILOSOPHICAL PERSPECTIVES

As managers struggle for help in mastering international ethics, they can turn to the field of philosophy for some direction. Ethics have been a topic philosophers have grappled with since before the time of the ancient Greeks. Most philosophers embrace one of three schools of thought in guiding ethical judgments: utilitarianism, contractarianism, and pluralism.[9] Each of these three perspectives evaluates ethics differently and as a result promotes potentially different responses to ethical decisions.

Utilitarianism is based on a foundation belief in "maximizing net expectable utility . . . for all parties affected by a decision or action."[10] Ethical decisions are those that maximize the overall welfare of stakeholders. Under utilitarianism, the costs and benefits of alternative decisions are weighed and actions taken that balance the interests of all participants.

An example of utilitarianism in action could include the following scenario. The general manager of a company is supervising the construction of a large assembly plant in Country A. The plant is essentially finished, except for a permit of occupancy. The Minister of Industry in Country A refuses to sign the permit leaving the plant unoccupied, thus idling 2,500 workers. The general manager hears that a contribution to the Minister's favorite "charity" will capture his attention and secure the desired signature. The general manager faces the dilemma of whether to make the contribution or see the plant mothballed. On the one hand, he is concerned about making a payment perceived as "unseemly" at home; on the other hand, he realizes that a $1,000 donation will ensure that a $500 million plant is opened, that 2,500 people will be employed, that the lives of 15,000 people (the estimated spillover impact on the broader economy) will be hugely improved including the health and welfare of thousands of children. What is the ethical thing to do? Under the utilitarian perspective, net expected utility is maximized by making the payment.

Contractarianism approaches ethics from a very different perspective. It is based on the belief that ethics are determined by overall fairness as specified in contracts. Decisions are fair when all participants are shown equal deference. Ethics are bound by the rules outlined in the laws of the land or negotiated contracts. If the laws are silent on a matter, then reason would suggest that action or inaction cannot be negatively judged. However, failure to live up to provisions of a contract or actions that break the laws of the land results in a loss of integrity.

Under contractarianism, decision making focuses on the rights of employees to be treated fairly, the rights of suppliers to fair compensation, and rights of consumers to be safe and effective products. An example of contractarianism at work could include the following scenario. The manager of an accounting department of a large manufacturer in Country B is facing a surprise tax audit of the company's books. Documents have to be submitted for review in three days' time. The manager, realizing that it will likely take more than five days of work to complete the task, orders his staff to "work around the clock" until the job is done. However, Country B has stringent employment laws that make it illegal to have female employees work "beyond sunset." The manager, while familiar with the law, believes the law is "unfair" to women, and besides, he has a deadline to meet. What is the ethical course of action? Under contractarianism, the ethical decision would be to allow the women employees to go home at sunset and either have the male employees pick up the slack or find some other means to meet the government deadline.

Pluralism is the third major perspective of ethical behavior. It is based on the "duty" of individuals to act morally. Rather than determining right and wrong by external criteria, pluralism focuses on the obligation of individuals to act in a decent, honorable way. The belief is that people everywhere know the difference between right and wrong and that ethics cannot be imposed through rules or expected utility curves.

An example of pluralism at work could include the following. The traffic manager of a shipping company in Country C believes she has discovered that one of her employees, Carlos, has been stealing radios. While she is not positive about it, she knows that the numbers on the manifests indicate full shipments of radios are being received into the company's warehouse. Forty-eight hours later, the radios are reloaded for shipment out of the country. The number of radios leaving the warehouse is between 5 and 10 percent lower than the numbers being received. The "shrinkage" only occurs when Carlos has been on the receiving dock. Furthermore, on days where the shrinkage has been noticed, Carlos has booked off work early. The traffic manager has heard "through the grapevine" that there is a thriving black market in Country C for consumer electronics like radios. She puts two and two together and concludes that Carlos is guilty. Company policies on theft are clear: immediate dismissal without recourse. These policies are normal in Country C and given Carlos's lack of status in the company, the manager knows that dismissing Carlos would be expected by others in the company and that if she did not act aggressively it could promote further stealing in the plant. Before deciding to act, the manager reviews Carlos's employment record. She learns that Carlos has been working for the company for 24 years, has an unblemished record, and has a dependent family with six children at home. Last year Carlos made $3,240 and took only three days off for sick leave. What would the "ethical" decision be? Under pluralism, the "right" and moral thing to do would be to treat Carlos with respect and dignity. It would be to gather more information and wait on a final decision until all the information was in. And even if it was proven that Carlos was to blame, attempts at rehabilitation should be made before a final termination decision was made.

Each of these three approaches to ethics helps managers make tough decisions. Each has its place and each contributes to an understanding of ethical conduct. In a domestic context, managers would more likely have a reflexive response to the above scenarios. No doubt some expatriate managers would make snap decisions overseas. But, most would struggle with deciding what to do. Without understanding the nuances of local cultures and norms, it is easy to get thrown off balance and be at a loss at deciding what to do. In these cases, different analytical frameworks can be very helpful.

While utilitarianism, contractarianism, and pluralism all help in making sound ethical judgments, not all are equally valuable. All have substantial weaknesses or problems. A major problem with utilitarianism is the accurate determination of "utility," both now and in the future. Understanding and measuring social welfare across multiple countries is essentially impossible. Take the factory start-up example cited above. While it can be argued that a $1,000 "donation" is nothing compared to the huge benefits of the factory, what is not known is the impact of corruption on the government and people of Country A. If companies stopped making payments like this, perhaps the government would fall, a new, more egalitarian government would emerge and people would be even better off. Future utility can never be accurately predicted. Furthermore, how can effective judgments be made around social benefits? There are always trade-offs involved. In many cases stakeholder interests are in serious conflict. What is more "valuable": full employment, profits, education, or health care? The benefits are almost always incommensurate, leading to judgment based on imperfect and often biased data.

Contractarianism and pluralism also have problems, but on balance they may be more useful in a global context. The problem for contractarianism is that while it recognizes rights, whose rights are paramount? When multiple countries are involved, it is often difficult to agree to legal jurisdictions. Are expatriate managers bound only by laws of the foreign country or by laws at home as well? And what happens when the laws are in conflict? Also, contracts and laws are often less than helpful on unanticipated issues. When market conditions change faster than the legal and contractual rules, making ethical decisions can be immensely difficult. Finally, managers need to differentiate between what is ethically defensible and what is good business. The Steve Parker and the SA-Tech Venture case study provides the foundation for a rich discussion of ethics and relationships in joint venture partnerships.

Pluralism also has its problems. Duty, as addressed by pluralism, can also be context-dependent. Duty to whom? To your family? To your employer? To your work team? And for what cause? Does the pursuit of profits represent a duty, and if so, does that duty supercede other duties like obeying the law? While one person might find paying kickbacks and bribes his or her "duty" as a manager, others would be appalled by this interpretation. In the final analysis, integrity is difficult to define in a world where duty has so many different connotations and objectives. The Sicom GmbH and CD Piracy case study provides an excellent vehicle to address company duty in an environment where home and host country norms differ widely.

AN INDIVIDUAL RESPONSIBILITY

Ethics can either be easy or difficult. Those who take the easy approach will use one interpretative framework and determine one set of irrevocable policies for everyone everywhere. Those who take the more difficult approach will start with a core of rigid principles but build from there using a combination of analytical frameworks and allowing for varying degrees of local interpretation. In both approaches, the trade-offs involve the efficiency of clear, irrevocable policies with the effectiveness of policies with higher levels of fluidity. At the end of the day, every leader has the responsibility to determine what is ethical and unethical and what is negotiable and what is "etched in stone." Because managers make decisions for broader organizations, they need to take the responsibility of defining ethical behavior very seriously.

Ethical leadership means more than establishing policies and standards. It requires a proactive approach so that future problems are avoided. In reality, most people do not fully recognize the moral dilemmas around them.[11] They go about their daily activities either unperceptive of the ethical conflicts around them or so convinced of the "rightness" of their standards and ability to interpret actions and intentions that the need for moral judgment is foreign to them. This can be dangerous, in part because global companies—and their managers—are attractive targets for the unscrupulous. The failure to take an aggressive, proactive approach to ethics raises the risks of falling into ethical traps and should be avoided at all cost.

Effective global managers exhibit their integrity by being fearless in confronting ethical dilemmas. To do this requires not only a commitment to ethical leadership, but action and direct personal leadership. In organizations with consistently high ethical standards, managers seem to be particularly good at doing three things: passive learning, active learning, and teaching.

Passive Learning Demonstrating integrity requires the ability to effectively observe and interpret behaviors and practices. Because integrity is embedded in actions and intent, managers need a healthy dose of introspection and external awareness. By understanding different values and beliefs, global managers can better anticipate ethical problems and provide more effective counseling and coaching.

Ethics have a huge contextual component that cannot be understood or appreciated without strong observation skills. Knowledge about the background of individuals, country laws and norms, and relationship histories is critical in developing an objective understanding of context. While some of this knowledge comes through deliberate study, much of it comes from passive learning—observing, absorbing, and filtering information. The knowledge that results is invaluable in determining the correct way of communicating company standards, role-modeling company standards, and enforcing company standards.

Strong observation skills can only come when there is a fondness for the subject in question. Those managers who try to understand people invariably feel closer to them. Emotionally connecting with people is important for a number of reasons. First, it encourages the manager to recognize his or her employees as real people with real feelings. This in turn reduces the likelihood of patronization or other forms of abuse. Second, when employees feel the manager cares about their welfare, they are much more likely to open up and share the challenges they face. This not only leads to more effective business decisions, but provides a format for managers to "teach" the company's values in a nonthreatening setting. Managers need large amounts of employee trust if they are ever going to be successful in heading off future ethical problems.

Active Learning Global managers are constantly aware of the risk of falling into ethical traps. Indeed, if managers are not proactive, they will invariably find themselves in situations that lead to unethical decisions or actions. In order to avoid these situations, effective global managers are active learners who constantly ask tough, probing questions about what is right and wrong. Nor are they prone to take things at face value. To assist in interpreting events and making the "right" decisions, they use trusted advisors liberally. They also feel comfortable referring tough decisions to internal and external legal counsel for advice. They ask lots of questions and are acutely aware of inconsistent responses.

In asking tough questions, global managers set the example for the rest of the organization. Most not only want to ask tough questions for themselves, but to promote a culture that thrives on openness and candor. One tool often used to promote ethical behavior throughout the organization is an ethics forum. Ethics forums are used to openly review tough ethical issues and weigh the pros and cons of possible actions. They can also be used as a decision-making forum that includes a range of technical, legal, and cultural experts.

Teaching   Global managers understand the importance of reinforcing company values and are mindful of the importance of " walking the talk" when it comes to their behaviors. But they also promote an ethics-oriented culture through in-house education and training programs. These programs can be used to teach and flesh out company values, to educate employees on nonnegotiable policies, and to impress upon employees the importance of ethical behavior. Motorola has created 83 different case studies that it uses to train managers in ethical conduct. The cases are presented in selected in-house management programs, managers are grilled on appropriate responses to tough ethical problems, and solutions are provided by professional ethicists and Chairman Bob Galvin.[12] At General Motors Asia Pacific, employees go through a three-step process. First, they are informed of the laws governing corruption throughout the region. Second, employees are given clear guidelines on the company's standards regarding accepting or making facilitating payments. And third, under the direction of Chief Executive for GM Asia Pacific, the General Counsel's office for the region regularly sponsors workshops on ethics for top managers in the region.

INTEGRITY IS GOOD FOR BUSINESS

In matters of internal and external activities, ethics are often complex and always require considerable judgment. Global managers must be believed and trusted by their employees if they are to be effective. But they must also ensure that the companies for which they work have appropriate standards that transcend national boundaries. Effective global managers constantly watch their employees for patterns of troubling behavior. And they are self-critical and introspective in evaluating their own conduct.

A manager who lacks personal morals and who acts in ways that are inconsistent with company standards can destroy a company much faster than a manager who picks a bad strategy. Lapses in ethical judgment are invariably motivated by short-term thinking—immediate gratification or one-time improvements in the numbers. But in the long run, a lack of integrity can undermine relationships with, and the confidences of, employees, customers, suppliers, and governments. Reputations take years to build and can be destroyed in moments.

In the final analysis, unethical behavior—whether real or perceived—can jeopardize a leader's position and bring huge negative consequences for the company. But the flip side is also true. The commitment of global managers to high personal and company standards also promotes numerous benefits. It is only through the exercise of integrity that a leader can bring out the most in employees. When employees view the internal systems as fair and open, and when they believe their leader has sound ethical judgment, the huge discretionary power of individuals and teams can be unleashed. Mastering global ethics, while difficult, can bring huge rewards for both managers and companies.

Supplementary Reading

Andelman, D. "Bribery: the New Global Outlaw," *Management Review,* 87 (4), 1998, pp. 49–51.

Banai, M., & Sama, L. M. "Ethical Dilemmas in MNCs' International Staffing Policies: A Conceptual Framework," *Journal of Business Ethics,* 25 (3), 1998, pp. 221–235.

Badaracco, J. and Webb, A. "Business Ethics: A View from the Trenches," *California Management Review,* 37 (2), 1995, pp. 8–28.

Black, S., Morrison, A., and Gregersen, H. *Global Explorers: The Next Generation of Leaders.* New York: Routledge, 1999.

Brandt, R. *A Theory of the Good and the Right.* Oxford University Press, London, 1979.

Cockcroft, L. "Transnational Bribery: Is It Inevitable?" *Business Strategy Review,* 7 (3), 1979, pp. 30–39.

England, G. "Managers and Their Value Systems: A Five Country Comparative Study," *Columbia Journal of World Business,* 1978.

Goodpaster, K. "Some Avenues for Ethical Analysis in General Management," Teaching note #383-007 (Harvard Business School, Cambridge, MA, 1982).

Hare, R. *Moral Thinking.* Oxford University Press, London. 1981.

Husted, B. W. "Toward a Model of Cross-Cultural Business Ethics: The Impact of Individualism and Collectivism on the Ethical Decision-Making Process," *Academy of Management Proceedings,* 2000, pp. 11–16.

Lee, K. "Ethical Beliefs in Marketing Management: A Cross-Cultural Study," *European Journal of Marketing,* 1982, pp. 58–67.

McCoy, B. "The Parable of the Sadhu," *Harvard Business Review,* September–October 1983, pp. 103–108.

Nash, L. "Ethics Without the Sermon," *Harvard Business Review,* November–December 1981, pp. 78–90.

Nyaw, M. and Ng, I. "A Comparative Analysis of Ethical Beliefs: A Four Country Study," *Journal of Business Ethics,* 13, 1994, pp. 543–555.

Prasad, J. *Impact of the Foreign Corrupt Practices Act of 1977 on U.S. Export.* New York: Garland. 1993.

Presbey, G. M., Struhl, K. J., & Olsen, R. (Eds.). *The Philosophical Quest: A Cross-Cultural Reader* (2/E.). New York: McGraw-Hill, 1999.

Yeung, A. and Ready, D. "Developing Leadership Capabilities of Global Corporations: A Comparative Study in Eight Nations," *Human Resource Management,* Vol. 34 (4), Winter 1999, pp. 529–547.

Endnotes

1. For more on these two perspectives, see A. Morrison, "Integrity and Global Leadership," *Journal of Business Ethics,* vol. 31, 2001, pp. 65–76.
2. P. Wilhelm, "International Validation of the Corruption Perceptions Index: Implications for Business Ethics and Entrepreneurship Education," *Journal of Business Ethics,* February 2002; A. Goldsmith, "Democracy, Property Rights and Economic Growth," *Journal of Development Studies,* Vol. 32, 1995, pp. 157–175.
3. As reported by Nicholas Moss. "Who Bribes Wins." *The European,* December 11, 1997, pp. 26–27.
4. P. Voyer, "The Effect of Corruption on Japanese Foreign Direct Investment." Working paper, Ivey Business School, University of Western Ontario, 2002.
5. "A Global War Against Bribery," *The Economist,* January 16, 1999, p. 22.
6. M. Nyaw, and I. Ng, "A Comparative Analysis of Ethical Beliefs: A Four Country Study," *Journal of Business Ethics,* 13, 1994, pp. 543–555.
7. For a review, see A. Morrison, "Integrity and Global Leadership," Op cit.
8. Amanda Tucker, director of business compliance at Nike, as quoted by T. Vickery, "Social Accountability in Central America," *World Trade,* Vol. 15 (4), April 2002, pp. 48–53.
9. For a more complete review of these three perspectives, see K. Goodpaster, "Some Avenues for Ethical Analysis in General Management," Teaching note #383-007 (Harvard Business School, Cambridge, MA, 1982).
10. Goodpaster, 1982, p. 5.
11. B. McCoy, "The Parable of the Sadhu," *Harvard Business Review,* September–October 1983, pp. 103–108.
12. For a review of this program, see S. Black, A. Morrison, and H. Gregersen, *Global Explorers: The Next Generation of Leaders,* (New York: Routledge, 1999).

Chapter Fifteen

Managing the New Global Workforce

The explosion of foreign direct investment (FDI) has been one of the most important economic trends of the past 15 years. As recently as 1985, FDI stood at about $60 billion per year. By 1997, flows of new FDI surpassed $400 billion; by 1998 FDI reached $600 billion; and by 2000 new flows of investment stood at $1.2 trillion. In 2001, after the stock market bubble burst and worldwide recession curtailed economic activity, flows of FDI still amounted to more than $700 billion. The underlying trends are clear: companies in almost all industries, small as well as large, are undertaking foreign direct investment. And they are pursuing all sorts of FDI: greenfield factories and design centers, cross-border acquisitions, joint ventures, as well as the expansion of existing activities.

Just as important, the geographic mix of foreign investment has changed. A decade ago, more than 80 percent took place among the major industrialized regions of Europe, North America, and Japan. Today, FDI increasingly reaches emerging markets of Asia, Latin America, and Central and Eastern Europe.

As a result, many companies have an increasing share of their sales and assets spread around the world. But another effect is less understood. Thanks to rapid foreign investment, many companies now have a much greater proportion of their workforce outside the home country. No longer are the great majority of employees located in the country of origin, or even in major industrialized countries. Increasingly they are spread broadly across the globe, and include a broad mix of nationalities, languages, and cultures.

Let's take a few examples. In 1991, ABB had 195,000 employees, with the greatest number in Switzerland, Sweden, Germany, and the United States. Over the next 10 years, employment declined in each of those countries, but doubled in Asia, Africa, and the Middle East. Once heavily centered in Europe, ABB's workforce is now spread broadly around the world.

In 1986, Matsushita Electric had 138,000 employees in Japan and 44,000 abroad. Ten years later, Japanese employment had risen 14 percent to 158,000,

This chapter was prepared by Philip Rosenzweig.

while foreign employment was up *245 percent* to 108,000. In 2001, Matsushita for the first time had a majority of employees outside Japan—149,000 overseas compared to 143,000 in Japan.

The same trends hold for major American firms. In the last decade, General Electric has expanded rapidly in Europe, Latin America, and Asia, setting up new factories and design centers. Between 1993 and 1997, while GE's U.S. workforce edged upward from 157,000 to 165,000, its workforce overseas almost doubled, from 59,000 to 111,000. By 2001, GE generated 41 percent of its revenues from outside the United States, and had a truly global workforce, with 70,000 employees in Europe alone. One of America's premier industrial firms entered the 21st century with a global position and a global workforce.[1]

These firms and many others, small as well as large, service as well as manufacturing, have workforces that are distributed broadly across continents, and increasingly in emerging markets of the world. They include people from many countries and cultures, speaking many languages and educated in very different systems.

How are companies responding to the changing shape of their workforce? Many have emphasized the need to manage *diversity*. Their newly diverse workforce should be, they maintain, a source of strength, not a weakness. Some issue statements are saying that "Our diversity is an opportunity." They look for ways that diversity can be used for competitive advantage. These efforts are well-intended, but they don't capture the full challenge. Why? Because in the face of accelerating international growth, companies have to do more than capture the benefits of workforce diversity. They also need its opposite: *consistency*. As companies expand into new markets, one of their greatest challenges has to do with hiring a local workforce and bringing about needed consistency in the performance of key tasks, the delivery of products and services, and the ways employees all over the world can work together.

In brief, the challenge facing multinational firms today is to *forge consistency* in a global workforce while also *fostering diversity*. It is a complex challenge and requires a delicate blending of opposing forces, yet it is of fundamental importance.

The balance of this chapter examines the concepts of diversity and consistency in multinational firms by exploring the concepts separately, then together. Some specific steps are provided, supported by examples from leading firms, for capturing the benefits of both consistency and diversity in a global workforce. These issues are explored in specific detail in the Rentsch in Poland and Mabuchi Motor Co. case studies later in the book.

WHAT DO WE MEAN BY "DIVERSITY"?

"Diversity" can refer to many things. When it comes to workforce management, it commonly has two meanings, one having to do with numerical composition and one having to do with inclusive behavior (see Exhibit 15.1).

EXHIBIT 15.1
Elements of Diversity

Diversity in numerical composition
- Numerical composition for legal compliance
- Numerical composition for market access

Diversity in behavior
- Better individual performance through inclusion
- Better group performance through knowledge exchange

Diversity as Numerical Composition

Most frequently, workforce diversity is thought of in terms of numerical composition. A "diverse workforce" is one that reflects the many different kinds of people in the community or society, usually meaning men and women of different ethnic origins, educational experiences, professional backgrounds, and so forth. When a firm says it must increase its workforce diversity, it usually means hiring more women and ethnic minorities, or citizens of different countries, and promoting them more fully into all levels of the company. The emphasis is on numbers.

Why is diverse composition of the workforce important? One reason has to do with legal compliance. In some countries, workforce diversity is mandated by law. Another reason is a sense of fairness—to many managers, it seems equitable and just to compose a workforce broadly. Much of the writing about diversity comes from the United States, where a diverse workforce commonly refers to racial and gender composition, and can also refer to age, sexual orientation, physical abilities, and religion. Many U.S. firms make a deliberate effort to recruit and promote women and ethnic minorities. For example, the largest American automakers—Daimler Chrysler, Ford, and General Motors—present in their annual reports the gender and racial composition of their workforces, showing the change from one year to the next. These firms and others find it important to show that their workforce reflects the broad diversity of American society.

Diversity in numerical composition is also important for access to specific market segments. For example, many companies have learned to put women into positions that interface with female clients, and similarly many companies in the United States hire Hispanic-Americans to reach the rapidly growing Hispanic community. The emphasis is still on numerical composition, but more for instrumental reasons than legal compliance or a sense of fairness.

Diversity as Inclusive Behavior

Diversity means more than just numerical composition—it also has to do with behavior. It suggests an attitude that respects individual differences, that values all employees, and that fosters an environment where all employees can succeed.

Why is it important to encourage and support diversity of behavior? First, so that all employees feel part of the firm and empowered to develop themselves fully. Intel Corporation is one firm that has defined diversity in this way. Its statement, "Workplace of Choice," explains:

We strive to be a workplace of choice in which people of diverse backgrounds are valued, challenged, acknowledged, and rewarded, leading to increasingly higher levels of fulfilment and productivity.[2]

A workplace that respects diverse behavior may bring the best out of each individual. But the benefits don't stop there. The combination of people from different backgrounds and with different ideas can lead to better overall performance. Groups consisting of people with different world views and experiences can share ideas and perspectives, inspiring new solutions to problems. To some observers, the greatest benefit to diversity has to do with sharing ideas and increasing organizational effectiveness. According to this view, capturing the full benefit of diversity means creating a whole that is more than the sum of its parts.

Diversity in numerical composition and *diversity in behavior* are of course related. It is hard to have one without the other. Diversity in composition is needed to achieve diversity in behavior—it's hard to get breadth of experience and perspective if employees are overwhelmingly of the same race, gender, education, and professional background. At the same time, diversity in behavior creates an inclusive work environment which can attract and retain a broad cross-section of employees, leading to diversity in numerical composition. Each reinforces the other.

Not surprisingly, many companies naturally think of "diversity" as a broad term that encompasses both numerical composition and information sharing. At Coopers & Lybrand, for example, gender diversity has been a major priority. Why the importance placed on women in partner positions? One executive put it this way: "The face of our buyer is changing and they expect people who serve them to represent them. And real diversity brings more creative solutions to our clients." To Coopers & Lybrand, the benefits of diversity are clear: diversity in composition helps mirror the client base, and diversity in behavior leads to improved decisions.[3]

DIVERSITY IN MULTINATIONAL FIRMS

Diversity is important in all firms but takes on particular importance in multinationals. As we saw above, the surge in FDI has created a new global workforce, with a more complex set of nationalities, cultures, and educational backgrounds. In terms of sheer numbers, workforces are already more diverse. But having a diverse workforce is one thing; capturing the full benefits of diversity is something else. In fact, it is more imperative than ever for multinational firms to think clearly about the nature of diversity and to take steps to make the most of diversity.

Diversity in numerical composition is critical for multinational firms for several reasons. Again, a first reason is legal. Many countries impose limits on the number or the proportion of expatriates. For example, Colombian law stipulates that the subsidiary of a foreign company must be 90 percent composed of Colombians. Just as important, operating successfully in national markets calls for a workforce that speaks the local language, understands traditions and rules of behavior, and interacts effectively with local customers, public officials, and other stakeholders. Expatriates may be helpful in getting a new subsidiary established and transferring practices to the local operation, but over time it is important to bring local managers into key decision-making roles. This is true whether indigenisation pressures (see Larson in Nigeria case) exist or not. At Gillette, diversity among its top managers is a high priority. Gillette's president, Michael C. Hawley, explained: "I don't think you can be a global company and say you have Americans running it."[4] Two of Gillette's four executive vice presidents are Europeans. Its business in the former Soviet Union, to offer just one example, is headed by a Frenchman, supported by an Egyptian controller, an English sales director, and officers from Pakistan and Ireland.

Just as important for multinationals is diversity in behavior. A first priority, critical to hiring and retaining employees, is creating an inclusive work environment. In rapidly growing markets, such as China and Central and Eastern Europe, competition for local talent is intense. Offering a higher salary is not enough—employees who are attracted by a high salary might one day leave for more money elsewhere. Providing opportunities for development and career advancement is a better bet to attract the best new talent. Firms that value and reward diversity will retain key employees, reducing costs associated with new hiring and training.

Diversity of behavior is also vital to stimulate creativity and innovation. Because it brings together people of different experiences, perspectives, and backgrounds, a diverse workforce has the potential to achieve higher performance than a homogenous workforce. Many multinationals recognize that the cultural diversity of their workforce is a major asset, bringing a wealth of viewpoints, traditions, and ways of solving problems. By leveraging diverse viewpoints and experiences, individuals can learn from each other and the company can increase effectiveness. One multinational that has thought explicitly about the benefits of diversity is the consulting firm, Cap Gemini. Its CEO, Geoff Unwin, noted: "Diversity brings a lot to the company. . . . When people think differently, it puts a different perspective on problems. We exploit that."[5]

THE LIMITS OF DIVERSITY

For all the reasons listed above, many multinational firms agree that diversity—both in numerical composition and in behavior—is a high priority. Yet in practice, benefiting from diversity has proven quite difficult. Why should this be so? One reason is that diversity in multinational firms is much more complex than in primarily domestic firms. In the United States, for example, a workforce may be diverse in race and gender but is still very homogeneous along a number of other dimensions: use of language, assumptions about the economic system, educational background, and in some basic cultural values. By contrast, multinationals confront diversity on a great many dimensions. For starters, they contend with differences in language—communication at its most basic level among employees may be problematic. They also face differences in culture, manifested in styles of management, attitudes toward hierarchy, approaches to teamwork, ways of expressing agreement and disagreement, participation in decision making, and so forth.

EXHIBIT 15.2
Elements of
Consistency

Consistency in output
- Consistent product quality
- Consistent service delivery

Consistency in behavior
- Consistency in how we communicate
- Consistency in how we interact

Moreover, employees in different countries may operate in markedly different economic systems, legal systems, educational systems, and labor markets.

These many dimensions present the multinational firm with a bewildering problem. Is diversity on *all* of these dimensions expected to be a source of advantage? Can they really imagine that more diversity on all these dimensions will be helpful? Or might differences on some dimensions be a source of fragmentation and conflict? Of the many dimensions we can identify, which are most worthy of attention—language, culture, education, race, gender, age, religion, or some others?

Whereas many U.S. firms begin at a point of relative employee homogeneity and try to promote greater diversity in racial and gender representation, the multinational firm begins from a point of relative heterogeneity. Given this starting point, multinational firms cannot push only for diversity; they must also try to establish and maintain some measure of consistency and cohesion among disparate parts. As they expand around the world, bringing local citizens into their workforce, they face an opposite and equally important challenge: how to forge consistency.

WHAT DO WE MEAN BY "CONSISTENCY"?

There are two elements of consistency: consistency of output and consistency of behavior. Consistency of output refers to the nature of goods and services provided to customers and stakeholders: quality, reliability, service delivery, and so forth. Achieving consistency in output is a basic requirement for any high-performing firm.

How do companies achieve consistency in output? By emphasizing consistency in behavior. By training employees in specific ways. By forging shared values and establishing common ways of communicating. By developing processes and practices that are used effectively throughout the organization, allowing employees to interact efficiently (see Exhibit 15.2).

Consistency in Multinationals

Forging consistency for any company is a challenge, but for multinationals, with operations spread across the world, it is a monumental challenge. Take Heineken, a leading international beer. Heineken is brewed and bottled at more than 120 sites worldwide, from Singapore to Capetown to its largest brewery in Zoeterwoude, outside of Amsterdam. The quality of its beer has to be absolutely consistent, batch after batch, year after year, no matter the continent or culture.

Brewery workers, scientists, technicians—Heineken's workforce has to do things the same way everywhere.

Consistency of output is also critical in multinational service firms. The customers at Accor's leading hotel brands, Sofitel and Novotel, are globally mobile. They expect the same level of service whether in France, Brazil, or Korea. Yet Sofitel and Novotel operate in more than 35 countries and on 6 continents. Other leading multinationals, like J.P. Morgan, and SAP, all have multinational firms as their clients. Excellent service on a consistent basis is essential.

How do these far-flung multinationals bring about consistency of output? By focusing on consistency of behavior. They all pay close attention to employee selection and place great emphasis on training. Heineken brings key employees to Zoeterwoude for technical training. Accor also relies on careful selection and offers extensive training, both at its Academie Accor in France and onsite at thousands of hotels around the world. The goal: to make sure that everywhere in the world, key tasks are performed in a similar manner.

ACHIEVING CONSISTENCY *AND* DIVERSITY

Any company seeks the benefits of diversity while also bringing about consistency in output and behavior. But for multinationals, with workforces increasingly dispersed around the world, the challenge is even greater. Greater geographic dispersion means a greater need to respect differences, to make use of divergent ideas, to attract and retain a wide variety of employees. At the same time, the broadly dispersed nature of the global workforces means that achieving consistency is more important than ever.

How well have multinationals adjusted to the new global workforce? The record so far is decidedly mixed. A few multinationals have expanded so quickly, and so dramatically, that they haven't been able to forge coherence and consistency among employees around the world. The result is erratic product quality or customer service, and poor international communications for the lack of clear processes and shared ways of making decisions. But even more common are multinationals so concerned with maintaining consistency, especially as they contend with geographic complexity, that they overlook the need for diversity. They train local employees according to the established ways of doing things, but miss opportunities to use new ideas. They find it hard to attract outstanding talent into their organization—after all, why would a talented local manager want to join a company that doesn't foster diversity? In either event, these firms may design brilliant global strategies but cannot fully implement them since they have not developed a workforce capable of achieving high consistency while also benefiting from diversity.

RECOMMENDATIONS FOR MULTINATIONALS

How can multinationals foster diversity in its global workforce while also forging consistency? There are no easy answers, but the experiences of several successful firms offer some practical guidelines:

1. Recognize that Diversity and Consistency are Two Sides of One Coin

For starters, multinationals must recognize that diversity and consistency are both essential for high performance. The challenge is not to promote diversity alone, for that could suggest that "anything goes" or that "all differences are good"; nor is it to insist upon rigid conformity of behavior around the world, which negates the benefits of diversity. Rather, it is to identify the key elements of consistency needed to succeed, and to make the most of diversity on other dimensions.

The place to begin is with a discussion of consistency. What, a company should ask, are the qualities of conduct and the elements of behavior that we all should share? What should all members of our firm have in common? This exercise can help clarify where consistency is important and where it is not. The point is to identify the common spine that holds the organization together. Of course, what also becomes clear is that most of these qualities have little to do with many dimensions of diversity, including national origin, religion, gender, or race.

One company that has explicitly identified a set of basic behavioral norms is Nestlé. The world's largest food company, Nestlé has 459 factories and 200,000 employees spread over the world. Given this broad dispersion of activities, the firm takes several measures to forge consistency. It describes clearly the qualities of a "Nestlé Manager," applicable the world over. It articulates its principles of organization. It states explicitly the "Basics of the Nestlé Culture," including a shared commitment to pragmatism, personal modesty, and product quality.

But Nestlé is not concerned solely with forging consistency. As a vast and decentralized organization, whose products must conform to local tastes, and where innovation is essential, it must encourage local decision making. In formulating beverages, in devising advertising campaigns for confectionery products, and in countless other cases, employees have to take account of local conditions. The nature of Nestlé's industry makes local initiative all the more important. Because food products are closely linked to local eating and social habits, they have to be tailored to each locale. Diversity is therefore an explicit policy:

> Nestlé makes an effort to integrate itself as much as possible into the cultures and traditions of the different countries where it operates. Nestlé, therefore, accepts cultural and social diversity and does not discriminate on ethnic, religious, or any other basis.[6]

For Nestlé, the emphasis on consistency in some things while supporting diversity in others is not a contradiction, but a pragmatic way to bring about coherence on a core of values as well as creativity and responsiveness on a range of issues.

2. Allow Greater Importance for Either Diversity or Consistency, Depending on Strategic Imperative

Although diversity and consistency are both important, at any given time one or the other may be more important. After all, firms are not monolithic. They are composed of many subsidiaries and business units, at different stages of evolution and facing different challenges. Depending on the circumstances, greater emphasis may be given to diversity or consistency.

Take initial entry to a new market. For many firms, the immediate priority is to forge consistency—that is, to make sure that local employees are trained on key tasks, that they comply with safety standards, and are able to deliver needed output. As we saw above, Heineken operates 120 breweries in 84 countries, some of which it owns fully, some owned partially, and others which it runs under licence. The need for workforce consistency at Heineken is obvious. Not surprisingly, when starting a new brewery the primary emphasis is on forging consistency. Sharing new ideas and making the most of diversity is less important, at the outset, than ensuring consistent output. As an example, Heineken created a joint venture in Vietnam in 1991, and over the next 18 months hired more than 200 people, most of whom had never worked in a private company, much less a brewery. Heineken's single most important task was to train these new employees so that rigorous global quality standards would be met. Forging consistency took precedence.

3. Allow Local Units to Identify Their Most Important Dimensions of Diversity

After forging initial consistency, fostering diversity may become more of a priority. But again, various divisions or countries may have different needs regarding diversity. While corporate headquarters may be tempted to define the key issues, some multinationals take a different approach, asking local business units to define the key dimensions of diversity for themselves. These units may be asked: *Where could active sharing of information and ideas be most fruitful?* And: *Where are relations among our employees most problematic?* Once local units define their most important dimensions of diversity, they may take steps to address misunderstandings and misperceptions, and thereby benefit not only their local unit but the broader multinational.

One leading firm with a strong commitment to making the most of employee diversity is British Petroleum. Rather than taking a centrally driven approach, BP has encouraged several local units to define for themselves their most pressing concerns about diversity. For one unit, the interaction between local nationals and expatriates was identified as an area for improvement. In another, gender relations were the key topic. For still another unit, the challenge of managing diversity involved the ethnic diversity of the local workforce. Each unit could then take steps to improve diversity—both in terms of numerical composition and also building an inclusive work environment—adhering to one overarching view of diversity, but allowing local adaptation. The result was not only a more fine-grained approach, sensitive to the needs of particular units, but also helped create a sense of confidence, as each unit could define its own priorities.

4. Emphasize Joint Problem Solving and Collaboration

One of the most important benefits of diversity in a multinational firm is the promise of collaboration and joint problem solving among units around the world. Getting employees from different nationalities and traditions to work well together sounds easy—but actual examples are not abundant. The need for consistency often results in a single approach, usually reflecting the dominant home country culture, applied everywhere in the world. Consistency is achieved, but there is a corresponding failure to capture the benefits of local experience and insight.

One company that made significant strides to capture the benefits of joint problem solving is Mercedes-Benz. Consistency is critical—its automobiles have to meet the highest standard of quality. "In Germany," said one manager, "we don't say we build a car. We say we build a Mercedes."[7] Until the early 1990s, Mercedes-Benz designed and built all its passenger cars in Germany. Achieving consistency was made easier by having relatively few plants, located close-by, where employees spoke German and shared a common culture. In 1993, Mercedes-Benz announced it would build a new sports utility vehicle plant in Vance, Alabama. Whether Mercedes could maintain its quality while manufacturing in a different part of the world, with a different set of workers, was not obvious. Its challenge: to achieve consistent quality while also capturing benefits of diversity. Over the next few years, Mercedes-Benz explicitly sought to bring about consistency in workmanship and quality, while also retaining and even building upon the particular capabilities of an American workforce. Rather than impose a German approach of hierarchy and rigidity on American workers at the new sports utility vehicle plant in Vance, Alabama, Mercedes made a concerted effort to blend its traditional emphasis on quality and workmanship with distinctly American norms of informality and openness. The result has been a successful new venture that builds on the strengths of both cultures. *"Not Invented Here"* has been replaced by *"We Invented It Together."* The successful experience in Alabama, in turn, has helped guide collaboration among Chrysler and Mercedes employees in the years following the 1998 merger.

5. Facilitate Constructive Discussions about Diversity

A diverse workforce inevitably introduces friction and misunderstanding. Even if the benefits of diversity are accepted by all, the day-to-day experience of working with people of different cultures, languages, and educational systems is often frustrating. Accordingly, multinationals must do more than assert the importance of a diverse workforce; they must take steps to facilitate communication, understanding, and exchange of ideas. One place to start is to create an environment where it is safe to discuss differences—that is, where differences may be talked about in a constructive and positive way.

An example of how companies can address the issue of national diversity head-on was found at Bull, the French-based computer company that acquired a division of Honeywell in the United States in the late 1980s. Misunderstanding between French and American employees persisted for some time after the acquisition. Rather than let these problems fester, Bull conducted employee discussion groups about cultural differences, bringing together American and French employees and allowing them to express their perceptions and feelings in their own language. The discussions were videotaped, edited, and used for teaching purposes throughout the firm. The effort had several intentions: to help teach and communicate about differences; to legitimize the open discussion of differences, and to let employees see that frustration and anxiety is often normal in the discussion of differences.[8]

6. Monitor Progress in Numerical Composition

As noted above, diversity in numerical composition and in behavior are both important, and in fact each is needed for the other. But if broad numerical composition is not *sufficient* to make the most of diversity, it is to some degree *necessary,* for without a good mix of managers there can be little hope of effectively sharing knowledge. Multinational firms should therefore monitor diversity in hiring and in management development. The point is not to promote based on narrow numerical criteria, but to be alert for signs that promotions tend to favor one group—whether nationality, gender, educational degree, or some other—more than another.

At one leading European industrial firm, several efforts have been made to encourage diversity in management ranks. To identify young managers and not rely too heavily on seniority, it is requested that any short list of candidates for key management positions should include at least one person under 35 years of age. This approach forces managers to think beyond seniority and helps bring talented young managers to the attention of executives. Any short-list of candidates must also include people of different nationalities. To break the continual reliance on expatriates, it is requested that at the time a manager is sent abroad, a local manager is designated as his or her successor. This way, the expatriate will not merely be replaced by another expatriate. These steps are not intended to produce a rigid quota system for managers, but to force executives to think broadly about potential candidates, and to break the mindset that the "right" manager must fit a certain mold.

7. Lead from the Top: It All Starts with the CEO

Finally, strong commitment from the chief executive is essential when embarking on any effort to forge consistency and to foster diversity. Without a clear message, sent strongly and repeatedly from the top, little success can be expected.

One multinational that has been successful in forging consistency while fostering diversity is Hewlett-Packard. Consistency is seen in the set of management principles known as the *HP Way.* Employees everywhere find a commitment to openness, to respect, to informality. These are the bonds that hold HP together. Consistency is also critical in the processes used for product design and manufacturing. Global customers call for a consistent approach to service and support. In all these areas and more, HP strives for consistency in its workforce. At the same time, there is an explicit emphasis on diversity. As one company document explained:

> Diversity is much more than a program or a legal requirement at HP; it's a business priority for several compelling reasons. We sell to a diverse, global customer base. We operate in many countries and cultures, where we need to attract and retain

outstanding employees and partners. In addition, a culture that fosters respect for and appreciation of differences among people clearly helps teamwork, productivity, and morale.[9]

Toward this end, successive chief executives at Hewlett-Packard—Lew Platt in the 1990s and then Carly S. Fiorina, CEO since 1999 (and notably the first woman chief executive at a Fortune 50 company in the United States) have personally and consistently exemplified a commitment to workforce diversity. Indeed, at HP in 2001, three of the top seven executives are women.

Summary

For large multinationals like Nestlé, Heineken, Mercedes-Benz, BP, and Hewlett-Packard, the importance of forging consistency and fostering diversity has long been apparent. For other firms, only recently multinational, the need is only now becoming clear. But with recent shifts in the global workforce, more and more firms are recognizing the challenge.

As global competition centers more and more on knowledge, creativity, and human talent, multinational firms are finding it more and more important to make full use of their entire workforce, tapping the creative energy and talents of all their employees. Their task is to find ways of succeeding not *in spite* of a diverse workforce, but *because* of it. At the same time, consistency is more important than ever. The integration of activities calls for close communication and reliable interaction. The presence of global customers requires a single integrated approach to product delivery. Consistency as well as diversity is key.

Striving for consistency and fostering diversity is a continual process. There is no final resting point where a firm attains high consistency and high diversity once and for all. Managers cannot grasp consistency and diversity in a single step; they have to continually improve both, now pushing consistency and then stressing diversity, emphasizing commonality and deriving the full benefits from differences. When the multinational sets up a foreign subsidiary and hires a local workforce, it emphasizes *consistency.* When it tries to make the most of capabilities around the world, it stresses *diversity.* Sharing expertise requires a common single language or a shared information system—that brings us back to *consistency.* Integrating local nationals into important management positions means *diversity.* But a company will only feel confident putting local nationals in key positions when they have sufficient experience, and sufficient credibility, to do a good job—when they are *consistent* with managers everywhere else.

The best multinationals know that forging consistency and fostering diversity is a continuing processes. They stress consistency in some functions and emphasize diversity in others; they emphasize diversity in some areas and demand consistency in others. They understand both as a never-ending process, as means not ends. Yet thinking explicitly about consistency as well as diversity, and coming to see them as complementary rather than as opposites to be balanced, is a vital step toward successfully managing the new global workforce.

Supplementary Reading

Distefano, Joseph J. and Martha Maznevski, "Creating Value with Diverse Teams in Global Management," *Organizational Dynamics,* Vol. 29, No. 1, 45-63, 2000.

Gentile, Mary C. *Managerial Excellence through Diversity: Text and Cases,* Chicago: Irwin, 1996.

Harvey, Michael G., Novicevic, Milorad, M., and Cheri Speier, "An Innovative Global Management Staffing System: A Competency-Based Perspective," *Human Resource Management,* Winter 2000.

Mendenhall, Mark E. and Gunter K. Stahl, "Expatriate Training and Development: Where Do We Go From Here?" *Human Resource Management,* Summer/Fall 2000.

Roberts, Karen, Kossek, Ellen E., and Cynthia Ozeki, "Managing the Global Workforce: Challenges and Strategies," *The Academy of Management Executive,* November 1998.

Ross, Rachael and Robin Schneider, *From Equality to Diversity: A Business Case for Equal Opportunities.* London: Pitman Publishing, 1992.

Thomas, David A., and Robin J. Ely, "Making Differences Matter: A New Paradigm for Managing Diversity," *Harvard Business Review,* September-October 1996.

Endnotes

1. This chapter was prepared by Philip Rosenzweig. It draws on the author's *European Management Journal* article of the same title. Vol. 16, No. 6, 1998, pp. 644–652.
2. *Intel Corporation 1997 Annual Report,* page 28. Also: www.intel.com/intel/community/workplace.
3. Ms. Iris Goldfein, Vice Chairman, National Human Resources, quoted in *Financial Times,* May 26, 1997, p. 8.
4. William C. Symonds, "Gillette's Edge," *Business Week,* January 19, 1998, p. 47.
5. *Financial Times,* April 21, 1998.
6. "The Basic Nestle Management and Leadership Principles," Nestlé company document.
7. Bill Vlasic, "In Alabama, the Soul of a New Mercedes?" *Business Week,* March 31, 1997.
8. *Cultural Diversity: At the Heart of Bull,* Yarmouth ME: Intercultural Press, Inc.
9. Letter to Shareholders *Hewlett-Packard 1994 Annual Report.*

Part Two

Cases on Internationalization

Chapter Sixteen

The Global Branding of Stella Artois

In April 2000, Paul Cooke, chief marketing officer of Interbrew, the world's fourth largest brewer, contemplated the further development of their premium product, Stella Artois, as the company's flagship brand in key markets around the world. Although the long-range plan for 2000–2002 had been approved, there still remained some important strategic issues to resolve.

A BRIEF HISTORY OF INTERBREW

Interbrew traced its origins back to 1366 to a brewery called Den Hoorn, located in Leuven, a town just outside of Brussels. In 1717, when it was purchased by its master brewer, Sebastiaan Artois, the brewery changed its name to Artois.

The firm's expansion began when Artois acquired a major interest in the Leffe Brewery in Belgium in 1954, the Dommelsch Brewery in the Netherlands in 1968, and the Brassiere du Nord in France in 1970. In 1987, when Artois and another Belgian brewery called Piedboeuf came together, the merged company was named

Anthony Goerzen prepared this case under the supervision of Professor Paul Beamish solely to provide material for class discussion. The authors do not intend to illustrate either effective or ineffective handling of a managerial situation. The authors may have disguised certain names and other identifying information to protect confidentiality.

Interbrew. The new company soon acquired other Belgian specialty beer brewers, building up the Interbrew brand portfolio with the purchase of the Hoegaarden brewery in 1989 and the Belle-Vue Brewery in 1990.

Interbrew then entered into a phase of rapid growth. The company acquired breweries in Hungary in 1991, in Croatia and Romania in 1994, and in three plants in Bulgaria in 1995. Again in 1995, Interbrew completed an unexpected major acquisition by purchasing Labatt, a large Canadian brewer also with international interests. Labatt had operations in the United States, for example, with the Latrobe brewery, home of the Rolling Rock brand. Labatt also held a substantial minority stake in the second largest Mexican brewer, Femsa Cerveza, which produced Dos Equis, Sol, and Tecate brands. Following this major acquisition, Interbrew went on, in 1996, to buy a brewery in the Ukraine and engaged in a joint venture in the Dominican Republic. Subsequently, breweries were added in China in 1997, Montenegro and Russia in 1998, and another brewery in Bulgaria and one in Korea in 1999.

Thus, through acquisition expenditures of US$2.5 billion in the previous four years, Interbrew had transformed itself from a simple Belgian brewery into one of the largest beer companies in the world. By 1999, the company had become a brewer on a truly global scale that now derived more that 90 percent of its volume from markets outside Belgium. It remained a privately held company, headquartered in Belgium, with subsidiaries and joint ventures in 23 countries across four continents.

THE INTERNATIONAL MARKET FOR BEER

In the 1990s, the world beer market was growing at an annual rate of 1 to 2 percent. In 1998, beer consumption reached a total of 1.3 billion hectolitres (hls). There were, however, great regional differences in both market size and growth rates. Most industry analysts split the world market for beer between growth and mature markets. The mature markets were generally considered to be North America, Western Europe and Australasia. The growth markets included Latin America, Asia, Central and Eastern Europe including Russia. Although some felt that Africa had considerable potential, despite its low per capita beer consumption, the continent was not considered a viable market by many brewers because of its political and economic instability (see Exhibit 1).

EXHIBIT 1
The World Beer Market in 1998

Source: Canadean Ltd.

Region	% of Global Consumption	Growth Index ('98 vs. 92)	Per Capita Consumption (in litres)
Americas	35.1%	112.6	57
Europe	32.8	97.7	54
Asia Pacific	27.2	146.2	11
Africa	4.6	107.7	8
Middle East/Central Asia	0.4	116.0	2

Mature Markets

The North American beer market was virtually stagnant, although annual beer consumption per person was already at a sizeable 83 litres per capita (lpc). The Western European market had also reached maturity with consumption of 79 lpc. Some analysts believed that this consumption level was under considerable pressure, forecasting a decline to near 75 lpc over the medium term. Australia and New Zealand were also considered mature markets, with consumption at 93 lpc and 84 lpc, respectively. In fact, volumes in both markets, New Zealand in particular, had declined through the 1990s following tight social policies on alcohol consumption and the emergence of a wine culture.

Growth Markets

Given that average consumption in Eastern Europe was only 29 lpc, the region appeared to offer great potential. This consumption figure, however, was heavily influenced by Russia's very low level, and the future for the large Russian market was unclear. Further, some markets, such as the Czech Republic that consumed the most beer per person in the world at 163 lpc, appeared to have already reached maturity. Central and South America, on the other hand, were showing healthy growth and, with consumption at an average of 43 lpc, there was believed to be considerable upside. The most exciting growth rates, however, were in Asia. Despite the fact that the market in this region had grown by more than 30 percent since 1995, consumption levels were still comparatively low. In China, the region's largest market, consumption was only 16 lpc and 20 to 25 lpc in Hong Kong and Taiwan. Although the 1997 Asian financial crisis did not immediately affect beer consumption (although company profits from the region were hit by currency translation), demand in some key markets, such as Indonesia, was reduced and in others growth slowed. The situation, however, was expected to improve upon economic recovery in the medium term.

BEER INDUSTRY STRUCTURE

The world beer industry was relatively fragmented with the top four players accounting for only 22 percent of global volume—a relatively low figure as compared to 78 percent in the soft drinks industry, 60 percent in tobacco and 44percent in spirits. This suggested great opportunities for consolidation, a process that had already begun two decades prior. Many analysts, including those at Interbrew, expected that this process would probably accelerate in the future. The driver behind industry rationalization was the need to achieve economies of scale in production, advertising and distribution. It was widely recognized that the best profit margins were attained either by those with a commanding position in the market or those with a niche position. However, there were several factors that mitigated the trend towards rapid concentration of the brewing industry.

One factor that slowed the process of consolidation was that the ratio of fixed versus variable costs of beer production was relatively high. Essentially, this meant that there was a limited cost savings potential that could be achieved by bringing more operations under a common administration. Real cost savings could be generated by purchasing and then rationalizing operations through shifting production to more efficient (usually more modern) facilities. This approach, however, required large initial capital outlays. As a result, in some markets with "unstable" economies, it was desirable to spread out capital expenditures over a longer period of time to ensure appropriate profitability in the early stages. A second factor that may have had a dampening effect on the trend towards industry consolidation was that local tastes differed. In some cases, beer brands had hundreds of years of heritage behind them and had become such an integral part of everyday life that consumers were often fiercely loyal to their local brew. This appeared to be a fact in many markets around the world.

INTERBREW'S GLOBAL POSITION

Through Interbrew's acquisitions in the 1990s, the company had expanded rapidly. During this period, the company's total volumes had increased more than fourfold. These figures translated to total beer production of 57.5 million hls in 1998 (when including the volume of all affiliates), as compared to just 14.7 million hls in 1992. Volume growth had propelled the company into the number four position among the world's brewers.

Faced with a mature and dominant position in the declining Belgian domestic market, the company decided to focus on consolidating and developing key markets, namely Belgium, the Netherlands, France and North America, and expansion through acquisition in Central Europe, Asia and South America. Subsequently, Interbrew reduced its dependence on the Belgian market from 44 percent in 1992 to less that 10 percent by 1998 (total volumes including Mexico). Concurrently, a significant milestone for the company was achieved by 1999 when more than 50 percent of its total volume was produced in growth markets (including Mexico). Interbrew had shifted its volume so that the Americas accounted for 61 percent of its total volume, Europe added 35 percent, and Asia Pacific the remaining four percent.

Taken together, the top 10 markets for beer accounted for 86 percent of Interbrew's total volume in 1998 (see Exhibit 2). The Mexican beer market alone accounted for 37 percent of total volume in 1998. Canada, Belgium, the United States and the United Kingdom were the next most important markets. However, smaller, growing markets such as Hungary, Croatia, Bulgaria, and Romania had begun to increase in importance.

Adding to its existing breweries in Belgium, France and the Netherlands, Interbrew's expansion strategy in the 1990s had resulted in acquisitions in Bosnia-Herzegovina, Bulgaria, Canada, China, Croatia, Hungary, Korea, Montenegro, Romania, Russia, the Ukraine, the United States, in a joint venture in South Korea, and in minority equity positions in Mexico and Luxembourg. Through these breweries, in addition to those that were covered by licensing agreements in Australia, Italy, Sweden and the United Kingdom, Interbrew sold its beers in over 80 countries.

EXHIBIT 2
Interbrew's 1998
Share of the World's
Top 10 Markets

Source: Canadean Ltd.

Rank	Country	Volume (000 HL)	Market Share
1	USA	3,768	1.6%
2	China	526	0.3%
3	Germany	-	-
4	Brazil	-	-
5	Japan	-	-
6	UK	3,335	5.5%
7	Mexico	21,269	45.0%
8	Spain	-	-
9	South Africa	-	-
10	France	1,915	8.4%
Total		30,813	3.6%

INTERBREW'S CORPORATE STRUCTURE

Following the acquisition of Labatt in 1995, Interbrew's corporate structure was divided into two geographic zones: the Americas and Europe/Asia/Africa. This structure was in place until September 1999 when Interbrew shifted to a fully integrated structure to consolidate its holdings in the face of industry globalization. Hugo Powell, formerly head of the Americas division, was appointed to the position of chief executive officer (CEO). The former head of the Europe/Africa/Asia division assumed the role of chief operating officer, but subsequently resigned and was not replaced, leaving Interbrew with a more conventional structure, with the five regional heads and the various corporate functional managers reporting directly to the CEO.

RECENT PERFORMANCE

1998 had been a good year for Interbrew in terms of volume in both mature and growth markets. Overall, sales volumes increased by 11.1 percent as most of the company's international and local brands maintained or gained market share. In terms of the compounded annual growth rate, Interbrew outperformed all of its major competitors by a wide margin. While Interbrew's 1998 net sales were up 29 percent, the best performing competitor achieved an increase of only 16 percent. Of Interbrew's increased sales, 67 percent was related to the new affiliates in China, Montenegro and Korea. The balance was the result of organic growth. Considerable volume increases were achieved also in Romania (72 percent), Bulgaria (28 percent), Croatia (13 percent), and the United States (14 percent). While volumes in Western Europe were flat, duty-free sales grew strongly. In the U.S. market, strong progress was made by Interbrew's Canadian and Mexican brands, and Latrobe's Rolling Rock was successfully relaunched. In Canada, performance was strong, fuelled by a 2 percent increase in domestic consumption. Labatt's sales of Budweiser (produced under license from Anheuser Busch) also continued to grow rapidly.

Given that the premium and specialty beer markets were growing quickly, particularly those within the large, mature markets, Interbrew began to shift its product mix to take advantage of this trend and the superior margins it offered. A notable brand success was Stella Artois, for which total global sales volumes were up by 19.7 percent. That growth came from sales generated by Whitbread in the United Kingdom, from exports, and from sales in Central Europe where Stella Artois volumes took off. The strong growth of Stella Artois was also notable in that it was sold in the premium lager segment. In Europe, Asia Pacific and Africa, Interbrew's premium and specialty beers, which generated a bigger margin, increased as a proportion of total sales from 31 percent in 1997 to 33 percent in 1998. This product mix shift was particularly important since intense competition in most markets inhibited real price increases.

Success was also achieved in the United States specialty beer segment where total volume had been growing at 9 percent annually in the 1990s. In 1998, Interbrew's share of this growing market segment had risen even faster as Labatt USA realized increased sales of 16 percent. The other continuing development was the growth of the light beer segment, which had become over 40 percent of the total sales. Sales of Labatt's Blue Light, for example, had increased and Labatt Blue had become the number three imported beer in the United States, with volumes up 18 percent. Latrobe's Rolling Rock brand grew by 4 percent, the first increase in four years. Interbrew's Mexican brands, Dos Equis, Tecate and Sol, were also up by 19 percent.

Following solid volume growth in profitable market segments, good global results were realized in key financial areas. Net profit, having grown for each of the previous six consecutive years, was 7.7 billion Belgian francs (BEF) in 1998, up 43.7 percent from the previous year. Operating profit also rose 7.9 percent over 1997, from 14.3 BEF to 15.4 BEF; in both the Europe/Asia/Africa region and the Americas, operating profit was up by 8.5 percent and 4.9 percent respectively. Further, Interbrew's EBIT margin was up 58.1 percent as compared to the best performing competitor's figure of 17.0 percent. However, having made several large investments in Korea and Russia, and exercising an option to increase its share of Femsa Cerveza in Mexico from 22 percent to 30 percent, Interbrew's debt-equity ratio increased from 1.04 to 1.35. As a result, interest payments rose accordingly.

Interbrew also enjoyed good results in volume sales in many of its markets in 1999. Although Canadian sales remained largely unchanged over 1998, Labatt USA experienced strong growth in 1999, with volumes up by 10 percent. There was a positive evolution in Western European volumes as well, as overall sales were up by 6.5 percent overall in Belgium, France and the Netherlands. Central European markets also grew with Hungary showing an increase of 9.6 percent, Croatia up by 5.5 percent, Romania by 18.9 percent, Montenegro by 29 percent, and Bulgaria with a rise of 3.6 percent in terms of volume. Sales positions were also satisfactory in the Russian and Ukrainian markets. Further, while South Korean sales volume remained unchanged, volumes in China were 10 percent higher, although this figure was still short of expectations.

INTERBREW CORPORATE STRATEGY

The three facets of Interbrew's corporate strategy, i.e., brands, markets and operations, were considered the "sides of the Interbrew triangle." Each of these aspects of corporate strategy was considered to be equally important in order to achieve the fundamental objective of increasing shareholder value. With a corporate focus entirely on beer, the underlying objectives of the company were to consolidate its positions in mature markets and improve margins through higher volumes of premium and specialty brands. Further, the company's emphasis on growth was driven by the belief that beer industry rationalization still had some way to go and that the majority of the world's major markets would each end up with just two or three major players.

Operations Strategy

Cross fertilization of best practices between sites was a central component of Interbrew's operations strategy. In the company's two main markets, Belgium and Canada, each brewery monitored its performance on 10 different dimensions against its peers. As a result, the gap between the best and the worst of Interbrew's operations had narrowed decisively since 1995. Employees continuously put forward propositions to improve processes. The program had resulted in significantly lower production costs, suggesting to Interbrew management that most improvements had more to do with employee motivation than with pure technical performance. In addition, capacity utilization and strategic sourcing had been identified as two areas of major opportunity.

Capacity Utilization

Given that brewing was a capital-intensive business, capacity utilization had a major influence on profitability. Since declining consumption in mature markets had generated excess capacity, several of Interbrew's old breweries and processing facilities were scheduled to be shut down. In contrast, in several growth markets such as Romania, Bulgaria, Croatia and Montenegro, the opposite problem existed, so facilities in other locations were used more fully until local capacities were increased.

Strategic Sourcing

Interbrew had begun to rationalize its supply base as well. By selecting a smaller number of its best suppliers and working more closely with them, Interbrew believed that innovative changes resulted, saving both parties considerable sums every year. For most of the major commodities, the company had gone to single suppliers and was planning to extend this approach to all operations worldwide.

Market Strategy

The underlying objectives of Interbrew's market strategy were to increase volume and to lessen its dependence on Belgium and Canada, its two traditional markets. Interbrew dichotomized its market strategy into the mature and growth market segments, although investments were considered wherever opportunities to generate sustainable profits existed. One of the key elements of Interbrew's market strategy was to establish and manage strong market platforms. It was believed that a brand strength was directly related to a competitive and dedicated market platform (i.e., sales and distribution, wholesaler networks, etc.) to support the brand. Further, Interbrew allowed individual country teams to manage their own affairs and many felt that the speed of success in many markets was related to this decentralized approach.

Mature Markets

Interbrew's goals in its mature markets were to continue to build market share and to improve margins through greater efficiencies in production, distribution and marketing. At the same time, the company intended to exploit the growing trend in these markets towards premium and specialty products of which Interbrew already possessed an unrivalled portfolio. The key markets in which this strategy was being actively pursued were the United States, Canada, the United Kingdom, France, the Netherlands and Belgium.

Growth Markets

Based on the belief that the world's beer markets would undergo further consolidation, Interbrew's market strategy was to build significant positions in markets that had long-term volume growth potential. This goal led to a clear focus on Central and Eastern Europe and Asia, South Korea and China in particular. In China, for example, Interbrew had just completed an acquisition of a second brewery in Nanjing. The Yali brand was thereby added to the corporate portfolio and, together with its Jingling brand, Interbrew became the market leader in Nanjing, a city of six million people.

In Korea, Interbrew entered into a 50:50 joint venture with the Doosan Chaebol to operate the Oriental Brewery, producing the OB Lager and Cafri pilsener brands. With this move, Interbrew took the number two position in the Korean beer market with a 36 percent share and sales of 5.1 million hls. The venture with Doosan was followed in December 1999 by the purchase of the Jinro Coors brewery. This added 2.5 million hls and increased Interbrew's market share to 50 percent of total Korean volume. Thus, the Interbrew portfolio in Korea consisted of two mainstream pilsener brands, OB Lager and Cass, the two local premium brands, Cafri and Red Rock, and Budweiser, an international premium brand.

In Russia, Interbrew expanded its presence by taking a majority stake in the Rosar Brewery in Omsk, adding the BAG Bier and Sibirskaya Korona brands. Rosar was the leading brewer in Siberia with a 25 percent regional market share, and held the number four position in Russia. New initiatives were also undertaken in Central Europe with acquisitions of a brewery in Montenegro and the Pleven brewery in Bulgaria, as well as the introduction of Interbrew products into the Yugoslavian market. Finally, although Interbrew had just increased its already significant investment in Mexico's second largest brewer from 22 percent to 30 percent, Latin America remained a region of great interest.

Brand Strategy

A central piece of Interbrew's traditional brand strategy had been to add to its portfolio of brands through acquisition of existing brewers, principally in growth markets. Since its goal was to have the number one or two brand in every market segment in which it operated, Interbrew concentrated on purchasing and developing strong local brands. As it moved into new territories, the company's first priority was to upgrade product quality and to improve the positioning of the acquired local core lager brands. In mature markets, it drew on the strength of the established brands such as Jupiler, Belgium's leading lager brand, Labatt Blue, the famous Canadian brand, and Dommelsch, an important brand in the Netherlands. In growth markets, Interbrew supported brands like Borsodi Sor in Hungary, Kamenitza in Bulgaria, Ozujsko in Croatia, Bergenbier in Romania, Jingling in China, and OB Lager in Korea. In addition, new products were launched such as Taller, a premium brand in the Ukraine, and Boomerang, an alternative malt-based drink in Canada.

A second facet of the company's brand strategy was to identify certain brands, typically specialty products, and to develop them on a regional basis across a group of markets. At the forefront of this strategy were the Abbaye de Leffe and Hoegaarden brands and, to a lesser extent, Belle-Vue. In fact, both Hoegaarden and Leffe achieved a leading position as the number one white beer and abbey beer in France and Holland. The Loburg premium pilsener brand also strengthened its position when it was relaunched in France. Further, in Canada, Interbrew created a dedicated organization for specialty beers called the Oland Specialty Beer Company. In its first year of operation, the brands marketed by Oland increased its volumes by over 40 percent. More specifically, sales of the Alexander Keith's brand doubled and the negative volume trend of the John Labatt Classic brand was reversed. The underlying message promoted by Oland was the richness, mystique and heritage of beer.

To support the regional growth of specialty beers, Interbrew established a new type of café. The Belgian Beer Café, owned and run by independent operators, created an authentic Belgian atmosphere where customers sampled Interbrew's Belgian specialty beers. By 1999, Belgian Beer Cafés were open in the many of Interbrew's key markets, including top selling outlets in New York, Auckland, Zagreb and Budapest, to name a few. The business concept was that these cafés were to serve as an ambassador of the Belgian beer culture in foreign countries. They were intended to serve as vehicles to showcase Interbrew's specialty brands, benefiting from the international appeal of European styles and fashions. Although these cafés represented strong marketing tools for brand positioning, the key factors that led to the success of this concept were tied very closely to the individual establishments and the personnel running them. The bar staff, for example, had to be trained to serve the beer in the right branded glass, at the right temperature, and with a nice foamy head. It was anticipated that the concept of the specialty café would be used to support the brand development efforts of Interbrew's Belgian beers in all of its important markets.

The third facet of Interbrew's brand strategy was to identify a key corporate brand and to develop it as a global product. While the market segment for a global brand was currently relatively small, with the bulk of the beer demand still in local brands, the demand for international brands was expected to grow, as many consumers became increasingly attracted to the sophistication of premium and super-premium beers.

THE EVOLUTION OF INTERBREW'S GLOBAL BRAND STRATEGY

Until 1997, Interbrew's brand development strategy for international markets was largely laissez faire. Brands were introduced to new markets through licensing, export and local production when opportunities were uncovered. Stella Artois, Interbrew's most broadly available and oldest brand, received an important new thrust when it was launched through local production in three of the company's subsidiaries in Central Europe in 1997. This approach was consistent with the company's overall goals of building a complete portfolio in high growth potential markets.

By 1998, however, the executive management committee perceived the need to identify a brand from its wide portfolio to systematically develop into the company's global brand. Although the market for global brands was still small, there were some growing successes (e.g., Heineken, Corona, Fosters and Budweiser) and Interbrew believed that there were several basic global trends that would improve the viability of this class of product over the next couple of decades. First, while many consumers were seeking more variety, others were seeking lower prices. It appeared that the number of affluent and poor consumer segments would increase at the expense of the middle income segments. The upshot of this socioeconomic trend was that eventually all markets would likely evolve in such a way that demand for both premium and economy-priced beers would increase, squeezing the mainstream beers in the middle. A second trend was the internationalization of the beer business. As consumers travelled around the world, consuming global media (e.g., CNN, Eurosport, MTV, international magazines, etc.), global media were expected to become more effective for building brands. A global strategy could, therefore, lead to synergies in global advertising and sponsoring. In addition, the needs of consumers in many markets were expected to converge. As a result of these various factors, Interbrew believed that there would be an increasing interest in authentic, international brands in a growing number of countries. Interbrew had a wide portfolio of national brands that it could set on the international stage. The two most obvious candidates were Labatt Blue and Stella Artois.

The Labatt range of brands included Labatt Blue, Labatt Blue Light and Labatt Ice. To date, however, the exposure of these brands outside of North America had been extremely limited and they were not yet budding global brands. Of the total Labatt Blue volume in 1998, 85 percent was derived from the Canadian domestic and U.S. markets, with the balance sold in the United Kingdom. The Labatt brands had been introduced to both France and Belgium, and production had been licensed in Italy, but these volumes were minimal. The only real export growth market for Labatt Blue appeared to be the United States, where the brand's volume in 1998 was some 23 percent higher than in 1995, behind only Corona and Heineken in the imported brand segment. The Labatt Ice brand was also sold in a limited number of markets and, after the appeal of this Labatt innovation had peaked, its total volume had declined by more than 25 percent since 1996. Total Labatt Ice volume worldwide was just 450,000 hls in 1998, of which 43 percent was sold in Canada, 33 percent in the United States, and 21 percent in the United Kingdom.

STELLA ARTOIS AS INTERBREW'S INTERNATIONAL FLAGSHIP BRAND

The other potential brand that Interbrew could develop on a global scale was Stella Artois, a brand that could trace its roots back to 1366. The modern version of Stella Artois was launched in 1920 as a Christmas beer and had become a strong market leader in its home market of Belgium through the 1970s. By the 1990s, however, Stella's market position began to suffer from an image as a somewhat old-fashioned beer, and the brand began to experience persistent volume decline. Problems in the domestic market, however, appeared to be shared by a number of other prominent international brands. In fact, seven of the top 10 international brands had experienced declining sales in their home markets between 1995 and 1999 (see Exhibit 3).

Stella Artois had achieved great success in the United Kingdom through its licensee, Whitbread, where Stella Artois became the leading premium lager beer. Indeed, the United Kingdom was the largest market for Stella Artois, accounting for 49 percent of total brand volume in 1998. Stella Artois volume in the U.K. market reached 2.8 million hls in 1998, a 7.6 percent share of the lager market, and came close to 3.5 million hls in 1999, a 25 percent increase over the previous year. By this time, over 32,000 outlets sold Stella Artois on draught.

EXHIBIT 3
Domestic Sales History of Major International Brands (million hectolitre)

	1995	1996	1997	1998
Budweiser (incl. Bud Light until '98)	69.48	71.10	72.43	40.00
Bud Light	n/a	n/a	n/a	30.00
Heineken	3.87	3.78	3.85	3.78
Becks	1.68	1.71	1.72	1.78
Carlsberg	1.47	1.39	1.31	1.22
Stella Artois	1.08	1.00	0.96	0.92
Fosters	1.48	1.11	1.40	1.43
Kronenbourg	5.65	5.53	5.35	5.60
Amstel	2.30	2.23	2.21	2.18
Corona	12.89	14.09	14.80	15.18

Apart from the United Kingdom, the key markets for Stella Artois were France and Belgium, which together accounted for a further 31 percent of total brand volume (see Exhibit 4). With these three markets accounting for 81 percent of total Stella Artois volume in 1999, few other areas represented a significant volume base (see Exhibit 5). Beyond the top three markets, the largest market for Stella Artois was Italy, where the brand was produced under license by Heineken. Stella Artois volume in Italy had, however, declined slightly to 166,000 hls in 1998. Licensing agreements were also in place in Sweden and Australia, but volume was small.

Stella Artois was also produced in Interbrew's own breweries in Hungary, Croatia and Romania, with very pleasing 1998 volumes of 84,000 hls, 120,000 hls, and 60,000 hls, respectively. After only three years, the market share of Stella Artois in Croatia, for example, had reached four percent—a significant result, given that the brand was a premium-priced product. In all Central European markets, Stella Artois was priced at a premium; in Hungary, however, that premium was lower than in Croatia and Romania where, on an index comparing Stella's price to that of core lagers, the indices by country were 140, 260 and 175 respectively.

Promising first results were also attained in Australia and New Zealand. Particularly in New Zealand, through a "seeding" approach, Interbrew and their local partner, Lion Nathan, had realized great success in the Belgian Beer Café in Auckland where the brands were showcased. After only two years of support, Stella Artois volume was up to 20,000 hls, and growing at 70 percent annually, out of a total premium segment of 400,000 hls. Interbrew's market development plan limited distribution to top outlets in key metropolitan centres and priced Stella Artois significantly above competitors (e.g., 10 percent over Heineken and 20 percent over Steinlager, the leading domestic premium lager brand).

EXHIBIT 4
1999 World Sales Profile of Stella Artois

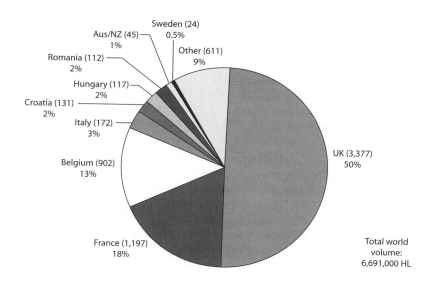

Sweden (24) 0.5%
Aus/NZ (45) 1%
Other (611) 9%
Romania (112) 2%
Hungary (117) 2%
Croatia (131) 2%
Italy (172) 3%
Belgium (902) 13%
France (1,197) 18%
UK (3,377) 50%

Total world volume: 6,691,000 HL

EXHIBIT 5
Stella Artois Sales
Volume Summary
(000 Hectolitre)

	1997	1998	1999
Production:			
Belgium	965	921	902
France	1,028	1,110	1,074
Hungary	59	84	117
Croatia	54	120	133
Romania	17	60	112
Bulgaria	-	-	3
Bosnia-Herzegovina	-	-	2
Montenegro	-	-	0
Total Production	**2,123**	**2,295**	**2,343**
License Brewing:			
Italy	162	166	172
Australia	6	11	22
New Zealand	7	11	22
Sweden	29	27	24
Greece	7	7	10
UK	2,139	2,815	3,377
Total Licensed	**2,350**	**3,037**	**3,627**
Export:			
USA	-	-	7
Canada	-	-	5
Other Countries	92	49	202
Duty Free	245	389	507
Total Export	**337**	**438**	**721**
Overall Total	**4,810**	**5,770**	**6,691**

The evolution of the brand looked very positive as world volumes for Stella Artois continued to grow. In fact, Stella Artois volume had increased from 3.4 million hls in 1992 to a total of 6.7 million hls in 1999, a rise of 97 percent. Ironically, the only market where the brand continued its steady decline was in its home base of Belgium. Analysts suggested a variety of reasons to explain this anomaly, including inconsistent sales and marketing support, particularly as the organization began to favor the rising Jupiler brand.

Overall, given Interbrew's large number of local brands, especially those in Mexico with very high volumes, total Stella Artois volume accounted for only 10 percent of total Interbrew volume in 1999 (14 percent if Femsa volumes are excluded). Interbrew's strategy of nurturing a wide portfolio of strong brands was very different as compared to some of its major competitors. For example, Anheuser-Busch, the world's largest brewer, focused its international strategy almost exclusively on the development of the Budweiser brand. Similarly, Heineken sought to centre its international business on the Heineken brand and, to a lesser extent, on Amstel. While the strategies of Anheuser-Busch and Heineken focused primarily on one brand, there were also great differences in the way these two brands were being managed. For example, Budweiser, the world's largest brand by volume, had the overwhelming bulk of its volume in its home U.S. market (see Exhibit 6). Sales of the Heineken brand, on the other hand, were widely distributed across markets around the world (see Exhibit 7). In this sense, Heineken's strategy was much more comparable to that of Interbrew's plans for Stella Artois. Other brands that were directly comparable to Stella Artois, in terms of total volume and importance of the brand to the overall sales of the company, were Carlsberg and Foster's with annual sales volumes in 1998 of 9.4 million hls and 7.1 million hls, respectively. While Foster's was successful in many international markets, there was a heavy focus on sales in the United Kingdom and the United States (see Exhibit 8). Carlsberg sales volume profile was different in that sales were more widely distributed across international markets (see Exhibit 9).

EXHIBIT 6
Top 10 Brewers by
International Sales

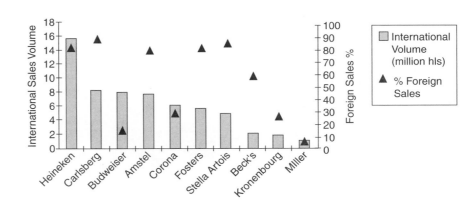

EXHIBIT 7
1998 Heineken World
Sales Profile

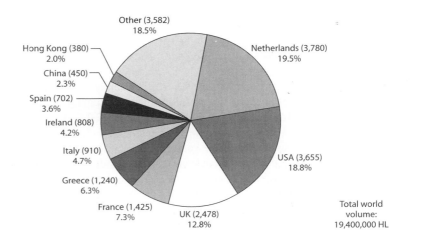

EXHIBIT 8
1998 Foster's World
Sales Profile

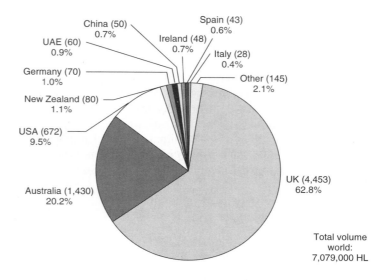

China (50) 0.7%
UAE (60) 0.9%
Germany (70) 1.0%
New Zealand (80) 1.1%
USA (672) 9.5%
Australia (1,430) 20.2%
Spain (43) 0.6%
Ireland (48) 0.7%
Italy (28) 0.4%
Other (145) 2.1%
UK (4,453) 62.8%

Total volume world: 7,079,000 HL

EXHIBIT 9
1998 Carlsberg
World Sales Profile

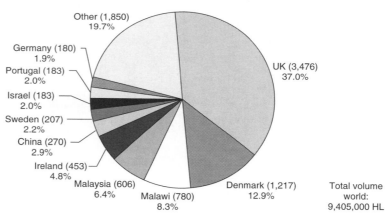

Other (1,850) 19.7%
Germany (180) 1.9%
Portugal (183) 2.0%
Israel (183) 2.0%
Sweden (207) 2.2%
China (270) 2.9%
Ireland (453) 4.8%
Malaysia (606) 6.4%
Malawi (780) 8.3%
Denmark (1,217) 12.9%
UK (3,476) 37.0%

Total volume world: 9,405,000 HL

STELLA'S GLOBAL LAUNCH

In 1998, Interbrew's executive management committee settled on Stella Artois, positioned as the premium European lager, as the company's global flagship brand. In fact, the Interbrew management felt that stock analysts would be favorably disposed to Interbrew having an acknowledged global brand with the potential for a higher corporate valuation and price earnings (P/E) multiple.

As the global campaign got under way, it became clear that the organization needed time to adapt to centralized coordination and control of Stella Artois brand marketing. This was, perhaps, not unexpected given that Interbrew had until recently operated on a regional basis; the new centralized Stella brand management approach had been in place only since September 1998. In addition, there were often difficulties in convincing all parties to become part of a new global approach, particularly the international advertising campaign that was the backbone of the global plan for Stella Artois. Belgium, for example, continued with a specific local advertising program that positioned Stella as a mainstream lager in its home market, and in the United Kingdom, Whitbread maintained its "reassuringly expensive" advertising slogan that had already proved to be so successful. For other less-established markets, a global advertising framework was created that included a television concept and a series of print and outdoor executions. This base advertising plan was rolled out in 1999 in 15 markets, including the United States, Canada, Italy, Hungary, Croatia, Bulgaria, Romania, New Zealand and France (with a slightly changed format) after research suggested that the campaign had the ability to cross borders. The objective of this campaign was to position Stella Artois as a sophisticated European lager. It was intended that Stella Artois should be perceived as a beer with an important brewing tradition and heritage but, at the same time, also as a contemporary beer (see Exhibit 10).

In 1998, an accelerated plan was devised to introduce Stella Artois to two key markets within the United States, utilizing both local and corporate funding. The U.S. market was believed to be key for the future development of the brand since it was the most developed specialty market in the world (12 percent specialty market share, growing 10 percent plus annually through the 1990s), and because of the strong influence on international trends. Thus, Stella Artois was launched in New York City and Boston and was well received by the demanding U.S. consumer and pub owner. Within 1999, over 200 pubs in Manhattan and 80 bars in Boston had begun to sell Stella Artois on tap. To support the heightened efforts to establish Stella Artois in these competitive urban markets, Interbrew's corporate marketing department added several million dollars to Labatt USA's budget for Stella Artois in 2000, with commitments to continue this additional funding in subsequent years.

EXHIBIT 10 **Global Positioning** **Statement**	**Brand Positioning** To males, between 21 to 45 years of age, that are premium lager drinkers, Stella Artois is a European premium lager beer, differentially positioned towards the product. Stella Artois offers a modern, sophisticated, yet accessible drinking experience with an emphasis on the very high quality of the beer supported by the noble tradition of European brewing. The accent is on the emotional consequence of benefit: a positive feeling of self esteem and sophistication. **Character, Tone of Voice** Sophistication Authenticity, tradition, yet touch of modernity Timelessness Premium quality Special, yet accessible Mysticism European

CURRENT THINKING

Good progress had been made since 1998 when Stella Artois was established as Interbrew's global brand. However, management had revised its expectations for P/E leverage from having a global brand. The reality was that Interbrew would be rewarded only through cash benefits from operational leverage of a global brand. There would be no "free lunch" simply for being perceived as having a global brand. In addition, in an era of tight fiscal management, it was an ongoing challenge to maintain the funding levels required by the ambitious development plans for Stella Artois. As a result, in early 2000 the prevailing view at Interbrew began to shift, converging on a different long-range approach towards global branding. The emerging perspective emphasized a more balanced brand development program, focusing on the highest leverage opportunities.

The experience of other brewers that had established global brands offered an opportunity for Interbrew to learn from their successes and failures. Carlsberg and Heineken, for example, were two comparable global brands that were valued quite differently by the stock market. Both sold over 80 percent of their total volumes outside their domestic market, and yet Heineken stock achieved a P/E ratio of 32.4 in 1999 versus Carlsberg's figure of only 17.1. According to industry analysts, the driving force behind this difference was that Heineken maintained a superior market distribution in terms of growth and margin (see Exhibit 11). The key lesson from examining these global brands appeared to be that great discipline must be applied to focus resources in the right places.

In line with this thinking, a long range marketing plan began to take shape that made use of a series of strategic filters to yield a focused set of attractive opportunities. The first filter that any potential market had to pass through was its long-term volume potential for Stella Artois. This volume had to trace back to a large and/or growing market, the current or potential sizeable premium lager segment (at least five percent of the total market), and the possibility for Stella Artois to penetrate the top three brands. The second screen was the potential to achieve attractive margins after an initial starting period of approximately three years. The

EXHIBIT 11
A Comparison of Carlsberg and Heineken

		Low	High
Market Return	High	Carlsberg = 19% Heineken = 2%	Carlsberg = 22% Heineken = 46%
	Low	Carlsberg = 56% Heineken = 2%	Carlsberg = 3% Heineken = 50%
		Market Growth	

third filter was whether or not a committed local partner was available to provide the right quality of distribution and to co-invest in the brand. The final screen was the determination that success in the chosen focus markets should increase leverage in other local and regional markets. For example, the size and stature of Stella Artois in the United Kingdom was a significant factor in the easy sell-in of Stella Artois into New York in 1999.

Once filtered through these strategic market development screens, the global branding plans for Stella Artois began to take a different shape. Rather than focus on national markets, plans emerged with an emphasis on about 20 cities, some of which Interbrew was already present in (e.g., London, Brussels, New York, etc.). This approach suggested that the next moves should be in such potential markets as Moscow, Los Angeles and Hong Kong. Some existing cities would receive focused efforts only when distribution partner issues had been successfully resolved to solidify the bases for sustained long term growth. The major cities that fit these criteria provided the right concentration of affluent consumers, who would be attracted to Stella's positioning, thus providing scale for marketing and sales, investment leverage, as well as getting the attention and support of motivated wholesalers and initial retail customers. These venues would thereby become highly visible success stories that would be leveragable in the company's ongoing market development plans.

Thus, the evolving global branding development plan required careful planning on a city-by-city basis. Among the demands of this new approach were that marketing efforts and the funding to support them would have to be both centrally stewarded and locally tailored to reflect the unique local environments. A corporate marketing group was, therefore, established and was charged with the responsibility to identify top priority markets, develop core positioning and guidelines for local execution, assemble broadly based marketing programs (e.g., TV, print advertising, global sponsorships, beer.com content, etc.), and allocate resources to achieve the accelerated growth objectives in these targeted cities. To ensure an integrated development effort the company brought all pivotal resources together, under the leadership of a global brand development director. In addition to the brand management team, the group included regional sales managers who were responsible for licensed partner management, a customer services group, a Belgian beer café manager, and cruise business management group. Another significant challenge that faced the corporate marketing group was to ensure that all necessary groups were supportive of the new approach. This was a simpler undertaking among those business units that were wholly owned subsidiaries; it was a more delicate issue in the case of licensees and joint ventures. A key element of managing brands through a global organizational structure was that the head office team had to effectively build partnerships with local managers to ensure their commitment.

Fortunately, much of the initial effort to establish Stella Artois as a global brand had been done on a city-by-city basis and, as such, there was ample opportunity for Interbrew to learn from these experiences as the new global plan evolved. In the late 1990s, for example, Stella Artois was introduced to various Central

European cities (e.g., Budapest, Zagreb, Bucharest and Sofia). In each of these cities, Interbrew's marketing efforts were launched when the targeted premium market was at an early stage of development. Further, distribution and promotion was strictly controlled (e.g., product quality, glassware, etc.) and the development initiatives were delivered in a concentrated manner (e.g., a media "blitz" in Budapest). In addition, results indicated that the presence of a Belgian Beer Café accelerated Interbrew's market development plans in these new areas. These early successes suggested that brand success could be derived from the careful and concentrated targeting of young adults living in urban centres, with subsequent pull from outlying areas following key city success.

The key lessons of these efforts in Central Europe proved to be very valuable in guiding the market development plan in New York City. In this key North American city, the rollout of Stella Artois was perceived by the analysts as "one of the most promising introductions in New York over the last 20 years" and had generated great wholesaler support and excitement. Among the tactics used to achieve this early success was selective distribution with targeted point of sale materials support. In addition, a selective media campaign was undertaken that included only prestigious outdoor advertising (e.g., a Times Square poster run through the Millennium celebrations). Similarly, the sponsoring strategy focused only on high-end celebrity events, Belgian food events, exclusive parties, fashion shows, etc. Finally, the price of Stella Artois was targeted at levels above Heineken, to reinforce its gold standard positioning. This concerted and consistent market push created an impact that resulted in the "easiest new brand sell" in years, according to wholesalers. The success of this launch also built brand and corporate credibility, paving the way to introductions in other U.S. cities as well as "opening the eyes" of other customers and distribution partners around the world.

To pursue this new global development plan over the next three years, a revised marketing budget was required. Given that the corporate marketing department was responsible for both the development of core programs as well as the selective support of local markets, the budget had to cover both of these key elements. To achieve these ends, total spending was expected to more than double over the next three years.

While great progress had been made on the global branding of Stella Artois, Cooke still ruminated on a variety of important interrelated issues. Among these issues was the situation of Stella Artois in Belgium—would it be possible to win in the "global game" without renewed growth in the home market? What specific aspirations should Interbrew set for Belgium over the next three years? Further, what expectations should Interbrew have of its global brand market development (e.g., volumes, profit levels, number of markets and cities, etc.)? How should global success be measured? With respect to Interbrew's promotional efforts, how likely would it be that a single global ad campaign could be successful for Stella Artois? Was there a particular sponsorship or promotion idea that could be singled out for global leverage? And what role should the Internet play in developing Stella Artois as a true global brand?

Chapter Seventeen

Sesame Workshop and International Growth

In August 2001, Martha Van Gelder, the group vice president of products and international television at Sesame Workshop, was faced with various issues. Sesame Workshop was the producer of *Sesame Street,* the highly acclaimed children's educational show. Since its American debut more than 30 years ago, *Sesame Street* had achieved great success in many other countries. In virtually every country where it was introduced, *Sesame Street,* or a locally produced version of the show, had become an immediate success. By 2001, the show was broadcast in almost 150 countries, making Sesame Workshop the largest single teacher of young children in the world. The show was co-produced in the local language in 20 countries with local actors, writers, musicians, animation, and sets. In the other countries, the show was either the English-language American version or the American version with some segments dubbed in the local language. International revenue represented about 20% of total revenue.

Within Sesame Workshop, there was a consensus that many interesting international growth opportunities existed. For example, *Sesame Street* was not broadcast in Brazil, France, or India. There were also opportunities for co-productions in many of the countries where the English-language version of the show was broadcast. However, capitalizing on the opportunities had to be balanced with various factors. Sesame Workshop's mission was to educate children and their families globally. But, even though Sesame Workshop was a not-for-profit

organization, creating a financially viable and growing organization was a necessity. Van Gelder described it this way:

> How do we take all the wonderful ideas and convert them into a real business? We often have broadcasters asking us to do special programs for outreach or to develop a special video. But, when we look at the time and resources, we have to come back to the main charge of developing the business and the brand. The most important thing is to deliver on the promise of what the brand and mission are; that means doing things well and may mean doing less.
>
> We face the dilemma every day: why is the preschooler in India more important than the one in France? They are not different. Our mission does not say that we should focus more on developing markets. We want to help all children. It really comes down to the opportunity and the feasibility; whether we have the staff and resources to do it; and how near or long-term it is.

BACKGROUND

In 1966 Joan Ganz Cooney was commissioned by the Carnegie Corporation, an American foundation, to do a study on the feasibility of using television for the education of preschool children. At the time, Cooney was a successful producer in educational television. Based on the study's findings, Cooney urged that an experimental television series devoted to preschool children be established. The Carnegie Foundation agreed, and with the support of the Ford Foundation and the U.S. Office of Education, a grant of $8 million was raised from government and private sources. The grant was to be used for pre-broadcast research and production, a seven-month broadcast period, and national evaluation of the broadcast season.

The Children's Television Workshop was founded in 1968 to conduct the study. A set of curriculum goals was developed in various categories: social, moral, and affective development; language and reading; mathematical and numerical skills; and reasoning, problem-solving, and perception. Research was conducted to determine how to best develop an operational model. Five test shows were developed and evaluated in August 1969. Based on the results of the tests, the first show, called *Sesame Street,* aired in November 1969 on stations of the Public Broadcasting Service, a commercial-free television network supported by government and private funding. The show was an immediate success and in the first season, the estimated audience was about seven million of the 12 million target audience. Over the next several decades the show became a fixture on American television and in 1999, *Sesame Street* was in its 31st season in the United States. In 2000, Children's Television Workshop changed its name to Sesame Workshop.

THE MISSION OF SESAME WORKSHOP

According to Sesame Workshop, "Our mission is to create innovative, engaging content that maximizes the educational power of media to help all children reach their highest potential."[1] Sesame Workshop core values were described as:

Innovation: We seek new ways to make the world of media more valuable for children, with a keen appreciation of children's imagination and inquisitive spirit.

Optimism: We champion the educational potential of media in the lives of children.

Knowledge: We ground our work in research to expand our understanding of what appeals to children and what helps them learn, develop, and grow.

Diversity: We create places where all children can see themselves and appreciate others.[2]

Sesame Workshop was a not-for-profit company chartered by the Board of Regents of the University of the State of New York under the Education Law of New York. Income generated by educational activities was exempt from taxation. Income generated by activities unrelated to Sesame Workshop's educational mission was taxable. Sesame Workshop's board of trustees had 16 members and included Joan Ganz Cooney.

Sesame Workshop had three financial goals. The first was to assemble public and private funding partnerships to support educational initiatives. For example, the development and production of the Israeli/Palestinian co-production of *Sesame Street* had a diverse group of funders, including the Netherlands Ministry of Foreign Affairs, the Ford Foundation, and the Israeli Ministry of Education. The second goal was to support educational activities with self-generated revenues. Various revenue-generating activities were undertaken: foreign and domestic product licensing, foreign licensing and distribution of local language adaptations and co-productions of Sesame Workshop programs, syndication of *Sesame Street* and other series, magazine and book publishing, and interactive software. These activities supported more than 80% of the cost of *Sesame Street.* The third financial goal was to establish underlying financial stability by maintaining an investment portfolio to cover operating deficiencies when necessary and to ensure the long-term financial viability of *Sesame Street.*

Sesame Street

In the United States, a six-month broadcast season for *Sesame Street* consisted of 130 hour-long programs. Each program was made up of 30–40 segments. The segments were in four categories: street scenes produced in a studio, animation, live action from outside the studio, and puppet scenes. Street scenes contained both the series' live cast of characters and such popular puppet characters as Big Bird, Elmo, and Oscar the Grouch. Each show closed with a 15-minute segment called *Elmo's World.* The puppets were Muppet characters that were originally created by the late Jim Henson. Muppet characters were integral to *Sesame Street,* and according to Joan Ganz Cooney, "The most fortunate thing that happened to us was when Jim Henson walked through the door. His puppets made us viable in the marketplace."[3] In 2000, Sesame Workshop acquired complete control over the rights of all Sesame Street characters; previously, they were shared with the Jim Henson Company, which was acquired by the German company EM.TV & Merchandising AG in 2000.

Each segment of the show addressed at least one highly specific educational goal. Extensive testing (*Sesame Street* has been the subject of more than 1,000 studies) found that viewers of *Sesame Street* made significantly greater gains than nonviewers in most tested areas of the series' curriculum. Three of the more recent studies demonstrated that the show made a significant and lasting contribution to preschoolers' cognitive and social development. Studies also showed that children who watched more learned more and that gains were made by children from both middle- and low-income backgrounds. Following its debut, *Sesame Street* won numerous awards in the United States and other countries. In the United States, *Sesame Street*'s 76 Emmy Awards were the most ever awarded to a single program.

THE GLOBALIZATION OF *SESAME STREET*

Soon after *Sesame Street* premiered in 1969, Children's Television Workshop began receiving inquiries from producers in Canada, Australia, New Zealand, and other English-speaking countries about the rebroadcast rights to the series (Exhibit 1 shows international milestones). In addition, producers from other countries where English was widely spoken approached Children's Television Workshop with requests to rebroadcast the series with slight modifications. In Israel, for example, the series first aired in English with occasional commentary in Hebrew. In Japan, the American version of *Sesame Street* was broadcast until 1998 unedited and unaltered, with the purpose of teaching English as a second language to children, teenagers, and adults. In 1998, NHK, the Japanese broadcaster, began offering a dubbed version of the show. Similarly, countries in the Caribbean used the series as a means of teaching English. As was the case for any television show, international distribution was quite profitable. For Children's Television Workshop, the only real incremental costs for re-broadcasting were for duplicating tapes and residuals for actors and musicians.

EXHIBIT 1
Sesame Workshop International Milestones

1968:	Children's Television Workshop formed.
1969:	*Sesame Street* premieres on U.S. public (commercial-free) television.
1969:	Sesame Workshop launches licensed product program.
1971:	U.S. version of *Sesame Street* debuts in Australia and in Japan.
1972:	First international co-production of *Sesame Street* in Germany.
1975:	*Barrio Sésamo* launched in Spain; *Plaza Sésamo* launched in Mexico.
1983:	U.S. version of *Sesame Street* debuts in U.K.
1996:	*Sesame Street* wins Japan Prize for best program in preschool education category; *Ulitsa Sezam* begins in Russia; *Ulica Sezamkowa* begins in Poland; *Sesame Park* begins in Canada.
1997:	*Sacatruc*, a French language co-production of *Big Bag*, premieres in France.
1998:	*Zhima Jie* launched in China; Rechov Sumsum/Shara' a Simsim premieres on Israeli and Palestinian television.
1999:	*Open Sesame* premieres in Pakistan and Italy.
2000:	Children's Television Workshop changes its name to Sesame Workshop; *Takalani Sesame* launched in South Africa; *Alam Simsim* launched in Egypt.
2001:	Mediatrade, Italy's largest commercial broadcaster, licenses *Tiny Planets*.

In addition to requests to rebroadcast the series in English, requests to alter the linguistic content for foreign audiences increased rapidly after the show's U.S. introduction. As a result, Children's Television Workshop needed policies and procedures for proposed international adaptations of *Sesame Street*. In late 1969, Children's Television Workshop created an international division charged with the responsibility of overseeing *Sesame Street's* licensing abroad. Four main licensing policies were developed:

- All non-U.S. versions of *Sesame Street* must be commercial-free.

- Changes to the series must meet the highest production standards.

- All non-U.S. versions of *Sesame Street* must reflect the values and traditions of the host country's culture.

- Any proposed changes to the series must be approved, initiated, and supervised by a local committee of educators working with Children's Television Workshop.

In 1970, a German network, NDR, began broadcasting *Sesame Street* dubbed in German. In 1971, NDR began producing and inserting a few segments that incorporated elements of the German national educational curriculum. In Canada and New Zealand, local segments also were produced and inserted into the show. In Canada, the segments focused on bilingualism, and in New Zealand, the focus was the heritage of the local Maori population.

In 1973, the international evolution continued with the introduction of a new series of 130 half-hour episodes entirely in Spanish for the Mexican market. Half the material came from the U.S. series and the other half was produced in Mexico. To avoid duplicating the look of the American series, a distinctive Latin American-looking set was designed around a neighborhood square. New music was recorded, and writers and producers were hired from Mexico and other Latin American countries. Two new puppet characters were created exclusively for the series. Financial support came from several Latin American sources and a grant from Xerox Corporation. Xerox received an institutional credit before and after each show but had no influence over content or distribution. *Plaza Sésamo's* debut in 1973 achieved the highest audience share of any television program ever broadcast in Mexico.

Based on the model pioneered in Mexico, 18 other *Sesame Street* co-production agreements were developed over the subsequent two decades. In Norway, for example, *Sesam Stasjon* immediately became the country's most popular children's show. In Portugal, *Rua Sesamo* became the most widely viewed children's program in the history of Portuguese television. In the Arab states, *Iftah Ta Simsim*, coproduced in Kuwait, was the top-rated preschool program for 15 years.

In 2000, *Talakani* (which means "be happy") *Sesame* debuted on South African television and, for the first time in *Sesame Street's* history, on radio. *Talakani Sesame* was initiated by Sesame Workshop, United States Agency for International Development (USAID), and the South African Department of Education. The street in *Talakani Sesame* combined aspects of both rural and urban South Africa and was designed as a street where all South African children could feel welcome and safe. Given the diversity of languages in South Africa, it was decided that the characters would be multilingual. Also in 2000, *Alam Simsim* debuted on Egyptian television as a daily series. *Alan Simsim* was co-produced with Karma Productions, a new firm formed solely to produce *Alan Simsim* and other programs. USAID was involved in the initiation of *Alan Simsim* and the official sponsor was Americana, a leading Middle East food company.

The Co-Production Model

Co-productions were set up as follows (Exhibit 2 shows the different countries in which *Sesame Street* co-productions have been aired). First, Sesame Workshop worked with local co-producers, usually a local broadcaster, to establish a board of advisors to set local curriculum standards. Based on the establishment of local goals and standards, Sesame Workshop collaborated extensively with co-producers

EXHIBIT 2 International Co-Productions of *Sesame Street*

Country	Series Title	Language	Year First Broadcast	Number of Seasons Produced	Currently in Production and/or Broadcast
Brazil	Vila Sésamo	Portuguese	1972	2	No
Canada*	Sesame Park	English (with some French segments)	1973	27	Yes
China	Zhima Jie	Mandarin	1998	1	Yes
Egypt	Alam Simsim	Arabic	2000	2	Yes
France	1, rue Sésame	French	1978	2	No
Germany	Sesamstrasse	German	1973	29	Yes
Israel	Rechov Sumsum	Hebrew	1983	4	Yes
Israel/Palestinian Territories	Rechov Sumsum/ Shara's Simsim	Hebrew and Arabic	1998	1	Yes
Kuwait**	Iftah Ya Simsim	Arabic	1979	3	No
Mexico***	Plaza Sésamo	Spanish	1972	7	Yes
Netherlands	Sesamstraat	Dutch	1976	24	Yes
Norway	Sesam Stasjon	Norwegian	1991	4	Yes
Philippines	Sesame!	Tagalog and English	1983	1	No
Poland	Ulica Sezamkowa	Polish	1996	2	No
Portugal****	Rua Sésamo	Portuguese	1989	3	No
Russia	Ulitsa Sezam	Russian	1996	2	Yes
South Africa TV	Takalani Sesame	Multi-lingual	2000	1	Yes
South Africa Radio	Takalani Sesame	Zulu, Xhosa, Sepedi with English segments	2000	1	Yes
Spain	Barrio Sésamo	Castilian, Catalan	1979	7	Yes
Sweden	Svenska Sesam	Swedish	1981	1	No
Turkey	Susam Sokagi	Turkish	1989	2	No

*The U.S. version of *Sesame Street* with some Canadian segments began broadcasting in 1973. The Canadian coproduction, Sesame Park, began in 1996.
**Also broadcast to 16 Arab-world countries.
***Also broadcast in Spanish-speaking Latin America and Puerto Rico.
****Also broadcast in Angola, Mozambique, Guinea, Cape Verde, and São Tomé.

on all production issues: writers, musicians, animation, sets, etc. Because Sesame Workshop believed that good writing was the key to success, about 25–30 people would be brought to New York for training on writing educational and entertaining segments for the show. Sesame Workshop also constructed puppets for local productions that reflected local cultures and customs. For example, in Israel, the main body puppet was a porcupine representing the Israeli culture: prickly on the outside and soft on the inside. In Germany, the puppet was a bear, and in Mexico, a parrot. In South Africa, puppets included a Zulu-speaking meerkat called Moshe, chosen in part because male and female meerkats share the task of looking after their young.

Sesame Workshop owned the characters and licensed them to the foreign productions. About half the shows' content came from Sesame Workshop and was dubbed into the local language. Typically, street scenes were 100% local production. Live action and animation were 50% Sesame Workshop and 50% local. Muppet segments, such as Bert & Ernie and Cookie Monster, were drawn from Sesame Workshop material and dubbed. The co-producer could also use material from Sesame Workshop's library of culturally neutral international segments.

Contractual arrangements with broadcasters had many variations. In Portugal, the broadcaster had the right to broadcast in Angola and Mozambique. The Netherlands partner had the right to broadcast in places like Aruba, in the Caribbean, where Dutch was spoken. With *Plaza Sésamo,* the Mexican show, Sesame Workshop retained the right to distribute the show in Latin America. With all international agreements, when the broadcast term expired, all rights reverted to Sesame Workshop.

Open Sesame was another international television product broadcast in international markets (Exhibit 3 shows the countries where *Open Sesame* was broadcast). *Open Sesame* was much cheaper to produce because it relied on dubbing the local language. *Sesame Street* could not be dubbed in its entirety because of the segments using live actors. For example, if the actors were talking about the letter *b,* and *b* was for *book,* it could not be easily dubbed. However, other segments were easy to dub. Live action, such as showing a farm where milk came from, could easily be dubbed. Animations and puppet scenes could be dubbed, although Sesame Workshop insisted on final approval for the voices chosen. *Sesame English,* created in association with Berlitz International, was introduced in 2000 in China and Taiwan as a daily series focused on conversational English. The series was supplemented by print, audio, video, and CD-ROM products.

Sesame Street in China

Entry into China began when Sesame Workshop contacted four Chinese universities with the message that Sesame Workshop was interested in China and would like to visit to discuss education and children's programming. Several people from Sesame Workshop went to China and conducted three-day seminars about Sesame Workshop, writing for children's programming, and possible partnerships. The seminars were sponsored by universities and their departments of education. The result of the trip was that almost every broadcaster contacted was interested in

EXHIBIT 3
Open Sesame
International
Productions

Country	Date First Broadcast	Currently in Production and/or Broadcast
Arab World	2001	Yes
Armenia	1997	No
Australia	2000	Yes
Canada	1998	No
Czech Republic	1997	Yes
Denmark	1997	No
Finland	1996	Yes
France	1974	No
Greece	1999	Yes
Hong Kong	1999	Yes
Hungary	1998	No
Iceland	1993	No
Indonesia	1997	No
Italy	1999	Yes
Korea	1999	No
Malaysia	1999	Yes
Morocco	1996	No
New Zealand	1999	No
Pakistan	1999	Yes
Philippines	2000	Yes
Singapore	1997	Yes
South Africa	1998	No
Spain	1979	Yes
Sweden	1996	Yes
Thailand	1997	Yes
Turkey	1989	No

partnering with Sesame Workshop. Eventually, the firm signed a contract with Shanghai Television, which broadcast to about 100 million people. The contract, negotiated over a year, included a provision for syndication throughout China, which at the time was a difficult process. The contract also required that Sesame Workshop find $5 million for the co-production. Eventually, Sesame Workshop secured General Electric as the primary sponsor for the Chinese coproduction.

Even though Sesame Workshop preferred to use locally created puppet characters in its co-productions, the Chinese partner insisted on Big Bird, a mainstay of the U.S. show. A compromise was made with the creation of Da Niao as the Chinese cousin to Big Bird. The Chinese show, *Zhima Jie,* became the only non-U.S. production to use a puppet similar to Big Bird. A 21-year-old former auto mechanic was selected to play the character. The other two main puppet characters were Hu Hu Zhu (Snoring Pig), an ageless, furry, blue pig who loved to sing, was very punctual, and had recently moved from the country to the city, and Xiao Mei Zi (Little Plum), a bright red, three-year-old monster.

In February 1998, the first show aired in China and was an immediate success. Later in the year a syndication deal was signed (China had more than 2,000 broadcasters). For the first season, 130 half-hour shows were developed with plans to develop new shows. With China Educational Television in Beijing, Sesame Workshop also produced 200 15-minute educational shows called "I Love Science." The first *Sesame Street* season was syndicated in 39 markets, including Beijing and several other large cities. In 2001, a second series of *Sesame Street* shows was being planned with a new sponsor.

Sesame Street in Russia

Sesame Street in Russia was initiated as part of a USAID program to the former Soviet Union. The program had three objectives: democratization, business principles, and education. *Ulitsa Sezam,* Sesame Workshop's Russian co-production, was launched in 1996 after six years in the making. Many issues, such as transportation, communications, office accommodations, and electricity proved to be major hurdles. A grant from George Soros and sponsorship by Nestlé S.A. made the production possible.

The initial production included 52 half-hour shows, which created the first educational television series produced in Russia. About 70% of the show was written, filmed, and produced in Russia. The *Ulitsa Sezam* set was a Russian courtyard—part city, part village, and more rural than the American *Sesame Street* set. Aunt Dasha was a central figure in the courtyard. She lived in a traditional Russian cottage and loved folklore and dispensing homespun wisdom. The main puppet character, named Zeliboda, was a seven-foot tall creature covered in blue feathers, with a large orange nose. Other Muppet characters, conceived in Russia and produced in New York, were pink Busya and orange Kubik. Bert and Ernie were also regular characters in their dubbed versions of Vlas and Yenik. In 2001, Sesame Workshop was in negotiations for a third series of shows, with Nestlé playing a key role in the negotiations with the broadcasters.

SESAME WORKSHOP IN 2001

Sesame Workshop was involved in multiple activities. Television, film, and video included television programming, feature films, home video, and various products on cassette and CD. Noggin, a joint venture between Sesame Workshop and the cable channel Nickelodeon, was launched in 1998 as the first commercial-free 24-hour cable television channel and online service dedicated to educating and entertaining children. In 1999, Sesame Workshop launched *Dragon Tales,* a half-hour animated fantasy-adventure program designed to encourage children to approach new experiences with confidence. *Dragon Tales* quickly became a huge success in the United States and markets such as Australia, U.K., and Hong Kong. *Dragon Tales* was being dubbed for markets such as Brazil and Mexico. A new series called *Sagwa, The Chinese Siamese Cat* would premiere in 2001. *Sagwa,* an animated series inspired by a book by Amy Tan, was targeted to children ages 5 to 8 years old. *Tiny Planets,* a multimedia learning system targeted to children 3 to 5 years old was to be launched online and on television in 2002.

The publishing and media division produced a variety of magazines with a readership of more than 12 million children and adults. Sesame Workshop's publishing library included more than 150 *Sesame Street*-based books. Sesame

Workshop also produced curriculum-related materials for elementary school children. Sesame Workshop was actively expanding its Internet presence through *SesameStreet.com* and developing new Web-based content, much of it tied to television shows. Sesame Workshop's Interactive Technology Group developed CD-ROMs, video games, and DVD content. *Sesame Street* CD-ROMs were among the best-selling educational titles.

Including co-productions and the U.S. version of programs, Sesame Workshop's television programs were shown in almost 150 countries. International product licensing tended to follow the introduction of the television show. As a country became more familiar with *Sesame Street,* it then became possible to introduce products based on *Sesame Street* characters. Sesame Workshop's licensing agreements stipulated that products could not be advertised on television if the audience was more than 10% preschoolers. The products were required to meet strict quality and safety standards. *Sesame Street* characters themselves could not be used in advertising to sell products.

With more than 400 licenses, Sesame Workshop licensed its brands throughout the world, with the revenue generated used to support Sesame Workshop's educational projects. Tens of thousands of Sesame Workshop products were available globally, produced in partnership with firms like Mattel, Sony, Kmart, Keebler, and Procter & Gamble. Mattel was the primary toy company partner with about 50% of Sesame Workshop's business. Target markets spanned all age groups. In 1996 and 1997, Sesame Workshop had the leading toys in the United States: Tickle Me Elmo and Sing & Snore Ernie. In 2000, *Sesame Street* brand cookies were rolled out successfully in the United States.

There were also *Sesame Street* theme parks in four locations: Pennsylvania; Monterrey, Mexico; São Paulo, Brazil; and Tokyo, Japan. Finally, Sesame Workshop's Outreach and Strategic Partnership division extended the use of *Sesame Street* as an educational resource. Outreach products were created through national and community partnerships and were designed to reach children in need and low income and minority families. Outreach programs included *Sesame Street Fire Safety Program; Sesame Street A is for Asthma Awareness Project* and *Sesame Street Beginnings: Language to Literacy.*

2000 Operations

Financial results for 2000 are shown in Exhibits 4 and 5. After an operating surplus in 1998, Sesame Workshop's first since 1992, Sesame Workshop returned to deficit positions in 1999 and 2000, although the 2000 deficit was significantly less than in 1999. The 1999 deficit, the largest in the firm's history, resulted in various new product initiatives and fundraising efforts.

In 2000, the *Sesame Street* show and related products accounted for the majority of revenue generated by Sesame Workshop. Revenue in 2000 grew by 19%, mainly as a result of the introduction of *Dragon Tales.* Publishing and product licensing revenues increased 1% and 2%, respectively. Reductions in corporate staff resulted in a decrease in general and administrative costs. The total number of employees was about 300, down from more than 400 in 1999.

EXHIBIT 4   **Consolidated Statement of Activities**

For the years ended June 30 (000s omitted)	2000	1999
Revenues		
Grants and contracts in support program production	$14,276	$5,923
Publishing, program and product licensing and royalties	132,766	117,925
Total operating revenues	$147,042	$123,848
Expenses		
Program production	$36,552	$26,563
Publishing, product licensing, development and distribution	91,816	84,275
Educational research, marketing and communications	14,429	13,631
General and administrative	10,901	11,796
Other expenses	4,008	2,813
Total operating expenses	**$157,706**	**$139,078**
Excess (deficiency) of operating revenues over operating expenses	**$(10,664)**	**$(15,230)**
Net investment income and change in unrealized appreciation	$15,958	$9,553
Other income, net	(5,411)	(3,323)
(Provision) benefit for income taxes	(1)	(17)
Increase in net assets	$(118)	$(9,017)

Source: Sesame Workshop Annual Report.

THE INTERNATIONAL ORGANIZATION FOR TELEVISION

Until 1992, Sesame Workshop had separate international sales forces for the English language show, co-productions, and product licensing. In 1992, the international television sales group was created to eliminate the problem of having different sales forces targeting the same broadcasters. Also in 1992, markets and customers were categorized as follows:

1. Current customers.

2. Broadcasters that had shown a real interest in televising *Sesame Street.* For these potential customers, funding issues were a major element in continuing discussions. About $5-8 million was necessary for a co-production of 130 half-hours of programming that could be used for 2–3 years. This category included countries like Poland.

3. Countries that had been in co-production and had stopped producing, such as Brazil and France.

4. Countries that Sesame Workshop would like to enter but where few, if any, established relationships existed.

EXHIBIT 5 **Consolidated Statement of Financial Position**

For the years ended June 30 (000s omitted)	2000	1999
Assets		
Current assets:		
Cash and short-term investments	$13,338	6,930
Receivables-		
Subscriptions, program and product licenses, less allowance for doubtful accounts, of $6,411 in 2000 and $5,279 in 1999	34,286	33,230
Grants and contracts in support of programs	2,296	1,132
Other	551	729
	37,133	35,181
Programs in process	16,028	10,547
Prepaid publishing costs	1,520	2,485
Other current assets	1,145	967
Total current assets	69,164	56,110
Deferred tax asset, less valuation allowance of $3,977 in 2000 and $4,212 in 1997	1,196	1,196
Marketable securities	174,928	180,914
Investment in Sesame Workshop Publishing Company LLC	88	3/4
Furniture, equipment, capitalized information systems, and leasehold improvements, at cost, net of accumulated depreciation and amortization of $16,257 in 2000 and $13,115 in 1999	11,983	9,753
Total assets	**$260,447**	**$248,468**
Liabilities and net assets		
Current liabilities:		
Accounts payable	11,387	5,686
Accrued expenses	31,547	32,562
Deferred subscription, program and product license revenues	35,710	29,895
Total current liabilities	**78,644**	**68,143**
Deferred rent payable	4,572	2,979
Total Liabilities	83,216	71,119
Net assets:		
Unrestricted	175,124	174,818
Temporarily restricted	2,107	2,531
Total net assets	177,231	177,349
Total liabilities and net assets	$260,447	$248,468

Source: Sesame Workshop Annual Report

Entry Strategies

Market-entry decisions through co-production typically were initiated by a broadcaster that had seen the English version of *Sesame Street* and wanted the show for its country. Various issues would then be considered by Sesame Workshop: 1) What is the level of television penetration? 2) Does Sesame Workshop have a relationship at the government level and, if not, can a relationship be established? 3) Does the market have financial viability, i.e., is it at least a breakeven proposition? 4) Does Sesame Workshop have people available to develop the show? 5) Are Sesame Workshop's license and publisher partners, Mattel and Random House, established in that market?

Initially, co-productions were funded entirely by local broadcasters. Assuming a decision was made to move forward and a contract was signed with a broadcaster, a co-production could take from a year to four or more years to produce. During this phase, Sesame Workshop would work with the product partners to develop a product strategy, which would follow the launch of the television show once the brand was established.

1996 Reorganization

A reorganization of international operations in 1996 resulted in a new structure headed by a group president for products and international television. A group vice president for international and two regional vice president positions were created: one for Latin America and Asia and one for Europe, Africa, and the Middle East. There was also a vice president for co-production. Each regional vice president had profit and return-on-investment responsibility for all Sesame Workshop business. For each region, there were regional directors responsible for television and licensing. Given the size and complexity of the China activities, there was also a senior director responsible for the television activities in China. The reorganization resulted in a revised classification of markets and countries. Non-U.S. markets in which Sesame Workshop either broadcast or planned to broadcast could be broken down as follows:

1. Large growth potential markets in which Sesame Workshop had strong recognition, e.g., U.K., Germany, Japan.

2. High potential markets that could generate more revenue, e.g., China, Mexico.

3. Maintenance markets, smaller markets that were currently generating revenue but had limited growth potential, e.g., Australia, Canada, Netherlands.

4. Social impact markets, e.g., Israel/Palestine, South Africa.

The reorganization of international activities resulted in a decision to reduce the managerial time spent on smaller markets and focus on the larger markets with high potential. However, selling the English version of *Sesame Street* or doing a co-production required roughly the same amount of effort regardless of the market size. As well, many of the smaller markets were some of Sesame Workshop's oldest customers, which raised the issue whether relationships with smaller customers should be scaled back. Within Sesame Workshop, the obvious answer was no, but there was a consensus that priority markets had to be established. As well, some market-entry decisions did not fit neatly into this model. For example, after the successful launch in Russia, USAID asked Sesame Workshop to consider Egypt, which was not initially considered a high potential market.

1999 Changes

In 1999, the group president for products and international television resigned. As of mid-2001, the position remained unfilled. A new division was created to manage projects that involved governments and NGOs, such as in South Africa, Egypt, and Israel. This division, called project management, consisted of four directors and focused on issues such as educational outreach, fundraising, and government contacts. These projects had limited product licensing opportunities. With the creation of this new division, the products and international television group headed by Martha Van Gelder, which consisted of 16 people, concentrated on developing markets in which both a product license and television businesses could be supported. However, there were close linkages between the groups, as Van Gelder explained:

> Every market we are in is mission—there is no market where *Sesame Street* is not reaching and teaching kids. When we go to meetings, we don't say, 'How will we make the most money?' We say, 'How will we reach the most kids?' This is a concept that is very comfortable to everybody.

In 2001, Sesame Workshop had no offices outside the United States. Agents were used to manage day-to-day business relationships in international markets. The firm began shifting away from having different agents in each country. *Sesame Street* now had one agent for all of Europe, which helped streamline decision-making. The same approach was being implemented in Latin America. Sesame Workshop was considering how to more effectively use alliances to support marketing and advertising while still maintaining control over the brand and program content.

NEW MARKETS

A Sesame Workshop manager described the challenge of identifying new markets:

> We need to be a profitable enterprise because if we are not profitable, we won't be around for very long. Even if we are not-for-profit, we compete against for-profit companies. We need good people, great shows, and good business systems and planning. We look at Sesame Workshop like a normal business: I have a certain overhead, I have production costs and marketing expenses and profit. We have to hit those numbers and we have to operate in a way that is as smart and professional as Warner Bros. or Disney. The difference between us and Disney is that we don't have to look for a certain profitability target in order to make a decision.
>
> Social responsibility is critical for us. We have pure mission countries, such as South Africa, that the company has decided are strategically important. We can and

do vary costs and pricing for poorer countries. In these countries, there is not a self-sustaining model around licensing. That means we have to come up with a different model that may have government or corporate sponsorship. In contrast, in a territory like Germany, the combination of the broadcaster and licensing makes this a great market.

Sesame Workshop celebrates diversity because it is at the heart of what we do. We believe the *Sesame Street* co-productions in China and Israel/Palestine help bring the world together. In Israel and Palestine, we saw that there was such a need for people to learn how to get along. For the Israel and Palestine show, there are two streets, one Arab and one Israeli. The same for Egypt—there was such a need for education on the role of women in society. By producing in Cairo, we end up with a series that can be broadcast throughout the whole Arab-speaking region. In South Africa—a total need for education for the masses.

India was a country that was considered a potentially interesting market, as another Sesame Workshop manager explained:

We have some English being shown on cable and maybe 5–6 million viewers. But from a licensing perspective, India is not very interesting because there are limited distribution channels. With television there is tremendous potential for reaching people and even getting some reasonable licensing fees. But given the language and cultural differences, how can one show play to the whole country? We have had discussions with Indian organizations. But it comes down to the problem that we only have a certain amount of people who can do co-production development. When South Africa comes along and we have millions of dollars of funding and only so many hours and bodies, India and other markets have to wait.

Brazil, France, and Italy were also obvious target markets:

The big holes in Europe have been France and Italy. We had versions of the series on the air back in the 1970s that did not work very well and did not leave us with a strong relationship. Both countries are known as difficult markets for American programming. Clearly, those are two markets that are very important for us with great potential. We recently signed a deal in Italy to broadcast *Sesame English* and *Elmo's World* on Rai and RaiSat. In Latin America, Brazil has great potential. We are always trying to find ways to enter new markets appropriately. But, it is a time-consuming process and every market is different. We cannot just take the same people and throw them against multiple projects that require an intense amount of work. That is why our head of global distribution focuses more on understanding markets than on actual selling.

Another manager summed up her views on Sesame Workshop's international strategy:

We make decisions differently from other companies developing children's programming. That's what makes it so interesting to be here and sometimes frustrating. There are some huge markets for co-production opportunities, such as Brazil and India. It's a little hard for me to fit together how we make the decision about allocating resources to these different markets. What drives our willingness to make commitments to these markets? We are still in the process of trying to figure out what we want financially and what we want the business to look like.

It is not feasible to do co-productions in every market. But because we are a not-for-profit, we have the freedom to go into new markets and break even. For example, I could have a great project for a small market and it would be as well received as a project for a huge market like China or Brazil. We want to do unique small projects. For example, we are doing a conflict resolution series for Cyprus using live action with an organization called Search for Common Ground. The producers could not even meet in Cyprus so they went to London. There is no profit in the project but it is consistent with the mission.

INVESTMENT CRITERIA

The usefulness of specific investment criteria as the basis for guiding new international investments had been debated, as an executive explained:

Several years ago, I felt we were not making decisions in a consistent manner. We need consistent breakeven on ongoing operations. I tried to establish criteria such as mission, cash flow, financial return, and management time involved. What I wanted was a consistent list so that we understood the implications of doing a project. The problem was how to weight the criteria. Which ones are the most important?

We need to look at the overall property and what can be generated from the property. We have not done this so well, or at all, in the past. A show that production-wise is at the highest level but that nobody can afford—how valuable is that? Is *Elmo's World* so successful because of the high-quality production or because of *Elmo* and the simple story lines? There is probably a bit of both and it is very hard to test.

We are being pushed to find new revenue sources while staying true to our brand and mission. Now, when we look at new properties as we develop them, we are looking at all its tentacles. It is not just revenue—there are outreach components and online ways to extend the experience. Trying to capture all the revenue and all the expense around the property is something we have to get better at.

BROADCAST COMPETITION

When Sesame Workshop internationalized in the 1970s and 1980s, television in most countries was dominated by public broadcasters. Many of these broadcasters were prepared to pay Sesame Workshop fees to cover production and other costs. In the 1990s, especially with the growth of commercial broadcasting via satellite and cable, the television industry worldwide became much more competitive. With new competition, audiences dropped for individual broadcasters and especially for the former monopoly public broadcasters. As well, the children's programming area was not a primary area for most commercial broadcasters.

In some markets, such as Taiwan, cable reached 80% of the households. In other markets, only a small percentage of households had cable. To deal with situations where cable and terrestrial (traditional broadcasters) coverage both existed, Sesame Workshop was beginning to structure deals whereby one company was given terrestrial rights and another company cable rights, with both rights exclusive and separate. However, co-productions were only done with terrestrial broadcasters.

A Sesame Workshop manager explained the new competitive challenges:

> In the old days we were it. We invented education through entertainment and we always took for granted that people knew who we were. We had a quality property that we were putting on the screen. People kept watching the show and the broadcaster said, "This is great." As competition has increased and the windows for the show are shrinking, the audience we are going after is also shrinking. So, with the number of programs that are available to the shrinking audience continuing to increase, if your program loses popularity, it is hard to come back.
>
> There are two different kinds of competition we face. We can no longer assume that *Sesame Street* will be the broadcaster's first choice. There are now dozens of preschool programs, not just on PBS. To be successful, a show has to be good, the product has to be on the cutting edge, and there must be a fabulous product offering in every category. There is increased competition from preschool shows across the board. Shows like *Teletubbies* and *Rugrats* are financed and designed for global exploitation from the beginning. We have taught the world how to do that. At one of the major conferences, broadcasters were saying to us, "We know you make *Sesame Street,* but I have tons of preschool shows. What do you have in live action for 7-12-year-olds?"
>
> Although there are now more channels and options for programming, license fees [paid by broadcasters] around the world have been going down and down. We have broadcasters who are willing to pay zero but still want us to deliver a fully produced show, promote it, and guarantee a percentage of ancillary revenue. If *Sesame Street* is too expensive, broadcasters will take something else. When U.S. broadcasters can fill their educational requirement by airing *GI Joe* because it shows good over evil, how much more would you pay for *Sesame Street* if your goal is just to satisfy a mandated educational requirement and you cannot use advertising on *Sesame Street*? Unfortunately, the marketplace does not always put the same value on our product as it costs us to produce it.
>
> The other competitive situation is that many broadcasters in the United States and globally own the shows and own the airtime. That means broadcasters like Nickelodeon, Disney, and Time Warner can decide they want to back a show like *Rugrats.* They own the rights and can keep it on the air, let it incubate, and slowly develop an audience. It is a lot more difficult if you don't own a channel, which is one of the strategic reasons why we launched *Noggin* on the Nickelodeon channel. We have to have strategic alliances with the broadcasters and we have to become a more flexible and creative partner. We also have to become more innovative in developing funding sources for co-productions. And we can no longer view 130 shows per season as essential. We can do 65 shows and perhaps get better quality shows.

Historically, most government-owned channels were not allowed to interrupt programming for young children with commercials. However, the increase in cable and satellite broadcasting was putting pressure on Sesame Workshop's commercial-free philosophy.

> If you are PBS or another public broadcaster, commercial-free television is accepted. But increasingly we are talking to commercial channels that want a commercial break. It is becoming difficult to ask somebody to show an entire hour

commercial-free. In Mexico, we started a commercial break in the show as an experiment because they have been asking for it for so long. We were worried the kids wouldn't be able to make the distinction between the show and the commercial. The research that has come back from Mexico shows that kids clearly understand where the commercial is. I think in many markets the company will have to rethink its stance on commercial breaks.

OPPORTUNITIES AND CHALLENGES

Looking towards the future, the managers of the international group saw many opportunities and plenty of challenges. For example, Japan provided an interesting situation. Unique for Sesame Workshop, a large market in Japan was teenage girls and young women. Because the show until recently had been broadcast in English (in 1998 a dubbed version was introduced which was very successful), *Sesame Street* was watched primarily as a vehicle for learning English, which was never Sesame Workshop's intention for Japan. As well, Japanese girls were very fond of characters on products like clothing, purses, T-shirts, key chains, earrings, etc. The *Sesame Street* characters were very popular, and many offers for product licenses had to be turned down because they were deemed inconsistent for the brand. More recently in Japan, opportunities for wireless Internet were emerging, especially for English language training.

Production deals were also changing, which meant an increasingly complex network of partners, customers, sponsors, and other relationships.

> To make the co-production model work, we need first-run revenues, syndication if possible, international sales, and international product sales. The old model was that broadcasters paid for everything, including a management fee and some profit for us. A few years ago we started going into markets where there was government money available and where we had to raise sponsorship money. The broadcaster was not paying for the whole thing. Ultimately, Sesame Workshop was taking the risk if sufficient money could not be raised. Now, we have some broadcasters, who used to pay for the whole co-production, telling us they can no longer pay and asking us to help raise sponsorships for them.

Another manager expressed concerns about the heavy reliance on *Sesame Street:*

> We need new programs. We are a one-hit wonder that's been wonderful worldwide. But we need a follow-up success. We have had some other shows that have done pretty well but nothing near the global scale of *Sesame Street.* We have put a lot of energy into *Dragon Tales,* which is beautifully animated.

Product licensing was also an area that offered interesting challenges. Products could go from hot to cold very quickly, as a manager explained:

> We saw that happen with Tickle Me Elmo. Sesame Workshop was considered 'fashion' for awhile through Tickle Me Elmo. Moms and dads were buying Elmo ties, Elmo boxer shorts, and Elmo this and that. It was the hot brand. Then all of a

sudden the fashion side of it went away and we lost 60% of the business in less than six months time. Where did it go? It went to other licensee and new properties like *Teletubbies.*

We have to work very hard to make sure the brand does not erode to the point where moms and dads say, "I don't want junior to watch the show anymore." If that ever happens, you are out of business. The show is what drives everything we do at Sesame Workshop. People can tell you all day long that our products sell on their own because they are cute and fun. But eight out of every ten people buy our products because their children have seen this property on the TV show.

In some markets, we are severely limited by being with a public broadcaster in terms of television commercials and exploiting the brands the way other companies do. We can sell toys but we cannot promote them on television.

Our goal is to find ways to sustain our licensing activities but do it in a way that sets us apart from most other licensee/licensors. Our television competitors often pay for their television programming just to feed the licensing program. When Sesame Workshop enters international markets we don't say, "Here's *Mickey Mouse,* take him; here's *Teletubbies*—you can't do anything to change it." We can make our products local because our show is local.

CONCLUSION

Final comments from two Sesame Workshop executives:

In international, we have grown so quickly over the last few years that we worry about overextending ourselves. *Sesame Street* is a very powerful series and a lot of people want to work with us. But, we cannot respond to everybody. That's why we came up with things like *Open Sesame.* Our challenge is to remain true to our roots and develop programming that's enticing and educational. We need to address where we are as a brand today because that should underpin everything that we do.

We are a small firm with limited resources and unlimited dreams. Our mission of educating children is so important to us. But how many mission projects can we take on? I think what will drive it is what makes sense for our own survival and what it does to the overall health of the organization, both mission and financial health.

Endnotes

1. Sesame Workshop 2000 Annual Report.
2. 2000 Annual Report.
3. Cynthia Crossen, "Class Act: *Sesame Street,* at 23, Still Teaches Children While Amusing Them," *The Wall Street Journal,* Feb. 21, 1992, A1.

Chapter Eighteen

Where Have You Been? An Exercise to Assess Your Exposure to the Rest of the World's Peoples

Professor Paul Beamish prepared this note solely to provide material for class discussion. The author does not intend to provide legal, tax, accounting or other professional advice. Such advice should be obtained from a qualified professional.

INSTRUCTION

1. On each of the attached worksheets, note the total number and names of those countries you have visited, and the corresponding percentage of world population which each country represents. Sum the relevant regional totals on p. 316.

2. If used as part of a group analysis, estimate the grand total for the entire group. Then consider the following questions:

   • Why is there such a high variability in individual profiles (i.e., high exposure vs. low exposure)?

   • What are the implications of each profile for one's career?

   • What would it take to get you to personally change your profile?

Region: Africa

	Country	2000 Population (in millions)	% of World Total
1)	Nigeria	126.9	2.1
2)	Ethiopia	64.2	1.1
3)	Egypt	63.9	1.1
4)	Congo (Dem. Rep)	50.9	0.8
5)	South Africa	42.8	0.7
6)	Tanzania	33.6	0.6
7)	Sudan	31.0	0.5
8)	Algeria	30.3	0.5
9)	Kenya	30.0	0.5
10)	Morocco	28.7	0.5
11)	Uganda	22.2	0.4
12)	Ghana	19.3	0.3
13)	Mozambique	17.6	0.3
14)	Côte d'Ivoire	16.0	0.3
15)	Madagascar	15.5	0.3
16)	Cameroon	14.8	0.2
17)	Angola	13.1	0.2
18)	Zimbabwe	12.6	0.2
19)	Burkina Faso	11.2	0.2
20)	Mali	10.8	0.2
21)	Niger	10.8	0.2
22)	Malawi	10.3	0.2
23)	Zambia	9.8	0.2
24)	Senegal	9.5	0.2
25)	Tunisia	9.5	0.2
26)	Somalia	8.7	0.1
27)	Rwanda	8.5	0.1
28)	Chad	7.6	0.1
	Subtotal	**730.1**	

Source of all Statistics, except for Taiwan: 2002 World Bank World Development Indicators

Region: Africa
Concluded

	Country	2000 Population (in millions)	% of World Total
29)	Guinea	7.4	0.1
30)	Burundi	6.8	0.1
31)	Benin	6.2	0.1
32)	Libya	5.2	0.1
33)	Sierra Leone	5.0	0.1
34)	Togo	4.5	0.1
35)	Eritrea	4.0	0.1
36)	Central African Republic	3.7	0.1
37)	Liberia	3.1	0.1
38)	Congo, Rep.	3.0	0.0
39)	Mauritania	2.6	0.0
40)	Lesotho	2.0	0.0
41)	Namibia	1.7	0.0
42)	Botswana	1.6	0.0
43)	Gambia, The	1.3	0.0
44)	Gabon	1.2	0.0
45)	Mauritius	1.1	0.0
46)	Guinea-Bissau	1.1	0.0
47)	Swaziland	1.0	0.0
48)	Djibouti	0.6	0.0
49)	Comoros	0.5	0.0
50)	Equatorial Guinea	0.4	0.0
51)	Cape Verde	0.4	0.0
52)	São Tomé and Principe	0.1	0.0
53)	Mayotte (Fr)	0.1	0.0
54)	Seychelles	0.1	0.0
	Subtotal	**794.8**	**13.2**

Region: North America and Caribbean

	Country	2000 Population (in millions)	% of World Total
1)	USA	281.5	4.7
2)	Mexico	97.9	1.6
3)	Canada	30.7	0.5
4)	Guatemala	11.3	0.2
5)	Cuba	11.1	0.2
6)	Dominican Republic	8.3	0.1
7)	Haiti	7.9	0.1
8)	Honduras	6.4	0.1
9)	El Salvador	6.2	0.1
10)	Nicaragua	5.0	0.1
11)	Puerto Rico (U.S.)	3.9	0.1
12)	Costa Rica	3.8	0.1
13)	Panama	2.8	0.0
14)	Jamaica	2.6	0.0
15)	Trinidad and Tobago	1.3	0.0
16)	Bahamas	0.3	0.0
17)	Barbados	0.2	0.0
18)	Belize	0.2	0.0
19)	Netherlands Antilles	0.2	0.0
20)	St. Lucia	0.1	0.0
21)	Virgin Islands (U.S.)	0.1	0.0
22)	St. Vincent & the Grenadines	0.1	0.0
23)	Grenada	0.1	0.0
24)	Aruba (Neth.)	0.1	0.0
25)	Dominica	0.1	0.0
26)	Antigua and Barbuda	0.1	0.0
27)	Bermuda (UK)	0.1	0.0
28)	St. Kitts and Nevis	0.1	0.0
29)	Cayman Islands	0.1	0.0
	Subtotal	**482.6**	**8.0**

Region: South America

	Country	2000 Population (in millions)	% of World Total
1)	Brazil	170.4	2.8
2)	Colombia	42.2	0.7
3)	Argentina	37.0	0.6
4)	Peru	25.6	0.4
5)	Venezuela	24.1	0.4
6)	Chile	15.2	0.3
7)	Ecuador	12.6	0.2
8)	Bolivia	8.3	0.1
9)	Paraguay	5.4	0.1
10)	Uruguay	3.3	0.1
11)	Guyana	0.7	0.0
12)	Suriname	0.4	0.0
	Subtotal	**345.2**	**5.7**

Region: Western Europe

	Country	2000 Population (in millions)	% of World Total
1)	Germany	82.1	1.4
2)	United Kingdom	59.7	1.0
3)	France	58.8	1.0
4)	Italy	57.6	1.0
5)	Spain	39.4	0.7
6)	Netherlands	15.9	0.3
7)	Greece	10.5	0.2
8)	Belgium	10.2	0.2
9)	Portugal	10.0	0.2
10)	Sweden	8.8	0.1
11)	Austria	8.1	0.1
12)	Switzerland	7.1	0.1
13)	Denmark	5.3	0.1
14)	Finland	5.1	0.1
15)	Norway	4.4	0.1
16)	Ireland	3.7	0.1
17)	Luxembourg	0.4	0.0
18)	Malta	0.3	0.0
19)	Iceland	0.3	0.0
20)	Channel Islands (U.K.)	0.1	0.0
21)	Isle of Man	0.1	0.0
22)	Andorra	0.1	0.0
23)	Greenland (Den.)	0.1	0.0
24)	Faeroe Islands (Den.)	0.1	0.0
25)	Monaco	0.1	0.0
26)	Liechtenstein	0.1	0.0
27)	San Marino	0.1	0.0
	Subtotal	**388.4**	**6.4**

Region: Eastern Europe

	Country	2000 Population (in millions)	% of World Total
1)	Russian Federation	145.5	2.4
2)	Ukraine	49.5	0.8
3)	Poland	38.6	0.6
4)	Romania	22.4	0.4
5)	Yugoslavia, F.R. (Serb/Mont)	10.6	0.2
6)	Czech Republic	10.2	0.2
7)	Belarus	10.0	0.2
8)	Hungary	10.0	0.2
9)	Bulgaria	8.1	0.1
10)	Slovak Republic	5.4	0.1
11)	Croatia	4.3	0.1
12)	Moldova	4.2	0.1
13)	Bosnia and Herzegovina	3.9	0.1
14)	Lithuania	3.6	0.1
15)	Albania	3.4	0.1
16)	Latvia	2.3	0.0
17)	Macedonia, Fyr	2.0	0.0
18)	Slovenia	1.9	0.0
19)	Estonia	1.3	0.0
	Subtotal	**337.2**	**5.6**

Region: Central Asia and Indian Subcontinent

	Country	2000 Population (in millions)	% of World Total
1)	India	1,015.9	16.8
2)	Pakistan	138.0	2.3
3)	Bangladesh	131.0	2.2
4)	Afghanistan	26.5	0.4
5)	Uzbekistan	24.7	0.4
6)	Nepal	23.0	0.4
7)	Sri Lanka	19.3	0.3
8)	Kazakhstan	14.8	0.2
9)	Azerbaijan	8.0	0.1
10)	Tajikistan	6.1	0.1
11)	Turkmenistan	5.1	0.1
12)	Georgia	5.0	0.1
13)	Kyrgyz Republic	4.9	0.1
14)	Armenia	3.8	0.1
15)	Mongolia	2.3	0.0
16)	Bhutan	0.8	0.0
17)	Maldives	0.2	0.0
	Subtotal	**1,429.4**	**23.6**

Region: Middle East

	Country	2000 Population (in millions)	% of World Total
1)	Turkey	65.2	1.1
2)	Iran	63.6	1.1
3)	Iraq	23.2	0.4
4)	Saudi Arabia	20.7	0.3
5)	Yemen	17.5	0.3
6)	Syrian Arab Republic	16.1	0.3
7)	Israel	6.2	0.1
8)	Jordan	4.8	0.1
9)	Lebanon	4.3	0.1
10)	United Arab Emirates	2.9	0.0
11)	West Bank and Gaza	2.9	0.0
12)	Oman	2.3	0.0
13)	Kuwait	1.9	0.0
14)	Cyprus	0.7	0.0
15)	Bahrain	0.6	0.0
16)	Qatar	0.5	0.0
	Subtotal	**233.4**	**3.9**

**Region: Asia
Pacific**

	Country	2000 Population (in millions)	% of World Total
1)	China (Excl. HK & Macao)	1,262.4	20.9
2)	Indonesia	210.4	3.5
3)	Japan	126.8	2.1
4)	Viet Nam	78.5	1.3
5)	Philippines	75.5	1.2
6)	Thailand	60.7	1.0
7)	Myanmar	47.7	0.8
8)	South Korea	47.2	0.8
9)	Malaysia	23.2	0.4
10)	Taiwan	22.4	0.4
11)	North Korea	22.2	0.4
12)	Australia	19.1	0.3
13)	Cambodia	12.0	0.2
14)	Hong Kong (SAR - China)	6.7	0.1
15)	Lao PDr	5.2	0.1
16)	Papua New Guinea	5.1	0.1
17)	Singapore	4.0	0.1
18)	New Zealand	3.8	0.1
19)	Fiji	0.8	0.0
20)	Macao (SAR-China)	0.4	0.0
21)	Solomon Islands	0.4	0.0
22)	Brunei	0.3	0.0
23)	Samoa	0.2	0.0
24)	French Polynesia (FR.)	0.2	0.0
25)	New Caledonia (FR.)	0.2	0.0
26)	Vanuatu	0.1	0.0
27)	Guam (U.S.)	0.1	0.0
28)	Micronesia, Fed. Sts.	0.1	0.0
29)	Tonga	0.1	0.0
30)	American Samoa (U.S.)	0.1	0.0
31)	Kiribati	0.1	0.0
32)	Marshall Islands	0.1	0.0
33)	Northern Mariana Islands	0.1	0.0
34)	Palau	0.1	0.0
	Subtotal	**2,036.2**	**33.7**

Summary

Region	# of Countries	Which You Have Visited	2000 Population (millions)	Region's % of World Population	% of Population You Have Been Exposed To
Africa	54	_____	794.8	13.2	_____
North America and Caribbean	29	_____	482.6	8.0	_____
South America	12	_____	345.2	5.7	_____
Western Europe	27	_____	388.4	6.4	_____
Eastern Europe	19	_____	337.2	5.5	_____
Central Asia and Indian Subcontinent	17	_____	1,429.4	23.6	_____
Middle East	16	_____	233.4	3.9	_____
Asia Pacific	34	_____	2,036.2	33.7	_____
Grand Total	**208**	_____	**6,047.2**	**100.0**	_____

Chapter Nineteen

MTN: Investing in Africa

On a sunny afternoon in late 1999, senior executives gathered at the head offices of Mobile Telephone Networks plc (MTN) in Johannesburg to discuss the company's international strategy.

MTN was one of two mobile telephone operators in South Africa. It had grown rapidly since its founding in 1993, and by 1999 offered mobile telephony to more than 1.3 million subscribers throughout the country. Known for its high-quality service, MTN was one of only three network operators worldwide to receive ISO 9001 certification. During the past year, it had expanded beyond its home market, setting up mobile telephone networks in three other African countries: Rwanda, Uganda and Swaziland. Most recently, it had won a license to operate in Africa's most populous country, Nigeria. These were the first steps in MTN's strategic vision: *"To be the leading telecommunications operator on the African continent."*

Now MTN was considering further international growth. At the request of CEO Robert Chaphe, MTN's international business development department had identified 11 additional countries where MTN might set up mobile telephone networks. Timing was critical. Several of these countries were soon offering licenses for bid, and if MTN didn't enter now it could find itself shut out.

Yet the attractions of further international growth were balanced by serious concerns. Domestic growth had already stretched the company's resources. Some managers were concerned that foreign expansion might divert managerial attention from the critical home market, where MTN was locked in a head-to-head battle with Vodacom.

The topic for discussion at the meeting of MTN's investment subcommittee was a simple question: How should MTN proceed with its strategy of international growth?

Professor Philip M. Rosenzweig developed this case as a basis for class discussion rather than to illustrate either effective or ineffective handling of an administrative situation.
Copyright © 2000 by **IMD**—International Institute for Management Development, Lausanne, Switzerland. Not to be used or reproduced without written permission directly from **IMD**.

IMD
INTERNATIONAL
LAUSANNE · SWITZERLAND

THE MOBILE TELEPHONE INDUSTRY

Mobile telephones using analog technology had been commercially available in the 1980s in the United States and a few other markets. These first mobile phones were relatively expensive, and tended to be used by professionals with critical needs for mobile communication.

By the mid-1990s the advent of digital technology made mobile phones available to just about everyone. A virtuous cycle followed: powerful small handsets with low prices led to higher usage; growing numbers of subscribers led to even lower prices, which led to even more growth. The advent of prepaid services further stimulated demand. Traditionally, subscribers had received monthly rental charges and service contracts. Handsets now came with prepaid cards, obviating the need for time-consuming credit checks and monthly billing. With prepaid services came a change in the mode of distribution, as any retailer or distributor could sell mobile phones along with other fast moving consumer goods.[1] In some countries, mobile phones were becoming a fashion accessory, as young people owned multiple telephones of different colors, sometimes swapping them with friends.[2]

The number of mobile phone users doubled every year during the 1990s. By 1998, the percentage of the population using mobile phones—known as teledensity—exceeded 30 percent in 10 countries (refer to Exhibit 1). In Finland, where teledensity had reached 57 percent, mobile phone users now outnumbered fixed network users.[3] During the first six months of 1998 alone, Europe added more than 13.3 million users, with users in France, the Netherlands, Germany, Great Britain and Portugal doubling from 1997 to 1998.[4] Growth was just as dramatic in Asia. In Japan, despite persistent economic difficulties, the number of subscribers reached 20 million in 1998, up from just 1.3 million in 1994.[5] Korea, China and other countries also surged. Rapid growth worldwide was expected for several years, with penetration of mobile phones expected to reach 50 percent in many industrialized countries by 2005.[6]

While mobile telephony grew most rapidly in the industrialized markets of Europe, Asia and North America, its impact was even more important in the developing world, where fixed line telephones were often either outdated or nonex-

EXHIBIT 1
Chart of Leading Countries in the World by Percentage of Population that has Cellular Phones (as of December 31, 1998)

1. Finland	57.4%
2. Norway	48.1
3. Sweden	48.0
4. Hong Kong	44.0
5. Iceland	38.3
6. Italy	36.3
7. Israel	35.4
8. Denmark	33.8
9. Australia	32.2
10. Portugal	31.5

Source: Stanley, Alessandra. "In Italy, They Just Love Their Cellular Telephones." *International Herald Tribune*, 6. August 1999: 4.

istent. In Latin America, in the Middle East and in Africa, mobile telephony offered a way for millions of people to take part in economic and social life. Villages that had never been able to communicate directly could now link up. Patients could speak with their doctors; citizens could call their elected officials and law enforcement agencies; and merchants could contact each other as well as their customers. For these countries, mobile telephones weren't a fashion accessory—they were a lifeline, a component of economic development. One African commented, "Mobile phones allow us to be connected to each other, and to the world. They will allow the poor to participate in the new millennium."

NETWORK OPERATORS: GROWTH AND EXPANSION

The mobile telephone industry consisted of three main actors. First were *equipment manufacturers,* who built the handsets, base stations and switching equipment. Prominent equipment manufacturers included Ericsson, Siemens, Alcatel, Nokia and Motorola. Second were *service providers,* who signed up customers, provided them with service, and handled billings. These firms were primarily local and often small. Third were *network operators,* who installed and managed the entire network under licenses granted by the local telecommunications authority. This case study focuses on network operators.

Network operators incurred high initial costs as they bought or leased equipment to build a network of base stations, switches and control centers. In addition, they paid a license fee to the government, software license fees, and had substantial personnel costs. But once the network was up and running, variable costs were low. New subscribers added virtually no cost to running the network. One manager observed, "Once you cover your costs, there are huge margins." Running a successful network therefore depended on attracting a large number of subscribers. Network operators spent large sums on branding building and marketing, sometimes spending up to 30 percent of revenues on marketing alone.

Competition for Network Licenses

The number of network operators varied from country to country, based on the number of licenses issued by government telecom ministries. Japan issued a single network operator license, to NTT DoCoMo, a subsidiary of NTT. Its dominance of the Japanese market made it the world's largest mobile phone operator.[7] Similarly, China Telecom was the sole network operator in the People's Republic of China. Korean authorities issued licenses to five network operators, setting off intense competition among them for users.[8] The UK had four operators—Vodafone, Orange, Cellnet and One-2-One—each with between 15 percent and 30 percent of the total market.

Countries without domestic firms capable of running mobile networks looked to foreign companies. Often the result was a joint venture between the local state-owned telecom company and a foreign company. Brazil, for example, issued separate licenses for each of 10 geographic areas, and awarded licenses to network

EXHIBIT 2
Global Top 20
Cellular Operators
Ranked by Number
of Equity Subscribers
(as of end-June 1998)

Company	Country	Total	Domestic	Int'l
NTT DoCoMo	Japan	19,357,000	19,357,000	0
China Telecom*	China	18,600,000	18,600,000	0
Telecom Italia Mobile	Italy	12,385,705	11,440,000	945,705
AirTouch**	US	11,846,896	7,572,000	4,274,896
BellSouth	US	7,093,736	4,400,000	2,693,736
AT&T	US	6,945,266	6,484,000	461,266
Bell Atlantic	US	6,911,954	5,707,000	1,204,954
SBC Wireless	US	6,593,357	5,831,000	762,357
Vodafone	UK	6,514,992	3,637,000	2,877,992
T-Mobile	Germany	5,296,513	4,550,000	746,513
GTE	US	5,279,230	4,631,000	648,230
SK Telecom	S. Korea	5,140,159	5,140,159	0
France Telecom	France	5,082,029	3,914,800	1,167,229
Mannesmann Mobilfunk	Germany	4,600,000	4,600,000	0
DDI	Japan	4,517,400	4,517,400	0
Telefonica	Spain	4,327,250	3,726,000	601,250
Omnitel Pronto Italia	Italy	4,000,000	4,000,000	0
Telstra	Australia	3,100,000	3,100,000	0
BT***	UK	3,037,807	1,893,600	1,144,207
IDO	Japan	3,035,000	3,035,000	0

*Includes China Telecom (Hong Kong).
**Merged with Vodafone Group Plc on January 15, 1999.
***BT owns 60% of Cellnet.
Source: Global Mobile Subscriber Database.

operators from six countries: Bell South (US), Telia (Sweden), SK Telecom (South Korea), STET (Italy), DDI (Japan) and Bell Canada.

For their part, many network operators were rushing to sign contracts around the world. In addition to its entry in Brazil, Bell South operated networks in Chile, Denmark, Ecuador, Germany, India, Israel, Nicaragua, Panama, Peru, Uruguay and Venezuela. France Telecom ran networks in Slovakia, Greece, Romania, Poland, Russia, Lebanon, Congo and India. Spain's Telefonica had networks in Argentina, Chile, Peru, Puerto Rico and other Spanish-speaking countries. Many of the largest network operators in the world, listed in Exhibit 2, had significant international subscribers in addition to a strong domestic position.

MOBILE TELEPHONES IN SOUTH AFRICA

The most developed African nation in terms of mobile telephony was the Republic of South Africa. With an area of 1,226,000 square km, it was bordered by Namibia, Botswana, Zimbabwe, Mozambique and Swaziland (refer to Exhibit 3). Its population of 42 million made it one of the most largest countries in Africa, trailing only Nigeria, Ethiopia and Egypt. It was a highly diverse country, composed of blacks (76.3 percent), whites (12.7 percent), mixed race or "colored" (8.5 percent) and

EXHIBIT 3   Map of South Africa

Asian (2.5 percent). It had 11 official languages: Afrikaans, English, Ndebele, Pedi, Sotho, Swazi, Tsonga, Tswana, Venda, Xhosa and Zulu.

During the decades of official racial separation, known as *apartheid,* South Africa had been out of the economic mainstream. Government policy shifted in the late 1980s, first with the release of political prisoners including African National Congress leader Nelson Mandela in 1990, and then with a transition to democratic rule with universal suffrage. Following Mandela's election as president in 1994, foreign firms resumed investment in South Africa, and South African firms began to do business abroad.

By the end of the 1990s South Africa was a study of contrasts. It had several major cities—Johannesburg, Capetown, Port Elizabeth, Durban, Pretoria, Bloemfontein—yet 55 percent of the population lived in rural areas. It boasted a modern banking sector, a first-rate transportation infrastructure in many parts of the country and excellent universities, yet also had significant poverty, crime, unemployment and low education. Furthermore, as South Africa was more economically advanced than the rest of sub-Saharan Africa, it was a magnet for illegal immigration from all over the continent, which added to its woes.

Mobile Telephone Licenses: Vodacom and MTN

The South African government's Ministry of Telecommunications issued a first mobile telephone license in May 1993. It was awarded to Vodacom, a joint venture among three firms: Telkom SA, South Africa's monopoly telephone provider, Vodafone, a leading telecom operator from the UK, and Rembrandt, a cigarette and luxury goods conglomerate. Telkom was the largest shareholder, with 50 percent ownership. Local minority investors, known as Black Empowerment Shareholders, subsequently acquired a 5 percent holding.

A second network operator license was soon made available through a tender process. The winning bid went to a joint venture composed of Cable & Wireless, a UK-based firm with a 25 percent share, M-Net, a South African pay-TV channel, Transnet, the state-owned transport company, through its telecommunications division, Transtel, and two Black Empowerment Shareholders. The new company was called Mobile Telephone Networks, or MTN.

YEARS OF RAPID GROWTH

MTN began with a capital investment of 500 million rand (R), worth about US$150 million at the time. Key technology was provided by Cable & Wireless. The initial staff included some key expatriate managers from Cable & Wireless and a number of local employees, many from Telkom.

MTN's first task was to build a network of base stations across the country. Within six months it had set up 400 base stations, and could offer mobile telephony to the main urban areas of Johannesburg/Pretoria, Capetown, Durban and a number of other major cities. The network "went live" for testing in March 1994 and was launched commercially in June 1994. It met with immediate success. MTN's business plan projected 50,000 subscribers in the first year of operation; in fact, it achieved 95,000 subscribers in its first year. It was profitable after 22 months.

Building the Domestic Business

Over the next years, MTN built a network of 2,200 base stations at a cost of R 5 billion. The resulting network stretched from Capetown to the border with Zimbabwe, connecting all major cities and towns, and operating along 13,000 kilometers of national highway. It was the largest GSM network in the world, covering an area of 650,000 square kilometers, or 48 percent of the country—an area 50 percent greater than all of Germany. More than 75 percent of all South Africans were within MTN's coverage. MTN also made a point of extending its network to rural and under-privileged areas. Its community-service program offered subsidized mobile telephone services to under-privileged areas. By 1998 more than 8,500 community-service pay phones had been installed.

MTN's initial business model, based on Cable & Wireless's experience in the UK, called for it to build and maintain its network, and to handle marketing. Providing customers with service was left to local "service providers," some of which offered access only to MTN's network, while others also offered access to Vodacom. Over time, as some service providers failed or encountered difficulties, MTN acquired them and began to offer direct service.

Rapid growth presented a particular challenge in building a first-class workforce. In its first year of operation MTN had 200 employees; by 1999 it had more than 2,200. Almost 1,500 worked at the head office in Johannesburg's Sandton district. Others staffed regional offices in KwaZulu Natal, Western Cape, Gauteng and elsewhere. The largest numbers of employees worked in subscriber operations, the network group, sales and customer service. (Refer to Exhibit 4 for a distribution of employees by department and by location.)

Hiring and training the workforce was a constant concern. The workforce was young, with an average age of 29, and most managers were in the most responsible position they had ever held. Technical positions posed a special challenge, as engineers and technicians were in short supply in South Africa. Attracting highly qualified technical employees was difficult, and retaining them was just as hard. The worldwide demand for GSM meant that an employee in South Africa could easily find a job elsewhere. Multinational firms came to South Africa with the express goal of hiring away employees to fill positions around the world. Some competitors set up shop in hotels across from MTN to lure employees with attractive packages.

Maintaining a large network of base stations was another tall order. MTN ran a central network control center from the top floor of its Johannesburg offices, with a series of computer screens showing the operational status of every base station in the country. The network was monitored 24 hours a day, 365 days a year. The slightest problem set off alarms and sent technicians off to solve it. Reflecting its dedication to quality in production, delivery, training and servicing, MTN was the first telecommunications operator in the southern hemisphere to receive ISO 9001 accreditation.

EXHIBIT 4 MTN Group Headcount (as of 31 March 1999)

	Head Office	KwaZulu Natal	Western Cape	Central	Gauteng	Eastern Cape	Transvaal	Total
Human Resources	23	0	0	0	0	0	0	23
Marketing	62	4	6	2	0	3	0	77
Finance	194	24	24	11	19	7	0	279
Subscriber Operations	406	0	0	0	0	0	0	406
Network Group	302	38	32	28	46	0	38	484
Sales	52	90	61	34	111	28	0	376
IS	155	0	0	0	0	0	0	155
Corporate Relations	7	0	1	0	0	0	0	8
CEO	4	0	0	0	0	0	0	4
COO (Mtel)	3	0	0	0	0	0	0	3
Int'l Business Development	20	0	0	0	0	0	0	20
New Business Development	15	0	0	0	0	0	0	15
Customer Services	237	0	0	0	0	0	0	237
Service Center	0	34	28	18	78	12	0	170
Regional Management	0	2	3	3	0	2	0	10
Total	1,480	192	155	96	254	52	38	**2,267**

Source: MTN company documents.

MTN'S INTERNATIONAL EXPANSION

Even as it was building a successful domestic position, MTN had its eyes on international growth. Its focus was the African continent. With 700 million inhabitants, Africa was more populous than Europe or North America, yet it had very low teledensity. By one estimate, 70 percent of all Africans had never used a telephone. The company stated:

> The incredible potential for cellular telephony within the African market has driven us to explore the opportunities available in each country. In terms of securing the future success of our company, expansion in Africa came as a natural decision.

Africa was attractive not only for its growth potential, but because it offered MTN a potential competitive advantage. MTN's deep understanding of Africa's people, its cultures and its economic challenges suggested that it might fare better than European or American companies, most of which had little or no experience in Africa. Conversely, being close to MTN's home might make African countries easier to manage than more distant markets. MTN was also interested in mobile telephony as a way to spur development on the African continent. This was more than an altruistic objective, since the development of other African nations was vital to creating local employment and reducing the flow of illegal immigrants to South Africa, as well as to provide markets for South African exports. (Refer to the map of Africa on Exhibit 5.)

EXHIBIT 5   Map of Africa

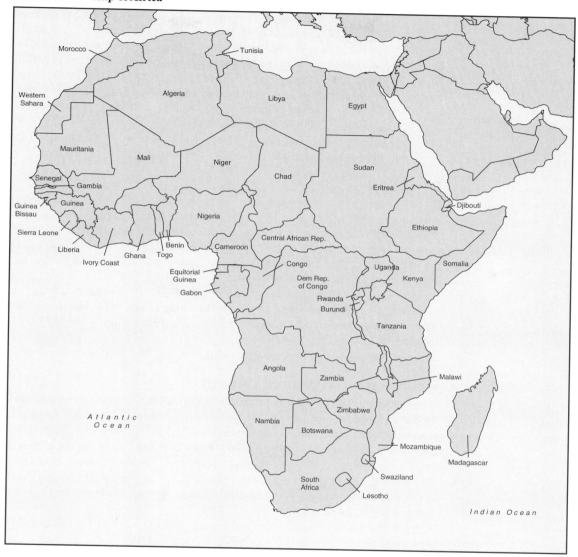

The International Business Development Department

To identify opportunities and prepare bids in foreign markets, MTN created a department of international business development. One of MTN's original hires, Ross Macdonald, was placed in charge. He was known around MTN's offices as the "hunter" whose job was to bring in new licenses.

Supporting Macdonald were "bid teams" that devised business plans and prepared bids. Bid teams analyzed a variety of factors: the host country's geography, its population, degree of urbanization, level of economic development, potential for growth, possible joint venture partners and more. Through this process, MTN determined if it wished to bid for a network license, and if so, what it was willing to pay. Most host governments were interested in more than the license fee—they favored business plans that promised mobile telephone coverage for a large fraction of the population, at low prices, in a short time. For their part, network operators needed to formulate bids that took into account risks, reasonable timetables and a satisfactory rate of return. MTN's International Business Development Department considered all of these factors as it devised bids for new markets.

Entry Modes

MTN planned to enter foreign markets through joint ventures with local telecom companies. In some instances, MTN would include additional partners who could provide specific expertise or technology, or could help with staffing. One MTN manager suggested that the "ideal" joint venture would involve a 40 percent stake for MTN, 30 percent for another operating company (a strategic equity partner) and 15 percent each for local investors.

Although it didn't require majority ownership, MTN insisted on being the lead partner in all its joint ventures. During the planning phase, MTN identified "material decisions" over which it needed to retain decision authority, including capital expenditures and the appointment of top executives. Keeping authority over those key decisions was a necessary condition of any tender offer.

Financing International Growth

International growth posed major financial requirements. Each new entry would call for the construction of a network of base stations, sometimes over a very large geographic area. As a rule, each base station might initially serve a few hundred customers, and could cost $200,000 to $300,000—which translated to an investment of about $1 million per 1,000 customers. In addition, MTN would have to hire a staff for marketing, administration and other functions. After significant outlays to construct the network and begin operations—known as "peak funding"—MTN could begin to generate a return.

Exchange controls posed additional complications. In an effort to retain its foreign exchange, the South African Reserve Bank (SARB) restricted the flow of funds to foreign countries. South African companies could invest up to R 250 million ($43 million at 1999 exchange rates) in countries within the South African Development Community, a group of nations in Southern Africa that included Mozambique, Zimbabwe and Botswana, but only R 50 million ($8 million) in countries outside SADC.

This limitation made it impossible to fund the installation and initial operation of mobile telephone networks directly from South Africa. MTN's chief financial officer, Rob Nisbet, remarked: "In telecom, 50 million rand is extremely low." MTN therefore needed to finance foreign investments with funds raised from outside South Africa. Fortunately, it could secure foreign loans with its South African assets. A few foreign funding options were available, including international lending agencies and international commercial banks. Nisbet observed that if a venture was expected to be profitable, finding capital was not usually a major obstacle—investors both inside and outside South Africa were ready to commit funds to a profitable venture.

Bidding for New Licenses

In 1996 MTN's board created the Investment Subcommittee (ISC) to assess opportunities for growth outside South Africa and approve investment decisions. It carefully examined the many opportunities available for network licenses, and determined which were most attractive. In some instances, such as in neighboring Botswana, MTN declined to bid for a license even though it had specifically been invited to do so by the host government. The reason? Botswana, a country of less than one million inhabitants, was making two licenses available, and MTN believed that a country of this size justified only one network. If it could not be the sole operator, it preferred not to bid at all. In other countries, MTN was unsuccessful in securing licenses, at times edged out by European rivals.

Soon, however, its efforts were successful. During 1998 MTN was awarded licenses to operate networks in three countries: Rwanda, Uganda and Swaziland. A synopsis of MTN's three successful bids is described here:

1. MTN RwandaCell

In April, 1998 MTN was awarded a license to operate the first GSM network in Rwanda, a small central African country with a population of seven million. The new company, MTN RwandaCell, was a joint venture owned 26 percent by MTN, 28 percent by Rwandatel, the state-owned telecommunications company, and the balance by a local investment holding company called Tristar. MTN's 26 percent stake was large enough to ensure that it could not be outvoted in special resolutions, but was relatively low in recognition of high-perceived political risk.

Over the next months, MTN sent a network implementation team to Rwanda. Working closely with Ericsson, the lead supplier of network equipment, MTN built in just three weeks a network of 20 base stations that included the capital city of Kigali and a few other towns. On July 4, Rwanda's National Liberation Day, the first mobile-to-mobile call was officially made. MTN RwandaCell launched commercial service in September 1998 and offered prepaid service three months later. At first, the number of subscribers was a bit low because only postpaid (i.e., contract) services were available, and because initial coverage was limited in scope. But with the introduction of prepaid services and the expansion of coverage, the company grew rapidly and was profitable after one year of operation.

2. MTN Uganda

MTN received a second network foreign operator license in Uganda, a nation of 19 million inhabitants located on Rwanda's northern border. A first mobile license had been awarded in 1996 to Cel-Tel, a joint venture between MSI, Vodafone and local investors. By 1998, Cel-Tel had 7,000 subscribers in and around the capital city, Kampala. The Ugandan government decided to award a second license, and MTN prepared a winning bid. Since its license called for fixed line as well as mobile telephony, MTN joined with Telia, a Swedish firm that provided fixed lines. The resulting company, MTN Uganda Ltd., was a joint venture between MTN with 50 percent, Telia with 30 percent and local partners owning the balance.

MTN Uganda began full commercial service on October 21, 1998, six months after the license had been issued. At launch, MTN Uganda covered an area of more than 2,800 square kilometers, including the capital city, Kampala, and the key towns of Entebbe and Jinga, as well as their connecting roads. More than 1.5 million people gained access to telecommunications.

Success was immediate. In five business days, MTN Uganda had a fully functional recharge-card-based prepaid system, a customer base of 3,500 subscribers, 50 distribution outlets, 2 interconnect agreements, and 10 international roaming agreements. The level of quality was excellent, with a "dropped call" rate of less than 2 percent and a congestion rate of less than 3 percent. Additional base stations were built during the first six months of operation to include the key cities of Mbarare, Masaka, Inganga, Mbale, Tororo and Kabale, as well as their linking roads. A next phase of network roll-out was planned to provide coverage to most of Uganda's population within two years. Just five months after its launch, MTN Uganda had 30,000 subscribers, twice the number projected in the business plan.

3. MTN Swaziland

MTN's third foreign license in 1998 was in Swaziland, a small country with a population of 900,000 nestled between South Africa and Mozambique. The bidding process pitted MTN against its domestic rival, Vodacom. In May 1998, MTN was selected as the preferred partner to the Swaziland Posts & Telecommunications Corporation (SPTC). The Government chose MTN as it had proposed a better technical solution and more aggressive roll-out. MTN and the SPTC signed the license on July 31, forming MTN Swaziland, a joint venture owned 30 percent by MTN and the remainder by SPTC and local black empowerment groups.

Roll-out followed briskly, and in early September the King of Swaziland made the first call on the network. Over the next months, MTN Swaziland allowed 100 customers to test the network on a non-commercial basis. Full commercial launch followed in December. A further roll-out expected to provide coverage to 41 percent of the population and 39 percent of the geographical area of the country by the year 2002.

Financial Challenges

Making MTN's African operations profitable was a complicated matter. Given the restriction on foreign investment, MTN had to find supplementary sources of funding. In Uganda, for instance, an initial investment of R 90 million was needed, prompting MTN to borrow R 40 million from an offshore South African bank. The result was a debt burden that demanded profitability in the short term, both through increased revenues and lower costs.

In terms of revenues, MTN's foreign operations paid it a management fee as a payment for technical know-how. This fee was a cost to the joint venture, not a share of profits, and began immediately. These fees were often sufficient to pay interest charges on debt incurred during the peak funding period. Later, as local operations were expected to reach profitability, additional funds would be generated, sufficient to pay back borrowed capital and also return a profit to MTN. As for costs, MTN's African subsidiaries looked for ways to help each other. Located in adjacent countries, Rwanda and Uganda shared a technical staff and a network control center. They could also combine their call volume and negotiate for better rates on international calls.

MTN IN 1999

By May 1999 MTN had a domestic customer base of 1.3 million, giving it a market share of about 45 percent. It had grown at close to 200 percent annually for the previous five years. MTN was recognized for its high quality by independent surveys. Its dropped call rate between 1.5 percent and 2.5 percent was half of that achieved by many European operators, and substantially better than its main South African competitor. Congestion rates were low, and indoor coverage was excellent.

Its financial position was strong. Revenues for the year ending March 31, 1999, reached R 4.45 billion, up from R 2.86 billion in 1998 and R 1.96 billion in 1997. Net profit for the year ending March 31, 1999, was R 363 million, an 82 percent increase over profits of R 199 million in the previous year. (Refer to financial statements on Exhibits 6A and 6B.) CFO Rob Nisbet noted that MTN's leverage of 60 percent was considerably lower than most telecom firms, some of which were levered at close to 150 percent. As for further investments, he commented: "We could invest 300 to 400 million rand this year and still be in a good position, balanced with shareholder cash flow requirements."

Ownership Structure and Organization Design

MTN's ownership structure changed in 1998, when Cable & Wireless and South-West Bell sold their shares to South African investors. Following a review of its global positions, Cable & Wireless decided to focus on Asia and markets where it had management control, and decided to sell its stake in MTN. SouthWest Bell, meanwhile, took a position in Telkom, which owned 50 percent of Vodacom, leading to a decision to divest its shares of MTN. After 1998, ownership of the MTN Group was divided among M-Cell, Ltd. (39.7 percent), Transnet Ltd. (30 percent) and a number of local investors, including black empowerment groups. MTN was now fully owned by South African investors, and was the largest "black empowerment" company in the country. Some observers speculated that these changes in ownership could affect the management of the company. Rather than being owned by multinational firms, with a deep commitment to the industry, an international outlook and deep pockets, the new ownership structure was local, less international in outlook, and had a greater desire for generation of dividends. (Refer to Exhibit 7 for a breakdown of ownership and profiles of major shareholders.)

In 1999 MTN was organized as a holding company—MTN Holdings (Pty) Ltd.—with three wholly owned subsidiaries. MTN (Pty) Ltd. was the network

EXHIBIT 6A   Mobile Telephone Networks Holdings (Proprietary) Limited Balance Sheets—March 31, 1999

	Company		Group	
	1999 **R m**	**1998** **R m**	**1999** **R m**	**1998** **R m**
Capital Employed				
SHARE CAPITAL	5	5	5	5
SUBORDINATED SHAREHOLDERS' LOANS	1,495	1,495	1,495	1,495
NON DISTRIBUTABLE RESERVE				
Foreign currency translation reserve	—	—	13	—
RETAINED INCOME				
(ACCUMULATED DEFICIT)	(112)	(112)	276	(87)
Total shareholders' interest	1,388	1,388	1,789	1,413
DEFERRED TAXATION	—	—	202	57
LONG TERM LIABILITIES	137	41	1,102	872
	1,525	1,429	3,093	2,342
Employment of Capital				
FIXED ASSETS	—	—	2,857	2,211
DEFERRED EXPENDITURE	—	—	154	147
INTEREST IN SUBSIDIARY COMPANIES	1,388	1,388	—	—
OTHER INVESTMENTS AND ADVANCES	141	43	193	61
	1,529	1,431	3,204	2,419
CURRENT ASSETS:				
Inventory	—	—	165	84
Accounts receivable	13	4	678	439
Bank and cash	—	—	63	—
Total current assets	13	4	906	523
CURRENT LIABILITIES:				
Bank overdraft	—	—	29	—
Accounts payable and accrued liabilities	13	4	962	550
Taxation	—	—	1	—
Current portion of long term liabilities	4	2	25	50
Total current liabilities	17	6	1,017	600
Net current liabilities	(4)	(2)	(111)	(77)
	1,525	1,429	3,093	2,342

Source: Arthur Andersen & Co. *Mobile Telephone Networks Holdings (Proprietary) Limited, Annual Financial Statements and Group Annual Financial Statements.* March 31, 1999.

operator in South Africa. It owned the license, ran the network, handled operations and all technical activities, as well as marketing, finance and human resources. M-Tel (Pty) Ltd. was the wholly owned cellular service provider. MTN (Africa) held ownership shares in the three African subsidiaries. So far, MTN (Africa) was a holding company with just one employee, Campbell Utton, a manager with considerable African experience who served as its acting head. All other employees of the MTN Group were either located in MTN (Pty) Ltd., M-Tel (Pty) Ltd. or in the three Africa subsidiaries. (Refer to Exhibit 8 for the organization chart of MTN.)

EXHIBIT 6B
Mobile Telephone Networks Holdings (Proprietary) Limited Income Statements for the Year Ended March 31, 1999

Source: Arthur Andersen & Co. *Mobile Telephone Networks Holdings (Proprietary) Limited, Annual Financial Statements and Group Annual Financial Statements.* March 31, 1999.

	Group	
	1999 R m	1998 R m
TURNOVER	4,453	2,859
OPERATING PROFIT before finance charges	685	354
FINANCE CHARGES, net	(176)	(98)
NET PROFIT before taxation	509	256
TAXATION	(146)	(57)
NET PROFIT for the year	363	199

EXHIBIT 7A
Ownership of MTN, 1999

Source: MTN documents.

M-Cell	34.71%
Transnet	30.03
Naftel	11.76
Johnnic	18.50
Black Empowerment Groups	3.50
National Empowerment Forum	1.50

EXHIBIT 7B
Profile of Major Investors

Source: MTN company reports.

M-Cell Limited was controlled by various media groups in South Africa. It was listed on the Johannesburg Stock Exchange and had a market capitalization of R 2.7 billion ($438 million).
Transnet Limited was wholly owned by the South African Government. It was a dominant player in transportation in Southern Africa—not only in terms of the transport and handling of freight and passengers but also in the provision and maintenance of a highly sophisticated transport infrastructure. Transnet's assets totaled R 42.8 billion ($6.9 billion) with annual turnover of R 21.7 billion ($3.5 billion).
National African Telecommunications (Pty) Limited (Naftel) was controlled through New Africa Investments Ltd. by Corporate Africa Ltd., a consortium of influential black businessmen. New Africa Investments Ltd. was listed on the Johannesburg Stock Exchange.
Johnnie's Industrial Corporation Limited (johnnic) was an industrial holding company that manages Omni Media Corporation (Omni Media) and johnnic properties. It had board and executive committee representation over its other strategic industrial interests, including South African Breweries and the Premier Group. The majority shareholder of johnnic was the National Empowerment Fund, a consortium of black controlled businesses and labor groups. Johnnic's turnover for the year ended 30 June 1998 was R 488.6 million ($78.1 million). It was listed on the Johannesburg Stock Exchange with a market capitalization of R 5.5 billion ($886 million).

EXHIBIT 7C
Subordinated Shareholders' Loans

Source: Arthur Andersen & Co. *Mobile Telephone Networks Holdings (Proprietary) Limited, Annual Financial Statements and Group Annual Financial Statements.* March 31, 1999.

	Company and Group	
	1999 R m	1998 R m
Johnnies Industrial Corporation Ltd	202	—
Cable & Wireless S.A. (Pty) Ltd	—	373
M-Cell Ltd	594	441
National African Telecommunications (Pty) Ltd	176	150
Transnet Ltd	449	299
SBCI International (S.A.) (Pty)	—	232
Black Economic Empowerment Groups	74	—
	1,495	1,495

EXHIBIT 8   **MTN Holdings Organization Chart**

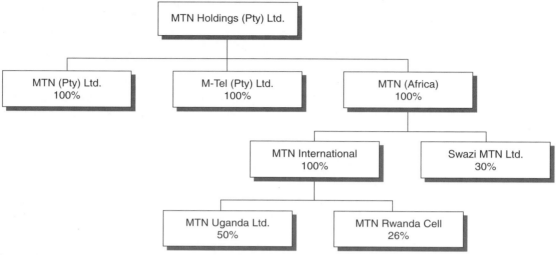

Source: MTN documents.

Domestic Position and Competition

MTN was locked in a tough competitive battle with Vodacom, the market leader with 55 percent of the market. Both companies provided excellent coverage and offered similar products and services. New service features, such as free voice mail and vehicle tracking, were copied quickly. Competition therefore took place mainly in marketing. Vodacom spent lavishly on high-profile sponsorships, supporting motor sports, rugby, golf and soccer. It brought the "Three Tenors"—Luciano Pavarotti, Placido Domingo and José Carreras—to Johannesburg for a highly publicized concert. MTN also spent large amounts on sponsorships, supporting tennis, cricket and soccer. The largest performing arts arena in Johannesburg was the MTN Dome. The head-to-head competition between MTN and Vodacom was obvious as soon as travelers landed at Johannesburg's international airport—after passing through customs, one found an MTN rental counter on one side, and a Vodacom counter on the other.

By May 1999 there were signs that MTN was losing ground to its major rival. Vodacom had secured a larger share of the booming prepaid market, and its pricing was more aggressive than MTN's. Thanks to its earlier start and larger market share, Vodacom enjoyed greater economies of scale and could pour more money into advertisements, sponsorships and promotions. Some managers at MTN worried about slipping further behind: "We could be running third in a two-horse race!"

There were, in addition, questions about the future of the South African market. It was still growing briskly, but eventually would level off. Some managers thought the domestic market could plateau within five years, while others thought it would take longer. One explained:

> It's hard to know when South Africa will flatten. Out of 40 million people, half are children, and of the rest, how many will want a cell phone?

As final concern, the South African government had recently approved the licensing of a third network operator. Whereas MTN and Vodacom had competed on services and marketing, a third entrant might compete on price. Both MTN and Vodacom charged by the minute—a new entrant could decide to charge by the second, effectively lowering the price to customers. MTN possessed the technology to follow suit and could charge by the second, too, but so doing would reduce its revenues.

Even without the prospect of a third entrant, maintaining the level of investment at home would be expensive. MTN was still adding base stations at a rapid clip, mainly to increase capacity as the number of domestic subscribers continued to grow. More than 80 were added per month in 1999.

EVALUATING FURTHER INTERNATIONAL GROWTH

Following MTN's entry into Rwanda, Uganda and Swaziland in 1998, and with its new license in Nigeria in 1999, some of the firm's managers were more confident than ever about future international growth. Ross Macdonald, head of International Business Development, elaborated:

> The African market is characterized by massive under-investment in telephony, and this presents us with tremendous opportunity to extend our business outside the South African borders.

But if most managers were supportive of further expansion in the long run, how to proceed in the next few years was an open question. A few remained very ambitious for rapid growth. As one remarked: "When a network license is available, you have to go for it."

Keeping up with domestic growth alone placed a strain on financial resources. One manager commented: "The funding requirements for South Africa are frightening." The strain on human resources was perhaps even greater. Most employees were working at the highest level of responsibility they had ever handled, and felt stretched very thin. One complained: "The amount of resources needed at home is still high, and we keep sending pioneers abroad!"

Yet to others, the intensity of domestic competition made foreign expansion all the more important:

> We're obviously good at managing foreign expansion. Our ability to get deals and roll-out is a competitive advantage.
>
> Vodacom hasn't managed to get any foreign licenses. We went head-to-head in Swaziland, and we beat them. It's not clear they have a clear strategy for Africa. Vodacom isn't focused on an African strategy, like MTN is.

Still others argued that new markets would not match South Africa in market size. One commented: "Aside from Nigeria, which could be big, I don't expect African revenue to match South African revenue for the foreseeable future." Rob Reynolds, COO for M-Tel, warned that MTN shouldn't be seduced by foreign markets: "If we forget about M-Tel, while we're chasing after foreign markets, we'll have a real problem." Another manager cautioned: "If we lose share in South Africa, we may never make it up." Even if other African countries offered possibilities for growth, South

Africa—far and away the most developed among sub-Saharan African countries—would still account for more than half the sales for many years. One manager estimated that at the most optimistic, revenues outside South Africa could reach about R 3 billion in five years, by which time domestic revenues would reach R 5 billion. Perhaps in 10 years, he speculated, could revenues from outside South Africa equal those of the domestic market.

Bidding for a New License in Nigeria

In late 1999 MTN was on the verge of adding a fourth license in Nigeria, Africa's most populous country. MTN planned for an extensive roll-out in the main centers of Lagos, Abuja and Port Harcourt. The Nigerian government was still engaged in its review of the telecommunications industry, but signs were positive, and MTN planned to "go live" in Nigeria six months after the license was confirmed.

The new venture in Nigeria would be considerably bigger than the three previous foreign ventures combined. The investment, exclusive of the up-front license fee, was expected to exceed $100 million. In addition, staffing would call for between 20 to 30 expatriates sent immediately to Nigeria. MTN had already identified these employees—some chosen from within the company and others recruited from the outside—and they were ready to be sent to Nigeria. They would, however, roughly double the total number of MTN expatriates.

Identifying New Markets

To help chart MTN's next steps, the International Business Development Department compiled a list of opportunities throughout Africa. Eleven additional countries were planning to offer GSM licenses in the near future: Cameroon, Ethiopia, Gabon, Ghana, Kenya, Malawi, Mauritius, Mozambique, Senegal, Zambia and Zimbabwe. The list included countries that were large and populous (Ethiopia) as well as small (Mauritius and Malawi); relatively well-off and very poor; and ranging from the west to the east to the south of the continent. Important facts about each country were assembled for analysis, including its size (square km), population, urbanization, GDP and GDP per person, as well as information regarding its existing telecom providers. (Refer to Exhibit 9.) Some countries were offering a second license, while others were offering a third. Existing competitors included France Telecom, Portugal Telecom, Telecel, MSI, Investcom, Vivendi, GTE, Telkom SA, Vodacom, Vodafone, Telecom Malaysia and Western Wireless.

THE INVESTMENT SUBCOMMITTEE MEETING

In late 1999 the Investment Subcommittee scheduled a meeting with the International Business Development Department to review the African strategy. The ISC consisted of CEO Bob Chaphe, CFO Rob Nisbet and Campbell Utton, the acting head of MTN Africa, as well as representatives of MTN Holdings shareholders, including representatives from Johnnic, Transnet and M-Cell. Some of these shareholders were reluctant to raise additional monies for foreign investment, preferring

EXHIBIT 9A

Country	Country Size (km)	Population (m)	Population Growth Rate	GDP Total	GDP per Capita	GDP Real Growth Rate	Capital City	Urbanization	Language Spoken	Telephone Lines Capacity	Telephone Lines Connected	Lines per 100 People
(1) Cameroon	475,442	14.3	2.8	9.1	650	5.1	Yaounde	46	French and English (both official)	134,600	120,000	0.84
(2) Ethiopia	1,100,000	58.7	2.1	6.1	110	8.0	Addis Ababa	13	Amharic (official), Tigrinya, Oromifa, English, Somali	194,378	154,615	0.20
(3) Gabon	267,667	1.2	2.5	5.2	4,230	4.1	Libreville	50	French (official)	42,445	35,000	3.27
(4) Ghana	239,460	18.0	2.7	6.8	370	3.0	Accra	36	English (official), Asante, Fante, Ewe, Ga, Dagombe	129,068	98,000	0.54
(5) Kenya	582,646	28.0	2.6	7.0	330	1.4	Nairobi	28	English and Swahili (both official)	384,000	264,000	0.81
(6) Malawi	118,484	10.3	2.7	2.4	220	3.3	Lilongwe	15	English and Chewa (both official), Lomwe, Tumbuka	70,960	36,974	0.35
(7) Mauritius	2,040	1.1	1.2	3.9	3,800	5.3	Port Louis	41	English and French	257,290	230,000	19.52
(8) Mozambique	801,590	18.7	4.2	2.8	90	12.4	Maputo	30	Portuguese (official)	104,556	61,175	0.39
(9) Senegal	196,722	9.0	2.6	4.9	550	5.0	Dakar	41	French (official)	160,000	115,000	1.32
(10) Zambia	752,614	9.4	2.7	4.0	380	3.5	Lusaka	44	English (official)	135,000	94,000	0.91
(11) Zimbabwe	390,759	11.5	2.3	8.9	750	3.2	Harare	32	English (official)	299,000	249,000	1.74

Source: MTN company documents.

335

EXHIBIT 9B

Country	OPERATOR 1	Ownership	Equipment Suppliers	Subscribers	OPERATOR 2	Ownership	Equipment Suppliers	Subscribers	OPERATOR 3	Ownership	Equipment Suppliers	Subscribers
(1) Cameroon	Camtel-Mobile	100% MINPOSTEL	Siemens	5,500	SCM	100% France Telecom						
(2) Ethiopia	ETC	100% Government										
(3) Gabon	Gabtel	100% OPT	Motorola	9,300	Telecel Gabon	Telecel Int. & local partners	Motorola		Celtel	100% MSI Cellular		
(4) Ghana	Milicom Ghana (Mobitel)	90% Milicom, 10% Commonwealth Development Corp.	Motorola	38,000	Celtel	95% Kludjeson Int'l, 5% AT&T	AT&T and Lucent	6,300	Scancom	80% Investcom Holding SA (Sweden), 20% local/Swedish	Ericsson	6,500
(5) Kenya	KPTC Tacs	100% KPTC	NEC	3,900	KPTC GSM (Safaricom)	70% KPTC, 30% Vodafone Airtouch	Siemens	7,700				
(6) Malawi	Telekom Networks of Malawi	60% Telekom Malaysia, 40% MPTC	Alcatel	12,700	MSI (Celtel)	70% MSI & 30% MDC	Siemens					
(7) Mauritius	Emtel Ltd	54% Bharti Cellular (Currumjee Group (local)), 46% Milicom	Motorola	37,100	Cellplus Mobile Communications	100% Mauritius Telecom	Alcatel	37,500				
(8) Mozambique	TDM-Mcel	74% TDM, 26% DETECON	Alcatel	9,200								
(9) Senegal	Sonatel Cellular	33% France Telecom, 34% Government, 33% Public ownership	Siemens	34,000	Sentel	70% Millicom & 30% local partners	Siemens	11,500				
(10) Zambia	Zamtel	100% Zamtel	NEC, Mitsui, Motorola	11,500	Telecel Zambia	90% Telecel Int'l, 10% Local partners	Motorola	8,300	Zamcell	80% MSI, 10% Mitsui, 10% IFC	Motorola	11,100
(11) Zimbabwe	Net One	100% PTC	Siemens, Motorola	64,600	Econet	100% T.S. Masiyiwa Holdings	Ericsson	122,600	Telecel	50% Telecel (USA), 50% Zimbabwe Wealth Creation & Empowerment Council	Siemens	8,650

Source: MTN company documents

instead to fund international expansion through cash flows. Others were keen to pay out any profits dividends rather than re-invest in new African ventures.

The debate centered on a few main themes. First, should MTN attempt additional foreign entries at this time? Given its domestic competition, the recency of its African initiatives, including Nigeria, and the timing of further bids, was this a time to move ahead? Second, if MTN did go ahead, how should it assess the 11 countries open for bid in the next year? Which were most promising for MTN? Third, more generally, what should MTN do to prepare for successful international growth?

Endnotes

1. Price, Christopher. "Market is revitalised with lure of pre-paid packages." *Financial Times,* March 18, 1999.
2. Ibid.
3. Black, George. "Promise of a 'wire-free future' heralds progress." *Financial Times,* March 11, 1999.
4. Cane, Alan. "Millennium forecast is for 1 bn cellular users." *Financial Times,* November 18, 1999.
5. Ibid.
6. Black, George. "Promise of a 'wire-free future' heralds progress." *Financial Times,* March 11, 1999.
7. Cane, Alan. "Millennium forecast is for 1 bn cellular users." *Financial Times,* November 18, 1999.
8. Ibid.

Chapter Twenty

The Chinese Fireworks Industry

In February 1999, Jerry Yu was spending the Chinese New Year holidays in Liuyang (lee-ou-yang), a city known as "the home of firecrackers and fireworks," located in Hunan Province in China. Jerry was an ABC (America-Born-Chinese). With an MBA, he was running a small family-owned chain of gift stores in Brooklyn, New York. Liuyang was his mother's hometown. During his visit, his relatives invited him to invest in a fireworks factory that was owned by a village. Mr. Yu had been impressed by the extravagant fireworks shows he had seen during the festival, however, he wanted to assess how attractive the Chinese fireworks industry was before he even looked at the financial details of the factory.

HISTORY OF FIREWORKS AND FIRECRACKERS

Fireworks referred to any devices designed to produce visual or audible effects through combustion or explosion. The art of making fireworks was formally known as pyrotechnics. Firecrackers were a specific kind of fireworks, usually in the form of a noisemaking cylinder. Firecrackers were often strung together and fused consecutively, a staple of Chinese New Year celebrations, weddings, grand openings, births, deaths and other ceremonial occasions.

IVEY

Richard Ivey School of Business
The University of Western Ontario

Ruihua Jiang prepared this case under the supervision of Professor Paul Beamish solely to provide material for class discussion. The authors do not intend to illustrate either effective or ineffective handling of a managerial situation. The authors may have disguised certain names and other identifying information to protect confidentiality.

The main ingredients of fireworks had remained almost the same over the past thousand years: 75 parts-by-weight potassium nitrate, 15 parts charcoal and 10 parts sulfur. It burned briskly when lighted, but did not erupt or make any noise. When it was found that a projectile could be thrust out of a barrel by keeping the powder at one end and igniting it, black powder became known as gunpowder. Today, smokeless powder has replaced black powder as the propellant in modern weaponry, but black powder remains a main ingredient in fireworks, both as a propellant and as a bursting charge.

It was generally believed that the Chinese were the first makers of fireworks. The Chinese made war rockets and explosives as early as the sixth century. One legend said that a Chinese cook, while toiling in a field kitchen, happened to mix together sulfur, charcoal and saltpetre, and noticed that the pile burned with a combustible force when ignited. He further discovered that when these ingredients were enclosed in a length of bamboo sealed at both ends, it would explode rather than burn, producing a loud crack. This was the origin of firecrackers. In fact, the Chinese word for firecrackers—*bao-zhu*—literally means "exploded bamboo."

The loud reports and burning fires of firecrackers and fireworks were found to be perfect for frightening off evil spirits and celebrating good news at various occasions. For more than a thousand years, the Chinese had been seeing off past years and welcoming in new ones by firing firecrackers.

Fireworks made their way first to Arabia in the seventh century, then to Europe sometime in the middle of the 13th century. By the 15th century, fireworks were widely used for religious festivals and public entertainment. Most of the early pyrotechnicians in Europe were Italians. Even today, the best-known names in the European and American fireworks industry were Italian in origin. From the 16th to the 18th century, Italy and Germany were the two best known areas in the European continent for fireworks displays.

In 1777, the United States used fireworks in its first Independence Day celebration, and fireworks have became closely associated with July Fourth celebrations ever since.

Up until the 1830s, the colors of the early fireworks were limited, but by 1999, there were six basic colors used in fireworks.

LIUYANG—THE HOMETOWN OF FIRECRACKERS AND FIREWORKS

According to historical records in China, firecrackers and fireworks "emerged during the Tang dynasty (AD 618–907), flourished during the Song Dynasty (AD 960–1279), and originated in Liuyang." For more than a 1,000 years, Liuyang had been known as the "hometown of firecrackers and fireworks of China," a title that was officially conferred to Liuyang by the State Council of China in 1995. As early as 1723, Liuyang fireworks were chosen as official tributes to the imperial family and were sold all over the country. Exports started early: by 1875, firecrackers and fireworks were being shipped to Japan, Korea, India, Iran, Russia, Australia,

EXHIBIT 1
Liuyang Firecrackers and Fireworks: Total Revenue and Export Sales (US$000)

	1992	1993	1994	1995	1996
Total Revenue	49,639	55,542	86,747	126,606	134,940
Tax Revenue	5,099	7,010	11,829	15,422	18,434
Export Sales	15,100	30,200	51,240	84,030	85,560

Source: Liuyang Firecrackers and Fireworks Exhibition, 1998.

England, U.S., and other countries. In China, the name Liuyang had become almost synonymous with firecrackers and fireworks. Liuyang-made firecrackers and fireworks won numerous awards over its long history of fireworks making.

The long history and tradition had made fireworks more than just a livelihood for the Liuyang people. Almost every native person in the area knew something about fireworks making, or had actually made firecrackers or fireworks in their lifetime. As a result, Liuyang claimed an impressive pool of skilled labor. Firecrackers and fireworks had become the pillar industry of Liuyang, employing more than 400,000 people in peak seasons, or about one-third of the total population in the Liuyang District (including Liuyang City and the surrounding counties). Liuyang claimed more than 500 fireworks manufacturers. Among them, only one was a state-owned-enterprise (SOE) with more than 1,000 workers. The rest were owned either by villages or families. Among them, about a dozen or so were medium to large factories with employment between 100 to 500 workers. The rest were small workshops employing anywhere from 10 to 50 people, depending on market demand.

Liuyang was the top fireworks exporter in the world, making up 80 percent of fireworks export sales of Hunan Province, and 60 percent of that of China (see Exhibit 1 for information on revenue and export sales of Liuyang fireworks). The trademarked brand "Red Lantern" had become well known to fireworks-lovers around the world.

The Product

Fireworks could be classified into two categories: display fireworks and consumer fireworks. The display fireworks, such as aerial shells, maroons, and large Roman candles, were meant for professional (usually licensed) pyrotechnicians to fire during large public display shows. They were devices that were designed to produce certain visual or audio effect at a greater height above the ground than the consumer fireworks, which the general public could purchase in convenience stores and enjoy in their own backyards. Display fireworks were known as Explosives 1.3 (Class B prior to 1991) in the U.S. The consumer fireworks belonged to Explosives 1.4 (Class C prior to 1991). The difference lay mainly in the amount of explosive components contained in the product. Canada had a similar classification system. In the U.K., it was more carefully divided into four categories: indoor fireworks; garden fireworks; display fireworks; and display fireworks for professionals only.

There were many varieties of fireworks. Liuyang made 13 different types with more than 3,000 varieties. The major types included fountains, rockets, hand-held novelties, nail and hanging wheels, ground-spinning novelties, jumping novelties, floral shells, parachutes and firecrackers.

Historically, firecrackers made up 90 percent of the total production and sales. Over the past 50 years or so, however, there had been a shift away from firecrackers to fireworks. In 1999, firecrackers made up only about 20 percent of the total sales. The skill levels of fireworks-making had been greatly improved. For instance, the old-day fireworks could reach no more than 20 metres into the sky, while the new ones could go as high as 400 metres.

Not much had changed in fireworks-making. Over the last few decades, numerous novelties were added to the fireworks family. However, innovation had never reached beyond product variations. The ingredients had remained more or less the same. The process technology had not changed much either, although some manual processes, such as cutting the paper, rolling the cylinders, mixing powder, and stringing the cylinders could now be done by machines.

Safety Issues

The fact that fireworks were made with gunpowder and listed under explosives brought about the issue of safety. Numerous accidents related with fireworks had resulted in tragic human injuries and considerable property damages. As a result, fireworks had become heavily regulated in most countries.

According to the manufacturers, fireworks were the most dangerous during the production process. Powder mixing and powder filling, in turn, were the two most dangerous procedures. The workers had to abide by strict safety measures. Even a tiny spark caused by the dropping of a tool on the floor or the dragging of a chair could start a major explosion. The quality of the ingredients was also of significant importance. Impure ingredients could greatly increase the possibility of accidents. In Liuyang, almost every year, there would be one or more accidents that resulted in deaths and damages.

Once the fireworks were made, they were relatively safe to transport and store. Even in firing, good quality fireworks rarely caused any problems if everything was done properly. Most of the fireworks-related accidents occurred during private parties or street displays, and quite often involved children playing with fireworks that needed to be handled by adults, or adults firing shells that required professional expertise. Most accidents were linked to consumer backyard events rather than to public displays.

According to the United States Consumer Products Safety Commission's (CPSC) data, injuries related to fireworks had declined by 44 percent, even though their use had increased (see Exhibit 2). For 1997, there were an estimated 8,300 fireworks-related injuries, 32 percent of which were caused by firecrackers. Of all the injuries related to firecrackers, 42 percent involved illegal firecrackers.

Children from ages five to 14 were the most frequently involved in fireworks-related injuries. However, fireworks were not the only consumer product that might cause injuries to this age group. According to a 1997 CPSC Injury Surveillance

EXHIBIT 2

Total Fireworks Consumption and Estimated Fireworks-Related Injuries in U.S.: 1994 to 1998

Source: American Pyrotechnics Association.

Year	Fireworks Consumption, Millions of Pounds	Estimated Fireworks-Related Injuries	Injuries per 100,000 Pounds
1994	117.0	12,500	10.7
1995	115.0	10,900	9.4
1996	118.0	7,800	6.2
1997	132.8	8,300	6.2
1998	112.6	7,000	6.2

EXHIBIT 3

Estimated Emergency Room Treatment per 100,000 Youths (ages 5 to 14)

Source: American Pyrotechnics Association.

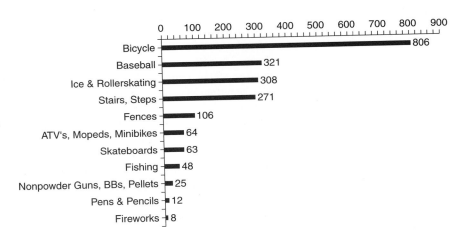

Report, fireworks were actually safer than some much more benign-looking products, like baseballs, pens and pencils. However, fireworks-related injuries were usually the most dramatic and the most widely publicized accidents, which partly explained the fact that fireworks was the only category among the products listed in Exhibit 3, for which prohibition, instead of education and adult supervision, was often urged.

In the United States, multiple government agencies were involved in regulating fireworks. The Bureau of Alcohol Tobacco and Firearms (BATF) controlled the manufacture, storage, sales and distribution of explosives, i.e., Class B fireworks. The CPSC regulated Class C consumer fireworks, and the Department of Transportation dealt with the transportation of fireworks. Although at the federal level, fireworks and firecrackers were allowed as long as the safety features were up to the standard, local governments would have their own different regulations regarding fireworks consumption. Out of the 50 states, 10 would not allow any fireworks, five would allow novelty fireworks, 18 would allow "safe and sane" fireworks, while the remaining 17 would allow essentially all consumer fireworks. For display fireworks, permits would have to be obtained from federal and local authorities and fire departments.

All legal consumer fireworks offered for sale in the United States had been tested for stability by the Bureau of Explosives and approved for transportation by the U.S. Department of Transportation. Because of the limited amount of pyrotechnic composition permitted in each individual unit, consumer fireworks would not ignite spontaneously during storage, nor would they mass-explode during a fire. Therefore, no special storage was required.

In most of Europe, similar regulations were in place for safety considerations, only the requirements were regarded as less stringent. In Canada, however, regulations were extremely restrictive. On the list of fireworks companies that were allowed to sell fireworks to Canada, no Chinese companies were found.

THE FIRECRACKERS AND FIREWORKS INDUSTRY IN CHINA

The firecrackers and fireworks industry in China was dominated by small family-owned-and-operated workshops. It was essentially a low-tech, highly labor-intensive industry. After 1949, government-run factories replaced the family-owned workshops. The increased scale and government funds made possible the automation of some processes. However, the key processes like installing powder, mixing color ingredients, putting in fuses, were still manually done by skilled workers.

The factories themselves were made up of small workshops that stood away from each other, so that in case of an accident the whole factory would not explode. For the same safety consideration, the workshops were usually located near a water source and in sparsely populated rural areas, to reduce the noise and explosion hazard.

After the reform towards market economy started in 1979, most of the factories were broken up and became family-run units of production again. It was hoped that this privatization might help to motivate people better, to increase their productivity and consequently raise the output. However, this move also served to restrict further technological innovations. There were hardly any research and development (R & D) facilities, nor human and capital resources allocated to R & D in most fireworks companies. The few resources that were available were all spent on product varieties. Even in Liuyang, out of the 400,000 or so people working in the industry, only four were engineers with advanced professional training and titles. The 40 some research facilities scattered in Liuyang area were poorly funded and equipped.

In fact, the majority of the workers were regular farmers who had learned how to make fireworks just by watching and following their elders. They would come to work in fireworks workshops when there were jobs to be done, and return to till their fields if there were none. In Liuyang, for instance, only four to five factories were operating year-round. The rest of the 500 plus workshops would operate as orders came in. Since the fireworks-making communities were very concentrated geographically and had lasted for generations, only a few places (like Liuyang) came to claim a large pool of skilled fireworks-makers.

Although Liuyang was by far the most well-known place for making fireworks in China, it faced increasing competition within the country. Also located in Hunan

Province, Liling was another major manufacturing community of fireworks. Liling fireworks might not enjoy the same reputation and variety as Liuyang products, but they were fierce in price competition. In the neighboring Jiangxi Province, Pingxiang and Wanzai fireworks had become strong competitors both in price and quality, especially on the low- and medium-priced market. In the high-end product market, especially in large-type display fireworks and export market, Dongguan in Guangdong Province, had taken advantage of its closeness to Hong Kong and more sophisticated management and marketing practices, and snatched market share from Liuyang.

The initial capital requirement for starting a fireworks-manufacturing facility was relatively low. To set up a factory with the necessary equipment for making large display shells would require RMB1,000,000.[1] However, setting up a small family workshop making consumer firecrackers and fireworks would require less than RMB100,000. Consequently, the number of small manufacturers mushroomed after the government started to encourage private business ventures.

The labor cost was low in the area. Skilled workers engaged in major processes would earn an average of RMB800 to RMB1,000 per month. A non-skilled worker would be paid only RMB300 to RMB400 every month. Therefore, the labor cost took no more than 20 percent of the total cost. For the small private workshops, the percentage would be around 10 percent.

The main raw materials for fireworks were gunpowder, color ingredients, paper, fuse and clay soil. None would be difficult to procure. The prices and supply were both quite stable. The one possible problem in supply was quality. Major manufacturers would usually establish long-term relationships with their suppliers to guarantee the quality of the materials. The small workshops would often go with the lowest prices, sometimes at the cost of quality, which could lead to fatal results.

The emergence of the small companies intensified competition. The private workshops were flexible and quick in responding to market demand. They did not entail much administrative cost. Compared to government-owned or some collectively-owned factories, they did not have the social responsibilities of health care, retirement benefits and housing. They usually did not do any product research or design. Oblivious to intellectual property protection, they would copy any popular product design and sell it for much less. The resulting price drop had become a serious problem for the whole industry. As the profit margin kept shrinking, some workshops would hire cheap unskilled workers, use cheap equipment and raw materials to cut down on cost. The results could be disastrous. Fireworks-related damages and injuries and factory accidents were reported every year, pushing the authorities to impose stricter regulations.

THE DOMESTIC MARKET

Firecrackers and fireworks had long been an integral part of any ceremonies held in China. Until recently, demand had been stable, but had risen in the past two decades because of increased economic development and living standards. Economically, market reform and unprecedented growth had given rise to the daily appearance of multitudes of new companies and new stores. As people's income level and living standards kept rising, fancier and pricier fireworks and firecrackers were desired over the cheap simple firecrackers, thereby creating more profit opportunities for fireworks manufacturers. Almost every household would spend at least a couple of hundred yuan on firecrackers and fireworks during the Spring Festival.

However, since the beginning of the 1990s, increased concerns over environmental pollution and safety of human life and property led more and more cities to regulate the consumption of fireworks and firecrackers. Every year, high profile fireworks-related accidents were reported and emphasized on mass media before and after the traditional Spring Festival. Some articles even condemned firecrackers and fireworks as an old, uncivilized convention that created only noise, pollution and accidents. In a wave of regulations, city after city passed administrative laws regarding the use of fireworks. By 1998, one-third of the cities in China had completely banned the use of firecrackers and fireworks. Another one-third only allowed fireworks in designated places. This led to a decline in domestic market demand.

In the meantime, domestic competition grew intensely. The reform towards a market economy made it possible for numerous family-run workshops to appear. They competed mainly on price. Almost every province had some fireworks-making workshops or factories, many set up and run with the help of skilled workers who had migrated from Liuyang. These small establishments usually were located in rural, underdeveloped areas where labor cost was minimal. The manufacturing was done manually, sometimes without safety measures, using cheap raw materials and simplified techniques. The products were sold locally at low prices, making it difficult for Liuyang fireworks to sell in those areas. To make things worse, these products would often copy any new or popular product designs coming out of Liuyang or other traditional fireworks communities, even using their very brand names.

In the past, fireworks were sold through the government-run general merchandise companies. Eventually, private dealers took over a large part of the business. Overall, the distribution system was rather fragmented. The old government-run channels were not very effective, especially for general merchandise. In the new distribution channels, wholesale dealers would get shipments directly from the manufacturers, and then resell to street peddlers and convenience stores.

In the countryside, wholesale markets would appear in focal townships, with wholesale dealers and agents of the manufacturers setting up booths promoting their products. Small peddlers in the surrounding areas would get supplies from the market and then sell them in small towns or villages. The wholesale markets in China were important outlets for distributing general merchandise like fireworks.

In the display fireworks market, the buyers were often central and local governments, who would purchase the product for public shows on national holidays or special celebrations. Obviously, a local company would have advantages in supplying to local government in its area. Large fireworks shows usually would use invited bidding to decide on suppliers. The amount of fireworks used could range from RMB100,000 to several million yuan, depending on the scale of a fireworks show.

Account receivables and bad debt control was a problem not just for fireworks manufacturers, but for all businesses in China. Bad debts and lack of respect for business contracts had created a credit crisis in China. The bad debt problem greatly increased transaction costs, slowed down the cash turnover, and had become a headache for fireworks manufacturers. Some had chosen to withdraw from selling in the domestic market, although the profit margin was higher than in the export market.

Legal restrictions, local protectionism, cutthroat price competition, hard-to-penetrate distribution channels and bad debt were impacting negatively on the domestic sales of Liuyang fireworks. In 1997, seeing the decline of its fireworks sales, Liuyang Firecrackers and Fireworks Industry Department, the government agency in charge of the overall development of the pillar industry, decided to start an offensive strategy. First, it opened local offices in most of the 29 provinces, major cities and regions to promote Liuyang fireworks. Second, it regulated the prices that Liuyang fireworks companies could quote and sell in export sales. Third, it resorted to a government-to-government relationship in order to secure contracts for large public fireworks displays in each province. One year after introducing the offensive strategy, Liuyang fireworks sales had increased.

THE EXPORT MARKET

Since the opening of the Chinese economy in 1979, exporting had become a major market for the Chinese fireworks industry. As one of the most celebrated products out of China, export sales of fireworks had risen between 1978 and 1998. According to government statistics, the recorded export sales of firecrackers and fireworks reached US$143 million and US$172 million in 1994 and 1995 respectively. The estimate for 1998 was about US$200 million.

The general belief was that China-made fireworks actually made up about 80 percent to 90 percent of the world's fireworks market. The products from China were rich in variety and low in price, but also had a lower reputation in quality control, packaging and timing control, compared to the products made in Japan and Korea. China-made fireworks also would wholesale for much lower prices, usually 80 percent lower than similar products made in Japan or Korea.

There was little overall coordination of export sales. As more and more companies were allowed to export directly, competition kept intensifying and the profit margins on export sales kept slipping. Some manufacturers would even sell at or below cost, just to get the tax refund that the government set aside to encourage export, which could sometimes reach 20 percent. As a result, underpricing each other became a common practice. Therefore, despite its dominant share of the world market, the Chinese fireworks export industry enjoyed limited profitability. Exhibit 4 provides a comparison of the free on board (FOB) prices quoted by the Chinese companies to U.S. markets versus the prices quoted by the U.S. importers and wholesalers to the retailers and end users on some consumer and display fireworks items. The importers enjoyed a high markup even after paying the 12.5 per-

EXHIBIT 4
Comparison of FOB Import Prices from China and Wholesale Prices of Chinese Fireworks in U.S.

Source: China Sunsong Fireworks Corp. and websites of various firework wholesalers in U.S.

Product Type	Packing	FOB China[1] US$	Wholesale in U.S.[2] US$
Thunderbombs	12/80/16	12.40	42.00
Tri-Rotating Wheel	24/12	15.50	48.50
Changing Color Wheel	72/1	20.70	57.60
Jumping Jack	20/48/12	16.70	60.00
Cuckoo	24/6	14.50	50.40
Ground Bloom Flower	20/12/6	16.40	62.40
Color Sparkler	24/12/8	16.60	66.74
Moon Traveller	25/12/12	9.20	40.00
Crackling Whips	72/12	16.99	50.40
Aerial Display	4/1	19.40	68.00
Evening Party	12/1	12.60	60.00
Assorted Fountain	18/4	10.30	64.20
Assorted Rockets	36/12	24.20	68.00
4″ Display Shell w/Tail	36/1	52.65	165.00
6″ display	10/1	41.82	160.00
8″ display	6/1	54.53	190.00
12″ display	2/1	60.95	190.00

[1]FOB major ports in South China. Cost, Insurance, Freight to major ports in U.S. world be $3.00 to $4.00 more per carton.
[2]U.S. import duty rate for fireworks from China was 12.5 percent.

cent U.S. import duty. Of course, the importers had to absorb the cost of getting permits, shipping, storing and carrying the inventory for three to four months before making the sales.

Besides suffering from low profit margin, the Chinese fireworks makers were also risking losing their brand identities. Given the low cost and reasonably good quality of the Chinese fireworks, many large fireworks manufacturers and dealers in the West started to outsource the making of their brand name fireworks. Failing to see the importance of brand equity, the Chinese fireworks manufacturers were sometimes reduced to mere manufacturing outfits for foreign companies, gradually losing their own brands. There were also fireworks merchants in Korea, Japan or Spain, who would buy the products from China, and then repackage them, or replace the fuses with better quality ones, then resell them for much higher prices.

The export market was usually divided into five blocks: Southeast Asia, North America, Europe, South America and the rest of the world. The most popular market had been Europe, where the regulations on fireworks were less stringent, and orders were of larger quantities and better prices. The United States was considered a tough market because of complex regulations and high competition, nevertheless a necessary one if a company wanted to remain a viable world-player. The Canadian market was virtually closed to the Chinese fireworks due to its regulations, although most of the fireworks consumed in Canada were imported, and had probably originated in China before being repackaged in other countries. The result of the stricter regulations in Canada was higher prices for consumers. It was estimated that a fireworks display that cost less than $3,500 in the U.S. would cost Canadians $8,000.

The foreign importers were powerful buyers for several reasons. First, they were very well informed, both through past dealings with China and the Internet. Second, they were able to hire agents who were very familiar with the industry in China. Third, they could deal directly with the factories that were willing to take lower prices. Fourth, there were basically no switching costs, so they could play the suppliers against each other.

The diversity of the cultures in the destination countries greatly reduced the seasonality of the fireworks production and sales. As a result, orders evened out throughout the year. However, the peak season was still towards the end of the year. For the U.S., it was before July 4. Usually, the importers would receive the shipment two or three months beforehand.

The Internet was gradually becoming a marketing outlet for Chinese fireworks. According to a fireworks company's office in Shenzhen, 20 percent to 30 percent of the business inquiries they got were through the Internet. However, export sales were still made mainly through foreign trade companies or agents.

In recent years, foreign investments were also funneled into the fireworks industry. In Liuyang, four of the large fireworks factories had foreign investments, made mainly by the fireworks trading companies in Hong Kong.

In 1999, about four-fifths of the 5,000 or so containers of fireworks exported from China annually, were consumer fireworks. However, demand for display fireworks was growing at a faster pace. It was predicted that the demand for display fireworks would increase as organized public shows grew more popular; at the same time, demand for consumer fireworks was expected to decline as regulations were getting stricter. Fireworks shows were increasingly being used in promotional campaigns, and were finding customers among amusement parks, sports teams and retailers for store openings, anniversaries and holiday celebrations.

The Future of the Fireworks Industry in China

The managers of the Chinese fireworks companies that Jerry talked to expressed mixed feelings towards the future outlook of their industry. One pessimistic view was that this was a sunset industry and held that regulations were killing the industry. Moreover, as people became more environmentally conscious and more distracted by the endless diversities of modern entertainment, traditional celebrations using firecrackers and fireworks would die a gradual death. As to the function of attracting public attention for promotional purposes, fireworks also faced challenges from new technologies, such as laser beams combined with sound effects.

In fact, "make-believe firecrackers" already appeared as substitutes in China. These were made of red plastic tubes strung together like firecrackers with electric bulbs installed inside the tubes. When the power was turned on, the lights would emit sparks, accompanied by crackling reports that sounded like firecrackers. These were being used at weddings and grand openings in cities where firecrackers and fireworks were banned. More interesting substitutes were spotted at some weddings in Beijing, where people paved the road with little red balloons, and made the limousine carrying the bride and groom run over the balloons to make explosive cracking sounds as well as leave behind red bits and pieces of debris. Also, more and more young couples were getting married in western styles, in a church or a scenic green meadow outdoors, where serene and quiet happiness prevailed over the traditional noisy way of celebrating. Therefore, some managers believed that firecrackers and fireworks were doomed to fade off into history.

The more optimistic view, however, was that the industry would not die at all. If the right moves were made by the industry, it could even grow. Some said that tradition would not die so easily. It was in their national character for the Chinese to celebrate with an atmosphere of noisy happiness. Moreover, even in the West, the popularity of fireworks was not suffering from all the regulations. No real substitutes could replace fireworks, which combined the sensual pleasures of visual, audio and emotional stimuli. For instance, the U.S. Congressional resolution in 1963 to use bells to replace fireworks in celebrating Independence Day never really caught on.

Fireworks were also being combined with modern technologies like laser beams, computerized firing and musical accompaniment to make the appeal of fireworks more irresistible. The safety problem was not really as serious as people were made to believe, and would only improve with new technological innovations like smokeless fireworks.

However, both sides agreed that the Chinese fireworks industry would have to change its strategy, especially in international competition, to stay a viable and profitable player.

THE DECISION

Meanwhile, Jerry had to decide whether it was worthwhile to invest in the fireworks industry. He wondered whether he could apply the industry analysis framework he had studied in his MBA program.

Endnote

1.   In 1999, the exchange rate was around 8.30 yuan per US$1.00.

Chapter Twenty-One

Swatch and the Global Watch Industry[1]

In early June 1999, the management of the Swatch Group could be satisfied with the company's accomplishments over the last 15 years. Thanks to its 14 brands and unusual approach to marketing, and with 116 million finished watches and movements produced in 1997, the Swatch Group had helped resuscitate the Swiss watch industry and become, in value terms, the world's largest watch manufacturer. Despite an enviable track record, there was a growing sense of anxiety over the future of the company in an industry that seemed to be in a perpetual state of change.

EARLY HISTORY

Until 1957, all watches were mechanical. The aesthetics of the exterior visible elements (dials, hands and case) as well as the reliability and accuracy of a traditional timepiece depended on the meticulous care and precision that had been dedicated to its manufacturing and assembling processes. Mechanical watches consisted of between 100 and 130 components that were fitted together in the

Richard Ivey School of Business
The University of Western Ontario

Cyril Bouquet prepared this case under the supervision of Associate Professor Allen Morrison solely to provide material for class discussion. The authors do not intend to illustrate either effective or ineffective handling of a managerial situation. The authors may have disguised certain names and other identifying information to protect confidentiality.

Ivey Management Services prohibits any form of reproduction, storage or transmittal without its written permission. This material is not covered under authorization from CanCopy or any reproduction rights organization. To order copies or request permission to reproduce materials, contact Ivey Publishing, Ivey Management Services, c/o Richard Ivey School of Business, The University of Western Ontario, London, Ontario, Canada, N6A 3K7; phone (519) 661-3208; fax (519) 661-3882; e-mail cases@ivey.uwo.ca.

EXHIBIT 1
Watch Production in Switzerland

Source: FH, Federation of the Swiss Watch Industry

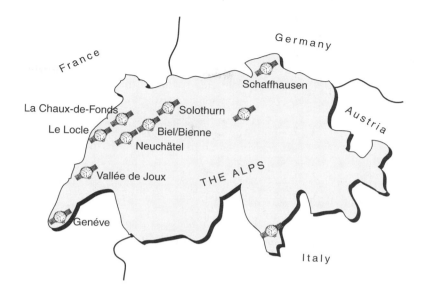

ébauche (winding stem, gear train) and regulating parts (mainspring, escapement, balance wheel). Most expensive watches contained at least 15 jewels (very hard stones such as synthetic sapphires or rubies that had been drilled, chamfered and polished), which were inserted in places that were most subject to metal wear. The tiny dimensions of a watch case did not leave much room for approximation, and watchmakers were required to have a great deal of micro-mechanical engineering expertise, craftsmanship spirit, patience, experience and ingenuity.

By most accounts, the first reliable pocket watch was invented in 1510 by Peter Henlein, a locksmith from Nuremburg, but the promising art of watchmaking in Germany was rapidly killed by the Thirty Years War (1618 to 1648). Starting in the late 1500s, the development of the watchmaking industry in Europe traced its roots to the flight of protestant Huguenots who were driven out of France by a series of religious persecutions. The Huguenots found refuge in Geneva, bringing with them skills in numerous handicrafts. For centuries, Geneva had been a centre of ornate jewelry making, but it was left with little industry after John Calvin's famous *Sittenmandate* edicts against luxury and pleasure had progressively put an end to the goldsmiths' activities in the city. Looking for a new source of income, and with their knowledge of metals, skills in jewelry making and artistic flair, many Genevan goldsmiths embraced the watchmakers' profession.

As they were becoming more and more numerous, watchmakers decided to regulate their activities, and incorporated into a guild in 1601. The development of the industry in Geneva and the surrounding Jura mountains was rapid. By 1686, there were 100 masters in Geneva; 165 in 1716; and 800 in 1766 employing some 3,000 people. By 1790, Geneva exported more than 60,000 watches throughout Europe. Many of the Genevese moved north along the French frontier in the Vallée de Joux, Neuchatel and La Chaux-de-Fonds (see Exhibit 1).

The emergence of the watch industry in Switzerland was a blessing for the local farmers who could extract only modest agricultural revenues from their mountainous terrain. In fact, many families—who had been educated through a close-knit system of community schools—were looking for an additional source of income, particularly during the long and snow-filled winters. Thanks to advances in new machine powered watchmaking tools, individual Swiss families began to specialize, some in the production of single components, others in assembly. The small size of watches and watch components allowed for relatively easy transportation from mountain farms and villages to commercial centres.

Swiss watches were sold exclusively through jewelry and upscale department stores, which were also fully responsible for repair and aftersales services. Watches were purchased as lifetime investments and were often handed down from generation to generation. Swiss watches found ready acceptance throughout Europe and later in the U.S., in part because of their promotion by jewellers who saw them as a source of ongoing revenues through their repair services.

In the 18th and 19th centuries, English competitors were a constant challenge for the Swiss who undertook serious efforts to overcome early British supremacy. First, the Swiss invested in education and training, establishing several watchmaking academies at home and watch-repair schools in major foreign markets. Second, to strengthen their image internationally they created a "Swiss made" label, which would become by 1920 an important symbol of quality, style and prestige. Third, the Swiss significantly improved process technology, setting up the world's first mechanized watch factory in 1839. British watchmakers made no attempt to mass manufacture watches until much later. Seeing mass production techniques as a threat to their craft, they persuaded Parliament to pass a law barring the use of specialty production tools in the British watch industry, and devoted themselves to the production of very expensive marine chronometers. As a result, the British watch industry steadily declined during the 19th century, while the Swiss industry was on its way to achieving world dominance, thanks to significant advances in design, features, standardization, interchangeability of parts and productivity. In 1842, Adrien Philippe introduced complicated watches featuring perpetual calendars, fly-back hands and/or chronographs. Other early Swiss names included Beaume & Mercier (1830), Longines (1832), Piaget (1874), Omega (1848), Movado (1881) and Rolex (1908).

The U.S. watch industry appeared in the middle of the 19th century. Local production consisted of high-volume, standardized products manufactured in machine-driven factories. U.S. watches—such as the US$1 *Turnip* pocket watch introduced under the Ingersoll brand name by the Waterbury Clock Company—were cheap but also of very poor quality. Anyone who wanted a "real" watch bought Swiss.

In the early 20th century, the hard economic times (collapsing sales and soaring unemployment) following the First World War, led to a profound reorganization of the Swiss watch industry. Almost 2,500 distinct watchmaking firms grouped together into three associations, namely the Federation of the Swiss Watch Industry (FH) in 1924, the Ebauches SA in 1926, and the group Union des

Branches Annexes de l'Horlogerie (UBAH) in 1926. The associations agreed to coordinate activities (for example, watch components had to be bought from members of the associations only) and maintain high prices. The Swiss Laboratory for Watchmaking Research (CEH) was also founded in 1924, with the objective of strengthening the country's technological advantage. Finally, and in response to the world depression at the time, the Swiss government pushed several important watch assembly firms to form a holding company, ASUAG, in 1931.

POSTWAR COMPETITIVE CHANGES (1945 TO 1970)

By 1945, the Swiss accounted for 80 percent of the world's total watch production, and 99 percent of all U.S. watch imports. Swiss watch production was divided among nearly 2,500 distinct companies, 90 percent of which employed fewer than 50 people. Despite the 200-year dominance of Swiss watchmaking companies, much would change in a short period of time.

U.S. Competitors

The main source of competition for the Swiss arose from two American watchmakers, Timex and Bulova. Using a combination of automation, precision tooling and simpler design than that of higher-priced Swiss watches, U.S. Time Corporation introduced in 1951 a line of inexpensive (US$6.95 to US$7.95), disposable, yet stylized and highly durable Timex watches, whose movements had new hard alloy bearings instead of traditional and more expensive jewels. Hard alloy metals allowed for the creation of durable watches at lower costs than jewelled lever timepieces. They also allowed U.S. Time to more effectively automate its production lines, further lowering costs.

Traditional jewellers were very reluctant to carry the brand for a variety of reasons. Its prices and margins were slim compared to those offered by the Swiss, while the watches' riveted cases could not be opened, thereby eliminating the possibility for jewellers to generate aftersales repair revenues. Locked out of jewelry stores, Timex had no choice but to innovate in its marketing and distribution strategy. Their first extensive worldwide advertising campaign on television, "Took a licking and kept on ticking," was to become a legend in marketing history. Consumer demand soared after John Cameron Swazey, a famous U.S. news commentator, was featured in live "torture tests" commercials emphasizing the watch's low cost and incredible durability. The disposable aspect of Timex watches (no local repair involved) pushed the company to develop new distribution channels, including drugstores, discount houses, department stores, catalogue showrooms, military bases and sporting goods outlets. By 1970, Timex (having changed its name from U.S. Time) had established a manufacturing and/or marketing presence in over 30 countries and become the world's largest watch manufacturer in terms of units sold.

Bulova was the leading U.S. manufacturer of quality, jewelled-lever watches. Integrating the highly accurate tuning fork technology bought from a Swiss engineer in 1959, after the main Swiss companies had turned down the technology, Bulova introduced *Accutron* in 1962. Five years later, *Accutron* was the best selling watch over $100 in the United States. Bulova also formed a partnership with Japan's Citizen Watch Company to produce the movements for the *Caravelle* line, designed to meet the low-cost/high quality challenge imposed by Timex. By 1970, Bulova had expanded its international presence all around the world, and become the largest seller of watches, in revenue terms, in both the United States and the world overall.

Japanese Competitors

Like the U.S. industry, the Japanese watch industry was highly concentrated. In 1950, three main competitors, K. Hattori (which marketed the Seiko brand), Citizen and Orient accounted for 50 percent, 30 percent, and 20 percent of the Japanese market respectively. Their positions were protected by the 70 percent tariff and sales tax imposed on all imported watches by the Japanese government.

As the Japanese market became saturated in the 1960s, Hattori and Citizen moved aggressively into other Asia Pacific countries. After first exporting from Japan, Hattori and Citizen established component and assembly operations in low cost Hong Kong, Singapore and Malaysia. With hundreds of millions of unserved consumers, the region was also a highly attractive market. From a position of strength in Asia, the Japanese watch companies began in earnest to push into Europe and North America.

The Swiss response to the growing power of U.S. and Japanese competitors was limited. In 1962, the Swiss FH and ASUAG created a research organization, the Centre Electronique Horloger (CEH) to develop a competitive alternative to the tuning fork technology patented by Bulova. These efforts were unsuccessful, in part because of only lukewarm support from member companies. A rising worldwide demand for watches did little to slow the steady decline in the Swiss share of the world market (from 80 percent in 1946 to 42 percent in 1970).

CHANGING TECHNOLOGIES (1970 TO 1990)

The advent of light-emitting diodes (LED) and liquid crystal display (LCD) watches constituted a true revolution in the world of watchmaking, as they allowed the digital display of time. In 1970, Hattori Seiko became the first to develop and commercialize a quartz watch named *Astron,* based on LED technology.

Despite their novelty, LED watches had many flaws. A button had to be pushed to activate the display of LED watches, a process that consumed a lot of electrical energy and wore out batteries quickly. Additionally, most people felt that LEDs were distracting and inconvenient to use. In 1973, Seiko introduced the world's first LCD quartz watch with six-digit display and by the late 1970s, LCDs dominated the digital segment. However, digital watches remained largely plagued by quality problems, and consumers never fully embraced the style. Quartz analogue watches, which involved a more delicate manufacturing, and conserved—with their hands and gear train—the traditional appearance of mechanical timepieces, increasingly gained consumers' acceptance. By 1984, over 75 percent of all watches sold around the world were based on quartz technology, versus only three percent in 1975. The large majority of quartz watches were analogue.

Quartz watches used an integrated circuit, made up of numerous electronic components grouped together in the space of a few square millimetres. Extremely accurate, thanks to their high frequency of vibrations (32 kHz), they were accurate to less than one second per day. Generally more sophisticated—in terms of functions—than their mechanical counterparts, they were also far less expensive to manufacture. The average production cost of a standard quartz watch fell from US$200 in 1972 to about US$0.50 in 1984, the cost of components being constantly driven down by the main U.S. chipmakers such as National Semiconductor and Texas Instruments.

Faced with soaring international competition, the Swiss abolished all internal regulations in 1981, and the industry began to consolidate. Many firms merged in an attempt to leverage their marketing and/or manufacturing capabilities. The largest operation resulted in the creation of the Société Suisse pour L'Industrie Horlogère (SSIH), which controlled brands such as Omega and Tissot, among others.

THE JAPANESE INDUSTRY

Convinced that technologically sophisticated watches could allow Swiss prices at Timex costs, Hattori Seiko and Citizen made important efforts to promote the new quartz technology. Large investments were made in plant and equipment for fully automated high-volume production of integrated circuits, batteries and LCD panels. Hattori's production lines were designed to produce up to 1,000,000 watches per year per product line. Manufacturing/assembly facilities were set up all around the world (Japan, the United States, western Europe, Australia, Brazil, Hong Kong, Korea, Mexico). To ease the transition, employees were retrained, relations with distributors were reinforced, and advertising budgets were increased.

By 1979, Hattori produced about 22 million watches annually and became the world's largest watch company in terms of revenues, with sales approaching US$1.2 billion, versus only US$503 million for the Swiss ASUAG. Citizen launched the world's first wristwatch movement with a thickness of less than one millimetre in 1978, and became the global leader in both movement and finished wristwatch production volumes in 1986.

Casio entered the watch market in 1974 with a digital model priced at US$39.95. Its subsequent low-cost, multifunction digital plastic watches were rapidly fitted with gadgetry such as timers and calculators. By 1980, the company had captured 10 percent of the Japanese digital watch market, and became the world's second most important player in the under US$50 world watch market, behind Timex.

Hattori, Casio and Citizen were largely integrated companies. Most operations, from the production of movements and components to the assembly and distribution of finished watches, were carried out through wholly owned subsidiaries and/or majority joint ventures. In 1980, Japan produced about 67.5 million watches, up from 12.2 million in 1970.

THE U.S. INDUSTRY

U.S. competitors were relatively slow to get on the electronic bandwagon. Neither Bulova nor Timex's facilities easily allowed the production of quartz crystal or integrated circuits. In fact, they were rapidly becoming obsolete in light of those new technologies sweeping the industry. In addition, Timex was struggling with management problems as Mr. Lehmkuhl—who had run the business for almost 30 years with no clear successor—fell ill and could no longer work. Nevertheless, both companies finally entered the quartz watch market in the mid-1970s, sourcing their quartz components from a variety of suppliers and backing their product lines with full-scale advertising and promotion campaigns. The Timex model was priced at US$125, which was 60 percent below Seiko's least expensive watch on the market at that time.

About 100 semiconductor firms such as National Semiconductor, Texas Instruments (TI), and Litronix, were also attracted to the promising market for digital watches and circuits for electronic movements in the mid-1970s. Most started as suppliers of quartz movements and components, then invested in high-volume, fully automated watch-manufacturing plants. The belief was that their huge existing distribution channels for consumer electronics products would give them a strong competitive advantage. Watches were introduced at very aggressive prices (TI's retailed at $19.95 in 1976 and $9.99 in 1977). In 1978, TI's digital watch sales reached $100 million, for a pretax profit of US$28 million. However, stagnant demand coupled with continuous price wars and numerous distribution problems led all semiconductor firms to exit the market one by one. In the end, most customers felt uncomfortable buying watches in electronic stores where the semiconductor firms had a distribution advantage.

The price wars following the arrival of these semiconductor firms were also largely detrimental to the main U.S. watchmaking companies. Although it was constantly underpriced by Texas Instruments, Timex turned down a number of propositions to form manufacturing partnerships with several chipmakers. Some observers argued that Timex was probably too proud to accept the idea of cooperation. Timex lost US$10 million in 1980, being surpassed by Seiko as the world's largest watch manufacturer company (both in units and total sales), while its share of the U.S. market fell to under 33 percent. The two other U.S. players remaining in the industry were not in a much better situation. Bulova experienced three years of significant losses before being purchased by Loews Corporation; Hamilton lost $15 million in 1970 and went bankrupt in 1978: the Pulsar rights were bought by Seiko and the remaining assets purchased by SSIH.

WATCHMAKING ACTIVITIES IN HONG KONG AND KOREA

By the end of the 1970s, Hong Kong had become the highest volume producer of timepieces in the world. Japanese, American and European watchmakers had all established assembly plants (mechanical, digital and quartz analogue watches) in the city to take advantage of highly skilled, cheap labor and favorable tax conditions. Numerous local semiconductor firms had also engaged in the production of low-cost digital quartz watches that were then distributed through local retail chains and department stores, or exported, mainly to mainland China.

The timepiece industry in Korea also experienced considerable growth in the 1970s. By 1988, the country's total watch exports amounted to US$39 million, along with a rising reputation in the eyes of the world for quality assembling capabilities.

The Hong Kong and Korean watch industries benefited from their flexible manufacturing systems, capable of handling small quantity orders in different styles. However, downward pressures on prices and low profit margins discouraged local watch producers from investing in technology and branding.

THE SWISS INDUSTRY RESPONDS SLOWLY

Although the Swiss pioneered quartz technology, they were particularly reluctant to adopt the new technology. Contrary to the Japanese, their industry structure was very fragmented and, therefore, not adapted to high-volume mass production procedures. Besides, electronic watches were regarded as being unreliable, unsophisticated, and not up to Swiss quality standards. Consequently, digital and analogue quartz watches were regarded as just a passing fad, and in 1974, accounted for only 1.7 percent of the 84.4 million watches exported from Switzerland. Instead, the Swiss focused on the high-end, mechanical segment of the industry, where traditional craftsmanship remained the deciding factor.

As SSIH and ASUAG regularly increased prices to maintain profitability, foreign competition rapidly established a strong foothold in the low and middle price ranges where the Swiss were forced to abandon their leadership, virtually without a fight. Compounding the problems faced by the Swiss, the U.S. dollar more than halved its value against the Swiss franc during the 1970s. The appreciating Swiss franc effectively raised the export prices of Swiss watches (see Exhibit 2).

The Swiss industry experienced a severe crisis in the late 1970s and early 1980s. Its exports of watches and movements decreased from 94 million in 1974 to 43 million in 1983, while its world market share slid from 43 percent to less than 15 percent during that same period. Employment fell from 90,000 (1970) to 47,000 (1980) to 34,000 (1984) and bankruptcies reduced the number of firms from 1,618 to 860 to 630 respectively. These competitive changes resulted mainly from the seeming inability of the Swiss to adapt to the rapid emergence of new watch technologies.

EXHIBIT 2
Exchange Rate to the U.S. Dollar (Annual Average)

	1950-1970	1971	1972	1974	1976	1978	1980
Swiss Franc	4.37	4.15	4.15	3.58	2.89	2.24	2.18

Source: International Monetary Fund Yearbook of Statistics.

Near Death Experience

In the early 1980s, Swiss watch production hit an all time low. SSIH and ASUAG faced liquidation and a profound restructuring of the Swiss industry became necessary. The Swiss government provided financial assistance and initiated the "electronic watch" program in 1978 to promote new technologies as well as the production of electronic watch components in Switzerland. But this initiative was not sufficient, and in 1981 SSIH reported a loss of SFr142 million, giving the company a negative net worth of SFr27.4 million. The Swiss creditor banks—which had just taken over the country's two largest watchmaking groups—were getting ready to sell prestigious brand names, such as Omega, Tissot or Longines to the Japanese. But Nicolas Hayek, the already well-known founder and CEO of Hayek Engineering, a consulting firm based in Zurich, was convinced he could revive the Swiss industry and regain lost market share, primarily in the lower-end segment. He invested $102 million—mostly his own money—and led a group of 16 investors in buying back the two groups, before orchestrating their merger in 1983.

SMH and Swatch

Hayek teamed with Dr. Ernst Thomke to head the new group, Société Micromécanique et Horlogère (SMH). After the merger, SMH owned many of the country's famous watchmaking names, such as Omega, Tissot, Longines and Rado. Five years later, the group had become the world's largest watchmaking company. Its first product initiative, Swatch, was to become an enormous commercial success, as well as the main instrument behind the revitalization of the entire Swiss industry.

The Swatch mania marked the 1980s for the Swiss industry. The Swatch (contraction of "Swiss" and "watch") was conceived as an inexpensive, SFr50 (US$40), yet good quality watch, with quartz accuracy, water and shock resistance, as well as a one-year guarantee. The concept was challenging. Particular efforts were needed to reduce production costs down to Asian levels. Watch engineers slashed the number of individual parts required in the production of a watch from 91 to 51, and housed them in a standardized plastic case that could be produced on a fully automated assembly line. For the first time ever, it became possible to produce cheap watches in high cost Switzerland. By 1985, production costs were decreased to under SFr10 per unit, and only 130 people were needed to assemble the first eight million Swatch models. By comparison, 350 people were still required to assemble 700,000 Omega watches.

Swatch was an immediate success. Within two years of its 1983 launch, sales were averaging 100,000 units a month, for a cumulative total of 13 million sold. In 1985, Swatch accounted for over 80 percent of SMH's total unit sales, and by 1989, just six years after its debut, the company had placed 70 million Swatches on customers' wrists.

Marketing was key to the watch's success. Franz Sprecher, an independent consultant, and Max Imgrüth, a graduate of New York's Fashion Institute of Technology, helped SMH position the watch as a lifestyle symbol and fashion accessory, not as a traditional timekeeping instrument. With their trendy and colorful designs, models were created for every occasion.

Initially, the media appeared to be mesmerized by Hayek's charismatic style and unusual approach to marketing. This resulted in lots of free media coverage and publicity. The company also spent liberally on special events and public relation activities. SMH budgeted about SFr5 million per Swatch product line per year in promotional money, and used celebrity endorsements extensively. Swatches were sold through nonconventional channels of distribution such as discount houses and department stores, where variety and low prices constituted the main selling points. Swatch made a few attempts to diversify, but its line of accessories (casual clothing and footwear, umbrellas, sunglasses, and cigarette lighters) experienced mixed success and was discontinued in 1988.

COMPETING IN REAL TIME (1990s)

Global watch production grew steadily in the 1990s, at a rate of about four percent per annum, and reached 1.3 billion watches in 1998, equivalent to 22 percent of the world's population (see Exhibit 3). The production of mechanical watches (and to a lesser extent, that of digital watches) gradually decreased over the years, while that of analogue quartz watches rose 11 percent per year on average. In 1998, quartz watches—digital and analogue—accounted for about 97 percent of the worldwide industry's production in volume. On average, annual watch purchases were about one unit per person in North America, and 0.6 unit per person in Europe and Japan. Together these three regions—which accounted for 14 percent of the world's population—generated about 56 percent of global watch demand (see Exhibit 4).

EXHIBIT 3   Global Watch Production; 1984 to 1998 (in thousands)

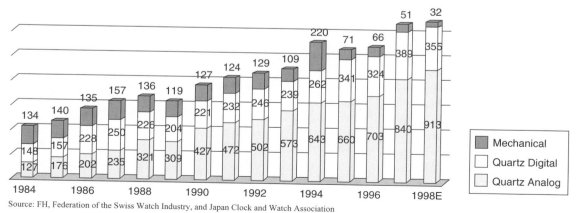

Source: FH, Federation of the Swiss Watch Industry, and Japan Clock and Watch Association

EXHIBIT 4
Per Capita GNP and Annual Watch Purchases, By Region

Source: Japan Clock and Watch Association, *United Nations Demographic Yearbook,* The World Bank.

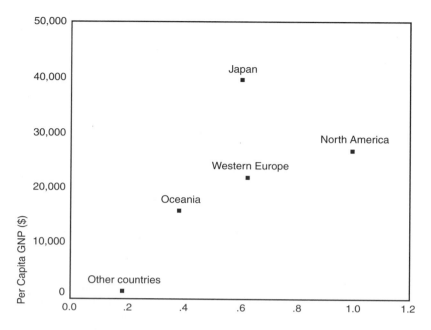

Industry Restructuring

The global watch industry experienced downward profit pressures in the 1990s, as many watchmakers incessantly cut prices—driven in part by a push for economies of scale. Overcapacity and tough head-to-head competition led prices of basic watch movements to be slashed by over 30 percent in 1998 alone. By the end of the decade, consolidation had reduced the number of watch movement manufacturers from 30 to just three (the Swatch Group—having changed its name from SMH—as well as Seiko and Citizen). The achievement of a critical mass was becoming a necessity to compete globally in all segments of the industry.

Several types of internal reorganizations allowed companies to realize economies of scale and/or maintain profitability. These included:

Restructuring Initiatives

Many watchmaking companies reacted to declining prices in their core business by increasing productivity and shifting manufacturing overseas. With the exception of the Swatch Group, most watch companies manufactured in Southeast Asia exclusively.

Pursuing Acquisitions

In tune with its strategy to reinforce its position in the luxury or prestige brands, the Swatch Group acquired Blancpain in 1992, thereby also taking control of Frederic Piguet, a company admired for its complex, high-quality mechanical movements. In January 1999, the Swatch Group purchased the total shares of Favre and Perret, the highly reputed producer of quality Swiss watchcases. As another example, Gucci, the luxury Italian company, acquired Severin Montres, its 23-year Swiss watch manufacturer, for $150 million in November 1997. The following year, Gucci's watch sales increased by 160 percent to $60.1 million. "There is no question that Gucci is destined to become more than a shoe and bag business," said De Boisgelin, an equity analyst with Merrill Lynch in London.[2]

Accessing New Distribution Channels

Watchmakers traditionally used independent agents to sell products around the world. However, increasing difficulties controlling the merchandising and pricing policies used by local retailers led many of them to alter their strategies. In 1997, the Swatch Group opened 61 new free-standing Swatch stores (mostly operated as franchisees), bringing the total to 120 (including five megastores) in more than 20 countries. Despite the risks involved, the strategy was promising: sales at New York's Swatch Time Shop boutiques approached 100,000 units in 1998, up 32 percent over 1997. By taking over 85 percent of its distribution network, Tag Heuer increased its gross margins from 45 percent to 65 percent, which more than offset the cost of running local subsidiaries. According to CEO Christian Viros, the move allowed "greater control of our destiny, better control of the implementation of our marketing programs, better understanding of local issues, and greater reactiveness to new developments."[3]

Creating New Niche Products

Despite ongoing consolidation, there was a viable place for niche companies with clearly defined brands and images. By the late 1990s, Switzerland had about 600 watchmaking companies, employing 34,000 employees, in addition to the big four (The Swatch Group, The Vendôme Luxury Group, Rolex and Tag Heuer), which together accounted for 75 percent to 80 percent of Swiss industry turnover. As examples of niche players, St. John Timepieces entered the industry in 1997 with a collection of Swiss watches specifically designed for sophisticated women, retailing from $450 to $18,000. Breitling scarcely deviated from the aerial image it established in 1884. In 1999, it equipped Breitling Orbiter 3's pilots, Bertrand Piccard and Brian Jones, with wristwatches for their successful, first nonstop 26,602 miles balloon flight around the world.

Increasing Advertising

The overabundance of supply in the industry implied that watchmakers had to find ways to distinguish their offerings from those of their competitors. Advertising expenditures reached unprecedented levels. In the 1990s, 40 percent of the value of all Swiss advertisements in international media promoted wristwatches, not banking institutions. Seiko's 1998 *Electricity* campaign was backed with a 60 percent increase in media spending, while Timex allocated about US$8 million in 1999 to market its *Turn 'n' Pull* Alarm watches.

Huge advertising budgets were not, per se, a guarantee of success. The campaigns also needed to be creative in order to get consumers' attention. Companies turned down conservative ads in favor of eye-popping, humorous, and thought-provoking messages that obtained an emotional reaction from viewers. For example, Bulgari formed a one-year partnership with Alitalia, Italy's national airline, to have a personalized Boeing 747 fly around the world with a three-dimensional image of its latest cutting-edge aluminum timepiece painted on the fuselage. Audemars Piguet's ad crusade, "Who is behind an Audemars Piguet Watch?" featured mysterious men and women showing off their watch faces while their own faces remain obscured. Other watchmakers tried to get exposure in action-packed movies such as *Men in Black* and *Lethal Weapon 4* (Hamilton), James Bond (Omega), or *Armageddon* (Tag Heuer). Strong marketing muscle was also put behind sports partnerships. For example, Tag Heuer and Hugo Boss had long been associated with Formula One auto racing, and Spanish-based Festina with cycling events such as the Tour de France.

Emphasizing Quality

Faced with strong competition from independent, low cost Asian producers, many European and U.S. watchmakers chose to gradually reposition their brands in the upper market, and proposed increasingly expensive and sophisticated watches. According to the Federation of the Swiss Watch Industry, the average price of a Swiss wristwatch, taking account of all materials, rose from US$132 in 1996 to US$157 in 1997. A growing number of customers were becoming aware of quality and increasingly wanted a watch with lasting value.

Emphasizing Technology

The end of the 1990s looked promising in terms of technological breakthroughs. Bulova's *Vibra Alarm* watch featured dual sound and vibrating alarms. In Seiko's *Kinetic,* an oscillating weight was set in motion by the slightest movements of the wearer's arm ("If you're going to create electricity, use it!"). Timex's *DataLink* pioneered the utilization of wristwatches as wearable information devices. Following Timex's lead, various watch manufacturers introduced multifunctional watches that could be interfaced with personal computers. Other manufacturers designed watches with built-in global positioning systems (Casio, Timex), or offered fast, customized and reliable access to Internet services.

Accentuating Fashion

Another noticeable trend was the entry of fashion house designers. By 1999, and partly thanks to the Swatch revolution, people increasingly believed that they were judged by what they wore on their wrists. Fashion designers strove to create new watch brands to meet every one of their possible fashion needs. Some decided to put their signatures on stylized watches produced in cooperation with major specialist manufacturers. Examples included Emporio Armani (Fossil), Calvin Klein (The Swatch Group), Guess (Timex) and Yves St Laurent (Citizen). Others, such as Bulgari, Hermes, and Dior set up their own in-house manufacturing operations.

EXHIBIT 5
World Production of Finished Watches: 500 Million Pieces (1997)

Source: Federation of the Swiss Watch Industry

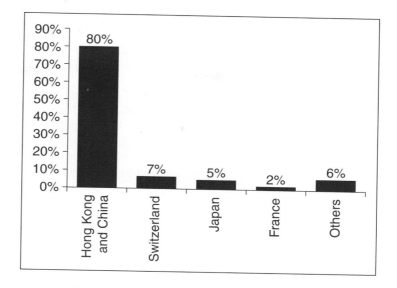

"We have very high expectations for this side of the business," said Guillaume de Seynes, director of Hermes Montres. "Watches are already our fourth biggest product in sales terms after leather, silk, and ready-to-wear. We've made a significant investment in the new factory because we expect even faster growth in the future."[4]

DEVELOPMENTS IN THE HONG KONG AND JAPANESE INDUSTRIES

In the late 1990s, Hong Kong was the world's dominant centre for watch assembly. In 1998, about 80 percent of all watches produced worldwide were assembled in the city (see Exhibit 5).

Japanese watch manufacturers saw their combined domestic and overseas watch production rise about 14 percent per year in the 1990s. Particularly strong in the sports watch segment, the Japanese offered an impressive range of multi-function chronographs for virtually any type of outdoor activity, including diving, mountain climbing and flying. However, sales and profitability deteriorated between 1993 and 1996 due to a rapid appreciation of the yen. In addition, the average unit price of analogue quartz movements fell by nearly 50 percent to ¥234 in the first half of the decade, and by over 30 percent in 1998, as major companies boosted production. This collapse severely shook the industry, and many manufacturers, such as Orient Watch, had to exit the market. Throughout the last half of the 1990s, Seiko and Citizen began cutting production in order to hold prices firm.

Citizen maintained its world's volume leadership with 2,500 new models released every year and 311 million timepieces produced in 1997 (about 25 percent of the world's total and 36 percent of the global market for analogue quartz watches). Sales were mainly dependent upon Japan (38 percent), Asia (32 percent), America (15 percent) and Europe (14 percent). Two new collections—the light-powered *Eco-Drive* watches and the affordable luxury *Elegance Signature* dress watches—marked the company's desire to move from traditional sports watches towards more sophisticated or expensive timepieces.

Seiko introduced a few technological marvels in the early 1990s, such as the *Perpetual Calendar* watch, with the first built-in millennium plus (1,100 years) calendar, *the Scubamaster,* with the first integrated computerized dive table, and the *Receptor MessageWatch,* with paging functions and built-in antenna that allowed access to specialized information services and incoming alphanumeric messages. In 1995, Seiko introduced the *Kinetic* series, backed with a $20 million advertising campaign. The futuristic line became the driving force behind the company's growth in the late 1990s, accounting for 25 percent of Seiko's $3 billion global sales. Great hopes were also placed on *Kinetic*'s lower-cost cousin, the $200 *Pulsar* solar-powered quartz watch, which was launched at the end of 1996.

Casio enjoyed a significant expansion of its wristwatch division, thanks to the successful launches of the *G-shock* and *Baby-G* product lines. The company was particularly strong in the U.S. (second largest market share after Timex), but also heavily dependent on domestic Japanese sales, which made up two-thirds of total *G-shock* and *Baby-G* sales. A depressed Japanese economy in the late 1990s had a profound negative effect on the company's profits, which were estimated to have dropped from ¥38 billion in 1998 to ¥19 billion in 1999.[5]

THE U.S. INDUSTRY

The biggest single watch market in the world was also the one with the largest trade deficit. In 1991, exports amounted to $73.4 million compared to an import total of $1.84 billion. Thanks to a factory in Little Rock, Arkansas, Timex was the only U.S. watch company with any domestic production in the late 1990s.

Timex

From sports watches and classic styles to watches featuring *Star Trek* and Walt Disney characters, Timex offerings strove to address a variety of consumer trends in the 1990s. The production of watches for Guess, Timberland, Nautica, and Reebok further emphasized Timex's willingness to reach a mass audience. Two innovations distinguished the company. The first was the durable, multi-function *Ironman Triathlon* watch, named after the gruelling annual Hawaiian sports event. Initially positioned as an instrument for serious athletes, the watch rapidly appealed to a wider audience of pedestrian customers. By the late 1990s, it was the word's best selling sports watch with more than 25 million units sold since its 1986 introduction. The second was *Indiglo,* a patented luminescent dial technology launched in 1992, and credited with more than doubling the company's sales by 1994. *Indiglo* received considerable attention in 1993 after a group of people

EXHIBIT 6
Share of Purchasers by Brand in the U.S. Market—1999

Source: Euromonitor

Brand	Share	Brand	Share
Timex	30.6%	Gitano	2.0%
Casio	7.8%	Gucci	1.9%
Seiko	7.4%	Swatch	1.6%
Guess (Timex)	5.0%	Rolex	1.1%
Armitron (Gluck)	4.5%	Movado	1.0%
Citizen	4.0%	Tag Heuer	0.8%
Fossil	3.5%	Hamilton (Swatch)	0.7%
Pulsar (Seiko)	3.1%	Tissot (Swatch)	0.7%
Lorus (Seiko)	2.5%	Omega (Swatch)	0.5%
Bulova	2.2%	Rado (Swatch)	0.2%

trapped in the World Trade Center bombing had been led to safety by an *Indiglo* owner, who guided them down 34 flights of pitch-black stairs through the glow of his Timex watch. Other technological innovations rapidly followed, with Timex *DataLink,* a $139 wristwatch allowing wireless transfer to and from a desktop PC, and *Beepwear,* a $160 alphanumeric pager wristwatch developed and commercialized in partnership with Motorola.

Timex's annual sales exceeded $600 million in the late 1990s, one-quarter of which came from the U.S. market where the company remained the top selling watch company, far ahead of its main competitors. By 1999, with a 30 percent market share in its hands, Timex had sold more watches in the U.S. than the next five competitors combined (see Exhibit 6). However, the huge majority of these watches were manufactured in Asia.

NEW ENTRANTS IN THE 1990s

By the early 1990s, mainland China and India had emerged among the fastest growing watch markets in the world. With a combined population of 2.1 billion people, these markets could not be ignored, especially after a series of government decisions to liberalize trade and investment in those countries. A number of reputable watchmaking companies had established a presence in India and mainland China, despite the threat of counterfeiting (about 50 percent of wristwatches sold in those markets were either counterfeited or smuggled in). Most came in via the trading route, appointing local distributors such as Dream Time Watches in India. This strategy was ideal for the Swiss, who could capitalize on the well-appreciated label "Swiss made." Others such as Timex, Seiko and Citizen established their own production facilities, often in cooperation with key local partners.

Titan Industries was probably one of the most remarkable industry success stories of the 1990s. The group was established in 1987, with a greenfield investment of $130 million from giant Indian conglomerate Tata Group and the government of Tamil Nadu state, where Titan built one of the world's biggest integrated watch factories, near India's technological centre Bangalore. Constantly scanning the

EXHIBIT 7
World Production of Finished Watches in Value Terms: 16 Billion Swiss Francs (1997)

Source: Federation of the Swiss Watch Industry

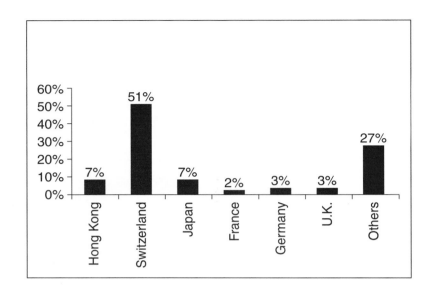

world for best practices, Titan sourced designs and technology from France, Switzerland and Germany, watchstraps from Austria, and cases from Japan. This world-class strategy created a remarkably successful company. During its first year of operation, 750,000 high-quality finished timepieces were produced and, in 1997, the company enjoyed a dominant 60 percent share of the organized Indian watch market, with pretax profits amounting to US$7.5 million on turnover of US$96 million. Titan's management believed the company had little choice but to internationalize, partly to defend its own domestic position. Mr. Desai, Titan's vice-chairman and managing director commented on the need to globalize: "India is being globalized and the whole world is now turning up in India. So the kind of protection we've enjoyed will go. It's going to get very crowded."[6] By 1997, the company exported over 600,000 watches annually and had established offices in Dubai, London, New York and Singapore. However, by the end of the 1990s and despite the company's recent $20 million advertising campaign, it was difficult to predict international success. Seducing consumers into buying $120 to $700 Indian-made wristwatches was challenging given the country's poor reputation for the quality of its exports.

THE SWISS INDUSTRY IN THE LATE 1990s

In the late 1990s, watch production in Switzerland was the country's third most important industry behind the chemical-pharmaceutical and electronic industries. In 1998, 34 million timepieces were produced in Switzerland for a total value of SFr8.2 billion.[7] Of those, 90 percent were exported, positioning the country as the world's leading exporter—in value—of finished watches (see Exhibit 7).

EXHIBIT 8
Luxury, Prestige and Top Range: Global Market Players (1998)

Source: Bank Leu estimates, Vendôme Group Data

	Turnover in SFr. Million	Market Share
Rolex	2,200	28%
Vendôme*	1,540	20%
Swatch Group**	1,000–1,100	14%
Gucci	620	8%
TAG Heuer	470	6%
Patek Philippe	250	3%
Bulgari	215	3%
Chopard	195	3%
Jaeger LeCoultre	180	2%
Audemars Piguet	120	2%
Other (Ebel, IWC, Breguet, . . .)	910	12%
Total	7,750	100%

*(Cartier, Piaget, Vacheron and Constantin, Beaume & Mercier)
**(Blancpain, Omega, Rado, Longines)

The Swiss industry had the ability to provide consumers with a comprehensive choice of products in all market segments. Whatever their needs and preferences (mechanical versus quartz technologies; diamond set watch of precious metals versus stainless steel, plastic or ceramic; classic appearance versus trendy design), consumers could always find a "Swiss made" solution when shopping for their wristwatches. Of course, the Swiss industry stood apart in the upper market range where its watches had gained an unequalled reputation for quality, styling, reliability and accuracy. In 1998, the average price of watches exported by Switzerland was SFr235, four times higher than the average of the world industry (see Exhibits 8 and 9). The "Swiss made" label remained one the oldest examples of a registered and fiercely protected national branding name, which could be used only on watches and clocks containing at least 50 percent Swiss-manufactured components by value.

The Vendôme Luxury Group accounted for about 20 percent of Swiss industry turnover, privately-held Rolex for 15 percent, and Tag Heuer—which sold over 673,000 units in 1997, for seven percent. The Swatch Group was the main player with a third of industry turnover. Thanks to its 14 brands (Blancpain, Omega, Rado, Longines, Tissot, Calvin Klein, Certina, Mido, Hamilton, Pierre Balmain, Swatch, Flick Flack, Lanco, and Endura), the group had gained a presence in all price and market categories.

Swiss watches were sold all around the world. Exports to the United States increased by more than 10 percent in 1998 for the third consecutive year. Sales in Europe were also on the rise, especially in Spain (+41.3 percent), Italy (+18 percent) and France (+16 percent). In Asia, the ongoing economic crisis depressed demand and put downward pressures on prices (the demand in Hong Kong, Singapore, Thailand and Taiwan dropped by 23 percent or SFr500 million in 1998). In 1997, Tag Heuer saw Asian sales drop by 21.4 percent from SFr130 million to SFr102.9 million, accounting for the brand's overall 5.4 percent decrease.

EXHIBIT 9
Average Price of Watches in 1998 (in Swiss francs)

Source: Federation of the Swiss Watch Industry

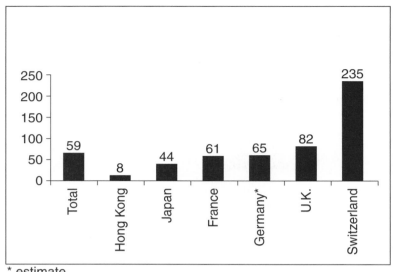

* estimate

The Swatch Group

In value terms, the Swatch Group was the world's leading manufacturer of watches (14 percent share of the world market). In 1998, the Swatch Group increased its gross sales and net profits by 7.1 percent and 7.5 percent respectively. With a growth averaging 15 percent to 25 percent per year, Omega had been a major profit driver for the group (see Exhibit 10), thanks to a successful repositioning strategy initiated in the early 1990s. To rejuvenate the brand, cheaper, silver-plated gold was used to replace more expensive metals (platinum, titanium, solid gold and special steel alloys).

The company also streamlined its models from 2,500 to 130 representing four distinct product lines. Other major initiatives consisted of integrating distribution and launching a new advertising campaign (with Cindy Crawford, Michael Schumacher, Martina Hingis and Pierce Brosnan as high-profile "ambassadors"). The strategy was quite successful and with an average price point 50 percent lower than its main competitor, Rolex, Omega seemed to have plenty of room to grow.

Despite the success of the Omega brand, the Swatch Group was facing several issues. Management problems were plaguing the organization. Key figures such as Klaus Schwab, a professor at the University of Geneva and founder of the World Economic Forum in Davos, Drs. Stephan Schmidheiny, Pierre Arnold and Walter Frehner all stepped down from the board of directors in the mid-1990s. Several managing directors also left the group in the last two years. Hayek's management style was resulting in growing criticism in the company. Dr. Ernst Thomke, a former partner, had less-than-flattering comments about Hayek: "He has to be the big boss alone, and can never share opinions. He was a consultant all his life and he wanted to become a marketer and product developer. But he never learned that job."[8]

EXHIBIT 10

The Swatch Group's Turnover and Margin Estimates for 1998

Source: Bank Leu estimates

	Units in Thou.	Average Price in SFr.*	Turnover in SFr. Million	% of Total	EBIT in SFr. Million	% Total	Margin in %
Omega	550	1,200	670	28%	147	47%	22%
Swatch	26,000	36	925	38%	79	25%	9%
Tissot	1,600	100-150	210	9%	20	6%	10%
Rado	300	570	170	7%	31	10%	18%
Longines	550	270	150	6%	23	7%	15%
Calvin Klein	600	130	75	3%	4	1%	5%
Blancpain	10	6,500	65	3%	6	2%	9%
Other	1,500	80	145	6%	3	1%	2%
Total	31,110	80	2,410	100%	312	100%	13.0%

*Factory gate price

EXHIBIT 11

U.S. Market and Swatch Group's Market Share—1999

Source: Dresdner Kleinwort Benson estimates

	Units	%	Value	%	Swatch Market Share
Mass (under $50)	124,653	78%	2,056	34%	9%
Middle market ($50-299)	31,840	20%	2,219	37%	4%
Upper/Luxury ($300)	2,705	2%	1,771	29%	21%
Total	159,198	100%	6,046	100%	11%

The Swatch Group was also experiencing persistent difficulties in establishing a strong foothold in the U.S. market, where it faced stiff competition from Timex, Casio, Seiko and Citizen. Even the Swatch Group's role as the official timekeeper of the 1996 Summer Olympic Games in Atlanta failed to significantly boost interest in the company's offerings. Although, the group generated about 19 percent of its sales in the U.S. its market share in the basic and middle-priced segments was particularly weak (see Exhibits 6 and 11). Finally, its highly successful and emblematic Swatch brand appeared to be at a crucial crossroads.

The brand had sold a total of 200 million watches since its introduction in 1983. A Collectors' Club (100,000 members worldwide) was founded in 1990 to create an international link between fans around the world. Limited edition watches, special events, and the quarterly *Swatch World* journal also contributed to reinforce the value of the brand. Demand rapidly exceeded supply for a number of special launches and collectors started to compare the rarity of their collections, to trade and to speculate around Swatches during auction sales. In the early 1990s, it looked as if Swatch's expansion had no limit. So great was management's confidence that the group even decided to actively contribute to the development and market introduction of the small ecological smart car.

Despite the growing interest of many, Swatch sales had plateaued at 18 million to 20 million units a year. In 1998, sales and profit margins were well below the levels achieved in the early 1990s as Swatch was facing increased competition from the likes of Fossil and Guess. One concern was whether there were too many Swatch products on the market. Another concern centred on the product mix. Many young Swatch fans of the past wanted more expensive and sophisticated watches as their incomes increased. A proliferation of products also led to a growing problem with Swatch distributors. Many retailers were dropping Swatch from their shelves. The number of stores selling the trendy watch decreased from 3,000 in the early 1990s to 1,200 in 1998. For Steven Rosdal, co-owner of Hyde Park Jewelers, expressed the views of some retailers: "Swatch came out with more products than the market could bear, and the consumers seemed to back off. I guess if you use the word 'fad' for anything, it could be used for Swatch."[9]

The group was undertaking several steps to revamp and differentiate the brand. First, Swatch was trying to reposition itself from a low-margin, high-volume business involved in day-to-day fashion watches to a high-margin, high-volume enterprise focusing on watches fitted with state-of-the-art electronic gadgetry. As an example of its repositioning efforts, it launched the *Access* watch in 1995, which could be programmed to function as a pass to access ski lifts, hotel chains, public transport and numerous other applications. Although the watch had yet to achieve its commercial potential, there were promising signals: Swatch equipped the Lisbon universal exhibition with one million units and about 200 ski resorts in some 17 countries. Also, with assistance from German Electronics giant Siemens, Swatch developed *Swatch Talk,* a Dick Tracy type wristwatch with an integrated mobile telephone. Finally, Swatch created the *Swatch Beat,* as a completely new global concept of time, as well as a whole new area of market potential. With *Swatch Beat,* time was the same all over the world "No Time Zones, No Geographical Borders." People using the same clock could agree to a phone call at "500," without time zone arithmetic required. The day was divided into 1,000 units (each one being the equivalent of one minute and 26.4 seconds) with a new BMT meridian created in Bienne, home of the Swatch Group.

As a second initiative, Swatch launched a new advertising campaign ("Time is what you make of it") designed to reinforce the brand's primary message ("Innovation, provocation, fun. Forever.") Sponsorship was primarily focused on new and youth-oriented sports or events with an offbeat lifestyle, such as snowboarding, mountain biking, bungee jumping, and rock climbing.

However, in October 1998, Swatch sold its minority 19 percent shareholding of Micro Compact Car, the vehicle producer, to manufacturing partner Daimler-Benz. Although the group was still looking for key partners to develop the hybrid electric *Swatchmobile,* management made it clear that its core business remained the watch industry and microelectronics.

STRATEGIC DECISIONS

In early June 1999, Hayek was under growing pressure to clarify the company's strategy. Many observers and shareholders were wondering whether the original management philosophy that shaped the company's success remained viable.

EXHIBIT 12
Watch Production and Value Added Chain

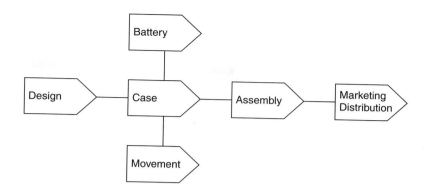

Conventional wisdom suggested that all watch companies should locate manufacturing activities in countries that offered low-cost production solutions. The Swatch Group had always remained committed to its Swiss home base, leaving the bulk of its technology, people and manufacturing in the isolated villages surrounding the Jura Mountains. Those places possessed hundreds of years of experience in the art of watchmaking. Employees had spent generations in the factories controlled by the Swatch Group, where they developed a special feel and touch for this business along with a true sense of organizational commitment. However, the company's junior secretaries in Switzerland earned more than senior engineers at competitors in Thailand, Malaysia, China or India. Maybe it was time to move on and stop building watches in one of the most expensive countries in the world. But which, if any, of the value-added chain activities should be moved (see Exhibit 12)?

With its huge domestic demand and low-cost labor, India offered interesting sourcing opportunities. Many industry analysts believed that Titan Industries was looking for key foreign partners, after the demise of an early alliance with Timex. Would a partnership with a company like Titan make sense, or if and when the company were to move, should it go it alone?

Another trend management had to address was the movement of many watch companies into ever-more narrow or differentiated market niches. The Swatch Group was present in all market segments and price categories, but its performance depended mainly on four brands names, Omega, Swatch, Tissot and Rado, which together accounted for 82 percent of total sales and 88 percent of operating profit in 1998 (see Exhibit 10). Perhaps it was time to reorganize the company's portfolio. Advertising budgets had already been reallocated towards the luxury and high-tech markets, where the company was also constantly looking for key partners and acquisition targets. However, for many industry observers, this product market strategy (luxury-high tech and/or globalization) was becoming too complex for the company's internal capabilities, as indicated in the failure of the smart car project.

Endnotes

1. This case has been written on the basis of published sources only. Consequently, the interpretation and perspectives presented in this case are not necessarily those of the Swatch Group or any of its employees.
2. *Women's Wear Daily,* March 20, 1998.
3. Chief Executive, 1998.
4 *Financial Times,* April 24/25 1999
5. In June 1999 US$1 = ¥119
6. Financial Times London Edition. *Financial Times.* September 10, 1997; 43.
7. In June 1999, SFr. 1 = US$0.66.
8. *Time,* March 28, 1994.
9. Jewellers' Circular-*Keystone,* December 1998.

Chapter Twenty-Two

Selkirk Group in Asia

From their modern brick building in Victoria, Australia, it seemed a long way from the economic crisis that had engulfed Asia in the past 18 months. At one side of the board table sat Bernie Segrave, the Managing Director of the Selkirk Group of Companies and the person who had taken direct charge of the group's export marketing strategy across Asia. On the other side, and with a view of the large brick chimney that announced Selkirk Brick's presence in the local community, sat Peter Blackburn, Export Manager and the person being groomed to progressively take over the exporting responsibilities. Both were looking at the export performance graphs of the group over the past five years as background preparation for their forthcoming trip.

Ahead of them (in late October 1998) was an overseas tour to meet their existing network of agents and potential customers in Singapore, Thailand, Hong Kong and Taiwan. Their largest market, Japan, was not included in this tour. The reasons for the tour were quite straightforward in Segrave's mind:

> We have made a strategic decision to continue developing and building relationships in Asia in these bad times. We went to Japan earlier this year. In this downturn, we are very lucky we have good agents in Japan. If Japan goes, we don't want to think about it—but I guess the rest of the world goes as well.

Richard Ivey School of Business
The University of Western Ontario

Lambros Karavis prepared this case under the supervision of Professor Paul Beamish solely to provide material for class discussion. The authors do not intend to illustrate either effective or ineffective handling of a managerial situation. The authors may have disguised certain names and other identifying information to protect confidentiality.

Asia is very important in the long term because we continue to develop products of excellent technical quality which are appreciated by Asians. It's very important to us in terms of sales and output. Within five years we expect to have either a subsidiary or a selling arm in an Asian destination.

At issue was how to continue developing their business in Asia. Both Segrave and Blackburn were wondering about the business opportunities they would uncover and whether it was time to review their export strategy and organisation for the region.

SELKIRK BRICK—A FAMILY BUSINESS FOR OVER 100 YEARS

Selkirk Brick was established in 1883 when the gold rush in colonial Victoria brought together fortune seekers and entrepreneurs from across the world. Chinese, Scots, Irish and even Californians were among the immigrants who saw the opportunity to prosper in the colony. Among them was Robert Selkirk, a Scottish stonemason, who sought to capitalise on the building boom accompanying the wealth generated from gold and wool. He started making bricks using a local clay deposit in Allendale but moved to nearby Ballarat in 1900 where suitable clay deposits had been identified on ten hectares of land in Howitt Street, the present-day site of the works and head office.

Though clay bricks and pavers were often seen as a low-tech product, there was, in fact, considerable technical expertise required to produce a high quality product. Apart from selecting the right clays as the raw material for firing into bricks and pavers, a number of other factors needed to be managed carefully. The moisture content in the clay was critical to both moulding and firing outcomes achieved. Various oxides and other additives were used to achieve specific colors and finishes. Kiln temperature, length of time in the kiln and airflows also needed to be carefully controlled to achieve consistency in strength and color characteristics.

The high quality of Australian clay bricks and pavers has led to their extensive use as a building material for external cladding. Many houses had been traditionally built with double brick walls, particularly in the more temperate climate zones in Australia ranging from New South Wales, through Victoria, South Australia and Tasmania (refer to Exhibit 1 for geographic locations in Australia). In recent years, the use of brick had declined as brick veneer, steel frames, timber, concrete and even mud-brick homes gained popularity with the home buyer. Increasingly, clay bricks and pavers were being used as architectural features rather than simply as a construction material.

From a study of the company's history (see Appendix 1), Selkirk Brick could be characterised as a company which was managed in a financially conservative manner but which embraced (world-class at the time) technological innovation to maintain technical superiority and cost efficiency in the marketplace. It was a company which had resisted buyouts and generational fragmentation in the process.

The shareholders were well aware that by the time a family company reached the fifth generation, it was unlikely to accommodate the needs of all who might

EXHIBIT 1
Geographic
Locations

expect to work there. Robert Selkirk, who became Chairman in 1985 and was in charge of marketing, commented on the roles of the working shareholders:

> It's something that you have to work at every day of your life. There are conflicts; we all see things differently. The challenge is to try to put personal and family disagreements to one side when in the office.

Jim Selkirk, Finance Director since 1986, suggested a few basic requirements for a family company: no gamblers, squanderers or alcoholics; no tendency to over-borrow or be over-acquisitive; be prepared to spend most of your time with the company; and no expensive or messy divorces.

Overall, the Selkirk family believed their success stemmed from a number of features: a mix of family and non-family directors, conservative finance, market leadership through technology, maintaining a good reputation in the market and a belief that nothing happens until you make a sale. They saw themselves as adaptable, able to make decisions quickly, having a close rapport with repeat customers, and constantly examining their strategies to produce long-term success.

THE SELKIRK GROUP—DIVERSIFICATION IN THE 1980s AND 1990s

Between 1982 and 1992, the company made three major acquisitions, none of which were cheap but all of which were easily absorbed into the balance sheet:

- Phillips Bricks and Pottery Pty Ltd was acquired in 1982. This Bendigo-based company had a strong market-presence in north-western Victoria and was converted from the traditional extruded to the higher-priced pressed brick production in 1986. (Segrave became Managing Director of Phillips in 1983).

- In 1987, Selkirk purchased Hick Timbers in Altona (a suburb of Melbourne) in a move that took it outside bricks but still serving the needs of the building industry. Hick was a specialised supplier of structural timber importing softwoods from the USA, Canada, New Zealand and Finland and supplying engineered timber beams.

- Shepparton Bricks and Pavers, one of Victoria's largest concrete building and landscaping products manufacturers was acquired in 1992. While Selkirk had been supplying clay pavers since 1983, this acquisition took the company into the less expensive concrete paver business in a booming market for pavers.

At a time when Australian entrepreneurs like (the subsequently convicted) Alan Bond and (the fugitive) Christopher Skase had created conglomerates through leveraged acquisitions, Selkirk Brick had been tempted to the brink of over-expansion, according to Jim Selkirk, but was saved at the eleventh hour by a bidder with deeper pockets. To date, its diversification had been within the confines of its perceived area of expertise, the building industry. Each of the acquisitions was valuable for adding manufacturing capacity and for providing additional sales outlets. Each office and outlet sold the complete range of Selkirk products.

Hick Timbers was closed down in 1997 though the company name was retained. Margins in the timber business were falling for players and the company was being outmuscled in the marketplace by large integrated timber and hardware groups such as Bunnings (which had established a series of home/trade superstores across the Melbourne metropolitan area). The Board of Selkirk had taken a common-sense but courageous strategic decision to quit while they were ahead.

While diversifying through acquisition, Selkirk Brick also embarked on a three-stage, A$5 million program of modernisation between 1982 and 1986 which resulted in world-class product quality outcomes. This investment program involved modernising the processes for extrusion and material preparation in the first stage, improving the productivity and energy efficiency of the drying tunnel in the second stage, and replacing the 25-year-old tunnel kiln with an energy-efficient one in the final stage.

By 1988, pavers had come to represent 20 percent of the company's production volume and Selkirk Brick was recognised as the only brick company supplying products compliant with Australian Products Standard AS1225. While most of the product sales were in Victoria, the sales region was progressively being extended into the South Australian and New South Wales marketplace where product quality and service were being used to overcome price and transport barriers to competition. Selkirk was reputed to have a 15 percent share in the Victorian clay building products market and was the largest privately owned brick company in Australia.

Selkirk Brick survived the severe economic recession that hit Victoria in the early 1990s by halving production at one stage and closing one plant for ten months in 1991. By late 1993, utilisation had recovered to 75 percent and by 1998 the plants were operating again at full capacity. Selkirk Brick acquired Stratblox, a manufacturer of quality concrete building products located in the Gippsland region of Victoria in 1998. This acquisition meant that Selkirk had geographically encircled the Melbourne metropolitan area through a series of country acquisitions and had established itself as the dominant player in rural Victoria.

The capacity of the Selkirk Group of Companies exceeded 70 million bricks and pavers prior to that acquisition. Production capacity at Bendigo was 10 million units (bricks and pavers) per annum while Shepparton capacity was 23,000 tonnes per annum. The Gippsland acquisition added 27,000 tonnes per annum of capacity. Total Victorian sales were in the range of A$25 million and A$30 million per annum (refer to Exhibit 2 for external estimates of group revenue). The company employed 170 people, 100 people at the Ballarat head-office and operations alone. With the acquisition of Stratblox, Selkirk Brick could no longer be seen as a specialist clay brick and paver company (refer to Appendix 2 for additional information on the Australian Brick and Paver Industry) but as a more broadly diversified company in the clay and concrete brick and paver business.

Company documents indicate that each of the acquisitions was a wholly owned subsidiary of Selkirk Brick Pty Ltd but they were managed autonomously, each with its own Board of Management and Board of Directors. In 1998, Robert Selkirk was Non-Executive Chairman of the Board, Bernie Segrave was the Managing Director,

EXHIBIT 2
Group Sales Estimates

Note: Estimates derived from industry data.

Year	Sales Revenue (A$millions)
1987/88	$19.9
1988/89	$24.8
1989/90	$25.5
1990/91	$20.7
1991/92	$19.0
1992/93	$23.5
1993/94	$24.9
1994/95	$25.8
1995/96	$23.2
1996/97	$22.2
1997/98	$27.8

Jim Selkirk was the Finance Director, and Iain Selkirk was the Works Director. In 1994, Jamie Selkirk (son of the Chairman) became the first of the fifth-generation to join the family company.

ASIA—A SELKIRK SUCCESS STORY OF THE 1990s

The export trading activities of Selkirk Brick began in earnest in 1992 when Robert Selkirk attended a Global Business Opportunities Convention in Osaka, Japan. A Japanese company had been looking at securing a supply of sandstone from Australia and had seen Selkirk pavers extensively used at Bond University in Queensland. (A major Japanese construction and development company was a joint-venture partner in the university at the time). Selkirk pavers had been selected for their ability to withstand the high traffic and high humidity requirements of Australia's first private university in 1988. Following a visit of Japanese personnel to the plant in Ballarat, a trading alliance was formed and Selkirk began to export to Japan. As Robert Selkirk reminded people within the company, not everybody had approved of the move at the time:

> Six years ago, we wouldn't have believed where we are now. It was all done on an exploratory "try it and see" basis. We had (Prime Minister) Paul Keating telling us that Australian companies had to be in Asia. There was considerable criticism at the time on the expense and management attention being directed to the export efforts. We were advised that we had to be patient. Then we got the first order within twelve months and it was done on a handshake.

Total exports had grown strongly from the first export order to Japan of 49,000 paving units (approximately six containers) in 1992. Exports to all destinations increased by 735 percent in 1993, followed by a 69 percent increase in 1994 and a 150 percent increase in 1995. Flat sales in 1996 and 1997 were followed by a massive increase in 1998 to approximately four million units. While initial sales were to Japan, by 1998 Selkirk Brick was exporting pavers and some bricks across Asia

EXHIBIT 3
Export Pricing Nomenclature and Value-Added

ex-Factory Gate	
Goods in vehicle at factory gate.	**A$3,500/container**
Free Alongside Ship (F.A.S.)	
Goods unloaded off vehicle on wharf at port of origin.	**A$3,800/container**
Free on-Board (F.O.B.)	
Goods loaded on vessel at port of origin.	**A$4,000/container**
Cost, Insurance and Freight (C.I.F.)	
Goods on vessel at port of destination with insurance premiums included.	**A$5,000/container**
Market Price	
Price of goods at final consumer market.	**A$12,000 to $17,500/container**

to countries such as Hong Kong ('94) and Taiwan ('96) as well as Singapore, Indonesia, New Zealand and Malaysia. Japan was the largest export destination but healthy sales were beginning to be experienced in Taiwan where product quality and service were considered to be key selling features.

By 1998, Asian exports had become a small but increasingly important part of Selkirk Brick's business. Exports accounted for just under 10 percent of total sales volume (slightly higher in terms of sales value) in the 1997/98 financial year and that figure was expected to increase. Well over 25 percent of paver manufacturing volume was now being exported. The clay paver market had been facing low growth and market share losses in the highly competitive Australian market to cheaper pavers made from concrete and other composite materials. Exports were an important sales outlet for the company.

Selkirk had a policy of appointing non-exclusive distributor agents in the marketplace and currently had 18 distributors across Asia: five in Japan, four in Hong Kong, three in Taiwan, two in Singapore, and one each in Malaysia, Indonesia, Thailand and New Zealand. Letters from overseas parties interested in purchasing directly and offering their local services were inevitably referred back to the nearest agent. Product was usually sold C.I.F. (Cost, Insurance and Freight to Destination Port). Prices ex-factory and loaded into containers were generally 70 percent of the C.I.F. price. Anecdotal data suggested that a unit price of A$0.47 F.O.B. (Free on Board at Shipping Port) for shipped products could be sold for as high as A$2.00 per unit in Japan to end-users (refer to Exhibit 3 for Export Pricing Nomenclature and Value-Added). The use of agents did mean, however, that there was a lack of information on who was the ultimate user of products and what margins were being charged locally.

Information on the clay brick and paver market across Asia was otherwise limited and generally anecdotal in nature. Housing construction materials varied considerably across the region and clay bricks were not traditionally used. Local brick manufacturers in countries such as Malaysia ran "cottage-industry" facilities using kilns with inadequate temperature controls and with a poor understanding of quality control mechanisms. Brick walls were often rendered and thus considered a "filler" material which did not require high quality standards. Clay brick and pavers were being increasingly seen in large "upper middle class" housing estates across the region where developers were taking the lead in developing suburban housing and shopping communities.

Exports to the region came from a number of countries, with Canada, the United States, the United Kingdom, South Africa and Australia mentioned frequently. Export data often lumped clay bricks and pavers with other construction materials such as timber and composite materials. The Australian data on exports were derived from shipping data collected at ports of origin but some ports used different classification methods, making accurate information difficult to ascertain. Australian brick and paver products were reputed to have more durability, better water repelling capability and more vibrant color attributes than the cheaper product sourced from local or imported Asian producers.

SALES DISTRIBUTION AGREEMENT IN JAPAN

Exports to Japan had grown steadily from 900,000 units in 1995/96 to 1.8 million units in 1996/97 and 3.5 million units in 1997/98. One reason for the growth was a five-year distribution agreement that had been signed in 1997 with a leading Japanese building products company and that agreement was expected to triple current export figures within two years. Segrave commented on his experiences in doing business with their Japanese agents:

> We find the Japanese are very tough negotiators—but also very fair. We are thrilled they fully appreciate the technical qualities of our products. So often here in Australia, aesthetic requirements dominate a specifier's consideration. Mind you, we have been developing a clay brick with smaller width dimensions and new colors to suit the Japanese market (in conjunction with the Stonehenge Group, a major builder in urban Victoria.) Our wide variety of pavers and special shapes also meets their needs.
>
> Understand that the Japanese do not tolerate mediocrity which means you must send your most senior people to negotiate with them. In 1992 we had employed a retired General Manager of a large clay brick and paver company in Western Australia who had the requisite seniority, technical knowledge and excellent sales skills to become our first Export Manager.
>
> One must also be courteous, pleasant and respectful with the Japanese and become practised in Nemawashi: the art of building relationships and personal trust over time. Our success can be measured by the fact that the 1997 distributor agreement had everybody from the Managing Director down to the most senior functional managers attending the Agreement Signing ceremony. What may look like a simple commercial arrangement to us was a symbol of strategic intent and business partnering in their eyes.

While exact details of the 1997 Sales License Agreement were confidential, certain aspects of the Agreement have been disclosed (refer to Appendix 3).

Selkirk retained the brand and trademark for its range of products in Japan, prohibited the transfer of distribution rights to other companies without its approval, had the ability to terminate the agreement with 90 days' notice and ensured any arbitration was done through "officially approved" channels. The term of the agreement was for five years and required 90 days' written notice on either side to terminate. Advertising and sales promotions in Japan were at the expense of the agent.

The Japanese agent had secured a number of conditions in the agreement as well. No new agents were to be appointed without their prior agreement. The primary language of the agreement was English but it was to be interpreted under Japanese commercial law. The bricks and pavers were to carry a Japanese logo and meet the requirements of the Japanese Industrial Standard but to be labelled as "Made in Australia". All products were to be inspected and certified by Selkirk Brick as meeting the product and shipping standards specified in the agreement, with the agent being able to reject shipments in Japan if these conditions were not met.

THE EXPORT FUNCTION IN SELKIRK BRICK

The Group Managing Director, Bernie Segrave, was directly responsible for overseeing all export matters including communication with the main agents, creating new relationships across Asia and being one-half of the trade show that travelled to Asia every four to five months. He spent approximately 15 percent of his time on export-related matters across a year but this time allocation varied between 100 percent and zero percent on a weekly basis. Having started in sales and marketing with Selkirk Brick in 1968, Segrave brought significant experience and credibility to the role. He reported directly to the Board of Directors (see Exhibit 4: Organisation Chart).

The Export Manager, Peter Blackburn, spent between five and 20 percent of his time on export matters during the course of a week. He reported directly to the Group Managing Director on these export matters. The rest of the time, Blackburn was officially the Regional Sales Manager for Western Victoria. In addition to maintaining relationships with agents across Asia, Blackburn was involved in developing products for export markets and ensuring that products exported met the highest technical standards. One of his current projects was working with an Australian residential building group to develop smaller, thinner bricks for the Japanese market.

Blackburn had joined Selkirk Brick four years ago though he had extensive industry experience with NuBrik. He was in the process of gradually assuming responsibility for all export business matters and had accompanied Segrave on all the recent overseas export development tours. In his view, Selkirk had been successful in Asia because it spent time building relationships with its agents, delivered products required in the marketplace on the basis of technical excellence and service rather than price alone, was committed to helping agents secure orders and maintained face-to-face relationships in order to avoid "long-distance communications and language" barriers.

EXHIBIT 4 **Organisation Chart**

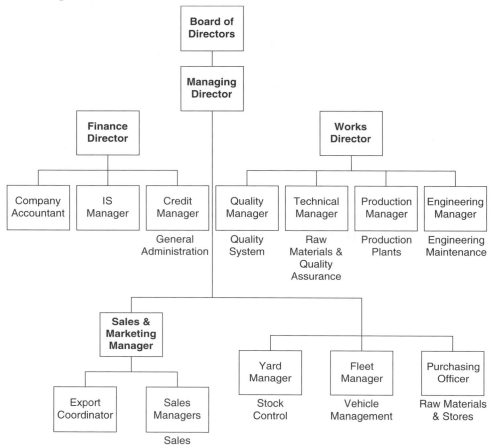

Assisting the senior export marketing duo was Clare McGuinness, Export and Agency Sales Coordinator, who spent some 80 percent of her time specifically on export matters. Among her responsibilities were receiving export orders, arranging all aspects of an export order (stock, shipping, letters of credit and export documents) and preparing all correspondence for Segrave on export related matters. All product for export markets was palletised and containerised at the brick yard adjacent to the head office in Ballarat. Selecting the appropriate bricks and pavers to ensure that they met required quality and aesthetic standards was considered to be critical in meeting customer needs. The Yard Stock Controller, Steve Banks, played an important role in this.

Overseas trips to visit agents and develop new business opportunities were generally scheduled every four to five months with Segrave and Blackburn travelling together to visit two to three countries over a two- or three-week period. Accompanying them on these trips was a technical reference manual, "The Selkirk Technical Advantage", that contained over 400 pages of technical specifications, photos of significant building projects where Selkirk bricks and pavers had been used across Asia, and a whole range of information on Frequently Asked Questions. This manual was provided for the exclusive use of agents in each country as a selling tool but was not to be distributed further.

The cost of these overseas trips was substantial for a small family-owned company, each in the range of A$15,000 to A$25,000 depending upon the countries visited and the length of the trip. Typically, these trips involved more than meeting with existing agents. They included talking to customers, meeting with architects and providing technical information on products and services offered. Often these visits coincided with local trade fairs and with Austrade government missions to specific countries. The company tried to see each overseas agent at least once per annum. Most of the agents had visited Selkirk Brick's operations at head-office at least once and some of the Japanese agents had visited three or four times each.

LOOKING TO THE FUTURE OF ASIA

The future of the Australian export business to Asia was in some doubt in early October 1998. According to the internationally respected newsmagazine Business Week, Asia was experiencing a widespread social backlash to the collapsing economic situation and stringent conditions imposed by the IMF (International Monetary Fund). The headlines of one issue (August 17, 1998) were quite pointed:

- Joblessness is soaring in Japan.

- Bitterness is growing in Korea.

- Political opposition is rallying in Thailand.

- Will the repercussions of recession scuttle Asia's economic reforms?

The Asian crisis had, in fact, spread to create global financial risk from collapsing economies and the flight of capital needed to underpin economic growth. Malaysia had already imposed currency controls on the Ringgit, and in China there was strong evidence that Beijing was resorting to import controls and other measures to keep the Asian crisis at bay. Indonesia was still an open currency economy (despite moves earlier that year to establish a Currency Board) but the value of the Rupiah (R12,000 to the US$1.00) meant that imports were effectively priced out of the market.

During the months of August and September, the Australian dollar had suffered a significant decline against the U.S. dollar, dropping to a low of US$0.56 per A$1.00 before recovering to US$0.63. In 1997 the Australian dollar had traded at US$0.73. Though not suffering as high a devaluation as the Thai Baht or the Indonesian Rupiah, the Australian dollar had devalued in line with the decline in the Japanese Yen and Korean Won against the U.S. dollar because Japan and South Korea were the major export market destinations for Australian products. The Australian balance-of-trade data suggested that a falling Australian dollar rate and an aggressive shift to European and North American markets had reduced the (potentially negative) impact of the Asian crisis on the Australian economy.

In this global economic context, the prospects for future export business were difficult to predict. Segrave was expecting a large export order from the Greater China triangle (China, Hong Kong and Taiwan) but the strength of home startups in the local building industry in Victoria meant that export orders would be competing with local orders in the short term. The forthcoming trip would be useful in providing first-hand evidence on the future prospects for their export business across Asia. This would be another factor to consider in developing a strategy and organisational structure for their Asian export business.

At this stage, Selkirk did not have any licensing agreements, joint-venture operations or subsidiaries overseas. Segrave thought it was an interesting question:

> These types of strategic alliances are all useful. In fact, we have a new product right now which we are considering licensing to Asian companies.
>
> We would consider a licensing agreement (for bricks and pavers) if someone wanted to do it on their own in Asia. We would joint-venture if that was more appropriate (and it was commercially viable). These both have great benefits as we don't really know much about the Asian marketplace. Establishing an Asian subsidiary would depend upon the state of our core business in Australia.
>
> It also depends upon the state of Asia and the business opportunities that arise. We have thought of dedicating one plant here in Ballarat to meeting (the higher standard) needs of the Asian marketplace. This would allow us to ensure product quality and still take advantage of our unique clay deposits.

Thus far Selkirk Brick had concentrated on exporting product to Asia and using existing production capacity to meet market needs. The current strategy of appointing export agents made sense in that context.

Nevertheless, there was some concern that increasing exports to the region and a future recovery of the Asian marketplace would change the economics of competing locally as brick and paver utilisation increased. In that case, product and brand licensing would become attractive alternatives and technical support agreements would become viable. Segrave was also concerned that new technologies could make "mini-kilns" economically viable and change the economic attractiveness of local production. This would require a change not only in their international export strategy but also to their whole way of doing business in Asia.

Appendix 1   Historical Highlights of Selkirk Brick

Extracted from a profile of Selkirk Brick, one of eight companies examined by Edna Carew and published in *Family Business: The Story of Successful Family Companies in Australia.*

- In 1883, Robert Selkirk began making bricks using a clay deposit in Allendale, Victoria. Bricks were hand-made using moulds. A brick press and engine purchased in 1892 signalled the beginning of mechanised production.

- In 1905, Selkirk was using coal-fired kilns to produce five brick types in batches. During that year, they began continuous firing of bricks on a three-shift, 24-hour, seven-day a week basis.

- In 1921, James Selkirk assumed control of Selkirk Brick (upon the death of his father) and was assisted by Bill Gillman, his brother-in-law, as company secretary.

- In 1935, James Selkirk suffered a heart attack and was ultimately succeeded by his two sons, Bill and Ron Selkirk. They managed the business until they enlisted and handed over control to Bill Gillman (Uncle Willy) during the war years.

- The post-WWII years saw Bill and Ron return to the family business, with Bill managing operations and staffing while Ron handled management and accounting.

- The late '40s and '50s were years of a great (re)building boom for Australia and Selkirk often needed to resort to a lottery to allocate bricks to customers. Innovation was central to its continued success; mechanised claypit in 1952, forklifts in 1953, its own transport company in 1954, "packaged" bricks in 1955 and the appointment of its first Sales Rep in 1959.

- By 1962, the brick works was completely redeveloped and a tunnel-kiln was built that allowed a clean-burning butane gas and an automated plant, both of which substantially enhanced the quality of bricks produced but also left the company with debt that stretched it financially for the next decade.

- During the '60s, the boom market evaporated and Selkirk Brick began to market its bricks across state boundaries into New South Wales and Canberra (the national capital). In 1969, Bill and Ron Selkirk became joint chairmen of the company.

- In 1974, production capacity was doubled to 50 million bricks a year with Plant No. 2 commissioned in Ballarat and in 1978 the fourth generation of Selkirks (Robert, Iain and Jim) was appointed to the Board.

- Bill and Ron Selkirk retired from day-to-day management in 1981; Ian McCoy (who had joined the company in 1951) became Chairman and several other long-term employees, who had joined the Board in 1969, were also promoted.

Appendix 2 The Australian Clay Brick Manufacturing Industry in 1998

The Australian clay brick industry was small, accounting for 0.09 percent of GDP in 1997/98. Products included clay bricks and pavers used in new housing construction (70 percent), housing renovations (15 percent) and commercial construction (15 percent). The state of New South Wales had the largest market share (36.3 percent) followed by Queensland (18.9 percent), Western Australia (17 percent) and Victoria (16.9 percent). Exports were low at 2.3 percent of turnover in 1997/98 and imports were negligible.

Market Demand and Prices

Industry turnover reached A$906 million in 1992/93 but then declined to A$728 million in 1996/97 before climbing to A$780 million in 1997/98. Clay brick production was estimated to be 1,532 million bricks in 1997/98. Approximately 87 percent of housing was constructed using clay brick (typically as brick veneer, with the external walls using brick and interior walls using plaster or fibre board). Premium bricks (used in exterior walls) cost approximately A$500 per 1,000 bricks while seconds (used as fill-in) cost in the order of A$300 per 1,000. Pavers represented 15 percent of production but less than 10 percent of sales revenue.

The outlook for 1998/99 was for a solid increase in sales to A$880 million due to a strong residential housing construction demand fuelled by low mortgage interest rates, a strong domestic economy (despite the Asian crisis) and widespread concerns that the proposed 10 percent value-added tax in July 2000 would increase housing costs. (Clay bricks and pavers were currently exempt from wholesale sales tax). The long-term market demand was expected to decline as new materials (concrete bricks, steel panels, and prestressed concrete) and new construction techniques (steel frames in particular) acted as substitutes. Steel-framed buildings using steel or corrugated iron cladding were reputed to cost about two-thirds the cost of brick-veneer.

Prices across markets were believed to be stable with competition based on product differentiation and distribution networks. High transportation costs and fear of price wars in a concentrated marketplace led to careful geographic competition. The industry cost structure had been estimated as follows:

• Material Purchases	9%	• Repairs and Maintenance	7%
• Electricity and Fuel	12%	• Wages and Salaries	22%
• Freight and Cartage	8%	• Other (Overheads/Profits)	42%

INDUSTRY COMPETITION

Industry concentration was considered to be relatively high with the top five competitors accounting for 85 percent of sales: the top four competitors also accounted for 35 of the 75 enterprise units in the Australian market.

Company	Market Share	Industry Revenue
Boral Limited	33%	A$235 million
CSR Limited	21%	A$150 million
Pioneer International	13%	A$95 million
Futuris Limited	10%	A$72 million
Brickworks Limited	8%	A$56 million

The industry could be divided into three strategic groups:

National Competitors   Boral, Pioneer and CSR were competitors nationally with operations in a number of states. They were all diversified building products companies with manufacturing interests in related markets and with significant overseas manufacturing interests. Boral and CSR were each reported to have brick manufacturing capacity of 500 million to 550 million bricks across Australia. Boral, Pioneer and CSR had recently been penalised by the Australian Consumer and Competition Commission for collusive pricing in the Queensland cement market.

Regional Competitors   Futuris (Western Australia), Brickworks (NSW/Queensland) and Selkirk (Victoria) were considered to be regional players. They were specialist clay brick and paver companies, with a number of plants and brands under their umbrella. Futuris had a manufacturing capacity of 200 million bricks.

Local Competitors   A number of small companies with local distribution and very small production capacities. Pioneer was the dominant player in Victoria with a 50 percent market share followed by Boral with 25 percent. Victoria's share of national production had fallen from 21 percent in 1990/91 to less than 17 percent in 1993/94. Overcapacity was considered to be high. Production in 1997/98 had reached 2,177 million bricks.

International Business

Australian bricks were gaining export markets across Asia due to their natural colors and strength. Boral was successfully exporting through its Western Australian subsidiary, Midland Bricks. Exports had risen to A$14.9 million in 1993/94 but had fallen subsequently to A$14.0 million in 1994/95 and remained at that level in the two years that followed. The three largest companies all had overseas brick-making operations though the scale and importance of these varied considerably.

Appendix 3   Outline of Distributor Sales Agreement

1.1	Definitions
1.2	Appointment Period
1.3	Terms and Conditions of Sale
1.4	Trademarks
1.5	Advertising and Sales Promotions
1.6	Management Reports
1.7	Product Specifications
1.8	Acceptance Test and Inspections
1.9	Termination, Extensions and Revisions
1.10	Transfer of Rights
1.11	Business Secrecy
1.12	Force Majeure
1.13	Arbitration
1.14	Notice Addresses
1.15	Governing Laws

Chapter Twenty-Three

Looks.com (A)—
A Gray Issue

Ian Smith, founder and managing director of looks.com—a soon-to-be-launched Hong Kong-based e-commerce site for brand name cosmetics, fragrances, skin care products and fashion aimed at Asian women—had run into a potentially serious issue in the implementation of his business plan. He had just finished a call with a high profile buyer with over a decade of industry experience in Asia, Robbie Jessel. Jessel had stated in no uncertain terms that he would not compromise his hard-earned reputation to be associated with a parallel importer—regardless of his confidence in the concept.

Parallel importing, sourcing products wholesale from unauthorized distributors through the "gray" market, was a popular practice in Asia in most industries, including cosmetics. It allowed retailers to offer products at up to 70 percent off retail, and, thus, consumers loved it. When authorized distributors complained about gray market intrusions and the consequent erosion of their margins, manufacturers took a tough stance against those responsible. Yet, driven by a desire to increase sales, at least in the short run, some brand owners looked the other way when it came to gray market sales. The "official" manufacturer disposition to gray markets was one of contempt.

IVEY

Richard Ivey School of Business
The University of Western Ontario

Donna Everatt prepared this case under the supervision of Professor Kersi Antia solely to provide material for class discussion. The authors do not intend to illustrate either effective or ineffective handling of a managerial situation. The authors may have disguised certain names and other identifying information to protect confidentiality.

According to Smith's business plan, looks.com would source products on the gray market. However, given Jessel's reticence, he now felt compelled to reconsider this decision—one of the most important strategic elements of the whole plan. Smith's business plan had been extraordinarily well received among the investment and Internet community. As a matter of fact, he had secured so much seed capital that his initial offering was oversubscribed, and in order to maintain his target equity level in the company, he was forced to return the last few subscriptions of US$100,000 each. Partnerships had been established with one of the most well known websites in the region, China.com. The latest technology would support the site and a locally renowned and award-winning design team had created an exciting site design and layout. Smith was poised to capitalize on a first-mover advantage—a critical success factor in the Internet industry—planning on launching the site just in time for the 1999 Christmas shopping season. "Dot-com fever" had caught on in Hong Kong, and e-commerce promised vast new opportunities, as Asian consumers adopted the Internet as a viable retail channel, repeating the pattern of rapid adoption of the Internet in the United States.

THE INTERNET INDUSTRY IN ASIA HEADING INTO THE NEXT MILLENNIUM

The e-commerce boom experienced in the United States was expected to hit Asia with full force in 2000. "While 1998 was the year that online shopping first rose to prominence in the United States, the 1999 holiday season is shaping up to be the launching point for an expansion of global consumer e-commerce" according to a senior analyst for the Gartner Group, a high profile Internet consulting firm.

It was estimated that in 1999 there were between 20 million to 30 million Internet users throughout the Asia-Pacific region (almost half of whom were located in Japan) (see Exhibit 1). Though growth of the Internet had surged from a year earlier—up from 8.6 million users in 1997—this number accounted for only about 15 percent of the world's total Internet-user population.[1] Internet usage in the region, however, was expected to rise significantly in the foreseeable future, coinciding with development of supporting infrastructure,[2] and as consumers overcame their initial skepticism and fears regarding security (a key concern globally with regard to e-commerce). Thus, in 1999 e-commerce in Asia accounted for just 7 percent of the worldwide total of over US$12 billion (whereas the United States accounted for 70 percent of online purchases and Europe 23 percent). Asia, however, was forecast to be the second largest Internet growth opportunity in the world (after western Europe) and by 2002, the region was widely expected to have 50 million users, whose purchase activity would account for almost 10 percent of the value of global e-commerce activity.

Several environmental factors would encourage increased e-commerce activity in Asia. Beyond the sheer size of several key markets,[3] regional governments were expected to gradually loosen restrictions, opening markets to foreign competition paving the way for knowledge transfer of information technology (IT), as well as reducing tariffs. Public sector initiatives to strengthen the IT infrastructure[4] of

EXHIBIT 1
Industry Statistics

Source: Market Tracking
International, Euromonitor

INDUSTRY STATISTICS

Growth in Number of Internet Users
  1997—8.6 million
  1998—14 million
  1999—20 million
  2000e—26 million
  2001e—35 million
  2002e—48 million

Internet Spending in Asia
  1998—US$700 million
  2003—US$32 billion

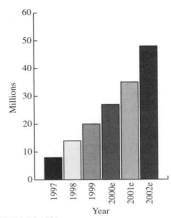

E-COMMERCE REVENUES IN ASIA

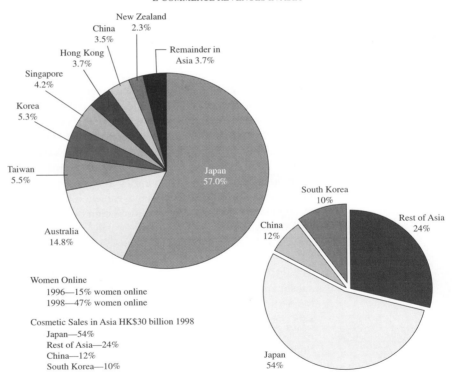

Women Online
  1996—15% women online
  1998—47% women online

Cosmetic Sales in Asia HK$30 billion 1998
  Japan—54%
  Rest of Asia—24%
  China—12%
  South Korea—10%

many regional economies had also been developed. Pent-up demand among consumers and businesses alike for imported goods and services (especially those from the Western Hemisphere) would be unleashed over the next couple of years, aided by the increased adoption of e-commerce, making products and services readily available that had previously been sold predominantly in western markets.

Many Asian consumers and retailers alike welcomed this trend. Companies engaged in e-commerce were afforded several competitive advantages over their "bricks and mortar" competitors, including minimal leasing, leasehold improvement and overhead costs, centralized and highly efficient order processing and inventory controls, and lower cost, highly targeted marketing campaigns.[5] These competitive advantages, combined with a first-mover advantage, and the attractive margins associated with the cosmetic industry convinced Smith that looks.com was a tremendous opportunity.

LOOKS.COM

Smith's business plan stated that looks.com would offer a secure site[6] that sold "the most popular brands of cosmetics, fragrances, skin-care and fashion-related products at competitive prices." In addition to an "aggressive pricing strategy," Smith's approach for building customer loyalty involved providing an extensive range of free giveaways, ranging from lipsticks and other cosmetic samples, to toiletry bags, perfumes and bigger ticket items. Smith planned on obtaining these give-aways "free of charge from the cosmetics companies as per standard industry practice." Looks.com offered "fast delivery to any destination around the world" (though Smith expected that at least 50 percent of looks.com initial sales would be in the Hong Kong market). Taiwan and Singapore were other targeted key markets, though sales would come from other Southeast Asian countries as the site gained a higher profile throughout the region, and as Internet usage gained higher penetration among consumers throughout the Asia Pacific or as looks.com expanded into new markets.

One of the first market expansion plans was for Japan, where Smith planned on expanding in early 2000 with the development of a "mirror" site (in Japanese), with a company-owned server housed at a Japanese Internet service provider (ISP). Though he planned on organizing the Japanese site as a wholly or majority-owned subsidiary of Looks.com Holdings Limited, Smith did not rule out the possibility of the participation of a Japanese joint venture partner. In looking at initial target markets (including Singapore and Taiwan), Smith did not foresee duty and import tariffs as major constraints to sales. However, Japan was a high tariff market. Therefore, Smith planned on establishing a distribution center within Japan, which would also significantly reduce distribution costs and delivery times in that market.

According to Smith, while China remained another attractive market for the sale of consumer products, it remained a challenge for online sales. The combination of a lack of credit card processing facilities, post-sale distribution logistics, low Internet penetration and adoption rates, and high tariffs, posed significant hurdles to effective penetration in the short term.

EXHIBIT 2 **Sample Pages from the Looks.com Site www.looks.com**

Receive a
FREE
superslim
looks.com
mirror ...

FREE
SHIPPING
ACROSS ASIA

Beautiful
hand-made
bracelets made
with semi-precious
stones.

Pashmina
Shawl
Promotion
(size: 36" x 80")

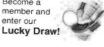

Become a
member and
enter our
Lucky Draw!

Back to Basics
how to look
your best!

Cordelia for Starz People   IKE Photography

looks
Boutique

Your great online
shopping experience.

● Gift Sets
● Skincare
● Makeup
● Body & Hair
● Fragrance
● Accessories

looks
Zone

Your beauty and
fashion e-zine.

● Back to Basics 4 -
  Irresistible Eyes
● Hairstyle DIY
● Personality Quiz(2)
● All About
  Fragrance (II)
● 10 Tips Diet Plan
● Spring Radiance

Looking for
a specific product?
Click here for product search.

| Browse By Brand ▾ |

Looking for a special brand?
Simply click on the pull down
menu.

download
Screen
Saver

中 文   日 本 語

My Account
My Shopping Bag
Check My Order
Join Our Club
Delivery & Returns
looks' Guarantee
Site Map
Feedback
About Us
Legal

our partners
china.com
hongkong.com
taiwan.com
cww.com
● aol
womenjapan.com
Redskirt.com
the web connection
24/7 asia
starz people

Source: Company website, October 1999.   *(continued)*

Though looks.com would initially focus on the markets in Hong Kong, Singapore, and Taiwan, as e-commerce transcended geographic boundaries, Smith considered the five million women with middle to high incomes, aged 17 through 35 in the Asia Pacific region, to be looks.com's target market. Smith felt that this segment of women was more likely to have Internet access, and to be early adopters of online shopping. Smith grouped the target market into four market segments—"Trendies," "New Women," "Mothers," and "Sophisticates."

The so-called Trendies were at the younger end of target market demographic, sought new trends, and had a relatively high share of disposable income. Availability of new products, extensive choice and value were meaningful benefits to Trendies. The New Women had careers, relationships, and family commitments, with hectic lives and a wide range of interests and, thus, valued the benefits of convenience, quality, and value. Mothers and Sophisticates were considered secondary target markets. Though the latter group gravitated toward the higher end brands and was less concerned with value, they both sought quality and convenience. The design and functionality of the site would appeal to each of these market segments, offering two fully integrated and complementary components: the "looks Boutique" and the "looks Zone" (see Exhibit 2).

EXHIBIT 2 **Continued**

The looks Boutique, the retail component of the site, would offer brand name cosmetics and fragrances, and health and beauty products and fashions at competitive prices, with extensive product descriptions, photos, and where appropriate, digital demonstrations. The looks Zone was the entertainment component, and was designed to promote repeat visits to "solidify looks.com as a Web-based community" by providing information on issues concerning Asian women, including, but not limited to, health and beauty. Various articles focusing on self-help and self-improvement, image consulting, fashion and trend reports would be written by looks.com in-house writers, and other articles would be written by contracted dermatologists, gynecologists, and other medical people, augmented with content that was aggregated from other sites. Smith's objective was to become a portal[7] for Asian women, selling health and beauty-related products—anything from baby and maternity products and services to vitamins and fashion accessories, for example. Beyond the spectacular forecast growth of e-commerce in Asia, looks.com's ability to evolve into a portal aimed at the lucrative and fast-growing market of Asian females was a key consideration in why Smith chose to sell cosmetics over the Internet in the first place.

WHY COSMETICS?

Smith explained that he had "no particular affinity for cosmetics" and no prior experience in the industry (or the Internet for that matter). However, he had been working in Asia for over a decade, since he was 24, and had been surfing the Net for almost as long. Most recently, Smith had worked for several years with a Hong Kong-based investment firm as an associate director, after a two-year term as the managing director (Asia) of a car park operation. Working in Asia was a natural move after having graduated with a degree in Asian Management Studies from the University of Hawaii. In 1998, Smith had enrolled in a two-year Executive MBA program at the Hong Kong campus of the Richard Ivey School of Business at The University of Western Ontario. Feeling a strong pull toward something entrepreneurial, Smith felt he wanted to "strike while the iron was hot" to capture a first-mover advantage in the rapidly growing e-commerce industry in Hong Kong and throughout Asia, and began research into what type of site he would launch. After examining "30 or 40 different site concepts, including pure portal plays, auction sites, and e-commerce opportunities for products and services, such as real estate, Asian art, sporting goods, and factory direct stuff out of China for example," Smith found that cosmetics offered the most promising e-commerce opportunities:

> In cosmetics, 80 percent of the sales are repeat purchases—customers are highly brand loyal. Moreover, cosmetic brands are particularly recognizable—the industry spends about the highest percentage of revenue on promotion, so most of the products that would be listed on the site would already have a high profile in many other Asian markets. Fraud was not as much of an issue as with other e-commerce sites—you can't download cosmetics, and statistics have proven that sites catering to males were much more susceptible to fraud.
>
> Moreover, health and beauty products are very small generally, so they're easily shipped and received (a consideration especially in Asia where most people have very small mail boxes in apartment buildings) and they had a high value-to-weight ratio. Inventory management is made easier with such small products, and styles change each season so you don't have to carry products 10 years old (like Amazon does with books). One of the most enticing things attracting me to cosmetics was the fact that manufacturers are doing their damnedest to keep prices high; it was the profit margins that ultimately convinced me to sell cosmetics online.

Another important factor persuading Smith to launch a cosmetics website was the fact that in 1999, direct competition to looks.com was limited. Though several manufacturers of cosmetics and health and beauty products had created their own website, and a myriad of sites had been created that sold name brand cosmetics, none catered specifically to Asian women, and few U.S.-based sites shipped outside of North America. Smith considered traditional cosmetic retail outlets including department, drug, and variety stores as well as beauty salons, supermarkets, and discount cosmetic outlets to be indirect (as opposed to direct) competition, as he felt that looks.com held a particular competitive advantage over more traditional distribution channels. Thus, Smith considered the concept behind looks.com an "overlooked Internet opportunity in Asia" and set out to develop a business plan. One of his most important considerations, therein, was whether he would source his products for sale on the site from the "gray" market or deal with authorized distribution channels.

THE GRAY MARKET

Gray marketing activity—often confused with the illegal activity of counterfeiting, the sale of fake goods—was not universally illegal per se. However, the transport of goods between markets was often done cross-border, without proper licences or contrary to trade regulations.[8] By definition, gray marketing (also known as product diversion and parallel importing) occurred whenever the same product was sold at different prices in different markets, through authorized or unauthorized distribution channels. Thus, gray marketers were parties that capitalized on price differences between markets—their margins were made in the sales of those goods in the higher-priced markets, and as such gray market activity was arbitrage, conducted by parties outside the established supply-chain agreements.

Over the past decade, gray market activity had become ever more common across a variety of industries, ranging from watches, cameras, and health and beauty products to heavy industrial equipment. By some accounts, such unauthorized sales were increasing at a rate of over 20 percent annually, in tandem with the increase in the level of cross-border trade, aided partly by the availability of market-by-market pricing information and crumbling trade barriers around the globe. While precise figures were difficult to come by, research suggested that gray market sales occurred to the tune of billions of dollars worldwide, and Asian markets accounted for some of the most prevalent gray marketing activity (see Exhibit 3).

There were several advantages in obtaining goods through the gray market. Being a parallel marketer would allow looks.com to offer deep discounts. Combined with the convenience of online shopping, Smith felt looks.com could gain a significant competitive advantage over "bricks and mortar" cosmetic retailers who dealt with authorized distribution channels (and, therefore, offered products within a narrowly defined range of the manufacturers suggested retail price [MSRP]). Smith felt, however, that as an online retailer, he could undercut not only full-price competitors, but also the discounters. Smith felt this would be key in securing a leadership position.

EXHIBIT 3
**Estimated Regional
Gray Market Activity**

Source: *Business Horizons,*
Elsevier Science, Inc., NY,
November–December 1999.

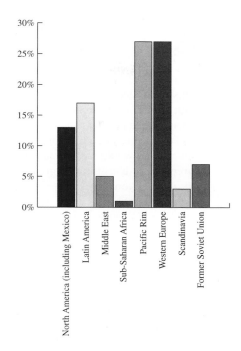

Naturally, if Smith sourced products in the gray market, another key advantage was that he would not have to gain each manufacturer's permission to list their lines for sale on looks.com. Several positive consequences flowed from this. First, Smith would be free to set not only the price at which products were offered, but also the variety of products listed on the site. A key factor driving the success of the site was not only the breadth of product offerings, but also that looks.com offered many of the most sought-after brands. Another advantage in bypassing the manufacturer was that Smith could control the presentation and positioning of all products listed within the site. This meant that Smith was free to consider the overall branding of looks.com, without the particular positioning and branding of each individual product, allowing him to develop a more comprehensive looks.com brand. This was important, given that in Asia, e-commerce was not fully understood or adopted by the general public and Smith was eager to establish looks.com as "a premier, top-of-mind e-commerce site." The looks.com business plan also stated that looks.com would be "the lowest priced retailer in Asia in its category." By sourcing products through the gray market, Smith had more flexibility with regard to pricing as well. The business plan qualified this low pricing strategy, indicating:

> Because of the sheer number of products available, it will be impossible to ensure that looks.com is the price leader for all products. However, utilizing the customer and purchase analysis tools available on the Internet, looks.com will be able to ensure that it has the lowest prices on the products that are of the greatest interest to our customers.

A MODEL PARALLEL IMPORTER IN HONG KONG— SA SA COSMETICS

Products sourced in gray markets were sold at a significant discount on manufacturer's suggested retail prices to gain competitive advantage. Thus, even though Smith's costs would be lower, often his retail markup would be less than if he dealt with authorized dealers and sold items at close to full MSRP. Moreover, Smith explained that the added link (or links) added to the value chain (and, hence, another level of cost) would also decrease profit margins. Smith stated that if he chose to source his products through gray markets, "the game would be to drive up the volume, and get your profit that way." This was a key part of the business model of a very successful bricks and mortar cosmetics retailer—Sa Sa.[9]

Sa Sa's 25 locations throughout Hong Kong and the New Territories had the distinctive character of a discount retailer. Sa Sa's stores were located in very high pedestrian traffic locations, in a confined "no frills" environment, where cosmetics counters and bins brimmed with health and beauty products retailed at 25 percent to 70 percent off the MSRP. This business model had served the company well—1998 profits were HK$250 million on sales of HK$1.25 billion. With a 20 percent after-tax profit, Smith referred to Sa Sa as "the best-known and most successful parallel importer in Asia."

Smith explained that Sa Sa obtained their products through a variety of channels, including manufacturers who were eager to get rid of last season's lines, products that were close to their expiry date, or excess inventory. Often, products were acquired in other regions and imported to Hong Kong, through either authorized distributors from a region outside of Hong Kong or an unauthorized party with access to the goods. They also bought product at retail at a bulk discount, or from a liquidation sale of another retailer (either in the region or internationally and then imported) or without the manufacturer's consent from the authorized distributor at a discounted rate. The UPC[10] code of products sold through parallel importers like Sa Sa had been covered or otherwise made illegible, making it impossible to trace the product's origin. The inventiveness of parallel importers left Sa Sa, and similar companies, with a myriad of sources to purchase their product, allowing them a distinct competitive advantage over drug and department stores and retailers who sourced their health and beauty products from locally authorized distributors.

Thus, Smith explained that the effect of parallel importing, which allowed retail sales at significantly below MSRP, had been hotly contested by brand name manufacturers of cosmetics for years. However, because parallel importing was "not really illegal," according to Smith, manufacturers had little recourse:

> Parallel importers pose a huge threat to manufacturers in Asia, and, therefore, most distributor contracts included a clause that forbade sales to discounters such as Sa Sa. If a manufacturer was to somehow find that a distributor was selling to Sa Sa (i.e., knowing that the product will be sold at a deep discount) in order to increase their numbers, they would likely run into trouble, but really, there is little that can be done to stop the practice.

Smith recounted the example of a large cosmetics manufacturer that took a parallel importer to court in Australia—and lost. According to Smith, the court said "hey, if you can't control the distribution of your product outside of Australia, then that's outside the jurisdiction of the Australian courts." The U.S. Supreme Court came to a similar conclusion when they ruled unanimously in favor of a distributor (Quality King Distributors, an $800 million company). The appellant was Robert L'anza, the founder and CEO of a US$20 million company, L'anza Research International. Though many other manufacturers had filed similar suits in lower courts in the United States, L'anza was the first professional beauty product manufacturer to take his cause all the way to the Supreme Court and, thus, the case received extensive media coverage. Many interested parties across a myriad of industries viewed the decision of the case as a landmark, feeling that it would embolden Quality King and other gray marketers. In March 1998, L'anza summarized the court's decision saying:[11]

> A company that exports its U.S.-manufactured products is not protected under federal copyright laws from having them sold and shipped back into the country for sale by another firm.

This was certainly the case in Asia, where, according to Smith "there's essentially no such thing as MSRP for most products, not only cosmetics." He continued:

> When Sa Sa came to the market, it really caused problems. Local distributors would consistently be frustrated and angry at seeing their lines at their local Sa Sa store, knowing that they did not sell the products to Sa Sa. It gave a bad name to the industry—but the consumers love it.
>
> Many of the products bought on the gray market are highly sought after brands, including Christian Dior, Shiseido, and Lancome among others. Consumers don't really care about where the product came from if it means they can buy their favorite brands at significant discounts, for what appeared to be authentically branded products in their original wrapping, prior to (or close to) the date of expiry in most cases.

Smith described one perspective, saying that it's a good deal for consumers.

> There's one school of thought that says 'If Sa Sa can make money by parallel importing, then why not?' It's the manufacturer's responsibility to monitor the distribution, and if they can't do it, then in a highly entrepreneurial society as found throughout Southeast Asia, many people say 'tough luck.' Of course, in Asia, it is very difficult—if not impossible—to control distribution, given the widespread use and acceptance of parallel importing.

On the other hand, Smith stated that the practice could compromise a brand's quality positioning, as often (though not always) products were sold that were close to, or exceeded the suggested date of expiry, or that had not been stored or transported in optimal conditions, adversely affecting product quality. Moreover, the placement of the products on shelves or in bins, or the condition of its packaging, was generally at odds with the quality positioning that the manufacturers had invested heavily in to promote. Thus, manufacturers openly condemned Sa Sa and other parallel importers like them as a blight on the Asian retailing landscape. Smith was reluctant to position looks.com in this league, but was daunted by the considerable disadvantages in dealing directly with manufacturers and felt that on the whole, the advantages of parallel importing outweighed the disadvantages—at least while looks.com was becoming established. After the site had earned a reputation as an industry player and could meet minimum order lots, Smith planned on dealing directly with manufacturers. However, that day could come sooner than he had originally thought.

DECISIONS, DECISIONS

Smith felt compelled at this juncture to consider the implications of being a parallel importer. Would other highly sought-after industry professionals, as well as potential suppliers, strategic partners, and investors take the same stance as Jessel and refuse to deal with looks.com if they were a parallel marketer? Yet, so many issues arose if Smith decided to source products through authorized distribution channels. Not only would approaching each manufacturer be a time-consuming proposition, Smith expected that many manufacturers would not be interested in dealing with a relatively smaller player.[12]

Moreover, by supplying looks.com, there was a risk of antagonizing their distributors, fearing that sales through looks.com would cannibalize their existing distribution arrangements, even if Smith positioned the site as a duty-free retailer. If looks.com were to source its product line from local distributor(s), the firm's margins would decline precipitously. This extra layer could erode profit margins so that it could be virtually impossible to achieve an acceptable return on investment. However, if manufacturers were attracted to list with the site, looks.com's margins would be higher than if they dealt in the gray market, and they would establish themselves with arguably a more favorable reputation among manufacturers right from the beginning.

In the final analysis, though, there were clear advantages for manufacturers to list their products on the site, including increased sales and support of the brand. If several of the most sought-after brands decided not to sell to looks.com, it could be the ultimate demise of the site. Nonetheless, Smith felt strongly that Jessel's decade of industry experience managing the distribution in Asia of products from high profile manufacturers such as Orlane, Club Monaco, Benetton, Ahava (a popular brand from Israel), Nina Ricci, Paco Robane, and Giorgio Fragrances would prove invaluable. Jessel would apply his knowledge of markets, pricing and the structure of deals to the looks.com venture, and would establish key contacts with various international suppliers through his extensive personal network.

During their discussions, Jessel had stated many times that his position would be the general sentiment of the most talented buyers in the industry, and Smith's initial inquiries seemed to support this. As Smith hung up from the videoconference, he mulled over whether he should revise the entire business model of looks.com. Smith considered the decision regarding whether or not to be a parallel importer, perhaps the single most important decision he could make, one that could have the largest impact on the success—or failure—of his dream.

Endnotes

1. Despite the fact that almost half of the world's population lived in the region.
2. Specifically, many Asian-based websites still did not have payment gateways—electronic paths that directed credit card charges to the card's bank, from an electronic site, which made sites more secure. Without an electronic payment gateway, customer service representatives typed credit card numbers into a terminal, which then relayed the data to a bank.
3. Including Australia, China, Japan, Hong Kong, Taiwan, and South Korea for example.
4. Including Singapore's "wired island," Malaysia's "Multimedia Super Corridor," and Hong Kong's "Cyberport."
5. Web-based technologies allowed sites to capture a tremendous amount of knowledge on customer buying habits and preferences, as well as valuable demographic information that could be obtained through registration with the site.
6. Using an electronic payment gateway.
7. A portal is a website that is intended to be the first place people see when using the Web. Typically, a "portal site" has a catalog of websites, a search engine, or both. A portal site may also offer email and other services to entice people to use that site as their main "point of entry" (hence "portal") to the Web.
8. In 1999, legislation in the European Union (EU) banned gray market activity (resulting in an increase in legal actions taken against retailers and importers dealing in such activity) however, this is not the case in most other regions.
9. Though Sa Sa did purchase some brands directly from the manufacturer, they purchased the prestige brands – Lancome, Estée Lauder, and Polo Ralph Lauren for example—on the gray market.
10. Uniform Product Code, a numerical sequence identifying individual products or SKUs (stock-keeping units).
11. *Professional Beauty,* Issue Number One, Creative Age Communications Inc., Van Nuys, CA., 1998
12. Minimum wholesale orders for L'Oreal product lines were US$100,000 for example.

Chapter Twenty-Four

Intel's Site Selection Decision in Latin America

Ted Telford faced a dilemma. As the only full-time member of Intel Corporation's worldwide site selection team, he had to make a recommendation about where Intel should locate its first manufacturing plant in Latin America.[1] After months of analysis, involving both desk research and numerous field trips to potential country locations, the site selection team had narrowed the choice to four countries: Brazil, Chile, Mexico, and Costa Rica. All were attractive in different ways, but now it was October 1996, and Ted had to write his final report for the headquarters office in Santa Clara. Headquarters would want his recommendation and evidence to support it. He shifted uneasily in his chair. At stake was a long-term investment decision involving $300–$500 million, a substantial amount of money even for a company like Intel, with over $20 billion in annual revenues. Ted hunched over his files, and began reviewing the data one more time.

INTEL AND THE SEMICONDUCTOR INDUSTRY

Microprocessors are the brains of personal computers. They are composed of millions of microscopically small transistors—essentially, tiny electronic switches—grouped and interconnected with each other on individual chips of silicon to store and manipulate data.[2] This is why microprocessors are often referred to as chips, as in "the Pentium II chip." Computer software enables microprocessors to perform specific functions with the stored data. As a result, microprocessors today are

found not just in computers, but in virtually any inanimate object that can "think" (be programmed to perform certain tasks): traffic lights, cars, cellular telephones, airplanes, etc.

This enormous range of applications for microprocessors spawned a huge industry—the semiconductor industry—with well over $120 billion in sales in 1995, and a projected growth rate of over 20 percent per year.[3] Intel, as the first company in the world to introduce microprocessors in 1971, quickly established a dominant position in this industry and, in 1996, remained the dominant player with over 85 percent of microprocessor sales worldwide.

Although Intel had a number of competitors, the company invested billions each year in Research and Development (R&D) in order to retain its lead in innovation and design of new chips. As a result, Intel was constantly introducing faster and more powerful microprocessors in order to stay ahead of the competition. Intel's former CEO, Andy Grove, noted that in a high-technology industry such as semiconductors, "only the paranoid survive."[4]

The contrast between Intel's first microprocessor, the 4004, with only 2,300 transistors, and the one it planned to assemble and test in the proposed Latin American plant, the Pentium II—with over 7.5 million transistors—illustrated this dramatic rate of growth in computing power. Gordon Moore, one of Intel's founders, highlighted the fast-paced nature of competition and innovation in the semiconductor industry when he devised his famous "Moore's Law": driven by competitive market forces, the power of microprocessors will double every 18 months. This law had been fairly consistent with developments in the industry, and Intel had been leading the way since the beginning.

Given the speed of developments and growth in the industry, Intel needed to open a new plant at a rate of almost one every nine months.[5] Doing this, as well as maintaining high levels of spending on R&D, was very expensive—a serious disadvantage when the company had to deal with competitors who could imitate its product designs, then offer similar products at a lower cost. Clearly, if Intel wanted to remain competitive, it could not pass on these costs to consumers in the form of higher prices. Early on, then, Intel's management realized that the company would have to build at least some plants in countries where costs (especially labor costs, which in assembly and testing facilities amount to between 25 percent to 30 percent of total costs) would be lower than in the United States.[6]

Intel's first overseas plant was built in Malaysia in 1972. Later plants followed in Israel, the Philippines, Ireland, and mainland China. But now, in 1996, Ted knew that there was a sense among management that the next plant should be in Latin America. Excessive investment in one region could create risks. For example, although Intel's plant in Malaysia had been productive for many years, in 1996 the plant faced problems resulting from a shortage of qualified labor. As a result, turnover among employees was approaching 30 percent to 40 percent, training was becoming expensive and difficult, and salaries were rising. It made sense to diversify the geographic location of the plants. The company already had a number of plants in Asia, but absolutely none in Latin America. The region offered relatively low labor costs, as well as logistical advantages for exporting production to the United States or Europe.[7]

INTEL'S PROPOSED LATIN AMERICAN PLANT: CHARACTERISTICS

Ted knew that the plant Intel had in mind would be an assembly and testing facility, rather than a more sophisticated fabrication plant ("fab"). Still, when it came to making microprocessors, assembly and testing was an involved, complex process, requiring significant technical and engineering expertise, clean rooms, advanced knowledge of chemical processes, and considerable expense. The site selection committee already knew that the plant or plants would employ about 2,000 technicians and engineers initially; this number would eventually increase to 3,500. It would also require the participation of significant numbers of expatriate personnel for extended periods, at least during the startup phase.

While all of these considerations would influence the site selection process, the size of the selected country's market would be irrelevant. This was because Intel planned to export 100% of the product assembled and tested at the plant; almost all of that would be going to the United States.

THE SITE SELECTION PROCESS, PHASE 1: DESK RESEARCH—AND COSTA RICA MAKES THE SHORT LIST

As Ted reviewed the data before him, he reflected on the long, highly systematic site selection process. It had all started with several weeks of desk research. During that time, a group of Intel employees had gathered as much information as they could on a long list of countries in Latin America. The group gathered data on such issues as political and economic stability, labor unions and labor regulations (a particular concern of Intel's), infrastructure, and the availability of an educated workforce (after all, the plant would need trained technicians and engineers).

After this desk research, Ted had been able to eliminate some countries altogether. Venezuela, for example, seemed to be too unstable financially; the desk research phase quickly ruled it out as a serious candidate. But three countries stood out as seeming to have necessary conditions for Intel's planned investment: Mexico, Chile, and Brazil. Costa Rica was added later.

Ted recalled that Costa Rica had *not* been on the original short list. It was only after officials at *Coalición Costarricense de Iniciativas para el Desarrollo* (CINDE, Costa Rica's Investment Promotion Agency) had given presentations to Silicon Valley executives in late 1995 about Costa Rica's potential as a center for high technology investment that Intel executives in California had considered this possibility.

CINDE had been created in 1982 with financial assistance from the United States Agency for International Development (USAID). Its original purpose was to serve as a private, nonprofit export promotion center. Its Board of Directors was (and still is) composed almost entirely of businessmen from the Costa Rican private sector. CINDE was a collaborative effort between USAID and civicminded businessmen in Costa Rica to promote nontraditional exports (in Costa Rica, this meant anything that was *not* bananas or coffee) and enhance economic development in Costa Rica.

At the time CINDE was created, the Reagan administration was hoping to strengthen the private sector in Central America and the Caribbean to prevent the spread of political instability in these regions. The Administration's Caribbean Basin Initiative (giving preferential access to the U.S. market for manufactured goods from Central America and the Caribbean) was one way to do this. US-AID's creation of CINDE was a separate policy but was consistent with the overall strategy.[8]

Over the years, especially after the end of the Cold War in the early 1990s and the fall of the Sandinista regime in Nicaragua in 1990, USAID reduced its funding to Costa Rica and finally closed its offices in the country in 1996. CINDE, with new funding from the World Bank and a trust fund of its own to finance its activities, continued—but with a different emphasis.

Following advice from a consultant with the highly successful Irish Development Authority (IDA)—Ireland's investment promotion agency—as well as from the World Bank, CINDE's directors realized that they should focus on promoting investment from specific firms in specific industries.[9] Professors at the *Instituto Centroamericano de Administración de Empresas* (INCAE), Costa Rica's premier business school, gave CINDE similar advice. Founded by Harvard University, IN-CAE was influenced by Harvard professor Michael Porter, a frequent visitor to the school and a close adviser to Costa Rica's president, Jose Maria Figueres (himself a Harvard graduate). INCAE recommended that CINDE pursue Porter's idea of promoting clusters of firms in particular industries as a way to accelerate national economic development.[10]

In a detailed study, the World Bank recommended to CINDE that it should target the electronics industry.[11] The Bank argued that the level of technical education in Costa Rica, and the number of electronics firms already located there, made it a suitable location for attracting a number of companies and creating clusters of firms in this industry. Others in CINDE had already made similar arguments, but the World Bank study confirmed these views.[12]

While not a government organization itself, CINDE was fortunate that it had support for its plans at the highest levels of government. Costa Rica's President, Jose Maria Figueres (1994–98), was very interested in promoting high-technology investment in Costa Rica.[13] Educated at West Point (with later graduate study at Harvard), Figueres had a vision of making Costa Rica a haven for high-technology investment. He believed very strongly that the country would be left behind in its quest for economic development if it remained principally an exporter of bananas and coffee, with only some manufacturing investment in low-tech, low-wage, low-value-added industries such as textiles. Costa Rica's gradual increase in Gross Domestic Product (GDP)/capita, education levels, and living standards, combined with the end of political unrest in neighboring Central American countries, had already resulted in a migration of investment out of Costa Rica's textile sector. New investment in this industry was going to countries like Nicaragua, where wages were much lower.

Clearly, changes in the world economy meant that Costa Rica would have to change its strategy, as well. As Figueres explained his government's plan:

> We wanted to incorporate Costa Rica into the global economy in an intelligent way. Globalization was more than simply opening the country to foreign trade. We needed a national strategy not based on cheap labor or the exploitation of our natural resources. We wanted to compete based on productivity, efficiency and technology . . . . many textile firms [had] left the country, and the government received severe criticism for not trying to sustain the maquila industry . . . . [but] the foreign investment attraction strategy had changed. We wanted to attract industries with higher value-added, that would allow Costa Ricans to increase their standard of living.[14]

All of these factors, including the high level of support from the Figueres administration, made CINDE eager to approach Intel when they heard, in 1995, that the company was planning to put a plant somewhere in Latin America. CINDE officials paid a special visit to Intel's headquarters in Santa Clara and were able to persuade management there that Costa Rica should be on the list. During the actual country visits, the site selection team decided to visit Costa Rica on their way to Brazil.

THE SITE SELECTION PROCESS, PHASE 2: INITIAL COUNTRY VISITS

Actually visiting the countries on the short list was crucial to get a sense, beyond all the data and statistics the team already had, of whether a plant would be a viable investment for a given country. For example, would the country's roads and airport facilities be adequate to transport the product quickly and efficiently to foreign markets? Did the country pose a security risk, to expatriate personnel or to the product? After all, silicon wafers containing hundreds of chips were very valuable—indeed, they were literally "worth more than their weight in gold." (Intel executives used this phrase often in interviews when referring to silicon wafers.) If trucks transporting hundreds or thousands of these on a daily basis were likely to be robbed, the site should be ruled out.

Other questions Intel wanted answered were even more difficult to glean from secondhand written reports. For example, would Intel executives be able to negotiate effectively with government officials in the country in question? Could a good working relationship be established? Finally, would expatriate managers be happy living in the country?

Ted was in charge of making the initial contacts with the relevant government officials in each of the countries the site selection team planned to visit. In setting up the visits for the team, he wrote detailed letters explaining what the team hoped to learn during its visit. Central concerns, he stressed, included the following:

- availability of technical personnel and engineers to staff the proposed plant;

- labor unions and labor regulations;

- transportation infrastructure and costs (roads and airports only, since Intel would export all of its product via air);

- the availability and reliability of the electrical power supply;

- the government's corporate taxation rates—and more specifically—whether the government offered any tax incentives for investments of the kind Intel proposed to make.

Ted had been confident in asking about incentives, for he knew that his requests for meeting with the relevant government officials would be well received. In the past, governments in Latin America had adhered to ideas of protectionism and economic nationalism, but by the late 1990s those ideas were a thing of the past. The proposed investment was something that would be attractive to almost any government in Latin America. After all, Intel's $300 million to $500 million investment would bring with it thousands of good jobs for technically trained workers and engineers.

In addition, rather than displacing indigenous producers by selling in the domestic market, Intel's product would be 100 percent exported. This would also contribute to the country's balance of payments. Finally, there was the possibility that Intel would use at least some locally produced components or products, thus creating so-called "linkage effects" and contributing to local economic development. If anything, Ted knew, Intel's proposed plant was the kind of project that countries would compete with one another to attract.

As it had turned out, the site selection team's initial experiences in each of the four countries were very important in making their decision. The team's first visit was to Costa Rica, then Brazil, Chile, and Mexico. Ted opened the first file, and began reviewing what he had learned.

Costa Rica

At first, despite CINDE's lobbying, Costa Rica had seemed an unlikely prospect. The country was simply too small. With only 3.5 million people and a tiny (if reasonably healthy) economy, the Intel executives feared that their investment would overwhelm the small nation. As Bob Perlman said, they were concerned that if Intel did invest in Costa Rica, it would be like "putting a whale in a fish bowl."[15] But the CINDE officials had been persistent, and the site selection team was willing to give the country a closer look.

When it came to luring foreign investors, Costa Rica had many advantages. One was its well-deserved reputation for political stability and democratic government. Surrounded by other countries that had been engulfed in political turmoil and war for much of the 1980s, Costa Rica, in contrast, had abolished its military in 1948 and had been stable, peaceful, and democratic ever since. Costa Rican President Oscar Arias (1986–90) won the Nobel Peace Prize for brokering a peace among the warring Central American nations, thus enhancing Costa Rica's reputation as a center of peace and stability in a chaotic region. Since 1948, the nation had devoted its main government activities toward providing social welfare for the populace and improving education and health care. The government had even set aside over 25 percent of its national territory as national parks in order to preserve its astonishingly rich biodiversity (and to promote ecotourism).

But for Intel, more important than any of this was the role CINDE played in attending to their concerns. CINDE, autonomous from the government and administered by private business people, was by the mid-1990s a streamlined, efficient, flexible organization. One factor in CINDE's success was that its private status allowed it to pay its employees far more than they could have made working for the government. As a result, CINDE had bright, highly competent employees who were able to pursue Intel aggressively and creatively.

During the visit to Costa Rica, the site selection team was deeply impressed with how prepared CINDE was to receive them and answer their questions quickly and efficiently. The CINDE officials had clearly done their homework. For the harried team, trying to get information as quickly as possible so that a decision could be made and a plant could be built fast, this quality made a very favorable impression indeed.

Following specific advice from Michael Porter, and also from the World Bank's Foreign Investment Advisory Service (an agency at the World Bank that provides less-developed countries with advice on investment promotion), CINDE knew that for a high-tech company like Intel, quick, speedy responses to questions were essential. Therefore, Enrique Egloff, CINDE's General Director, assigned three investment promotion specialists to the task of working only on the upcoming Intel visit. Because of the magnitude of the Intel project and the considerable benefits for the country if Costa Rica could land it, Egloff decided that these CINDE employees would be responsible only for the Intel project for the duration of the site selection team's decision-making process.

The three CINDE staff members on the project were Danilo Arias, Julissa Bravo, and Marcella Mora. Danilo, a lawyer by training, was assigned to handle any Intel issues related to legal matters or taxation. Julissa dealt with questions about human resources and education, and Marcela with questions of real estate, construction, and permits. It is significant that Intel executives were so impressed with these CINDE employees that all three were later offered jobs with the company. Danilo Arias became a Director of Public Relations, and Julissa Bravo accepted a position as a Human Resources manager with Intel. Although Marcella Mora was also offered a job at Intel, she chose to accept a job as Microsoft's Sales Manager for Latin America and the Caribbean.[16]

Rather than waiting for the site selection team to arrive and then responding to questions, each of these CINDE officials researched potential questions *in advance* to *anticipate* what Intel might ask. Then, if asked, they were exceptionally well prepared with facts, figures, etc. Also, together the three organized visits for the Intel executives with all of the key government officials that they knew the team would want to meet.

When Ted and his colleagues arrived in Costa Rica, CINDE had a well-planned, extensive agenda already laid out for them. During this and later visits, the Intel team was able to have in-depth discussions on relevant issues with, among others, the head of the ICE (the Costa Rican Electric Utility Company, still state-owned); the Minister of Transport and Public Works; the Minister of Education; the Minister of Science and Technology; the Dean of the *Instituto Tecnológico de Costa Rica* (ITCR); two separate accounting and consulting firms; and a number of other high-technology companies already established in Costa Rica, including Motorola, DSC Communications, and Baxter Healthcare. (Although Baxter had nothing to do with microprocessors, Intel found that it was useful to consult with this company during site selection. Like Intel, Baxter had operations all over the world and had similarly high standards in its production processes, such as the use of clean rooms.)

During the site selection team's initial visit to the country, CINDE officials arranged a visit with Jose Rossi, Minister of Foreign Trade, and President Figueres himself. Figueres impressed the team with his level of personal interest in the company, and his willingness to get involved in details of the negotiating process. But Figueres' level of personal involvement really hit home when the team casually mentioned that they were interested in getting to know Costa Rica's central valley better, since that was where the proposed plant would be located. Figueres said that if they could show up at 7:00 A.M. the next day, he could arrange a helicopter tour. When Ted and his colleagues showed up early the next morning, they were astonished to find Figueres himself at the controls.

Despite the high level attention and the apparent willingness the government had to work with Intel, the site selection team still had several very serious concerns about Costa Rica. The main issues were:

Education

Although Costa Rica appeared to have a sufficient number of engineers, it was lacking in mid-level technicians, crucial for staffing the assembly and testing plant. While the engineers needed to keep the plant operating might number in the several hundreds, the need for mid-level technicians would be in the thousands. Finding enough people with the right training was clearly going to be a problem in Costa Rica.

In discussing this problem with Figueres, the Minister of Education, and the Dean of the Costa Rican Technological Institute (ITCR), the virtues of Costa Rica's small size quickly became evident. All of these officials made clear that they could adapt to Intel's needs, modifying the curriculum of the ITCR and even creating a special certification program to produce the requisite numbers of technicians.

Adapting to Intel's need in this way raised a potential problem. The site selection team had emphasized from the beginning that Intel did not want special treatment, no matter how much Costa Rica wanted its investment project. A major concern was that any special deals or special incentives offered by the Figueres government, and not done in a transparent, legal way, would create problems for Intel in the future, should the next president want to withdraw this special support. Intel was very explicit from the beginning, therefore, that the government not try to offer anything like this.

But the Costa Rican government took care to make sure that the agreement to modify the ITCR's curriculum did not fall into this category. Although the new curriculum would be created in direct response to Intel's concerns, adapting the

ITCR's curriculum to Intel's rigorous standards would make the school's graduates better-trained overall, and thus better-equipped to work for *any* high technology firm. The modifications were not just for Intel—they were strengthening the ITCR generally.

In addition to investigating the technical preparedness of Costa Rica for the proposed plant, Ted and his colleagues also observed the level of English language proficiency in the general population, which they perceived to be much higher than it was in other Latin American countries. Ted and his colleagues observed that in Costa Rica, even cab drivers seemed to have a high degree of proficiency in English. Clearly, the general population was relatively well educated, and this was just one indication of that. In addition, the team noted that the current government had made English a required subject in the public school system. While a relatively minor point, English proficiency would be important when expatriates arrived to train local workers, especially since most technical manuals were in English.

Labor Issues

Labor unions were a major concern of Intel's. It did not want them in any of its plants, anywhere in the world, even if they were weak or labor unions in name only. In large part this had to do with the company's complex, highly technical production processes, which simply could not function properly with work stoppages or other kinds of union-related disruptions. These kinds of issues appeared to present few problems for Intel in Costa Rica. In fact, only about 7 percent of Costa Rica's private-sector workers belonged to labor unions.[17]

Labor unions had not had much power in Costa Rica since the end of the civil war in the late 1940s, when the new government banned the largest labor confederation in the country because of its affiliation with the Communist Party. Later, when the *Partido Liberación Nacional* (PLN) government was elected in the 1950s, it established *Solidaridad* (Solidarity), a government-sponsored movement to create special voluntary associations as an alternative to more confrontational, industry-wide unions.

Workers who belonged to these *solidarista* associations received numerous benefits, including participation in special savings plans (with contributions made by employers as well as employees), low-interest loans, and profit-sharing. (The profit-sharing was with the association, not the company.) *Solidarista* associations were quite different from labor unions in that they allowed management as well as workers to participate, and had no negotiating power of their own. Some believed that this system had contributed greatly to "labor peace" in the workplace.[18] Over 19 percent of multinational corporations in Costa Rica, including Firestone, McDonalds, and Colgate-Palmolive, had *solidarista* associations.[19]

In addition to the Solidarity movement, other factors also prevented the development of more traditional, combative labor unions in Costa Rica. One was the government's establishment of a national collective bargaining system, using wage boards to establish wage levels—thereby eliminating an important role for such unions. Still another was the law stating that unions could call a strike only if 60 percent of affected members signed a petition in favor of doing so, and a judge decided that the reason for the strike was valid. While the judge was deciding, the employer could fire any workers who were involved.[20]

Clearly, labor unions in Costa Rica would not be a major concern for Intel. Moreover, wages in Costa Rica were low in comparison with those in the United States, even for technical workers or skilled technicians. However, this was also true of the other countries on Intel's short list, with the exception of Chile (more on that below).

Transportation

While the roads from most potential sites for the plant to the airport were in excellent condition, and San Jose's international airport was acceptable, Intel's main concern was that the airport did not offer sufficient daily flights. This presented a very serious problem, because Intel would need to export all of its chips by air. After discussing the problem at length with Intel's executives, Costa Rica's Ministry of Transportation and Public Works was willing to be flexible in creating an "open skies" program. It began issuing more licenses and encouraging many other airlines to use the national airport. Again, while this might have seemed a special concession to Intel, it benefited other companies and other industries, especially the tourism industry, as well.

Electrical Energy

Because Costa Rica was not accustomed to industrial projects of the size Intel proposed, it did not have adjusted rates for heavy industrial users. The rate for industrial users varied only between $0.07 and $0.09 per kilowatt-hour—much more expensive, for example, than Mexico's rate of about $0.02 per kilowatt-hour.[21]

After discussion of this issue, ICE agreed to create a new rate for especially heavy users of electricity: $0.05 per kilowatt-hour. This rate would apply to any company using more than 12 megawatts of electricity (more than any other user of electricity in the country). Again, this was *not* a special concession to Intel—because *any* large industrial user that chose to invest in Costa Rica could also take advantage of this heavy use rate.

Investment Incentives

Costa Rica already offered generous incentives to companies located in its eight industrial parks with free trade zone status. Companies in the *Zona Franca* not only did not pay duties on imported parts or components, but were also completely exempt from income tax for eight years, and 50 percent exempt for four years after that. Intel wanted even more than this and the Costa Rican government was willing to negotiate. After all, other multinational corporations operating in the free trade zones, such as Baxter and Conair, had expressed concern about paying the higher tax rate at the end of their eight-year exemption, even if they planned to reinvest in the country.

Jose Rossi, the Minister of Foreign Trade, agreed to lobby the Costa Rican legislature for a change in the legislation. The new law would give a company a 75 percent exemption after eight years, provided that it reinvested more than 25 percent of its initial investment after the fourth year. Again, this would benefit not just

Intel but other multinational corporations as well. Jose Rossi emphasized to Intel executives that he would do his best to push for the new policy to become law, but that he could promise no more than that.[22] Working its way through the slow but democratic legislative process, this law finally passed in 1998.

Clearly, there were reasons to be concerned about putting the plant in Costa Rica. But the government did seem willing to work with Intel without breaking any of its own laws by offering special deals. The prospects at least looked promising. But the next country the team planned to visit, Brazil, seemed potentially to offer a lot more.

Brazil

The site selection team's experience in Brazil was in marked contrast to what had happened in Costa Rica. Brazil's size alone was an enormous contrast: 160 million people in contrast to Costa Rica's relatively puny 3.5 million. Also, unlike Costa Rica's simple, unitary political system, where power was centered in the national legislature and the president, Brazil offered another layer of complexity: it had a federal system. This meant that Intel could pick and choose among Brazil's 26 states for just the right investment deal. Under Brazil's decentralized system, states and even municipalities had some control over taxation policy and could offer individual incentives in order to lure investment. This practice had grown to such an extent that in Brazil it had come to be known as the *guerra fiscal* or "taxation war." Some states had actually driven themselves to the point of bankruptcy in their efforts to compete with other states in offering the most generous exemptions from the state value-added tax, the ICMS.[23]

At the federal level, Brazil provided a tax incentive specifically directed toward the computer industry through the *Processo Produtivo Básico* (PPB), or Basic Productive Process law. In order to receive this incentive (which included a reduction of up to 50 percent of corporate income tax, as well as reductions in some other taxes), companies had to invest 5 percent of total revenue in research and development. At least 2 percent of this had to be invested in universities or other government-approved institutions; the rest could be invested internally.[24]

While the PPB potentially seemed interesting, the fiscal incentives at the state level turned out not to be very relevant. The site selection team had already decided that the best location for a plant would be in the state of São Paulo—where the governor, Mario Covas, had explicitly rejected offering any special tax incentives.[25] In any case, the ICMS tax itself would not apply to Intel, since this tax was not levied on exported products.[26]

Covas's reason for not being generous about incentives was that São Paulo did not need to do much to lure investment. For after Brazil had finally stabilized its economy with the implementation of the *Plano Real* in 1994, billions of dollars of foreign investment were flowing into the country every year. And the lion's share of this investment went to São Paulo, the most heavily populated and economically developed state in the entire country.

What intrigued Intel about São Paulo was that the state had already succeeded in attracting numerous high technology firms. In fact, within a couple hours' drive from the capital, the megacity of São Paulo (population: 16 million people), were the much smaller cities of São Jose dos Campos and Campinas. In these cities, hundreds of high-technology firms had already established themselves. São Jose dos Campos was the home of EMBRAER and many other high-technology firms. Campinas, of particular interest to Intel, had managed to attract IBM, Compaq, Hewlett Packard, DEC, and Texas Instruments, to name just a few. Significantly, while São Paulo state did not offer any special tax incentives, Campinas's municipal government did provide them. Specifically, it granted exemption from city property and service taxes for any high-technology companies that established manufacturing plants in either of two industrial parks in the city, both specifically oriented toward high-technology firms.[27]

Clearly, Brazil had a lot to offer. In terms of *adequate numbers of technical personnel,* there was no question that the numbers in Campinas (home of the famed technological university, the *Universidade Estadual de Campinas,* or UNICAMP) would be far superior to what Intel could find in Costa Rica. *Infrastructure* was more than adequate; electrical power was readily available at reasonable costs, and the airports were already capable of meeting Intel's needs.

But other issues worried Intel's site selection team. *Security* was of some concern; according to some reports, hijacking of trucks in the São Paulo area was on the rise.[28] Another concern was *labor unions,* which, while not as powerful as they were in some Latin American countries, could be more militant than those in Costa Rica. In Brazil, all workers paid union dues, whether they were formal union members or not (of Brazil's total workforce, about 20 to 25 percent was unionized). A single union represented all workers in a particular industry in a given geographic area. These unions were organized at the federal level into labor federations. The *Central Única dos Trabalhadores* (Central Workers' Union, or CUT), the more combative of Brazil's two principal labor federations, was linked to the *Partido dos Trabalhadores* (Workers' Party, or PT), which controlled some state and municipal governments in Brazil. While workers' base wages were relatively low, overall labor costs in Brazil tended to be higher than in other Latin American countries because mandatory benefits for full-time employees, such as paid vacations, lengthy maternity (also paternity) leaves, and social security taxes, added 50 percent to 80 percent to the total cost.[29]

But perhaps the biggest problem that the site selection team encountered in their visit to Brazil was that, after their highly favorable experience with CINDE, and all the personal attention to their concerns lavished upon them from Figueres, Brazilian government officials seemed indifferent to their concerns. Foreign firms were so eager to get into Brazil to get access to its huge internal market that state and national government officials did not need to concern themselves with addressing special concerns of individual corporations—even of an industry giant like Intel. Moreover, on balance, the federal government's policies did not seem all that favorable. While the federal government did offer the specific PPB incentive for firms investing in R&D, it offered no general exemption from corporate income tax—and it had a high rate of taxation.

After the Costa Rica experience, all of this left a negative impression. Certainly Brazil did have a huge and very attractive domestic market. But for this particular project, Intel had no interest whatsoever in the domestic market of the country where its plant would be located. 100 percent of the product manufactured in the plant would be exported.

In addition to the lack of special incentives in São Paulo state, and the required income tax at the federal level, there were still more additional costs associated with doing business in Brazil. There seemed to be numerous other taxes, such as the infamous tax on financial transactions, and other expenses that all added up to what expatriate executives referred to as "the Brazil cost"—the extra cost of doing business in Brazil. Extra costs might be worth enduring if the tradeoff was access to a huge local market. But when a company intended to produce exclusively for export, as in Intel's case, these costs could be prohibitive. After all, aside from the (at the time) overvalued exchange rate, the "Brazil cost" was one of the chief reasons Brazilian firms themselves had difficulty exporting and why Brazil's current account deficit was so large.

Chile

After Brazil, the site selection team visited Chile. The team was very impressed with Chile's modern infrastructure and the country's technical training programs. But they immediately encountered four problems: distance, labor costs, capital controls, and lack of government incentives.

Distance

The site selection team was struck by the sheer amount of travel time to get from the United States to Santiago, Chile (almost 12 hours, given the scarcity of direct flights). Aware of the number of expatriate executives who would have to be travelling to the plant, at least in the startup phase, the team saw that this could present a problem. Costa Rica, in contrast, was only a three-hour flight from Texas or California.

Labor Costs

One legacy of the dictatorship of General Augusto Pinochet in Chile (1973–89) was a labor code that inhibited the development of powerful, confrontational labor unions. Only about 12 percent of the workforce was unionized. Unions that included members from more than one company were allowed to engage in collective bargaining only if the company in question agreed to this arrangement—which few companies ever did.[30]

Partly as a result of these rules, labor costs for unskilled workers were low in Chile, even though the country had one of the highest GDPs/capita in all of Latin America. However, salaries for technically trained personnel, which Intel needed most, were relatively high. The starting salary for an engineer in Chile was between $30,000–$40,000—not very different from what it would be in the United States. Intel could hire engineers in Costa Rica or Mexico for almost half that amount.

Capital Controls

At the time of Intel's visit in 1996, Chile's Central Bank had a policy designed to control capital flight during times of market volatility. This policy stated that for portfolio capital investments (*not* for direct foreign investments, such as what Intel planned), investors would be restricted from withdrawing their investment from Chile for one full year. In addition, investors would be required to deposit an amount, called the *encaje,* equivalent to 30 percent of their overall investment in a special account at Chile's Central Bank during that time period.[31]

This policy was a legacy of an earlier era, when capital controls were common throughout Latin America. Most Latin American countries had already eliminated this kind of policy, considering it to be counterproductive, in line with the overall "Latin American consensus" in favor of market-oriented policies. Even though Intel presumably would not be affected, since the proposed plant would be a *direct* foreign investment (as opposed to portfolio investment, e.g., investment in the Chilean capital markets), Intel executives were spooked by this policy. One government official was struck with how often the Intel executives brought up this issue, in meeting after meeting.[32]

Government Incentives

Beyond these other concerns, the Chilean government simply was not able to offer any significant investment incentives to Intel. Government officials at *Corporación de Fomento de la Producción* (CORFO), Chile's government development agency, explained to the site selection team that the market-oriented "Chilean model" was designed not to interfere with market forces, i.e., *not* to give special incentives for investment in selected industries.[33]

CORFO *was* authorized to offer incentives if the investment were to be located in an especially poor region of the country in need of economic development. CORFO officials went so far as to suggest a location for Intel's plant that would meet these criteria, a poor region of Chile not far from Valparaiso. But the site selection team made very clear to CORFO that they did not want to be outside of the general vicinity of Santiago.[34]

Mexico

The final country on the team's itinerary, Mexico, offered an especially promising location for Intel's plant: the Silicon Valley of Mexico, Guadalajara. The second-largest city in the country, Guadalajara had by the mid-1990s established itself as a center for high technology firms, particularly in the electronics sector. Beginning with Motorola and IBM in the 1960s, hundreds of electronics firms had established plants in and around Guadalajara, the capital of the relatively prosperous Mexican state of Jalisco.

The site selection team was highly impressed with Guadalajara. They talked to a number of executives in high-technology firms, including Motorola and Lucent, which were already there. The *Secretaría de Promoción Económica*

(SEPROE), or Jalisco State Economic Development Agency, was extremely well prepared with eye-catching brochures and detailed information that rivaled what the Intel executives had encountered at CINDE. SEPROE, too, prepared a detailed agenda, just as CINDE had done; and the site selection team had plenty of opportunities to speak to several expatriate executives on their own, just as they had done in Costa Rica.

The response from all of the site selection team's interviews was highly favorable about Guadalajara.[35] As part of Mexico's fabled "Golden Triangle," infrastructure in the city and surrounding area was more than adequate. The airport's number of flights and capacity was sufficient. Labor costs were low, yet there appeared to be a relatively large supply of skilled engineers and technicians. Finally, energy in Mexico, produced from abundant supplies of natural gas, was relatively inexpensive. As mentioned before, electrical power in Mexico was only about $0.02 per kilowatt-hour—significantly cheaper than Costa Rica's rate, even after implementation of the ICE's new policy granting special rates to heavy industrial users.

Unlike the indifference the site selection team had encountered in São Paulo, the Jalisco state government was eager to work with Intel. SEPROE officials explained that, in collaboration with the governor of Jalisco (renowned for his honesty and effectiveness), the agency was actively pursuing a strategy of encouraging high-technology investment. It was doing this indirectly by subsidizing numerous technical training schools so that there would be an adequate supply of skilled labor in the region. Also, like CINDE in Costa Rica, SEPROE officials traveled frequently (sometimes accompanied by the governor) to spread the word about Guadalajara overseas and encourage foreign investment by high-technology firms, particularly in the electronics sector. The governor, Alberto Cardenas, was a member of the *Partido de Acción Nacional* (PAN), a business-friendly political party with market-oriented economic views.

SEPROE had a complex formula that it used to determine the number of jobs a company's investment project would be likely to produce, and the capital that the project would bring to the state. On the basis of this formula, SEPROE was prepared to offer Intel free land for the plant's site, and subsidized training for Intel employees for an extended period. But despite all of these positive factors, Intel had two serious concerns.

Lack of Government Incentives at the Federal Level

For all of the incentives the Jalisco state government was prepared to offer at the state level, the federal government of Mexico refused to budge on giving income tax exemptions at the federal level. Also, the extreme centralization of the budget process in Mexico meant that, while the states could provide incentives such as free land and subsidized training for employees, state officials had no ability to offer fiscal incentives of their own, even if the federal government had allowed them to do so. As one top SEPROE official remarked in frustration, "The federal government receives 100 percent of the tax revenues, but then only redistributes about 20 percent of that revenue to the states."[36]

Labor Unions

Mexican federal law also contained certain rules about unions that worried the site selection team. Intel had a policy about not having unions anywhere in the world. But Mexico's federal law[37] stated that if a minimum of 20 employees in a given company decided to form a union, the company would be required to recognize it. If only two employees chose to affiliate with a union from outside the company, the company would be required to recognize and work with that union, provided that it was already recognized by the Mexican labor authorities. However, the workers would have to decide which form of representation they wanted, because only one union was allowed to represent the workers in a specific company. Most workers belonged to unions that were members of Mexico's nine largest national labor confederations, which had close ties to the dominant *Partido Revolucionário Institucional* (PRI) party.

Although companies were not required to have unions, in practice union organizers from outside the company would often work with company employees to organize a union or recruit them to affiliate with outside unions. This meant that most large companies in Mexico had to deal with unions, and that the country had a high rate of unionization. Of Mexico's total workforce, nearly 40 percent was unionized; of industrial workers in companies with more than 20 employees, the figure was closer to 80 percent.[38]

Many companies in Mexico ensured harmonious labor relations by working with company unions referred to as *sindicatos blancos* ("white unions"). In some cases, these unions were not really representative of the workers, but served only to comply technically with Mexico's legal requirements. Outside organizers would not be able to come in and form a more combative union (unless a majority of the workers voted for this), because the company would technically already have union representation. Other white unions were more genuinely representative of the workers, but worked in a collaborative way with management. In any case, white unions were much easier to work with than the more combative, confrontational unions that existed in many industries in Mexico.

But even if Intel were able to negotiate an agreement with a white union, this would still go against Intel's worldwide policy not to have unions in its plants. Intel would no longer be able to tell its employees elsewhere that the company had no unions whatsoever, at any plant in the world.

IBM managed to get around this problem at its own plant in Guadalajara by contracting out the majority of its workforce. Although 10,000 people worked at the IBM plant in Guadalajara, only about 500, all nonunionized management-level personnel (engineers and executives), were actually IBM employees. The rest worked *at* the IBM plant but were actually employed by other companies that were contract manufacturers, doing specific projects on a temporary basis for IBM. (Of course, all of these companies had unions.) This arrangement gave IBM flexibility in terms of its payroll, because during times of slack demand it could simply hire fewer contract manufacturers without having to worry about dismissing its own personnel and dealing directly with Mexican labor law issues.

Knowing about these different ways of working around Mexico's labor laws, SEPROE officials told Intel's site selection team not to worry. The company would not need to have a labor union. Intel could very easily be an exception to the general norm in Mexico.

But this very willingness on the part of government officials in Mexico even potentially to make an exception in Intel's case alarmed the site selection team even more. If the rules were not clear-cut, objective, and adhered to in a straightforward manner, then this created an unpredictable, nontransparent environment. This potential for lack of predictability and transparency in the rules of the game was of grave concern to Intel. It smacked of the "special deals" that the company had tried so much to avoid in Costa Rica.

Ted closed the last file and rubbed his eyes. He really had to finish that report.

References

1. The principal members of the site selection team were Ted Telford, International Site Selection Analyst; Chuck Pawlak, Director, New Site Development; and Bob Perlman, Vice President for Tax, Customs, and Licensing. Telford and Pawlak worked out of Intel's Chandler, Arizona, office; Perlman was based at the headquarters office in Santa Clara, California. Beyond these three members, there was an extended group of about 15 Intel employees all over the world who participated in detailed assessment of countries on issues such as energy availability, construction, operations, security, etc. Frank Alvarez, Vice President of the Technology and Management Group, was also based in Santa Clara and ultimately had final say over the site selection decision, along with Mike Splinter, Vice President of Worldwide Manufacturing and, of course, Craig Barrett, Intel's CEO.

2. Silicon is used because it is a semiconductor. Semiconductors are materials that can be altered either to be conductors of electricity or insulators—a useful quality in a material used for constructing the complex electronic circuitry of microprocessors. "Silicon Valley" is a nickname for the region around Stanford University, which includes many towns that serve as a home to important high-technology companies (including Santa Clara, where Intel headquarters were located).

   Using sophisticated chemical processes and engineering techniques, microprocessors are manufactured by the hundreds on extremely thin layers of silicon known as wafers. Each wafer is about 6-8 inches in diameter. The microprocessors are tested while they are still on the silicon wafer. Later, these wafers are cut into individual pieces or chips, each containing one microprocessor. The microprocessors are then tested again, packaged, and sent to customers for installation in many different kinds of automated devices.

3. World Bank, Foreign Investment Advisory Service, *FDI News,* December 1996, p. 5.

4. Grove later wrote a book with this title.

5. Debora Spar, "Attracting High Technology Investment: Intel's Costa Rican Plant," Foreign Investment Advisory Service, World Bank, Occasional Paper #11, April 1998, p. 4.

6. Ibid., p. 8.

7. Interview with Ted Telford, Site Selection Analyst, Intel, Glendale, Arizona, September 10, 1998.

8. Mary A. Clark, "Transnational Alliances and Development Policy in Latin America: Non Traditional Export Promotion in Costa Rica," *Latin American Research Review,* Vol. 32, No. 2, 1997, p. 91.

9. Interviews with CINDE officials, San Jose, Costa Rica, October-November 1998.

10. Thomas T. Vogel, "Costa Rica's Sales Pitch Lures High-Tech Giants Like Intel and Microsoft," *Wall Street Journal,* April 2, 1998, p. A-18; interviews with CINDE officials, San Jose, Costa Rica, October-November 1998.

11. The World Bank, "Costa Rica: A Strategy for Foreign Investment in Costa Rica's Electronics Industry" (Washington, D.C.: The World Bank), 1996.

12. Interview with Rodrigo Zapata, former Vice President of CINDE (now General Manager for GE-Costa Rica), San Jose, Costa Rica, October 1998. The study was conducted by the World Bank's Foreign Investment Advisory Service. Although the final version was published in 1996, CINDE was well aware of its main points long before that time.

13. Jose Maria Figueres was the son of Jose (Pepe) Figueres Ferrer, who led a civil war in 1948 when the Costa Rican legislature had nullified the outcome of a presidential election for a candidate who had won a legitimate election victory. During a brief period as interim president immediately following the war, Pepe Figueres succeeded in writing a new constitution and abolishing Costa Rica's military entirely, an unprecedented feat in Latin America (or virtually anywhere else, for that matter). He then turned power over to the rightful victor in the 1948 presidential election. He was elected president of Costa Rica himself several years later (1953–57).

14. Excerpt from interview with Jose Maria Figueres, quoted in Nils Ketelhohn, "The Costa Rican Electronics and Information Technology Cluster," unpublished manuscript, 1998, p. 6.

15. Telephone Interview with Bob Perlman, Intel's Vice President for Tax, Customs, and Licensing, August 1998.

16. Interviews with all three individuals in San Jose, Costa Rica, October–November 1998.

17. Bruce M. Wilson, *Costa Rica: Politics, Economics, and Democracy* (Boulder, CO.: Lynne Rienner Publishers, 1998), p. 70.

18. CINDE website, www.cinde.or.cr.

19. Ibid.

20. Wilson, *Costa Rica,* pp. 69–70.

21. Interview with Danilo Arias, Public Relations Director, Intel-Costa Rica, San Jose, Costa Rica, October 1998.

22. Interview with Jose Rossi, former Minister of Foreign Trade, San Jose, Costa Rica, November 1998.

23. I use only the acronym for the state value-added tax here because the full name is quite a mouthful. ICMS stands for *Imposto sobre as operações relativas a*

Circulação de Mercadorias e sobre a prestação de Serviços de transporte intermunicipal e de comunicação.

24. Renato Bastos, U.S. Department of Commerce, "Computer Hardware and Peripherals," Industry Sector Analysis for Brazil, São Paulo, Brazil, October 1998, p. 15.

25. Although São Paulo did allow an exception for the computer industry by reducing its relatively high ICMS from 18 percent to 12 percent for computer products only, this was still a high rate. See Bastos, p. 15.

26. American Chamber of Commerce-São Paulo, "How to Undertstand Corporate Taxation in Brazil" (informational pamphlet), São Paulo, 1999, p. 17.

27. Município de Campinas, Lei N. 8003 de agosto de 1994, in "Incentivos Fiscais do Município de Campinas - SP," provided by Prefeitura Municipal de Campinas, November 1998.

28. Interview with Intel executive, Glendale, Arizona, October 1998.

29. "Brazil: Investing, Licensing, and Trading," The Economist Intelligence Unit (London: The Economist Intelligence Unit), January 1999.

30. Matt Moffett, "Pinochet's Legacy: Chile's Labor Law Hobbles Its Workers and Troubles the U.S.," *Wall Street Journal,* October 15, 1997, p. A-10.

31. Technically, the policy still exists. However, currently, the rate is set at 0%—so portfolio investors do not have to put any money in this special account. Some in Chile, and all foreign investors, would like to see the end of this policy once and for all. The fact that the policy still remains, even if the rate is set at 0 percent, means that a higher percentage could be re-imposed at any time.

32. Interview with Francisco Troncoso, Director, International Relations Division, CORFO, Santiago, Chile, December 1998.

33. Ibid.

34. Ibid., and interview with Mario Castillo, Deputy Director, Strategic Planning Division, CORFO, Santiago, Chile, December 1998.

35. Interview with Ted Telford, Phoenix, September 1998. Information from this section is also based on my interviews with officials at SEPROE, with executives at Lucent, Motorola, SCI, and IBM, and with others in Guadalajara, Mexico, December 1998, and August 1999.

36. Comments by SEPROE official, Guadalajara, Mexico, August 1999.

37. Edward G. Hinkelman (ed.), *Mexico Business: The Portable Encyclopedia for Doing Business with Mexico* (San Rafael, CA: World Trade Press), 1994, p. 15.

38. "Mexico: Investing, Licensing and Trading," The Economist Intelligence Unit (London: The Economist Intelligence Unit Limited), September 1998.

Chapter Twenty-Five

Cameron Auto Parts (A)—Revised

Alex Cameron's first years in business were unusually harsh and turbulent. He graduated from a leading Michigan business school in 1991 when the American economy was just edging out of recession. It was not that Alex had difficulty finding a job, however; it was that he took over the reins of the family business. His father timed his retirement to coincide with Alex's graduation and left him with the unenviable task of cutting back the workforce to match the severe sales declines the company was experiencing.

HISTORY

Cameron Auto Parts was founded in 1965 by Alex's father to seize opportunities created by the signing of the Auto Pact between Canada and the United States. The Auto Pact permitted the Big Three automotive manufacturers to ship cars, trucks and original equipment (OEM) parts between Canada and the United States tariff free, as long as they maintained auto assembly facilities on both sides of the border. The Pact had been very successful with the result that a lot of auto parts firms sprang up in Canada to supply the Big Three. Cameron Auto Parts prospered in this environment until, by 1989, sales had reached $60 million with profits of

Professor Harold Crookell prepared this case solely to provide material for class discussion. The author does not intend to illustrate either effective or ineffective handling of a managerial situation. The author may have disguised certain names and other identifying information to protect confidentiality. Revised by Professor Paul Beamish.

Richard Ivey School of Business
The University of Western Ontario

$1.75 million. The product focus was largely on small engine parts and auto accessories such as oil and air filters, fan belts and wiper blades, all sold as original equipment under the Auto Pact.

When Alex took over in 1991, the company's financial position was precarious. Sales in 1990 dropped to $48 million and for the first six months of 1991 to $18 million. Not only were car sales declining in North America, but the Japanese were taking an increasing share of the market. As a result, the major North American auto producers were frantically trying to advance their technology and to lower their prices at the same time. It was not a good year to be one of their suppliers. In 1990, Cameron Auto Parts lost $2.5 million, and had lost the same amount again in the first six months of 1991. Pressure for modernization and cost reduction had required close to $4 million in new investment in equipment and computer-assisted design and manufacturing systems. As a result, the company had taken up over $10 million of its $12 million line of bank credit at an interest rate which stood at 9.5 percent in 1991.

Alex's first six months in the business were spent in what he later referred to as "operation survival". There was not much he could do about working capital management as both inventory and receivables were kept relatively low via contract arrangements with the Big Three. Marketing costs were negligible. Where costs had to be cut were in production and, specifically, in people, many of whom had been with the company for over fifteen years and were personal friends of Alex's father. Nevertheless, by the end of 1991, the workforce had been cut from 720 to 470, the losses had been stemmed and the company saved from almost certain bankruptcy. Having to be the hatchet man, however, left an indelible impression on Alex. As things began to pick up during 1992 and 1993, he added as few permanent workers as possible, relying instead on overtime, part timers, or sub-contracting.

RECOVERY AND DIVERSIFICATION

For Cameron Auto Parts, the year 1991 ended with sales of $38 million and losses of $3.5 million (see Exhibit 1). Sales began to pick up in 1992 reaching $45 million by year-end with a small profit. By mid-1993, it was clear that the recovery was well underway. Alex, however, while welcoming the turnaround, was suspicious of the basis for it. Cameron's own sales hit $27 million in the first six months of 1993 and company profits were over $2 million. The Canadian dollar had dropped as low as 73 cents in terms of U.S. currency and Cameron was faced with more aggressive competition from Canadian parts manufacturers. The short-term future for Cameron however, seemed distinctly positive, but the popularity of Japanese cars left Alex feeling vulnerable to continued total dependence on the volatile automotive industry. Diversification was on his mind as early as 1991. He had an ambition to take the company public by 1997 and diversification was an important part of that ambition.

Unfortunately, working as an OEM parts supplier to the automotive industry did little to prepare Cameron to become more innovative. The auto industry

EXHIBIT 1

INCOME STATEMENTS
For Years Ended December 31, 1991, 1992, 1993
($000's)

	1991	1992	1993
Net Sales	$38,150	$45,200	$67,875
Cost of goods sold:			
Direct materials	6,750	8,050	12,400
Direct labor	12,900	10,550	12,875
Overheads (including depreciation)	16,450	19,650	27,600
Total	36,100	38,250	52,875
Gross Profit	2,050	6,950	15,000
Expenses:			
Selling and administration			
(includes design team)	3,150	3,800	6,200
Other (includes interest)	2,400	2,900	3,000
Total	5,500	6,700	9,200
Net Profit before Tax	(3,500)	250	5,800
Income Tax	(500)	-	200
Net Profit after Tax	$(3,000)	$ 250	$5,600

Note: Alex expected total sales to reach $85 million in 1994 with profits before tax of $10 million. Flexible couplings were expected to contribute sales of $30 million and profits of $5 million on assets of $12 million.

tended to standardize its parts requirements to the point that Cameron's products were made to precise industry specifications and consequently, did not find a ready market outside the industry. Without a major product innovation it appeared that Cameron's dependence on the Big Three was likely to continue. Furthermore, the company had developed no "in-house" design and engineering strength from which to launch an attempt at new product development. Because product specifications had always come down in detail from the Big Three, Cameron had never needed to design and develop its own products and had never hired any design engineers.

In the midst of "operation survival" in mid-1991, Alex boldly decided to do something about diversification. He personally brought in a team of four design engineers and instructed them to concentrate on developing products related to the existing line but with a wider "nonautomotive" market appeal. Their first year together showed little positive progress, and the question of whether to fund the team for another year (estimated budget $425,000) came to the management group:

Alex: Maybe we just expected too much in the first year. They did come up with the flexible coupling idea, but you didn't seem to encourage them, Andy (production manager).

Andy McIntyre: That's right! They had no idea at all how to produce such a thing in our facilities. Just a lot of ideas about how it could be used. When I told them a Canadian outfit was already producing them, the team sort of lost interest.

John Ellis: (Finance) We might as well face the fact that we made a mistake, and cut it off before we sink any more money into it. This is hardly the time for unnecessary risks.

Alex: Why don't we shorten the whole process by getting a production licence from the Canadian firm? We could start out that way and then build up our own technology over time.

Andy: The team looked into that, but it turned out the Canadians already have a subsidiary operating in United States—not too well from what I can gather—and they are not anxious to licence anyone to compete with it.

Alex: Is the product patented?

Andy: Yes, but apparently it doesn't have long to run.

At this point a set of ideas began to form in Alex's mind, and in a matter of months he had lured away a key engineer from the Canadian firm with an $110,000 salary offer and put him in charge of the product development team. By mid-1993, the company had developed its own line of flexible couplings with an advanced design and an efficient production process using the latest in production equipment. Looking back, in retrospect, Alex commented:

> We were very fortunate in the speed with which we got things done. Even then the project as a whole had cost us close to $1 million in salaries and related costs.

MARKETING THE NEW PRODUCT

Alex continued:

> We then faced a very difficult set of problems, because of uncertainties in the market place. We knew there was a good market for the flexible type of coupling because of its wide application across so many different industries. But, we didn't know how big the market was nor how much of it we could secure. This meant we weren't sure what volume to tool up for, what kind or size of equipment to purchase, or how to go about the marketing job. We were tempted to start small and grow as our share of market grew, but this could be costly too and could allow too much time for competitive response. Our Canadian engineer was very helpful here. He had a lot of confidence in our product and had seen it marketed in both Canada and the United States. At his suggestion we tooled up for a sales estimate of $30 million—which was pretty daring. In addition, we hired eight field sales representatives to back up the nation-wide distributor and soon afterwards hired several Canadian-based sales representatives to cover major markets. We found that our key Canadian competitor was pricing rather high and had not cultivated very friendly customer relations. We were able to pay the modest (and declining) Canadian tariffs and still come in at, or slightly below, his prices. We were surprised how quickly we were able to secure significant penetration into the Canadian market. It just wasn't being well-serviced.

During 1993, the company actually spent a total of $2.5 million on equipment for flexible coupling production. In addition, a fixed commitment of $1.5 million a year in marketing expenditures on flexible couplings arose from the hiring of sales representatives. A small amount of trade advertising was included in this sum. The total commitment represented a significant part of the company's resources and threatened serious damage to the company's financial position if the sales failed to materialize.

"It was quite a gamble at the time," Alex added. "By the end of 1993, it was clear that the gamble was going to pay off."

	Sales by Market Sector ($millions)			
	OEM Parts Sales	**Flexible Couplings Sales**	**Total Sales**	**After Tax Profits**
1989	60	Nil	60	1.75
1990	48	Nil	48	(2.50)
1991	38	Nil	38	(3.50)
1992	45	Nil	45	.25
1993	58	10 (six months)	68	5.80

Cameron's approach to competition in flexible couplings was to stress product quality, service and speed of delivery, but not price. Certain sizes of couplings were priced slightly below the competition but others were not. In the words of one Cameron sales representative:

> Our job is really a technical function. Certainly, we help predispose the customer to buy and we'll even take orders, but we put them through our distributors. Flexible couplings can be used in almost all areas of secondary industry, by both large and small firms. This is why we need a large distributor with wide reach in the market. What we do is give our product the kind of emphasis a distributor can't give. We develop relationships with key buyers in most major industries, and we work with them to keep abreast of new potential uses for our product, or of changes in size requirements or other performance characteristics. Then we feed this kind of information back to our design group. We meet with the design group quite often to find out what new types of couplings are being developed and what the intended uses are, etc. Sometimes they help us solve a customer's problem. Of course, these 'solutions' are usually built around the use of one of our products.

FINANCING PLANT CAPACITY

When Alex first set his diversification plans in motion in 1991, the company's plant in suburban Detroit was operating at 50 percent capacity. However, by early 1994, sales of auto parts had recovered almost to 1989 levels and the flexible coupling line was squeezed for space. Andy McIntyre put the problem this way:

> I don't see how we can get sales of more than $85 million out of this plant without going to a permanent two-shift system, which Alex doesn't want to do. With two full shifts we could probably reach sales of $125 million. The

problem is that both our product lines are growing very quickly. Auto parts could easily hit $80 million on their own this year, and flexible couplings! Well, who would have thought we'd sell $10 million in the first six months? Our salespeople are looking for $35 to 40 million during 1994. It's wild! We just have to have more capacity.

There are two problems pressing us to consider putting flexible couplings under a different roof. The first is internal: we are making more and more types and sizes, and sales are growing to such a point that we may be able to produce more efficiently in a separate facility. The second is external: The Big Three like to tour our plant regularly and tell us how to make auto parts cheaper. Having these flexible couplings all over the place seems to upset them, because they have trouble determining how much of our costs belong to Auto Parts. If it were left to me I'd just let them be upset, but Alex feels differently. He's afraid of losing orders. Sometimes I wonder if he's right. Maybe we should lose a few orders to the Big Three and fill up the plant with our own product instead of expanding.

Flexible couplings were produced on a batch basis and there were considerable savings involved as batches got larger. Thus as sales grew, and inventory requirements made large batches possible, unit production costs decreased, sometimes substantially. Mr. McIntyre estimated that unit production costs would decline by some 20 percent as annual sales climbed from $20 million to $100 million, and by a further 10 percent at $250 million. Scale economies beyond sales of $250 million were not expected to be significant.

John Ellis, the company's financial manager, expressed his own reservations about new plant expansion from a cash flow perspective:

We really don't have the balance sheet (Exhibit 2) ready for major plant expansion yet. I think we should grow more slowly and safely for two more years and pay off our debts. If we could hold sales at $75 million for 1994 and $85 million for 1995, we would be able to put ourselves in a much stronger financial position. The problem is that people only look at the profits. They don't realize that every dollar of flexible coupling sales requires an investment in inventory and receivables of about 30 cents. It's not like selling to the Big Three. You have to manufacture to inventory and then wait for payment from a variety of sources.

As it is, Alex wants to invest $10 million in new plant and equipment right away to allow flexible coupling sales to grow as fast as the market will allow. We have the space on our existing site to add a separate plant for flexible couplings. It's the money I worry about.

FOREIGN MARKETS

As the company's market position in North America began to improve, Alex began to wonder about foreign markets. The company had always been a major exporter to Canada, but it had never had to market there. The Big Three placed their orders often a year or two in advance, and Cameron just supplied them. As Alex put it:

EXHIBIT 2

	BALANCE SHEETS **For Years Ended December 31, 1991, 1992, 1993** **($000's)**		
	1991	1992	1993
Assets			
Cash	$ 615	$ 430	$ 400
Accounts Receivable	5,850	6,850	10,400
Inventories	4,995	4,920	7,500
Total Current Assets	11,460	12,200	18,300
Property, plant and equipment (net)	10,790	11,800	13,000
Total Assets	22,250	24,000	31,300
Liabilities			
Accounts Payable	4,850	5,900	9,500
Bank loan	11,500	12,000	10,000
Accrued Items (including taxes)	450	400	500
Total Current Liabilities	16,800	18,300	20,000
Common Stock (Held by Cameron family)	500	500	500
Retained Earnings	4,950	5,200	10,800
Total Equity	5,450	5,700	11,300
Total Liabilities	$22,250	$24,000	$31,300

It was different with the flexible coupling. We had to find our own way into the market. We did, however, start getting orders from Europe and South America, at first from the subsidiaries of our U.S. customers and then from a few other firms as word got around. We got $40,000 in orders during 1993 and the same amount during the first four months of 1994. This was a time when we were frantically busy and hopelessly understaffed in the management area, so all we did was fill the orders on an FOB, Detroit basis. The customers had to pay import duties of 5 percent into most European countries (and a value added tax of about 20 percent) and 20 percent to 50 percent into South America, on top of the freight and insurance, and still orders came in.

Seeing the potential in Europe, Alex promptly took an European Patent from the European Patent Office in the United Kingdom. The cost of the whole process was $30,000. The European Patent Office (EPO) headquartered in Munich, Germany received more than 50,000 patent applications each year. Since the EPO opened in 1978, additional countries had joined the EPO, often in step with joining the European Economic Community, now known as the European Union (EU). However, the EPO was not part of the EU, rather it was an autonomous organization. The current 17 member states of the EPO are Austria, Belgium, Denmark, Finland, France, Germany, Greece, Ireland, Italy, Luxembourg, Monaco, Netherlands, Portugal, Spain, Sweden, Switzerland (including Liechtenstein) and United Kingdom. The official filing fees, although high, were much less than the fees which would be encountered by filing separate patent applications before the individual national patent offices.

A LICENSING OPPORTUNITY

In the spring of 1994, Alex made a vacation trip to Scotland and decided while he was there to drop in on one of the company's new foreign customers, McTaggart Supplies Ltd. Cameron Auto Parts had received unsolicited orders from overseas amounting to $40,000 in the first four months of 1994, and over 10 percent of these had come from McTaggart. Alex was pleasantly surprised at the reception given to him by Sandy McTaggart, the 60-year-old head of the company.

Sandy: Come in! Talk of the devil. We were just saying what a shame it is you don't make those flexible couplings in this part of the world. There's a very good market for them. Why my men can even sell them to the English!

Alex: Well, we're delighted to supply your needs. I think we've always shipped your orders promptly, and I don't see why we can't continue. . . .

Sandy: That's not the point, lady! That's not the point! Those orders are already sold before we place them. The point is we can't really build the market here on the basis of shipments from America. There's a 5 percent tariff coming in, freight and insurance cost us another 10 percent on top of your price, then there's the matter of currency values. I get my orders in pounds (£)[1] but I have to pay you in dollars. And on top of all that, I never know how long the goods will take to get here, especially with all the dock strikes we have to put up with. Listen, why don't you license us to produce flexible couplings here?

After a lengthy bargaining session, during which Alex secured the information shown in Exhibit 3, he came round to the view that a license agreement with McTaggart might be a good way of achieving swift penetration of the U.K. market via McTaggart's sales force. McTaggart's production skills were not as up-to-date as Cameron's, but his plant showed evidence of a lot of original ideas to keep manufacturing costs down. Furthermore, the firm seemed committed enough to invest in some new equipment and to put a major effort into developing the U.K. market. At this point the two executives began to discuss specific terms of the license arrangements:

Alex: Let's talk about price. I think a figure around 3 percent of your sales of flexible couplings would be about right.

Sandy: That's a bit high for an industrial license of this kind. I think 1½ percent is more normal.

Alex: That may be, but we're going to be providing more than just blueprints. We'll have to help you choose equipment and train your operators as well.

EXHIBIT 3
Data on McTaggart
Supplies Ltd.

1993 Sales	£35 million (down from £44 million in 1991).
Total assets	£11 million: Equity £6.5 million
Net profit after tax	± £1.5 million
Control	McTaggart Family
Market coverage	15 sales representatives in U.K., two in Europe, one in Australia, one in New Zealand, one in India.
Average factory wage rate	£5.00 per hour (which is below the U.K. mean of £6.70 due to the factory being located in a depressed area (versus $11.70 in America).
Factory	Old and larger than necessary. Some very imaginative manufacturing knowhow in evidence.
Reputation	Excellent credit record, business now 130 years old, good market contacts (high calibre sales force).
Other	Company sales took a beating during 1991–92 as one of the company's staple products was badly hurt by a U.S. product of superior technology. Company filled out its line by distributing products obtained from other manufacturers. Currently about one-half of company sales are purchased from others. Company has capacity to increase production substantially.

Pricing	Index
Cameron's price to McTaggart	100
(same as net price to distributor in America)	
+ Import duty	4
+ Freight and insurance	11
Importer's Cost	115
+ Distributor's (McTaggart's) Margin (30%)	35
+ Value Added Tax (17.5% on cost plus margin)	26
= Price charged by McTaggart	176
vs Price charged by American distributor in U.S.	120

Note: Under the European Union agreement, all imports from non-EU countries were subject to common external tariffs (CET). In 1994, the CET for the flexible coupling had an import duty of 4 percent. (It was expected that with the GATT agreement, CET would be totally abolished by AD 2000.) In addition to the import duty, all imported items were subjected to the value added tax (VAT) which was applied on all manufactured goods—both imported as well as locally made. The VAT was going through a harmonization process but was expected to take some years before a common VAT system was in place. As of 1994, the VAT for United Kingdom was 17.5 percent, and France 20.6 percent. Sweden had the highest VAT at 25 percent.

Sandy: Aye, so you will. But we'll pay you for that separately. It's going to cost us £500,000 in special equipment as it is, plus, let's say, a $100,000 fee to you to help set things up. Now you have to give us a chance to price competitively in the market, or neither of us will benefit. With a royalty of 1½ percent I reckon we could reach sales of £500,000 in our first year and £1 million in our second.

Alex: The equipment will let you produce up to £4 million of annual output. Surely you can sell more than a million. We're getting unsolicited orders without even trying.

Sandy: With the right kind of incentive, we might do a lot better. Why don't we agree to a royalty of 2 1/2 percent on the first million in sales and 1 1/2 percent after that. Now mind you, we're to become exclusive agents for the U.K. market. We'll supply your present customers from our own plant.

Alex: But just in the U.K.! Now 2 percent is as low as I'm prepared to go. You make those figures 3 percent and 2 percent and you have a deal. But it has to include a free technology flow-back clause in the event you make any improvements or adaptations to our manufacturing process.

Sandy: You drive a hard bargain! But it's your product, and we do want it. I'll have our lawyers draw up a contract accordingly. What do you say to a five year deal, renewable for another five if we are both happy?

Alex: Sounds good. Let's do it.

Alex signed the contract the same week and then headed back to America to break the news. He travelled with mixed feelings, however. On the one hand, he felt he had got the better of Sandy McTaggart in the bargaining, while on the other, he felt he had no objective yardstick against which to evaluate the royalty rate he had agreed on. This was pretty much the way he presented the situation to his executive group when he got home.

Alex: . . . so I think it's a good contract, and I have a cheque here for $100,000 to cover our costs in helping McTaggart get set up.

John: We can certainly use the cash right now. And there doesn't seem to be any risk (finance) involved. I like the idea, Alex.

Andy: Well, I don't. And Chuck (head of the Cameron design team) won't either when (production) he hears about it. I think you've sold out the whole U.K. market for a pittance. I thought you wanted to capture foreign markets directly.

Alex: But Andy, we just don't have the resources to capture foreign markets ourselves. We might as well get what we can through licensing, now that we've patented our process.

Andy: Well, maybe. But I don't like it. It's the thin edge of the wedge if you ask me. Our know-how on the production of this product is pretty special, and it's getting better all the time. I hate to hand it over to old McTaggart on a silver platter. I reckon we're going to sell over $20 million in flexible couplings in the United States alone during 1994.

Endnote

1. One pound was equivalent to US$1.50 in 1994.

Chapter Twenty-Six

Time Warner Inc. and the ORC Patents

In early July 1992, John Adamson, president of Optical Recording Corporation (ORC), sat depressed and second-guessed his company's decision to sue Time Warner Inc. for patent infringement. An in-house patent counsel from the U.S. Philips Corporation, whose parent firm developed and licensed the compact disc (CD) technology in partnership with Sony Corporation, had just finished his testimony in the Wilmington, Delaware, courtroom.

The Philips attorney had just advised the court that Philips International N.V. had indeed signed a license agreement with ORC but only to "get rid of ORC with a modest nuisance payment." He had gone on to say that in spite of their decision to accept a license from ORC, the Philips engineers and attorneys had never believed that the Russell patents owned by ORC were valid nor that any compact disc products infringed these patents. Adamson watched in shock as the Philips man made his way out of the courtroom.

Given that Time Warner had mounted a very credible defense and that ORC's entire licensing program might be at risk, Adamson needed to decide whether he should make a modest settlement with Time Warner, just to save the licensing program.

Ivey

Richard Ivey School of Business
The University of Western Ontario

BACKGROUND

Optical Recording Corporation (ORC) was incorporated in 1984 to exploit a technology invented by James T. Russell, an American inventor, then working in laboratories in Salt Lake City, Utah. Due to the desperate financial straits of SLC[1], his employer, Russell had made little progress in the previous two years and both he and SLC were anxious to secure a buyer for the technology.

Through Wayne White, a fellow MBA 1972 graduate from the University of Western Ontario, then working with Dominion Securities in Toronto, John Adamson was put in contact with Dr. R. Moses and Dr. A. Stein. These two Toronto businessmen had been working for close to a year to buy Russell's technology. By happenstance, Adamson had contacted White looking for business opportunities to start his next business, preferably in electronics or software, just days after Moses and Stein had advised White that they were going to throw in the towel on their Russell project. In spite of the considerable time that they had spent, it appeared unlikely that they would be successful in securing the necessary finances to proceed.

Adamson negotiated an option with these gentlemen to assume their "interests" in the Russell project, on the condition that he secure the necessary funding for a technology transfer by April 1, 1985, a propitious date as it would turn out. In return, Adamson agreed to reimburse their expenses to date and to give to each, a 5 percent equity interest in the incorporation formed to exploit the Russell project in Toronto.

After completing a "due diligence" investigation of the Russell technology, with the assistance of Warner Sharkey, an alumnus and friend from the Royal Military College of Canada and a senior technology consultant, who operated from offices in New York and Toronto, Adamson began planning in earnest. He wanted to transfer the Russell technology to Toronto, where he expected a well qualified team of scientists and engineers could be assembled to pursue a cost-effective development of a pocket-portable digital storage device.

For the next nine excruciating months, he worked to find investors for an issue of special debentures from his Toronto start-up. These debentures also offered a very attractive cash-back feature under a research tax credit program of the Canadian government. Funding was secured and the technology transfer agreements were signed on March 28, 1985, only three days before the option agreement with Moses and Stein would have expired. Adamson had resisted the temptation to request an extension of time on his option agreement with Moses and Stein. He feared that, better informed, they might rekindle their interest in the Russell technology and work to obstruct what little chance he still had to find funding prior to the option expiry on the first of April.

With the debenture funding and the transfer agreements signed, the new Toronto company, soon to be called Optical Recording Corporation (ORC), was now ready to hire Russell and transfer SLC's technology to Toronto.

JIM RUSSELL

By 1984, Jim Russell had worked for close to 20 years toward an improvement in recorded music beyond what was possible with the analog magnetic tape technology. This quest was motivated in part by his love of opera and a desire to listen to more accurate playbacks of recorded performances. When Adamson first visited Russell's lab in Salt Lake City, he was treated to the playback of a recording of Richard Wagner's "Ride of the Valkyries" (or "Die Walkure" in the original German). It was a most rousing introduction to a technology!

Russell had accomplished this playback by shining an argon ion laser beam onto a prerecorded glass plate, the size of an index card. This was the latest of his laboratory prototypes designed to demonstrate his patented techniques. These techniques were claimed in his extensive portfolio of 26 U.S. patents with corresponding foreign issues in seven other countries.

In Russell's way of recording music, the acoustic signal of the music was first preprocessed into a single *digital* bit stream from a series of time-coincident frequency samples. A laser, an *optical* device, was then used as the energy source to mark the music, as digital bits, onto a glass plate in the recording step and then used to read the music, as digital bits, in the playback step. This technology was known as *digital optical* audio recording.

Adamson was not the first to visit Russell's lab, far from it. Over the course of the previous 10 years, both at SLC in Salt Lake City, and at Battelle Northwest Laboratories in Richland, Washington, electronics manufacturers around the world beat a path to Russell's laboratory door and at his invitation. SLC had been trying to sell technology licenses to the Russell technology but with virtually no success. Prominent among the visitors to SLC's labs were representatives from Philips International N.V., the multinational electric/electronics giant headquartered in Eindhoven, the Netherlands. They had made three separate visits over that 10-year period.

Prior to the commercial availability of the diode laser in the early 1980s, Russell's recording and playback devices were operated with the use of a gas ion laser and as such could be made no smaller than the dimensions of an office desk. Gas ion lasers were too bulky, complicated and expensive to be used in consumer products. This may explain SLC's lack of success in licensing and their resultant financial distress. With the advent of the diode laser, essentially a powerful light source on a silicon chip, a light, compact and economical consumer product such as the compact disc was possible. Although never well funded, SLC's money troubles really began in 1981, just as the mass commercialization of a digital optical audio recording device became feasible.

From Adamson's viewpoint, Russell's greatest achievement was not any one of his inventions, but his success in demonstrating the technical feasibility of recording a digital audio signal optically. Before Russell had successfully demonstrated this technical feat in 1975, no one else had even attempted it. By early 1984, however, the electronics trade papers were reporting that Sony and Philips were developing a so-called compact disc player. SLC and Russell must have felt that they were being left on the sidelines in Salt Lake City, a bitter fate for the inventor and his investors who had all contributed so much.

In bringing Russell and his technology to Toronto, Adamson had decided that there was little point in continuing audio research toward a digital optical tape recorder. The opportunity to develop a massive random access data storage device using credit card-sized media was seen a less ambitious technical challenge and possibly of greater commercial value than a music device like the CD. With the insight of Russell, Adamson envisioned books, medical records, equipment schematics, maintenance instructions and records on this type of device—and all pocket-portable.

In order to determine what protection the existing Russell patents would provide to the new research focus, Adamson employed the services of John Orange, a patent agent, then with the Toronto law firm of McCarthy & McCarthy. (Orange was recommended by Daniel Cooper, a corporate attorney with the same law firm, who earlier had prepared all of the financing and technology transfer agreements for ORC.)

After working with Russell for several months, Orange advised Adamson in early 1986 that the Russell patents may not provide much protection to the new company's research focus, as the most relevant patents appeared to be limited in their claims to audio applications. Adamson had already understood that it was the precise language of the claims within a patent that determined the patent's intellectual property rights.

DISCOVERING A TREASURE

In completing his study of ORC's patents with the assistance of Russell, Orange also concluded that the newly released compact disc players and discs might infringe one or more of the claims in the Russell patents. What a finding! Russell had mentioned this possibility to Adamson during their first meeting in the Salt Lake City lab; however, Adamson had put little faith in Russell's remark at the time, as no consumer electronics firm had bothered to license the technology, in spite of SLC's efforts. Furthermore there were no CD products on the market then and its commercial success could not be anticipated.

Encouraged by the report from Orange and the early market success of the compact disc by the spring of 1986, Adamson retained the services of Adrian Horne, an established patent licensing professional of Dolby acoustic research fame. With Horne's assistance, ORC set out to advise every electronics firm likely to market a compact disc player anywhere in the world that "they may infringe the Russell patents" by doing so. Horne was most clear on the point that ORC must not appear to threaten legal action in their notice, as it may give grounds to the recipients to file a preemptive request for Declaratory Judgment and thereby force ORC into premature legal proceedings that ORC could ill afford.

In conjunction with the initial contact of alleged infringers, Adamson prepared cost estimates for the licensing effort and started to gain some early information on what it would cost to sue for patent infringement. He knew that once launched, any investment in the licensing program was certain to be incurred, whereas the return by way of royalty revenues would be anything but certain. He also made early estimates of the royalty potential for the licensing program, but these royalty estimates carried an enormous emotional impact.

Simple arithmetic established that if 100 million CD players were sold in ORC's patent-protected territories at an average manufacturer's selling price of US$100 and if ORC licensed their patent rights for this product at 2 percent of revenues, ORC's projected royalties would total US$200 million. And this figure ignored the royalties to be earned on the manufacture and sale of the compact disc media itself! It was clear that a successful licensing program could be mounted given these simple estimates. Adamson chose not to dwell on these figures, however, as his typical reaction oscillated between a measured excitement and a raw fear of the business of licensing beyond what little he knew.

ORC's first meeting with a suspected infringer took place in the early summer of 1986 in Tarrytown, New York, in the offices of N.A. Philips Corporation. Legal representatives for both N.A. Philips and their Philips parent in Eindhoven, the Netherlands, and for the DuPont Corporation of Wilmington, Delaware, were in attendance. For ORC there were Cooper, Orange, and Adamson and a lawyer from Battelle Laboratories of Columbus, Ohio, Jim Russell's first employer, and the original owner and assignor of the Russell patents, first to SLC and then to ORC.

This first meeting with the Philips and DuPont people ended three and one-half hours later, after a full exchange of views and some acrimony, but no progress toward a licensing agreement. The attorneys representing both Philips and DuPont were of the view that no patents were infringed and further that there was some question about the validity of the Russell patents in the first place. There seemed little point in a further meeting and it seemed very likely that ORC might get no further without filing a patent infringement suit.

In August 1986, Adamson made a first trip to Tokyo on behalf of ORC, with Horne and Russell. A week-long series of company presentations had been arranged by Horne, with the assistance of Far East Associates, a technology licensing agency based in Tokyo, with whom Mr. Horne had collaborated in his Dolby days. Only one prominent manufacturer was invited to each meeting.

On Horne's advice, ORC had booked conference room space at the prestigious Okura Hotel, located directly across from the American Embassy in Minato-ku, a district of central Tokyo. Adamson choked on the daily expense of US$2,000 per day for a meeting room that comfortably held only six people. Horne, however, had stressed the importance of the location to ensure that the status-sensitive Japanese gained the best initial impression of ORC and its business offering.

The ORC team was overwhelmed by the turnout to their presentations. Each firm sent at least four executives and engineers; and in two instances, a group of over 10 people arrived, forcing the ORC team to scramble for a larger meeting room. Many guests recognized Horne from his previous Dolby research licensing days and more than a few appeared quite knowledgeable of Russell's research and patents. In fact, three firms clearly had comprehensive files on Russell's work and appeared very familiar with the technology.

The ORC presentations were made in English. Horne had advised that the executives in the international departments of all Japanese companies were invariably fluent in English. The younger members, however, tended to be more at ease in English, while some of the more experienced guests appeared to be there simply to witness the process and tone of the meeting and to gage the visitors as adversaries. Adamson concluded that some of the groups had arrived en masse, ready to take notes, in order to do a team translation, once they returned to their corporate offices. This would explain the large numbers of guests from some companies.

Nonetheless, this initial series of meetings convinced the ORC team that their patent infringement claims were being taken seriously by the Japanese firms. Apart from Philips, only the Japanese had announced CD player products by the fall of 1986.

During this initial trip by the ORC team to Tokyo, Yoshihide (Josh) Nakamura, then senior general manager, Intellectual Property, Sony Corporation invited the ORC team to Sony's headquarters for another meeting on their next visit to Japan.

Adamson returned to Tokyo with Orange and Horne in November 1986, for another series of presentations and meetings, but this time at each company's offices as prearranged again by Far East Associates. The most important of these meetings was with Sony Corporation, as the ORC team felt certain that Sony's decision on whether to license the Russell patents, would predetermine ORC's success with all other firms in Japan. (It was a Philips-Sony partnership that had launched the compact disc and taught an industry how to make them.)

On a schedule of two and even three meetings each day, including shuttles between companies located around Tokyo and Osaka, the ORC team made 12 more presentations. All discussions were held in English, again with only a perfunctory objection from the Japanese hosts. Everyone appreciated that the United States represented the largest domestic market for the compact disc industry and as Jim Russell had first filed his patents in the United States, it was also likely to be the site of ORC's most comprehensive patent protection.

In fact, ORC's patents were most comprehensive in the United States, Britain and Canada, but appeared to provide a weaker protection in Germany, France and the Netherlands. The prosecution of ORC's patents before the Japanese Patent Office had been stalled for many years, partly due to SLC's lack of funds. As such, while virtually all of the CD players were being manufactured in Japan, apart from those made by Philips, the greatest exposure of these Japanese manufacturers to ORC's claims of infringement lay in their export shipments to North America and Europe. Their shipments within Japan and to the rest of the world would only be exposed if ORC succeeded in getting the Japanese Patent Office to issue a key patent. (ORC never succeeded at having their Japanese patent issued.)

Some firms, including Sony, had gone to the expense of having an U.S. patent attorney present at all meetings with ORC, but Sony appeared the most ready to enter into substantive discussions. In this second round of discussions, Sony's team of six or seven engineers and executives presented ORC with a package of over 25 U.S. patents, all cited as Prior Art against the Russell patents.

PUBLISHING THE "BLUE BOOK"

Adamson had been warned by both Horne and Orange to expect such a patent defense from Sony. He understood that if the techniques that Russell had claimed in his patents as inventions could be found in any reference that had been published or made public prior to the filing of his patents (i.e. Prior Art), Russell's patents would be found "invalid" and unenforceable. In spite of the warnings, Adamson was highly alarmed and wondered whether ORC was in for a challenge.

On returning to Toronto and on the suggestion of Orange, Adamson tasked him to collaborate with Russell in a review of documents that Sony had provided. Orange prepared a technical response for each reference and compiled these results in a bound booklet for distribution to each prospective licensee. Thus, the so-called "Blue Book" was born. It was thought that by making a general distribution of the "Blue Book," any duplication of effort from one set of technical discussions to another could be minimized, while hopefully speeding all talks toward the signing of licenses.

Adamson had no sense whether one or other of the Prior Art references might hold a "golden arrow" that would pierce the assumed validity for the Russell patents. He knew that a patent was generally assumed to be valid as issued, and therefore enforceable before the courts, but any unanswered Prior Art reference could quickly dispose of ORC's credibility and their licensing prospects.

DISTRACTIONS ALONG THE WAY

Adamson had another more urgent reason to wish the licensing talks to progress quickly. As a research firm, ORC was funding its operations from its initial financing, gained through a tax credit program of the Canadian government. With an initial net investment of just Cdn$6.5 million and a monthly "burn-rate" approaching Cdn$250,000 for the research program, Adamson knew that ORC would likely run out of cash by the end of 1987, at the latest. (Luckily for ORC, the mid-1980s were a period of rampant inflation and ORC was earning 10 percent, and 12 percent per annum on its cash hoard.)

To add to the general instability of the situation, the Canadian government, SLC (the firm that had transferred the Russell technology to ORC) and the inventor himself, Russell, were now all objecting to the terms of the agreements that had brought the technology to Toronto. The Canadian government wished to rescind their tax credits and were demanding an immediate cash reimbursement while SLC and Jim Russell were both interpreting their respective agreements in their favor, to secure some respective right to ORC's potential licensing windfall from the compact disc industry.

Adamson remained of the view that all claimants were incorrect in their positions and vowed privately to resist their claims even into bankruptcy. Despite all of these distractions, he also knew that ORC had to maintain the appearance of complete stability, control and competence, in order to avoid "losing face" before their Japanese prospective licensees. Many hours of sleep were lost during this desperate period.

THE SONY PROTOCOL

By their second meeting with ORC, the Sony team were stating that they wished to deal directly with ORC and not through Far East Associates, as Sony reportedly had for their patent license with the Dolby firm. They also indicated that if Sony agreed to a license, they would want the right to act as ORC's exclusive agent to license all other manufacturers based in Japan, for their CD player production. As only Japanese manufacturers were then making CD players, apart from Philips in the Netherlands, this was difficult to agree to, given that ORC had resisted a similar proposal from Far East Associates.

Both the services of Horne and Far East Associates had been contracted on a fee-for-service basis, with ORC retaining all licensing rights to the Russell patents. Both could be terminated without cause in the normal course of business. As consultants, their services were required only as long as the client thought they were adding value. Far East Associates had indicated a desire to assume a full agency role on behalf of ORC with the full authority to license ORC's patents on behalf of ORC, but Adamson had resisted this overture, convinced that ORC would be better served by dealing with each manufacturer directly.

Now Sony was asking ORC to terminate Far East Associates and to make presentations directly to Japanese manufacturers, in anticipation of Sony agreeing to a patent license. This license, however, would only apply to CD players, with Sony assuming the role of exclusive agent, possibly for all of Asia. Adamson accepted this protocol with Sony, but he had to trust that Sony was in earnest in their desire to be the exclusive agent and not just leading ORC toward a dead end.

Further, as with Far East Associates, he had no idea how ORC was to monitor the work and licensing progress of an exclusive agent based in the Far East, directly licensing Asian manufacturers. How was one to know when a license was signed and royalties collected, if not by the exclusive agent? In any case, as co-licenser with Philips of the CD technology, Sony's support was clearly paramount to ORC.

So a pattern developed. Every four to eight weeks, Adamson and Orange traveled to Tokyo, Osaka and other cities in Japan to hold patent infringement and licensing discussions with the major Japanese consumer electronics firms such as Matsushita (Panasonic), Toshiba, Hitachi, Sanyo, Pioneer, Sharp and particularly Sony.

With each visit, new Prior Art references were put forward by one or other of the manufacturers, and ORC, in the person of Orange, would respond "on the fly" if an obvious separation from the art could be discerned. If not, ORC would fax a response to all participants upon returning to Toronto.

As the months passed, it was becoming increasingly clear to all that the Russell patents as presented by the ORC team, could withstand the invalidity challenges from the Prior Art. Equally important, the compact disc technical standard that ensured manufactured compatibility across all compliant CD products included techniques claimed in the Russell patents. To comply with this CD standard was to infringe the Russell patents! In short it appeared that the Russell patents were valid and infringed by all CD products!

To balance this rosy picture, however, it was equally clear that, month by month, ORC's cash was disappearing into its research program. The company had lost any of the financial strength with which to mount a credible court challenge against even one of the established manufacturers: Sony, Philips or any of the twenty other firms of similar bulk.

THE END GAME?

Finally in the fall of 1987, Adamson realized that neither Sony nor any other firm was likely to accept a license without more pressure being applied and more pressure than ORC could bring to the negotiating table. With nothing left to lose, Adamson flew to Tokyo in mid-January 1988, for a final meeting with Sony Corporation. No other firm was as advanced in discussions with ORC as Sony and Adamson reasoned that Sony had become fairly certain of the profit potential as ORC's master licensee for Japan. Sony would also have something to lose if the talks with ORC failed.

To add to this pressure, he could advise Sony that ORC was close to bankruptcy and, if ORC went into bankruptcy, the Russell patents would revert to their former owner, SLC, a firm that, in his direct experience, proved to be very litigious. The Sony team requested a lunch break.

Over lunch Josh Nakamura asked Adamson whether he would continue to be involved with the Russell patent licensing if ORC went bankrupt. Adamson replied that while his ownership of the patents would be lost, he could no doubt strike a deal with SLC such that the licensing program would not "skip a beat." However the program would then be well financed by a very litigious American backer and, under the circumstances, Adamson would have little interest in favoring Sony in any way. Given his rocky relations with SLC, Adamson painted a most optimistic view of his future.

Returning to the Sony offices after lunch, the Sony team requested a further break and Adamson and Cooper sat quietly for an hour and a half in the meeting room at the Sony corporate head offices in Kita-Shinagawa; Adamson pondering his fate.

ORC'S FIRST LICENSE

Back in the meeting, Nakamura advised that Sony would be ready to sign a license with ORC. The license, however, would only cover CD players, not compact disc media. Further, ORC had to significantly reduce their royalty demands, accept Sony as the exclusive agent with full authority to license all CD player manufacturers based in Asia and pay Sony an administrative fee for their exclusive agency representation out of the royalties to be received. The proposal also required that ORC transfer the right to sue Asian CD player manufacturers for patent infringement to Sony as their exclusive agent. Adamson felt he had no choice but to accept this proposal if he wished to maintain his control of the Russell patents.

It was then agreed that the outline of the license and agency agreements be developed that very afternoon with a final negotiation of royalty rates to occur by telephone in the following week. Cooper took on the task of drafting the required changes to ORC's standard patent license agreement. Negotiations were then completed by telephone the following week and the Sony CD player agreement was signed in early February 1988.

From this shaky last-minute effort, Adamson had managed to retain his full ownership of the Russell patents through ORC. By licensing Sony, ORC now had a royalty cash flow with which to maintain the research program underway in Toronto, as well as the resources to fend off the lawsuits from the Government of Canada and SLC. For the first time in its existence, ORC was cash flow positive and in that sense, time was now on ORC's side; however, when measured against industry norms, the license with Sony cost ORC plenty. Nakamura and the Sony team had done their job well.

Apart from Sony's hard bargain, they were always gracious but now as business partners, Nakamura and Sony's negotiating team seemed to relish this role even more.

Adamson came to look forward to an invitation to dine at one restaurant in particular. High above Akasaka in central Tokyo, directly overlooking the Diet, Japan's national parliament, there was a restaurant laid out in a series of private dining rooms, each in a unique Western décor of a particular color and at least one Monet or similar Old Master painting dominating the room. Their chefs were trained at the Paul Bocuse culinary school in France and the wine list read like a vintners' award booklet.

Adamson also came to realize that the superb ambiance and staff service of the Hotel Okura was very habit-forming and in spite of the expense, he opted to stay there whenever he was in Tokyo. Horne had been right. Being invited to lunch or dinner at the Hotel Okura, was also a great treat for ORC's licensing prospects and other business associates in Tokyo.

ONWARD

Among the more difficult challenges that ORC faced in mounting the licensing program was the determination of the size of the infringing production unit volumes and sales revenues. A prospective licensee is not about to divulge this data, as it would impair their negotiating position and possibly increase their chances of being sued before one of their competitors. Nevertheless in the case of CD media, it was pretty obvious that the five sisters of sound; Philips (Deutsche Grammophon), Sony (Columbia), Time Warner (Warner), EMI (London and Angel) and Bertelsmann (RCA) were the largest manufacturers of CD media. After Philips and Sony, Time Warner was likely to be the largest compact disc maker in the United States.

Government agencies and industry trade associations publish trade statistics, but this data is usually on an industrywide basis (not by company) and for broad product categories, not for individual products, such as a CD player. Beyond these sources, there are industry consultants of varying usefulness and reliability. Nevertheless the licenser must develop estimates of the production and sales volumes for the infringing product by manufacturer and for each year from the start of the infringement to the expiry of the patent or the end of the infringement, whichever comes first.

Without such numbers it is not possible to decide which companies are the more lucrative licensing prospects and more importantly whether a licensing program is even feasible. Without this data the licenser cannot know which infringer to sue or in which jurisdiction to bring the suit, to ensure the most favorable cost-benefit ratio for such an action.

In the ensuing 12 months, Sony sub-licensed over 50 percent of the remaining Japanese production for CD players and ORC began to develop a substantial "war-chest." Still unresolved were ORC's equivalent infringement claims against the manufacturers of the discs, the compact disc media. Sony had refused to include this item in the initial license as they advised that they needed more time to study the matter. They also stated the view that the Russell patents were less likely to be infringed by the discs.

In the summer of 1988, however, ORC succeeded in licensing the Philips Corporation for both CD players and media and with this success, somewhat confirming Sony's earlier license commitment, Sony agreed to sign a license for CD media in November 1988. By the end of 1988, ORC had a cash position well in excess of US$10 million and the licensing program was on a roll.

The next largest manufacturer of CD media in the United States, by production volume, after American subsidiaries of Sony and Philips-Dupont, was known to be WEA Manufacturing, a subsidiary of Time Warner Inc. Commencing in 1987, Adamson held several discussions, by mail, telephone and face-to-face meetings, with Time Warner's in-house counsel. These discussions led nowhere however as Time Warner's often-repeated view was the standard "non-infringement and invalid patents" position of an alleged infringer.

ENFORCING ORC'S PATENT RIGHTS

In early 1990, ORC had retained Davis Hoxie Faithfull & Hapgood, a patent law firm, just next door to Time Warner's corporate head office in the Rockefeller Centre in New York City. Charles Bradley, a senior patent litigating attorney with Davis Hoxie had been recommended to Adamson on a chance encounter, while in Tokyo, with an American attorney who had the misfortune of opposing Bradley in a previous patent case. Bradley and Lawrence Goodwin, his partner, were engaged to pursue ORC's interests with the respect to the alleged infringement by WEA Manufacturing, a subsidiary of Time Warner Inc. Goodwin became the "lead" attorney on the ORC file with Bradley providing oversight, senior counsel and strategic advice to Goodwin.

On ORC's behalf, the Davis Hoxie firm filed a patent infringement complaint against WEA Manufacturing in the Federal District Court in Wilmington, Delaware, in June 1990. Like many other major American corporations, Time Warner and its subsidiary, WEA Manufacturing, were incorporated in the State of Delaware.

Not the least of Adamson's concerns in deciding to sue Time Warner in early 1991, was a looming patent expiry date in July 1992, for a U.S. patent, the key to ORC's infringement claims against CD media manufacturers.

The greatest threat that a patent-holder has against a recalcitrant infringer is a court injunction to stop the infringer's production lines. By 1991, this threat was all but lost to ORC as the July 1992 expiry date of ORC's key U.S. patent was likely to pass before any court could rule on the matter.

Without the threat of a court order to stop an infringing production, the patent-holder's leverage is reduced to the probability of a favorable court award being considerably more arduous for the infringer than the royalty payable if a license had been accepted. Even this leverage is diminished by the reality that, at any time prior to an appeal court ruling on a lower court award, the infringer is free to negotiate a settlement with the licenser, even well past a court decision which declares them to be infringing. The infringer can also hope that the patent-holder will capitulate before the end of a full trial, for lack of sufficient funds.

These considerations were very much on Adamson's mind in March 1992 as he drafted a letter (see Exhibit 1) to be sent directly to Time Warner's in-house counsel with a copy to Goodwin. Goodwin had advised against sending the letter, given that ORC had filed their patent infringement suit against Time Warner almost two years earlier, however, Adamson felt certain that Time Warner should be willing to settle for the modest sum of US$3 million, just to avoid the patent infringement trial now scheduled for June 1992, with all of its costs and disruption. Of no surprise to Goodwin, Time Warner politely declined ORC's settlement proposal, perhaps thinking that the letter was a clear indication that ORC was about to capitulate, if they had not already, with their modest US$3 million settlement offer.

WILL THEY LIKE US IN WILMINGTON?

Now faced with the certainty of a trial in the United States, Adamson had to deal with a personal overriding concern. Could an American jury be prejudiced against a Canadian company such as ORC? Goodwin had told him not to worry about it, but Adamson was concerned that Goodwin simply did not know.

Too embarrassed to advise Goodwin of his continuing concern with a potential American prejudice toward a Canadian company, Adamson hired the New York office of Goldfarb Consultants, a Canadian market survey firm. Their assignment was to conduct an opinion survey on attitudes, toward Canadian companies, of people drawn from the "jury-pool" population around Wilmington, Delaware. The Goldfarb team suggested that they conduct this survey with focus group interviews based on a set of questions pre-cleared by ORC.

In April 1992, Adamson traveled to Wilmington to witness the interviews first-hand by watching the proceedings on a video monitor in an adjacent room. There

EXHIBIT 1   Draft Letter to Time Warner's In-house Counsel

CONFIRMATION ONLY

FACSIMILE MESSAGE OF TWO PAGES TO: 1 (212) 522-1252

March 4, 1992

WITHOUT PREJUDICE

Dear

RE: ORC vs Time Warner Inc.

Over the past week, we have prepared estimates on the costs and probable outcome of this case. We share this information with you now, in the hope of developing a common understanding from which a mutually satis-factory settlement might result. Our New York counsel is aware of this communication but, the views ex-pressed here may not necessarily coincide with theirs.

Assuming that your costs to date equal ours, Time Warner has spent US$1,000,000 in out-of-pocket expenses alone. Assuming that we will each spend another US$1,000,000. to the end of trial and then another US$200,000 on an appeal, we will each have spent another US$1,200,000. for a total of US$2,200,000 on this case. Give or take a few $100,000, these costs have a 100% probability of being incurred, if we proceed.

As to the outcome, it is our view that ORC has a significantly stronger case, as Justice Farnan's recent rulings might suggest. Further, we have substantial confidence in our representation. Nevertheless, we accept that the trial process is highly unpredictable. Therefore, we would attach a conservative estimate of perhaps 50% to the probability of ORC winning at both, trial and appeal.

Our licensing program had been based on the royalty rate of US$0.015 per disk and against the estimated and actual production totals for WEA and Allied of 400 million disks, a royalty amount of US$6,000,000 can be estimated. The size of award by the court could vary up or down from this royalty estimate but, it is our view that US$6,000,000 is a good average to assume of all possible court awards. If we assume a 50% probability that ORC will win, then it follows that there is a 50% probability that Time Warner will be required to pay the average award of US$6,000,000.

OPTICAL RECORDING CORPORATION

141 JOHN STREET, TORONTO, CANADA M5V 2E4 • TELEPHONE (416) 596-6862 • FAX (416) 596-0452

EXHIBIT 1 (Continued)

OPTICAL RECORDING CORPORATION

-2-

To summarize, at this point in time, Time Warner has a 50% probability of paying out $6,000,000 in award and a 100% probability of paying $1,200,000 in continuing litigation costs, if we proceed.

We believe that a final attempt at settlement is in the interest of both companies at this time. Therefore, we now propose a patent license to Time Warner for their manufacture of Compact Disc in the United States, for $3,000,000.: that is, for 50% of the $6,000,000. which we contend that Time Warner has at least a 50% probability of incurring as a court award.

This offer will remain open until 5:00 pm, Friday, March 6, 1992, after which, this and all previous offers will be withdrawn.

We would appreciate your comments on the logic presented here, particularly if you have a significantly divergent view on any point. Please feel free to call me directly if you wish to discuss any point in this letter.

Yours very truly,

G. John Adamson
President

GJA/gj

Source: Company files.

were three sessions comprising a total of 35 participants, who gave up a part of their evening for the survey in return for dinner and a modest stipend.

The interviews were conducted in two parts. The first part was designed to solicit an unprompted reference to Canada, in its role as a trading partner of the United States. The second part was designed to solicit directly any opinions that they may hold toward Canadian companies and then specifically a Canadian company's right to protect their American rights by suing an American company in Delaware.

The survey was of great benefit to Adamson as it quickly became clear that he should not be concerned about an American prejudice toward Canadian companies. If a prejudice did exist, it could only be positive because the survey, in every focus group, turned into a love-fest for Canada and Canadians.

Each focus group became frustrated with the first part of the survey. In trying to find the trading partner that they might be concerned about, Canada was never mentioned, even in their desperate attempts to finally yell out the "correct answer."

This desperation was then followed by groans when Canada was finally noted by the session moderator at the beginning of the second part of the survey. Very few of those surveyed knew that Canada was indeed the largest trading partner of the United States.

With Canada now on the table and not hiding as in a trick question, many positive views were openly expressed. In fact more than a few had vacationed in Canada, some had close Canadian relatives and one woman was so effusive as to simply say, "I love Canadians," quickly adding that she and her husband vacationed regularly in the Montreal area.

A little sheepishly, Adamson returned to Toronto and phoned Goodwin to advise him that "the ball was now in his court" and that ORC would see the Time Warner case through to appeal, if necessary. He did not mention the survey.

THE RUBBER MEETS THE ROAD

Lead by Goodwin, the Davis Hoxie team was comprised of one other full-time attorney, Robert Cote, and a support staff of three, all of whom stayed in Wilmington for the duration of the trial (with some weekends at home in New York). This Delaware team worked from the offices of a Wilmington law firm. This law firm in turn provided its own legal and support staff to ORC's team on an as-required basis. At Davis Hoxie in New York, at least one additional full-time attorney, Peter Bucci, and various other support staff were employed in research and document preparation for the duration of the trial. This entire trial effort was monitored and when appropriate, coached by Charles Bradley.

The trial began in the last days of May 1992, and it was to run for five and one-half weeks. Throughout the trial period, the Davis Hoxie team worked a daily double shift, one in courtroom and then a second in their law offices and hotel rooms, debriefing the day's events and preparing for the next day's court sessions. This preparation included a review of salient facts, prior affidavits, deposition testimony and then general court procedures with each individual witness, in preparation for the court appearance.

It also included a daily review of defendant witness testimony for discrepancies. The review of the court plan for the following day might include witness questioning, preparing motions that pulled together now-important facts and revising presentation materials imperiled by the day's events.

Adamson had decided to remain in Wilmington and attend every court session, given the importance of its outcome for ORC. Having watched the jury selection a few days before, he was highly stressed on the morning of the first day of the trial. He took some comfort in the size and evident competence of the Davis Hoxie team until the Time Warner team appeared.

Either by chance or design, 20 minutes prior to the official court start-time, opposing attorneys began to file into the courtroom. First they filled to overflowing the small defendant's bench in front of the commons rail, and then gradually they occupied the entire commons observer section on the defendant side of the courtroom, spacing themselves comfortably. Adamson sat as a lone observer for ORC directly behind the Davis Hoxie team of five on the plaintiff's side until three more groups of attorneys whom he had never met, filed in to sit behind him, also on the plaintiff's side.

Possibly the entire recording industry, including a few Japanese firms with still unlicensed CD plants in the United States, had sent attorneys, some 30 in all, to observe the start of the trial. The contrast between the sizes of the defendant and plaintiff legal teams was so evident that, prior to the jury entrance, lead counsel for Time Warner told the attorneys behind him to scatter into the plaintiff's observer benches.

Apparently unfazed by the obvious imbalance, a few minutes later, Goodwin stood up to address judge, jury and courtroom on behalf of ORC in a calm, humble but masterful tone. He was to continue as he had started through five and one-half weeks of trial, through surprise, setback, equipment failure, client panic and one or two staff confusions.

ORC's case was further strengthened by the skill of a superb expert witness, Leonard Laub. Laub was responsible for explaining ORC's highly technical infringement case, to a jury with no technical training except for one retired man with an engineering degree dating back to the 1930s. This was accomplished with Laub's testimony guided by questioning from Goodwin and with the use of circuit diagram blow-ups and point summaries on white three feet by five feet storyboards. Adamson was satisfied that if there were a chance that the jury could come to understand ORC's case, it would be solely through the ample teaching skills of Goodwin and Laub.

ORC asked the court and jury for an award in lieu of royalty of six cents per disc against Time Warner and their American subsidiaries and a tripling of that award in punitive damages for willful infringement. The decision to ask for six cents per disc was partly based on ORC's initial licensing request of three cents per disc. Legally, licensers are able to change their royalty demands at any point in a negotiation, before or after the filing of a suit, just as infringers are free to agree to previously unacceptable terms.

(In normal licensing practice, it is simply wise to give active infringers, some substantial incentive to sign a license prior to the filing of a suit. This is usually accomplished by increasing the royalty rate by some multiple of the original, say 2, 3, 5 or even 10 times. The practical upper limit of a royalty rate is, of course, at that point where the manufacturer can make little profit after paying the royalty, as it is unlikely that any judge or jury would endorse a more onerous royalty request.)

Hearing Goodwin make this request for six cents per disc in open court was a thrilling moment early in the trial. Weeks later the Time Warner attorney was obliged to produce for the court, the unit volumes of their subsidiary's infringing production of compact discs. Their infringement for the period covering the start of production in 1986 through July 1992, the month of the expiry of ORC's patent, totalled over 450 million discs and, at six cents per disc, represented a potential court award for ORC of over US$27 million. The addition of pre-judgment interest and a possible tripling of those damages were more than Adamson could fathom or entertain.

In spite of the good efforts of the Davis Hoxie team with Laub and several other strong witnesses, including Russell, the inventor, and the prospect of an enormous court award, all was not well. After the court appearance by the Philips attorney, Adamson believed that ORC's decision to sue Time Warner might have been taken too lightly.

Goodwin had warned that corporate litigation in the United States was a very expensive enterprise. It was also very demanding of management time, given the need to find, assemble and organize relevant business records, to educate the attorneys in the minutiae of events that usually had happened long ago and to attend court hearings as observers and witnesses. He had also noted that, in the normal course of a robust cross-examination, the combatants and their witnesses could expect personal insults and general verbal abuse. Adamson observed somewhat ruefully that Goodwin had been correct on all counts.

Preliminary motions, production and review of plaintiff and defendant business records and correspondence files, witness depositions, private investigators and trial preparations for the attorneys, company personnel and expert witnesses had already consumed close to US$750,000 of ORC's hard won royalties all before the actual trial had begun. Adamson had budgeted an additional US$1.5 million for fees and expenses to be incurred from the trial itself; however, after the first three weeks of the trial, Adamson saw no end in sight to the trial or its expense.

As was its right as the plaintiff, ORC had chosen to have its case against Time Warner heard before a jury. Even this decision seemed to backfire as it was clear that the jury was putting a good deal of attention and apparent credence into what the defendant's attorneys had to say. The Time Warner litigating team had mounted a very credible defense. They seemed to cloud the technical issues of patent validity and product infringement as these related to the Russell patent claims and the compact disc technology, so that even Adamson found himself confused with ORC's claims from time to time. He had little hope left that the jury would be able to sort through the haze.

With this technical complexity and possible jury confusion, Adamson worried that the direct and damning statements of the Philips attorney toward the Russell patents and ORC's infringement claims could be disastrous for ORC, as these arguments gave the jury, a reasonable and easy "out," from all the confusing technical jargon. Perhaps he was simply someone who knew better about these matters than they could ever hope to know.

Adamson also reflected on the fact that he had been forced to curtail the ongoing licensing program for the other CD manufacturers. He had been concerned that some event within ORC's licensing program, such as an agreement with a royalty rate for CD discs below the six cents per disc demanded in the court case, might affect the outcome of the case; however this concern was made moot by the simple fact that the other CD manufacturers had displayed little interest in signing a license with ORC as long as a major record company such as Time Warner was challenging ORC's infringement claims in court.

Should the court case result in anything less than a complete endorsement of ORC's infringement claims, ORC's entire licensing program could collapse including the all important quarterly payments from Sony. The CD player license with Sony may have been a "done deal." As a matter of practicality, Adamson wondered whether ORC would be prudent to take Sony to court, should Sony simply stop paying royalties to ORC after a jury verdict had cleared Time Warner of ORC's patent infringement claims.

Over the course of the six years from 1986 to 1992, Adamson had been drawn away from ORC's research effort and future prospects and ever deeper into patent licensing and then this litigation struggle. As he had testified in the Time Warner trial, "there seems little point in investing in the creation and development of new intellectual property rights if major industrial firms are prepared to ignore and infringe existing patent rights that you already own." Playing somewhat to the jury, he knew that he had purposefully overstated his predicament but the basic truth of his simple observation resonated in the momentary silence of the court that day.

Adamson had made the very difficult decision early in 1991, to temporarily shelve ORC's research program and to reduce the Company's technology development team to a skeleton staff of five team leaders. This move had been made for reasons other than the need to focus the Company's resources on the Time Warner litigation. Nonetheless as he sat in that Delaware courtroom, watching the door close after the hasty exit of the Philips attorney, Adamson felt that he had bet ORC's entire future on the outcome of the court case against Time Warner.

Endnote

1. Due to a series of commercial lawsuits lasting 10 years with Russell's former employer, the author prefers to omit any real name reference to this company that had been a party to the technology transfer agreements with ORC. It is referred to here as "SLC." In all other references herein to persons, places or businesses, the actual names are used.

Chapter Twenty-Seven

General Motors and AvtoVAZ of Russia

To compete on technology, you have to spend on it, but we have nothing to spend. Were there a normal economic situation in the country, people wouldn't be buying these cars.

Vladimir Kadannikov, Chairman, AvtoVAZ of Russia.

There are 42 defects in the average new car from AvtoVAZ, Russia's biggest carmaker. And that counts as the good news. When the firm introduced a new model last year, a compact salon called the VAZ-2110, each car came with 92 defects—all the fun of the space station Mir, as it were, without leaving the ground.

"Mir On Earth," *The Economist,* August 21, 1997.

In June 2001, David Herman, President of General Motors (GM) Russia, and his team arrived in Togliatti, Russia for joint venture negotiations between GM and OAO AvtoVAZ, the largest automobile producer in Russia. GM and AvtoVAZ had originally signed a memorandum of understanding (MOU)—a nonbinding commitment—on March 3, 1999, to pursue a joint venture in Russia. Now, nearly two years later, Herman had finally received GM's approval to negotiate the detailed structure of the joint venture (JV) with AvtoVAZ to produce and sell Chevrolets in the Russian market.

THUNDERBIRD
THE AMERICAN GRADUATE SCHOOL
OF INTERNATIONAL MANAGEMENT

The Russian car market was expected to account for a significant share of global growth over the next decade. Herman was increasingly convinced that if GM did not move decisively and soon, the market opportunity would be lost to other automakers. Ford, for example, was proceeding with a substantial JV in Russia and was scheduled to begin producing the Ford Focus in late 2002 (it was already importing car kits). Fiat of Italy was already in the construction phase of a plant to build 15,000 Fiat Palios per year beginning in late 2002. Daewoo of Korea had started assembly of compact sedan kits in 1998 and were currently selling 15,000 cars a year.

However, Herman also knew that doing business in Russia presented many challenges. The Russian economy, although recovering from the 1998 collapse, remained weak, uncertain, and subject to confusing tax laws and government rules. The Russian car industry seemed to reel from one crisis to another. The second largest automobile producer, GAZ, had been the victim of an unexpected hostile takeover only three months ago. GAZ's troubles had contributed to GM's fears over the actual ownership of AvtoVAZ itself. In addition, AvtoVAZ had been the subject of an aggressive income tax evasion case by Russian tax authorities in the summer of 2000. Finally, from a manufacturing point of view, AvtoVAZ was far from world class. AvtoVAZ averaged 320 man-hours to build a car, a stark comparison against the 28 hours typical of Western Europe and 17 hours in Japan.

Further complicating the situation was a lack of consensus within different parts of GM about the Russian JV. GM headquarters in Detroit had told Herman to find a third party to share the risk and the investment of a Russian JV. Within Adam Opel, GM's European division, there were questions about the scope and timing of Opel's role. Prior to becoming GM's vice president for the former Soviet Union, Herman had been chairman of Adam Opel. Now, Herman needed Opel's support for the Russian JV and had to convince his former colleagues that the time was right to enter Russia. As he prepared for the upcoming negotiations, Herman knew there were many more battles to be fought, both within GM and in Russia.

GENERAL MOTORS CORPORATION

General Motors Corporation (US), founded in 1908, was the largest automobile manufacturer in the world. GM employed more than 388,000 people, operated 260 subsidiaries, affiliates, and joint ventures, managed operations in more than 50 countries, and closed the year 2000 with $160 billion in sales and $4.4 billion in profits.

John F. "Jack" Smith had been appointed Chairman of GM's Board of Directors in January 1996, after spending the previous five years as President and Chief Executive Officer. Taking Jack Smith's place as President and CEO was G. Richard "Rick" Wagoner, Jr., previously the director of strategic and operational leadership within GM. GM's International Operations were divided into GM Europe, GM Asia Pacific, and GM Latin America, Africa, Middle-East. GM Europe, headquartered in Zurich, Switzerland, provided oversight for GM's various European operations including Opel of Germany and the new initiatives in Russia.

Although the largest automobile manufacturer in the world, GM's market share had been shrinking. By the end of 2000, GM's global market share (in units) was 13.6 percent, with the Ford group closing quickly with a 11.9 percent share, and Volkswagen a close third at 11.5 percent. Emerging markets, like that of Russia, represented so-called "white territories" which were still unclaimed and uncertain markets for the traditional Western automakers.

THE RUSSIAN AUTOMOBILE INDUSTRY

The Russian auto industry lagged far behind that of the Western European, North American, or Japanese industries. Although the Russian government had made it a clear priority to aid in the industry's modernization and development, inadequate capital, poor infrastructure, and deep-seated mismanagement and corruption resulted in outdated, unreliable, and unsafe automobiles.

Nevertheless, the industry was considered promising because of the continuing gap between Russian market demand and supply and because of expected future growth in demand. As illustrated in Exhibit 1, between 1991 and 1993 purchases of cars in Russia had grown dramatically. But, this growth had been at the expense of domestic producers, as imports had garnered most of the increase in sales, largely because of a reduction in automobile import duties. With the reduction of import duties in 1993, imports surged to 49 percent of sales and Russian production hit the lowest level of the decade. Domestic producers reacted by increasing their focus on export sales, largely to former Commonwealth of Independent

EXHIBIT 1   The Russian Automobile Industry, 1991–1999 (units)

Russian Production	1991	1992	1993	1994	1995	1996	1997	1998	1999
AvtoVAZ	677,280	676,857	660,275	530,876	609,025	684,241	748,826	605,728	717,660
GAZ	69,000	69,001	105,654	118,159	118,673	124,284	124,339	125,398	125,486
AvtoUAZ	52,491	54,317	57,604	53,178	44,880	33,701	51,411	37,932	38,686
Moskovich	104,801	101,870	95,801	67,868	40,600	2,929	20,599	38,320	30,112
KamAZ	3,114	4,483	5,190	6,118	8,638	8,935	19,933	19,102	28,004
IzhMash	123,100	56,500	31,314	21,718	12,778	9,146	5,544	5,079	4,756
DonInvest	0	0	0	0	321	4,062	13,225	4,988	9,395
Other	14	14	6	7	1	41	3,932	3,061	1,307
Total	1,029,800	963,042	955,844	797,924	834,916	867,339	985,809	839,608	955,406
Percent change	−6.6%	−6.5%	−0.7%	−16.5%	4.6%	3.9%	13.7%	−14.8%	13.8%
Russian Exports	411,172	248,032	533,452	143,814	181,487	144,774	120,551	67,913	107,701
Percent of production	39.9%	25.8%	55.8%	18.0%	21.7%	16.7%	12.2%	8.1%	11.3%
Imports into Russia	26,649	43,477	405,061	97,400	69,214	54,625	42,974	62,718	55,701
Percent of sales	4.1%	5.7%	49.0%	13.0%	9.6%	7.0%	4.7%	7.5%	6.2%
Auto Sales in Russia	645,277	758,487	827,453	751,510	722,643	777,190	908,232	834,413	903,406
Percent growth		17.5%	9.1%	−9.2%	−3.8%	7.5%	16.9%	−8.1%	8.3%

Source: www.just-auto.com, February 2001.

States (CIS) countries. Exports ranged between 18 percent and 56 percent of all production during the 1991–95 period.

With the reimposition of import duties in 1994, the import share of the Russian marketplace returned to a level of about 7 percent to 10 percent. Domestic production began growing again and fewer Russian-made cars were exported. Unfortunately, just as domestic producers were nearly back to early-1990s production levels, the 1998 financial crisis sent the Russian economy and auto industry into a tailspin. Domestic production of automobiles fell nearly 15 percent in 1998. Auto sales in Russia as a whole fell 8 percent. The industry, however, experienced a strong resurgence in 1999 and 2000.

Russian auto manufacturing was highly concentrated, with AvtoVAZ holding a 65 percent market share in 2000, followed by GAZ with 13 percent, and an assorted collection of what could be called "boutique producers."[1] Although foreign producers accounted for less than 2 percent of all auto manufacturing in Russia in 2000, estimates of the influx of used foreign-made cars were upwards of 350,000 units in 2000 alone.

Although much had changed in Russia in the 1990s, much had also remained the same. In the Russian automobile market, demand greatly exceeded supply. Russians without the right political connections had to wait years for their cars. Cars were still rare, spare parts still difficult to find, and crime still rampant. It was still not unusual to remove windshield wipers for safekeeping from cars parked on major city streets. Cars had to be paid for in cash, as dealer financing was essentially unheard of as a result of the inability of the Russian financial and banking sector to perform adequate credit checks on individuals or institutions. And once paid for, most Russian-made new cars were full of defects to the point that repair was often required before a new car could be driven.

AvtoVAZ

It's mind-blowingly huge. The assembly line goes on for a mile and a quarter. Workstation after workstation. No modules being slapped in. It's piece by piece. The hammering is incessant. Hammering the gaskets in, hammering the doors down, hammering the bumpers. On the engine line a man seems to be screwing in pistons by hand and whopping them with a hammer. If there's a robot on the line, we didn't see it. Forget statistical process control.

"Would You Want to Drive a Lada?" Forbes, *August 26, 1996.*

AvtoVAZ, originally called VAZ for Volzhsky Avtomobilny Zavod (Volga Auto Factory), was headquartered approximately 1,000 kilometers southeast of Moscow in Togliatti, a town named after an Italian communist. The original auto manufacturing facility was a JV (in effect, a pure turn-key operation) with Fiat of Italy. The original contract, signed in 1966, resulted in the first cars produced in 1970. The cars produced at the factory were distributed under the *Lada* and *Zhiguli* brands and for the next 20 years became virtually the only car the average Russian could purchase.

AvtoVAZ employed more than 250,000 people in 1999 (who were paid an average of $333 per month), and produced 677,700 cars, $1.9 billion in sales, and $458 million in gross profits. However, the company had a pre-tax loss of $123 million. AvtoVAZ was publicly listed on the Moscow Stock Exchange. The Togliatti auto plant, with an estimated capacity of 750,000 vehicles per year, was the largest single automobile assembly facility in the world. It had reached full capacity in 2000. But the company developed only one new car in the 1990s and had spent an estimated $2 billion doing so.

In the early 1990s, following the era of Perestroika and the introduction of economic reforms, AvtoVAZ began upgrading its technology and increasing its prices. As prices skyrocketed, Russians quickly switched to comparably-priced imports of higher quality. As a result, AvtoVAZ suffered continual decreases in market share throughout the 1990s (see Exhibit 1), although it still dominated all other Russian manufacturers.

The financial crisis of August 1998 had actually bolstered AvtoVAZ's market position, with the fall of the rouble from Rbl 11/$ to over Rbl 25/$. Imports were now prohibitively expensive for most Russians.

It's cynical to say, but in the case of a devaluation, the situation at AvtoVAZ would be better. There would be a different effectiveness of export sales, and demand would be different. Seeing that money is losing value, people would buy durable goods in the hopes of saving at least something.

Vladimir Kadannikov, Chairman of the Board, AvtoVAZ, May 1998.

In recent years, AvtoVAZ senior management had been discussing the development of a more modern car that could be exported to developed countries. This car, called the Kalina, would require an investment of as much as $850 million. AvtoVAZ Chairman Vladimir Kadannikov had stated publicly that he hoped commercial production of the Kalina could begin by 2004. He had also indicated that he was receptive to the Kalina being produced in a joint venture with an outsider automaker.

AvtoVAZ also suffered from tax problems and was called a "tax deadbeat" by the Russian press. In July 2000 the Russian Tax Police accused AvtoVAZ of tax fraud. The accusations centered on alleged under-reporting of automobile production by falsifying vehicle identification numbers (VINs), the basis for the state's assessment of taxes. The opening of the criminal case coincided with warnings from the Kremlin that the new administration of President Vladimir Putin would not tolerate continued industry profiteering and manipulation from the country's *oligarchs,* individuals who had profited greatly from Russia's difficult transition to market capitalism. AvtoVAZ denied the charges and less than one month later, the case was thrown out by the chief prosecutor for tax evasion. A spokesman for the prosecutor's office stated that investigators had found no basis for the allegations against AvtoVAZ executives.

EXHIBIT 2
AvtoVAZ's Webs of
Infuence and
Ownership

Source: Adapted from
www.just-auto.com

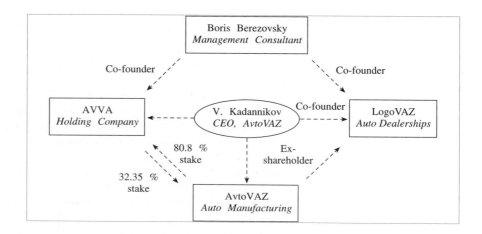

AvtoVAZ Ownership

One of the primary deterrents to foreign investment in Russia had been the relatively lax legal and regulatory structure for corporate governance. Identifying the owners of most major Russian companies was extremely difficult.

Although the exact ownership of AvtoVAZ remained unclear, two different management groups controlled the majority of AvtoVAZ shares. One group, the All-Russian Automobile Alliance (AVVA) was based in Moscow and led by Mr. Yuri Zektser. AVVA held 32.35 percent of total shares. A second group, the Automobile Finance Corporation (AFC), owned 19.19 percent. Two other groups, OAO Russ-Invest and ZAO Depository Center, owned 5.45 percent and 5.05 percent, respectively. The remainder of the shares were widely held. AvtoVAZ itself held an 80.8 percent interest in AVVA (see Exhibit 2 for an overview of the complex relationships surrounding AvtoVAZ). AVVA itself was in some way influenced, controlled, or owned in part by one of the most high profile oligarchs in Russia, Boris Berezovsky.

In 1989, prior to the implementation of President Boris Yelstin's economic reforms, Boris Berezovsky, a mathematician and management-systems consultant to AvtoVAZ, persuaded Vladimir Kadannikov to cooperate in a new car distribution system. Berezovsky formed an automobile dealer network, LogoVAZ that was supplied with AvtoVAZ vehicles on consignment. LogoVAZ did not pay for the cars it distributed (termed "re-export" by Berezovsky) until a date significantly after his dealer network sold the cars and received payment themselves. The arrangement proved disastrous for AvtoVAZ and incredibly profitable for Berezovsky. In the years that followed, hyperinflation raged in Russia, and Berezovsky was able to run his expanding network of businesses with AvtoVAZ's cash flow. (Mr. Berezovsky has admitted to the arrangement, and its financial benefits to him. He has also pointed out, correctly, that under Russian law he has not broken any laws.) LogoVAZ was also one of the largest auto importers in Russia.

In 1994, the Russian government began privatizing many state-owned companies, including AvtoVAZ. Boris Berezovsky, Vladimir Kadannikov, and Alexander

Voloshin, recently appointed Chief of Staff for Russian President Vladimir Putin, then formed AVVA. The stated purpose of AVVA was to begin building a strong dealer network for the automobile industry in Russia. AVVA quickly acquired its 32.35 percent interest in AvtoVAZ, in addition to many other enterprises. AVVA frequently represented AvtoVAZ's significant international interests around the world.

By 2000, Berezovsky purportedly no longer had formal relations with AVVA, but many observers believed he continued to have a number of informal lines of influence. In December 2000, AVVA surprised many analysts by announcing that it was amending its charter to change its status from an *investment fund* to a *holding company*. Auto analysts speculated that AVVA was positioning itself to run AvtoVAZ, which had reorganized into divisions (car production, marketing and sales, research and development).

Share ownership anxiety had intensified in November 2000 when the second largest automobile manufacturer in Russia, GAZ, had been the victim of a hostile takeover. Beginning in August 2000, Sibirsky Alyuminiy (SibAl) started accumulating shares in GAZ until reaching the 25 percent plus one share threshold necessary for veto power under Russian law. The exact amount of SibAl ownership in GAZ, however, was unknown, even to GAZ. Current regulations required only the disclosure of the identity and stake of stockholders of 5 percent equity stake or more. Only direct investors were actually named, and those named were frequently only agents operating on behalf of the true owners. Adding to the confusion was the fact that frequently the "nominees" named represented multiple groups of ultimate owners. The inadequacy of information about ownership in Russia was demonstrated by GAZ's inability to actually confirm whether SibAl did indeed have a 25 percent ownership position.

Rumors surfaced immediately that AvtoVAZ could be next, and the threat could arise from the Samara Window Company (abbreviated as SOK), AvtoVAZ's largest single supplier. Many industry players, however, viewed this as highly unlikely.

Besides Kadannikov, the brass at AvtoVAZ tend to keep a low profile, but they still rank among Russia's elite executives, and they are independent," said an official of a foreign supplier in Russia. "SOK may be powerful with AvtoVAZ, and AvtoVAZ may find SOK highly useful, but I doubt SOK ever could impact AvtoVAZ strategy, and I think SOK ultimately plays by rules set by AvtoVAZ.

> *"Domino Theory: AvtoVAZ following GAZ falling to new owner?",*
> *just-auto.com, December 12, 2000.*

Management of AvtoVAZ also felt they had an additional takeover defense, which strangely enough, arose from their history of not paying corporate taxes. In 1997, as part of a settlement with Russian tax authorities on $2.4 billion in back-taxes, AvtoVAZ gave the Russian tax authorities the right to 50 percent plus one share of AvtoVAZ if the firm failed—in the future—to make its tax payments. AvtoVAZ management now viewed this as their own version of a poison pill. If the

EXHIBIT 3
AvtoVAZ Suppliers
Owned or Controlled
by SOK

Source: just-auto.com

Supplier	Location	Parts
Avtopribor	Vladimir	clusters for instrument panels, gauges, speedometers
Avtosvet	Kirzhach	connectors, exterior and interior lights, reflectors, signals
DAAZ	Dimitrovgrad	electronics, lights, moldings, wheels
Osvar	Vyazniki	exterior and interior lights, reflectors, signals, warning lights
Plastik	Syzran	foam, plastics, sealants
Syzranselmash	Syzran	chemicals, headliners, sun visors, window lifters

target of a hostile takeover, management could stop paying taxes and the Russian government would take management control, defeating the hostile takeover.[2]

AvtoVAZ Suppliers

Unlike many former Communist enterprises, AvtoVAZ was not vertically integrated. The company depended on a variety of suppliers for components and subassemblies and an assortment of retail distributors. It had little control over its suppliers, and was prohibited by law from retail distribution. In recent years, AvtoVAZ' supplier base had been continually consolidated. The three biggest suppliers to AvtoVAZ were DAAZ, Plastik, and Avtopribor (see Exhibit 3), all of which had been purchased by SOK in the preceding years. *Sok* in Russian means "juice," but in the auto sector in Russia, the English-language joke was that SOK was SOKing-up the supplier industry.

Starting from a relatively small base, SOK had grown from a small glass window factory to a diversified enterprise of roughly $2 billion in sales in 1999, with businesses that included bottled water, building construction, medical equipment, plastic parts and windows, and most recently, AvtoVAZ' largest supplier and retailer. Although SOK officially purchased only 8,000 cars per year for distribution from AvtoVAZ, it was purportedly selling over 40,000 cars per year. The difference was rumored to be cars assembled by SOK from kits exchanged with AvtoVAZ. AvtoVAZ, often short of cash, frequently paid taxes, suppliers, and management in cars.

Dealerships and Distribution

In the early 1990s hundreds of trading companies were formed around the company. Most trading companies would exchange parts and inputs for cars, straight from the factory, at prices 20 percent to 30 percent below market value. The trading companies then sold the cars themselves, capturing significant profit, while AvtoVAZ waited months for payment of any kind from the trading companies. The practice continued unabated in 1996 and 1997 because most of the trading companies were owned and operated by AvtoVAZ managers. Russian law did not prevent management from pursuing private interests related to their own enterprises. Despite these issues, AvtoVAZ dealers across the country made up the only truly national distribution network for cars in Russia. The existence of a dealer network was viewed very positively by GM because building a dealer network from scratch was enormously difficult.

EXHIBIT 4   AvtoVAZ Exports

	1991	1992	1993	1994	1995	1996	1997	1998	1999
Baltic countries	8,392	3,895	3,325	590	8,832	2,648	1,101	716	487
CIS countries	126,440	42,900	19,644	4,491	1,601	1,074	962	108	331
Elsewhere	269,936	271,763	280,593	196,696	175,161	129,957	94,303	68,689	49,957
Total exports	404,768	318,558	303,562	201,777	185,594	133,679	96,366	69,513	50,775
Total sales	674,884	673,821	656,403	528,845	607,279	680,965	736,000	599,829	677,669
Export percentage	60%	47%	46%	38%	31%	20%	13%	12%	7%

Source: just-auto.com

Crime was also prevalent on the factory floor. Mobsters purportedly would enter the AvtoVAZ factory and take cars directly from the production lines at gunpoint. Buyers or distributors were charged $100 at the AvtoVAZ factory gates for protection. To quote one automobile distributor, "They were bandits. Nevertheless, they provided a service." By the fall of 1997 the intrusion of organized crime became so rampant that Kadannikov used Russian troops to clear the plant of thugs.

International Activities

AvtoVAZ was actually a multinational company, with significant international operations in addition to significant export sales.

As illustrated in Exhibit 4, in 1991 AvtoVAZ was exporting over 125,000 cars per year to the countries of the Soviet state. With the deconstruction of the old Soviet Union, sales plummeted to the now CIS countries as a result of the proliferation of weak currencies from country to country, as well as the imposition of new import duties at every border to Russia of 30 percent or more.[3] In the late 1990s, sales were essentially zero. Similarly, sales in the Baltic countries of Latvia, Lithuania, and Estonia had also essentially disappeared.

Brazil has been the site of substantial AvtoVAZ activity in the past decade, with starts and stops. AvtoVAZ had originally flooded the Brazilian market in 1990 with imports when the government of Brazil had opened it to imports. Despite 85 percent import duties, deeply discounted Ladas and Nivas sold well. However, in 1995, the Brazilian government excluded AvtoVAZ from a list of select international manufacturers which would be allowed much lower import duties. AvtoVAZ then withdrew from the Brazilian market. In November 2000, AvtoVAZ concluded the negotiation of an agreement with a Brazilian entrepreneur, Carlos de Moraes, for his company, Abeiva Car Imports, to begin assembly of Nivas in 2001. The target price, 17,000 Brazilian reals, about $8,900, would hopefully make them affordable for Brazilian farmers.

In the past decade, AvtoVAZ has exported to a variety of European countries as well, including Germany, Portugal, Spain, the United Kingdom, and Greece. These sales have typically been small special-order models of the Niva (diesel engines, Peugeot gas engines, etc.). Continued issues surrounding quality and reliability, however, had pushed the company toward an emerging market strategy. It was hoped that low-income markets such as Egypt, Ecuador, and Uruguay would reignite the export potential of the company. GM's strategy was based on extreme low prices to successfully penetrate local markets.

FOREIGN ENTRY INTO RUSSIA

GM interest in Russia extended back to the 1970s when Opel had proposed shipping car kits to Moscow for assembly. The plan foundered because of GM concerns about quality control. In 1991, GM renewed its interest in Russia, once again opening talks with a number of potential JV partners. But after more than a decade, few deals had materialized.

In December 1996 GM opened a plant in Elabuga, Tatarstan, in a JV with Yelaz to assemble Chevrolet Blazers from imported kits (complete knockdown kits or CKDs). The original plan had been to ramp up production volumes rapidly to 50,000 units a year. But the operation struggled. One problem was the product; the Blazers were 2-wheel drive with 2.2 liter engines. The Russian consumer wanted the 4-wheel-drive version widely sold in the United States, typically powered by a 3-liter engine. A second problem was the origin of the kits. The CKDs were imported from Brazil and most Russians did not have a high degree of respect for Brazilian products.

In September 1998 operations were suspended as a result of the Russian financial crisis. Only 3,600 units had been assembled. An attempt was made to restart assembly operations in 1999, this time assembling Opel Vectras, but when it became apparent that the market for a vehicle costing $20,000 would not succeed in the needed volumes, the JV's assembly operations were closed. GM still had over 200 Blazers in inventory in January 2001 and was attempting to close out the last vestiges of the operation.

There were a number of foreign automobile producers in various stages of entry into the Russian marketplace, as summarized in Exhibit 5. Daewoo of Korea, which had made major volume achievements in a number of former Eastern Block countries such as Poland, had begun assembly of compact sedan kits in 1998, and had quickly reached a sales level in Russia of 15,000 units in 1999. Similarly, Renault of France had followed the kit assembly entry strategy with

EXHIBIT 5   **Foreign Auto Producers in Russia**

Foreign Manufacturer	Russian Partner	Auto Model	Target Price Range	Capacity per year	Expected Startup
Daewoo (Korea)	Doninvest	Compact	$6,000–$8,000	20,000	1998
BMW (Germany)	Avtotor	523, 528	$36,000–$53,000	10,000	2000
Renault (France)	City of Moscow	Megane	$8,500–$13,500	100,000	1998
Ford (USA)	Bankirsky Dom	Focus	$13,000–$15,000	25,000	2002
Fiat (Italy)	GAZ	Palio, Siena	$7,000–$10,000	15,000	2002
GM (USA)	AvtoVAZ	Niva, T3000	$7,500–$10,000	75,000	2002

the Renault Megane in 1998, but had only assembled and sold 1,100 units by end of year 1999.

Others, like Ford Motor Company of the United States, had announced JVs with Russian manufacturers to actually build automobiles in Russia. The Ford Focus, priced on the relatively high side at $13,000 to $15,000, was planned for a production launch in late 2002. The facility planned was to produce 25,000 cars per year. The Russian government had given its blessing to the venture by allowing the elimination of import duties on imported inputs as long as the local content of the Focus reached 50 percent within five years of startup (2007 under current plans). Ford was already importing the Focus to begin building a market, but in the early months of 2001, sales were sluggish.

Fiat of Italy was potentially the most formidable competitor. Fiat planned to introduce the Fiat Palio and Fiat Siena into the Russian marketplace through a JV with GAZ in 2002. Although the planned capacity of the plant was only 15,000 cars per year, the Fiat Palio was considered by many auto experts as the right product for the market. The critical question was whether Fiat could deliver the Palio to the market at a low enough price. In its negotiations with the Russian government, Fiat announced its intentions to make the Palio a true Russian-made automobile which would quickly rise to over 70% in local content. If Fiat could indeed achieve this, and there were many who believed that if anyone could it was Fiat, then this would be the true competitive benchmark.

RENEWED INTEREST

For most Russians, price was paramount. The average income levels in Russia prevented automobile pricing at Western levels. As seen in Exhibit 6, prices over the past few years had dropped as a result of the 1998 financial crisis. For 2001, analysts estimated that almost the entire market in Russia was for cars priced below $10,000. Given that the average Russian's salary was about $100 per month, cars remained out of reach for the average Russian.

In a September 2000 interview, David Herman summarized GM's viewpoint on pricing and positioning:

> We could not make an interesting volume with a base price above $10,000. Such a vehicle would feature few specifications—ABS [anti-lock braking systems] and airbags plus a 1.6-liter 16-valve engine. But, if the car costs $12,000, it is only

EXHIBIT 6
Russian Auto Market Shares by Price

Source: General Motors.
Seg=segment,
cum=cumulative.

Price Range	1998		1999	
	Seg	Cum	Seg	Cum
Below $5,000	3%	3%	85%	85%
$5,001–$10,000	65%	68%	12%	97%
$10,001–$15,000	15%	83%	1%	98%
Above $15,000	17%	100%	2%	100%

$2,000 less than certain foreign imports, and this gap may be too small to generate enough sales to justify a factory. We knew we could make a vehicle cheaper with AvtoVAZ, but we need to ensure the price advantage of T3000 imports over competitive models is closer to $7,000 than $2,000.[4]

GM had originally considered the traditional emerging market approach of building complete cars in existing plants and then disassembling them by removing bumpers, wheels, and other separable parts, shipping the disassembled "kit" into Russia, and reassembling with local labor. The disassembly/assembly process allowed the automobile to be considered domestically produced by Russian authorities, thereby avoiding prohibitive import duties. The market assessment group at GM, however, believed that Russian buyers (as opposed to customs officials) would see through the ruse and consider the cars high-quality imports. But marketing research indicated the opposite: Russians did not want to buy cars reassembled by Russians. The only way they would purchase a Russian-made automobile was if it was extremely cheap, like the majority of the existing AvtoVAZ and GAZ product lines, which retailed for as little as $3,000 per car. GM, realizing that it could not deliver the reassembled Opel to the Russian marketplace for less than $15,000 per car, dropped the kit proposal.

GM's marketing research unveiled an additional critical element. Russians would gladly pay an additional $1,000 to $1,500 per car if it had a *Chevrolet* label or badge on it. This piece of research resulted in the original proposal that David Herman and his staff had been pursuing since early 1999: a two-stage JV investment with AvtoVAZ that would allow GM to both reach price targets and position the firm for expected market growth. In the first stage, GM would co-produce a four-wheel-drive sport utility vehicle named the Lada Niva II (VAZ-2123). The target price was $7,500 and plant capacity was to be 90,000 cars. The Niva II would be largely Russian-engineered and, therefore GM would avoid many of the development costs associated with the introduction of a totally new vehicle. The Lada Niva I had originally been introduced in 1977 and updated in new models in 1990 and again in 1996. It had been a successful line for AvtoVAZ, averaging 70,000 units per year throughout the 1990s.[5] Since the Niva II was largely Russian-engineered, GM would bring capital and name to the venture. Because the NIVA II supplier base was in place and component costs already established, GM would not have to deal with issues of local content compliance. In other parts of the world, such as China, local content requirements meant that multinational firms were often forced to source parts from technically unqualified suppliers unfamiliar with the demands of world standard competitive sourcing. As well, existing NIVA II suppliers would likely appreciate becoming GM suppliers because they would get paid on time and possibly receive technical support and advances for new tools.

The second stage of the project would be the construction of a new factory to produce 30,000 Opel Astras (T3000) for the Russian market. Herman's proposal was for AvtoVAZ to use a basic Opel AG vehicle platform as a pre-engineering starting point. Pre-engineering represented about 30 percent of the development cost of a vehicle. The remaining 70 percent would be developed by AvtoVAZ's 10,000 engineers and technicians who worked at a much lower cost than Opel's engineers in Germany. Herman's Russian Group estimated that even if GM and Av-toVAZ used AvtoVAZ's factory to build the existing Opel Astra from mostly im-ported parts and kits from Germany, the resulting price tag would have to fall to between $12,500 and $14,000 per car. This was still considered too expensive for substantial economic volumes. Using the Russian engineering approach, the car would be cheaper, but still fall at the higher end of the spectrum, retailing at about $10,000 per car. As seen in Exhibit 5, this would still put the higher-priced Chevro-let in the lower end of the foreign-made market.

By no means was there consensus within GM and Opel about the viability of the proposed JV. One concern was that as a result of the cash shortage at AvtoVAZ and the slow rate of negotiation progress, in order to build test-models of the new Niva, AvtoVAZ had to use 60 percent of the old Niva's parts. Although many of the consumers that tested the Niva II ranked it above all other Russian-built cars, the car was rough riding and noisy by Western standards. One Opel engineer from Germany who safety-tested the Niva II and evaluated its performance declared it "a real car, if primitive." Heidi McCormack, General Director for GM's Russian operations believed that with some minor engineering adjustments, better materi-als for the interior construction, and a new factory built and operated by GM, the quality of the Niva II would be "acceptable."

GM management was pleased AvtoVAZ appeared willing to contribute the re-juvenated Niva to the JV. "That's their brand new baby," said McCormack. "It's been shown in auto shows. And here's GM, typical big multinational, saying, 'Just give us your best product.' "[6] But in the end, AvtoVAZ's limited access to capital was the driver. Without GM, AvtoVAZ would probably take five years to get the Niva II to market; with GM the time could be cut in half.

NEGOTIATIONS

Negotiations between AvtoVAZ and GM had taken a number of twists and turns over the years, involving every possible dimension of the project. The JV's *market strategy, scope, timing, financing,* and *structure* were all under continual debate. GM's team was led by David Herman.

Herman had been appointed Vice President of General Motors Corporation for the former Soviet Union in 1998. Starting with General Motors Treasury as an at-torney in 1973, Herman had extensive international experience, including three years as GM's Manager of Sales Development in the USSR (1976–79), and other Managing Director positions in Spain (1979–82), Chile (1982–84), and Belgium (1986–1988). These were followed by Chief Executive positions for GM (Europe) in Switzerland and Saab Automobile. From 1992 to 1998, Herman had been Chairman and Managing Director of Adam Opel in Germany. Although Herman's new appointment as head of GM's market initiatives in Russia was described by the press as a Siberian exile, Herman actually requested the position in 1997. Her-man's parents were Belorussian and he had studied Russian at Harvard. In addi-tion to Russian and English, he was also fluent in German and Spanish.

Market Strategy

Back in Detroit, the JV proposal continued to run into significant opposition. GM President Rick Wagoner continued to question whether the Russian market could actually afford the Opel-based second car, the Opel T3000. Wagoner wondered whether the second phase of the project should not be cut, making the Niva the single product which the JV would produce. This could potentially reduce GM's investment to $100 million.

A further point of debate concerned export sales. As a result of the 1998 financial crisis in Russia, a number of people inside both GM and AvtoVAZ pushed for a JV which would produce a car designed for both Russian sales and export sales. After 1998 the weaker Russian rouble meant that Russian exports were more competitive. If the product quality was competitive for the targeted markets, there was a belief that Russian cars could be profitably exported. As a result, Herman expanded his activities to include export market development. The working proposal now assumed that one-third of all the Chevrolet Nivas produced would be exported. The domestic market continued to be protected with a 30% import duty against foreign-made automobiles, both new and used.

Herman brought AvtoVAZ senior management to the Detroit auto show in the spring of 2000 to meet with GM President Rick Wagoner and Vice Chairman Harry Pearce. The meetings went well. In March 2000, however, GM announced an alliance with Fiat. A key element of the alliance involved GM acquiring 20 percent of Fiat's automotive business. GM paid $2.4 billion using GM common stock for the 20 percent stake, which resulted in Fiat owning 5.1% of GM. In June 2000, GM and Fiat submitted a joint bid for Daewoo, which was part of the bankrupt Daewoo *chaebol*. The bid was rejected. Herman returned to Russia, once again slowing negotiations until any possible overlap between GM and Fiat ambitions in Russia were resolved.

Timing

In the summer of 1999, AvtoVAZ had formally announced the creation of a JV with General Motors to produce Opel Astras and the Chevrolet Niva. However, this announcement was not confirmed by GM. Later in 1999, GM's European management, primarily via the Opel division, lobbied heavily within GM to postpone the proposed Chevrolet Niva launch until 2004 to allow a longer period of economic recovery in Russia. Upon learning of this, Kadannikov reportedly told GM to "keep its money," that AvtoVAZ would launch the new Niva on its own. The two sides were able to agree on a tentative 2003 launch date.

Financing

In May 2000 Herman's presentation of the JV proposal to Wagoner and Pearce in Detroit hit another roadblock: the proposed $250 million investment was considered "too large and too risky for a market as risky as Russia—with a partner as slippery as AvtoVAZ."[7] Wagoner instructed Herman to find a third party to share the capital investment and the risk, as GM would not risk more than $100 million itself. Within three months Herman found a third party—the European Bank for

Reconstruction and Development (EBRD). EBRD was willing to provide debt and equity. It would lend $93 million to the venture and invest an additional $40 million for an equity stake of 17 percent.[8]

The European Bank for Reconstruction and Development was established in 1991 with the express purpose of fostering the transition to open market-oriented economies and promoting private and entrepreneurial ventures in Eastern Europe and the Commonwealth of Independent States (CIS). As a catalyst of change the Bank seeks to co-finance with firms that are providing foreign direct investment (FDI) in these countries in order to help mobilize domestic capital and reduce the risks associated with FDI. Recent economic reforms and the perceived stability of President Putin's government had convinced the EBRD's senior management that conditions were right.

GM management knew that $332 million would be insufficient to build a state-of-the-art manufacturing facility. However, given that AvtoVAZ contributions would include the design, land, and production equipment, $332 million was believed to be sufficient to launch the new Niva. The planned facility would include a car body paint shop, assembly facilities, and testing areas. AvtoVAZ would supply the JV with the car body, engine and transmission, chassis units, interior components, and electrical system.

Structure

A continuing point of contention was where the profits of the JV would be created. For example, AvtoVAZ had consistently quoted a price for cement for the proposed plant which was thought to be about 10 times what GM would customarily pay in Germany. Then, just prior to the venture's going before the GM Board for preliminary approval for continued negotiations, AvtoVAZ made a new and surprising demand that GM increase the price the JV would pay AvtoVAZ for Niva parts by 25 percent. (Vladimir Kadannikov demanded to know where the profits would be, "in the price of the parts each side supplied to the joint venture or in the venture itself?").[9] When Herman warned them this would scuttle the deal, AvtoVAZ backed-off. After heated debate, the two parties now agreed that they would not try to profit from the sale of components to the JV.

The structure for the management team and specific allocation of managerial responsibilities had yet to be determined. Although both sides expected to be actively involved in day-to-day management, GM had already made it clear that management control of the JV was a priority for going forward. GM also wanted to minimize the number of expatriate managers assigned to the venture. AvtoVAZ saw the JV as an opportunity for its managers to gain valuable experience and expected to have significant purchasing, assembly, and marketing responsibilities. AvtoVAZ expected GM to develop and support an organizational structure that ensured technology transfer to the JV. AvtoVAZ knew that in China GM had created a technical design center as a separate JV with its Chinese partner. The specific details as to how GM might be compensated for technology transfer to Russia remained unclear. Finally, the issue of who would control the final documentation for the JV agreement had yet to be agreed.

The JV would be located on the edge of the massive AvtoVAZ complex in Togliatti. It would utilize one factory building which was partially finished and previously abandoned. The building already housed much equipment in various operational states, including expensive plastic molding and cutting tools imported from Germany in the early 1990s which AvtoVAZ had been unable to operate effectively but could not resell.

Progress

Again, primarily out of frustration with the pace of negotiations, AvtoVAZ announced in January 2001 that it would begin small scale production of a SUV under its own Lada brand. Herman once again was able to intervene. Herman promised GM's Board that AvtoVAZ would actually build no more than a few dozen of the SUVs "for show." The two sides also continued to debate whether AvtoVAZ would be allowed to sell the prototypes of the new Niva that AvtoVAZ planned to build (approximately 500). GM was adamant, according to long-standing policy, that these should not find their way to the marketplace. AvtoVAZ countered that this was routine for Russian manufacturers and served as a type of "test fleet."

Finally, on February 6, 2001, Herman presented the current proposal to GM's board in Detroit. After heated debate, the board approved the proposal. The possibility of entering a large and developing market, with shared risk and investment, was a rare opportunity to get in early and develop a new local market. According to Rick Wagoner, "Russia's going to be a very big market."

> We'll sell it in former Soviet Union, and eventually export it and because of the cost of material and labor in Russia, we should reach a price point which gives us a decent volume. That will give us a chance to get a network and get started with suppliers and other partners in Russia in a way which I hope will make us amongst the leaders.[10]

David Herman had gained the approval of the General Motors Board to pursue and complete negotiations with AvtoVAZ. The negotiations themselves, however, represented an enormous undertaking, and both GM and AvtoVAZ had many issues yet to be resolved. The two sides at the negotiating table in June included David Herman and Heidi McCormack of GM Russia and Vladimir Kadannikov and Alexei Nikolaev representing AvtoVAZ.

Endnotes

1. Other Russian auto manufacturers included KAMAZ, Roslada, SeAZ, Izh-Mash, and DonInvest.
2. The Russian government was not, however, anxious for this series of events to unfold. It would also mean that AvtoVAZ would be entering an 18-month period in which it paid no taxes whatever to the government if the option were exercised by the Tax Police.
3. AvtoVAZ did attempt to restart CIS sales in 1997 with the introduction of hard-currency contracts. The governments of Uzbekistan, Byelorussia, and Ukraine, however, forbid residents from converting local currency into hard currency for the purpose of purchasing automobiles (in two cases, specifically the product of AvtoVAZ). AvtoVAZ accused the authorities in these countries of working in conjunction with Daewoo of Korea, who had production facilities in Uzbekistan and the Ukraine, of working to shut them out.

4. "Exclusive Interview: David Herman on GM's Strategy for Russia," just-auto.com, September 2000.
5. One of the primary reasons for the success of the Niva was the poor state of Russian roads. The four-wheel-drive Niva handled the pot-holed road infrastructure with relative ease.
6. Gregory L. White, "Off Road: How the Chevy Name Landed on SUV Using Russian Technology," *The Wall Street Journal,* February 20, 2001.
7. *The Wall Street Journal,* February 20, 2001.
8. The willingness of EBRD to invest was a bit surprising given that two of its previous investments with Russian automakers, GAZ and KamAZ, had resulted in defaults on EBRD credits. A third venture in which EBRD was still a partner (20 percent equity), Nizhegorod Motors, a JV between Fiat and GAZ, had delayed its car launch from late 1998 to the first half of 2002.
9. *The Wall Street Journal,* February 21, 2001.
10. "David Herman on GM's Strategy for Russia," just-auto.com, September 2000.

APPENDIX 1   OAO AvtoVAZ Profit and Loss Statement, 1996–1999

(Thousands of roubles)	1996	1997	1998	Jan–Oct 1999
Net sales less VAT	23,697,167	26,255,183	9,533,172	33,834,987
Less cost of goods sold	(18,557,369)	(21,552,999)	(7,650,161)	(25,998,011)
Gross profits	5,139,798	4,702,184	1,883,011	7,836,976
Gross margin	21.7%	17.9%	19.8%	23.2%
Less sales & marketing expenses	(638,739)	(497,540)	(168,381)	(603,170)
Operating income	4,501,059	4,204,644	1,714,630	7,233,806
Operating margin	19.0%	16.0%	18.0%	21.4%
Interest	—	—	—	—
Dividend income	3,366	3,392	159	8,749
Income on asset disposal	3,084,203	23,052,035	2,516,466	4,115,346
Loss on asset disposal	(3,935,990)	(21,718,864)	(3,430,751)	(5,716,732)
Income from core business	3,652,638	5,541,207	800,504	5,641,169
Non-operating income	400,185	372,340	69,415	252,713
Non-operating expenses	(1,136,225)	(1,033,305)	(299,123)	(1,124,448)
Income for period	2,916,598	4,880,242	570,796	4,769,434
Less income tax	(682,556)	(1,166,911)	77,268	(1,112,039)
Disallowable expenses	(409,906)	(7,069,333)	(251,574)	(1,674,947)
Net income	1,824,136	(3,356,002)	396,490	1,982,448
Return on sales (ROS)	7.7%	−12.8%	4.2%	5.9%
In U.S. dollars				
Exchange rate (roubles/US$)	5.6	6.0	9.7	24.6
Net sales	$4,231,636,964	$4,375,863,833	$982,801,237	$1,375,405,976
Gross profits	917,821,071	783,697,333	194,124,845	318,576,260
Income from core business	652,256,786	923,534,500	82,526,186	229,315,813
Income for period	520,821,071	813,373,667	58,844,948	193,879,431
Net income	325,738,571	(559,333,667)	40,875,258	80,587,317

Source: AvtoVAZ.

APPENDIX 2   AvtoVAZ Product Prices by City (February 2001, in roubles)

Code	Model	Type	Tolyatti	Moscow	St. Petersburg
21060	Lada Classic	1976 sedan	84,100	86,500	90,100
2107	Lada Classic	1982 sedan	86,700	91,700	94,400
21083	Lada Samara	1985 3-door hatch	111,900	117,500	115,800
21093	Lada Samara	1987 5-door hatch	112,200	119,700	115,800
21099	Lada Samara	1990 sedan	122,500	132,000	132,600
21102	Lada 2110	1996 sedan	146,500	150,700	151,700
21103	Lada 2110	1997 station wagon	161,100	164,800	162,300
21110	Lada 2110	1999 5-door hatch	157,200	161,900	168,900
2112	Lada Samara II	2001 3-door hatch	167,300	168,600	168,300
2115	Lada Samara II	1997 sedan	143,000	153,700	149,600
21213	Lada Niva	1997 SUV	103,500	111,300	111,100
Average (roubles)			126,909	132,582	123,582
Exchange rate (roubles/US$)			30.00	30.00	30.00
Average (US$)			$4,230	$4,419	$4,111

Source: AvtoVAZ.

APPENDIX 3   Russian Demographics and Economics, 1993-2005

				Actual			
Indicator	**1993**	**1994**	**1995**	**1996**	**1997**	**1998**	**1999**
Real GDP growth (%)	−8.7%	−12.7%	−4.1%	−3.5%	−0.8%	−4.9%	3.2%
GDP per capita (US$)	1,135	1,868	2,348	2,910	3,056	1,900	1,260
Consumer price index (%chg)	875%	308%	198%	48%	15%	28%	86%
External debt (bill US$)	112.7	119.9	120.4	125.0	123.5	183.6	174.3
Foreign direct investment (bill US$)	na	0.5	0.7	0.7	3.8	1.7	0.8
Population (millions)	148.2	148.0	148.1	147.7	147.1	146.5	146.0
Unemployment rate (%)	5.3%	7.0%	8.3%	9.3%	10.8%	11.9%	12.5%
Wages (US$/hour)						0.63	0.36
Exchange rate (roubles/US$)	1.2	3.6	4.6	5.6	6.0	9.7	24.6

			Estimates			
Indicator	**2000**	**2001**	**2002**	**2003**	**2004**	**2005**
Real GDP growth (%)	5.8%	3.5%	4.0%	4.0%	4.5%	4.2%
GDP per capita (US$)	1,560	1,760	1,970	2,170	2,390	2,610
Consumer price index (%chg)	21%	17%	14%	12%	11%	8%
External debt (bill US$)	160.6	171.2	176.8	182.8	186.2	188.8
Foreign direct investment (bill US$)	2.0	4.0	5.7	6.5	6.5	6.5
Population (millions)	145.4	145.1	144.8	144.5	144.2	143.2
Unemployment rate (%)	10.8%	10.1%	10.1%	9.8%	9.2%	9.1%
Wages (US$/hour)	0.44	0.52	0.60	0.70	0.80	0.90
Exchange rate (roubles/US$)	28.4	30.5	32.0	33.5	35.0	36.0

Source: Economist Intelligence Unit, February 2001.

APPENDIX 4   Foreign Automobile Manufacturers & Russian Partners in Russia

Manufacturer/ Partner	Price Range Model	Capacity Low	High	Per Year	Startup
Daewoo Doninvest	Compact sedan	$6,000	$8,000	20,000	1998 Assembly
BMW Group ZAO Avtotor	523 & 528 models	$36,450	$53,010	10,000	2000 Assembly
Renault City of Moscow	Clio Symbol Megane	$8,500 $13,500	$9,000 $16,000	100,000 3,000	1998 Assembly 2002 Assembly
Ford Motor Co ZAO Bankirsky Dom	Focus to >50% local in 5 yrs	$13,000	$15,000	25,000	2002 Staged
Fiat SpA OAO Gaz	Palio Siena	$9,000 $10,000	$10,000 $11,000	10,000 5,000	2002 Production
General Motors OAO AvtoVAZ	New Niva Astra T3000	$7,500 $10,000	$10,000 $12,000	75,000	2002 Production

Source: Compiled by authors.

APPENDIX 5   Russian Automobile Sales Forecasts by Scenario, 2000–2008 (millions)

Scenario	2000	2001	2002	2003	2004	2005	2006	2007	2008
Optimistic	1.317	1.387	1.439	1.498	1.538	1.560	1.615	1.650	1.710
Moderate	1.045	1.131	1.232	1.288	1.315	1.368	1.483	1.500	1.570
Pessimistic	1.017	1.090	1.099	1.125	1.145	1.153	1.174	1.191	1.135

Source: www.just-auto.com, September 2000. Average annual growth rates by scenario: 3.3%, 5.2%, and 1.4%, respectively.

APPENDIX 6 EBRD's Commitment to the GM-VAZ Joint Venture, Russia

The EBRD proposes to provide financing for the construction and operation of a factory to manufacture and assemble up to 75,000 Niva vehicles in Togliatti, Russia.

Operation Status: Signed

Board Review Date: 28 March 2000

Business Sector: Motor vehicle manufacturing

Portfolio Classification: Private sector

The Client: General Motors—AvtoVAZ Joint Venture is a closed joint-stock company to be created under Russian law specifically for the purpose of carrying out the project. Once the investment is complete, AvtoVAZ (VAZ) and General Motors (GM) will hold an equal share in the venture. GM is currently the world's top automotive manufacturer with production facilities in 50 countries and 388,000 employees world-wide. VAZ is the largest producer of vehicles in Russia, having sold approximately 705,500 (over 70 percent of the Russian new car market) in 2000.

Proposed EBRD Finance: The EBRD proposes to provide up to 41 percent of the financing of the venture in a combination of a loan of US$100 million (€108 million) and an equity investment of US$40 million (€43 million). The loan includes interest during the construction phase. Up to US$38 million of the loan may be syndicated after signing to reduce EBRD exposure.

Total Project Cost: US$338 million (€365 million)

Project Objectives: The construction and operation of a factory to manufacture and assemble up to 75,000 Niva vehicles per annum in Togliatti, Russia.

Expected Transition Impact: The transition impact potential of this transaction stems primarily from the demonstration effects associated with the entrance of a major Western strategic investor into the Russian automotive market. The fact that this investment has two well-known partners who are investing equally in the joint venture adds both to the visibility and the potential of the project. This complex project is one of the largest examples of foreign direct investment in post-crisis Russia in a period when many foreign investors are still adopting a wait and see approach. The use of Russian design and engineering skills together with the introduction of Western technologies, methods and processes and the related development of skills are further key sources of positive demonstration effect, especially given the huge modernisation needs of the Russian automotive sector. Other suppliers and client companies will also benefit from technological links or training programmes with the joint venture.

Environmental Impact: The project was screened B/1, requiring an audit of the existing facility and an analysis of the impact associated with the joint venture (JV). While typical environmental issues associated with heavy manufacturing are present at the main AvtoVAZ facility, there have been no prior operations at the site of the proposed JV. Potential liabilities arising from historic soil and ground water pollution were addressed as part of the due diligence, and no significant levels of contamination have been identified. The engine for the new Niva will meet Euro II (Russian market) and Euro IV (European market) standards for vehicle emissions. All vehicles will be fitted with catalytic converters. Safety standards for all vehicles will meet EU and GM standards in full. On formation, the JV will adopt GM management and operations systems and GM corporate practices for all aspects of environment, health and safety and will be in compliance with all applicable EU and best international environmental standards.

Source: http://www.ebrd.com/english/opera/psd/psd2001/483gm.htm

Chapter Twenty-Eight

Nora-Sakari: A Proposed Joint Venture in Malaysia

On the morning of Monday, July 13, 1992, Zainal Hashim, vice chairman of Nora Holdings Sdn Bhd[1] (Nora), arrived at his office about an hour earlier than usual. As he looked out the window at the city spreading below, he thought about the Friday evening reception that he had hosted at his home in Kuala Lumpur (KL), Malaysia, for a team of negotiators from Sakari Oy[2] (Sakari) of Finland. Nora was a leading supplier of telecommunications (telecom) equipment in Malaysia while Sakari, a Finnish conglomerate, was a leader in the manufacture of cellular phone sets and switching systems. The seven-member team from Sakari was in KL to negotiate with Nora the formation of a joint venture between the two telecom companies.

This was the final negotiation that would determine whether a joint venture agreement would materialise. The negotiation had ended late Friday afternoon, having lasted for five consecutive days. The joint venture company, if established, would be set up in Malaysia to manufacture and commission digital switching exchanges to meet the needs of the telecom industry in Malaysia and in neighbouring countries, particularly Indonesia and Thailand. While Nora would benefit from

Richard Ivey School of Business
The University of Western Ontario

R. Azimah Ainuddin prepared this case under the supervision of Professor Paul Beamish solely to provide material for class discussion. The authors do not intend to illustrate either effective or ineffective handling of a managerial situation. The authors may have disguised certain names and other identifying information to protect confidentiality.

Ivey Management Services prohibits any form of reproduction, storage or transmittal without its written permission. This material is not covered under authorization from CanCopy or any reproduction rights organization. To order copies or request permission to reproduce materials, contact Ivey Publishing, Ivey Management Services, c/o Richard Ivey School of Business, The University of Western Ontario, London, Ontario, Canada, N6A 3K7; phone (519) 661-3208; fax (519) 661-3882; e-mail cases@ivey.uwo.ca.

the joint venture in terms of technology transfer, the venture would pave the way for Sakari to acquire knowledge and gain access to the markets of Southeast Asia.

The Nora management was impressed by the Finnish capability in using high technology to enable Finland, a small country of only five million people, to have one of the fastest-growing economies in the world. Most successful Finnish companies were in the high-tech industries. For example, Kone was one of the world's three largest manufacturers of lifts, Vaisala was the world's major supplier of metereological equipment, and Sakari was one of the leading telecom companies in Europe. It would be an invaluable opportunity for Nora to learn from the Finnish experience and emulate their success for Malaysia.

The opportunity emerged when in February 1990, Peter Mattsson, president of Sakari's Asian regional office in Singapore, approached Zainal[3] to explore the possibility of forming a cooperative venture between Nora and Sakari. Mattsson said:

> While growth in the mobile telecommunications network is expected to be about 40 percent a year in Asia between 1990 and 1994, growth in fixed networks would not be as fast, but the projects are much larger. A typical mobile network project amounts to a maximum of a few hundred million Finnish marks, but fixed network projects can be estimated in billions. In Malaysia and Thailand, billion-mark projects are currently approaching contract stage. Thus it is imperative that Sakari establish its presence in this region to capture a share in the fixed network market.

The large potential for telecom facilities was also evidenced in the low telephone penetration rates for most Southeast Asian countries. For example, in 1990, telephone penetration rates (measured by the number of telephone lines per 100 people) for Indonesia, Thailand, Malaysia and the Philippines ranged from 1 to 11 lines per 100 people compared to the rates in developed countries such as Canada, Finland, Germany, United States, and Sweden where the rates exceeded 50 telephone lines per 100 people.

THE TELECOM INDUSTRY IN MALAYSIA

In November 1990, Syarikat Telekom Malaysia Sdn Bhd (STM), the government-owned telecom company, became a public-listed company, Telekom Malaysia Berhad (TMB). With a paid-up capital of RM2.4 billion,[4] TMB was given the authority by the Malaysian government to develop the country's telecom infrastructure. It was also given the mandate to provide telecom services that were on par with those available in developed countries.

In a corporate statement, TMB announced that it would be investing in the digitalization of its networks to pave the way for offering services based on the ISDN (integrated services digitalized network) standard, and investing in international fibre optic cable networks to meet the needs of increased telecom traffic between Malaysia and the rest of the world. TMB would also facilitate the installation of more cellular telephone networks in view of the increased demand for the use of mobile phones among the business community in KL and in major towns.

As the nation's largest telecom company, TMB's operations were regulated through a 20-year licence issued by the Ministry of Energy, Telecommunications and Posts. In line with the government's Vision 2020 program which targeted Malaysia to become a developed nation by the year 2020, there was a strong need for the upgrading of the telecom infrastructure in the rural areas. TMB estimated that it would spend more than RM6 billion between 1991 and 1995 on the installation of fixed networks, of which 25 percent would be allocated for the expansion of rural telecom. The objective was to increase the level of telephone penetration rate to 25 percent by the year 2000.

Although TMB had become a large national telecom company, it lacked the expertise and technology to undertake massive infrastructure projects. In most cases, the local telecom companies would be invited to submit their bids for a particular contract. It was also common for these local companies to form partnerships with large multinational corporations (MNCs), mainly for technological support. For example, Pernas-NEC, a joint-venture company between Pernas Holdings and NEC was one of the companies that had been successful in securing large telecom contracts from the Malaysian authorities.

NORA'S SEARCH FOR A JOINT-VENTURE PARTNER

In mid-1991, TMB called for tenders to bid on a five-year project worth RM2 billion for installing digital switching exchanges in various parts of the country. The project also involved replacing analog circuit switches with digital switches. Digital switches enhanced transmission capabilities of telephone lines, increasing capacity to approximately two million bits per second compared to the 9,600 bits per second on analog circuits.

Nora was interested in securing a share of the RM2 billion forthcoming contract from TMB and more importantly, in acquiring the knowledge in switching technology from its partnership with a telecom MNC. During the initial stages, when Nora first began to consider potential partners in the bid for this contract, telecom MNCs such as Siemens, Alcatel, and Fujitsu seemed appropriate candidates. Nora had previously entered into a five-year technical assistance agreement with Siemens to manufacture telephone handsets.

Nora also had the experience of a long-term working relationship with Japanese partners that would prove valuable should a joint venture be formed with Fujitsu. Alcatel was another potential partner, but the main concern at Nora was that the technical standards used in the French technology were not compatible with the British standards already adopted in Malaysia. NEC and Ericsson were not considered, as they were already involved with other local competitors and were the current suppliers of digital switching exchanges to TMB. Their five-year contracts were due to expire by the end of 1992.

Subsequent to Zainal's meeting with Mattsson, he decided to consider Sakari as a serious potential partner. He was briefed about Sakari's SK33, a digital switching system that was based on an open architecture, which enabled the use of standard components, standard software development tools, and standard software languages. Unlike the switching exchanges developed by NEC and Ericsson which required the purchase of components developed by the parent companies, the SK33 used components that were freely available in the open market. The system was also modular, and its software could be upgraded to provide new services and could interface easily with new equipment in the network. This was the most attractive feature of the SK33 as it would lead to the development of new switching systems.

Mattsson had also convinced Zainal and other Nora managers that although Sakari was a relatively small player in fixed networks, these networks were easily adaptable, and could cater to large exchanges in the urban areas as well as small ones for rural needs. Apparently Sakari's small size, compared to that of AT&T, Ericsson, and Siemens, was an added strength because Sakari was prepared to work out customized products according to Nora's needs. Large telecom companies such as AT&T, Ericsson and Siemens were alleged to be less willing to provide custom-made products. Instead, they tended to offer standard products that in some aspects, were not consistent with the needs of the customer.

Prior to the July 1992 meeting, at least 20 meetings had been held either in KL or in Helsinki to establish relationships between the two companies. It was estimated that each side had invested not less than RM3 million in promoting the relationship. Mattsson and Ilkka Junttila, Sakari's representative in KL, were the key people in bringing the two companies together. (See Exhibits 1 and 2 for brief background information on Malaysia and Finland respectively.)

NORA HOLDINGS SDN BHD

The Company

Nora was one of the leading companies in the telecom industry in Malaysia. It was established in 1975 with a paid-up capital of RM2 million. In 1991, the company's paid-up capital increased to RM16.5 million and recorded a turnover of RM320 million. Nora Holdings consisted of 30 subsidiaries, including two public-listed companies: Multiphone Bhd, and Nora Telecommunications Bhd. As at August 1991, Nora had 3,081 employees, of which 513 were categorized as managerial (including 244 engineers) and 2,568 as nonmanagerial (including 269 engineers and technicians).

The Cable Business

Since the inception of the company, Nora had secured two cable-laying projects, one in 1975 and the other in 1983. For the 1983 project worth RM500 million, Nora formed a joint venture with two Japanese companies, Sumitomo Electric Industries Ltd (held 10 percent equity share) and Marubeni Corporation (held 5 percent equity share). Japanese partners were chosen in view of the availability of a financial package that came together with the technological assistance needed by Nora. Nora also acquired a 63 percent stake in a local cable-laying company, Selangor Cables Sdn Bhd.

EXHIBIT 1   Malaysia: Background Information

Malaysia is centrally located in Southeast Asia. It consists of Peninsular Malaysia, bordered by Thailand in the north and Singapore in the south, and the states of Sabah and Sarawak on the island of Borneo. Malaysia has a total land area of about 330,000 sq km, of which 80 percent is covered with tropical rainforest. Malaysia has an equatorial climate with high humidity and high daily temperatures of about 26°C throughout the year.

In 1991 Malaysia's estimated population was 18 million, of which approximately 7 million made up the country's labor force. The population is relatively young, with 40 percent between the ages of 15 and 39 and only 7 percent above the age of 55. A Malaysian family has an average of four children and extended families are common. Kuala Lumpur, the capital city of Malaysia, has approximately 1.5 million inhabitants.

The population is multiracial; the largest ethnic group is the Bumiputeras (the Malays and other indigenous groups such as the Ibans in Sarawak and Kadazans in Sabah), followed by the Chinese and Indians. Bahasa Malaysia is the national language but English is widely used in the business circles. Other major languages spoken included various Chinese dialects and Tamil.

Islam is the official religion in Malaysia but other religions (mainly Christianity, Buddhism and Hinduism) are widely practiced. Official holidays are allocated for the celebration of Eid, Christmas, Chinese New Year, and Deepavali. All Malays are Muslims, followers of the Islamic faith.

During the period of British rule, secularism was introduced to the country, which led to the separation of the Islamic religion from daily life. In the late 1970s and 1980s, realizing the negative impact of secularism on the life of the Muslims, several groups of devout Muslims including the Malaysian Muslim Youth Movement (ABIM) undertook efforts to reverse the process, emphasizing a dynamic and progressive approach to Islam. As a result, changes were introduced to meet the daily needs of Muslims. Islamic banking and insurance facilities were introduced and prayer rooms were provided in government offices, private companies, factories, and even in shopping complexes.

Malaysia is a parliamentary democracy under a constitutional monarchy. The Yang DiPertuan Agung (the king) is the supreme head, and appoints the head of the ruling political party to be the prime minister. In 1992 the Barisan Nasional, a coalition of several political parties representing various ethnic groups, was the ruling political party in Malaysia. Its predominance had contributed to the political stability and economic progress of the country in the late 1980s and early 1990s.

The recession of 1985 through 1986 led to structural changes in the Malaysian economy that had been too dependent on primary commodities (rubber, tin, palm oil and timber) and had a very narrow export base. To reduce excessive dependence on primary commodities, the government directed resources to the manufacturing sector. To promote the establishment of export-oriented industries, generous incentives and relaxed foreign equity restrictions were introduced. A pragmatic approach toward foreign policy and heavy investments in modernizing the country's infrastructure (highways, air and seaports, telecommunications, industrial parks) led to rapid economic growth in 1988 through 1991 (Table 1). In 1991, the manufacturing sector became the leading contributor to the economy, accounting for about 28 percent of gross national product (GNP). Malaysia's major trading partners are Singapore, United States, United Kingdom, Japan, Korea, Germany, and Taiwan.

**Malaysia: Economic Performance
1988 to 1991**

Economic Indicator	1988	1989	1990	1991
Per capita GNP (in RM)	5,065	5,507	6,206	6,817
Real economic growth rate	9.5%	9.3%	11.4%	9.1%
Consumer price index	2.5%	2.8%	3.1%	4.4%

Source: Ernst & Young International. 1993. "Doing Business in Malaysia."

The Telephone Business

Nora had become a household name in Malaysia as a telephone manufacturer. It started in 1975 when the company obtained a contract to supply telephone sets to the Telecom authority, which would distribute the sets to telephone subscribers on a rental basis. The contract, estimated at RM130 million, lasted for 15 years. In

EXHIBIT 2   Finland: Background Information

Finland is situated in the northeast of Europe, sharing borders with Sweden in the west, Norway in the north and the former Soviet Union in the east. About 65 percent of its area of 338,000 sq km is covered with forest, about 15 percent lakes and about 10 percent arable land. Finland has a temperate climate with four distinct seasons. In Helsinki, the capital city of Finland, July is the warmest month with average midday temperature of 21°C and January is the coldest month with average midday temperature of −3°C.

Finland is one of the most sparsely populated countries in Europe. In 1991 Finland had a population of five million, 60 percent of whom lived in the urban areas. Currently the city of Helsinki has a population of about 500,000. Finland has a well-educated workforce of about 2.3 million. About half of the workforce are engaged in providing services, 30 percent in manufacturing and construction, and 8 percent in agricultural production. The small size of the population led to scarce and expensive labour. Thus Finland had to compete by exploiting its lead in high-tech industries.

Finland's official languages are Finnish and Swedish, although only 6 percent of the population speaks Swedish. English is the most widely spoken foreign language. About 87 percent of the Finns are Lutherans and about 1 percent Finnish Orthodox.

Finland has been an independent republic since 1917, having previously been ruled by Sweden and Russia. A president is elected to a six-year term, and a 200-member, single-chamber parliament is elected every four years.

In the 1980s, Finland's economy was among the fastest growing economies in the world, with gross domestic product increasing at an average rate of over 10 percent a year. Other than its forests, Finland has few natural resources. The country experienced a bad recession in 1991 leading to a drop in GDP (Table 2). Finland's economic structure is based on private ownership and free enterprise. However, the production of alcoholic beverages and spirits is retained as a government monopoly. Finland's major trading partners are Sweden, Germany, the former Soviet Union, and the United Kingdom.

Finland's standard of living is among the highest in the world. The Finns have small families with one or two children per family. They have comfortable homes in the cities and one in every three families has countryside cottages near a lake where they retreat on weekends. Taxes are high, the social security system is efficient and poverty is virtually nonexistent.

Until recently, the stable trading relationship with the former Soviet Union and other Scandinavian countries led to few interactions between the Finns and people in other parts of the world. The Finns are described as rather reserved, obstinate, and serious people. A Finn commented, "We do not engage easily in small talk with strangers. Furthermore, we have a strong love for nature and we have the tendency to be silent as we observe our surroundings. Unfortunately, others tend to view such behavior as cold and serious." Visitors to Finland are often impressed by the efficient public transport system, the clean and beautiful city of Helsinki with orderly road networks, scenic parks and lakefronts, museums, cathedrals, and churches.

Finland: Economic Performance 1988 to 1991

Economic Indicator	1988	1989	1990	1991
Per capita GDP (in FIM)	88,308	99,387	104,991	102,083
Increase in GDP	12.8%	12.2%	6.0%	−2.8%
Inflation	5.1%	6.6%	6.1%	4.1%
Unemployment	n.a.	3.5%	3.4%	7.6%

Source: Ernst & Young International. 1993. "Doing Business in Finland."

1980 Nora secured licenses from Siemens and Northern Telecom to manufacture telephone handsets and had subsequently developed Nora's own telephone sets—the N300S (single line), N300M (microcomputer controlled), and N300V (hands-free, voice-activated) models.

Upon expiry of the 15-year contract as a supplier of telephone sets to the government-owned Telecom authority (STM) in 1989, Nora suffered a major setback when it lost a RM32 million contract to supply 600,000 N300S single line telephones. The contract was instead given to a Taiwanese manufacturer, Formula Electronics, which quoted a lower price of RM37 per handset compared to Nora's RM54. Subsequently, Nora was motivated to move toward the high end feature phone domestic market. The company sold about 3,000 sets of feature phones per month, capturing the segment of the Malaysian market that needed more sophisticated sets than the ones supplied by STM.

Nora had ventured into the export market with its feature phones, but industry observers predicted that Nora still had a long way to go as an exporter. The foreign markets were very competitive and many manufacturers already had well-established brands. In 1989, exports amounted to RM2 million and were expected to increase to RM5 million after orders were filled for its N300M and N300V models from Alcatel and Tokyo Telecommunications Network. Nora's N300V had been recently approved in Germany and a shipment of 2,000 sets would be distributed through its subsidiary, Nora GmbH, to test the German market.

The Payphone Business

Nora's start-up in the payphone business had turned out to be one of the company's most profitable lines of business. Other than the cable-laying contract secured in 1975, Nora had a 15-year contract to install, operate, and maintain payphones in the cities and major towns in Malaysia. By 1992, Nora had started to manufacture card payphones under a license from GEC Plessey Telecommunications (GPT) of the United Kingdom. The agreement had also permitted Nora to sell the products to the neighbouring countries in Southeast Asia as well as to eight other markets approved by GPT.

While the payphone revenues were estimated to be as high as RM60 million a year, a long-term and stable income stream for Nora, profit margins were only about 10 percent because of the high investment and maintenance costs.

Other Businesses

Nora was also the sole Malaysian distributor for Northern Telecom's private automatic branch exchange (PABX) and NEC's mobile telephone sets. The company had ventured into the paging market through a subsidiary, Unikom Sdn Bhd, and was capturing 50 percent of the paging business in Malaysia. It was also an Apple computer distributor in Malaysia and Singapore. In addition, Nora was involved in: distributing radio-related equipment; supplying equipment to the broadcasting, meteorological, civil aviation, postal and power authorities; and manufacturing automotive parts (such as the suspension coil, springs, and piston) for the local automobile companies.

The Management

When Nora was established in 1975, Osman Jaafar, founder and chairman of Nora Holdings, managed the company with his wife, Nora Asyikin Yusof, and seven employees. Osman was known as a conservative businessman who did not like to dabble in acquisitions and mergers to make quick capital gains. He was formerly an electrical engineer who was trained in the United Kingdom and had held several senior positions at the national Telecom Department in Malaysia.

In 1980, Osman recruited Zainal Hashim to fill the position of deputy managing director at Nora. Zainal held a master's degree in microwave communications from a British university and had several years of working experience as a production engineer at Pernas-NEC Sdn Bhd, a manufacturer of transmission equipment. In 1984, he was promoted to the position of managing director and in 1990, the vice chairman.

Industry analysts observed that Nora's success was attributed to the complementary roles, trust, and mutual understanding between Osman and Zainal. While Osman "likes to fight for new business opportunities," Zainal preferred a low profile and concentrated on managing Nora's operations.

Industry observers also speculated that Osman, a former civil servant and an entrepreneur, was close to Malaysian politicians, notably the Prime Minister. Zainal, on the other hand, had been a close friend of the current Finance Minister since the days when they were both active in the Malaysian Muslim Youth Movement (a group that had developed a reputation for idealism, integrity and progressive interpretation of Islam). Zainal disagreed with allegations that Nora had succeeded due to its close relationships with Malaysian politicians and stressed that Nora's success was not due to its political skills. However, he acknowledged that such perceptions in the industry had been beneficial to the company.

Osman and Zainal had an obsession for high-tech and made the development of research and development (R&D) skills and resources a priority in the company. About 1 percent of Nora's earnings was ploughed back into R&D activities. Although this amount was considered small by international standards, Nora planned to increase it gradually to 5 percent to 6 percent over the next two to three years. Zainal said:

> We believe in making improvements in small steps, similar to the Japanese *kaizen* principle. Over time, each small improvement could lead to a major creation. To be able to make improvements, we must learn from others. Thus we would borrow a technology from others, but eventually, we must be able to develop our own to sustain our competitiveness in the industry. As a matter of fact, Sakari's SK33 system was developed based on a technology it obtained from Alcatel.

To further enhance R&D activities at Nora, Nora Research Sdn Bhd (NRSB), a wholly owned subsidiary, was formed, and its R&D department was absorbed into this new company. NRSB operated as an independent research company undertaking R&D activities for Nora as well as private clients in related fields. The company facilitated R&D activities with other companies as well as government organizations, research institutions, and universities. NRSB, with its staff of 40 technicians/engineers, would charge a fixed fee for basic research and a royalty for its products sold by clients. Thus far, NRSB had developed Nora's Network Paging System, which was the system presently used by the company's paging subsidiary, Unikom Sdn Bhd.

Zainal was also active in instilling and promoting Islamic values among the Malay employees at Nora. He explained:

> Islam is a way of life and there is no such thing as Islamic management. The Islamic values, which must be reflected in the daily life of Muslims, would influence their behaviours as employers and employees. Our Malay managers, however, were often

influenced by their western counterparts, who tend to stress knowledge and mental capability and often forget the effectiveness of the softer side of management which emphasizes relationships, sincerity and consistency. I believe that one must always be sincere to be able to develop good working relationships.

SAKARI OY

Sakari was established in 1865 as a pulp and paper mill located about 200 km northwest of Helsinki, the capital city of Finland. In the 1960s Sakari started to expand into the rubber and cable industries when it merged with the Finnish Rubber Works and Finnish Cable Works. In 1973 Sakari's performance was badly affected by the oil crisis, as its businesses were largely energy-intensive.

However, in 1975, the company recovered when Aatos Olkkola took over as Sakari's president. He led Sakari into competitive businesses such as computers, consumer electronics, and cellular phones via a series of acquisitions, mergers, and alliances. Companies involved in the acquisitions included: the consumer electronics division of Standard Elektrik Lorenz AG; the data systems division of L.M. Ericsson; Vantala, a Finnish manufacturer of colour televisions; and Luxury, a Swedish state-owned electronics and computer concern.

In 1979, a joint venture between Sakari and Vantala, Sakari-Vantala, was set up to develop and manufacture mobile telephones. Sakari-Vantala had captured about 14 percent of the world's market share for mobile phones and held a 20 percent market share in Europe for its mobile phone handsets. Outside Europe, a 50–50 joint venture was formed with Tandy Corporation which, to date, had made significant sales in the United States, Malaysia, and Thailand.

Sakari first edged into the telecom market by selling switching systems licensed from France's Alcatel and by developing the software and systems to suit the needs of small Finnish phone companies. Sakari had avoided head-on competition with Siemens and Ericsson by not trying to enter the market for large telephone networks. Instead, Sakari had concentrated on developing dedicated telecom networks for large private users such as utility and railway companies. In Finland, Sakari held 40 percent of the market for digital exchanges. Other competitors included Ericsson (34 percent), Siemens (25 percent), and Alcatel (1 percent).

Sakari was also a niche player in the global switching market. Its SK33 switches had sold well in countries such as Sri Lanka, United Arab Emirates, China, and the Soviet Union. A derivative of the SK33 main exchange switch called the SK33XT was subsequently developed to be used in base stations for cellular networks and personal paging systems.

Sakari attributed its emphasis on R&D as its key success factor in the telecom industry. Strong in-house R&D in core competence areas enabled the company to develop technology platforms such as its SK33 system that were reliable, flexible, widely compatible, and economical. About 17 percent of its annual sales revenue was invested into R&D and product development units in Finland, United Kingdom, and France. Sakari's current strategy was to emphasize global operations in production and R&D. It planned to set up R&D centres in leading markets, including Southeast Asia.

EXHIBIT 3
Ten Major
Telecommunication
Equipment Vendors

Source: International
Telecommunication Union.
1994. "World
Telecommunication
Development Report 1994."

Rank	Company	Country	1992 Telecom Equipment Sales (US$million)
1	Alcatel	France/Netherlands	19,359
2	Siemens	Germany	11,877
3	AT&T	United States	10,809
4	Northern Telecom	Canada	8,029
5	Ericsson	Sweden	7,742
6	Motorola	United States	7,724
7	NEC	Japan	7,591
8	Bosch	Germany	5,221
9	Fujitsu	Japan	3,738
10	Philips	Netherlands	3,412

Sakari was still a small company by international standards (see Exhibit 3 for a list of the world's major telecom equipment suppliers). It lacked a strong marketing capability and had to rely on joint ventures such as the one with Tandy Corporation to enter the world market, particularly the United States. In its efforts to develop market position quickly, Sakari had to accept lower margins for its products, and often the Sakari name was not revealed on the product. In recent years, Sakari decided to emerge from its hiding place as a manufacturer's manufacturer and began marketing under the Sakari name.

In 1988, Sakari's revenues increased but margins declined by 21 percent when integration of the acquired companies took longer and cost more than expected. In 1989 Mikko Koskinen took over as president of Sakari when Olkkola died. Koskinen announced that telecommunications, computers, and consumer electronics would be maintained as Sakari's core business, and that he would continue Olkkola's efforts in expanding the company overseas. He believed that every European company needed global horizons to be able to meet global competition for future survival. To do so, he envisaged the setting up of alliances of varying duration, each designed for specific purposes. He said, "Sakari has become an interesting partner with which to cooperate on an equal footing in the areas of R&D, manufacturing, and marketing."

In 1991, Sakari was Finland's largest publicly traded industrial company and derived almost 80 percent of its total sales from exports and overseas operations. However, export sales were confined to other Scandinavian countries, Western Europe and the former Soviet Union. Industry analysts observed that Finnish companies had a privileged relationship with the former Soviet Union, which was considered an easy market with minimal trading costs and high margins. As a result, until recently, these companies failed to invest in other parts of the world and were not making the most of their advantage in high-tech industries.

The recession in Finland which began in 1990 led Sakari's group sales to decline substantially from FIM22 billion[5] in 1990 to FIM15 billion in 1991. The losses were attributed to two main factors: weak demand for Sakari's consumer electronic products, and trade with the Soviet Union which had come to almost a complete standstill.

Consequently Sakari began divesting its less profitable companies within the basic industries (metal, rubber, and paper), as well as leaving the troubled European computer market with the sale of its computer subsidiary, Sakari Macro. The company's new strategy was to focus on three main areas: telecom systems and mobile phones in a global framework, consumer electronic products in Europe, and deliveries of cables and related technology. The company's divestment strategy led to a reduction of Sakari's employees from about 41,000 in 1989 to 29,000 in 1991.

In June 1992, Koskinen retired as Sakari's President and was replaced by Visa Ketonen, formerly the President of Sakari Mobile Phones. Ketonen appointed Ossi Kuusisto as Sakari's vice president.

THE NORA-SAKARI NEGOTIATION

Since mid-May 1990, Nora and Sakari had discussed the potential of forming a joint-venture company in Malaysia. Nora engineers were sent to Helsinki to assess the SK33 technology in terms of its compatibility with the Malaysian requirements, while Sakari managers travelled to KL mainly to assess both Nora's capability in manufacturing switching exchanges and the feasibility of gaining access to the Malaysian market.

In November 1991, Nora submitted its bid for TMB's RM2 billion contract to supply digital switching exchanges supporting four million telephone lines. Assuming the Nora-Sakari joint venture would materialise, Nora based its bid on supplying Sakari's digital switching technology. Nora competed with seven other companies short listed by TMB, all offering their partners' technology—Alcatel, AT&T, Fujitsu, Siemens, Ericsson, NEC, and Samsung. In early May 1992, TMB announced five successful companies in the bid. They were companies using technology from Alcatel, Fujitsu, Ericsson, NEC, and Sakari. Each company was awarded one-fifth share of the RM2 billion contract and would be responsible in delivering 800,000 telephone lines over a period of five years. Industry observers were critical of TMB's decision to select Sakari and Alcatel. Sakari was perceived to be the least capable in supplying the necessary lines to meet TMB's requirements, as it was alleged to be a small company with little international exposure. Alcatel was criticized for having the potential of supplying an obsolete technology.

The May 21 Meeting

Following the successful bid and ignoring the criticisms against Sakari, Nora and Sakari held a major meeting in Helsinki on May 21, 1992, to finalise the formation of the joint venture. Zainal led Nora's five-member negotiation team that comprised Nora's general manager for corporate planning division, an accountant, two engineers, and Marina Mohamed, a lawyer. One of the engineers was Salleh Lindstrom who was of Swedish origin, a Muslim and had worked for Nora for almost 10 years.

Sakari's eight-member team was led by Kuusisto, Sakari's vice president. His team comprised Junttila, Hussein Ghazi, Aziz Majid, three engineers, and Julia Ruola (a lawyer). Ghazi was Sakari's senior manager who was of Egyptian origin and also a Muslim who had worked for Sakari for more than 20 years while Aziz, a Malay, had been Sakari's manager for more than 12 years.

The meeting went on for several days. The main issue raised at the meeting was Nora's capability in penetrating the Southeast Asian market. Other issues included Sakari's concerns over the efficiency of Malaysian workers in the joint venture in manufacturing the product, maintaining product quality, and ensuring prompt deliveries.

Commenting on the series of negotiations with Sakari, Zainal said that this was the most difficult negotiation he had ever experienced. Zainal was Nora's most experienced negotiator and had single-handedly represented Nora in several major negotiations for the past 10 years. In the negotiation with Sakari, Zainal admitted making the mistake of approaching the negotiation applying the approach he often used when negotiating with his counterparts from companies based in North America or the United Kingdom. He said:

> Negotiators from the United States tend to be very open and often state their positions early and definitively. They are highly verbal and usually prepare well-planned presentations. They also often engage in small talk and 'joke around' with us at the end of a negotiation. In contrast, the Sakari negotiators tend to be very serious, reserved and 'cold'. They are also relatively less verbal and do not convey much through their facial expressions. As a result, it was difficult for us to determine whether they are really interested in the deal or not.

Zainal said that the negotiation on May 21 turned out to be particularly difficult when Sakari became interested in bidding a recently-announced tender for a major telecom contract in the United Kingdom. Internal politics within Sakari led to the formation of two opposing "camps". One "camp" held a strong belief that there would be very high growth in the Asia-Pacific region and that the joint-venture company in Malaysia was seen as a hub to enter these markets. This group was represented mostly by Sakari's managers positioned in Asia and engineers who had made several trips to Malaysia, which usually included visits to Nora's facilities. They also had the support of Sakari's vice president, Kuusisto, who was involved in most of the meetings with Nora, particularly when Zainal was present. Kuusisto had also made efforts to be present at meetings held in KL. This group also argued that Nora had already obtained the contract in Malaysia whereas the chance of getting the U.K. contract was quite low in view of the intense competition prevailing in that market.

The "camp" not in favor of the Nora-Sakari joint venture believed that Sakari should focus its resources on entering the United Kingdom, which could be used as a hub to penetrate the European Union (EU) market. There was also the belief that Europe was closer to home making management easier and that problems arising from cultural differences would be minimized. This group was also particularly concerned that Nora had the potential of copying Sakari's technology and eventually becoming a strong regional competitor. Also, because the U.K. market was relatively "open", Sakari could set up a wholly owned subsidiary instead of a joint-venture company and consequently, avoid joint-venture-related problems such as joint control, joint profits, and leakage of technology.

Zainal felt that the lack of full support from Sakari's management led to a difficult negotiation when new misgivings arose concerning Nora's capability to deliver its part of the deal. It was apparent that the group in favour of the Nora-Sakari joint venture was under pressure to further justify its proposal and provide counterarguments against the U.K. proposal. A Sakari manager explained, "We are tempted to pursue both proposals since each has its own strengths, but our current resources are very limited. Thus a choice has to made, and soon."

The July 6 Meeting

Another meeting to negotiate the joint-venture agreement was scheduled for July 6, 1992. Sakari's eight-member team arrived in KL on Sunday afternoon of July 5, and was met at the airport by the key Nora managers involved in the negotiation. Kuusisto did not accompany the Sakari team at this meeting.

The negotiation started early Monday morning at Nora's headquarters and continued for the next five days, with each day's meeting ending late in the evening. Members of the Nora team were the same members who had attended the May 21 meeting in Finland, except Zainal, who did not participate. The Sakari team was also represented by the same members in attendance at the previous meeting plus a new member, Solail Pekkarinen, Sakari's senior accountant. Unfortunately, on the third day of the negotiation, the Nora team requested that Sakari ask Pekkarinen to leave the negotiation. He was perceived as extremely arrogant and insensitive to the local culture, which tended to value modesty and diplomacy. Pekkarinen left for Helsinki the following morning.

Although Zainal had decided not to participate actively in the negotiations, he followed the process closely and was briefed by his negotiators regularly. Some of the issues of which they complained were difficult to resolve had often led to heated arguments between the two negotiating teams. These included:

1. Equity Ownership

In previous meetings both companies agreed to form the joint-venture company with a paid-up capital of RM5 million. However, they disagreed on the equity share proposed by each side. Sakari proposed an equity split in the joint-venture company of 49 percent for Sakari and 51 percent for Nora. Nora, on the other hand, proposed a 30 percent Sakari and 70 percent Nora split. Nora's proposal was based on the foreign equity regulations set by the Malaysian government that allowed a maximum of 30 percent foreign equity ownership unless the company would export a certain percentage of its products (see Exhibit 4 for these regulations). In addition, formal approval from the Malaysian authorities would have to be obtained to enable the foreign partner to hold an equity share of more than 30 percent. Nora was concerned that this would further delay the formation of the joint venture.

Equity ownership became a major issue as it was associated with control over the joint-venture company. Sakari was concerned about its ability to control the accessibility of its technology to Nora and about decisions concerning the activities of the joint venture as a whole. The lack of control was perceived by Sakari as an obstacle to protecting its interests. Nora also had similar concerns about its ability to exert control over

EXHIBIT 4
An Extract of the Malaysian Government's Policy on Foreign Investment

Source: Malaysian Industrial Development Authority (MIDA). 1991. "Malaysia: Your Profit Centre in Asia."

> The level of equity participation for other export-oriented projects are as follows:
>
> For projects exporting between 51 percent to 79 percent of their production, foreign equity ownership up to 51 percent will be allowed; however, foreign equity ownership of up to 79 percent may be allowed, depending on factors such as the level of technology, spin-off effects, size of the investment, location, value-added and the utilization of local raw materials and components.
>
> For projects exporting 20 percent to 50 percent of their production, foreign equity ownership of 30 percent to 51 percent will be allowed, depending upon similar factors as mentioned above; however, for projects exporting less than 20 percent of their production, foreign equity ownership is allowed up to a maximum of 30 percent.
>
> For projects producing products that are of high technology or are priority products for the domestic market, foreign equity ownership of up to 51 percent will be allowed.

the joint venture because it was intended as a key part of Nora's long-term strategy to develop its own digital switching exchanges and related high-tech products.

2. Technology Transfer

Sakari proposed to provide the joint-venture company with the basic structure of the digital switch. The joint-venture company would assemble the switching exchanges at the joint-venture plant and subsequently install the exchanges in designated locations identified by TMB. By offering Nora only the basic structure of the switch, the core of Sakari's switching technology would still be well-protected.

On the other hand, Nora proposed that the basic structure of the switch be developed at the joint-venture company in order to access the root of the switching technology. Based on Sakari's proposal, Nora felt that only the technical aspects in assembling and installing the exchanges would be obtained. This was perceived as another "screw-driver" form of technology transfer while the core of the technology associated with making the switches would still be unknown.

3. Royalty Payment

Closely related to the issue of technology transfer was the payment of a royalty for the technology used in building the switches. Sakari proposed a royalty payment of 5 percent of the joint-venture gross sales while Nora proposed a payment of 2 percent of net sales.

Nora considered the royalty rate of 5 percent too high because it would affect Nora's financial situation as a whole. Financial simulations prepared by Nora's managers indicated that Nora's return on investment would be less than the desired 10 percent if royalty rates exceeded 3 percent of net sales. This was because Nora had already agreed to make large additional investments in support of the joint venture. Nora would invest in a building which would be rented to the joint-venture company to accommodate an office and the switching plant. Nora would also invest in another plant which would supply the joint venture with surface mounted devices (SMD), one of the major components needed to build the switching exchanges.

An added argument raised by the Nora negotiators in support of a 2 percent royalty was that Sakari would receive side benefits from the joint venture's access to

Japanese technology used in the manufacture of the SMD components. Apparently the Japanese technology was more advanced than Sakari's present technology.

4. Expatriates' Salaries and Perks

To allay Sakari's concerns over Nora's level of efficiency, Nora suggested that Sakari provide the necessary training for the joint-venture technical employees. Subsequently, Sakari had agreed to provide eight engineering experts for the joint-venture company on two types of contracts, short term and long term. Experts employed on a short-term basis would be paid a daily rate of US$700 plus travel/accommodation. The permanent experts would be paid a monthly salary ranging from US$12,000 to US$15,000. Three permanent experts would be attached to the joint-venture company once it was established and the number would gradually be reduced to only one, after two years. Five experts would be available on a short-term basis to provide specific training needs for durations of not more that three months each year.

The Nora negotiation team was appalled at the exorbitant amount proposed by the Sakari negotiators. They were surprised that the Sakari team had not surveyed the industry rates, as the Japanese and other western negotiators would normally have done. Apparently Sakari had not taken into consideration the relatively low cost of living in Malaysia compared to Finland. In 1991, the average monthly rent for a comfortable, unfurnished three-bedroom apartment was US$920 in Helsinki and only US$510 in Kuala Lumpur.[6]

In response to Sakari's proposal, Nora negotiators adopted an unusual "take-it or leave-it" stance. They deemed the following proposal reasonable in view of the comparisons made with other joint ventures that Nora had entered into with other foreign parties:

Permanent experts' monthly salary ranges to be paid by the joint-venture company were as follows:

1. Senior expert (7–10 years experience) RM13,500–15,500
2. Expert (4–6 years experience) RM12,500–14,000
3. Junior expert (2–3 years experience) RM11,500–13,000
4. Any Malaysian income taxes payable would be added to the salaries.
5. A car for personal use.
6. Annual paid vacation of 5 weeks.
7. Return flight tickets to home country once a year for the whole family of married persons and twice a year for singles according to Sakari's general scheme.
8. Any expenses incurred during official travelling.

Temporary experts are persons invited by the joint-venture company for various technical assistance tasks and would not be granted residence status. They would be paid the following fees:

1. Senior expert .... RM750 per working day
2. Expert .... RM650 per working day
3. The joint-venture company would not reimburse the following:
   • Flight tickets between Finland (or any other country) and Malaysia.
   • Hotel or any other form of accommodation.
   • Local transportation.

In defense of their proposed rates, Sakari's negotiators argued that the rates presented by Nora were too low. Sakari suggested that Nora's negotiators take into consideration the fact that Sakari would have to subsidize the difference between the experts' present salaries and the amount paid by the joint-venture company. A large difference would require that large amounts of subsidy payments be made to the affected employees.

5. Arbitration

Another major issue discussed in the negotiation was related to arbitration. While both parties agreed to an arbitration process in the event of future disputes, they disagreed on the location for dispute resolution. Because Nora would be the majority stakeholder in the joint-venture company, Nora insisted that any arbitration should take place in KL. Sakari, however, insisted on Helsinki, following the norm commonly practised by the company.

At the end of the five-day negotiation, many issues could not be resolved. While Nora could agree on certain matters after consulting Zainal, the Sakari team, representing a large private company, had to refer contentious items to the company board before it could make any decision that went beyond the limits authorized by the board.

THE DECISION

Zainal sat down at his desk, read through the minutes of the negotiation thoroughly, and was disappointed that an agreement had not yet been reached. He was concerned about the commitment Nora had made to TMB when Nora was awarded the switching contract. Nora would be expected to fulfill the contract soon but had yet to find a partner to provide the switching technology. It was foreseeable that companies such as Siemens, Samsung and AT&T, which had failed in the bid, could still be potential partners. However, Zainal had also not rejected the possibility of a reconciliation with Sakari. He could start by contacting Kuusisto in Helsinki. But should he?

Endnotes

1. Sdn Bhd is an abbreviation for Sendirian Berhad, which means private limited company in Malaysia.
2. Oy is an abbreviation for Osakeyhtiot, which means private limited company in Finland.
3. The first name is used because the Malay name does not carry a family name. The first and/or middle names belong to the individual and the last name is his/her father's name.
4. RM is Ringgit Malaysia, the Malaysian currency. As at December 31, 1991, US$1 = RM2.73.
5. FIM is Finnish Markka, the Finnish currency. As at December 31, 1991, US$1 = FIM4.14.
6. IMD & World Economic Forum. 1992. The World Competitiveness Report.

Chapter Twenty-Nine

Euro-Air (A)

As Herman Miller read through the newly arrived fax, he swore quietly to himself. Minutes later, he asked Elizabeth Gold to join him. Miller and Gold were two of the senior regional representatives in a major city in the eastern half of North America for Euro-Air. Euro-Air, a major European-based commercial airline, operated daily service to its European hub from fourteen cities in North America and onward service to more than 300 locations in 90 countries around the world. The fax letter (see Exhibit 1) suggested that Euro-Air had recently caused a lot of problems for at least one of its passengers.

Passenger complaint letters were not unusual at any airline. What was unusual about this letter was the litany of problems described, the fact that a quick check had revealed that virtually all the listed complaints were valid, and the nagging question at the end of the letter that asked "What would Euro-Air as an organization learn from this saga?"

During this meeting, Miller and Gold agreed that Gold should probably take the unusual step of paying a personal visit to Peter Boyd, the passenger who had written. For Elizabeth Gold, the issues were: "If I do visit, what do I say to Mr. Boyd in response to the questions he's raised?" "What, if any, compensation should be offered?" "What can we do from a regional office perspective to learn from this experience?" "Should we even bother trying to change operating practices at Euro-Air at the headquarters (parent company) level?"

IVEY

Richard Ivey School of Business
The University of Western Ontario

Paul W. Beamish prepared this case solely to provide material for class discussion. The author does not intend to illustrate either effective or ineffective handling of a managerial situation. The author may have disguised certain names and other identifying information to protect confidentiality.

Ivey Management Services prohibits any form of reproduction, storage or transmittal without its written permission. This material is not covered under authorization from CanCopy or any reproduction rights organization. To order copies or request permission to reproduce materials, contact Ivey Publishing, Ivey Management Services, c/o Richard Ivey School of Business, The University of Western Ontario, London, Ontario, Canada, N6A 3K7; phone (519) 661-3208; fax (519) 661-3882; e-mail cases@ivey.uwo.ca.

EXHIBIT 1 Complaint Letter

International
Consulting
Practice

April 10, 1999

Mr. Herman Miller
Managing Director
Euro-Air Regional Office
L.F Hansen Building

Subject: Euro-Air Flights from North America-Europe-Egypt
on April 5/6/7, 1999

I am taking the unusual (for me) step of writing to you in regards to my trip to Cairo, Egypt from North America on Euro-Air. Euro-Air should be ashamed of the way it treated me. I have never seen so much airline mismanagement and poor service in such a short space of time. Before I go into detail, you should be aware of four things.

First, I am a very frequent flyer. I cross an ocean every month. I am a Platinum Elite (Crown Alliance Gold) member, and sometimes fly non-Crown Alliance airlines also.

Second, I have never had cause to write any member of the Crown Alliance before, despite having travelled over 1,000,000 flight miles in the past decade.

Third, I was travelling to Egypt for a very brief stay with only carry-on luggage. At my point of embarkation, I politely (as always) explained to desk and lounge staff that there was no point in my getting on the plane Monday night (or what became Tuesday morning) if they could not assure me that I would be in Cairo in time for my scheduled presentation on Wednesday morning to Government Ministers, and scheduled appearance on national television.

Fourth, I am the author of an International Business Newsletter. It is currently read by about 10,000 business people in over 20 countries. Thus, I have an abiding professional interest in firms operating internationally. I have particular interest in and expertise in alliances; this, in fact, was the reason I was asked to speak in Egypt. So my readers and I will be interested in your response.

<u>The Events</u>

On Monday April 5, 1999, I caught the 6:20 p.m. connector flight from my home town to your regional hub. It arrived on time, and I proceeded through security to the Business Class lounge to await the 9:30 p.m. departure on Euro-Air (code shared with Air North-Am) to your European hub. The Euro-Air flight was scheduled to arrive Tuesday April 6th at 11:00 a.m., with a two-hour and 50-minute hour layover before the Euro-Air flight to Egypt, scheduled to arrive in Cairo at 6:55 p.m. I was travelling Business Class. The cost of my ticket was $5,182.

By about 8:45 p.m., I asked the airline representative in the lounge why boarding had not commenced. She explained that your plane from Europe was in, but that there was "a problem." She did not know what the problem was. The Departure screen both inside and outside the lounge did not indicate any delay. (Despite the fact that this flight eventually left more than five hours late, the Departure screens <u>never</u> indicated anything other than on-time departure!)

EXHIBIT 1 *Continued*

Over the ensuing hours, the passengers were kept in the dark about the nature of the problem, how long it might take to rectify it, and whether the flight would even depart. The lounge staff were kept in the dark as well. It was not until after 10:00 p.m. that we learned that the delay had been the result of a "Pilot Error." As you are no doubt aware, the inbound Euro-Air pilot, after landing, taxied the plane off the pavement onto the grass and mud. There then was the need to have the plane towed back onto the area which it should not have left, and then to check for air worthiness. (This explanation was confirmed by the outbound Euro-Air pilot).

Your in-flight magazine April 1999 contained the following notice about delay information on page 50.

> We plan to provide passengers with better information about delays. Monitors will be positioned in central locations around airports and in lounges, and extra announcements about delays will be made both at the departure gates and on board.

Such a "plan" seems overdue!

Recommendation #1 — Even if the news is bad, or the solution uncertain, Communicate Early and Communicate Often.

By about 8:00 p.m., Euro-Air knew they had a problem due to the Pilot's Error, but they did not communicate this to airport staff, or passengers. If I had known that the flight was going to be delayed, I could have examined the feasibility of catching another flight across the Atlantic. The longer Euro-Air waited to share any information about the problem, the fewer the choices it left premium fare-paying customers like me.

As time passed that evening, it became increasingly evident that I would not be able to catch my connecting flight to Egypt. Consequently, I asked the (North-Am) lounge staff to please start investigating alternative routes. One member of the lounge staff said that the airline's office in Europe would work on a solution and have it for me when I arrived. I explained that this was not good enough because if there was not a feasible solution to get me to my destination for the start of my meeting, there was no point wasting money and time on the flight. Several possiblities emerged: (A) Euro-Air to Rome, Alitalia to Egypt, (B) Euro-Air back to Amsterdam, KLM to Egypt. When checking options, it became quickly evident that the lack of a Euro-Air route map, and timetable, in the lounge was slowing the search process.

Recommendation #2 — For each and every Crown Alliance partner, provide a copy of the current timetable and route map to the staff in each Business Lounge.

Eventually, the flight departed about 2:30 a.m. By then, most passengers were quite tired, in part from the late hour and in part from the stress associated with the uncertainty. Prior to departure, I asked if there was an airline telephone I could use to call my contact in Egypt and see whether I should even get on the plane given the complete uncertainty about whether I would make it on time. The lounge staff said no (but that I would be able to be reimbursed for the cost of the call I made).

When seated on the plane, and just prior to landing, all passengers received a very terse apology from the pilot. I have received longer and more sincere-sounding apologies for 20-minute weather delays from other airlines.

EXHIBIT 1 *Continued*

Recommendation #3 — In the case of delays — especially long delays caused not by weather or mechanical problems, but Pilot Error – Apologize, Apologize, Apologize.

The perception of many of the premium fare customers (and I was clearly not the only one who held this view) was that Euro-Air seemed almost indifferent to the trouble/disruptions they were causing.

After the flight was airborne, I immediately sought out the Chief Purser, and explained the difficult situation I was in. I asked him to contact your hub and to have someone meet me upon landing with a solution. When the flight landed, I again went looking for the Purser (he had not come back to me). He assured me that there would be someone to meet me when the transfer bus dropped us at the arrival hall.

I was on the first bus off the plane. There were no Euro-Air staff to meet me at the arrival hall. I waited a few minutes until all the passengers from my bus went upstairs — and still there were no Euro-Air staff. The hall was empty. I then proceeded to the gate where the flight to Rome was leaving from because the Purser had earlier indicated that this might, in fact, be the eventual solution. At the check-in counter they had no knowledge of me, but were eventually able to tell me that I was booked on a flight to Amsterdam. One of the women at the Rome check-in counter told me repeatedly that I must have been mistaken about no one meeting my bus. I politely explained that I know what an empty room looks like.

I was directed to a different area where I was issued with new tickets (backtracking to Amsterdam, and thence to Egypt). My new arrival time in Egypt was to be 1:20 a.m. The KLM (Martinair) flight arrived in the Middle East a few minutes early. No offer had been made by Euro-Air to meet me in the Cairo airport, or arrange ground transportation (since my own previously arranged transportation was no longer available given the late hour.)

In fact, no offer of any form of compensation was ever made by Euro-Air. I find it incredible that an airline's highest fare-paying customers can be treated this way. Other airlines have such things as On Board Compensation Forms — for travel voucher or frequent flyer points — for relatively minor inconveniences such as reading lights that do not function.

Recommendation #4 — Compensate when the airline is at fault.

What Euro-Air caused me was not a minor inconvenience. It was a major inconvenience. I arrived exhausted in Egypt. Further, I knew I would be able to get a maximum of three hours sleep before my workday began there.

So, I leave you with the following questions.

1. If you were the passenger, how would you expect to be treated?
2. What, if anything, can Euro-Air and Crown Alliance learn from the saga?
3. Why should I ever fly Euro-Air again?

Sincerely,

Peter Boyd
Director, International Consulting Practice

cc   North-Am

THE WORLD AIRLINE INDUSTRY[1]

Air transport was the largest component of the world's largest industry (travel and tourism). The world's airlines carried over a billion passengers annually. One in four flights was to an international destination. Most airlines, including Euro-Air and its alliance partners, belonged to the International Air Transport Association (IATA). The approximately 250 members of IATA were responsible for about 95 percent of international scheduled air traffic.

Because aircraft such as a Boeing 747 cost in the range of US$150 million, airlines had large fixed costs, and worked very hard to fill their planes. Most international flights operated at an average of about 70 percent of available capacity (referred to as load factor) and slightly less for domestic flights.

The marginal cost to an airline of carrying an additional passenger was very small. Consequently, airlines spent a lot of effort trying to increase load factors by such activities as brand definition and promotion, loyalty programs, strong route systems, etc. Airline managements had only limited control over costs of production/operation (see chart below), which reduced their ability to compete solely on price.

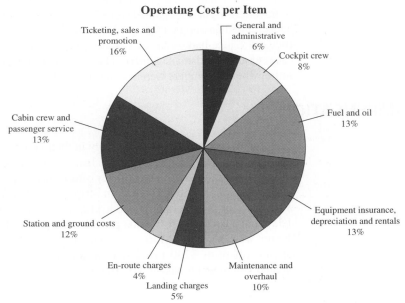

Operating Cost per Item

Ticketing, sales and promotion 16%

General and administrative 6%

Cockpit crew 8%

Fuel and oil 13%

Equipment insurance, depreciation and rentals 13%

Maintenance and overhaul 10%

Landing charges 5%

En-route charges 4%

Station and ground costs 12%

Cabin crew and passenger service 13%

Source: IATA, 1997.

Thus schedule, in-flight service and loyalty were the subjects of intense rivalry between airlines, and especially with the increase in interfirm collaboration. The most frequent flyers (such as Mr. Boyd) represented one half of 1 percent of passengers, but provided 40 percent of an airline's profits.

EURO-AIR

Originally state-owned, by the late 1990s, Euro-Air was completely privately owned and profitable. Euro-Air had a reputation for being safety-oriented and technically reliable. It had a stable work force, with union representation on the Euro-Air board of directors. In contrast to competitors such as Singapore Airlines, it was not known for its service culture. It had a fleet of over 200 aircraft, and was a member of the Crown Alliance network. According to its in flight magazine, this global partnership (one of several major groups which existed) had been formed to "make global travel easier and more convenient for its passengers." Euro-Air also operated a pilot training school, a catering service, and a major cargo freight business.

AIRLINE PASSENGER FAIR TREATMENT INITIATIVE

Complaints to the U.S. Department of Transportation about the airlines rose 20 percent in 1997 and 27 percent in 1998. In response to an escalating volume of complaints from outraged travellers, various consumer advocacy groups in the United States had sprung up. The impetus for lawsuits and legislation in support of travellers' rights had gained significant momentum in January when one airline had stranded passengers for up to eight hours on the runway during a snowstorm. Industry critics had observed that the current laws were punishing passengers in cases of airline mismanagement. The consumer groups were demanding compensation when passengers were inconvenienced.

COMPENSATION

The commercial airlines varied widely in their compensation practices. Three examples illustrate. Northwest Airlines had stranded passengers on planes for up to eight hours during a snowstorm. They offered passengers they had inconvenienced for more than 2½ hours a free round-trip ticket anywhere in the mainland USA, while Lufthansa merely provided a $125 credit on a future flight for a five-hour delay it had caused. Air Canada provided a $100 credit if the personal television did not work perfectly. Most passengers in North America were accustomed to receiving offers of $200 to $600 from airlines when they oversold a flight and wanted volunteers to take a later flight.

Endnote

1. This section draws from D. Reid, Mimeo on "Collaboration and Competition in the Global Airline Industry."

Part Three

Cases on Multinational Management

Chapter Thirty

Samsung China: The Introduction of Color TV

In October 1995, Mr. Chung Yong,[1] President of Samsung China Headquarters (SCH), was spearheading a major drive to integrate various business units in China into a single Samsung. Prior to the establishment of SCH in 1995, business activities in China had been conducted separately by each of Samsung's business units, based on its own business strategies. Mr. Chung was considering a recent meeting with the SCH marketing director, Hyun Young-Koo, who was responsible for developing a marketing strategy for the entire China market. The topic at the meeting was the marketing strategy for color TVs, which had been chosen as the flagship product for the China market. However, they had not yet agreed on a basic market strategy for China. The immediate decision was on the market segment and product line that SCH should target. Should SCH cover all the market segments and product lines? Or should SCH focus on the low-end market segment with a limited line of products, just as Samsung Electronics had done when it entered the U.S. market? Or should SCH target the high-end market segment, as most Japanese electronics companies had done in the United States and China markets?

Chang-Bum Choi prepared this case under the supervision of Professors Paul Beamish and David Sharp solely to provide material for class discussion. The authors do not intend to illustrate either effective or ineffective handling of a managerial situation. The authors may have disguised certain names and other identifying information to protect confidentiality.

THE CHINESE ECONOMIC ENVIRONMENT IN 1995

The Macro Environment

Although China had introduced many market-driven economic reforms, it was still primarily a centrally planned socialist economy. The most important lesson learned by foreign firms in China was that there was a huge gap between the stated plans and the actual ability of the government to manage and control the economy. Therefore, a tremendous amount of economic interaction took place outside the government's formal economic plan. In China's computer industry, for example, factories stood idle when printed circuit boards failed to be delivered as promised. The reason was either that circuit boards were diverted to another facility through the so-called "back door" or that the circuit board factory received the wrong order. Furthermore, smuggling and piracy were major issues in China as well as the USSR and other former Eastern Bloc nations.

Competition Among Governments: Self-Interest versus National Interest

There existed a high degree of competition among governments at both the central and local levels. This was due to a scarcity problem as well as the incomplete planning system. Governments tended to vie with one another to protect their already scarce resources. The self-interested competition among local governments caused another form of competition—"regional blockades". For example, one province or city might make an effort to utilize a foreign joint venture project as a means of expanding national market share. To counter what it called "market trespassing," government authorities in certain localities created various obstacles to block such competition. It was only after high level intervention from Beijing that the distribution channel would be opened up. Therefore, some MNEs targeting both the domestic market and the export market set up production bases in at least two places: typically, one in the south and the other in the north.

Difference in Emphasis on Economic Profitability versus Social Profitability

The Chinese government emphasized social profitability more than economic profitability when it evaluated the worthiness of a proposed project or the success of an existing project. The Chinese concept of social profitability referred to the benefits of a particular project in terms of "social factors" such as employment, the construction of a new building, the training of workers, the prestige or recognition that came from having a big, foreign-invested project located in one's province or city. These "soft" criteria could be a major source of confusion for foreign firms when determining whether or not a project would be attractive to their Chinese partner, because their socialist counterpart might be interested in something other than the basic ROI.

The Over-Employment Problem

Underlying the issue of social profitability was the fact that many socialist enterprises suffered from the problem of over-employment. Foreign managers visiting

Chinese factories often commented on the huge number of workers that seemed to be present, but not engaged in any real productive activities. Many foreign firms entering into joint venture agreements with socialist firms had found themselves in the position of having to inherit a large number of workers and staff, of which perhaps only 50 percent were needed to complete the production tasks at hand. While changes had been introduced to allow the streamlining of the work force, it was often politically difficult to release workers. Besides, China made it a compulsory rule to work only five days a week. The idea was that a five-day work week would make the company employ more workers.

The Micro Environment

The Chinese Color TV Industry

China was estimated to have an annual production capacity of 18 million color TV sets, with total output for 1995 hitting 16 million sets, including two million units exported to Europe, North America, Africa, and Australia. The Chinese government judged that its current TV production capacity was sufficient to fulfill demand in both domestic and export markets. On the demand side, the Chinese color TV market was the second largest after the U.S. and the third largest after NAFTA and EU in unit sales. As such, it had been the principal battleground for the major international color TV manufacturers. Therefore, the Chinese color TV industry was quite heterogeneous in terms of the composition of its supplying firms which came from many different nations, notably Japan, the Netherlands, France, and Germany. Exhibit 1 shows the market size of China, together with the other major markets.

Competition

Since the Chinese market was strategically important, competition in the color TV market was intense. In particular, Japanese firms stood out in the high-end market segment. Sony and Matsushita, with excellent brand recognition from high-income consumers, had a combined market share of about 75 percent in the high-end market segment. Their combined sales in 1994 were estimated to be around 1.5 million units. The next group of firms, including Sharp, Sanyo, Toshiba, Mitsubishi, JVC, and Hitachi had also established significant market share. On the production side, Japanese firms had already set up 19 production bases all over China. As part of their strategy to increase sales in China, they were said to have plans to increase the production bases from 19 to 30. On average, Japanese color TV manufacturers produced 69 percent of their production outside Japan. In the case of Sony, the overseas production ratio approached 90 percent.

China had more than 20 indigenous firms which focused on the low-end market segment. Some of them were competitive enough to attack the medium-end market segment. Changhong, Konka, and Panda were the three major local TV manufacturers in the country, with a combined domestic market share of nearly 35 percent. While Chinese firms were capable of competing with foreign firms in producing small and medium-sized sets, they were less competitive in large screen

EXHIBIT 1
The Demand for Color TVs in Selected Markets (in millions)

Source: JETRO, 1994

1990		1995		2000	
United States of America	20.8	NAFTA	29.4	NAFTA	28.7
Canada	1.6				
Mexico	1.2				
Germany	5.6	EU	20.5	EEA	22.9
United Kingdom	3.3				
Italy	2.8				
France	2.7	China	14.0	China	21.0
Netherlands	0.8	Japan	10.1	Japan	10.3
Spain	2.0	CIS	4.8	MERCOSUR*	7.6
China	7.7	Brazil	3.8		
Japan	9.6	Korea	2.1		
CIS	6.5	India	1.4	CIS	6.0
Brazil	2.3	Indonesia	1.2	ASEAN	4.7
Korea	2.0	Thailand	1.2		
India	0.7	Argentina	1.1	Korea	2.5
Thailand	0.9			India	2.0
Australia	0.9			Australia	0.8
Taiwan	0.8				
Poland	1.0				

*MERCOSUR is a common market in South America. Member countries are Brazil, Argentina, Paraguay, and Uruguay.

color TVs because of their low technology, insufficient capital, and lack of promotion. Furthermore, unlike the foreign firms which were notable for their global strategies, Chinese firms remained mostly national in the scope of their operations. Exhibit 2 shows the major Chinese firms and their product lines.

Market Size by Product Line

In the Chinese market, the small color TV (less than 17″) market was shrinking rapidly while the medium and large screen color TV markets were growing fast. As of 1995, the 18″, 20″ and 21″ sets made up the largest segments of the color TV market. Together the 20″ and 21″ screen sizes represented 60 percent of the total in 1994. The second largest screen-size category was 18″ which represented 23 percent of sales. Most Chinese firms marketed only a few of the most popular sizes of television sets, such as 18″, 20″ and 21″, because the large market size of these product lines facilitated the fast achievement of cost reduction not only through the experience curve but also through economies of scale. China's market size by product line was 29″—2 percent; 25″—11 percent; 21″—36 percent; 20″—24 percent; 18″—23 percent; 17″ or less—4 percent.

Market Penetration Level

In 1994, China had 300 million households. The percentage of households with a color TV set was just 41 percent. However, unlike the rural market, the urban market for color TV sets was nearing saturation. It was estimated that about 80 percent of China's 80 million urban households already owned a color TV, whereas

EXHIBIT 2
Major Chinese Color TV Manufacturers

Source: KORTA, 1995.

Brand Name	Product Size (in inches)
1. Changhong	18, 20, 21, 25, 29
2. Xiongmao (Panda)	18, 20, 21, 25, 29
3. Konka	18, 21, 25
4. Haiyan (Petrel)	18, 20
5. Hongmei	18, 20
6. Kongque (Peacock)	18, 20
7. Jingfeng	18, 20
8. Kaige	18, 20
9. Feiyao	18, 21
10. Changcheng (Great Wall)	18, 21
11. Xihu	18
12. Jingxing	18, 21
13. Xinghai	18
14. Shanyuan	18
15. Huanghe (Yellow River)	18
16. Beijing	20, 21
17. Shanghai	20, 21
18. Mudan (Peony)	18, 20

only 28 percent of 220 million rural households owned color TV sets. Though replacement demand in urban markets still remained, it did not offset the decreasing market potential for these products. This situation implied that the market strategy of depending on a low- and medium-end urban market segment was not a viable long-term option. However, the overall market was still expanding at a rate of 10 percent per year. The color TV market in China expanded rapidly from 12.6 million units in 1994 to 14 million units in 1995. In terms of unit sales, China's market size was one and half times as large as Japan's.

Consumer's Buying Power

McKinsey, the management consulting firm, determined that 60 million Chinese had per capita purchasing power exceeding US$1,000, an income level above which Chinese could start buying color TVs, washing machines, and imported clothing. By 1992, average per capita income levels in five urban areas had already topped the US$1,000 threshold. These were Shenzhen with US$2,000, Shanghai with US$1,700, Guangzhou with US$1,500, Beijing with US$1,400, and Tianjin with US$1,100. Exhibit 3 shows the cities where per capita income in 1995 exceeded Guangzhou's. Experts predicted that the list would grow to between 30 and 40 cities by the year 2000, and the number of Chinese above the US$1,000 threshold would hit 200 million.

Where were the Chinese getting all this money? First, many Chinese did not report all their income—they had more than the government knew about, thanks to a booming black market in labor, goods, services, and foreign exchange. Second, government housing subsidies meant that there were no mortgages in China. Hence, the

EXHIBIT 3
Cities above 1995
Guangzhou Level in
Per Capita Income

Source: China Statistical
Yearbook, 1995; McKinsey
analysis.

amount of household income the Chinese spent on housing and utilities was between
5 percent and 10 percent, compared with 20 percent to 40 percent in other East and
Southeast Asian countries. All this implies that the Chinese market had started to expand quickly in terms of high-end as well as low-end market segments.

First Mover Advantage

China was a market where the first mover enjoyed advantages over late comers.
Consumers had a tendency to be loyal to a first mover's products. This meant that
the first image of a product lasted long in the eyes of the consumer and that the
first to enter the market could gain the largest market share. In China, there was a
saying that "old friends are welcome," meaning that firms that came into the market early could be guaranteed that their initial "good will" would not be forgotten
when other firms entered the market. The first mover advantage effect can be evidenced by the market competition between Pepsi and Coca-Cola in China;

whichever firm had entered a city/province first, continued to have the dominant market share. In the color TV market, Japanese manufacturers that entered the China market first received the highest brand recognition from Chinese consumers. In particular, the Sony and Panasonic brands made up the largest market share in the high-end market segment.

Consumer Preferences

Consumers' color TV preferences in urban areas were different from those in rural areas. City dwellers were more concerned about brand names and the functionality of the products, while consumers in rural markets preferred color TVs with reasonable quality and lower prices. Consumers in rural areas preferred TVs with 21″ and 19″ screens which cost less than RMB 3,000 (US$361). Local manufacturers with the brand name of Panda shipped 21″ TVs at a price of RMB 3,000, whereas Japanese brand TVs cost well over RMB 4,000.

Protectionism

China was a highly protected market. Although the tariff for color TVs had decreased from 100 percent to 60 percent on average in 1995, it was still high. The tariffs for smaller than 15″, 17″, or 18″, and more than 19″ screen color TVs were 50 percent, 60 percent, and 65 percent respectively. In late 1995, the Ministry of Foreign Trade and Economic Cooperation (MOFTEC) announced that the tariff rates were scheduled to be lowered to 36 percent on average in 1997 and that it would make continuous efforts to lower its import tariffs to 15 percent, a level equal to that in most developing economies. Industry observers said that China strongly hoped to enter the World Trade Organization (WTO) which encouraged free trade among nations.

THE TV INDUSTRY

Product Differentiation

The importance of product differentiation through brand name recognition posed another barrier against firms relying on low prices for their unknown branded products. In the TV set industry, a few established firms such as Sony, Matsushita, and Philips had succeeded in making their brand names (Sony, Panasonic and Philips, respectively) well entrenched in many national markets through their global coverage. They had made significant up-front investments not only in advertising, but also in after-sales service facilities and dealer networks to support the brand image and to move from the low-end to the high-end market segment.

Economies of Scale and Learning Effects

Cost competitiveness obtained through economies of scale and the learning effect was a critical competitive weapon. Given that economies of scale always led to cost advantages for large scale firms over small scale firms and that the learning effect did the same thing unless the smaller firms came up with advanced production technologies, economies of scale and the learning curve effect functioned as other entry barriers in the TV set industry. In particular, Japanese giants in the consumer electronics industry were famous for exploiting these advantages on a large scale.

HOME COUNTRY (SOUTH KOREA)

Realities of the 1990s

One of the most significant threats Korean firms were facing by the mid-1990s was that Korea's major advantages in labor costs had been deteriorating not only in relation to advanced countries, but more importantly, in relation to its immediate competitors such as the Southeast Asian countries. Wages, averaging $1,144 a month, were now among the highest in Asia outside Japan. Considering the entry into the color TV industry of firms from the Peoples' Republic of China, the relative position of Korean firms as low cost suppliers would be increasingly endangered. Furthermore, The World Competitiveness Report of 1994, an annual assessment of relative economic prowess by Swiss business school IMD and the World Economic Forum, ranked South Korea sixth among 15 newly industrializing economies—behind even Malaysia and Chile. The South Korean economy was undergoing a fundamental restructuring. Moreover, the government, once so supportive of big business, had cut back on subsidies and export credits.

In short, Korean industries were no longer competitive in the low-end products. As an example, the market performance of Korean goods in the U.S. market, a representative global market, was poor. In particular, Korean goods were losing market share to Chinese goods. Korean share in the U.S. market declined from 3.7 percent in 1990 to 2.6 percent in 1996, whereas that of China went up from 2.0 percent to 6.4 percent in the same period. In order to make up for lost market share in low-end products and traditional industries, Korea had to catch up to developed countries in high-end products and in high-tech industries.

Market Liberalization

Another change in the home market was that the Korean domestic market witnessed new entries as it became more competitive. Thanks to deregulation of distribution channels in Korean markets, foreign firms were allowed to sell their products directly to consumers as of July 1993. Market entry barriers were supposed to be fully deregulated by 1996. By October 1995, foreign firms such as Sony, Matsushita, Sanyo, Sharp, Phillips, GE, Siemens, Whirlpool, and Laox were busy building their market competitiveness by developing distribution networks, professional sales forces, and after-sales services.

Existing firms would have to rely more on foreign business to compensate for potential losses in the domestic market. Samsung was facing increased competition in the home market as well as the global market.

SAMSUNG'S EXPERIENCE IN THE U.S.

Samsung Electronics Co. actively started to penetrate the U.S. market when it first set up its overseas marketing subsidiary there in 1979. The market strategy for the U.S. was to focus on the low-end market segment, based on its home country-specific comparative advantage in low labor costs. The low-end segment had two merits. One was that it had a large demand base and the other was that the market entry barriers were low.

Samsung particularly selected only a few of the most popular sizes of television sets, such as 13″ and 19″ sets, because the large market size of these two products enabled it to achieve cost reduction through economies of scale and the experience curve. In the market, traditionally the 13″ and 19″ sets had comprised the largest segments of the color TV market. The 19″ screen size represented 52 percent of total sales in 1983. The second largest screen-size category was 13″ which represented 19 percent of sales.

Furthermore, the competition in the low-end market segment was low because Japanese firms were changing their focus from the low-end to the medium- and high-end market segment. Investing heavily in advertising, Japanese firms were emphasizing color TV sets with innovative features suited to high-income markets.

At the beginning of U.S. market penetration, Samsung adopted mostly a "buyer brand name" product policy. It was understandable that, given its unknown brand names, the only way to create a volume large enough to achieve economies of scale was to adopt a "buyer brand name" policy, especially for large retailers or O.E.M.'s. By doing so, Samsung could rely on foreign buyers for marketing and physical distribution functions through the latter's established marketing networks.

However, Samsung tried to build its own brand image at the same time as it adopted a "buyer brand name" policy. Samsung retained its own brands mostly for small to medium-size buyers, and used buyers' brands for mass retailers and O.E.M. buyers. This dual branded-product policy was intended to reconcile both the short-term and long-term objectives of the firm. The short-term objective was high volume business initially to achieve the experience curve and economies of scale, and the long-term one was stable volume business with differentiated products through the establishment of its brand name.

In terms of production, it served the U.S. market by establishing a production subsidiary in 1984. According to the firm, the major reason was that the U.S. trade barrier, which it had thought to be temporary, turned out to be more or less a long-standing one, though not permanent. The clincher was the antidumping suit filed by a few U.S. domestic firms and labor unions in 1983. This charge, which would add extra costs in the form of antidumping duties if Korean firms were found guilty, would easily wipe out the already low margins of the export business. However, in anticipation of NAFTA, the assembly plant in New Jersey was moved to Tijuana, Mexico, in 1988. Samsung Electronics Mexicana (SAMEX) which had been expanded in 1992, produced 1.17 million color TVs in 1994. Exhibit 4 shows SEC's color TV production network in 1994.

In the U.S. market, Samsung Electronics grew to be one of the top 12 companies with approximately 3 percent of market share in 1995 (see Exhibit 5). However, Samsung Electronics's operating profit was much smaller than that of

EXHIBIT 4 Samsung Electronics' 1994 Color TV Production (1000's of units)

	Suwon (Korea)	SAMEX (Mexico)	SEH (Hungry)	SEMUK (UK)	SETAS (Turkey)	TSE (Thai)	TTSEC (China)	Total
13″	1	219				264	15	499
14″	1,188	43	71	97	9	109	55	1,572
16″	96					8		104
19″	12	610						622
20″	1,480	48	80	398	32	46		2,084
21″	454	62	12	160	12	25		725
25″	53	99	2	36				190
26″	23	5				1		29
27″		70						70
28″	6			51				57
29″	69	8	1					78
31″		3						3
33″	2	3						5
Others	14							14
Total	3,397	1,172	165	742	53	453	70	6,051

Source: Company data.

EXHIBIT 5
Color TV Market Share and Price Position in the U.S.

Source: Robert Lanich, *Market Share Reporter—1997,* Gale, New York, 1997.Gale Research Inc., Consumer Product and Manufacturer Ratings, Detroit, 1994

Company (Brand Name)	Market Share (1) (%)	Overall Price Position (2)
Thomson (RCA/GE)	21	72/65
North America Philips (Magnavox)	14	70
Zenith (Zenith)	13	75
Sony (Sony)	7	80
Sharp (Sharp)	6	69
Emerson (Emerson)	5	64
Sanyo Fisher (Sanyo)	5	69
Toshiba (Toshiba)	5	73
Matsushita (Panasonic/JVC)	4	72/73
Mitsubishi (Mitsubishi)	3	75
Samsung (Samsung)	3	67
LG (LG)	2	61
Others	12	

Note: 1. Market shares shown are based on 25.2 million units shipped in 1995.
2. Ratings are based on a scale of 0 to 100.
3. According to 1996 report of U.S. Bureau of Census, population and households are 265 and 98 million, respectively.

Matsushita (Panasonic) with 4 percent market share. The reason was that Samsung could not avoid intense competition in the low-end segment because products in that segment were not differentiated. However, Matsushita in the high-end market could avoid intense competition and so commanded a much higher price than Samsung, based on differentiating its products through brand name recognition (see Exhibit 6). Exhibit 7 shows Samsung's quality score in 1995 according to *Consumer Reports.* Samsung still seemed to pursue an aggressive pricing strategy.

EXHIBIT 6

Comparison of
Advertising Expenses
among Major
Electronics Firms in
the U.S. Market
(1968–94)

Source: Media Watch.

Brand	Cumulative Advertising Expenses (US$ million)
Sony	522
Matsushita (Panasonic)	413
Sharp	278
Samsung	27

EXHIBIT 7

The Comparison
between Quality
and Price

Source: *Consumer Reports,*
1995.

20″ Color TV—1995

Brand Name	Quality Index	Average Retail Price (US$)
Sharp 20-FM100	86	235
Zenith SMS2049S	83	235
RCA F20602SE	82	235
Zenith SMS1935S	82	225
GE 20GT324	81	215
Samsung TTB-2012	**80**	**210**
Sony KV-20M10	79	290
Sanyo AVM-2004	75	210
Zenith SMS1917GS	70	210
Panasonic CT-20R11	68	260
Emerson TC1972A	59	185

27″ Color TV—1995

Brand Name	Quality Index	Average Retail Price (US$)
Panasonic CT-27SF11	95	650
Samsung TXB2735	**94**	**430**
Sony KV-2756	93	740
Toshiba CF27D50	93	555
JVC AV-27BP5	90	615
Mitsubishi CS-27303	89	635
Toshiba CX27D60	89	630
RCA F27701BK	87	605
Magnavox TP2790 B101	86	565
RCA F27701BK	86	535
Zenith SM2789BT	85	620
Goldstar GCT2754S	83	405
Sony KV-27V10	82	615
Panasonic CT-27S18	79	590
Sanyo AVM-2754	79	380
GE 27GTR618	78	400
Zenith S2773BT	75	520

In 1995, Samsung Electronics' total color TV production volume was 6 million units, 44 percent of which were produced overseas. It had six overseas production bases: SAMEX (Mexico), SEH (Hungry), SEMUK (UK), SETAS (Turkey), TSE (Thailand), TTSEC (China). The largest production base was SAMEX in Mexico which produced 19 percent of overseas production. TTSEC of China produced 70,000 units, most of which were 14″ TV sets. TTSEC was originally intended as an export base. Besides six overseas production bases, four more production bases—SEDA (Brazil), SVEC (Vietnam), SEIL (India), and SESA (Spain)—were under construction.

Samsung Electronics, ranked 221st in Fortune's Global 500 in 1995, was the largest consumer electronics firm in Korea. It recorded US$21 billion in total sales in 1995, up 40 percent from the 1994 figure of $14.6 billion. Net income grew to $3.2 billion in 1995 from $1.2 billion in 1994.

Samsung Electronics was organized into four divisions—semiconductors, telecommunication systems, multimedia, and home appliances. In terms of sales contribution, the largest division was the semiconductor division which accounted for 47.9 percent of total sales in 1995, a big jump from 39.8 percent in 1994. The semiconductor division made Samsung the second largest DRAM chip producer in the world. Home appliances was Samsung Electronics' second largest division. In 1996, the sales of the home appliances division grew by 13.3 percent to 5,127 billion Korean won, thanks to a 31 percent increase in TV sales in emerging markets.

SAMSUNG'S MARKET PARTICIPATION IN CHINA

In 1985, when Chung first moved to Beijing to pioneer new businesses for the Samsung Group, his phone rarely rang. These days, he sat in a suite on the fifteenth-floor of the Beijing Bright China Chang An Building and his phone rang constantly. "Now we have more than 13 projects all over China and the list is getting longer all the time," he said, motioning towards the maps on his wall (see Exhibit 8). More than 16 projects throughout China projected Samsung both as a major investor in China and as a multinational company with a global vision.

However, Samsung's active move into the Chinese market had really started only after Beijing and Seoul established diplomatic relations in 1992. Before 1992, the Chinese market was indirectly penetrated through Hong Kong because the Korean government strictly regulated business investment in China. As a result, Samsung's market presence was far behind that of the Japanese electronics companies. Furthermore, prior to the establishment of SCH in 1995, Samsung's focus was on investment in production facilities all over China rather than marketing its own products in China. That was because the Chinese government strongly encouraged foreign companies in China to focus on exports rather than the domestic market.

EXHIBIT 8 Samsung Business Group's Production Facilities in China

Business Unit of Samsung Group	Location	Equity Position	Products	Investment Startup	Operation Startup
Samsung	Huizhou	90%	Audio system	Aug. 1992	Jul. 1993
Electronics	Tianjin	50%	VCR	Feb. 1993	Jun. 1993
Co., Ltd.	Standing, Weihai	62%	Telecommunication switching system	Aug. 1993	Sep. 1993
	Guangdong	90%	Compact disk player	Sep. 1993	
	Tianjin	50%	CTV	Jun. 1994	Jan. 1995
	Suzhou	100%	Semiconductor assembly	Dec. 1994	Jul. 1996
	Suzhou complex	80%	Refrigerator Microwave Oven Washing Machine Air Conditioner	Jul. 1995	Sep. 1996
Samsung Aerospace Industries Co., Ltd.	Tianjin	55%	Camera	Feb. 1994	
Samsung Corning Co., Ltd.	Tianjin	100%	Head drum for VTR	Apr. 1992	
Samsung Electro- Mechanics Co., Ltd.	Tianjin	91%	Electronic components for TV	Dec. 1993	
	Tianjin	91%	Assembly metal	Dec. 1995	
	Guangdong	100%	Speaker, Deck, Keyboard.	Jul. 1992	
	Guangdong	100%	Assembly metal	Dec. 1995	

Source: Company data.

In 1995, Samsung established SCH in Beijing to coordinate the more than 16 operations, each of which had been separately managed by the various business units of the Samsung Group. SCH would be responsible for coordinating all development, production, logistics, and marketing in China, most of which had previously been done in Seoul. SCH would also formulate the overall marketing strategy for China, in place of separate plans from each business unit headquarters in Seoul. The establishment of SCH would enhance Samsung's insider image in China because it showed Samsung's commitment to the Chinese market. The SCH would also speed up the accumulation of local knowledge of the market which had been acquired by each business unit. In April 1995 when Lee Kun-Hee, chairman of Samsung (the largest non-Japanese conglomerate in Asia with US$54 billion in sales), visited Beijing, he announced that the Samsung Group would invest an additional US$4 billion in China by the year 2000. Exhibit 9 shows the relationship of SCH to other business units in the Samsung Group and Exhibit 10 shows the organization chart of SCH.

EXHIBIT 9   **Organization Chart of Samsung Business Group**

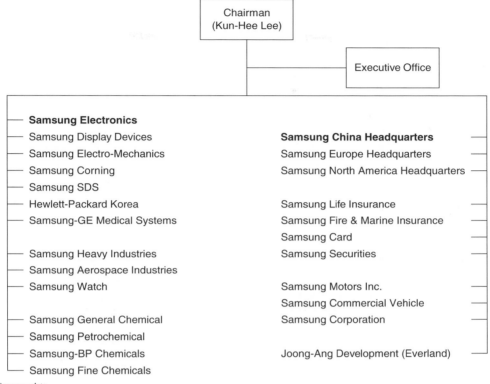

Source: Company data.

OPTIONS AND CONTROVERSIES

Mr. Chung, who was responsible for coordinating Samsung's business units in China, had proposed that Samsung introduce the high-end color TV first in order to position Samsung as a premium product producer. His argument for prioritizing a premium brand image was aligned with Samsung Group's recent commitment to its higher quality image. However, the idea had been met with skepticism from Samsung's Seoul headquarters. Many in Seoul questioned the idea of introducing a high-end product in a market with annual per capita income levels of US$353. China was stereotyped in Seoul as the land of "subsistence-level peasants, mystic sages on mountaintops, Chairman Mao's "Little Red Book", 89-year-old Deng Xiaoping and the events in Tiananmen Square."

Many in Samsung Electronics supported the low-end market strategy. It emphasized that the low-end market segment was still the largest market segment in China. It also pointed to the relatively faster growth in sales of small and medium-sized

EXHIBIT 10 Organization Chart of Samsung China Headquarters

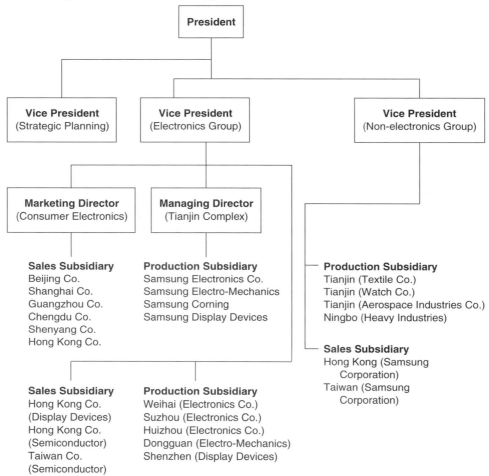

Source: Company data.

product lines. Moreover, it was argued that the Samsung brand could compete effectively with local TV manufacturers better than Japanese TV manufacturers. They asserted that these markets, where the largest demand existed, should be targeted.

Moreover, a premium-priced product would not sell in large volumes in the Chinese market, it was argued. Some of the Seoul-based people in Samsung Electronics, which was supposed to supply SCH with color TVs, were more interested in sales volume. Because Korean consumer electronics firms had invested in production capacities which far exceeded the domestic market size to realize scale economies, they had a high fixed cost. This led to a volume business-oriented strategy necessary to achieve break-even. In fact, the consumer electronics industry, including color TVs, was recognized as a global industry where scale economies in product development and manufacturing, rather than responsiveness to national market demands, were considered key success factors.

However, Mr. Chung thought that if Samsung did not establish a strong brand image in China, it would have to lower prices to offset the Japanese high brand image. In fact, Japanese firms that had a high quality brand reputation commanded a high price in both China and North America. Moreover, Japanese consumer electronics products which were produced in Southeast Asia were as competitive in terms of price as Korean consumer electronics products which were produced in Korea and Southeast Asia. Therefore, Mr. Chung thought, "if we do not build up a brand image equivalent to that of Japanese firms, we could not compete in China as well as in North America in the near future". Mr. Chung also thought that China was not going to stay in the low-end market even though the low-end market was currently the largest one. The product line Mr. Chung wanted to introduce to China was the latest 29″ model which had recent success in Korea. Mr. Chung wanted to present to the people in Seoul a clear reason why Samsung China should start with high-end products rather than low-end products.

Endnote

1. The name is written as it would be in Korean: family name first and first name last.

Chapter Thirty-One

Dubai Aluminium

دوبال
dubal

In 1994, Dubai Aluminium—known as Dubal—had built a reputation as a producer of high quality aluminium, including billet, ingot, and high purity products. Its capacity of 250,000 tonnes per annum (tpa) made it an important international producer, although much smaller in size than industry leaders such as Alcoa and Alcan.

Yet its financial performance was disappointing. By the early 1990s, after more than a dozen years of weak financial performance, there was serious discussion of closing the site. In 1993, Dubal's owners—the ruling family of the Emirate of Dubai—appointed a new vice chairman, Mohamed Alabbar. After an extensive audit, Alabbar reorganized the company, leading to the departure of several senior executives. The following year, Dubal hired a new chief executive officer, a veteran from Alcan named Ian Rugeroni.

Rugeroni joined an underperforming company with a demoralized management team. The situation, he recalled later, was desperate. Yet as he assessed Dubal's people, its manufacturing processes, and its geographic position, Rugeroni concluded that Dubal could achieve great things.

As he prepared to meet his top management team for the first time, Rugeroni faced some basic choices. Of all the changes he might make, which were most urgent, and which should be deferred? For instance, should he immediately change

Professor Philip Rosenzweig prepared this case as a basis for class discussion rather than to illustrate either effective or ineffective handling of a business situation.

Dubal's sales and marketing approach? Should he attempt to improve Dubal's efficiency at its present size, or should he undertake an expansion project? How should he try to revitalize Dubal's confidence and improve its company culture?

DUBAI AND THE UNITED ARAB EMIRATES

The Emirate of Dubai is one of seven states that comprise the United Arab Emirates (see map on Exhibit 1). Since becoming an independent nation in 1971, the UAE has prospered, thanks in large part to oil and gas revenues. The largest emirate, Abu

EXHIBIT 1 **Map of the Arabian Peninsula**

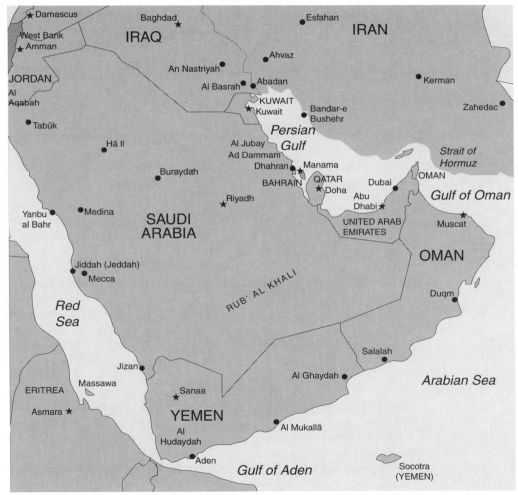

Source: Perry-Castañeda Library Map Collection: http://www.lib.utexas.edu/maps/ (originally produced by the US Central Intelligence Agency)

EXHIBIT 2   **Map of the United Arab Emirates with Dubai and Jebel Ali Port**

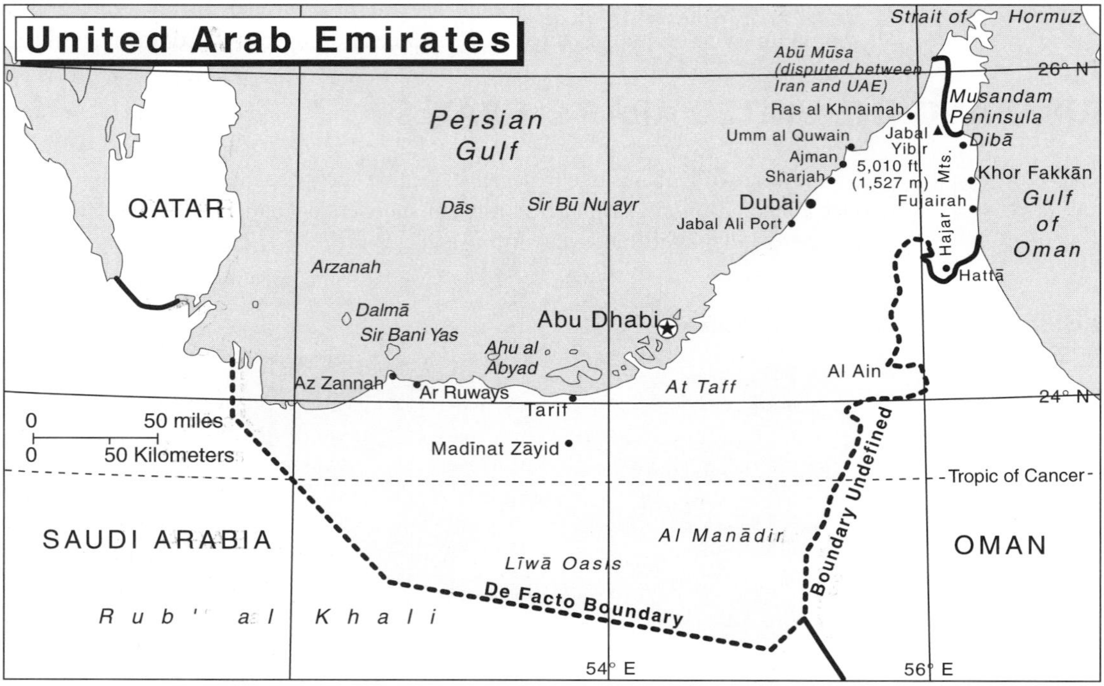

Source: www.mapquest.com

Dhabi, enjoys vast oil reserves. Dubai, the second largest emirate, has oil and gas revenues but on a smaller scale. Rather, Dubai's growth has been due to its unique history and to the vision of its rulers.

The Emirate of Dubai included the city of Dubai and a thin strip of land along the shore of the Arabian Gulf toward Abu Dhabi (see map on Exhibit 2). The city of Dubai grew up next to a natural harbor and has been, since the Middle Ages, a hub of trading and commerce. By the early 20th century, Dubai was a thriving commercial center and attracted settlers from Persia and India. In 1954, the British set up their administrative headquarters for the Persian Gulf in Dubai. One observer noted: "The international trade which flowed from these cosmopolitan contacts was the basis of rapidly growing prosperity."[1]

Until the 1950s, Dubai's economy was based on coastal activities of fishing, trade, and the harvesting of pearls, while the sparse inland population grew dates and raised goats and sheep. The discovery of oil in 1958 transformed the regional economy. Dubai's fortunes improved further with the rise of oil prices in the 1970s. Yet Dubai's rulers were determined not to let the Emirate become dependent on natural resources. Under the rule of Sheikh Rashid bin Saeed al-Maktoum, Dubai embarked on a path of economic diversification, using its oil wealth to transform itself into a modern center for trade, services, manufacturing, and tourism. By the time of Sheikh Rashid's death in 1990, Dubai had become the most dynamic and modern economic center in the region.

One by-product of Dubai's drive for economic growth was the need to augment its local population with expatriates. Thousands of people, often from India, Pakistan, the Philippines, came to Dubai for employment opportunities. By 2001, Dubai's population of almost one million included only 20 percent UAE Nationals.

FOUNDING DUBAI ALUMINIUM

A key element in Sheikh Rashid's development plan for Dubai was the creation of a free trade zone in Jebel Ali, 50 km (30 miles) south of the city. Many leading companies from Europe, Asia, and the Americas based their regional activities in Dubai. In the 1970s, Dubai built a deep-water port at Jebel Ali, capable of accommodating the largest oil tankers and container ships in the world.

Sheikh Rashid also encouraged the development of manufacturing, and identified aluminium as a priority. Aluminium made sense for several reasons. First, an aluminium company would benefit from the port at Jebel Ali by importing bulk raw materials in large quantities; and, conversely, it would become a major customer to the Jebel Ali port. Second, aluminium manufacturing is highly energy intensive and benefits from proximity to abundant sources of oil and gas. Third, waste heat from the power station could be used to run a desalination plant, providing fresh water to a growing community. Finally, Dubai's rulers wanted new industrial developments to provide career opportunities for its population.

Dubai Aluminium Company Ltd., known as Dubal, was founded in 1975 with a small amount of seed money. Financing for construction of the plant was secured through loans from international banks. The initial construction finance was either arranged or guaranteed by the owners. The resulting loans from financial institutions were repaid by the owners and treated as an advance from the owners on Dubal's books.

In 1977, an American company, NSA (National Southwire Aluminum), arrived to oversee the construction of the plant. At the outset, Dubal had a dedicated power plant, a carbon plant, a smelter with three potlines, a casthouse and an annual production capacity of 135,000 tpa. The first potline began operation on November 12, 1979.

Once the plant was operational, NSA departed and management of Dubal was turned over to a core of professionals, mostly British expatriates, many of whom had previously worked at Aluminium Bahrain. Dubai's rulers, the al-Maktoum family, were owners of Dubal, with Sheikh Hamdan bin Rashid al-Maktoum as chairman. Management, meanwhile, rested in the hands of British expatriates.

THE WORLD ALUMINIUM MARKET

Aluminium is a basic commodity, known for its qualities of high strength and light weight. Aluminium is produced by reducing raw materials, including alumina, coke, and carbon pitch, to a hot liquid through a highly energy intensive process

EXHIBIT 3 Aluminum Production Process

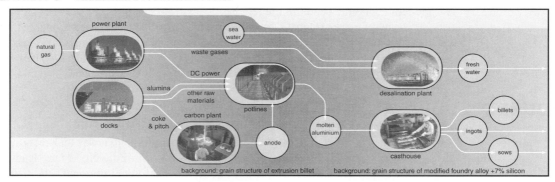

The production of aluminium involves several steps:

A. Aluminium production requires a great deal of power. Dubal uses natural gas to run its power plant, and is entirely self-sufficient in meeting its power needs.

B. Raw materials include high-grade alumina, calcinated petroleum coke, and tar coal pitch. Dubal imports these raw materials in large quantities to its own docks at Jebel Ali port.

C. At the carbon plant, coke and pitch are mixed together and compacted into anode blocks. These are then baked to retain only pure carbon.

D. Metal rods are then connected to the anode blocks to enable them to pass electrical current when immersed in the electrolyte in the pot.

E. Aluminium smelting brings together anode blocks, alumina and other raw materials, and DC power. Aluminium is produced in a reduction cell called a "pot" by the electrochemical reduction of aluminium oxide (alumina). Between 13 and 15 megawatt-hours of energy are needed to produce one tonne of liquid metal.

Anodes and cathodes used in the process are made from carbon. The anodes, which are consumed during the process, are made from high purity petroleum coke and coal tar pitch. The pot is a large metal shell lined with carbon, which acts as a reservoir for the molten metal. This metal is vacuum tapped every 32 hours into crucibles. The process is carried out at 960-970°C, at which temperature the electrolyte and metal are both molten.

F. Molten aluminium is transported to the casthouse, where it is cast into three categories of products: billets, ingots, and high purity aluminium.

G. Waste heat from power plants can be used to generate steam for the desalination of sea water.

Source: Company information.

called smelting, and finally casting the liquid into solid metal. There are three groups of products: *Billets* are long logs cast from aluminium alloy, used by aluminium extruders to make products such as window frames for the construction industry. *Ingots* are large blocks cast from foundry alloy, used to make such things

EXHIBIT 4   World Primary Aluminum Consumption: 1960–1994

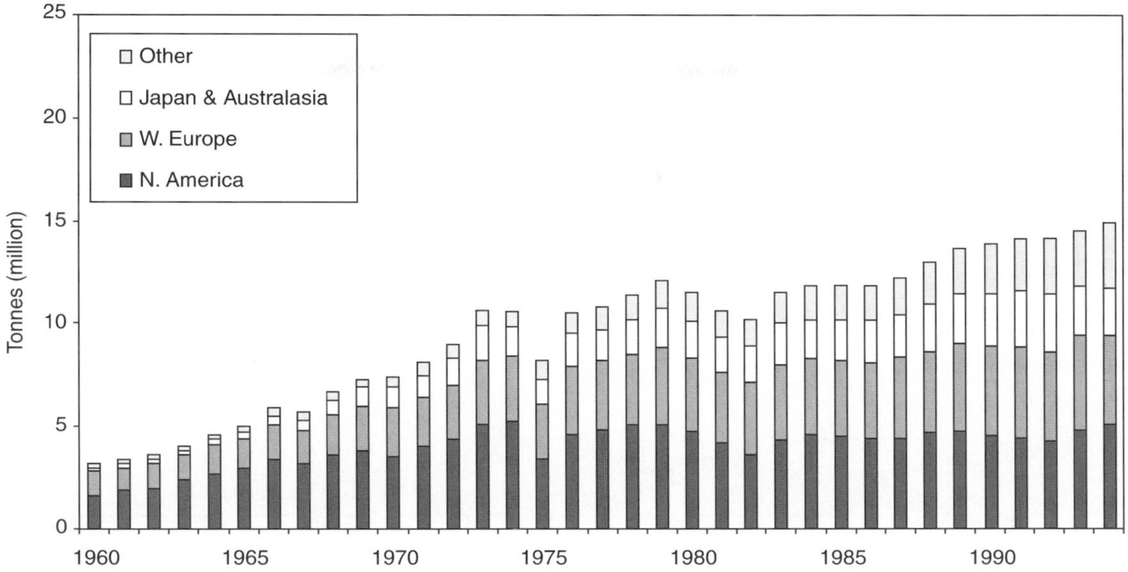

Source: Company information.

as wheels for cars. *High purity aluminium* is poured directly from crucibles into large molds called "sows," and is used for specialized applications such as computer hard disks and electrical components such as capacitors. (Refer to Exhibit 3 for a more detailed description of the production process.)

Demand for aluminium products had risen steadily over the past decades, with consumption growing in all parts of the world, as shown on Exhibit 4. Used in many industrial applications, aluminium was a highly cyclical commodity, subject to sharp swings in demand and volatility in price. Aluminium was traded on the London Metal Exchange (LME). In recent years prices had been fairly stable, although falling. The LME price for 99.7 percent pure aluminium had declined gradually in the 1990s, and had dipped below $1,200 per metric tonne in 1993 (see Exhibit 5).

Dubal's Activities

From the time it began operations in 1979, Dubal focused on the production of aluminium. Dubal's manufacturing site included a dedicated power generation plant, a carbon plant for the transformation of raw materials, potlines for smelting, and a casthouse. Each part of the manufacturing process was in balance with the others: the power plant generated sufficient electricity to run the smelters, whose output could be handled by the casthouse. As an added benefit, waste heat from the power plant was used to run a desalination plant.

Dubal received all raw materials at its own docks at the nearby Jebel Ali port. It bought raw materials on contract.

EXHIBIT 5   **LME Price: 1990–1994**

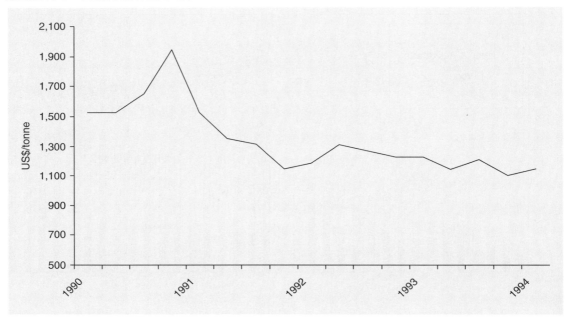

Source: Company information.

Dubal had no downstream sales and marketing activities, but sold its entire output to traders and was paid the LME price plus a small premium. The aluminium was in turn sold to companies that remelted it and used it for a variety of purposes. Some of Dubal's products, including semi-finished billet for extrusion, were worth more to certain end-users than 99.7 percent pure commodity aluminium, and could be sold by traders at a substantially higher price. In other instances, Dubal made products that included certain alloys, which were worth a further premium to end-users.

Yet Dubal was unable to capture higher value for its products, receiving only slightly more than the LME price from traders. One manager recalled that, on average, Dubal would have been able to earn 10 percent above the LME price for its output if it had been able to sell directly to customers. "We left 10 percent on the table—and 10 percent on 245,000 tonnes is a lot."

By 1994, Dubal relied on a group of 12 traders, 6 in Japan, Dubal's largest single market, and 6 elsewhere in Asia and Europe. These traders were the exclusive intermediary between Dubal and its final customer. Dubal had no direct knowledge of customer needs, nor could it predict future customer demands, whether in terms of quantity, specifications, or timing. One Dubal manager recalled: "The traders had all the advantage—they owned the customer relationship."

In addition to earning margins on the sale of aluminium, traders made money by buying and selling forward contracts. Options to buy, known as calls, allowed the purchase of a specified quantity of aluminium on a given date at an agreed

price. Options to sell, known as puts, allowed the sale of a specified quantity on a given date at an agreed price. By understanding market movements, traders could take forward positions and benefit from anticipated movements. Furthermore, by combining puts and calls, traders could hedge their positions and manage risk.

Dubal's Management

Dubal was organized by major functions, called divisions (see Exhibit 6). Reporting to the CEO were six divisional managers. Four were high-level staff positions: Technology, Finance, Corporate Services, and Human Resources. Sales and Marketing was a small group, with just six employees, responsible for facilitating sales to Dubal's traders. The final division, Operations, included all production activities, from power generation and desalination to smelting and casting, as well as the shared support services of engineering and maintenance. A single manager was in charge of each of these operational activities.

By organizing operations in this manner, Dubal aimed to share support services and avoid duplication, yet this approach had an unanticipated effect: Managers in charge of key processes, such as power generation, smelting, and casting, did not have control of all the resources necessary for them to meet their goals, but relied on shared engineering and maintenance support. The result was a culture of excuses, as managers could blame others for their lack of performance.

CORPORATE CULTURE

Since Dubal's founding, its style of management could be described as formal and tightly controlled. Many employees described it as a "command and control" culture. Each department had very clear performance targets, but aside from top management, no one saw the entire picture. Nor did managers in the various operations, such as smelting, casting, or marketing, have much direct contact with each other. Overall profit figures were not communicated, and information was shared on a "need to know" basis.

Many of Dubal's managers, both expatriates and Nationals, recalled a company culture that was neither open nor transparent. As one later commented:

> You didn't have a clue what was going on. It was: *Know your place.* There were no discussions about marketing, revenues, profits. No one saw a P/L.

EXHIBIT 6
Dubal Organizational Chart 1994

Source: Company information.

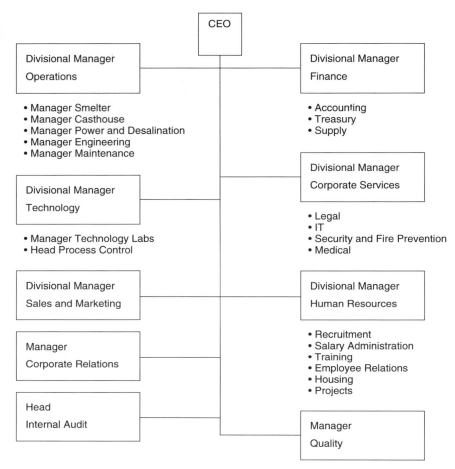

There was, in addition, no clear system of job ratings, no clarity about performance evaluation, and no standard approach to salary reviews. There had been no predictability about raises, no objectivity or transparency. Bonuses were paid in white envelopes at Christmas time, but no one was sure who was getting what or why. Not surprisingly, the lack of any clear system was a source of much concern.

A MULTINATIONAL WORKFORCE

Dubal's workforce numbered 1,700. Most workers came from India, Pakistan, or the Philippines. They had been recruited in their home countries and were brought to Dubal, where they tended to be long-term employees. Citizens of the UAE—

known as Nationals—held a variety of positions at Dubal, including front-line supervision in the power station, carbon plant, smelter, and casthouse, as well as many white-collar jobs in finance and administration. A number of Nationals had good technical training, including advanced degrees from Western universities, but so far none had been promoted above superintendent level. Senior management remained exclusively in the hands of expatriates. One National explained that many European expatriates believed that UAE Nationals weren't capable of senior management. Others believed that perceptions of competence were an excuse—expatriates naturally resisted nationalization since it signaled a loss of power. Either way, by the 1990s, there was a cohort of young Nationals who hadn't been properly developed.

The Early 1990s: Performance Worries

Dubal earned a reputation as a high quality producer of ingots, billets and high purity aluminium products. In 1990 it added a fourth potline, expanding its capacity to about 270,000 tpa. One manager recalled: "Each year we got a bonus, and output was good. So we thought everything was going well."

Yet in terms of financial performance, the company was struggling. Not only had it failed to earn a dividend, but it had also received a total of $1.5 billion in cash advances from its owners for working capital, mainly in the early years of operation. By the 1990s, the owners were running out of patience.

In 1993, Dubal's revenues were estimated at about $350 million, or 270,000 metric tonnes at an average LME price of $1,300 per tonne.[2] Costs were approximately the same. Dubal's cost structure, shown on Exhibit 7, included 44 percent for raw materials, 26 percent for electricity, 5 percent for production labor, 12 percent for depreciation, and 13 percent for all other expenses including sales, general and administrative expenses.

APPOINTMENT OF MOHAMED ALABBAR

In an effort to get greater control over the company, Dubal's owners turned to a bright and energetic UAE National named Mohamed Alabbar. In his early thirties, Mohamed Alabbar was not a member of the ruling family, but came from a family with long experience in business and entrepreneurship. He had studied and worked in the United States, where he expanded his business knowledge. Upon his return, Mohamed Alabbar was named director general of the Department of Economic Development. In 1993, he was also appointed vice chairman of Dubal.

Although he had no background in aluminium, Mohamed Alabbar was a shrewd businessman who could take charge of the company and make tough decisions. His objective was clear: Fix Dubal or close it. After 15 years of operation, and $1.5 billion invested, poor financial performance would no longer be tolerated.

One of Mohamed Alabbar's first actions was to assign a team of internal auditors to discover the source of problems. They found problems throughout the

EXHIBIT 7
Dubal Cost Profile:
1994

Source: Company estimates

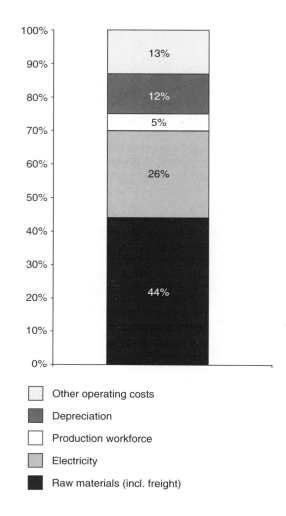

organization. As Abdullah Kalban, a long-time Dubal manager and a UAE National, recalled:

> On the front end, when it came to procuring raw materials, Dubal was paying too much. There were even allegations of improprieties. The manufacturing operation wasn't cost efficient—it was of high quality, but not efficient. And on the back end, traders captured substantial margins. We had an operation of high quality and with good people, but we weren't performing well financially.

Based on the internal auditors' report, Mohamed Alabbar reorganized the senior management team. The chief executive, deputy chief executive, chief financial officer, and marketing and sales manager soon left the company. An executive search firm found a new CEO. Soon, however, he was replaced by a long-time Dubal manager who acted as a caretaker chief executive for the next six months.

Internal candidates were promoted to fill the posts of chief financial officer and marketing manager.

Mohamed Alabbar next brought in the consulting firm, Arthur D. Little, to conduct a thorough analysis of Dubal's operations. ADL reported that Dubal had good technical operations, good control processes, and good people. In fact, ADL concluded the company's economic position could be improved by expanding capacity, which would provide significant economies of scale in procurement and manufacturing. Rather than undertake a major expansion all at once—very difficult given the capital costs involved, as well as the managerial challenge—ADL advised Dubal to expand in increments over the next few years. Dubal might first add power generation capacity, then expand the smelter operations, and finally add to the casthouse.

After his first year as vice chairman, Mohamed Alabbar decided that Dubal had to make a few fundamental changes. First, rather than rely on traders, Dubal needed to establish direct contact with customers. Not only would direct sales remove the margins earned by traders, but they would also provide direct information about customer needs and their buying patterns. Second, Dubal had to lower its costs of production, through the procurement of raw materials as well as throughout the production process. Finally, management needed to become increasingly composed of UAE Nationals, rather than continuing to rely on expatriates, and more broadly, the management environment of the company had to become open and dynamic. These three points became the centerpiece of Mohamed Alabbar's vision for Dubal.

A first priority, however, was to find a CEO who would be a strong leader. When Alabbar asked ADL for a recommendation, it suggested Ian Rugeroni, an experienced manager who was soon planning to retire from Alcan.

ARRIVAL OF IAN RUGERONI

Rugeroni was an Argentine-born Canadian citizen with 35 years of experience in the aluminium industry. Most recently he had managed all of Alcan's downstream activities in North America, which included 21 divisions and 50 plants. When Alcan decided to sell its downstream business, Rugeroni decided it was time to retire. Then came the call from Mohamed Alabbar.

Intrigued by the turnaround possibility at Dubal, Rugeroni flew to the UAE for a visit. As he flew across the Atlantic, Rugeroni reviewed the ADL report. "The report was very clear," he recalled. "It said, be careful, you have an excellent operation here."

Once in Dubai, Rugeroni met Mohamed Alabbar and was immediately impressed with the vice chairman's energy and commitment. He also met a number of Dubal managers. One of them, John Boardman, recalled their conversation:

> Ian asked me, "John, why are you still here? You're a talented manager, with good qualifications. Why haven't you left?"
>
> I told him: "I've been tempted, but we've got three good things. First is a first class asset: an excellent power station, smelter, and desalination plant. Second, we

have a wonderful workforce—they're skilled, they'll bend light for good leadership. Third, this is a great location for an aluminium smelter. We have a jewel here. If we had good leadership we could turn it around, and I want to be part of it."

After reflection, Rugeroni concluded that he could help turn Dubal around. In fact, after running an operation as complex as Alcan's downstream business, he believed that improving performance at a single-site operation shouldn't be too difficult. Yet he asked Mohamed Alabbar for no contract. As Rugeroni put it:

> If I don't like it here, I'll leave; and if you don't like me, you'll fire me. So there's no need for a contract.

Taking Charge

On May 1, 1994, Rugeroni became CEO of Dubal. He inherited a budget for 1994 that expected Dubal to break even, but not to earn a profit. He also inherited a set of managers who were demoralized after the recent performance problems and turnover of senior executives. As he later recalled:

> The situation in 1994 was desperate. The company hadn't made any money since the beginning. The mandate given to Mohamed Alabbar was, fix it or close it. That's how desperate it was.

As he prepared for the job ahead, Rugeroni identified a number of desired actions. One was for Dubal to move away from its reliance on traders and to begin direct sales and marketing, yet it wasn't clear if this was an immediate priority, or an action to be undertaken later. Changing the company's management style and building morale were vital, as well.

Much of his thinking centered on the ADL report and the implications of capacity expansion. There were a few major options. One was to stabilize the operation at its present capacity and focus on organizational and management problems. Improving the procurement process, perhaps using forward contracts to stabilize input costs, as well as more efficient supply chain management, could reduce raw material costs by up to 20 percent.

A second option was to follow the advice of ADL and embark on a course of expansion, raising capacity by 50 percent to 400,000 tonnes per annum over five years. ADL had recommended expanding in stages, first adding capacity to the power plant, then adding a new potline, later the casthouse, and so forth. Such an approach would call for up to $100 million in capital for each of the next five years.[3] Once Dubal achieved a larger scale, its total operating costs could decline on a per-unit basis by up to 20 percent. Rather than breaking even at $1,300 per metric tonne, Dubal would earn a solid profit.

A third approach was to undertake a more rapid expansion, adding 50 percent capacity in the next two years. The benefits of scale would accrue after two years. In that case, however, Dubal would need $500 million in capital all at once—quite a sum for a company with annual revenues of about $350 million and that had never performed. It was unclear how to gain support for such an expansion. It was also not obvious whether Dubal had the management capability to improve the performance of its existing operations while also undertaking a rapid expansion.

At the same time, the LME price for aluminium was rising steadily. The price at the start of 1994 was around $1,400 per tonne, but now was climbing steadily upwards. If prices held up, and if costs could be contained, Dubal might earn good returns in 1995. But relying on traders meant that Dubal earned the spot rate, which could swing sharply.

As Rugeroni prepared to meet with his top management team for the first time in May 1994, he wondered what actions to take.

Endnotes

1. *UAE: A Meed Practical & Business Guide,* London: EMAP Business International, 5th ed., 1999: 218.
2. Case writer's estimate. As a privately owned company, Dubai Aluminium did not publish its financial results.
3. Case writer's estimate.

Chapter Thirty-Two

Quest Foods Asia Pacific and the CRM Initiative

"Declan, we have to talk," said Mathijs Boeren, marketing director Foods, Asia Pacific, Quest International, as he walked into the Singapore office of Declan Mac-Fadden, regional vice president, Foods, Asia Pacific, in the early morning of February 28, 2000. Quest, which among other activities created flavors and textures for food and beverage companies, had about six months earlier begun implementing a business process re-engineering (BPR) project. This initiative involved the analysis of every facet of Quest's businesses with the objective of finding new and better ways of operating.

MacFadden was responsible for the implementation of the Foods Division BPR throughout Asia Pacific. As part of this effort, he was also championing the development of an information technology-based customer relationship management model (CRM), an initiative he felt was critical for Quest to gain a sustainable competitive advantage with customers in the region. This initiative would offer much more to customers than the company's current website, where customers could

Richard Ivey School of Business
The University of Western Ontario

Donna Everatt and Professor Allen Morrison prepared this case solely to provide material for class discussion. The authors do not intend to illustrate either effective or ineffective handling of a managerial situation. The authors may have disguised certain names and other identifying information to protect confidentiality.

simply obtain basic information on Quest's global operations and product offerings. Likely, it would contain interactive communications with some processes handled without human contact. MacFadden's ultimate goal was to bring Quest to the next phase of e-business—full interactivity.

Boeren took a seat and began talking:

> Declan, I've just come from a meeting with International Snackfoods.[1] The director of Procurement for Asia Pacific, Larry Wong, told me that one of our most formidable competitors had implemented CRM technology weeks earlier. Though Wong was somewhat reticent, he did hint to me that the new system addressed some of International Snackfoods' needs for increased transparency, responsiveness and information flow. As far as I can tell, this new system not only tracks orders, but is likely the first stage of a full Extranet. If so, our competitor will be able to give our key customers increased transparency, accelerate their product development, and link their research and development (R&D) facilities before we can.
>
> As you can well imagine, this makes me nervous. At this point, I don't know whether our competitor has implemented this system worldwide. But whether it has or not, I am still concerned about Quest's 'mission readiness' for a similar IT platform.

MacFadden sank back into his chair. He already felt pressure to move forward with CRM, hearing through the grapevine that some senior managers felt that the project was moving too slowly. But this pressure was not universal. In a recent regional directors' meeting, others had questioned whether CRM was even a worthwhile priority given the finite time and money resources available, especially if its development and implementation ran concurrent to the implementation of Quest's BPR.

"Still, Mathijs," MacFadden said, "the issue remains—what are our priorities?" MacFadden, Boeren and the executive team in charge of the implementation of Quest's BPR had considered the implications to that question for months. Although the elements of an initial CRM had been created, it was still in its early stages. And, although some of Quest's customers had expressed interest in using a CRM system, it remained unclear whether a fully deployed CRM would generate any new sales.

After Boeren had left his office, MacFadden swiveled his chair and took in the view of Singapore's financial district, contemplating the situation. Should he wait until the key components of the BPR process had been smoothly implemented, or should he respond to a potential need in the market and rush through the process of setting up a CRM? If the latter, should he focus the CRM initiative on just one customer in one region, one customer globally, or should he involve all customers that might be interested? Beyond this decision was the concern over the degree of sophistication offered by the system. The greater the sophistication, the longer the development time. The simpler the system, the less interest customers might have. Although MacFadden believed wholeheartedly that a CRM system could potentially hold the key to Quest's long-term competitive advantage, he was clearly troubled as to how he should proceed.

THE FOOD FLAVORING INDUSTRY

Consumers around the world had an almost insatiable appetite for new flavors incorporated into either new or existing products. Distinctive flavors had always given food and beverage manufacturers their competitive edge, and consumer demands for more convenient, healthful foods put enormous pressure on the flavorings industry for new and innovative products. Most flavor houses combined a wide range of artificial and natural products with a family of emulsifiers and stabilizers that provided "texture" for the food. Texture was important in creating "mouth feel"—for example, whether the final food product was creamy, sticky or smooth.

The flavorings industry consisted of two different market segments: the generic market (off-the-shelf flavors), and the custom flavoring market, which Quest focused on. Although occasionally Quest would approach its clients with a need that was identified through their marketing or R&D channels, responding to a customer's request for a particular product ingredient or flavoring generated the vast majority of its business.

In order to delineate the desired performance parameters of their new or improved product, food manufacturers issued a "brief" to Quest and other ingredients suppliers. Responding to the brief generally took between three to six months, and was a non-recoverable expense. At the deadline date, each company responding to the brief presented the specific performance details of its formulation to the client. Once accepted by a customer, the formulation that was developed could not be used for any other customer (though it remained the developer's intellectual property). Clients demanded strict confidentiality.

DELIVERING INCREASED VALUE-ADDED SERVICES

Boeren explained Quest's business model:

> We don't sell finished products. Quest sells food ingredients and flavors that are incorporated with other food components to become an end product. In this business you must have a core competency in the application of your products in a final food product. We cannot just give our customers large bags of white powder, and say 'here it is.' It's very important that we understand how our customers are using the ingredient. Moreover, achieving the desired performance or taste in a lab is usually very different from replicating it in a mass manufacturing environment. Flavor houses need real expertise in the scalability of their developments.

Over the past few years, global food and beverage manufacturers had leveraged their considerable purchasing clout, and had begun to ask for—and receive—more value-added services from their suppliers. According to MacFadden:

> Increasingly our customers want us to move further down the value chain and have Quest deliver something new to them. We are now becoming increasingly responsible for determining trends in consumer preferences, finding new flavors

and flavor substances, discovering new ingredients that maintain the integrity of the flavor.

Within the last three or four years, customers have been saying to Quest: 'Show me that you've got a winning new flavor—show me quantitative evidence for the preference for the flavor by consumers.' They've even begun to prescribe what type of statistical market analysis they want done.

Recognizing that Quest would lose credibility if it developed flavors that scored very low on consumer taste tests or if the products were taken off the market soon after introduction, Quest was strongly committed to conducting market research for its clients. Moreover, given that consumer tastes and demands always evolved, Quest was constantly seeking new ways to stay in tune with the market and enhance or re-fine existing products, or meet new consumer needs. Quest's extensive marketing re-search department provided key market information, including data on consumption patterns, trends, industry structure, and more importantly on consumer tastes and preferences, for various regions throughout the world. This was happening at a time when Quest's customers were becoming increasingly price-sensitive (most markedly in MacFadden's region since the onset of the Asian financial crisis). Thus, Quest (and its competitors) faced considerable pressure to develop ingredients and applications that were not only low cost but that delivered high efficacy.

With a view to eliminating redundancies and creating increased economies of scale, many of Quest's largest customers were globally organizing procurement, manufacturing, operational and administrative processes, as well as developing global brands. Despite these trends, strong national and regional differences con-tinued in the area of food flavorings and textures. Cheese flavor, for example, could have many different nuances—a spicy flavor in India and Indonesia or fish flavor in Japan. Even though large companies like International Snackfoods had invested heavily in global brands and global purchasing systems, when it came to matters of flavors and food textures, they faced the reality that subtle—and in some cases, distinct—demand differences existed from country to country.

THE COMPETITIVE LANDSCAPE

A dozen or so globally aligned companies dominated the food ingredients and fla-vors industry (comprised of hundreds of smaller firms). Companies that manu-factured flavors and texturising products were generally thought of as representing the highest value-added segment of the overall food ingredients industry.

Because of the role of chemical sciences and biotechnology in the flavorings industry, many industry players had strong ties to large, well-funded agricul-tural, chemical, and pharmaceutical companies. Quest's major competitors in-cluded Givaudan Roure (a division of the large Swiss-based pharmaceutical company Hoffman La Roche), Firmenich (also Swiss-based), New York-based International Flavors & Fragrances (IFF), and several major Japanese players in-cluding Takasako and Hasegawa. Increasingly, large chemicals and pharmaceu-tical companies were divesting non-core assets including their flavors and textures businesses. Some industry observers expected that these divestments would continue, followed over the next ten years by consolidation in the industry, resulting eventually in three or four huge global players.

The natural interdependence between the developers of flavors and textures and the food manufacturers themselves was expected to forge increasingly strong partnerships in the future. A noticeable trend was the blurring of boundaries between developer and manufacturer with arrangements including exclusive or preferential development and collaborative joint ventures. A prime example of this relationship was Frito-Lay's alliance with Procter and Gamble, which resulted in the development of a synthetic fat named Olestra for snack foods.

Another element altering the structure of the industry was a dramatic reduction in development times and a rapid stream of new products and ingredients, which made innovation more imperative than ever. MacFadden explained Quest's commitment with regard to innovation:

> The relationship we have developed and nurtured over the years with our key customers gets us into their labs to work on solutions together. We need to constantly design creative solutions to the problems they bring to us. The key to success is coming up with revolutionary ideas.
>
> Though innovations vary around the world, many are really product line extensions—mostly ethnic line extensions in the Western consumer markets. But, in countries like Japan, there is also phenomenal innovation, including new flavors, new foods, and nutritional benefits.
>
> In the past, researchers and marketers were essentially taking 'bad' elements out of food, like fats and sugar. Now they are working on adding back 'good' things—nutrients, fiber, and so on—to produce what are called 'functional foods.' Producers are also pushing convenience-food solutions—products that are prepared faster, with higher nutritional value, and that are more shelf-stable. These concepts are starting to spread worldwide.

QUEST INTERNATIONAL

Quest was based in Naarden, Holland and was a major division of UK-based ICI. By 1999, ICI employed almost 60,000 people worldwide, and sold over £5.6 billion of products, resulting in a net profit (before goodwill, amortization and exceptional items) of £267 million. Quest's 4,000 employees developed and manufactured an extensive product line that included not only flavors and textures, but also fragrances for perfume manufacturers of cosmetics, toiletries, dental products and household goods. In 1999, due to rising sales and further operational efficiencies, Quest realized a profit of £92 million on sales of £676 million, more than 18 percent more than the previous year.[2]

Flavorings and textures were part of the Food Division, which was organized around (1) products, (2) end users, and (3) geography. Quest's Food Division developed products for several categories, including the dairy and beverage industries, bakery and confectionery products, meals, soups, sauces and dressings, snack foods, meats, human nutrition, and cell nutrition (see Exhibit 1). In total, the Food Division

EXHIBIT 1
Flavors and Food Ingredients: Quest's Integrated Approach

Dairy Industry

Quest offered a comprehensive range of ingredients and flavors to improve the taste, texture, appearance, shelf-life and overall quality of dairy products, from ice-cream and frozen desserts to cheese and yogurt.

- Starter cultures
- Stabilizers and shelf-life extenders
- Whipping proteins
- Emulsifiers
- Natural and artificial flavors

Beverages

Quest flavors and ingredients enhanced beverages from soft drinks, teas and herbals to distilled spirits, beers, wines and cordials.

- Natural flavors
- Stabilizers
- Artificial flavors
- Vanilla extract
- Enzymes

Bakery and Confectionery Products

Quest technology improved the market appeal of bakery and confectionery products, from breads, cakes and crackers to candy and chewing gum.

- Heat-stable, natural and fat flavors
- Vanilla extract
- Fat replacement systems
- Shelf-life extenders
- Enzymes
- Cultures
- Emulsifiers
- Proteins

Meals, Soups, Sauces and Dressings

Quest ingredients and flavors gave sauces, gravies, prepared meals, dressings, soups and related products characteristics consumers preferred.

- Natural flavors
- Replacement ingredients
- Meat flavors
- Tenderizers
- Emulsifiers
- Dried vegetables
- MSG replacers
- Yeast extracts
- Stabilizers
- Cultures

(continued)

EXHIBIT 1
(Continued)

Snack Foods

Specialty snack foods benefited from Quest's distinctive flavors, spices and ingredient blends.

- Cheese flavors
- Cheese "plus" flavors
- Beef flavors
- Chicken flavors
- Seafood flavors
- Specialty blends

Meat Industry

Quest ingredients helped create the quality difference in meat products, from fermented items like pepperoni, to hams and meat spreads.

- Cultures
- Shelf extenders
- Carrageenans
- Enzyme tenderizers
- Flavors
  - Autolysed yeast
  - Hydrolysed vegetable proteins
  - Low fat flavors
  - Replacement flavors

Human Nutrition

Quest supplied specialized ingredients to supplement the nutritional value of products including functional foods/drinks, supplements, infant formula, enriched sports drinks and clinical foods.
- Lactose

Cell Nutrition

Proteins, hydrolysates (Peptones) and yeast extracts, for use in culturing micro-organisms, and laboratory and industrial fermentations (which provided essential peptides, amino acids, vitamins and minerals, as well as a complex mixture of yeast cell-wall derived carbohydrates).

had six different product groups, four end users (bakery, savory, beverage, dairy), and four geographic regions. Some observers wondered whether the Division's organizational structure was overly complex in an industry that was becoming increasingly global and where the ability to generate synergies was growing rapidly.

In 1999, Quest's Food Division grew at 5 percent, ahead of the market, with flavors doing particularly well. Many observers attributed the success of Quest's Food Division to its ability to leverage its global network, marketing acumen, and its use of world-class R&D and application skills. Top managers were proud of the Division's culture which encouraged regional managers, scientists and account managers to work together to seek creative answers to the challenges they faced. Senior employees were generally empowered to seek their own solutions, and many had developed close relationships with customers by creating special formulations that were especially effective.

QUEST'S BPR PROCESS

BPR represented an attempt to better serve customers by streamlining international operations. Within the Food Division, BPR represented a fundamental rethinking and radical redesign of business processes to achieve dramatic improvements in critical measures of performance, including cost, quality, service, and speed. The implementation of Quest's BPR had begun about six months earlier, after having obtained Board level support. Such high level support was critical, given the scope and strategic shift the initiative involved.

A new business model was at the heart of the BPR process, and the challenge was to find one that would truly differentiate Quest from its competitors. Paul Dreschler, chairman and CEO, Quest International, commented on the importance and direction of BPR:

> Having exited Y2K and looked at our priorities over the next two years, BPR is one of eight priorities we have set. Interestingly, BPR is a key enabler of the other seven initiatives, so it is important to us. At this stage, the over-riding priority is to strengthen our customer-driven focus. I am very flexible about the design and possibilities for BPR. I don't have a predisposed view of what it should look like. However, I can say that whatever we do has to be earnings enhancing. I need to deliver BPR without a one-year financial dip.

MacFadden was excited by the emphasis on customer intimacy and Quest's openness to new business models. He saw the BPR process as "not just a case of improving what we currently have." He continued,

> We have set an ambitious goal to double revenue within about five years and to strengthen our relationship with our valued customers around the globe. BPR can play a pivotal role in this process by helping us revolutionize our operations.
>
> Our first step is to align all our processes so that everybody works the same way, using the same processes. This means standardizing operations management, administrative and customer services functions, for example—every facet of the company—so that it is the same no matter which Quest operation you're working at. We are forecasting this will be a US$70 million to US$80 million project, which will take between two to three years to complete.

MacFadden's work on BPR put him in regular contact with various key managers from the Asia Division head office in Singapore, as well as Quest's four regional directors in Asia, one each for Australia and New Zealand, Japan and Korea, China, and all other Southeast Asian nations (based in Jakarta). Dreschler commented on the selection of MacFadden for this role:

> Each food executive takes charge of a key project or process around the business. MacFadden was given BPR because he really wanted to do it. He was hungry for it. In my view, we need a bias for action more than intellectual conversion.

KNOWLEDGE MANAGEMENT AT QUEST

A critical goal of BPR was a new ability to share data on best practices, competitors, and customers on a global basis. Quest relied on two methods of storing knowledge—in "employees' brains," and through the process of codifying data (either electronically, or through a written record). MacFadden explained:

> The majority of our processes are documented, somewhere or other, throughout the world. Our major challenge is to get this information into the hands of the people who need it. However, the reality is that getting it organized, codified and entered into compatible databases is a hell of a job.

Critical information in the Food Division was shared across geographies through word of mouth, documented processes, and cross-functional teams. On occasion, a specialist in a particular application—cheese flavoring on crackers, for instance—would visit the development team (located anywhere in the world) to apply his or her expertise personally to the brief. However, this had obvious time, space, and money resource restraints. As a result, the quality of information exchange varied significantly in detail and effectiveness depending on the scientist who prepared it.

Once data were transferred, the application specialists (scientists) applied both generalizable and specialty knowledge for each development, often adding their own special techniques or ingredients to create the desired result. Most who were involved in sharing data across geographies and product groups acknowledged that highly creative and innovative processes were very difficult to codify.

MacFadden felt that, although very challenging, data could be effectively collected and disseminated through what he dubbed an "elaborate global knowledge management system." He described the elements of such a system:

> It is almost impossible to transfer required knowledge through word of mouth alone, so we need to find some mechanism that puts the information at the fingertips of our technology people and key business decision-makers. For example, consider an applications guy. Suppose his job is to develop a new winning cookie flavor for a particular customer. The objective would be for him to be able to log onto the internal Quest systems, and ask it for 'any ideas for new cookies,' and it would offer him a range of new, innovative ideas for the latest cookie applications developed at other Quest facilities around the world.
>
> It would also give him any information-related activities like manufacturing processes, cost structures, market research regarding the performance of the cookie in various markets, particular ingredients and specific information regarding flavors, as well as subjective and interpretive information provided by the people involved in the cookie's development. It would help him get samples onto his desk within a very short period of time—essentially it would be designed *for* him and *by* him so that it would meet every need he had to do his job well. I want to make it so easy to use and helpful to him that his life rotates around it.

MacFadden felt such a system would provide the Food Division with a huge advantage in the marketplace. He explained:

tomers and to a lesser degree from Quest itself. The third and final requirements included testing (creating an internal interface, adding filters, beta-testing), and finally, full roll out to customers.

TIMING AND LOCATION ISSUES

It was believed by most managers associated with BPR that a highly sophisticated CRM system would help create Quest's sustainable competitive advantage. However, where there appeared to be less consensus was over the timing and appropriate speed of the rollout. Senior Quest managers had recently approached MacFadden asking why the process seemed to be moving so slowly, to which he responded:

> We are actually not moving slowly on this; when you consider what needs to be done, it's an immense initiative. Each of the steps of the CRM system is critically inter-dependent and of immense scope.
>
> Take, for example, the responsibility of universally coding internal data, never mind customer specific data. We have to find a very simple way of handling a very complicated process, and we have not yet done this. Even if it offers incredible benefits, our customers will not use our GUI if it is not easy to understand or if they get lost in it.

Others were concerned about CRM being championed out of the Singapore office, as the region was not yet a leader in Internet-based commerce or Web-based alliances. One expatriate manager at Quest with seven years' experience in the region explained:

> E-commerce will be slower in Asia than elsewhere. Our people in Asia who interface with customers don't see many benefits right now. If e-commerce is ever going to work, it's going to have to first be introduced in the United States or Europe. These regions should take the lead instead of Asia. Part of the problem is that right now in Asia the cost of trying to get synergies far outweighs the benefits. E-commerce is ultimately based on maximizing efficiencies, which is a big incentive in mature markets but not as big an issue in Asia.
>
> There are still lots of growth opportunities in Asia with the recent up-turn in national economies. We are all very busy and I don't believe it is in our best interest right now to be distracted by e-commerce. This is particularly problematic given weakness in management bench strength in Asia. Less than 10 percent of our customers in Asia are the kinds of multinational companies that would most benefit from CRM. Just because we are a global company doesn't mean we don't have lots of local customers.

Other managers were deeply worried about the lack of resources in Quest Asia to complete the task. Betty Tse, regional human resources director, Asia Pacific, for Quest had the following observation:

> In Asia Pacific, within Quest, keeping up with e-commerce and IT requires constant effort. The good news is that in many markets, customer demand for Extranets may not be there. This is a concern because it takes some of the pressure off our people.

UNDER PRESSURE

The challenges of providing CRM leadership were not lost on MacFadden. Prior to Boeren's meeting with International Snackfoods, MacFadden felt that Quest had "between half a year and two years" to implement a CRM system; now he was no longer certain. During their February 28 meeting, Boeren reviewed with MacFadden the details of his recent meeting with Larry Wong at International Snackfoods.

> Wong said that International Snackfoods had recently moved to a regional structure. This means that purchasing was being centralized for the region here in Singapore. Furthermore, I learned that while International Snackfoods had a relatively small sales base in Asia, it was growing at between 40 percent and 60 percent per year, which is far faster than many local customers.
>
> Moreover, I learned that International Snackfoods wants to continue to differentiate between Asian tastes and those from the U.S. and Europe. One example is that Americans continue to prefer flavors that are dairy-based; however, cheese flavors don't do well in Asia. Asians seem to like meat or fish-based flavors. Tastes also vary significantly within Asia. Wong pointed out that while International Snackfoods' BBQ-flavored chips had the same smoky taste in Australia as in the United States, they had a spicier flavor in Thailand and India. In China, he asserted that end-users prefer a more "meaty" flavor in potato chips. And within a big country like China, he pointed out that tastes vary from region to region. For example, in Northern China consumers seem to want a less salty flavoring than they do in the South.

It was Boeren's impression that International Snackfoods was pushing its suppliers not only to accommodate these local differences in taste, but also to mirror its push toward globalization. To support this view, Boeren again quoted Wong from their earlier meeting:

> It doesn't make sense for International Snackfoods to have global tastes—we cannot import the flavorings—they have to be produced locally. To be cost competitive and to lower lead times and reduce supply volatility, we must localize as much as possible. Therefore, we might as well make products locally flavored. However, it does make sense to globalize our quality standards—chip thickness, freshness guarantees, and the like. Importantly, we also globalize our top brands. Quest's structure must mirror our organization and be globally sophisticated, with local capabilities.
>
> For Quest to be successful, you must be transparent with us. If you want a long-term partnership, both sides must share information. This way we both win. We need trust and transparency. Our businesses are more volatile over here. Our forecasts are often less predictable than in the U.S. or Europe. We need each other's help.
>
> Right now we are in the process of setting up an Extranet with one of your competitors from Germany. The Extranet will allow us to track inventory, order status, and payments. This German supplier is linking up its Hanover facility with our R&D people here in the region.
>
> Other suppliers are also e-mailing us every month to tell us what they are doing around the world for International Snackfoods. They also keep us up-to-date on other generic developments. We don't see this kind of coordinated support from Quest.

MOVING FORWARD

MacFadden wondered how much time he had to respond to International Snack-foods. On the one hand, no one at Quest was comfortable being out-done by a competitor. Furthermore, the world was turning decidedly in favor of CRM linkages. On the other hand, International Snackfoods and other key clients were undergoing their own re-engineering efforts and were not yet strongly demanding CRM. Furthermore, its country-centered approach to product development suggested that linkages to Quest's regional and global technology might be less important to International Snackfoods than having access to strong in-country development teams at Quest. Some argued that it would be smarter for Quest to delay CRM and spend its efforts on building its technology skills in major countries like China, Korea, and Japan.

Despite having a relatively high degree of autonomy in Asia, MacFadden fully realized that any decisions he made would have global consequences—either positively or negatively. His colleague, Angel Dias de Leon, explained:

> Whatever Declan does with International Snackfoods in Singapore will impact what we do in the rest of the world with this customer. We have to assume that International Snackfoods shares information internally. If we open the door to them in Asia, we open the door worldwide. There are consequences beyond Asia in any decision that is made.

Although essentially every customer wanted maximum supplier transparency, responsiveness and information flow, MacFadden was not sure whether this would translate into a willingness to work with Quest in designing and implementing an Extranet. Partly because of this concern, MacFadden wondered whether Quest should focus its first CRM partnership on a global customer in Asia or on an up-and-coming second-tier food company.

Instead of focusing on a large, global account like International Snackfoods, some argued that Quest might be better served by partnering with a more nimble, technology-oriented food company. Evidence from other industries suggested that the greatest benefits came from partnering with tomorrow's industry leaders. However, if MacFadden decided to move in this direction, it was unlikely that Quest would easily find such a partner in Asia. MacFadden commented on the challenge:

> This is Asia and many of Quest's customers do not even have broadband Internet access to facilitate many of the more sophisticated electronic applications we have been discussing. Some of our larger customers in Asia are still using DOS. This is not to say that over the next couple of years they won't upgrade, but currently, their systems are not necessarily state-of-the-art.

Partner selection and roll-out strategy were closely linked. Under one scenario, Quest would implement an internal knowledge management system first, proceed with BPR, and then extend that model externally to its customers. This situation would certainly delay CRM for several years. It would also ensure that the internal systems worked before closely linking with a partner. A delay would also provide time for Asian customers to catch up on technology and help MacFadden better clarify partner selection criteria. MacFadden clearly had some leeway on this matter. Paul Dreschler put the decision in context:

> You have to look at your total business agenda and choose your priorities, make decisions, and allocate resources. There has been a lot of fantastic stuff done, but my question is, does it make money and will it make money? MacFadden's colleagues all have very different views about what CRM means. Declan has defined it one way but there are different ways of looking at it.

On the downside, MacFadden was deeply aware that in the Internet-era, everything changed overnight. Waiting until everything was internally aligned and everyone was in agreement was highly risky.

Under a second scenario, MacFadden could jump into CRM with a customer who would agree to act as a learning partner. Under this option, Quest would develop a model CRM system based on one strategic partner's needs, and then roll it out to other customers when demanded (but after BPR had progressed more completely). Under this scenario, MacFadden wondered how closely Quest's systems should be aligned with those of its learning partner. Would a more generic system be appropriate at this stage until the optimum level of technological sophistication became clearer? If Quest did develop a more generic CRM model, MacFadden wondered whether it would meet his goal of gaining a sustainable competitive advantage.

MacFadden summarized the reality of the context in which these decisions had to be made:

> These issues are a few of the many priorities I have. On a daily basis, Asia is a region that we need to hold together. I'm not sure if this is the most exciting opportunity Quest faces, or our most terrifying challenge.

Endnotes

1. International Snackfoods is a disguised name for a large, U.S.-based manufacturer of convenience food products.

2. In February 2000, £1.0 = US$1.55.

3. Within ICI, the term CRM was used quite differently. For example, ICI Paints used CRM to refer to sales force systems that were designed to provide information on customer visits, plans and actions. The CRM definition used by Quest was much broader and included systems to "improve customer relationships."

Chapter Thirty-Three

Blue Ridge Spain

Yannis Costas, European managing director of Blue Ridge Restaurants, found it difficult to control the anger welling up inside him as he left the meeting with the company's regional vice-president (VP) earlier in the day. That evening, he began to reflect on the day's events in the relative peace of his London flat. "Ten years work gone down the drain," he thought to himself, shaking his head. "What a waste!"

Costas recalled the many years he had spent fostering a successful joint venture between his company, Blue Ridge Restaurants Corporation, and Terralumen S.A., a mid-sized family-owned company in Spain. Not only had the joint venture been profitable, but it had grown at a reasonably brisk pace in recent years. Without a doubt, partnering with Terralumen was a key reason for Blue Ridge's success in Spain. Therefore, Costas was somewhat dismayed to find out that Delta Foods Corporation, Blue Ridge's new owner, wanted out. Yes, there had been recent tension between Terralumen and Delta over future rates of growth (see Exhibits 2 and 3), but the most recent round of talks had ended in an amicable compromise—he thought. Besides, Delta's senior managers should have realized that their growth targets were unrealistic.

They had gone over the arguments several times, and Costas tried every angle to convince his superiors to stick with the joint venture, but to no avail. To make matters worse, Costas had just been assigned the unpleasant task of developing a dissolution strategy for the company he had worked so hard to build.

Ivey

Richard Ivey School of Business
The University of Western Ontario

Jeanne M. McNett prepared this case under the supervision of David Wesley and Professors Nicholas Athanassiou and Henry W. Lane solely to provide material for class discussion. The authors do not intend to illustrate either effective or ineffective handling of a managerial situation. The authors may have disguised certain names and other identifying information to protect confidentiality.

BLUE RIDGE RESTAURANTS CORPORATION

Blue Ridge was founded in Virginia in 1959, and quickly established a reputation for quality fast food. In 1974, after establishing more than 500 food outlets in the United States and Canada, Blue Ridge was sold to an investment group for US$4 million.

Over the next five years, the company experienced sales growth of 96 percent annually. However, international sales were haphazard and there was no visible international strategy. Instead, whenever a foreign restauranteur wanted to begin a Blue Ridge franchise, the foreign company would simply approach Blue Ridge headquarters with the request. As long as the franchise delivered royalties, there was little concern for maintaining product consistency or quality control in foreign markets.

In 1981, Blue Ridge was acquired by an international beverages company for US$420 million. Under new ownership, the company made its first major foray into international markets, and international operations were merged with the parent company's existing international beverage products under a new international division.

The strategy at the time was to enter into joint ventures with local partners, thereby allowing Blue Ridge to enter restricted markets and draw on local expertise, capital and labor. Partnering also significantly reduced the capital costs of opening new stores. The strategy of local partnering combined with Blue Ridge's marketing know-how and operations expertise, quickly paid off in Australia, Southeast Asia and the United Kingdom, where booming sales led to rapid international expansion.

On the other hand, there were some glaring failures. By 1987, Blue Ridge decided to pull out of France, Italy, Brazil and Hong Kong where infrastructure problems and slow consumer acceptance resulted in poor performance. Some managers, who had been accustomed to high margins and short lead times in their alcoholic beverages division, did not have the patience for the long and difficult road to develop these markets and would tolerate only those ventures that showed quick results.

These early years of international expansion provided important learning opportunities as more managers gained a personal understanding of the key strategic factors behind successful foreign entry. The success of the company's international expansion efforts helped Blue Ridge become the company's fastest growing division. When Blue Ridge was sold to Delta Foods in 1996 for US$2 billion, it was one of the largest fast-food chains in the world and generated sales of US$6.8 billion.

Delta was a leading soft drink and snack food company in the United States, but at the time of the Blue Ridge acquisition, it had not achieved significant success internationally. It had managed to establish a dominant market share in a small number of countries with protected markets in which its main competitors were shut out. For example, one competitor was shut out of many Arabic countries after deciding to set up operations in Israel.

The company's senior managers disliked joint ventures, in part because they were time-consuming, but also because they were viewed as a poor way to develop new markets. Delta was an aggressive growth company with brands that many believed were strong enough to support entry into new overseas markets without the assistance of local partners. When needed, the company either hired local managers directly or transferred seasoned managers from the soft drink and snack food divisions.

Delta also achieved international growth by directly acquiring local companies. For example, in the late 1990s, Delta acquired the largest snack food companies in Spain and the United Kingdom. However, given that joint ventures had been the predominant strategy for Blue Ridge, and that some countries, such as China, required local partnering, Delta had no choice but to work with joint venture partners.

YANNIS COSTAS

Yannis Costas was an American-educated Greek who held degrees in engineering and business (MBA) from leading U.S. colleges. Although college life in a foreign country had its challenges, it afforded him an opportunity to develop an appreciation and understanding of American culture and business practices. Therefore, upon completing his MBA, Costas turned down several offers of employment from leading multinational corporations that wanted him to take management positions in his native country. Such positions, however appealing they may have been at the time, would have doomed him to a career as a local manager, he thought. He chose instead to accept a position in international auditing at Blue Ridge headquarters in Virginia, mainly because of the opportunity for extended foreign travel.

The transition from university to corporate life was a difficult one. Social life seemed to revolve around couples and families, both at Blue Ridge and in the larger community. Although Costas met some single women from the local Greek community, his heavy travel schedule prevented him from establishing any meaningful relationships. Instead, he immersed himself in his work as a way to reduce the general feeling of isolation.

Costas was fortunate to have an office next to Gene Bennett, the company's director of business development. Bennett had served as a lieutenant in the U.S. Navy before working in the pharmaceutical industry setting up joint ventures in Latin America and Europe. He was hired by Blue Ridge specifically to develop international joint ventures. As Costas' informal mentor, Bennett passed on many of the lessons Costas would come to draw on later in his career.

It was at the urging of Bennett that Costas applied for a transfer to the international division in 1985. Three years later, Costas was asked to relocate to London, England, in order to take on the role of European regional director for Blue Ridge. In this position, he became responsible for joint ventures and franchises in Germany, the Netherlands, Spain, Northern Ireland, Denmark, Sweden and Iceland.

In 1993, Costas was transferred to Singapore where, under the direction of the president of Blue Ridge Asia,[1] he advanced in his understanding of joint ventures,

EXHIBIT 1 Timeline

Year	Blue Ridge Restaurants	Yannis Costas
1959	Company founded in Virginia	
1974	Blue Ridge Sold for $4 million	
1975–1980	96 percent annual growth	Leaves Greece to study in United States
1981	Blue Ridge sold for $420 million	
1982	International expansion	Completes his B.S. in United States
1983	Begin negotiations for JV in Spain	
1984		Completes M.B.A. and is hired by Blue Ridge; moves to Virginia
1985	JV agreement with Terralumen S.A.	Applies for transfer to International Division
1986	Rodrigo appointed managing director of Blue Ridge Spain	
1987	Company pulls out of France, Brazil, Hong Kong, and Italy	
1988		Promoted to European regional director; moves to London
1988–1993	Spanish JV grows slower than expected	
1993	U.S. manager sent to oversee Spanish JV	Transfer to Singapore
1995	Rodrigo replaced by Carlos Martin	
1996	Blue Ridge sold to Delta for $2 billion	
1995–1998	Spanish JV grows more rapidly	
1998	5-year plan for 50 restaurants in Spain, Blue Ridge has 600 stores in Europe/ME	Costas asked to return to London
January 1999		Rescues JV in Kuwait
May 1999	Södergran hired as Delta VP for Europe	
June 1999	Directors meeting for Spanish JV	
December 1999	Dryden withholds Delta payment to JV; Alvarez sells prime Barcelona property	
January 2000		Asked to develop dissolution strategy for Spain

market entry and teamwork. Over the next five years, Costas built a highly productive management team and successfully developed several Asian markets. He was eager to apply these new skills when he returned to London in 1998 to once again take up the role of European director (see Exhibit 1 for a summary of Costas' career).

THE SPANISH DECISION

When the decision was first made to enter the Spanish market, Bennett was sent overseas to meet with real estate developers, construction companies, retail distributors, agribusiness companies, lawyers, accountants and consumer product manufacturers in order to gather the preliminary knowledge needed for such an undertaking. Bennett soon realized that Blue Ridge would need a credible Spanish partner to navigate that country's complex real estate and labor markets.

Few Spaniards among Bennett's peer generation spoke English. However, Bennett had a basic knowledge of Spanish, a language that he had studied in college, and this helped open some doors that were otherwise shut for many of his American colleagues. Still, Bennett knew that finding a suitable partner would be difficult, since Spaniards frequently appeared to distrust foreigners. The attitude of one investment banker from Madrid was typical:

> Many Spaniards do not want to eat strange-tasting, comparatively expensive American food out of paper bags in an impersonal environment. We have plenty of restaurants with good inexpensive food, a cozy atmosphere and personal service, and our restaurants give you time to enjoy your food in pleasant company. Besides, we don't even really know you. You come here for a few days, we have enjoyable dinners, I learn to like you, and then you leave. What kind of relationship is that?

Luckily, Bennett had a banker friend in Barcelona who recommended that he consider partnering with Terralumen.

TERRALUMEN S. A.

Terralumen was a family-owned agricultural company that had later expanded into consumer products. In doing so, Terralumen entered into several joint ventures with leading American companies. In recent years, Terralumen had also begun to experiment with the concept of establishing full-service restaurants.

Bennett was introduced to Francisco Alvarez, Terralumen's group vice-president in charge of restaurant operations and the most senior nonfamily member in the company. In time, Bennett had many opportunities to become well acquainted with Terralumen and its managers. On weekends he stayed at Alvarez's country home, attended family gatherings in Barcelona and had family members visit him in Virginia. Over the span of their negotiations, Bennett and Alvarez developed a solid friendship, and Bennett began to believe that Terralumen had the type of vision needed to be a successful joint venture partner.

After two years of negotiations, Blue Ridge entered into a joint venture with Terralumen to establish a Blue Ridge restaurant chain in Spain. Upon returning to Virginia, Bennett could not hold back his euphoria as he related to Costas the details of what he considered to be the most difficult joint venture he had ever negotiated.

BLUE RIDGE SPAIN

Alvarez hired Eduardo Rodrigo to head up the joint venture as its managing director. An accountant by trade, Rodrigo was a refined and personable man who valued his late afternoon tennis with his wife and was a professor at a university in Barcelona. He also spoke fluent English.

Before assuming his new role, Rodrigo and another manager went to Virginia to attend a five-week basic training course. Upon his return, Rodrigo's eye for detail became quickly apparent as he mastered Blue Ridge's administrative and operating policies and procedures. He knew every detail of the first few stores' operating processes and had an equally detailed grasp of each store's trading profile. As a result, Blue Ridge Spain began to show an early profit.

Profitability was one thing; growth was another. Although the Blue Ridge concept seemed to be well received by Spanish consumers, Rodrigo was cautious and avoided rapid expansion. Moreover, one of the most important markets in Spain was Madrid. Rodrigo, who was Catalan,[2] was not fond of that city and avoided travelling to Madrid whenever possible. As personal contact with real estate agents, suppliers and others was necessary to develop new stores, Blue Ridge's expansion efforts remained confined to the Barcelona area. Terralumen, becoming impatient with Blue Ridge's sluggish growth, decided to focus more resources on its consumer product divisions and less on the restaurant business.

For Costas, one of the challenges during his first assignment as European director was to convince Terralumen to focus more on the joint venture and support faster growth. Rodrigo positively opposed more rapid growth, even though Alvarez, his direct superior, voiced support for the idea. Although he had been very cordial in his interactions with his American counterparts, Rodrigo believed himself to be in a much better position to judge whether or not the Spanish market would support faster growth.

In 1993, shortly after Costas was transferred to Singapore, Blue Ridge decided to send one of its own managers to oversee the Spanish joint venture. Under pressure, Rodrigo began to ignore criticism about the company's lack of growth. On one occasion, Rodrigo decided to close the Blue Ridge offices for an entire month just as Blue Ridge's international director of finance arrived in Barcelona to develop a five-year strategic plan.[3]

Terralumen finally replaced Rodrigo with a more proactive manager who had just returned from a successful assignment in Venezuela. Under the new leadership of Carlos Martin, Blue Ridge Spain began to prosper. Soon everyone was occupied with the difficult task of acquiring new sites, as well as recruiting and training employees.

COSTAS RETURNS TO EUROPE

In late 1998, Costas was transferred from Singapore to London to resume the role of European managing director. The previous director had performed poorly and it was felt that Costas had the experience needed to repair damaged relations with some of Blue Ridge's Middle Eastern joint venture partners. By this time, Blue Ridge had more than 600 stores in Europe and the Middle East.

One of Blue Ridge's more lucrative joint ventures was in Kuwait. However, the partners were threatening to dissolve the enterprise after the previous managing director became upset that the Kuwaitis were not meeting growth targets. The partners were especially concerned when they discovered that he had begun to seek other potential partners.

Costas decided to schedule a visit to Kuwait in early January. The partners counselled against the visit since Costas would be arriving during Ramadan,[4] and therefore would not be able to get much work done. Nevertheless Costas went to Kuwait, but spent nearly all of his time having dinners with the partners. He recalled:

> Most American managers would have considered my trip to be a waste of time, since I didn't get much "work" done. But it was a great opportunity to get to know the partners and to re-establish lost trust, and the partners felt good about having an opportunity to vent their concerns.

Costas returned to London confident that he had reassured the Kuwaiti partners that Blue Ridge was still committed to the joint venture.

Costas was also happy to be working with his old friend Alvarez again, as the two began working on an ambitious plan to develop a total of 50 stores by 2002 (see Exhibit 2).[5] As Blue Ridge Spain continued to grow, stores were opened in prime locations such as the prestigious Gran Via in Madrid and Barcelona's fa-

EXHIBIT 2
Development Plan Agreed Between Blue Ridge Restaurants and Terralumen (as of December 1998) (in 000s U.S. dollars)

Source: Company files.

	1998	2000	2001	2002	2003	2004
Number of Stores	12	24	37	50	65	80
Average Annual Sales	700	770	847	932	1,025	1,127
Gross Sales	$8,400	18,480	31,339	46,600	66,625	90,160
Cost of Goods Food	1,680	3,322	5,474	8,141	11,639	15,770
Cost of Goods Direct Labor	1,680	3,323	5,641	8,374	11,646	15,766
Advertising/Promotion	504	1,109	1,880	2,796	3,998	5,410
Occupancy Costs	1,260	1,848	3,129	4,660	6,663	9,016
Fixed Labor	840	1,478	2,507	3,728	5,330	7,213
Miscellaneous	168	277	470	699	999	1,352
Royalties to Blue Ridge U.S.	420	924	1,560	2,330	3,331	4,508
Total Costs	6,552	12,281	20,662	30,728	43,606	59,035
Contribution to G&A	1,848	6,199	10,677	15,872	23,019	31,125
Salaries and Benefits	875	1,531	2,641	3,493	4,580	5,899
Travel Expenses	120	240	300	375	469	586
Other	240	312	406	527	685	891
Occupancy Costs	240	720	828	952	1,095	1,259
Total G&A	1,475	2,803	4,175	5,347	6,829	8,635
Earnings Before Interest/Tax	$ 373	3,396	6,502	10,525	16,190	22,490
Percent of Gross Sales	4.44	18.38	20.75	22.59	24.30	24.94
Office Employees (Spain)	10	20	30	35	40	45

Notes:
- This plan was agreed before Yannis Costas' appointment to Blue Ridge Europe in late 1998.
- End 2004 plan: 20 stores in Barcelona, 30 in Madrid, 30 in other cities.
- Capital Investment per store $700,000 to $1 million.
- Site identification, lease or purchase negotiation, permits, construction: 18 to 24 months. Key Money is a part of occupancy costs. It is a sum paid to property owner at signing; varies by site $100,000 plus. Up to 1999, many owners wanted Key Money paid off the books, often in another country.
- Store Staffing (at the average sales level):
  —One manager, two assistants full time (larger stores three to four assistants).
  —10 to 12 employees per eight-hour shift (40 hours per week); 980 employee hours per week.
- Store employees needed by end of 1999: 300; by the end of 2004: 2,250 (approx.).
- Store employee attrition: approximately 25 percent per year.
- Dividends from earnings were declared periodically and then were shared equally between partners.

mous Las Ramblas shopping district. Costas and Alvarez, both of whom had been involved from the beginning of the joint venture, were delighted to see how far the company had come.

EUROPEAN REORGANIZATION

Delta began to take a more direct and active role in the management of Blue Ridge. In Europe, for example, Delta created a new regional VP position with responsibility for Europe, the Middle East and South Africa. When Costas became aware of the new position, he asked whether or not he was being considered, given his extensive experience in managing international operations. The human resources department in the United States explained that they wanted to put a seasoned Delta manager in place in order to facilitate the integration of the two companies.

Although disappointed, Costas understood the logic behind the decision. He also considered that by working under a seasoned Delta manager, he could develop contacts in the new parent company that might prove favorable to his career at some future date.

In May 1999, Costas received a phone call from Bill Sawyer, Blue Ridge's director of human resources, whom Costas had known for many years.

Sawyer: We hired someone from Procter and Gamble. He's 35 years old and has a lot of marketing experience, and he worked in Greece for three years. You'll like him.

Costas: That's great. Have your people found anyone for the VP job yet?

The line was silent, then Sawyer replied in an apologetic tone, "He *is* the new VP." Costas was dumbfounded.

Costas: I thought you said you were planning to transfer a Delta veteran to promote cooperation.

Sawyer: Nobody from Delta wanted the job, so we looked outside the company. Kinsley (president, international division) wanted a "branded" executive, so we stole this guy from P&G.

Sawyer went on to explain that Mikael Södergran, who was originally from Finland, had no background in restaurant management, but had achieved a reputation for results in his previous role as a P&G marketing manager for the Middle East and Africa. He had recently been transferred from Geneva, Switzerland to P&G European headquarters in Newcastle upon Tyne.[6] Södergran was not happy in Newcastle and saw the Delta position both as an opportunity to take on greater responsibility and to move back to the civilization of London.

"You couldn't find anyone better than *that?*" Costas exclaimed. He was furious, not only for having been deceived about the need to have a Delta manager as VP, but also that he, with 10 years experience managing international operations, had been passed over in favor of someone with no experience managing operations, joint ventures or a large managerial staff. Nevertheless, the decision had been made, and Södergran was scheduled to start in two weeks.

THE DIRECTORS' MEETING

It was Södergran's first day on the job when he met with Blue Ridge Spain's board of directors to discuss a recently drafted consultants' report and negotiate new five-year growth targets (see Exhibit 3). The study, which was conducted by a leading U.S.-based management consulting firm, projected significant expansion potential for Blue Ridge in Spain, as well as in France and Germany, where Blue Ridge had no visible presence.[7] Delta also wanted to increase the royalties and fees payable from the joint venture partner in order to cover the cost of implementing new technologies, systems and services (see Exhibit 4).

Other Blue Ridge managers at the meeting included Yannis Costas and Donald Kinsley, Blue Ridge's new international president. Although Kinsley had formerly been president of a well-known family restaurant chain in the United States, this was his first international experience. Terralumen was represented by company president Andres Balaguer, Francisco Alvarez and Carlos Martin, Blue Ridge Spain's managing director.

Even before the meeting began, Delta's management team assumed that Terralumen was content to keep growth rates at their current levels and would have to be pressed to accept more aggressive targets. As expected, Martin protested that his team of 10 managers could not handle the introduction of 30 new stores a year, as suggested by the study. The meeting's cordial tone quickly dissolved when Södergran unexpectedly began to press the issue. His aggressive stance was not well received by Terralumen, who in turn questioned the ability of the consulting firm's young freshly minted American MBAs to understand the intricacy of the Spanish fast-food market. Balaguer simply brushed off the study as "a piece of American business school cleverness."

Södergran became visibly annoyed at Balaguer's refusal to consider Delta's targets. "The contract says that you are required to grow the markets," Södergran

EXHIBIT 3
Consultants'
Recommendations
Blue Ridge European
Expansion (Selected
Markets)

Source: Company files.

	1998	2000	2001	2002	2003	2004
Stores						
Spain	12	30	65	100	135	170
France	0	10	20	55	90	130
Germany	3	15	30	65	100	150
Total	15	55	115	220	325	450
Regional Managers (London)	1	15	20	22	24	26
Country Staff/Managers	12	40	90	180	220	250
Store Employees	215	1,650	3,450	6,600	9,750	13,500

EXHIBIT 4 Blue Ridge Spain Exceptional Term Highlights

	Blue Ridge U.S. Desired Objective	Blue Ridge Spain—Variance
Joint Venture Outlets		
Royalty	At least 4 percent	No royalty
Fees	$20,000	$5,000
Term	10 years	5 years
Exclusivity	Avoid exclusivity	Spain, Canary Islands, Spanish Sahara, Beleares Islands
Advertising	5 percent, right of approval	No obligations
Outlet Renewal	Renewal fee at least $2,000;	No fee or other specific
Requirements	Upgrading or relocation	requirements
Delta Products	Required	No requirement
Development Program	Schedule for required development of territory	No requirement
Non-Competition	Restrictions on similar business	No provision
Assignment	First refusal right; approval of assignee	No provision
Sub-Franchising		
Contract Privity	Blue Ridge U.S. should be a party and successor to franchisor	Blue Ridge cited; Blue Ridge succeeds on JV dissolution
Royalty	At least 4 percent	None
Fees	$20,000	None
Joint Venture Operation		
Equity Participation	More than 50 percent	50 percent
Profit Distribution	At least 50 percent	Additional 20 percent when profits are greater than 20 percent
Actual Management	Blue Ridge U.S. should appoint General Manager	General Manager is from JV partner
Board Control	Blue Ridge U.S. should have majority	Equal number of board members

Source: Company files.

demanded. Balaguer, a tall, elegant man, slowly stood up, lifted a sheaf of papers and replied, "If this is your contract, and if we rely on a contract to resolve a partnership problem, well, here is what I think of it and of you." He walked across the room and dropped the papers into a garbage can. Then upon returning to his seat, he remarked in Spanish, "If this meeting had been conducted in my language, you would have known what I *really* think of you," in reference to Södergran.

After a long pause, Costas tried to mend the situation by pointing out that Terralumen had already committed to considerable growth, and had therefore already come some way toward Delta's expansions goals. He suggested that the two companies break to consider alternatives.

A few weeks later, Costas sent an e-mail to Södergran outlining his recommendations (see Exhibit 5).

EXHIBIT 5   Costas' Recommendations

From: Yannis Costas [Costas@deltafoods.co.uk]
Sent: Wednesday, July 7, 1999, 10:16 AM
To: 'Sodergran@deltafoods.co.uk'
Subject: Key Issues—Here is what I believe we should be going for in Spain.

Mikael:
Here are my recommendations for Spain.

A. PRESERVE PARTNERSHIP
   • Need a "real" market success while developing markets elsewhere in Europe.
      • Fuel interest of potential partners elsewhere.
      • Keep Blue Ridge and Delta believing in European potential.
      • Market for real testing of concepts and ideas.
      • No complete reliance on U.K. for "successes."

B. REVERSAL NOT EASY TO OVERCOME
   • May have to pay a high premium to buy out joint venture.
   • Will lose all key managers (*no substitutes on hand*).
   • If we inherit "green field."
      • Down time close to two years.
      • Why? From decision to opening will take approximately nine months to one year.
      • In a new market this will be longer as we have no human resource experience to draw on.
      • Potential new partners need to be convinced about why we broke up with a "good" partner.
      • Real estate market does not want to deal with foreigners or raises to the price.
   • If the divorce is messy, we may be bound by the current contract for another year.

C. WORK TOWARD ACHIEVING ACCEPTABLE INTEGRATION WITH OUR DESIRABLE CONTRACT
    FRAMEWORK OVER CURRENT DELTA PLANNING HORIZON (FIVE YEARS)
   • Strong development schedule for joint venture.
   • Royalty integration over mutually acceptable period.
   • Designated "agency" for franchisees immediately, but fee flow indirectly to Blue Ridge only the amount *over* current
     terms with existing franchisees. Phase in higher flow on schedule similar to royalties.
   • Accept the notion of phasing in royalties as *we* phase in systems and services (If we *don't* phase them in there won't be
     much of a business anyhow!)

D. KEY RATIONALE
   • We may have the perfect contract, but no stores to apply it to for three years—hence no income to cover overheads.
     So . . .
   • Accept half the current growth targets with the full expectation that by year three or five, there will be a decent system
     for the contract's objectives to be meaningful.

EMERGING CONFLICTS

Costas tried his best to keep an open mind with regard to Södergran and to support him as best he could. However, as time went on, Costas began to seriously question Södergran's ability. He never seemed to interact with anyone except to conduct business. On one occasion Costas suggested that they have dinner with the joint venture partners. Södergran replied, "Oh, another dinner! Why don't we get some work done instead?"

Costas became more concerned after Södergran rented a suite two floors below the company offices "in order to have some peace and quiet." Some of the regional headquarters staff began to wonder if Södergran had taken on too much responsibility and whether he was avoiding them because of the pressure he was under. Costas also believed that Södergran was uncomfortable with him, knowing that he resented not being offered the VP position.

In October 1999, Delta sent a finance manager from the snack foods division to become the company's new VP of finance for Europe. Geoff Dryden had no overseas experience, but when he was in the United States, he had been involved in several large international acquisitions. Dryden, who was originally from North Carolina, was pleasant, well polished in his manners and dress, and very proud of his accomplishments at Delta. For him, the European assignment was an opportunity to move out of finance and, if all went well, to assume greater managerial responsibilities.

Costas, who had specialized in finance when doing his M.B.A., had always done his own financial projections and was not very fond of the idea of surrendering this responsibility to someone else. Still, he helped Dryden as much as needed to make accurate projections, taking into account the unique aspects of each market.

A NEW STRATEGY

Over the next six months, the joint venture board of directors met four times. In the end, Terralumen committed to half the growth rate originally proposed by Delta and agreed to make upward revisions if market conditions proved favorable. Delta's managers were clearly becoming frustrated by what they perceived to be their partner's entrenched position.

After the final meeting, Södergran and Costas met with their European staff to discuss the results. Dryden asked why they put up with it. "Why don't we just buy them out?" he asked, calling to mind Delta's successful acquisition of a Spanish snack food company. Costas reminded Dryden that not only were snack foods and restaurants two very different enterprises, but all the joint venture managers had come from Terralumen, and most would leave Blue Ridge if Delta proceeded to buy out the partners.

After the meeting, Dryden discussed the situation privately with Södergran. Noting that a major loan payment would soon be due to one of their creditors (a major Spanish bank), Dryden suggested holding back Delta's contribution, thereby forcing the joint venture company to default on the loan. If all went according to plan, the joint venture would have to be dissolved and the assets divided between the partners. This, he noted, would be much less expensive than trying to buy out their partner.

As expected, Terralumen requested matching funds from Delta, but Dryden simply ignored the request. However, unbeknownst to Dryden or anyone else at

Delta, Alvarez proceeded to sell one of the company's prime real estate properties and lease back the store as a means of paying the loan.

Costas happened to be in Barcelona working on Blue Ridge Spain's marketing plan with Carlos Martin. One evening, Costas was dining with his counterparts from Terralumen when Alvarez mentioned the sale of the company's Barcelona property. Costas, who at the time was unaware of Dryden's strategy, was dismayed. Real estate values in Barcelona were expected to appreciate significantly over the short term. Selling now seemed illogical. Furthermore, Costas was surprised to discover that Alvarez had been given power of attorney to make real estate transactions on behalf of the joint venture. Alvarez explained:

> Quite a few years ago, when you were in Singapore, Blue Ridge decided to give Terralumen this authority in order to reduce the amount of travel required by your managers in the United States. Besides, as you know, it is not often that good properties become available, and when they do, we must act quickly.

On his return to London, Costas discussed the real estate transaction with Dryden, who, upon hearing the news, furiously accused Costas of "siding with the enemy." Costas was quick to remind Dryden that he had not been privy to the dissolution strategy and, besides, the whole thing was unethical. Dryden retorted, "Ethics? Come on, this is strategy, not ethics!"

Dryden was clearly surprised by the news, especially given the fact that Delta would never have given such powers of attorney to a joint venture partner. The company's lawyers could have warned Dryden, but he had not been very fond of the "old hands" at Blue Ridge's legal affairs department, and therefore had chosen to not disclose his plan. Now that his strategy had failed, an alternative plan would have to be devised.

Costas felt torn between his responsibility to his employer and his distaste for the company's new approach. This whole thing was a mistake, he believed. Costas discussed his views with Södergran:

> We cannot hope to take over the stores in Spain while simultaneously developing new markets in Germany and France. Where are we going to find suitable managerial talent to support this expansion? People in Europe don't exactly see the fast-food industry as a desirable place to grow their careers. And besides, Delta hasn't given us sufficient financial resources for such an undertaking.
>
> Why don't we focus on France and Germany instead, and continue to allow Terralumen to run the Spanish operation? Revenue from Spain will help appease Delta headquarters while France and Germany suffer their inevitable growing pains. In the meantime, we can continue to press Terralumen for additional growth.

Södergran dismissed these concerns and instead gave Costas two weeks to develop a new dissolution strategy. Costas was furious that all his suggestions were so easily brushed off by someone who, he believed, had a limited understanding of the business.

On his way home that evening Costas recalled all the effort his former mentor, Gene Bennett, had put into the joint venture 16 years earlier, and all the good people he had had the privilege to work with in the intervening years. Just as all that work was about to pay off, the whole business was about to fall apart. Why hadn't he seen this coming? Where did the joint venture go wrong? Costas wondered what to do. Surely he had missed something. There had to be another way out.

Appendix 1 Management Styles for Selected Nationalities*

Spain

In Spain, a strong differentiation of social classes and professional occupations exists. Business communication is often based on subjective feelings about the topic being discussed. Personal relationships are very important as a means to establish trust, and are usually considered more important than one's expertise. Established business contacts are essential to success in Spain. Therefore, it is important to get to know someone prior to conducting business transactions. Only intimate friends are invited to the home of a Spaniard, but being invited to dinner is usual.

Spaniards are not strictly punctual for either business or social events, and once a business meeting is started, it is improper to begin with a discussion of business. National pride is pervasive, as is a sense of personal honor. To call someone "clever" is a veiled insult. Only about 30 percent of local managers speak English, while French is often the second language of choice for many older Spaniards.

Greece

Greek society employs a social hierarchy with some bias against classes, ethnic groups and religions. For Greeks, interpersonal relationships are very important when conducting business, and decisions are often based on subjective feelings. Much importance is placed on the inherent trust that exists between friends and extended families. Authority lies with senior members of any group, and they are shown great respect. They are always addressed formally.

While punctuality is important, it is not stressed. Greeks have a strong work ethic and often strive for consensus.

United States

Americans are very individualistic, with more stress placed on self than on others. Friendships are few and usually based on a specific need. Personal contacts are considered less important than bottom line results. Americans have a very strong work ethic, but a person is often considered to be a replaceable part of an organization. Great importance is placed on specialized expertise. Punctuality is important.

Business is done at lightning speed. In large firms, contracts under $100,000 can often be approved by a middle manager after only one meeting. Often companies and individuals have a very short-term orientation and expect immediate rewards. Small talk is very brief before getting down to business, even during dinner meetings and social gatherings.

Finland

Finns have a strong self orientation. More importance is placed on individual skills and abilities than on a person's station in life. Decisions are based more on objective facts than personal feelings. Privacy and personal opinions are considered very important. Finns often begin business immediately without any small talk. They are very quiet and accustomed to long periods of silence, but eye contact is important when conversing. Authority usually rests with the managing director. Punctuality is stressed in both business and social events.

* Based on *Kiss, Bow, or Shake Hands: How to do Business in Sixty Countries,* Adams Media, 1994. The descriptions do not account for individual differences within each nationality or culture.

Endnotes

1. At the time, Blue Ridge Asia was one of the company's most successful operations with nearly 800 restaurants in Singapore, Malaysia, Taiwan and Thailand.
2. Catalonia, a state in northeast Spain, had a distinct culture and language (Catalan).
3. In Spain, the month of August was traditionally set aside for vacations.
4. Ramadan is the holy month of fasting ordained by the Koran for all adult Muslims. The fast begins each day at dawn and ends immediately at sunset. During the fast, Muslims are forbidden to eat, drink, or smoke.
5. The plan to develop 50 stores was agreed to in 1998, prior to Costas' arrival.
6. Newcastle upon Tyne, United Kingdom, was an important industrial and transportation center located in northeast England (approximately three hours from London). It had a population of 263,000 (1991 census).
7. Large restaurant chains served only four percent of fast food meals in Spain, compared with 15 percent for the rest of Western Europe, and 50 percent for the United States.

Chapter Thirty-Four

Meridian Magnesium: International Technology Transfer

Len Miller was in the midst of planning a trip to Meridian Magnesium's U.S. and Italian production facilities. He was visiting the plants to learn how to improve Meridian's internal transfers of technology. While Meridian was the leading supplier worldwide of magnesium die-cast components to the automotive parts industry, differences in performance among Meridian plants were stark. Miller, a vice-president (VP) at Meridian, wondered what he might do to bring the performance of the U.S. and Italian facilities up to the same level as the Canadian facility. Part of the problem seemed to be that the U.S. and Italian facilities resisted the technological innovations that were benefiting the Canadian plant. Miller not only needed to understand the reasons for these differences, but also needed to develop a game plan that resolved the issues before Meridian's annual board meeting in two weeks' time.

Richard Ivey School of Business
The University of Western Ontario

Ken Cole prepared this case under the supervision of Professor Tima Bansal solely to provide material for class discussion. The authors do not intend to illustrate either effective or ineffective handling of a managerial situation. The authors may have disguised certain names and other identifying information to protect confidentiality.

Ivey Management Services prohibits any form of reproduction, storage or transmittal without its written permission. This material is not covered under authorization from CanCopy or any reproduction rights organization. To order copies or request permission to reproduce materials, contact Ivey Publishing, Ivey Management Services, c/o Richard Ivey School of Business, The University of Western Ontario, London, Ontario, Canada, N6A 3K7; phone (519) 661-3208; fax (519) 661-3882; e-mail cases@ivey.uwo.ca.

THE AUTOMOTIVE PARTS INDUSTRY

The global automotive parts industry, servicing the world's original equipment manufacturers (OEMs), was projected to have sales of over US$519[1] billion in 2000. Canadian manufacturers were expected to account for approximately US$39 billion of that amount.

In the 1990s, the automotive industry witnessed three major trends: consolidation, outsourcing and globalization. It had been predicted that by 2010, consolidation would result in as few as six global OEMs and approximately 50 major global parts suppliers. Consolidation and outsourcing provided automotive parts purchasers with incredible purchasing leverage that resulted in strong discount pressures on suppliers. In response, suppliers focused on developing value-added pre- and post-production services, including design, engineering, machining, finishing and assembly. For large international suppliers, the challenge was to ensure that all production facilities, regardless of geographic location, were using the most efficient, lowest cost technologies and processes.

The automotive parts industry was comprised primarily of three materials: steel, plastics and aluminum. These suppliers represented billions of dollars in annual sales, strong research and development (R&D) capabilities, and full customer design and engineering support. Magnesium autoparts suppliers, on the other hand, while growing quickly, were relatively small with just over one billion dollars cumulative global sales in 1999. Steel and aluminum autoparts generally competed on price, while magnesium and plastics autoparts generally competed on design, integration with other materials and quality. Magnesium was much lighter than steel and one-third lighter than aluminum. It was also stronger than either plastics or aluminum. However, recent alliances between plastics and steel companies, to produce a hybrid lighter-weight material, had left aluminum and magnesium die-casters uneasy and increased their sense of urgency to lower costs to remain competitive.

MERIDIAN MAGNESIUM INCORPORATED— CORPORATE HISTORY

Meridian Magnesium, originally Webster Manufacturing, began in the 1930s as a zinc die-casting operation based in London, Ontario, and focused primarily on small-machine parts. In the 1960s, with the signing of the automotive trade pact, the owner, John Webster, saw the opportunity to die-cast automotive parts. Webster's automotive business grew, and by the early 1970s, sales surpassed $20 million. At that time, Webster was approached by Ford to consider die-casting in magnesium, the lightest structural metal. Ford was interested in reducing the weight of vehicles due to the OPEC crisis and the emergence of corporate average fuel economy (CAFE) standards during that decade. In 1980, the company sold its first magnesium product: a "remote control mirror bezel" for the Ford Mustang.

The success of this first product convinced Webster to convert much of its zinc business to magnesium. In 1981, Webster built its first magnesium die-casting plant, moving four magnesium die-casting machines from London to Strathroy, Ontario. After John Webster's retirement in the early 1980s, the company changed hands several times, eventually becoming Meridian Magnesium Inc. and going public in 1989. Meridian attracted significant attention in the markets, particularly from two companies that, by 1998, had secured almost equal ownership. The first, with 49 percent of Meridian shares, was Norsk Hydro, the Norwegian public utility company and one of the world's largest producers of magnesium ingots and alloys. The second, with 51 percent ownership, was Teksid, an Italian-based world leader in the foundry (melting of metals) industry. In 1998, Norsk and Teksid took Meridian private once again and signed a shareholders' agreement providing for equal decision-making power on Meridian's board of directors. Both owners planned to provide Meridian with significant technological support; Norsk in areas related to magnesium metal and alloys, and Teksid in areas related to foundry processes.

MERIDIAN IN 2000

By the late 1990's, Meridian was the largest automotive supplier of magnesium die-cast components to both original equipment manufacturers (OEMs) and Tier 1 suppliers (major global suppliers), with approximately 40 percent of the global market for magnesium automotive parts. Meridian had sales in excess of $300 million and was a "big fish" in the "small pond" of magnesium automotive parts. Meridian's mission statement declared that, ". . . Meridian is committed to being the leading full service supplier of magnesium die-casting components and assemblies in the global automotive market."

The company had three plants, Magnesium Products Division (MPD) in Strathroy, Ontario, Magnesium Products of America (MPA) in Eaton Rapids, Michigan, and a smaller plant, Magnesium Products of Italy (MPI) in Valle D'Aosta in northeast Italy. Meridian was the industry's lowest-cost producer and the process technology leader. Meridian had a very strong market position in North America, with leading levels of magnesium know-how, strong shareholder support, good labor relations and few capital restraints due to a strong debt/equity position. The plants produced numerous products, including fully integrated instrument panels, cross-car beams, transfer cases and steering components. Meridian also had business development offices throughout North America and Western Europe. These offices developed and maintained contacts with customer engineering and design groups.

MERIDIAN'S GOALS

As part of its 10-year plan, Meridian had set some aggressive growth targets for 2010 including:

- Annual growth rate of 15 percent

- Return on capital employed exceeding 15 percent

- Maintaining a 40 percent share of global market

- Sales exceeding $1 billion

- Earnings of greater than $100 million

- Continuing to be the lowest-cost producer

Other more general goals included expanding operations to make sub-assemblies and modules; expanding product offerings into body, structural and powertrain applications; and the development of new technologies to provide Meridian with more sources of sustainable competitive advantage. In the short term, technological goals included the improvement of foundry systems and the development of "in-cell" recycling capabilities.

Recognized weaknesses in the Meridian organization included a lack of employee retention due to a very tight labor market. People with strong process and production knowledge were in very short supply. Furthermore, the Italian and U.S. facilities did not perform as well as the Canadian facility, which was partly attributable to the difficulty in retaining knowledgeable people.

LEN MILLER AND GTO

Upon assuming office in 1998, Meridian's chief executive officer (CEO), Paolo Maccario, had redesigned Meridian's management structure and appointed three VPs and a president (see Exhibit 1 for details). Based in Strathroy, Len Miller was responsible for Meridian's Global Technologies Organization (GTO). Miller had joined Meridian as the assistant general manager of MPD at the Strathroy plant in 1996, and had worked hard to improve operating efficiencies. In December of 1996, Miller was promoted to general manager and in early 1999, became VP of Meridian's recently created (January, 1998) GTO division.

As Meridian had expanded to a multiplant, international organization in the 1990s, it became apparent that the company could benefit from the centralization of some of the "knowledge" components within the business. At that time, each plant had its own R&D budget and developed its own technologies and solutions, and there was no formal system of communication between plants. GTO's mandate was to "facilitate the identification and communication of best practices between the plants" and to help the plants realize their business objectives as defined by the corporate strategy and growth targets. GTO was not a profit centre, and therefore it relied on the plants to finance its activities. GTO grew rapidly in its first three years of operations, from 11 to more than 55 employees. In 1998, GTO's budget was between $2 million to $3 million, but was increased to $7.5 million in 2000.

In the summer of 2000, GTO staff moved into a separate facility across the street from the MPD plant in Strathroy. The two-story, "Global Technology Centre (GTC)" was equipped with leading-edge technology solutions, sophisticated design program software, complete Intranet and Internet connectivity and powerful servers, accessible worldwide. Separated from the plants in this new facility, the organization quickly developed a reputation for being a "great place to

EXHIBIT 1 **Organizational Chart**

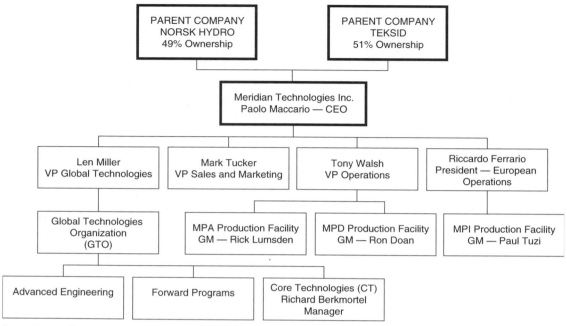

Source: Company files.

get promoted to," and many in the Meridian organization began to refer to GTC as the "Good Times Club."

When GTO was created, Miller had great hopes that the centralized development of best practices would generate significant benefits. He believed that the plants would readily participate in projects to improve operating efficiencies and lower costs. Instead, after more than two years of GTO operations, the plants continued to resist implementing some proven best practices. The NIH Syndrome (Not Invented Here), as Miller liked to call it, was pervasive at Meridian. But to Miller, the problem was even more complex than a mere question of where or how the technology was developed. Numerous organizational and cultural issues had developed as a result of Meridian's rapid international expansion, leaving Meridian struggling to develop and implement companywide standards.

There were other issues as well. According to Mark Tucker, Meridian's VP of sales and marketing, "One of the biggest things is that people don't understand the roles and responsibilities of GTO at the operations level, the business level . . . because today, I would bet, you go to any one of the plants and half the people there wouldn't even know what goes on here at GTO."

Miller also recognized that GTO had some other weaknesses that continually interfered with efforts to improve production efficiencies across all plants. According to Miller, ". . . The largest failure to date has been the failure to improve relationships

EXHIBIT 2
Core Technology
Objectives

- Serve as a Meridian "Centre of Expertise" and technical training resource for Business Units.
- Ensure a consistent application of Meridian's best process practices by coordinating and evaluating plant innovation and strong plant relations.
- Assist implementation of latest technology at Meridian plants.
- Research, benchmark and evaluate alternative technologies, products and materials.
- Gather and disseminate competitive intelligence.
- Set and achieve aggressive targets to speed to market—50 percent reductions for specific core technologies that can capture the heart of the industry.
- Relentless pursuit of low cost producer status within the process context to achieve a sustainable competitive advantage.

between GTO and the U.S. facility. This is a failure at the vice-presidential level, but it is also a failure at the organizational level, at the level of the plant employees and the GTO staff."

Despite these problems, Miller felt that overall, GTO had enjoyed success. The core technologies group within GTO had done an excellent job developing in-house recycling. All the plants had implemented the process and were realizing significant savings. According to Miller, "The true measure of success for GTO is in the value delivered."

CORE TECHNOLOGIES (CT)

Within GTO, Core Technologies was directly responsible for the centralized development and communication of best practices between the plants (see Exhibit 2 for CT objectives). CT also had a supporting role in other GTO functions, including assisting other GTO departments with business development, product engineering and product launch co-ordination. CT's primary focus, however, was on assisting with cost reductions, safety related projects and new technologies.

Miller had spent his first three months as VP trying to figure out how the Meridian organization really worked. He saw the need to build a strong CT team and find strong leadership. He envisioned a team that would be able to do anything technology-related within the fields of magnesium, die-casting and auto parts. Leadership was critical, and Miller chose Richard Berkmortel, a mechanical engineer with manufacturing and product engineering experience, and promoted him to manager of CT. Berkmortel had been at MPD for six years, his last two years as a business unit manager in Strathroy's operations.

The CT unit was comprised of Berkmortel, two PhD metallurgists, two process engineers with extensive "shop-floor" experience and three other engineers with specific areas of expertise. Four of the existing CT staff were promoted from the Strathroy production facility; three were external hires and one was hired from the U.S. facility. Three of the eight who were promoted internally had 15 or more years experience in the industry. Berkmortel himself had eight years of die-casting experience and the remainder of his team had, on average, five years of experience.

Communication between CT and the plants was largely informal, as it had been before GTO was formed. This informal style seemed to fit the practical "get the job done" mindset that was so prevalent at the plant level. Formal communication occurred at the monthly operations meetings where Miller often reviewed ongoing CT projects with the other VPs and the plant managers. On an irregular basis, GTO distributed an internal newsletter that highlighted developments and successes.

CT was respected for its development and implementation of in-house recycling of magnesium metal. This project, undertaken in 1998 and completed at all plants in late 2000, yielded significant savings to the plants and had been implemented companywide as quickly as possible.

Another project, gas displacement pumps, had not fared so well. While CT expended considerable resources to develop the pumps which were adopted by the Canadian facility, the U.S. facility independently developed siphon tubes. Despite some evidence that the gas displacement pumps were more efficient and led to cost savings, the U.S. facility continued to use siphon tubes. Other projects included "in-cell" recycling and the development of better systems for the delivery of SF6 (Sulpher Hexaflouride) that Meridian used as a cover gas to protect melted magnesium. The eventual replacement of SF6, a "greenhouse" gas, with a substitute cover gas was another ongoing CT project.

MERIDIAN PRODUCTS DIVISION (MPD)— STRATHROY, ONTARIO, CANADA

MPD began magnesium die-casting in 1981 and, by 1999, was the flagship of the Meridian organization. While employee retention at MPD was an issue, it was less so than at the other plants. Management believed that keeping good people from the predominantly rural farming communities surrounding the Strathroy facility was easier than in Michigan's extended suburbs and bedroom communities. Retention was a significant advantage since it took several years to develop significant levels of process expertise. MPD was non-union and had been since its inception. Relations between management and employees were strong and marked by frequent, frank and open communication. The plant had a strong relationship with GTO, and according to Ron Doan, the plant manager, collaboration on projects in the past had been fruitful.

MERIDIAN PRODUCTS OF AMERICA (MPA)— EATON RAPIDS, MICHIGAN

Approximately a three-hour drive from MPD, MPA was located in the heart of Michigan's famous automotive region. MPA began magnesium die-casting production in 1995 as an expansion project from MPD. From 1999 through 2005, MPA was slated to launch a number of new magnesium products. "Launch mode," with its numerous uncertainties, tough deadlines and growing pains, was predicted to significantly stretch plant resources.

MERIDIAN PRODUCTS OF ITALY (MPI)—
VERRES, VALLE D'AOSTA, ITALY

MPI began in 1995 as a joint venture between Teksid and Meridian to build the Fiat/Lancia "Epsilon" seat for SEPI, the seat division of Fiat Auto. Originally the business required four die-cast machines, but eventually production estimates resulted in expansion to 9 machines. Unfortunately, the seat project was subsequently cancelled, but Fiat chose Meridian to produce the cross-car beam for the Bravo Brava. The financial terms were highly unfavorable for Meridian, which had very little leverage, given MPI's significant excess capacity as a result of the cancellation of the seat project. After this inauspicious beginning, MPI struggled to turn a profit.

MPI was unionized, as were most Italian companies. Only 10 percent of the employees, however, were card-carrying union members, and the relationship between the union and management was "very smooth." The Aosta Valley was a newly developing industrial region, and the unions were pleased to have the jobs there. Salaries were similar across all industries in the region so the union had little effect on salary costs. But working conditions in the plant were always an issue, especially since the region's largest employer was the nearby casino, offering cleaner and "more glamorous" work. Of MPI's 130 employees, 20 were in business development or were GTO transferees assigned to MPI to help develop processes and technologies. In the future, MPI planned to expand production to 7,400 tonnes by 2003.

Plant Comparisons

Comparative figures for each of Meridian's three production facilities are as follows:

Comparative Figures 1999	MPD (Canada)	MPA (United States)	MPI (Italy)
Tonnes Mg Produced	14,000 gross metric tonnes	11,000 gross metric tonnes	3,000 gross metric tonnes
Die Cast Machines	20 from 800 to 2,500 tonnes	17 from 800 to 3,000 tonnes	9 from 420 to 2,500 tonnes
Employees	370	350	130
1999 Revenues (US$)	180 million	140 million	60 million
1999 EBIT* (US$)	40 million	12 million	(Loss)
Secondary Operations	Machining, finishing and assembly	Machining, drilling and assembly	None—Value added work currently outsourced

*EBIT—Earnings before Interest and Taxes.

NOTES FROM AN INTERVIEW WITH RICHARD BERKMORTEL

Miller had spoken to Berkmortel, the manager of Core Technologies, to understand his perspective on why the technologies developed by the CT division were not being adopted universally by Meridian plants. Several comments from his conversation with Berkmortel had stuck in Miller's mind.

PLANT ATTITUDES

According to Berkmortel, while CT was meant to be a centre of knowledge and best practices and to share information and innovations with the plants ". . . very little of this actually occurs in a formal, organized way and some of the plants are slightly proprietary about good ideas and innovations." Berkmortel believed that CT had failed to break down the "negative—NIH—attitudes at the plants" and to get the plants to adopt common values toward technological developments.

CHOOSING TECHNOLOGY PROJECTS

With respect to choosing the projects on which CT worked, Berkmortel reflected,

> A lot of innovations have to come from the plants. I think it is more efficient for them to do it. They have a specific need to resolve immediately, and that need, along with the time expediency, will drive innovation. A lot of the time, they are the best equipped to understand what their needs are and to resolve them.
>
> The plants may have an issue, and they have a lot of their own resources that they can put toward that issue. For MPA and MPI, it is more difficult since they are somewhat removed from us (CT) in terms of distance. Typically, I see that the plant managers find it difficult to ask for assistance from Miller since they are often unsure of GTO's role or are unwilling to accept support. Also at times, there is outside support that is better equipped to deal with a technical issue, such as the original equipment manufacturer could assist with their own piece of equipment.

A SUCCESSFUL PROJECT—IN-HOUSE RECYCLING

In-house recycling was a major success because everybody wanted it. The plants wanted it for financial reasons . . . the goals fit closely with plant philosophies, strength in foundries, and every part of the company wanted the project to go ahead . . . so there was full support and there was no disagreement as to what direction we should be taking. So that went a long ways to facilitating the initial steps of development. A pilot operation was set up at MPD. That facility was chosen due to location, location, location.

Today at MPD, all scrap is recycled . . . and that technology represents a significant savings on raw material costs. We had no problems in getting the other plants to adopt it. MPA wanted the project to go ahead immediately since it was seen as a corporate project, a Meridian project. MPA also had a relatively smooth transition. MPI came third since they had other priorities they needed to implement beforehand. Part of the delay at MPI was also related to resources, since the implementation team was working at MPA and had to finish there before they could begin working at MPI.

A MORE TYPICAL PROJECT—SF6 PULSE SYSTEM

Berkmortel discussed a typical project related to improving foundry design.

> The particular project was the SF6 pulse system. The plants, MPD in particular, had been complaining about corrosion on the pots and SF6 prices were rising. A study was done by CT on MPD's pots with the help of an outside gas analysing company. Plant participation from MPD and MPA was relatively minor. In the end, a new system was developed that reduced pot corrosion and SF6 consumption. The improvements were communicated directly from plant to plant at the operations meetings. MPA saw the positive effect on MPD's financials and requested the information directly from MPD. MPA is now probably at about 50 to 60 percent implementation. MPI has been very slow to react and does not have the process implemented yet . . . information and drawings have been sent several times, along with the equipment and they have yet to install the equipment, approximately one year later.

According to Berkmortel,

> MPI is not adopting SF6 pulse systems because their foundry knowledge is somewhat lacking. They do not yet understand their process enough for the pulse system to be useful since they have a number of other foundry issues to improve before the technology would help them to save money. I don't understand why their foundry technology is different from that of MPD and MPA since numerous people have been sent to assist and improve their systems.

A "FAILED" PROJECT—GAS DISPLACEMENT PUMPS

In speaking about CT's biggest disappointment to date, Berkmortel identified gas displacement pumps.

> Gas displacement pumps were a CT project and a plant project at MPD. Our work resulted in up to 25 percent improvement in some areas. At MPD these improvements were measurable and cost savings were evident. But the other plants refused to implement the technology. MPA did not accept it since they felt that they could get the same benefit from siphon tubes and that there would be less disruption in the plant since they would not have to reengineer their foundry processes. The financial benefits of gas displacement pumps were not as evident as they were with recycling. The process was a three-year process, and both the siphon tubes and the gas displacement pumps were being improved simultaneously . . . even if the data indicate that the fourth generation of gas displacement pumps are vastly superior for some products or some machines, it is unlikely that there will be enough evidence coming out of MPD to convince the other plants to make the investment.

COMMUNICATIONS

With respect to communications, Berkmortel indicated that cultural and language differences imposed barriers between North America and Italy, but that other problems existed between MPA and CT despite similarities in culture and language.

In the beginning, communication with MPI was difficult, but it has improved significantly over the last six months. The message that CT wants to give to the plants is that there is some benefit to seeking assistance from CT. CT definitely has the most success when the plant comes to CT with a problem to resolve. When they feel that they have a need and they come to us, it works. On projects, plant people are automatically respected . . . we have started to pull people from the "customers" to start to add credibility to the process.

IMPROVING CT

Berkmortel also believed that some of the issues were resource related.

Development of new processes, like in-house recycling, has consumed the majority of CT's resources, especially our human resources, or more so than expected, so our role in supporting the plants has been lower than 25 percent. I would say only 10 percent of our time has been spent on this and only when the plants have requested that we do so.

In terms of the future, Berkmortel believed that,

The focus needs to be on "big"—Meridian projects with direct financial impact. Smaller projects are harder to focus on because the resources have been allocated to priority items where we can have the most impact. We maybe need a slightly larger group of people where we can dedicate people to noncore projects. In terms of allocating people, there are millions of projects that the plant would like done, and often I don't have people with the right knowledge or enough people to respond to all of those needs.

Typically, CT works for a particular customer. We have looked at working in cross-plant teams. That goes back to communication—how we communicate with the plants. It has typically been done at operations meetings. The plant managers raise an issue that they believe CT should deal with, and CT reports back on how they could deal with the issue, and the teams are set up afterwards.

UNDERSTANDING THE PLANTS' PERSPECTIVES

Miller needed to find out why some technologies that had been adopted by MPD were not being adopted by the U.S. and Italian facilities. He had scheduled meetings with the managers of MPD, MPA and MPI over the next two weeks. Miller needed to get to the root of the problem and identify ways in which these issues could be resolved.

Endnote

1. Unless otherwise stated, all amounts are in Canadian dollars.

Chapter Thirty-Five

Honeywell Inc. and Global Research & Development

In mid-1997, Steve Wilson, a Honeywell Technology Center (HTC) manager, thought back to the previous week's visit from a Chinese delegation interested in Honeywell Inc. (Honeywell) technology and products. These visits were becoming increasingly frequent. Wilson and other HTC managers were certain that there were many international opportunities for Honeywell, not just in China but throughout Asia and Eastern Europe. The dilemma was that HTC, Honeywell's research and development (R&D) organization, was centralized in Minneapolis, a long way from the potential new markets.

Recently, a Honeywell manager based in Asia had raised the following issues:

There are several reasons for spreading R&D capability around the world. First, time to market in today's world is probably the most significant competitive advantage a company can have. One way to get quicker time to market is to do R&D in multiple locations around the world so you have a 24- hour R&D process. Second, there are talented people around the world and by not taking advantage of those skills and talents that may exist in China or India or other places, a company is putting itself at a competitive disadvantage. Third, in many countries, including China, personal contacts and connections are invaluable in the business world and there is a great loyalty among alumni of certain institutions. American companies that have established relationships with these institutions may get access to alumni in important government positions down the road. Fourth, its much easier to understand the unique product requirements of a country or region of the world if you spend time there. It's very hard to sit in Minneapolis and figure out the cooling

control requirement for a Chinese air conditioning system if you have never been in an apartment building in China that has poured concrete walls that you can't run thermostat wire through.

There was a growing consensus that HTC had to become more international to support Honeywell's growth opportunities. However, before anything could be done, many issues had to be addressed. How should Honeywell attempt to build effective global R&D capabilities? HTC had developed a unique entrepreneurial, interaction-based culture. Could this culture be replicated outside the United States? How quickly should HTC move? Who would manage new R&D organizations? How would these organizations be funded? Should international R&D sites be centers of excellence for specific technologies, or should they be application centers using technology developed in Minneapolis, or should they be a combination of both?

HONEYWELL BACKGROUND

Honeywell had a long history of engineering and scientific achievement. In 1885, Albert Butz invented the damper flapper, a device that opened furnace vents automatically. Butz formed the Butz Thermo-Electric Regulator Co. in Minneapolis to market the product. In 1927, the firm, now known as the Minneapolis Heat Regulator Company, merged with its main competitor, Honeywell Heating Specialties of Wabash, Indiana. The new public company, named the Minneapolis-Honeywell Regulator Co. and headquartered in Minneapolis, became the leading U.S. firm in home heating controls.

Throughout the 1930s, Minneapolis-Honeywell expanded and diversified. In 1930, the first international subsidiary was opened in Toronto and in 1934, the first European subsidiary was established in the Netherlands. Between 1900 and 1937, the company evolved from manufacturing one thermostat to producing more than 3,000 control devices and its engineers received more than 1,000 patents. During World War II, Minneapolis-Honeywell became involved in mass-production of military instruments and equipment. This work led to the development and production of an aircraft autopilot, positioning Minneapolis-Honeywell in the aeronautical engineering business. After the war, the firm reorganized its various defense-related businesses into the Military Products Group and by the late 1950s, military business represented one third of the company's sales. By the 1960s, the firm, now called Honeywell Inc., had become an important supplier for the U.S. space program.

In 1955, Honeywell formed a division called Datamatic to build computers. This division would eventually have a 10 percent market share. Honeywell's controls business also grew rapidly in the post-war period. In 1950, the firm acquired the Micro Switch Corporation, a manufacturer of switches, sensors, and manual controls used in myriad products such as cars, airplanes, appliances, air conditioning systems, and factory equipment. In 1953, Honeywell introduced its famous round thermostat, the Honeywell Round. Much of Honeywell's growth between 1960 and 1980 was the result of international growth and, in particular, demand from developing nations for home, building, and industrial controls.

The 1980s and early 1990s was a period of restructuring for Honeywell. Total employment dropped from 94,000 in 1985 to 50,000 in 1995. Cutbacks in U.S. defense spending had a dramatic effect on Honeywell's Space and Aviation Division. During a three-year period from 1991 to 1994, space and aviation revenue declined by $700 million to $1.4 billion. Space and aviation employment declined by half to about 11,000 and 3 million square feet of plant space was closed. In 1990, the defense business, which a few years earlier had accounted for almost half of total revenues, was spun off into a new organization. In 1986, Sperry Aerospace, a Phoenix-based firm manufacturing flight instrumentation, advanced avionics, and other electronics systems was acquired for $1.03 billion. The acquisition solidified Honeywell's position as the leader in aircraft navigation systems and flight controls. Also in 1986, after its market share dropped to 2 percent, the computer business was spun off into a joint venture of Compagnie des Machines Bull of France and NEC Corp. of Japan. In 1991, Honeywell exited the computer business.

Honeywell Sectors in 1997

Honeywell was organized around three industry sectors: home and building control, industrial control, and space and aviation control. Exhibit 1 shows summary financial information for Honeywell, Exhibit 2 shows a list of products, customers, and competitors, and Exhibit 3 shows segmented financial information by division and geographic region.

The home and building control division manufactured controls for heating such as thermostats, ventilation, humidification and air-conditioning equipment, home automation systems, lighting controls, building management systems and services, and home consumer products such as air cleaners and humidifiers.

The industrial control sector produced systems for the automation and control of process operations in industries such as oil refining, oil and gas drilling, pulp and paper manufacturing, food processing, chemical manufacturing, and power generation. For example, Honeywell controls were used in 24 of the world's 25 largest oil refineries. The industrial control sector also produced switches, sensors, and solenoid valves for use in vehicles, consumer products, data communication, and industrial applications.

The space and aviation sector was a leading supplier of avionics systems for the commercial, military, and space markets. Honeywell systems could be found on virtually every commercial aircraft produced in the Western world and were aboard every manned space flight launched in the United States. Products included automatic flight control systems, electronic cockpit displays, flight management systems, navigation, surveillance, and warning systems, and severe weather avoidance systems. In 1995, the Boeing 777 was launched, marking the successful launch of a new suite of Honeywell integrated avionics controls.

Of the three product sectors, home and building control was the most international because its products had potential applications in every country. The end customer was the homeowner and housing needs differed in every country. Most

EXHIBIT 1   Honeywell Inc. Financial Information

(Dollars and Shares In Millions Except per Share Amount)

	1996	1995	1994	1993	1992
SALES					
Home and Building Control	$ 3,327.1	$ 3,034.7	$ 2,664.5	$ 2,424.3	$ 2,393.6
Industrial Control	2,199.6	2,035.9	1,835.3	1,691.5	1,743.9
Space and Aviation Control	1,640.0	1,527.4	1,432.0	1,674.9	1,933.1
Other	144.9	133.3	125.2	172.3	152.0
Total sales	$ 7,311.6	$ 6,731.3	$ 6,057.0	$ 5,963.0	$ 6,222.6
OPERATING PROFIT					
Home and Building Control	$ 345.8	$ 308.6	$ 236.5	$ 232.7	$ 193.4
Industrial control	254.9	233.8	206.6	189.7	156.9
Space and Aviation Control	163.3	127.6	80.9	148.1	175.8
Other	6.2	2.8		(1.8)	(9.5)
Total operating profit	770.2	672.8	524.0	568.7	516.6
Operating profit as a percent of sales	*10.5%*	*10.0%*	*8.7%*	*9.5%*	*8.3%*
Interest expense	(81.4)	(83.3)	(75.5)	(68.0)	(89.9)
Litigation settlements				32.6	287.9
Equity income	13.3	13.6	10.5	17.8	15.8
General corporate expense	(91.9)	(97.6)	(89.3)	(72.6)	(95.7)
Income before income taxes	$ 610.2	$ 505.5	$ 369.7	$ 478.5	$ 634.7
ASSETS					
Home and Building Control	$ 2,144.3	$ 1,727.2	$ 1,529.8	$ 1,327.3	$ 1,302.4
Industrial Control	1,376.1	1,307.2	1,273.3	1,059.8	1,057.5
Space and Aviation Control	1,037.3	971.1	1,174.9	1,219.6	1,403.6
Corporate and Other	935.6	1,054.7	907.9	991.4	1,106.6
Total assets	$ 5,493.3	$ 5,060.2	$ 4,885.9	$ 4,598.1	$ 4,870.1
ADDITIONAL INFORMATION					
Average number of common shares outstanding	126.6	127.1	129.4	134.2	138.5
Return on average shareholders' equity	*19.7%*	*17.1%*	*15.6%*	*18.4%*	*13.8%*
Shareholders' equity per common share	$ 17.44	$ 16.09	$ 14.57	$ 13.48	$ 13.10
Price/Earnings ratio	20.7	18.6	14.7	14.3	11.5
Percent of debt to total capitalization	31%	28%	32%	28%	28%
Research and development					
Honeywell-funded	$ 353.3	$ 323.2	$ 319.0	$ 337.4	$ 312.6
Customer-funded	$ 341.4	$ 336.6	$ 340.5	$ 404.8	$ 390.5
Capital expenditures	$ 296.5	$ 238.1	$ 262.4	$ 232.1	$ 244.1
Depreciation and amortization	$ 287.5	$ 292.9	$ 287.4	$ 284.9	$ 292.7
Employees at year-end	53,000	50,100	50,800	52,300	55,400

Source: Honeywell 1996 Annual Report.

of the home and building control products sold in Europe were engineered and manufactured in European factories. For example, German homes were usually heated with hot water whereas in the U.S. forced air was the norm. As a result, various valves and boiler parts were developed in Germany for the German heating market. In other cases, the European products were close adaptations of products

EXHIBIT 2 Honeywell Products, Customers, and Competitors

Sector	Representative Customers	Competitors
HOME AND BUILDING CONTROL **Home and Building Products:** *Consumer Products:* Heaters; fans; humidifiers; vaporizers; electronic air cleaners; water filtration products; thermostats and home security systems. *Control Products:* Perfect Climate Comfort Center® System; SYSNet™ Facilities Integration System; thermostats; TotalHome® home automation system; HVAC equipment controls; integrated furnace and boiler controls; demand-side energy management systems; energy-efficient lighting equipment; utility services; water controls; direct-coupled actuators; zoning systems; media controls; heat recovery and energy recovery ventilators. **Building Solutions:** Installed systems; HVAC solutions (EXCEL 5000®); fire solutions (Excel Life Safety); security solutions (Excel Security Manager); open systems technology; performance contracting; compressed air management; isolation room controls; remove HVAC monitoring (ServiceNet®); and maintenance services.	Architects and developers; building managers and owners; consulting engineers; contractors; distributors and wholesalers; hardware and home center stores; heating, ventilation and air conditioning equipment manufacturers; home builders; physicians; consumers; airports; hospitals; hotels; manufacturing facilities; office and government buildings; restaurants; retail stores; education facilities; utilities; and security directors.	Johnson Controls; Siebe; Landis & Staefa; Emerson; White Rodgers, Holmes; Alerton; Siemens, ADT and regional companies such as Andover.
INDUSTRIAL CONTROL **Industrial Automation and Control Products and Solutions:** Advanced control software and industrial automation systems for control and monitoring of continuous, batch and hybrid operations; process control instrumentation; industrial control valves; recorders; controllers; flame safeguard equipment; supervisory cell controllers; product management software; equipment controls; programmable controllers; communications systems for industrial control equipment and systems; and professional services, including consulting, networking, engineering and installation. **Sensing and Control Products and Solutions:** Solid-state sensors for position, pressure, airflow temperature and current: vision-based sensors; precision electromechanical switches; PC-based device level control.	Chemical plants; computer and business equipment manufacturers; data acquisition companies; food processing plants; medical equipment manufacturers; oil and gas producers; pharmaceutical companies; pulp and paper mills; refining and petrochemical firms; textile manufacturers; heat treat processors; utilities; package and material handling operations; appliance manufacturers; automotive companies; and aviation companies.	Asea Brown Boveri; Elsag-Bailey; Fisher-Rosemount; Siebe (Foxboro); Siemens; Yokogawa; Allen-Bradley; Banner; Cherry; Omron; Sprague; Telemecanique; Turck.
SPACE AND AVIATION CONTROL **Major Products:** Integrated cockpit avionics, including automatic flight controls, electronic display systems, flight management systems: Global Positioning System (GPS) based avionics; communications systems: Traffic Alert and Collision Avoidance Systems (TCAS): automatic test systems; helmet-mounted display and sighting systems: space instruments and sensors; and data management and processing systems.	Airframe manufacturers; international, national and regional airlines; corporate operators; NASA; prime U.S. defense contractors; and the U.S. Department of Defense.	Allied Signal; Litton; Kaiser; Rockwell International; Sextant.

567

EXHIBIT 3   Segmented Financial Information

Home and Building Control

1996 Sales Mix

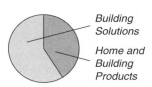

- Building Solutions
- Home and Building Products

- North America
- Europe
- Asia Pacific
- Latin America

Financial Results
(Dollars in Millions)

	1996	1995	1994
Sales	$3,327.1	$3,034.7	$2,664.5
Operating Profits	$345.8	$308.6	$265.2*
Margin	10.4%	10.2%	10.0%

Excluding special charges.

Industrial Control

1996 Sales Mix

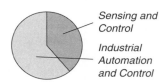

- Sensing and Control
- Industrial Automation and Control

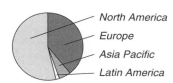

- North America
- Europe
- Asia Pacific
- Latin America

Financial Results
(Dollars in Millions)

	1996	1995	1994
Sales	$2,199.6	$2,035.9	$1,835.3
Operating Profits	$254.9	$233.8	$221.0*
Margin	11.6%	11.5%	12.0%

Excluding special charges.

Space and Aviation Control

1996 Sales Mix

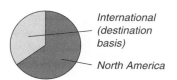

- Space Systems
- Commercial Flight Systems
- Military Avionics Systems

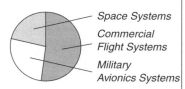

- International (destination basis)
- North America

Financial Results
(Dollars in Millions)

	1996	1995	1994
Sales	$1,640.0	$1,527.4	$1,432.0
Operating Profits	$163.3	$127.6	$100.5*
Margin	10.0%	8.4%	7.0%

Excluding special charges.

Source: 1996 Honeywell Inc., Annual Report.

sold in the United States. There were also products, such as thermostats sold in the Netherlands, that were imported directly from the United States.

With its worldwide standards, space and aviation was the best defined international sector. Aviation products did not have to be localized, which meant that aviation could be operated as a centralized global business. Industrial control products, although not standard worldwide, tended to be less localized than home and building products because customers wanted similar controls worldwide in their plants.

International Opportunities

Honeywell's international organization is shown in Exhibit 4. European operations were headquartered in Brussels and the Asia-Pacific region was based in Hong Kong. Non-U.S. sales were $2.8 billion, equal to 39 percent of 1996 total sales. By the year 2000, non-U.S. sales were expected to increase to 45 percent. Much of this growth was projected for China and Eastern and Central Europe. With their high levels of air and water pollution and poor record of energy efficiency, these areas were large potential markets for Honeywell home and building and industrial controls. As one HTC researcher indicated, "the mess in Eastern Europe is a huge market for us."

In particular, the area of district heating was a large potential market for Honeywell. In Eastern Europe and China, most people had never used a thermostat in their homes. Apartments generally had no heating controls and their temperatures were determined by outputs of a central district heating facility. During the winter it was not unusual to see open windows in apartment buildings as residents tried to cool their apartments. Hot water for domestic radiators was provided by a central boiler in each region. On a designated day of the year, an official turned the heating on for the whole city; on another, it was turned off. Often, there were no valves on the radiators. The plumbing was often arranged so that if one occupier turned down the heating, the entire building would be affected. With district heating, Honeywell's goal was to provide a complete system from the boiler to the individual apartment unit. Honeywell could provide monitoring and control systems to improve productivity, save energy, reduce air pollution and provide better temperature control. To do this would require Honeywell home and building control and industrial control units to work closely together as a team. As an early entrant, Honeywell, which opened a Moscow office in 1974, was a major supplier of district heating controls in Eastern Europe.

Although Honeywell's Asian business accounted for only about 8 percent of sales, CEO Michael Bonsignore indicated that "Asia represents the greatest growth opportunity for Honeywell in the next 20 years."[1] Bonsignore added that he would like Asian businesses to reach $1 billion in sales by 2000 and to grow at a 20 percent compound rate or better. Honeywell's Asia/Pacific business had operations in 17 Asian countries and Hong Kong. Its joint ventures included partnerships with South Korean conglomerate Lucky-Gold Star Group and China National Petrochemical, the world's third-largest petroleum refiner. About half of Honeywell's Asian sales were in China. Honeywell generated about $250 million

EXHIBIT 4 Honeywell International

President, Honeywell Asia Pacific	President, Honeywell Europe	Vice President and GM, Latin America	President, Honeywell Canada
HQ, Hong Kong	HQ, Brussels	HQ, Sunrise, Florida	HQ, North York, Ontario

Affiliates: Australia, China, Hong Kong, Malaysia, New Zealand, Pakistan, Singapore, Taiwan, Thailand

Manufacturing: Sydney, Auckland, Taipei, Shenzhen, Tianjin

Joint Venture Manufacturing: Pune (India), Fujisawa, Hadano, Kamata, Isehara, Shanan (Japan), Bupyong (South Korea)

Affiliates: Austria, Belgium, Bulgaria, Czech Republic, Denmark, Egypt, Finland, France, Germany, Hungary, Italy, Kuwait, The Netherlands, Norway, Oman, Poland, Portugal, Romania, Commonwealth of Independent States (Russia), Saudi Arabia, Slovak Republic, South Africa, Spain, Sweden, Switzerland, Turkey, Ukraine, United Arab Emirates, United Kingdom

Centers of Excellence and Manufacturing: Brussels, Belgium; Varkaus, Finland; Amiens and Grenoble, France; Amsberg, Maintal, Mosbach, Neuwied and Schönaich, Germany; Den Bosch and Emmen, The Netherlands; Port, Portugal; Newhouse, Scotland, Geneva and Zurich, Switzerland

Affiliates: Argentina, Brazil, Chile, Mexico, Panama, Puerto Rico, Venezuela, Colombia, Ecuador

Centers of Excellence and Manufacturing: Caracas, Venezuela; Chihuahua, Ciudad Juarez, Districto Federal and Tijuana, Mexico; São Paulo, Brazil

Manufacturing: Ontario, Quebec

in revenue in China and expected sales of at least $500 million by the end of the decade. In 1997, Honeywell began working with Beijing District Heating Co. to improve heating services for 20 percent of the capital's buildings, with the potential for expansion. As well, China needed more than 1,000 new aircraft over the next 15 years, which created opportunities for Honeywell avionics products.

Competition

Honeywell's home and building and industrial control competitors ranged from diversified global giants like Siemens and Asea Brown Boveri to small, specialized firms such as Andover Controls, a $70 million manufacturer of programmable, network-based building automation systems (see Exhibit 2). In the space and aviation control sector, the set of competitors was much smaller and primarily U.S.-based.

Competitors in the home and building and industrial control sectors were, like Honeywell, intent on international growth. For example, Johnson Controls,

Honeywell's largest U.S.-based competitor in home and building controls, had recently announced an R&D partnership with a Hong Kong university. In 1997, U.K.-based Siebe announced plans to establish a wholly owned subsidiary in India, which would include engineering centers for industrial process control equipment. White-Rodgers, a division of Emerson Electric with a worldwide base of 23 sales, distribution and manufacturing sites, had made a commitment to expand its international presence. Even tiny Andover, based in Andover, Massachusetts, operated three technical centers outside the United States in the United Kingdom, Germany, and Hong Kong.

In addition to increasing internationalization, the controls industry had seen a wave of mergers, acquisitions, and alliances. In 1996, Electrowatt Group, a Swiss-based holding company, announced the formation of Landis & Staefa, Inc., a worldwide combination of Landis & Gyr and Staefa Control System. Landis & Staefa competed with Honeywell in home and building controls. Later in 1996, it was announced that Siemens AG was acquiring a 44.9 percent share in Electrowatt Group. Siemens, a Honeywell competitor in various product markets, was one of the world's largest organizations. Siemens had sales of more than $60 billion, 250 manufacturing sites in 42 countries, and subsidiaries and affiliates in more than 190 countries. In the United States alone, Siemens had more than 46,000 employees in over 400 office locations, 40 research and development facilities, and 80 manufacturing and assembly plants. In 1991 Siebe acquired U.S.-based Foxboro for $656 million. The Siebe group employed over 42,500 people and consisted of more than 150 companies located in 40 countries. In 1992, Emerson Electric bought Fisher Controls for $1.4 billion, forming the Fisher-Rosemount family of companies.

RESEARCH AND DEVELOPMENT

R&D was a focal point throughout Honeywell with technology seen as the key to marketplace differentiation. About 30 percent of Honeywell's current sales were from products introduced in the past five years. Honeywell was involved in two main R&D activities: R&D that supported Honeywell's worldwide product divisions and contract research funded by outside government agencies and firms. Including R&D done both in the product divisions and by HTC, Honeywell funded $353 million of R&D in 1996 and contract work generated revenue of $341 million. Until the cutbacks in U.S. military spending in the early 1990s, most of the contract research was for military purposes. Although a significant amount of contract research still involved the Department of Defense, other funding agencies included NASA, Department of Commerce, and the Electric Power Research Institute. Increasingly, nondefense firms were forming alliances to jointly develop new technologies through contract research. Cooperative research with OEM customers also occurred. All of the outside contract funding was from U.S. sources, although several project applications were targeted outside the United States, such as a Department of Commerce power plant upgrade project in Ukraine.

HONEYWELL TECHNOLOGY CENTER

The Honeywell Technology Center (HTC) was Honeywell's primary research organization and supported the worldwide product divisions. As a corporate service organization, HTC's mission was to support the product divisions and develop technologies that had the potential to benefit multiple product divisions. This mission was expressed as:

> In partnership with Honeywell's businesses, we provide world-class technologies, processes, and product concepts that fuel Honeywell's global growth and profitability.

HTC, based in Minneapolis, employed about 575 people, including 300 engineer/scientists. Of these 300, 100 had Ph.D.s, and 180 had Bachelor's or Master's degrees. With the exception of about 40 employees in Phoenix and 5 in Prague, all HTC employees were in two locations in the Minneapolis area. In 1996, HTC's spending was $90 million, which came from several sources: 50 percent from outside contracts, 40 percent allocated to HTC by Honeywell corporate management, and 10 percent funded directly by divisions for near-term projects.

HTC Organization

Exhibit 5 shows the Honeywell corporate organization and Exhibit 6 shows the HTC organization. Prior to 1993, Honeywell operated two corporate R&D organizations: the Sensors and Systems Development Center (SSDC) for home, building, and industrial R&D and the Systems and Research Center for space and aviation R&D. The Systems and Research Center was primarily involved in military research and was oriented to outside contracts. Because there was comparatively less outside contract work in the non-defense related controls area, SSDC R&D was focused on commercial applications and product division problems. In 1993 the two R&D groups were merged for both cost and synergy reasons. There was also a realization that with government military spending declining, Honeywell-funded R&D had to become more application-oriented.

About 350 HTC technical employees worked in one of the four technology areas whose managers reported to the HTC technology director. These four areas, controls and navigation, sensors, information processing and displays, and systems and software, were in turn broken down into 19 sub-areas headed by section heads. For example, controls and navigation R&D was divided into home and building control systems, industrial control systems, space and aviation guidance and control systems, and navigation systems. The role of the technology section head was to facilitate interaction between the product divisions and corporate R&D performed by the HTC. As one section head indicated, "I try to be a broker of technology to the product divisions."

R&D development cycles and the maturity of technologies influenced HTC's organization. Because commercial control technologies were more mature than the space and aviation technology, research in this area was more oriented towards how to apply the technology in existing and new products. As a result, the controls

EXHIBIT 5   **Honeywell Organization**

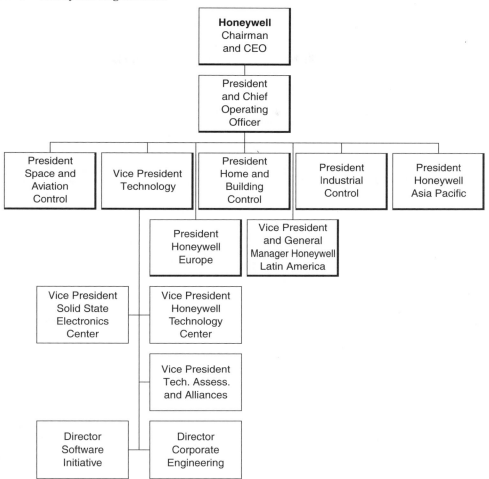

and navigation group was organized around markets and product lines. The other three groups were organized around technologies and engineers and scientists in these groups tended to identify with technologies rather than products.

HTC had two additional groups of managers called Business Development managers and Divisional Technology Managers (DTMs). The five Business Development managers were responsible for generating outside contracts. Six DTMs provided an interface between the divisions and HTC, working closely with the technology section heads and the product divisions. The DTMs had two main responsibilities: 1) to understand the divisional business strategy; translate that strategy into short- and long-term technology needs; and disseminate that information in HTC as the basis for influencing investments in R&D and 2) to

EXHIBIT 6 HTC Organization

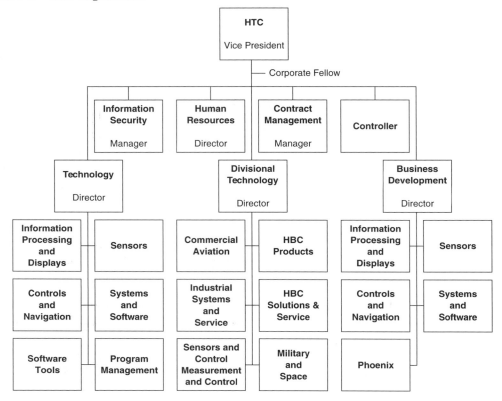

establish mechanisms for the transfer of mature technology from HTC to divisions. According to a DTM, the DTM's role was "to be a funnel for information transfer and dissemination."

Although HTC had a structure and clear lines of authority, HTC management believed that to operate effectively, the structure had to exist as a loose framework in order to support interaction among the engineers, scientists, and product divisions. According to an HTC manager:

> We are very good at quite a number of areas. I can bring together researchers in sensors, control theory, information processing, real time software and those are the guts of Honeywell products. We need to work from a systems perspective, which means we have to have interaction and networking.

HTC management saw their key role as ensuring that the interaction occurred.

> The researchers are the people that really make things happen here. As managers, our job is to make sure they have lights, food, and water to get things done.

THE RESEARCH PROCESS

Very little product development or product testing was done at HTC. HTC supported divisional product development by providing new technologies that could be incorporated into products and by developing concepts for new products. The actual development of new products was a divisional responsibility and each of Honeywell's product divisions had active engineering organizations. It was a divisional responsibility to turn new technology into something that was producible and salable. As such, most of the R&D done at the division level was product development and engineering work using existing technologies. Occasionally, if HTC was convinced a product should be developed immediately to create a market window and no division had the resources to react quickly, HTC might initiate product development. HTC might also approach a customer directly as the basis for generating divisional interest in a technology. As well, technology that would benefit only one division was normally viewed as R&D that should be funded at the division level rather than at corporate.

Within HTC, scientists and engineers competed for funding via various funding programs. The Home Run Program supported projects with low technical risk, an established market need, a large funding requirement, and an expectation of a rapid capital return. The Initiatives Program focused on innovative, technology-based funding with high risks and longer term payoffs. Technology Base Funding supported longer range division needs. Joint Projects provided for matching funds from divisions tied directly to divisional products needs.

There were many and varied linkages between HTC and the product divisions. In some cases, HTC engineers were assigned to divisions to support product development. The assignments could range from several weeks to a year. Nevertheless, it was acknowledged that it was difficult to get people to accept short-term assignments because of family and personal constraints.

Technology Transfer

Within the divisions, the perception of HTC had shifted in recent years as HTC increasingly stressed the importance of relevance and pushed this message deep within the organization. Relevance meant that HTC's goal should be to help the divisions serve their customers, as a manager remarked: "Our job in HTC is to transfer technology but we don't really transfer technology, we transfer solutions." As well, Honeywell was committing greater funds to technology transfer. Ten years ago, technology transfer was more ad hoc with fewer specific funding mechanisms available. This commitment to technology transfer was evident in the following comment from an HTC manager:

> We know that whatever we do is worthless until a division makes money from it. If they don't want the technology, we can't force them to take it.

The underlying philosophy of technology transfer was consistent throughout HTC. First, technology transfer required funding, which occurred through different mechanisms. Second, technology transfer was rarely a function of "how incredible the technology is." The technology had to be mature and its transfer had to be economically feasible in terms of cost effectiveness and ROI. Some successful technology transfers involved technology that had been developed five to ten years earlier. Third, there had to be an emotional commitment to the technology within a product division. The challenge for all technology transfers was to convince the product divisions that the technology was relevant and could provide customer solutions. The highest probability technology transfer occurred when HTC and a division identified a specific divisional need that HTC could meet. An HTC manager described the difficulty in transferring technology:

> Half the battle is how badly the product division managers and engineers want the technology. If they don't want it, they aren't going to get it. Tech transfer is about interaction and begins with trust between two people. . . . Some of the best engineers in Honeywell divisions think they don't need HTC because they can do it themselves and because they think HTC gets to do all the fun stuff. There is some implication that I [as a division engineer] am not capable of getting my part of the job done so the hired guns from HTC are being brought in to get it done for me. And, I have to pay for it.

The key to establishing a successful match between HTC and the division was the network and personal contact-based system that allowed individual researchers to determine the technological needs of Honeywell. Researchers were expected to generate funding for their projects, which could be either internal or external funding. This forced researchers to be in close contact with the divisions, the customers, other researchers, funding agencies, and so on. By getting an outside research sponsor, researchers could control the support for their research. The same held true for Joint Projects funded by divisions and HTC. For example, researchers might go to a divisional engineer and convince him(her) of the relevance of a project; the engineer might interact with the HTC DTM; and the DTM would work between the division and HTC to ensure that the project was funded. An HTC manager offered this view:

> The real success stories come out of these contact scenarios where a researcher sells an idea either internally or externally. If they sell it externally, it is with the end goal of eventually selling it internally. We don't do research for the good of science. We do research that will lead to customer solutions.

For software, technology transfer often involved transferring individuals to teach the software and adapt it to applications. For home and building controls and its more mature technology, technology transfer often meant the transfer of hardware solutions. For space and avionics applications, the cost of the technology might be less important than the contribution of the technology to safety or reliability. For home and building controls, the cost of the technology was always an issue since there was a belief that customers were very reluctant to spend more money for basic controls such as thermostats, even if the technology was significantly better.

Technology Transfer Example

Technology transfer occurred in many different forms depending on the technology, the product division involved, project funding, and so on. The following discussion illustrates one example of a successful technology transfer. The project began with an idea from a university student intern working at HTC. The project was initially funded under the Initiatives Program, the internal HTC funding mechanism for advanced, long-range thinking. The project involved fuzzy control theory that was not initially directed at a product. As the project progressed, the Home and Building Control Systems Group saw some potential applications for the technology in the boiler control area. Some additional internal funding of around $50,000 was provided to do some modeling and simulation of the concept. Although discussions with the product divisions had not yet occurred, there was a belief that the technology could be useful to one of the European divisions.

The next step was to show some examples of the technology to product divisions. The initiation of the HTC-division interaction could occur in various forms, such as a monthly HTC report on internally developed HTC programs, a DTM presentation to the divisions, or a specific request from a division for a particular technology. The HTC objective in interacting with the divisions was to develop divisional interest for the project. In this example, a division in the Netherlands was interested. This division sold valves and other components for boilers used in homes for heating and hot water. Based on a proposal prepared by HTC engineers, the division agreed to participate in a Joint Project, which meant that the division and HTC would share project funding equally. By getting the division involved, product and market specifications could be developed. At this point, the personnel involved in the project included the Home and Building Control Systems Group section head, HTC engineers, a division development engineer, and a DTM. At the division level, the engineer would work with sales and marketing people to justify the funding.

The next phase was called build-and-test and could have been done at HTC or in the division. This decision was negotiated based on various constraints: scheduling, funding, personnel, and R&D skills. In this example, the build-and-test phase was carried out in the division. Initial results were promising and it was hoped that the product could be marketed to boiler OEMs by the end of 1997. If so, the entire phase from idea to market would be about five years. From the time that the division became aware of the technology and saw it as a potential product application was about two years.

HTC'S RELATIONSHIP WITH HONEYWELL EUROPE

Technology transfer to the Honeywell Europe divisions had always been problematic. While the European divisions expected HTC to develop new technology, European managers often complained about the irrelevance of the technology for their markets, the cost of HTC, and their lack of contact with HTC. Although 25 percent of Honeywell sales were in Europe, a much smaller percentage of R&D was carried out either in Europe or in Minneapolis for European solutions. Until about 1990, there was very little Honeywell R&D being done for Europe even though Europe was supporting central R&D financially, creating some bitterness in the European operation. Central R&D was primarily focused on the U.S. market. New product development in Europe was originating in the European divisional engineering groups.

An HTC manager recounted his experience in making a presentation to a group of Honeywell managers in Brussels. After making the presentation and outlining current technology initiatives in HTC, the Europeans indicated that they were unaware that HTC was working on such leading technologies. The manager continued:

> When I first went to Europe a few years ago it was clear to me how angry they were at the U.S. notion that HTC was going to provide good stuff. They also believed that most of the Honeywell resources were being harbored in the United States. There was not a feeling that they were equal members in getting the same resources for development as the U.S. divisions. That said, in the past few years there have been some very good technology transfer projects and they were done in the same way as in the United States—personal interaction, people spending time in the divisions, some short term relocations to Europe. Increasingly, there is acceptance that the paradigm of R&D jointly sponsored by HTC and the divisions is the best approach.

Over the past few years, relationships with Europe had begun shifting and HTC was becoming more responsive in addressing the needs of European businesses. The current Honeywell COO was an Italian who was previously head of Honeywell Europe and the CEO had also been the head of Europe. The head of Divisional Technology responsible for the DTMs was also spending a great deal of time in Europe. As well, there was now an HTC organization based in Europe, HTC Prague.

HTC Prague

In the early 1990s SSDC (the R&D organization that preceded HTC) managers were considering how to strengthen European R&D. With the collapse of the Iron Curtain and expectations of new Honeywell markets developing in Eastern Europe, the viability of an R&D organization somewhere in eastern Europe was being debated. There was a belief that very strong technical skills could be found in countries like Poland and Russia. In 1992 an HTC scientist and former university professor in Czechoslovakia was attending a conference in Tampa. He met a Czechoslovakian from a research institute in Prague. With the Czech economy in transition and research funding drying up, the Czech scientist was interested in new opportunities. The HTC scientist returned to Minneapolis with reasonable assurance that a partnership with the Czech scientist could work. HTC Prague began with five former Czech university professors hired on a contract basis to do research in two areas: computational fluid dynamics, a technology area important for evaluating control product designs, and advanced boiler control technology. Honeywell's Eastern Europe office was moved from Vienna to Prague and by 1997, the Honeywell sales organization in Prague had grown to more than 60 employees. Prague was viewed as an excellent entry point for what could be a huge business in controls for district heating.

In 1995 the Prague professors became Honeywell employees. The professors were very entrepreneurial and had established a reputation for getting things done. Compared to their counterparts in the universities, they were pleased to have access to funding and equipment to continue their research. In 1997, one of the Prague researchers came to Minneapolis for nine months to work on a district heating project. All of the HTC senior management team had been to Prague.

Several objectives were established for HTC Prague: 1) to develop specific technologies for Europe; 2) to assist in HTC technology transfers to Europe; 3) to provide access to activities and opportunities in Eastern Europe; and 4) to help alleviate Honeywell Europe concerns about the lack of support from HTC. Projects in HTC Prague were to be coordinated through HTC to ensure that Prague became an integral part of HTC and not a separate entity.

In 1997, HTC management conceded that it was too early to make an evaluation of HTC Prague's viability and future within Honeywell. For one thing, HTC Prague consisted of only five researchers, which limited the potential impact. As a manager indicated, "With only five people, it is not clear what Prague really is or can be." There were concerns that HTC Prague might become an application center rather than a true R&D center. One manager suggested that the Europeans were too accustomed to looking to the United States for new technology and therefore, HTC Prague would have trouble building legitimacy. Still, other European divisions had questioned the decision to start an R&D organization in Prague rather than in say, Germany or Belgium. Other European managers offered a different perspective, suggesting that European divisions were already taking ownership of the technology being developed in Prague and viewed Prague as "their" technology center.

Several HTC managers were emphatic that Prague had to be expanded if it was to remain relevant. But, if Prague were to be expanded, when should it happen and could additional high quality technical talent be found for Prague? The model for HTC in the United States was to rely heavily on outside contracts. Would Prague be able to develop outside funding? Should Prague be given the tools and skills necessary to bid on outside contracts? If Prague were to be expanded, who would pay for the expansion: Honeywell Europe or HTC? Other managers suggested that perhaps Prague should remain at 5-6 people and additional R&D centers should be established close to other Honeywell operations, perhaps in Germany, Scotland or the Netherlands.

REASONS FOR CENTRALIZED R&D

Within Honeywell, reasons for and against centralized R&D were being actively debated. Reasons supporting centralized R&D included the following:

1. The complexity of Honeywell products and systems is such that a large team of R&D people is needed in one location to ensure interaction occurs between scientists. For example, the control system for a refinery incorporated hundreds of other products. It is easy to share information when almost all HTC employees

are in the same building and see each other regularly. Decentralization would reduce interaction and personal contacts.

Technology transfer is based on personal contacts. This is one of the biggest challenges we have in trying to operate on a global basis. We have a system in HTC that works quite well and we are comfortable with it. What does it mean to deal with things around the world when we need to maintain our contact-based system?

The strength of HTC is the world-class people we can bring to bear on a problem. How do we connect these people with the far-flung empire of Honeywell in order to bring together the expertise, know-how, and ability to make money?

The biggest logistical issue is communications. You can't invent science with only one scientist. You need multiple disciplines and interaction. The various distributed R&D organizations must communicate with each other the same way they would if they were all in Minneapolis and could meet in the hallways or the cafeteria. That is extremely difficult to do. We are looking at new information technology but you also have to have interchanges of people. Without communication, remote R&D will only work for a little while because people will get out of touch. Once people go native they lose the advantage of outside views and new ideas coupled with the connection with the marketplace.

2. One of the main functions of Honeywell's central R&D is to move ideas around the world. Decentralizing R&D would jeopardize this central dissemination function.

3. When the product is a system comprising various parts, a team can be built using people from different areas. Scattering people geographically would make this difficult.

   A product like abnormal situation management for oil refineries requires sensors, controls, human interface, and so on. We have all the people in one place to put these technologies together. No division of the company has all these parts.

4. If R&D scientists are too far from the central labs they risk becoming obsolete, migrating from R&D to the product divisions, or losing contact with central R&D. They may even think they are competing with central R&D.

   We have a group in Plymouth, which is only 15 miles from the Minneapolis location. When I talk to those guys, they feel like they are cut off from all kinds of things. To a degree, they are correct. We have a group in Phoenix that sometime feels like they are totally isolated.

5. If R&D is tied too closely with a division, there is the risk that the division will not have the long term orientation necessary for R&D, which could lead to complacency. Or, after assuming ownership of the R&D, the division may decide that a particular technology is no longer necessary and R&D efforts could decline. A central R&D organization can ensure stability in research efforts and implement controls to keep people motivated.

6. Engineers and scientists interested in R&D prefer to work in a central R&D organization.

7. What the non-U.S. and non-European divisions need now is localization of existing products, not new technology.

8. The HTC culture would be difficult to transfer.

   How do you transfer the HTC culture outside the United States? HTC has developed a unique culture based on openness and interaction across different levels and technologies. The kinds of people we hire and attract are very entrepreneurial down to the youngest engineers. How do you duplicate this culture in a place like like Prague? It is tough enough to do it in Phoenix.

9. Before R&D could be localized, Honeywell had to develop more incentives to transfer technology.

   Although a few years ago I was committed to the idea of global technology management, I am not so sure now. The problem is that within Honeywell there are still expectations that solutions will come from the United States. Until that changes and funding is in place to support technology transfer outside the United States, creating new R&D organizations makes no sense. Right now, we do not have the financial incentives in place to transfer technology to Europe.

REASONS FOR DECENTRALIZED R&D

1. Central R&D is too far removed from the customer, particularly customers outside the United States. It is impossible to develop customer solutions if you do not understand customer problems. The current remote sites in Phoenix and Prague benefit from being close to the divisions. Different parts of the world should logically be the focus for problems unique to their area. For example, tropical Asia has unique air conditioning requirements because of the heat and humidity.

   You need people immersed in all aspects of the culture to communicate with customers and other parts of Honeywell. There is a whole lot of networking that has to happen and it has to involve people from the HTC culture who know what is going on. People of this culture have to see with their own eyes what is going on outside the United States. We are not going to sell U.S. thermostats in Beijing. What they need and want is different, the amount of money the Chinese have to spend is different.

   You have to live with the culture to understand the opportunities. You cannot simply transfer technologies and product designs that are used in the United States. There have to be different solutions because the business models in different countries are different. Right now, the paradigm says that products come from the United States. There is a strong mix of prejudice and ignorance about international markets. For example, in the United States, air conditioning is the focus for home and building controls. In Europe, central air conditioning is much less common. We have a huge opportunity in district heating in Eastern Europe. In the United States, Honeywell has limited knowledge about district heating because it is hardly used here.

2. If the technology does not require interaction with other technologies, like the development of a particular sensor or flat panel displays, it may be better to

have it located where the local support structure is strongest. The support could come from the product division or in a geographic area known for a particular technology.

3. Application developments may require close interaction with a customer in the customer's facility.

4. Putting R&D people in geographic business units would increase the relevance of R&D and increase the information flow from business units to R&D.

5. Future sales will be growing faster outside the United States and, therefore, people from all parts of Honeywell must be in the growing areas of the business.

6. Traveling to Europe, China and other locations outside the United States is expensive and time consuming. It would be better to have people on the ground in these locations.

7. Remote R&D facilities would facilitate technology transfers outside the United States.

8. Remote locations in countries like China provide a foothold that gives Honeywell credibility and makes it look like a committed Chinese business. It could also help in hiring local engineers and scientists.

9. Remote locations show the product divisions that Honeywell is serious about a particular region.

Along with the basic question of centralized versus decentralized R&D, there were additional issues associated with R&D:

- Would remote locations have to focus on unique technologies? How would those technologies be identified? Are there technologies that are unique to specific locations?

- Outside funding was critical to HTC. As part of a U.S. corporation, could a remote location gain access to outside funding? With greater R&D presence, could HTC gain access to funding from agencies such as the World Bank and the Asian Development Bank?

- What kind of controls must be in place to ensure that a remote location remained part of *central* R&D rather than becoming an offshoot of a product division?

- In Europe and Asia, with its diversity of countries and markets, where should HTC have a stronger presence?

- With an increasing shift to software as the key to product differentiation, how would this influence future Honeywell R&D?

- Within Honeywell, the allocation of HTC costs were based on divisional revenues. Was this allocation system appropriate given that some regions within the firm were growing faster than others?

- How would remote R&D locations be staffed. Would it make sense to move HTC people out of Minneapolis to new locations? If not, were skilled scientists available in other parts of the world? As an HTC manager commented:

  The key thing about our culture is networking and sharing and bringing together different technologies. The only way you can create that culture in a remote R&D center is to take some of the HTC people and put them in China or Russia for a while. This would infect the new hires with "the way we do business." Then we will bring them back. We have had good luck getting people to go to different places.

FUTURE OPPORTUNITIES

In view of Honeywell's international growth opportunities, the issue of international R&D was becoming a high priority issue in HTC. For example, China's economy was growing so rapidly that some sort of HTC presence seemed inevitable. One line of thinking was that HTC should have employees based in China with a broad learning and exploration agenda. Another view was that until there was a clear understanding of the opportunities in China, it would not make sense to commit to expensive expatriate employees. A further issue was that in China, and Asia in general, there were no engineering staffs to adapt technologies for the local market. For the most part, products manufactured and sold in Asia were products transferred from American or European Honeywell divisions. Without an engineering staff in Asia, technology could not be transferred.

Further issues are evident in the following comments from HTC managers:

By the year 2000, sales outside the United States could be 60 percent of our business. At HTC we have to start experimenting in other parts of the world. Our mission is to help the divisions understand what they can do with our technology. If you ask them what they want, you will get the most ordinary ideas. If we work with their customers and understand that environment, we can link customers with our technology and come up with something completely different. If we are not out there looking at the world we will never grow the company. And, I can't hire someone in China to do this for me; someone from here has to go over there and get the HTC culture going.

Technology is technology; it is physical principles and science—there is nothing unique about the technology needed in Europe or Asia. However, the application needs seem to vary from region to region. Perhaps we should set up application groups around the world. The technology engine will remain in Minneapolis and Phoenix. These groups will be the selectors and appliers of those technologies given their knowledge of the region. If we go this way, we won't need the best researchers in Prague and other regions. We will need people who can apply technology and gain access to technology sources outside the United States. We have really not tapped into these non-U.S. sources.

The notion of distributed R&D is very important to me. I am convinced that HTC is going to become more distributed, not less. How we can create one large, global R&D organization and not 12 small ones is a big issue. Strategically, putting together other R&D centers in Beijing or Eastern Europe is going to become a way of life at HTC.

It is difficult enough making HTC work. Trying to replicate it somewhere else in the world is even more difficult. That is one of the reasons that Prague has remained small—we are not sure what to do with it. My view of what Prague should be will probably be radically different from other people's. In the United States, 20 years of evolution has allowed HTC to develop some unique capabilities. Can we wait for Prague or some other remote R&D center to naturally evolve over 20 years? What is the best way for a non-U.S. R&D organization to have an impact?

Endnote

1. DeSilver, D., "Honeywell Plans Asian Forays," *Minneapolis-St. Paul City Business,* June 21, 1996, p. 11.

Chapter Thirty-Six

Whirlpool Corporation's Global Strategy

> We want to be able to take the best capabilities we have and leverage them in all our companies worldwide.
>
> *David Whitman, Whirlpool CEO, 1994*
> *Quoted in the* Harvard Business Review

In 1989, Whirlpool Corporation (Whirlpool) embarked on an ambitious global expansion with the objective of becoming the world market leader in home appliances. Beginning with the purchase of a majority stake in an appliance company owned by Philips, the Dutch electronics firm, Whirlpool purchased a majority stake in an Indian firm, established four joint ventures in China, and made significant new investments in its Latin America operations.

However, by the mid-1990s, serious problems had emerged in the company's international operations. In 1995, Whirlpool's European profit fell by 50 percent and in 1996, the company reported a $13 million loss in Europe. In Asia, the situation was even worse. Although the region accounted for only 6 percent of corporate sales, Whirlpool lost $70 million in Asia in 1996 and $62 million in 1997. In Brazil, Whirlpool found itself a victim in 1997, and again in 1998, of spiraling interest rates. Despite the company's investments of hundreds of millions of dollars throughout the 1990s to modernize operations there, appliance sales in Brazil

plummeted by 25 percent in 1998. Whirlpool expected that 1999 would be the third straight year of declining sales for the Brazilian subsidiary.

In response to these problems, Whirlpool began a global restructuring effort. In September 1997, the company announced that it would cut 10 percent of its global workforce over the next two years and pull out of two joint ventures in China. In announcing the cuts, Whirlpool's CEO David Whitwam said, "We are taking steps to align the organization with the marketplace realities of our industry."[1] In Latin America, 3,500 jobs were abolished, and significant investments were made to upgrade plants and product lines.

After the optimism of the early 1990s, what went wrong with Whirlpool's global strategy? Was the company overly ambitious? Was there a lack of understanding about how to create an integrated global strategy? Or, were the problems the result of changes in the competitive and economic environments in Europe, Asia, and Latin America? Should Whirlpool have foreseen the problems and reacted earlier?

THE APPLIANCE INDUSTRY IN THE LATE 20TH CENTURY

Approximately 120 million home appliances are sold in developed countries each year.[2] The appliance industry is generally classified into four categories: laundry, refrigeration, cooking, and other appliances. Appliances are constructed in capital intensive plants and design usually varies among countries and regions.

The North American Industry

Although it was estimated that 46 million appliances were sold in North America annually, the market was expected to grow little in the late 1990s. Saturation levels were high, with virtually 100 percent of households owning refrigerators and cookers and over 70 percent owning washers. Because of the limited growth opportunities, competition was fierce. In the United States, the industry had consolidated in the 1980s, leaving four major competitors: Whirlpool, General Electric, Electrolux, and Maytag (see Exhibit 1 for more detail). These four firms controlled about 80 percent of the market.[3] Each firm offered a variety of products and brands segmented along price lines. Distribution of these appliances was generally through sales to builders for new houses or to retailers, such as department stores and specialty resellers.

In a *Harvard Business Review* article in 1994 called "The Right Way to Go Global," David Whitwam, Whirlpool's CEO, described the competitive situation that existed in the early 1990s:

> Even though we had dramatically lowered costs and improved product quality, our profit margins in North America had been declining because everyone in the industry was pursuing the same course and the local market was mature. The four main players—Whirlpool, General Electric, Maytag, and White Consolidated, which had been acquired by Electrolux—were beating one another up everyday.[4]

With limited growth opportunities and a handful of major players in the United States, it was critical that firms focus on cost reduction, productive efficiency, and product quality. Product innovation was also critical, although few major innovations had occurred in recent years. The apppliance firms segmented

EXHIBIT 1
**Major Competitors
in the United States**

Sources: Hoovers Online.
Accessed 2/9/00.

GE Appliance

General Electric Appliance was the second-largest manufacturer of household appliances in the U.S. (behind Whirlpool). Other brand names produced by the company included Monogram, Profile, Profile Performance, Hotpoint, and some private brands for retailers. GE Appliance comprised approximately 6 percent of the parent company's sales and had the top market share position in India and Mexico. In addition, the company had a 50–50 joint venture with General Electric Co., the leading appliance firm in the United Kingdom.

Maytag

Maytag's products were generally aimed at the mid-to-high end of the market and commanded a premium price based on product quality and reliability. Other brand names produced by Maytag included Jenn-Air, Magic Chef, Performa, and Hoover. Maytag entered the European market in 1989, but after a decline in profits, pulled out of Europe in 1995. Maytag had a limited international presence in China.

AB Electrolux

AB Electrolux was the world's largest producer of household appliances. Other Electrolux brand names included Frigidaire, Tappan, and Kelvinator. The Swedish company had the number one market share in Europe and number four market share in North America. Electrolux entered the United States when it bought White Consolidated Industries in 1986. The firm was actively expanding overseas into Eastern Europe, China, India, South East Asia, and Latin America.

Remich, Norman C. "A Kentucky Thoroughbred that is Running Strong," *Appliance Manufacturer,* July 1995: GEA-3. Steinmetz, Greg and Carl Quintanilla. "Tough Target: Whirlpool Expected Easy Going in Europe, and It Got a Big Shock," *Wall Street Journal,* 10 April 1998: Sec. A:1.

their products according to different consumers' needs, and each strived to achieve greater economies of scale. Still, by the end of the 1990s, the competitive landscape remained unattractive. Profit margins continued to decline for most firms. Many analysts believed that the market for appliances was saturated and that there would be little increase in growth rates. This saturation had left the distributors focusing primarily on replacement purchases and purchases for new housing developments.

The European Industry

In the early 1980s, there were approximately 350 producers of household appliances in Europe. With consolidation in the industry, by the late 1980s the number had shrunk to about one hundred.[5] By early 1995, it was estimated that five of the companies, including Electrolux (with a 25 percent market share), Philips Bauknecht, and Bosche-Siemens, controlled over 70 percent of the market.[6] The industry was highly regionalized, with many of the companies producing a limited number of products for a specific geographic area.

The European market consisted of more than 320 million consumers whose preferences varied by country and by region. For example, Swedes preferred galvanized washing machines to withstand the damp salty air.[7] The British washed their clothes more often than the Italians did, and wanted quieter machines. The French liked to cook on gas at high temperatures, splattering grease on cooking surfaces, and so preferred self-cleaning ovens, while the Germans liked to cook on electric stoves at lower temperatures and did not need such features.[8]

Distribution of the appliances in Europe was different than in the United States. Most appliances were sold through independent retailers, who had become organized in buying groups or as multiple store chains.[9] A smaller channel was through independent kitchen specialists who sold complete kitchen packages, including appliances.[10]

The Asian Industry

Asia, the world's second-largest home appliance market, was also the fastest growing market of the 1980s. By the mid-1990s, it was growing at a rate of between 8 percent and 12 percent annually, a rate that was expected to continue well past the year 2000.[11] The industry was highly fragmented, consisting of manufacturers primarily from Japan, Korea, and Taiwan. Matsushita, the market leader, held less than 10 percent market share outside Japan.

Asian consumer preferences were different from those in Europe or North America. Kitchen appliances needed to be smaller to fit in Asian kitchens. Lack of space sometimes required the consumer to store the appliance in an outside hallway and transport it into the kitchen for use.[12] Therefore, high value was placed on appliances that were portable, usually lightweight and on wheels, and easily hooked up to electrical and water supplies. Refrigerators also tended to be smaller and more colorful. Indeed, when Asian countries first began to experience significant economic growth, some East Asians viewed their refrigerators as status symbols and liked to display them prominently, perhaps even in the sitting room. Clothes dryers and dishwashers were uncommon in most Asian countries, but most homes had microwaves.

Appliances in Asia were traditionally sold through small retail shops. However, the industry was beginning to witness a shift away from these small shops and towards distribution through national, power retailer organizations, especially in China and parts of Southeast Asia.

The Latin American Industry

The economic stability in Latin America in the 1990s made the region an attractive growth proposition. The appliance makers hoped that the days of hyperinflation and economic mismanagement were over, and they were pleased to see that governments were reducing tariffs. Distributors in Latin America were generally responsible for marketing a company's appliances to small independent retailers in the region.[13] In 1994, there were over 65 competitors in the Latin American market, many of them subsidiaries of U.S. parents.

WHIRLPOOL CORPORATION

Whirlpool was founded in 1911 as The Upton Machine Co. in St Joseph, Michigan, to produce an electric motor-driven wringer washer. The company merged with The Nineteen Hundred Washer Company in 1929 and began to sell their first automatic washing machine through Sears, Roebuck & Co. in 1947. The Whirlpool brand was introduced in 1948 and steadily built a strong retail relationship with Sears. Through a series of acquisitions and mergers, the company emerged as a leading force in the U.S. appliance industry with annual revenue reaching $2 billion in 1978 (see Exhibit 2 for more detail on Whirlpool's history). Whirlpool's headquarters was in Benton Harbor, Michigan.

EXHIBIT 2 Whirlpool History

1911	Upton Machine Co. is founded in St. Joseph, Michigan, to produce electric motor-driven wringer washers.
1916	First order for washers is sold to Sears, Roebuck and Co.
1929	Upton Machine merges with Nineteen Hundred Washer Company of Binghamton, New York. The new firm, Nineteen Hundred Corp., operates plants in Michigan and New York until Binghamton is closed in 1939.
1942	All facilities are converted to wartime production until end of World War II in 1945.
1947	The company's first automatic washer is introduced to the market by Sears.
1948	A Whirlpool brand automatic washer is introduced, thus establishing dual distribution—one line of products for Sears, another for Nineteen Hundred.
1950	Nineteen Hundred Corporation is renamed Whirlpool Corporation. Automatic dryers are added to the product line.
1951	LaPorte, Indiana, plant is acquired. It will become the company's parts distribution center. Whirlpool merges with Clyde (Ohio) Porcelain Steel and converts the plant to washer production. All washers eventually will be produced here.
1955	Manufacturing facilities are purchased in Marion, Ohio, from Motor Products Corp., and dryer production is transferred there. Whirlpool merges with Seeger Refrigerator Co. of St. Paul, Minnesota, and the Estate range and air conditioning divisions of R.C.A. RCA Whirlpool is established as the brand name; Whirlpool-Seeger Corporation, as the company name. A refrigeration plant is acquired in Evansville, Indiana, from International Harvester.
1956	First full line of RCA Whirlpool home appliances is introduced. RCA will be used with the Whirlpool brand name until 1967. New administrative center is completed on 100-acre site in Benton Harbor.
1957	Company name is changed back to Whirlpool Corporation. Appliance Buyers Credit Corporation is established as a wholly owned finance subsidiary. It will be renamed Whirlpool Financial Corporation in 1989.
1957	Whirlpool invests in Brazilian appliance market through purchase of equity interest in Multibrás S.A. It is renamed Brastemp S.A. in 1972.
1966	The Norge plant in Fort Smith, Arkansas, is acquired, adding more than one million sq. ft. of refrigeration manufacturing space.
1967	Toll-free Cool-Line® Telephone Service begins. Renamed the Consumer Assistance Center in 1990, it gives customers direct, 24-hour access to Whirlpool. The company's first totally new manufacturing facility is completed in Findlay, Ohio. Dishwashers and, later, ranges will be manufactured there.
1968	The Elisha Gray II Research & Engineering Center is completed in Benton Harbor. For the first time, annual revenues reach $1 billion.
1969	The company enters the Canadian appliance market through purchase of an equity interest in Inglis Ltd. Sole ownership is established in 1990.
1970	Construction is completed on a new plant in Danville, Kentucky. Production of trash compactors and, later, vacuum cleaners is transferred there.
1976	Whirlpool increases its investment in the Brazilian market through purchase of equity interests in Consul S.A., an appliance manufacturer, and Embraco S.A., a maker of compressors.
1978	Annual revenues reach $2 billion.
1983	The company announces a phaseout of washer assembly at St. Joseph. All washers will be made at Clyde.
1984	The St. Paul Division is closed. Production of freezers and ice makers moves to Evansville.
1986	Whirlpool purchases the KitchenAid division of Hobart Corporation. A majority interest is purchased in Aspera s.r.l., an Italian compressor manufacturer. Whirlpool will become sole owner before the business is sold to Embraco of Brazil in 1994. Whirlpool closes most of its St. Joseph Division. The remaining machining operation is renamed the Benton Harbor Division.
1987	Whirlpool and Sundaram-Clayton Limited of India form TVS Whirlpool Limited to make compact washers for the Indian market. Whirlpool will acquire majority ownership in 1994.

(continued)

EXHIBIT 2 (Continued)

1988	A joint venture company, Vitromatic S.A. de C.V., is formed with Vitro, S.A. of Monterrey, to manufacture and market major home appliances for Mexican and export markets. Whirlpool acquires the Roper brand name, which it will use to market a full line of value-oriented home appliances.
1989	Whirlpool and N.V. Philips of the Netherlands form a joint venture company, Whirlpool Europe B.V., from Philips major domestic appliance division, to manufacture and market appliances in Europe. Whirlpool will become sole owner in 1991. Appliance operations in the United States, Canada, and Mexico are brought together to form the North American Appliance Group (NAAG). Annual revenues catapult over the $6 billion mark.
1990	A program is launched to market appliances in Europe under the dual brands Philips and Whirlpool. Whirlpool Overseas Corporation is formed as a subsidiary to conduct marketing and industrial activities outside North America and Western Europe. An Estate brand of appliances targeted to national accounts is introduced.
1991	The company commits globally to its Worldwide Excellence System, a total quality management program dedicated to exceeding customer expectations. NAAG repositions its refrigeration business. The Port Credit, Ontario, plant is closed. Top- and bottom-mount refrigerators are consolidated at Evansville, side-by-side refrigerators at Fort Smith.
1992	Whirlpool assumes control of SAGAD S.A., of Argentina. Whirlpool Hungarian Trading Ltd. is formed to sell and service appliances in Hungary. Whirlpool Tatramat is formed to make and sell washing machines and market other major home appliances in Slovakia. Whirlpool will take controlling interest in 1994. A Small Appliance Business Unit is formed to operate on a global basis. Revenues top $7 billion. The South American Sales Co. (SASCo), a joint venture with Whirlpool's Brazilian affiliates, begins directing export sales to 35 Latin American countries.
1993	Whirlpool Overseas Corporation is replaced by two separate regional organizations: Whirlpool Asia and Whirlpool Latin America. Whirlpool Asia sets up headquarters in Tokyo with regional offices in Singapore, Hong Kong, and Tokyo. Sales subsidiaries are opened in Poland and the Czech Republic, adding to Whirlpool Europe's growing presence in Eastern Europe. Whirlpool wins the $30 million Super Efficient Refrigerator Program sponsored by 24 U.S. utilities. Inglis Ltd. becomes Canada's leading home appliance manufacturer.
1994	Whirlpool Asia and Teco Electric & Machinery Co. Ltd. form Great Teco Whirlpool Co. Ltd. to market and distribute home appliances in Taiwan. Whirlpool becomes a stand-alone brand in Europe. Brazilian affiliates Consul and Brastemp merge to form Multibrás S.A. Electrodomésticos. Whirlpool breaks ground in Tulsa, Oklahoma, for a new plant to make freestanding gas and electric ranges. Whirlpool's Asian headquarters is moved to Singapore, and the number of operating regions is increased from three to four. Whirlpool exits vacuum cleaner business. To strengthen competitiveness, a major restructuring is announced in North America and Europe. One U.S. and one Canadian plant close. Total revenues top $8 billion.
1995	An executive office is formed in Whirlpool Asia to lead the company's rapid growth and manage strategic deployment in the region. Whirlpool acquires controlling interest in Kelvinator of India Ltd., one of India's largest manufacturers and marketers of refrigerators. TVS Whirlpool Ltd. changes name to Whirlpool Washing Machines Ltd. (WWML). Construction is completed on a new plant in Greenville, Ohio. KitchenAid small appliances will be manufactured there. Whirlpool begins to sell appliances to Montgomery Ward. Whirlpool Europe opens representative office in Russia. Whirlpool Financial Corporation (WFC) is established in India. Whirlpool assumes control of Beijing Whirlpool Snowflake Electric Appliance Group Co. Ltd., a refrigerator and freezer manufacturing joint venture. Beijing Embraco Snowflake Compressor Co. Ltd., a compressor manufacturing joint venture, is formed between Embraco and Beijing Snowflake. Whirlpool has a minority position in the joint venture. Whirlpool acquires controlling interest in Whirlpool Narcissus (Shanghai) Co. Ltd., a washing machine manufacturing joint venture. Whirlpool acquires majority ownership of SMC Microwave Products Co. Ltd., a microwave oven manufacturing joint venture. Shenzhen Whirlpool Raybo Air-Conditioner Industrial Co. Ltd., an air conditioner manufacturing joint venture, is formed with Whirlpool having a majority stake. Whirlpool investments in Asia increase to over US$350 million, and employees total more than 9,300.
1996	Whirlpool Europe opens sales subsidiaries in Romania and Bulgaria. Production of electric and gas ranges officially begins in Whirlpool's new plant in Tulsa, Oklahoma. The company's new Greenville, Ohio, plant, which manufactures KitchenAid small appliances, begins production. The Ft. Smith Division in Arkansas begins production of trash compactors. Whirlpool Asia employees total more than 12,000. Whirlpool Europe acquires the white goods business of Gentrade of South Africa. The acquisition provides Whirlpool a sales and manufacturing base in this country.

Source: <http://www.whirlpool.com>

As of 1998, Whirlpool Corporation manufactured in 13 countries and marketed its products under 11 major brand names (including Kenmore, Sears, KitchenAid, Roper, Inglis, and Speed Queen) to over 140 countries. Whirlpool's sales were $8.2 billion in fiscal year 1997.

THE GLOBALIZATION OF WHIRLPOOL

Whirlpool's first international investment was in 1957 when the firm acquired an equity interest in Multibras S.A., a Brazilian manufacturer of white goods. In 1969, the company entered the Canadian market by purchasing an equity interest in Inglis Ltd. and acquired sole ownership in 1990.

By the mid-1980s, Whirlpool saw that, despite increasing efficiencies and product quality, its profit margins were rapidly decreasing in North America. Top management believed that if the company continued to follow its current path, the future would be "neither pleasant nor profitable."[14] They considered restructuring the company financially or diversifying into related businesses but eventually settled on further global expansion for two main reasons: the company wished to take advantage of less mature markets around the world and it did not want to be left behind by its competitors, which had already begun to globalize.

Whitwam's Vision and Platform Technology

David Whitwam joined Whirlpool in 1968 as a marketing management trainee and rose through the sales and marketing ranks to succeed Jack Sparks as CEO in 1987. Although Whitwam admitted that he had never actually run a multinational company until Whirlpool bought Philips in 1989, he believed that:

> The only way to gain lasting competitive advantage is to leverage your capabilities around the world, so that the company as a whole is greater than the sum of its parts. Being an international company—selling globally, having global brands or operations in different countries—isn't enough.[15]

Whitwam was convinced that most companies with international divisions were not truly global at all, as their various regional and national divisions still operated as autonomous entities rather than working together as a single company. He believed that the only way to achieve his vision of an integrated international company, or one company worldwide, was through intensive efforts to understand and respond to genuine customer needs and through products and services that earn long-term customer loyalty.

Whitwam talked about his vision of integrating Whirlpool's geographical businesses so that the company's expertise would not be confined to one location or product. He forecast appliances such as a World Washer, a single machine that could be sold anywhere, and he wanted to standardize the company's manufacturing processes. According to Whitwam,

> Today products are being designed to ensure that a wide variety of models can be built on the same basic platform . . .Varying consumer preferences require us to

have regional manufacturing centers. But even though the features . . . vary from market to market, much of the technology and manufacturing processes involved are similar.[16]

Given this view that standardization should be the focus, Whirlpool planned to base all its products, wherever they were built or assembled, on common platforms. These platforms would produce the technological heart of the product, the portion of the product which varied little across markets. The products could then be diversified to suit individual and regional preferences. In this way, the parts that the customer sees—the dimensions of the appliance, the metal case, and the controls—could be varied by segment or market to fulfill consumers' needs. The products would also have to meet rigorous quality and environmental standards to ensure that they could be used in different countries around the world.

Whitwam believed that the platform technology would bring a $200 million annual savings in design and component costs by the time it was fully implemented in the year 2000.[17] In addition, management was convinced that the platform strategy would put the company two to three years ahead of its competitors.

Platform technology, however, represented only the beginning of Whirlpool's globalization strategy. According to Whitwam in the 1994 interview, Whirlpool could not truly achieve its goal of globalization until:

> . . . we have cross-border business teams . . . running all of our operations throughout the world . . . There will also come a day when we'll identify a location where the best skills in a certain product area should be concentrated, and that place will become the development center for that type of product . . . [but] while we may have only one major design center for a given product, not everyone associated with that product will have to be located there.[18]

DEVELOPING AND IMPLEMENTING THE GLOBAL STRATEGY

By 1987 Whirlpool had adopted a five-year plan to develop a new international strategy. The company's 1987 Annual Report included the following statement:

> The U.S. appliance industry has limited growth opportunities, a high concentration of domestic competitors, and increasing foreign competition. Further, the United States represents only about 25 percent of the worldwide potential for major appliance sales. Most importantly, our vision can no longer be limited to our national borders because national borders no longer define market boundaries. The marketplace for products and services is more global than ever before and growing more so every day.

Recent industry forecasts indicated that approximately three-quarters of the growth in domestic appliance sales between 1995 and 2000 would be in East Asia (including Australia), Eastern Europe, and South and Central America. According to the forecasts, by 2000 these three regions (excluding Japan) would account for about 34 percent of sales.

European Expansion

In 1989, Whirlpool bought a major stake in N.V. Philips, a struggling Dutch appliance operation, and then purchased the remaining equity in 1991 for a total of $1.1 billion.[19] Whitwam believed that the U.S. and European markets were very similar and hoped that Whirlpool would be able to replicate their successes in the United States in the new market through implementation of a pan-European strategy. Whirlpool management also believed that the European market was becoming more "American." Research performed by the company indicated that European integration was making it more difficult for smaller companies to survive and that the industry was ripe for consolidation. Whirlpool's plan was to be one of the big players following this consolidation, and Whitwam was expecting a 20 percent share of the $20 billion market by the year 2000.[20] Whirlpool's strategy was to focus on brand segmentation and operational efficiency. It was believed that the company that produced the most innovative products while reducing costs would capture the market.

The European subsidiary, Whirlpool Europe BV (WEBV), created a brand portfolio segmented by price. Bauknecht (Philip's German brand) served as the company's high-end product while Ignis served as the lower-end, value brand. The Philips/Whirlpool brand filled the middle range.[21] However, the company decided to heavily market the Whirlpool brand name at the expense of managing its other European brands. Managers at Bauknecht in Germany saw their marketing budgets slashed and Bauknecht's market share fell from 7 percent to 5 percent.[22] By 1995, however, consumer research showed Whirlpool to be the most recognized appliance brand name in Europe, despite the fact that many Germans, Italians, and French had a problem pronouncing the name.

To better manage sales and service throughout the region, Whirlpool set up two centralized distribution centers: one in Cassinetta, Italy, and one in Schorndorf, Germany. Operations were streamlined in order to achieve reduced costs through economies of scale, and considerable efforts were put toward product innovation and increasing operational efficiency. This strategic focus was overlaid with a global outlook, and managers were regularly rotated between Europe and the United States. The rotation generated a crossover of ideas but annoyed retail clients who felt that they had no continuity when dealing with senior managers.

The early years of European expansion were successful. Sales and profits increased steadily, and Whirlpool made a profit of $129 million in Europe in 1993. The company was able to cut costs by reducing the number of suppliers it dealt with and by using common parts in its appliances.

However, Whirlpool was not the only company aggressively attacking the market, and competition subsequent to Whirlpool's entry grew fierce. Electrolux and Bosch-Siemens both greatly improved their efficiency, along with many of the smaller European companies. The European companies laid off large numbers of workers, built up their core businesses, and concentrated on generating profits. Bosch-Siemens expanded its overseas operations while keeping production local and the company managed to raise its non-German revenue by more than 30 percent in five years. Electrolux shed all of its nonappliance businesses and cut its workforce by 15,000, closing 25 factories. Electrolux invested in new factories and achieved higher efficiency. Both Electrolux and Bosch-Siemens increased their profitability.

Across the industry, European plants doubled their output from 1990 to 1998 and cut the time needed to build a washing machine from five days to eight hours. Companies embraced computer aided design techniques to speed the development of products. In 1997, it was reported that a new washing machine could move from the ideas stage to the shops in just 2½ years, twice as fast as only a few years before. The "value gap" which existed between appliances in the United States and Europe also closed by an estimated 15 percent to 20 percent for all appliances.[23]

The state of the retail sector also changed. Traditionally, the producers had determined price in the European appliance industry. These producers had been able to reduce their costs through greater operational efficiencies and had allowed the retailers to keep their margins constant. However, by the 1990s, the number of retail outlets across Europe had fallen significantly, giving the larger surviving retailers more power when dealing with manufacturers. Recession in Europe also caused consumers to become more cost-conscious, and brands such as the low-price firm Indesit won considerable market share.

With all companies becoming more efficient as producers, there was a shift toward product innovation as the basis for competition. For example, Whirlpool increased the size of the entrance of its front-loading washing machines, thus allowing clothes to be pushed into the machine more easily and contributing to increased sales. Companies also attempted to improve customer service and to create appliances that were more friendly to the environment. Such changes were not going unnoticed, but the industry appeared to be extremely mature. Not only were new entrants, such as Whirlpool, GE, Daewoo of South Korea, and Malaysia's Sime Darby, trying to build up sales from a small base, but the traditional European producers had become more aggressive. More than that, few were making tactical or strategic errors. Seeing the increased costs of competition and the growing intensity of rivalry, Maytag left the European market in 1995, selling its Hoover unit at a $130 million loss. Leonard Hadley, Maytag's chairman, commented, "Europe isn't an attractive place to try to go in and dislodge the established players."[24]

Eastern Europe was seen as the next great battleground and Whirlpool expanded its operations in 1996 to newly developing countries in Eastern and Central Europe. In 1997, Whirlpool opened new offices in Romania, Bulgaria, Turkey, Morocco, and South Africa from its European headquarters. Sales in the initial years were disappointing.

PROBLEMS FOR WHIRLPOOL

Whirlpool's sales leveled off in the mid-1990s and profits began to fall. Sales only increased 13 percent from 1990 to 1996, which was far from the levels management had expected. The company initiated a major restructuring in 1995

EXHIBIT 3 **Whirlpool Share Price***

StockMaster
5 year chart of WHR – Apr 1 1999   (c) 1998 StockMaster.com

*The Whirlpool share price is on the bottom.

and laid off 2,000 employees. The restructuring did not solve the problems and in 1996, the company's European operations recorded a loss of $13 million. Between 1995 and 1997, the company also witnessed a rise in materials and labor costs. Exhibit 3 shows Whirlpool's stock prices versus the S&P 500. Exhibits 3 and 4 show Whirlpool corporate and business unit financial information.

Whirlpool announced a second restructuring in 1997. The company planned to cut a further 4,700 jobs worldwide, or about 15 percent of its workforce, mostly in Europe. In 1998, WEBV had a 12 percent market share and held the number three market position. However, in 1998, the profit margin had reduced further to 2.3 percent, compared to 10 percent in the United States.

Whirlpool's managers blamed a number of causes—reduced consumer demand, poor economic growth, the rising Italian lira, intense competition, and even the European Monetary Union—for its poor performance in Europe but shareholders were unimpressed. Indeed, Scott Graham, analyst at CIBC Oppenheimer, commented in 1998, "The strategy has been a failure. Whirlpool went in big [into overseas markets] and investors have paid for it."

In 1998, Whirlpool's goals remained the same, but the timeframes for delivery grew. Whitwam attributed the performance to temporary problems in the newer regions of activity and believed that Whirlpool was now "coming through the challenges." He and the rest of his management team remained resolute:

We were convinced when we first bought [the Philips operation] and we're convinced now. The benefits from Europe have begun to flow. But they have yet to be recognized.[25]

EXHIBIT 4
Whirlpool Financial Statements

Sources: Whirlpool Annual Reports.

Balance Sheet	Dec-98	Dec-97	Dec-96	Dec-95
	US$MM	US$MM	US$MM	US$MM
Cash	636	578	129	149
Securities	0	0	0	0
Receivables	1,711	1,565	2,366	2,117
Allowances	116	156	58	81
Inventory	1,100	1,170	1,034	1,029
Current Assets	3,882	4,281	3,812	3,541
Property and Equipment, Net	5,511	5,262	3,839	3,662
Depreciation	3,093	2,887	2,041	1,883
Total Assets	7,935	8,270	8,015	7,800
Current Liabilities	3,267	3,676	4,022	3,829
Bonds	1,087	1,074	955	983
Preferred Mandatory	0	0	0	0
Preferred Stock	0	0	0	0
Common Stock	83	82	81	81
Other Stockholders' Equity	1,918	1,689	1,845	1,796
Total Liabilities and Equity	7,935	8,270	8,015	7,800

Income Statement	Dec-98	Dec-97	Dec-96	Dec-95
	US$MM	US$MM	US$MM	US$MM
Total Revenues	10,323	8,617	8,696	8,347
Cost of Sales	9,596	8,229	8,331	6,311
Other Expenses	39	377	65	31
Loss Provision	45	160	63	50
Interest Expense	260	168	165	141
Income Pre Tax	564	−171	130	242
Income Tax	209	−9	81	100
Income Continuing	310	−46	156	209
Discontinued	15	31	0	0
Extraordinary	0	0	0	0
Changes	0	0	0	0
Net Income	325	−15	156	209
EPS Primary	$4.09	($0.20)	$2.08	$2.80
EPS Diluted	$4.06	($0.20)	$2.07	$2.76

ASIAN EXPANSION

Whirlpool's strategy in Asia consisted of five main points: partnering to build win-win relationships; attracting, retaining, and developing the best people; ensuring quality in all aspects of the business; exceeding customer needs and expectations; and offering four key products (refrigerators, washers, microwaves, and air conditioners). Although Whirlpool announced in 1987 a full-scale cooperation with Daiichi, a department store retailer in Japan, the company decided to focus its efforts in Asia primarily on India and China. There were two main reasons for this decision. First, recent changes in government regulations in both countries made it possible for foreign corporations to own a controlling interest in a manufacturing company. Second, the large populations of India and China reduced the risk of establishing large-scale operations there.

Whirlpool decided that the best way to enter the Asian market was through joint ventures, as they would allow the company to quickly establish a manufacturing presence in Asia. Once it had accomplished this goal, Whirlpool planned to build its own manufacturing facilities in the region. In 1987, Whirlpool announced an agreement with Sundram Clyton of India to manufacture compact washers for the Indian market, a joint venture which later became known as Whirlpool Washing Machines Limited. In 1993, the Asian group established regional headquarters in Tokyo and a pan-Asian marketing, product development, and technology center in Singapore.

Whirlpool intensified its Asian acquisition strategy in 1995 with various acquisitions and joint ventures in both India and China. The company bought controlling interest in Kelvinator in India, combined it with Whirlpool Washing Machines Limited, and renamed the new entity Whirlpool of India (WOI). In addition to giving Whirlpool a 56 percent interest in WOI, the Kelvinator purchase gave the company direct access to more than 3,000 trade dealers in India. Between 1994 and 1995, the company also set up four joint ventures in China, as it believed that China's market for appliances was likely to equal or surpass that of North America within ten years. By 1996, Whirlpool's investment in Asia had reached $350 million and they employed over 12,000 people. In 1997, the Asian businesses generated over $400 million in sales.

Despite its investments, however, the company suffered operating losses in Asia of $70 million in 1996 and $62 million in 1997. In 1997, Whirlpool decided to restructure its Chinese operations when overcapacity in the refrigerator and air-conditioning markets drove prices down significantly. In 1997, Whirlpool decided to find strategic alternatives for the two money-losing joint ventures which catered to these two markets.

Smaller Chinese companies were also seizing considerable market share away from the multinational foreign competition. Haier, a Chinese producer of air conditioners, microwave ovens, refrigerators, and dishwashers publicly announced plans to become a global brand by 2002 and had already expanded into Indonesia and the Philippines. In addition, the Chinese government was strongly encouraging consumers to "buy Chinese."[26] Too many producers were making similar goods, and production soon outpaced demand. For example, although Whirlpool believed it would take approximately five to six years for the market to become saturated, the refrigerator and air conditioning markets were deemed saturated just two years after Whirlpool established its joint ventures in China. In addition, the company's Asian operations produced products of poorer quality than its Japanese rivals.[27]

Competition and overcapacity were not the only problems for Whirlpool. The company had overestimated the size of the market. The Chinese middle class that could afford new home appliances numbered only about 120 million and there was no tradition in China of changing appliances that worked properly.

Once in China, Whirlpool also realized that it had not properly understood the distribution system. The company discovered that there were huge geographical distances between Chinese cities and that the country lacked strong distribution channels. The company had not expected to face major problems with telecommunications and, despite the country's huge labor supply, Whirlpool had difficulties finding qualified people for its factories.

The situation in India was similar. Despite having invested heavily in advertising and promotions, Whirlpool blamed overcapacity and difficult trading conditions in the refrigerator sector for its losses. Nevertheless, Whitwam remained confident:

> Our lower cost structure and focus on the remaining majority-owned joint ventures in China, combined with our strong market position in India and Asia-Pacific sales subsidiaries, leave Whirlpool well positioned for future growth and profitability in this region... Our growing knowledge of Asia and ability to draw on the other global resources of Whirlpool will lead to continued improvement in our operating performance in 1998 and beyond, especially as we manage through a difficult market and economic environment.[28]

Whirlpool continued to invest money in India and committed over $100 million to build a new plant near Pune to produce chlorofluorocarbon-free and frost-free refrigerators for the Indian market. The company began construction of the new facility in 1997 and the factory began commercial production in the first quarter of 1998.

LATIN AMERICAN EXPANSION

Throughout most of the 1990s, Brazil was Whirlpool's most profitable foreign operation.[29] The company first bought into the Brazilian market in 1957 and held equity positions in three companies: Brasmotor S.A., Multibras, and Embraco. These companies held a 60 percent market share and after 40 years of operating in Brazil, had extremely high brand recognition and brand loyalty. Whirlpool took over Philip's Argentine subsidiary, SAGAD, in 1992. In the mid-90s, sales and profit figures were good, with sales up 28 percent in 1994–1995, and 15 percent in 1996. In 1997, Brazilian operations recorded approximately $78 million in earnings.

Because Latin America had lower appliance penetration rates than Europe and the United States (e.g., only 15 percent of Brazilian homes owned microwaves, compared with 91 percent in the United States), the region appeared to be a good target for expansion. By the mid-1990s, Latin America was beginning to achieve economic stability, and growth was sure to follow. Consumers felt the same way. Many consumers were now able to replace old and worn-out appliances using budget plans and credit arrangements.

In 1997 in Brazil, Whirlpool spent $217 million to increase its equity share in Brasmotor from 33 percent to 66 percent. Whirlpool then invested another $280 million in 1997 and 1998 to renew plants and product lines. The company introduced data transfer systems, flexible production lines, and launched new products. Shortly after Whirlpool made these large investments in Brazil, however, interest rates in the country began to climb. The Brazilian government doubled interest rates in October 1997 and again in 1998. As a result, the currency depreciated and the economy suffered. In real terms, the *real* fell more than 50 percent in the six

EXHIBIT 5
Whirlpool Business Unit Sales and Operating Profit

Sources: Whirlpool Annual Reports.

Sales *(in millions of US dollars)*

	Dec. 97	Dec. 96	Dec. 95	Dec. 94
North America	5263	5310	5093	5048
Europe	2343	2494	2428	2373
Asia	400	461	376	205
Latin America	624	268	271	329
Other	−13	−10	−5	−6
Total	8617	8523	8163	7949

Operating Profit *(in millions of US dollars)*

	Dec. 97	Dec. 96	Dec. 95	Dec. 94
North America	546	537	445	522
Europe	54	−13	92	163
Asia	−62	−70	−50	−22
Latin America	28	12	26	49
Restructuring charge	−343	−30		−248
Business dispositions	−53			60
Other	−159	−158	−147	−154
Total	11	278	366	370

months prior to January 1999. Total foreign investment in Brazil slumped, and the country was eventually forced to request a $41.5 billion credit line from the International Monetary Fund in order to help rescue the economy.

Worse yet, Whirlpool's market research told them that consumers had reacted quickly to the economic problems. Many were afraid of job cuts in the worsening economy and were wondering whether Brazil would resort to the traditional solution of printing money to solve the economic problems. Consumers foresaw inflation and realized that they would not be able to afford to purchase Whirlpool's appliances, especially on credit. As Antonio da Silva, a 37-year-old maintenance worker said, "I'm afraid to pay over many months because you don't know if interest rates or inflation will rise again."[30]

In 1998, Whirlpool's Brazilian sales fell by 25 percent, or $1 billion.[31] Equally important, Whirlpool's *real* reserves had shrunk in value against the dollar, and the company was expecting inflationary pressures. As a result, in late 1998 the company announced more restructuring to its Latin American operations. Whirlpool immediately cut 3,200 jobs (about 25 percent of the workforce) to improve efficiency, and the company planned to cut out levels in the production chain in its seven factories in Brazil, Argentina, and Chile. At the same time, the company increased its marketing efforts in the region.

As of 1998, Whirlpool was still confident of a return to profitability in Latin America. The company believed that industry shipments to Brazil in 1999 would equal those in 1997. *Business Week* characterized the company as bullish:

> The experience of surviving Brazil's many debt crises, bouts of hyperinflation, and military governments has given Whirlpool a been-there, done-that aura of confidence.[32]

But, given Whirlpool's poor showing in the earlier phases of its globalization plan, it still had far to go in convincing the many sceptics and disappointed shareholders that globalization was the best strategy. Many analysts were unsure whether Whirlpool's self-confidence was actually deserved or if it was little more than self-delusion.

Endnotes

1. C. Quintanilla and J. Carlton, "Whirlpool Announces Global Restructuring Effort," *The Wall Street Journal,* 19 Sept. 1997: A3, A6.

2. Weiss, David D. and Andrew C. Gross, "Industry Corner: Major Household Appliances in Western Europe," *Business Economics,* Vol. 30, Issue 3, July 1995: 67.

3. Echikson, William. "The Trick to Selling in Europe," *Fortune,* 20 Sept. 1993: 82.

4. Maruca, Regina Fazio. "The Right Way to Go Global: An Interview with Whirlpool CEO David Whitwam," *Harvard Business Review,* March-April 1994: 137.

5. Weiss and Gross.

6. Jancsurak, Joe, "Holistic Strategy Pays Off," *Appliance Manufacturer,* Feb. 1995: W-3, W-4.

7. Steinmetz, Greg and Carl Quintanilla. "Tough Target: Whirlpool Expected Easy Going in Europe, and It Got a Big Shock," *The Wall Street Journal,* 10 April 1998: Sec. A:1.

8. Schiller, Zachary, et al., "Whirlpool Plots the Invasion of Europe," *Business Week,* 5 Sept. 1988: 70.

9. Jancsurak, Joe, "Group Sales: Channel Focused," *Appliance Manufacturer,* Feb. 1995: W-14.

10. "Group Sales," W-14.

11. Babyak, Richard J, "Strategic Imperative," *Appliance Manufacturer,* Feb. 1995: W-21.

12. Babyak, Richard J, "Demystifying the Asian Consumer," *Appliance Manufacturer,* Feb. 1995: W26.

13. Janesurak, Joe, "South American Sales Co.: Linking the Americas, Europe," *Appliance Manufacturer,* Feb. 1995: W-39.

14. Maruca, p. 136.

15. Maruca, p. 137.

16. Maruca, p. 136.

17. Whirlpool Corporation, Annual Report, 1997.

18. Maruca, p. 145.

19. Steinmetz and Quintanilla, A:6.

20. Steinmetz and Quintanilla, A:1, A:6.

21. "Holistic Strategy," W-3.

22. Steinmetz and Quintanilla, A:6.

23. Jancsurak, Joe, "Marketing: Phase 2," *Appliance Manufacturer,* Feb. 1995: W-10.

24. Steinmetz and Quintanilla, A:6.
25. Ibid.
26. Shuchman, Lisa, "Reality Check," *The Wall Street Journal,* 1998 April 30: Global Investing Section: 1.
27. Vlasic, Bill and Zachary Schiller. "Did Whirlpool Spin Too Far Too Fast?" *Business Week,* 24 June 1996: 136.
28. Whirlpool Corporation. Annual Report, 1997.
29. Katz, Ian, "Whirlpool: In the Wringer," *Business Week,* 14 Dec. 1998: 83.
30. Katz, 83.
31. Ibid.
32. Katz, 87.

Chapter Thirty-Seven

Bristol Compressors, Asia-Pacific

On Monday, August 4, 1997, Trevor Woods, President of Bristol Compressors, Asia-Pacific, chaired a meeting of his top management team to discuss the company's on-going management challenges in the region. The Hong Kong-based team, known as the Management Committee (MC), included Woods, aged 46, and seven other senior functional managers. Despite attractive markets in the region, Bristol Compressors' growth in Asia-Pacific had not met expectations. A broad consensus had emerged among MC members that lack of management depth was a major factor contributing to the company's weak performance. Although everyone present was convinced that something had to be done, a specific plan had not yet been developed. Woods' charge to MC members was to come up with a set of recommendations to increase significantly management bench strength in the region.

COMPANY BACKGROUND

Bristol Compressors was founded in 1913 by Peter Watson, who invested £4,000 to set up a machine shop on the eastern outskirts of Bristol, England. Watson, who was just 26 years old at the time, was heavily involved in purchasing equipment for a new steel fabrication plant and had been shocked at the prices of air compressors. After some research, he became convinced that existing suppliers were

Drs. Allen Morrison and Stewart Black prepared this case solely to provide material for class discussion. The authors do not intend to illustrate either effective or ineffective handling of a managerial situation. The authors may have disguised certain names and other identifying information to protect confidentiality.

inefficient and that the industry had huge growth prospects. With borrowed money, Peter set out on his own and Bristol Compressors was born.

The company initially manufactured air-compressing machines that were used as a blast for iron forges. In 1923, Bristol Compressors began what would become a tradition of aggressive product and international expansion by acquiring a Swiss company that specialized in the production of hammer tools used in tunnelling. By 1996, Bristol Compressors had sales revenues of £2.1 billion, and operating profits of £94 million. The company had 17 manufacturing plants in nine countries, sales and service offices in 42 countries, and over 22,000 employees worldwide. In two-thirds of its product lines, Bristol Compressors was either number one or number two in worldwide market share, making it the largest compressor manufacturing company in the world.

Bristol Compressors was organized into four product divisions. These included: (1) AirCom, which manufactured portable and stationary air compressors used in powering pneumatic tools such as wrenches and drills; (2) CleanCom, which made oil-free compressors that eliminated hazardous contaminants in the gas stream. Oil-free compressors were most commonly used in food production, scientific laboratories, hospitals, and the military, as well as in filling Scuba and fire-fighting tanks; (3) FrigCom, which made condensing equipment used in large air conditioning units for apartment, commercial, and industrial buildings. The division also made evaporative coil units and condensers for commercial refrigerators and freezers; and (4) DrillCom, which developed, manufactured and marketed a range of pneumatic tools including jackhammers and mechanical boring machines used in rock drilling, tunnelling, quarrying, and well drilling.

A division president who had full, worldwide profit and loss responsibility ran each of these four divisions. Although divisional headquarters were located in the same corporate offices in Bristol, each division operated with a relatively high level of autonomy. Product development, manufacturing, sales and marketing activities were all run independently. In 1989, purchasing activities and core research were centralized.

Until the late 1980s, the company's efforts to expand outside Europe centered almost exclusively on North America. In 1989, 84 percent of Bristol Compressors' sales came from Europe and North America. Under the direction of Stewart Egan, Bristol Compressors' Chairman and Managing Director since 1987, the company began seriously exploring market opportunities in Asia-Pacific. It was believed that the easiest way to enter new Asian markets was through the sale of portable and stationary compressors. In 1992, the Asia-Pacific region was formally organized in Hong Kong and given responsibility for the company's operations in India, Pakistan, Bangladesh, China, Taiwan, Japan, Korea, the Philippines, Vietnam, Indonesia, Malaysia, Thailand, and Singapore. The president of Asia-Pacific reported to Clive Brooks, 49, who was the president of AirCom. The thinking was that AirCom would take the lead in setting up manufacturing plants and representative offices throughout the region. Initially, the representative offices would also help sell and manage the importation of CleanCom, FrigCom and DrillCom products. In due time, it was anticipated that each of these divisions would establish its own facilities in the region.

INITIAL EXPANSION EFFORTS

In 1994, Bristol Compressors spent £11 million on a 50/50 joint venture factory in Indonesia with the Modir Group. In 1995, approximately £7 million was spent to renovate Asia-Pacific's existing headquarters and upgrade the company's Hong Kong warehouse facilities. In addition, in 1995, another £9 million was spent setting up a new compressor plant in Hong Kong.

In October 1995, Trevor Woods was appointed President of Bristol Compressors, Asia-Pacific. Before his appointment, Woods had served as Vice President Marketing and Sales for AirCom Europe (1992 to 1995), and senior marketing executive for AirCom Canada (1988 to 1990). Overall, he had spent nineteen years with the company.

In AirCom Europe, Woods worked closely with Clive Brooks (and would continue to do so in Hong Kong). Woods' promotion to President, Asia-Pacific was in part a recognition of his work launching the LiteCom line of highly portable compressors for use on construction sites. The compressors were used to power a wide range of pneumatic tools and were noteworthy for their lightweight, quiet operation and highly efficient gasoline-powered engines. To promote LiteCom compressors, AirCom organized a small army of field representatives that visited construction sites and offered convenient product demonstrations. In 1994, LiteCom was AirCom's number-one selling product line in Europe with sales of £72 million.

ASIA-PACIFIC INFRASTRUCTURE IS ESTABLISHED

Woods continued with the ongoing expansion efforts in Asia-Pacific. In 1996, £4 million was invested in a 50/50 joint venture with Zhou Ling Industries in Shekou, China (near Hong Kong). An additional £20 million was authorized for a second joint venture compressor plant in Shanghai, China. The output from these manufacturing plants (as well as the earlier investments in India and Hong Kong) was largely intended to meet anticipated demand from Asia-Pacific countries. A modest amount of exports to Europe and North America was also planned.

To build revenues, representative offices were also opened up throughout the region. From 1995 to 1997, offices were opened in Malaysia, Thailand, Taiwan, Korea, South Africa, and Hong Kong/China. Each office had between 25 and 50 employees who focused on marketing, sales, and service.

SLOW BEGINNINGS

Despite promising market research and substantial new plant capacity, Bristol Compressors' sales growth in the Asia-Pacific was slower than expected. By the summer of 1997, the company's manufacturing plants throughout Asia were operating at less than 30 percent capacity. Opinions varied as to why sales had not met expectations. With four years of service in Asia (and 17 years of experience with the company), Bombay-based Charles Withers, General Manager of Bristol Compressors India, had been in the Asia-Pacific region longer than any other expatriate manager in the company. He provided some important background on the investment decisions.

> We wanted to invest in Asia for global strategic purposes. We all knew doing business here would be hard. But if we had let our competitors continue to grow as they had in Asia, Bristol Compressors would have lost its number one position in worldwide compressor sales by 2005. We also thought that strength in Asia would help in the development of lower cost products for Europe and North America.
>
> Despite the strategic logic, you cannot get capital in this company without showing a three-to-four year payback. So that is what the budget numbers reflected. You cannot fault Woods for this. Most of the investment decisions were made before he arrived in January 1996.

Numerous formal and informal discussions were held within the MC over the cause of weak sales. Most discussions centered on three factors: (1) weaker markets than anticipated in the region, (2) unexpectedly fierce competition, and (3) ineffective strategy and execution.

Weak Markets

While sales of stationary compressors to factories had largely met projections, sales of portable compressors had been very weak in the region. By 1997, marketing managers had become leery of the earlier research that showed booming markets for portable compressors in Asia. In China, for example, it was believed that huge sales would be generated by the enormous construction projects underway in boom cities like Shanghai, Beijing and Guangzhou. For example, in 1996 it was estimated that there were more construction cranes operating in Shanghai than in the entire United States. How could there not be a gigantic market for portable compressors? However, further investigation revealed that many of the buildings were empty, unfinished shells. Unfortunately, compressors were more often used in interior finishing work than in heavy construction. Even when interior work was being done, compressors were rarely used in countries like China where labor was cheap compared to capital and where full employment was more important than labor productivity.

Fierce Competition

Others felt Bristol Compressors' disappointing performance was the result of fierce competition. Most company veterans underestimated the competitive response in Asia. Philip Dewer, Vice President of Marketing for Asia-Pacific and a member of the MC, put it this way:

> Competition in Asia has been brutal. We have been successful taking share from our competitors in Europe and North America and they are bound and determined not to let it happen again in Asia. Asia has become a fierce battleground in the global compressor industry.

Bristol Compressors' key competitors in the region included two Japanese companies, a Korean company, a German company, and two U.S. companies. Each was either a stand-alone multi-billion dollar company or a division of an even larger multinational corporation. In most Asian countries, local companies held between 25 percent and 35 percent of the market. Local manufacturers were generally viewed as relatively unsophisticated and vulnerable to the aggressive moves of multinational competitors.

The competition was unrelenting. For example, in 1996, one major competitor unilaterally cut its prices in Japan on stationary compressors by 20 percent. Bristol Compressors followed with a similar price cut. The competitor then cut prices by another 15 percent and signaled more cuts if Bristol Compressors followed. In addition to dramatic price cuts, competitors used a range of blocking strategies that, while perfectly legal in Asia, would be against the law in many of Bristol Compressors' traditional markets. For example, one competitor was notorious for shutting off supplies or cutting advertising incentives to distributors that added Bristol Compressors' products. This created substantial barriers to entry in distribution.

Strategy and Execution Missteps

Initially, Bristol Compressors sought to end-run the competition by downplaying distribution channels in favor of the pull strategy it perfected in Europe. When Woods first arrived in Hong Kong, he pushed the national sales and marketing offices to focus on the LiteCom brand of portable compressors and build sales by sending teams to construction sites and auto repair shops. Initially, the strategy seemed immensely successful. Local workers loved the site visits and seemed eager to try the pneumatic equipment and receive free T-shirts and key chains emblazoned with the LiteCom logo.

Surprisingly, though, few sales materialized. After months of tinkering with the concept, the national marketing and sales staffs began to realize that the way portable compressors were purchased in some parts of Asia was fundamentally different from Europe. In Europe, professional users typically either owned their own business or knew the owner. As a result, they either bought LiteCom products themselves or were influential in buying decisions. In contrast, in many parts of Asia, professional users had limited influence on buying decisions. In Singapore, for example, the vast majority of construction workers came from countries like India, Pakistan, and the Philippines. These people had no direct input in buying decisions. In other parts of Asia, construction workers or auto repair technicians were employed by large corporations or government-owned enterprises with independent buying offices. As a result, in many cases, worker interest in the "events" might have been driven more by curiosity and handouts than by an interest in actually purchasing compressors.

To complicate matters, the actual buyers were often large distributors. In China, for example, Bristol Compressors worked with approximately 20 distributors who handled the importation and distribution of portable and stationary compressors in different local markets. Not only were these distributors far removed from end users, but also compressors represented a fraction of each distributor's product line. As a result, it was often difficult to gain their full attention.

As their understanding of the buying criteria increased, Bristol Compressors' managers began to shift their emphasis towards developing deep relationships with major buyers. The "pull" strategy that was so effective in moving the Lite-Com line in Europe was gradually deemphasized in several major Asian markets. With this change in strategy came the need for sales people with different skills than had been anticipated. Winston Baxter, Sales Manager for China and Hong Kong, explained:

> In Asia, we need sales people who are skilled at finding the decision-makers. The decision-makers are not typically hanging around construction sites and auto repair shops. Once they find them, our people need to be excellent at building relationships with senior business people. These are different skills than we are promoting in our European sales people.

Although Bristol Compressors' strategy was still being sorted out, sales throughout Asia-Pacific had risen steadily over the past two years. In many Asian countries, Bristol Compressors was the only compressor manufacturer that was increasing its market share. In China, Bristol Compressors climbed to number four in market share for both portable and stationary compressors. However, despite encouraging growth, it still had a long way to go to match the market share it enjoyed in Europe and North America.

INCREASING MANAGEMENT BENCH STRENGTH

In order to accelerate sales and better manage existing business, members of the MC were convinced that Bristol Compressors, Asia-Pacific had to significantly increase both the number and quality of managers in the region. Better management would help Bristol Compressors find new markets, compete more effectively, and avoid strategy missteps.

The challenge was to determine the best approach to increasing management bench strength. Three options had begun to emerge: developing managers from within, hiring skilled local managers, and significantly increasing the number of expatriate managers in the Asia-Pacific. Each option had supporters and detractors.

Developing Managers from Within

Developing managers from within primarily meant working closely with employees to mold and shape their skills and abilities so that, over time, they would be competent in managing critical activities. In Europe as well as North America, Bristol Compressors hired most of its future leaders out of graduate schools. It then spent ten or more years developing them through a combination of in-house training, teamwork, travel, and new assignments. Exposure to these different developmental activities tested and developed managers and virtually guaranteed the company a steady stream of loyal and competent managers.

A similar approach to management development was thought by some to be essential if Bristol Compressors was ever to develop a strong market position in

Asia-Pacific. The advantage of this approach was that it was built on the natural strengths of host country nationals. These were the people who knew the markets, spoke the language, and had the local connections. Over time, they could develop a deep understanding of Bristol Compressors' products, values, culture and policies. They could also establish long-term relationships with other managers throughout Bristol Compressors' regional and global organization. Such relationships were essential in establishing and maintaining quality, two-way communications and in effectively formulating and implementing country and regional strategies.

Margaret Reeve, Director of Marketing for China and Hong Kong, believed Bristol Compressors had an excellent track record in developing people.

> A lot of people in Hong Kong and China want to work for an MNC because they generally provide good training. Bristol Compressors is very good at giving people significant responsibilities early in their careers. We are also a very good marketing company. People can learn an awful lot about marketing by working for us.

Despite the advantage of developing people from within, several senior Asia-Pacific managers were concerned that this approach was too little, too late. Charles Withers was one of them.

> It takes time to develop local people. The competition won't give us five years to get our act together.
>
> Bristol Compressors has a company culture that encourages people to develop themselves, to take personal responsibility for their own career progress. In Asia, the culture is 'company, look after me. Tell me what to do.' The model we have used to develop people in Europe and North America will likely fail in Asia.

Others cited different concerns with a "build from within" strategy. Hong Kong-based Anthony Yip was the Human Resource Manager responsible for management training in the Asia-Pacific. His major concern was attrition:

> Job turnover is high in Hong Kong and Singapore because demand exceeds supply. Losing people through poaching is a very big problem at all levels of the company. Lower level employees switch easily. If you fire them, they can find a job in a day. They will quit if the working conditions aren't perfect or for a little more money. Senior people also quit because they want a promotion or a better working environment.

Once trained, local managers faced attractive opportunities outside the company. Poaching was a huge problem for Bristol Compressors throughout Asia. Hong Kong-based Henry Lee, Director of Logistics for Bristol Compressors China and Hong Kong, explained that the situation in China was particularly tough:

> Our biggest problem in China is retaining quality people. The Chinese think out one to two years into the future only. They want immediate rewards—pay, power, and benefits. Senior Chinese managers, in particular, are very mobile. Typically, when we train these people, we put them under a contract to continue working for us for a certain period of time after the training is over. However, even when they are bound by a contract, some still leave. There is essentially no way to track them down or to enforce the contract in a Chinese court. One of our

competitors sent 24 Chinese managers to the U.S. for a 6-week, intensive training course. The course cost $20,000 per person. After two years, only one person was still with the company. The other 23 quit and got better offers with other companies in China.

Another reason for the high turnover is that many people—Chinese, in particular—don't like working under pressure. If the company pushes too hard to make the numbers, many Chinese get uncomfortable. They do not think the company should be that concerned with making the numbers but instead should focus on building relationships where things get worked out more slowly. Many expatriates we have over here do not understand this and are surprised when people simply quit. The Chinese will never complain and the reason they leave will never be brought up.

Others believed that the retention of trained managers was not as serious a concern as it might appear. Winston Baxter argued:

Retention is currently a problem for Bristol Compressors throughout the region. However, it is not as big a problem with some of our customers. Many of our customers have employees who have worked for them their entire careers. People want to work for a company they can count on. They want to be proud of their company. Bristol Compressors is new here. It does not have a track record. In time, it will, and the retention problem will largely look after itself.

Some questioned whether Bristol Compressors was starting off with the right group of local managers. Many of the best and the brightest were attracted to the large multinational companies like Sony, General Motors, Coca-Cola, and Unilever. These companies tended to have substantial national organizations that offered distinct career tracks and household names that looked good on a résumé. Some wondered whether Bristol Compressors' existing local management pool was strong enough to support a "build from within" strategy.

Cultural differences also raised serious questions about the efficacy of management development programs. Many potential Asia-Pacific managers were ethnic Chinese; in some cases, Chinese cultural norms interfered with Bristol Compressors' efforts to accelerate management development. The way in which many ethnic Chinese often approached decision making and delegation illustrated the issue. The typical structures of Western and Chinese business organization are shown in Exhibit 1. In most cases, Western business organizations were built on the principles of delegation and teamwork. Typical Chinese organizations followed very different principles. They tended to have large numbers of people who reported directly to the General Manager. Power was tightly guarded at the top of the organization and teamwork was not valued to the same degree it was in most Western organizations. It was not unusual for general managers in Chinese organizations to nominally supervise hundreds or even thousands of employees including drivers, loading dock workers, and clerical staffs. The problem was that Bristol Compressors' approach to management development placed a high emphasis on experiential learning through delegation and teamwork. As a result, some argued that Bristol Compressors faced huge cultural barriers in quickly developing large numbers of ethnic Chinese managers.

EXHIBIT 1 **Building Bench Strength in Bristol Compressors-Asia-Pacific**

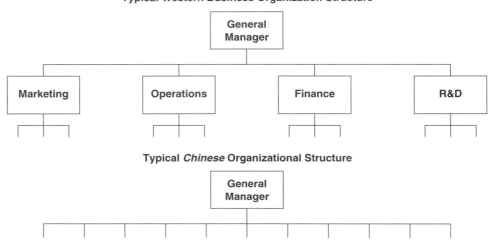

Typical *Western* Business Organization Structure

Typical *Chinese* Organizational Structure

Some also pointed out that accelerating the development process was inherently risky. The more rapid the learning process, the less grounded any individual would be in his or her current assignment. Costly mistakes would almost certainly follow. Several members of the MC wondered whether Bristol Compressors actually had the forbearance required to develop managers effectively. Hong Kong-based Paul Wang, Director of Finance for Asia-Pacific and the only non-British national on the MC, explained this concern:

> If you take a guy with no general management experience and put him in a job, and six to nine months later sales are still flat and nothing is happening, we'll likely replace him. Competition is so severe and members of the MC are so preoccupied putting out fires that we don't have the time or the attention span to effectively develop our replacements. It is a real problem. The question is, does Bristol Compressors have the patience to actually develop people?

One final obstacle to management development was the seeming unwillingness or inability of many Asians to move away from their countries of birth. Because developmental opportunities were limited in any one country, local managers often needed foreign assignments to gain exposure to the full array of issues facing Bristol Compressors in Asia-Pacific. While some welcomed the opportunities for promotions or lateral transfers outside their home countries, most were very hesitant to move. Woods explained:

> Most local nationals are much less mobile than Americans and Europeans. Many don't want to leave their home countries. Family is a big reason. In many cases, parents put huge pressures on them to stay nearby. In addition, religion can be a factor. For example, Muslims from Malaysia may be uncomfortable moving to

countries where Islam is not generally practised. Others simply fear the unknown. Short-term assignments and travel help but are usually not enough. We have developmental opportunities for people outside their home countries, but are restricted as to what we can do within the country.

Paul Wang had another perspective of developmental opportunities in the region:

Hong Kong is a great place to live. Who wants to give this up to move to Manila or Shanghai? Furthermore, Hong Kong nationals get much smaller relocation "packages" when they move to mainland China than the British. There is less incentive for us to move.

Hiring the Best and the Brightest Local Managers

A second option to building management bench strength was to simply hire the best local managers. This would circumvent the five-to-ten-year management development cycle and allow Bristol Compressors to build sales volumes in the region more quickly.

Paying top dollar for the best and the brightest local talent had many advantages. First, even the most expensive local managers were cheaper than expatriates. Elizabeth Higgens, Director of Human Resources for Asia-Pacific and a member of the MC, estimated that top talent in Singapore and Hong Kong would cost between £60,000 and £100,000 per year in 1997.[1] This was higher than Bristol Compressors paid for UK-based managers with comparable skills (about £40,000 to £55,000 per year). However, when a British national was brought to Asia as an expatriate, his or her total compensation package averaged about three times base salary (£120,000 or much more, depending on the position). As a result, hiring local talent was much more cost effective than using expatriates. The compensation differential was even more pronounced in countries like China where top local people cost between £20,000 and £35,000 per year.

The best and the brightest local managers often had established relationships with customers, distributors, and government officials. They also frequently had relationships with competent workers in other companies who could be tapped to join Bristol Compressors. Finally, they had the potential to serve as credible role models for other local employees.

Despite the clear advantages of this approach, several shortcomings were evident. Philip Dewer shared his views:

When you pay serious money to hire someone, you often don't get the experience required. They may have been great working as part of a big team in a well-established company with proven processes and Asian strategic experience. However, will they be effective as part of our team to develop the appropriate new strategies and processes Bristol Compressors needs to be capable and achieve success in Asia?

Margaret Reeve was also concerned that while Bristol Compressors could always hire top people, no one really knew what they were getting until it was too late.

It's hard to find talented people here in Hong Kong. I hired a guy who has worked in the compressor industry for many years. He had been a manager for one of our competitors. We are paying him about £65,000 per year and so far, I am not very happy with his performance. I have to follow up with him everyday on what he is doing. It seems that he needs to be told what to do all the time.

Charles Withers had a similar story:

We had a great guy we hired into the China/Hong Kong office. We hired him away from another large MNC. He was a Hong Kong national with an MBA from the London Business School. He looked great on paper. Unfortunately, he didn't last long. We had to let him go. He did not know either the industry or Bristol Compressors. We need a balance of both to succeed.

Winston Baxter felt that many of those who wanted to hire senior local managers were motivated by the desire to hire someone who "looked" as if they could do the job. The thinking was that if they wore a suit and had a good education they could be trusted. Baxter explained:

I have a fabulous sales representative who barely graduated from high school, speaks no English, has never worn a tie, has grease under his fingernails. I know some expats here are bothered by his appearance. But, he is great. He works extremely hard and is very successful. What I've found is that while hiring a 'suit' may be consistent with Bristol Compressors' culture, it doesn't always get the job done.

Flooding Asia-Pacific with Expatriate Managers

The third option under consideration was the most aggressive. The thinking went along the following lines. Bristol Compressors dominated the portable and stationary compressor industry in Europe and North America. Some competitors had been seriously hurt in these markets and were now focusing on Asia, the last major competitive battleground in the global compressor industry. Bristol Compressors could not permit these companies to succeed in the booming economies of Asia. To do so would allow the competition to build production volumes that would underwrite research and development and produce economies of scale that would lower per unit costs. If the company's competitors were allowed to dominate the growing markets of Asia, AirCom's established markets would eventually be at risk. In addition, Asian profits in portable and stationary compressors would strengthen competitors in market share battles with Bristol Compressors' other lines of business.

In order to ensure that this never happened, some argued that Bristol Compressors should flood Asia-Pacific with expatriates. Although expensive, expatriates had proven highly valuable throughout the Asia-Pacific. They had excellent functional skills; they knew how to run a marketing campaign and organize a sales force; they could efficiently run factories, they understood international logistics, and so on. They also had considerable industry knowledge. They knew who the competitors were, what their strategies were, etc. They were also familiar with Bristol Compressors' products including how compressors worked and how they could be used in a range of industries. They understood Bristol Compressors' values, culture, policies, and organization structure. Finally, Bristol Compressors' expatriates were highly loyal employees. The poaching of expatriates had never been a major problem.

At any point in time, Bristol Compressors had about twenty expatriates working in the Asia-Pacific region. Their contributions had proven invaluable. Charles Withers had seen this first hand. He believed that "well prepared expats can have a huge impact." Margaret Reeve concurred, "I would feel a lot better with ten more expatriates here. Things would happen much faster." Others shared similar views.

Under an expatriate strategy, Bristol Compressors would literally flood Asia-Pacific with professionals from outside the region. It was estimated that an additional forty to fifty expatriates would profoundly impact operations in the region. Less experienced locals would be moved out and would be replaced with seasoned expatriates. Under this scenario, all country general managers and virtually all of their direct reports would be expatriates. Local assistants would help in matters of cultural interpretation, language, cross-cultural negotiations, and so on.

Although this would be a novel strategy for Bristol Compressors, Japanese companies had for decades relied heavily on expatriates in managing international operations. Paul Wang had spent considerable time observing how Japanese firms were using expatriates:

> Some of our Japanese competitors are filling management bench strength in Asia with expatriates. An advantage Japanese companies have over us is that their expats are cheaper than British expats. They cost less, in part, because Japanese managers will go where they are told to go and, in part, because they are coming from Japan, which is far more expensive than most countries in the region. In many cases, Japanese companies pay less keeping expats in China or Indonesia than they would keeping them in Tokyo.

No one who promoted the expatriate strategy option believed that local managers were not needed. Rather, it was an issue of timing. The view was, "let's first win the war. In five years, then we'll get serious about developing local management."

Although the expatriate strategy seemed to have a certain logic, it had numerous detractors. Charles Withers identified a range of concerns.

> There are a number of reasons why relying on expats isn't a good idea. First, expats are very expensive. On average, each expat costs us well over £140,000 fully loaded. Second, I don't think we could find 40 quality expats in either Europe or North America who would come over here. Just because we ask doesn't mean they will come. Third, what do we do with the expats who go home? We don't have a program to deal with mass repatriation. Fourth, Bristol Compressors is essentially a marketing and sales company. To be effective, we need to understand local customers. No matter what is said about the strengths of expats, locals are far better at understanding customers.

Philip Dewer strongly agreed with Withers.

> We need quality management at home. Europe and North America would suffer if we moved 40 to 50 people overseas. Even if we had plenty to spare, many don't want to go overseas. They are comfortable with their familiar business environments and personal lifestyles. Some do not desire an international assignment for personal or family reasons. Finally, neither British nor Americans are insiders in Asia. Many of our skills simply don't work here.

Frank Lau, Finance Director for China and Hong Kong, was equally skeptical of the potential contribution of expatriates. From his perspective, expatriates were largely a negative influence:

> People in Hong Kong and China quit, in part, because they see such high turnover of expats. They get disoriented with such turnover. Sometimes people also feel disillusioned when they don't get the job but the company brings in another expat to the job that the local feels he or she could do better. It is bad for morale.

MOVING FORWARD

The stakes for Bristol Compressors were enormous. With substantial assets now in the region, every member of the MC was under mounting pressure to aggressively move the organization forward. All agreed that a new generation of competent, savvy managers was required.

Management bench strength affected each MC member personally. Seven of the eight members of the MC were British nationals. While most would eventually return home, they all shared a strong desire to build bench strength and nationalize management in Asia-Pacific. They also all understood that the greater the quantity and quality of local managers, the greater the impact each MC member could have on his or her own organization. Where they disagreed was over the timing and approach to be taken.

The August 4, 1997, meeting of the MC brought no clear solutions to a huge challenge for the Asia-Pacific region. With the meeting drawing to a close, everyone present had a new awareness of the need for a unifying approach to building management bench strength. After summarizing the discussion, Woods proceeded with the following request:

> The time for action is upon us. I want from each of you a two-page summary of the bench strength issue and a set of recommendations. You have two weeks to get me your input. Once I've heard from all of you, we can make some decisions and move forward.

Endnote

1. In September 1997, one British pound was equal to approximately 1.60 US dollars.

Chapter Thirty-Eight

Larson in Nigeria

David Larson, vice-president of international operations for Larson Inc., was mulling over the decisions he was required to make regarding the company's Nigerian operation. He was disturbed by the negative tone of the report sent to him on January 4, 1994, by the chief executive officer (CEO) of the Nigerian affiliate, George Ridley (see Exhibit 1). Larson believed the future prospects for Nigeria were excellent and was concerned about what action he should take.

COMPANY BACKGROUND

Larson Inc. was a New York-based multinational corporation in the wire and cable business. Wholly-owned subsidiaries were located in Canada and the United Kingdom, while Mexico, Venezuela, Australia, and Nigeria were the sites of joint ventures. Other countries around the world were serviced through exports from the parent or one of its subsidiaries.

IVEY

Richard Ivey School of Business
The University of Western Ontario

Professor Paul Beamish and Harry Cheung revised this case (originally prepared by Professor I. A. Litvak) solely to provide material for class discussion. The authors do not intend to illustrate either effective or ineffective handling of a managerial situation. The authors may have disguised certain names and other identifying information to protect confidentiality.

EXHIBIT 1   The Ridley Report

In response to the request from head office for a detailed overview of the Nigerian situation and its implications for Larson Inc., George Ridley prepared the following report in December, 1993. It attempts to itemize the factors in the Nigerian environment that have contributed to the problems experienced by Larson's joint venture in Nigeria.

The Nigerian Enterprises Promotion Decrees

1. There can be no doubt that the Nigerian Enterprises Promotion Decree of 1977 represents very severe and far-reaching indigenization legislation. The cumulative damaging effects of the decree have been exacerbated by some aspects of its implementation. In particular, the valuation of companies by the Nigerian Securities and Exchange Committee has in many cases been unrealistically low. This has represented substantial real-capital asset losses to the overseas companies concerned, which had no opportunity of appeal to an independent authority. Although the Decree was amended in 1989 to remove some of these problems, companies have experienced difficulties and delays in obtaining foreign currency for the remittance of proceeds from the sale of shares. A disquieting feature has been the enforced imposition, in certain cases, of a requirement to issue new equity in Nigeria instead of selling existing shares, with the consequent ineligibility to remit even part of the proceeds from Nigeria and dilution of value to both Nigerian and foreign shareholders. Another aspect causing great concern is related to the time constraint for compliance, particularly as the Nigerian authorities concerned appear to be literally snowed under with applications.

Remittance

2. In addition to the problems of remittances of the proceeds from the sale of shares, there has been a steadily increasing delay in the granting of foreign exchange for remittances from Nigeria, such as payment for supplies and services from overseas. Whereas early this year delays of about one year were being reported, delays of up to five years or even more are now not unusual. Larson Nigeria cannot continue to operate effectively if it is unable to remit proceeds and pay bills in a reasonable time frame. It is in the position of importing $5.5 million in products and services annually. These delays in remittances, coupled with delays in payments (see paragraph 4(a)), also raise problems related to export guarantees, which normally are of limited duration only.

3. A problem regarding remittances has arisen as a result of the Nigerian Insurance Decree No. 59, under which cargoes due for import to Nigeria have to be insured with a Nigerian-registered insurance company. For cargoes imported without confirmed letters of credit, claims related to cargo loss and damage are paid in Nigeria; however, foreign exchange for remittance to pay the overseas suppliers is not being granted on the grounds that the goods have not arrived.

Problems Affecting Liquidity and Cash Flow

4. A number of problems have arisen during the last two years that are having a serious effect upon liquidity and cash flow, with the result that the local expenses can be met only by increasing bank borrowing, which is not only an additional cost but also becoming more difficult to obtain.
    (a) Serious delays exist in obtaining payment from federal and state government departments for supplies and services provided, even in instances where payment terms are clearly written into the contract concerned. This is particularly true for state governments where payment of many accounts is 12 months or more in arrears. Even after payment, further delays and exchange-rate losses are experienced in obtaining foreign currency for the part that is remittable abroad. This deterioration in cash flow from government clients had, in turn, permeated through to the private clients.
    (b) There is a requirement that a 100 percent deposit be made on application for foreign currency to cover letters of credit.
    (c) In order to clear the cargo as soon as possible and to avoid possible loss at the wharf, importers normally pay their customs duty before a ship arrives.

The parent company was established in 1925 by David Larson's grandfather. Ownership and management of the company remained in the hands of the Larson family and was highly centralized. The annual sales volume for the corporation worldwide approximated $575 million in 1993. Revenue was primarily generated from the sale of power, communication, construction and control cables.

Technical service was an important part of Larson Inc.'s product package; therefore, the company maintained a large force of engineers to consult with customers and occasionally supervise installation. As a consequence, licensing was really not a viable method of serving foreign markets.

BACKGROUND ON NIGERIA

Nigeria is located in the west-central part of the African continent. With 105 million people in 1993, it was the most populous country in Africa and the ninth most populous nation in the world. From 1970 to 1993, population had grown by 2.4 percent annually. About 47 percent of the population was under 15 years of age.

Seventy-five percent of the labor force in Nigeria worked in agriculture. About 20 percent of the population lived in urban centres.

The gross national product in 1993 was about $33 billion. While per capita GNP was only about $310, on a purchasing power parity basis it was substantially higher at $1,480. GNP had grown from 1987 to 1993 at over 5 percent annually— one of the highest rates in the world. This increase was fuelled in part by the export sales of Nigeria's large oil reserves.

During the 1988 to 1992 period, Nigeria's annual inflation rate had ranged between 8 and 51 percent. This fluctuation had contributed to the change in the value of the naira from 4.5 to the U.S. dollar in 1988 to 17.3 to the U.S. dollar in 1992.

THE NIGERIAN OPERATION

Larson Inc. established a joint venture in Nigeria in 1984 with a local partner who held 25 percent of the joint venture's equity. In 1989, Larson Inc. promised Nigerian authorities that the share of local ownership would be increased to 51 percent within the next five to seven years. Such indigenization requests from developing country governments were quite common.

Sales revenue for the Nigerian firm totalled $28 million in 1993. Of this revenue, $24.5 million was realized in Nigeria, while $3.5 million was from exports. About 40 percent of the firm's Nigerian sales ($10 million) were made to various enterprises and departments of the government of Nigeria. The company was making a reasonable profit of 10 percent of revenue, but with a little bit of luck and increased efficiency, it was believed it could made a profit of 20 percent.

The Nigerian operation had become less attractive for Larson Inc. in recent months. Although it was widely believed that Nigeria would become one of the key economic players in Africa in the 1990s and that the demand for Larson's products would remain very strong there, doing business in Nigeria was becoming more costly. Furthermore, Larson Inc. had become increasingly unhappy with its local partner in Nigeria, a lawyer who was solely concerned with quick "paybacks" at the expense of reinvestment and long-term growth prospects.

David Larson recognized that having the right partner in a joint venture was of paramount importance. The company expected the partner or partners to be actively engaged in the business, "not businesspeople interested in investing money alone." The partner was also expected to hold a substantial equity in the venture. In the early years of the joint venture, additional funding was often required and it was necessary for the foreign partner to be in a strong financial position.

The disillusionment of George Ridley, the Nigerian Firm's CEO, had been increasing since his early days in that position. He was an expatriate from the United Kingdom who, due to his background as a military officer, placed a high value upon order and control. The chaotic situation in Nigeria proved very trying for him. His problems were futher complicated by his inability to attract good, local employees in Nigeria, while his best expatriate staff requested transfers to New York or Larson Inc.'s other foreign operations soon after their arrival in Nigeria. On a number of occasions, Ridley was prompted to suggest to the head office that it reconsider its Nigerian commitment.

THE DECISION

David Larson reflected on the situation. He remained convinced that Larson Inc. should maintain its operations in Nigeria; however, he had to design a plan to increase local Nigerian equity in the venture to 51 percent. Larson also wondered what should be done about Ridley. On the one hand, Ridley had been with the company for many years and knew the business intimately; on the other hand, Larson felt that Ridley's attitude was contributing to the poor morale in the Nigerian firm and wondered if Ridley had lost his sense of adaptability. Larson knew Ridley had to be replaced, but he was unsure about the timing and the method to use, since Ridley was only two years away from retirement.

Larson had to come to some conclusions fairly quickly. He had been requested to prepare an action plan for the Nigerian operation for consideration by the board of directors of Larson Inc. in a month's time. He thought he should start by identifying the key questions, whom he should contact, and how he should handle Ridley in the meantime.

Chapter Thirty-Nine

HCM Beverage Company

It was 7:45 A.M. on Friday, September 19, 1997, and the marketing office was still dark. Sitting in a small adjacent conference room, Mark Johnson, age 31, General Manager of HCM Beverage Company, wondered where everyone was. Johnson had a meeting scheduled with Mr. L. M. Dinh, the Marketing Manager, at 8:00 A.M. for the first of what Johnson planned would become a routine pattern of weekly updates. At 7:55 A.M., staff members started to trickle in one by one. At slightly past 8:00 A.M., Dinh walked into his office, put his briefcase on his desk, placed his cellular phone on the charger, and walked back out of the office. As Dinh reached for the doorknob to let himself out of the building, Johnson stepped out of the conference room and waved. Dinh said he would be right back and, before Johnson could reply, was out the door. Johnson looked at his watch and shook his head. He turned to Ms. L. P. My, a member of the marketing staff, and asked, "Where is Mr. Dinh going?" "To eat breakfast," My replied.

As Johnson walked back to the conference room, he could not help thinking that Dinh's behavior was indicative of the local marketing staff's indifference to their jobs. Johnson was deeply concerned about a steady deterioration in the company's performance, but he seemed to be the only one—besides his boss, Kevin Patterson. Patterson, Asia Pacific Regional Vice President, had made it clear to Johnson that Asia had been targeted by the company for rapid growth over the next

Drs. J. Stewart Black and Allen J. Morrison prepared this case solely to provide material for class discussion. The authors do not intend to illustrate either effective or ineffective handling of a managerial situation. The authors may have disguised certain names and other identifying information to protect confidentiality.

Ivey Management Services prohibits any form of reproduction, storage or transmittal without its written permission. This material is not covered under authorization from CanCopy or any reproduction rights organization. To order copies or request permission to reproduce materials, contact Ivey Publishing, Ivey Management Services, c/o Richard Ivey School of Business, The University of Western Ontario, London, Ontario, Canada, N6A 3K7; phone (519) 661-3208; fax (519) 661-3882; e-mail cases@ivey.uwo.ca.

ten years. Furthermore, Patterson stressed that this first venture into Vietnam was just the beginning of what could amount to tens of millions of dollars of investment in the country over the next several years. But, despite Johnson's best efforts, sales and profits had been down every month since he arrived. In two days, Johnson was to fly to Hong Kong to review HCM's performance with his boss. He was not looking forward to the meeting.

COMPANY BACKGROUND

Formed as a joint-venture (JV) bottling company in the summer of 1994 by a large multinational food and beverage firm headquartered in the United States (49 percent equity) and a local state-owned bottling company (51 percent equity), HCM Beverage Company was the U.S. firm's first investment in Vietnam. What the JV promised to provide to the American company was access to a potentially large and rapidly growing market. What it promised to provide to the state-owned bottler was access to Western technology, capital, and marketing savvy.

Given the mutual benefits, the JV was quickly granted a license to produce soft drinks to sell in the Vietnamese market. During the first year, the U.S. firm invested just over $US 2 million in new bottling equipment. By 1996, HCM Beverage Company had become the second largest bottler of carbonated beverages in Vietnam. The largest bottling company in Vietnam, and HCM Beverage Company's major competitor, was Vietnam Beverage Company (VBC), a state-owned company located in Hanoi.

HCM Beverage Company was headquartered in a small town on the outskirts of Ho Chi Minh City (HCM City). This was also where the factory was located. To ease distribution problems, the warehouse and the sales and marketing departments were located about 25 miles away inside HCM City.

HCM Beverage Company had 300 full-time factory employees and about 200 additional temporary factory workers. The factory ran 24 hours a day with three eight-hour shifts, each with a one-hour break for meals. Because there was no place to eat within the vicinity of the plant, meals were served free at HCM Beverage Company's cafeteria inside the factory. Due to poor public transportation from the city out to the factory, a company bus picked up employees at one central location in the city, dropped them off at the plant, and took them back after their shift.

Top management of HCM Beverage Company consisted of five full-time managers, three of whom were members of the Board of Directors. (See Exhibit 1 for HCM Beverage company's organizational chart.) The management team held staff meetings once a week to provide updates on their department's current activities and future plans. Given that the general manager, plant manager, and vice president of accounting all had offices either at or adjacent to the plant, staff meetings were typically held in a boardroom at the plant.

Mr. P. V. Luong was Chairman of the JV's Board of Directors. He was a government official who had worked in the Ministry of Industry prior to being appointed as chairman of the JV. During the JV negotiations in Hanoi, Mr. Luong had been a key representative for the government. Johnson commented on the Chairman's involvement with day-to-day operations:

EXHIBIT 1   **HCM Beverage Company's Organization Chart**

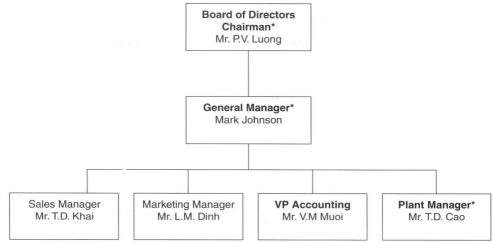

*Members of the Board of Directors

Normally, Mr. Luong doesn't involve himself in daily operating decisions. In general, he seems to be largely uninterested in the JV. However, with declining operating results, Mr. Luong had become more involved of late. More precisely, he has complained louder and more frequently at board meetings. Still, he is not active in the management of the JV nor can we rely on him for unique insights relating to our problems.

Mr. T. D. Cao, age 47, was a senior operations manager of the state-owned bottling company prior to the JV's formation. He had been with the company for over 20 years, and his family had lived in the south of Vietnam for several generations. When the JV was formed, HCM Beverage Company took over control of the former state-owned facility, and Mr. Cao was named plant manager. In addition to serving as plant manager, Mr. Cao also supervised the personnel department, covering not only the plant but the company's accounting, marketing and sales activities. Since the formation of the JV, Mr. Cao had made significant increases in overall output and efficiency of the plant. He readily acknowledged that the new equipment supplied by the U.S. partner had made a major difference in both quality and production capacity.

Mr. L. M. Dinh, age 51, had come to the JV soon after its formation. From 1963 to 1990, Mr. Dinh worked in Hanoi for VBC in a range of mid-to-upper level management jobs. From 1990 to 1994, he worked as a regional bureaucrat in the Ministry of Industry in the south of Vietnam. His appointment in late 1994 as marketing manager for HCM Beverage Company had been championed by Chairman Luong.

Mr. T. D. Khai, age 42, was the sales manager and, in theory, reported directly to Johnson. However, he was several years junior to Mr. Dinh, and Mr. Dinh treated him as though Mr. Khai was a direct report.

Mr. V. M. Muoi, age 38, was the VP of accounting. Mr. Muoi had little professional training, but had worked in the accounting section of the Vietnamese partner before the formation of the JV.

Mark Johnson had been in Vietnam as the General Manager for about six months. He had joined the U.S. parent in 1992, fresh out of graduate school with an MBA from a well-known U.S.-based business school. After a series of promotions, he was most recently national brand manager for the company's fifth best-selling soft drink product. HCM Beverage was his first international assignment. He explained the circumstances surrounding his appointment as the JV's general manager.

> I had been searching for an unusual assignment for the past couple of years. When I heard about the opening in Vietnam, I was intrigued. I contacted Kevin Patterson, Asia Pacific Regional Vice President of Marketing—someone I had known for a few years—about the position. He told me that despite a successful start-up, performance at the Vietnamese JV had begun to slip. He seemed very excited to learn I might be interested in the position.
>
> With nearly 80 million people, Vietnam seemed like a huge potential market. I really wanted some international experience. Asia was a strategic growth area for the company and I wanted some P&L responsibility to add to my marketing background.
>
> I met with my boss, Frank Carpano, and told him about the opening. He told me he thought I had great potential to move up in marketing and asked me if I was sure I wanted to leave headquarters to run some JV half way around the world. I gave him my rationale, and arranged for him and Patterson to talk. Within a few days, Kevin [Patterson] called me and offered me the job. The package was excellent—a 30 percent pay raise, cost of living adjustment, a furnished three-bedroom apartment in an up-scale, Western-oriented compound in HCM City, a new Mercedes and full-time driver, maid service, paid home leave. The works.
>
> My wife was excited by the opportunity. Neither of us had lived overseas. She had taken the past six months off to stay at home with our new daughter and seemed happy to stay out of the corporate grind for two or three years.
>
> The move happened so fast. Between the time we made the decision and when we arrived in Vietnam, we had just eight weeks. We barely had time to put our furniture in storage and contract with a property management company to take care of renting our house while we were gone.
>
> When we arrived here in February, our driver met us at the airport. The ride in from the airport was an eye opener. Bicycles and mopeds were everywhere. The heat and humidity were stifling. We had been warned about it, but until you experience it, you can't quite imagine it. Good thing our apartment was nice. Thank heavens for air-conditioning.

Johnson had felt he had no time for training prior to his departure for Vietnam and thought he had been too busy since his arrival for any follow up. He had picked up a couple of books on the country, but one was tough reading and went into all sorts of details about the economic and political history of the country that Johnson felt were a bit removed from his day-to-day management challenges.

VIETNAM

Vietnam's history and strong Chinese cultural influences date back to the third century BC, when early ancestors from China migrated into the Red River Delta. Located in the Indochina peninsula, Vietnam in 1996 had a population of just over 75 million people. In modern times, its people had experienced rule as a former French colony, the tragedy of the Cultural Revolution of 1945, the frustration of being a divided nation at the 17th parallel for 30 years (1945 to 1975), the devastation of the Vietnam War until the fall of Saigon in 1975 (renamed Ho Chi Minh City to honor the country's founding father, Ho Chi Minh), and the challenges of being reunited as an independent country and member of the United Nations since 1977.

Although Vietnam had been reunited almost as long as it was divided, many of the effects of the division remained. For almost 30 years, the North practised socialism with support from the former Soviet Union while the South followed capitalism with the support of the United States. The differences in these systems and their impact on the people of Vietnam had been profound.

Vietnam's Economic System

From 1945, the North operated a centrally planned economy modeled on those of the Soviet Union and Eastern Europe. The North's leaders believed that a centrally planned system was essential for war conditions, because resources were scarce and consumption had to be limited, stable, and equitable. The system allowed the state to control all land and natural resources and maintain ownership of virtually all productive activities; the state allocated equipment and raw materials for production, and it organized agriculture under a collective system, meaning no private ownership of agricultural land. The state, under a system of egalitarian rationing, also controlled the distribution of agricultural products and consumer goods for personal consumption. It created monopolies in foreign trade and in critical industries. Central plans set production quotas, ignored the requirements for profit-making and eliminated competition among enterprises. Managers were considered effective if they met state quotas regardless of the quality of the product or whether it simply sat in warehouses after it was finished.

Jobs were guaranteed for everyone willing to work, but severe restrictions were placed on the size, number of employees, and capitalization of non-state enterprises. As a consequence, most factory employees worked in state-owned and controlled enterprises and most "private" enterprises were small in size.

The implementation of the centrally planned system to mobilize human and material resources during the 30-year battle for national independence and reunification resulted in economic distress and hindered economic growth. Large enterprises were run like government agencies, with little concern for profits and losses. Virtually no incentives existed to develop management skills in marketing, quality control, product development, or finance. In most enterprises, labor surpluses were retained even if there was no work for employees to perform. State enterprises were vertically integrated and accumulated large inventories in the face of chronic uncertainty.

For nearly 10 years after reunification in 1975, the North tried to impose its centrally planned system on the whole country. To some extent, the North was successful in creating an "iron rice bowl" mentality throughout the whole country. People came to see a job, and more particularly a certain level of income, as an entitlement. However, while neighboring countries such as Taiwan, Hong Kong, and Singapore were growing and prospering, Vietnam stagnated economically.

EXHIBIT 2 Vietnam Economic Data, 1990 to 1996

	Measure	1990	1991	1992	1993	1994	1995	1996
Population	Millions	67.7	68.6	70.4	72.0	73.5	73.9	75.1
Labor Force	Millions	37.6	38.8	39.9	40.8	41.8	42.8	43.1
GDP (current price)	Trillions Dong	38.2	70.0	101.9	136.0	174.0	222.8	254.5
GDP (constant '89 price)	Trillions Dong	27.0	28.6	31.0	33.3	36.0	39.3	43.1
Industrial Output (constant '89 price)	Trillions Dong	14.0	15.5	17.8	19.7	21.9	21.5	22.3
Exchange Rate (D:$US)	Thousands Dong	N/A	N/A	11.18	10.64	10.98	11.04	11.05

As a result of problems arising from central planning and state ownership, in 1986 the Congress of the Vietnam Communist Party adopted the policy of restructuring (*doi moi*) in order to turn the country from a bureaucratic centralized state-subsidy system to a regulated market economy. In the late 1980s, the government began deregulating the state-owned industrial sector and moving toward privatization.

A lack of capital and hard currency for the economic restructuring forced the government to welcome foreign investors. As a result of these policy changes, foreign direct investment flows into Vietnam rose to an estimated $US 6.3 billion in 1994 from an estimated $US 3.5 billion in 1993. Most foreign investments took the form of JVs, with local partners typically contributing about 30 percent of the capital and foreign investors kicking in about 70 percent. These capital contributions, however, did not directly reflect equity ownership. In many of the JVs, local Vietnamese partners retained 51 percent ownership even if their capital contributions were less. Often plant, equipment, land, and "goodwill" were assigned valuations that made up the difference.

After the implementation of *doi moi* in 1986, Vietnam experienced rapid economic growth. In 1992, for example, Vietnam's gross domestic product (GDP) grew by 8.7 percent and real national income increased by 5.3 percent. Vietnam expanded its industrial sector by 14.5 percent and its agricultural output by 4 percent. The country stabilized its currency, the *dong,* and reduced inflation to 38 percent in 1992 from more than 67 percent the previous year. Inflation had remained basically between 8 percent and 9 percent through 1996.

The government expected this economic growth to continue. (See Exhibit 2 for data on the Vietnamese economy.) However, the government also realized that rapid growth would only be possible with continuing international aid, improved access to international borrowing, reductions in the country's massive budget deficit, and improved controls over inflation. Another roadblock to continued economic growth was government bureaucracy. The government was prone to assess high taxes on foreign investments, which had driven some foreign companies out of Vietnam. Most Western economists believed that Vietnam's long-term development depended on the government's ability to create a

EXHIBIT 3 Map of Vietnam and Area

favorable trade and investment environment, stable economic conditions, and an improved general standard of living.

Infrastructure

Vietnam's infrastructure had suffered from years of inadequate investment and before that, decades of war. Geography also added to the problem. Vietnam stretches 1,600 kilometers from north to south and from a temperate climate in the North to a tropical one in the South (see Exhibit 3). The central areas of the country are covered with dense forests. Vietnam has more than 2,000 rivers over 10 kilometers long. In the early 1990s, only 10 percent of Vietnam's 105,600 kilometers of roads were sealed with asphalt or concrete, and even the best roads were considered to be of very low quality. Given the poor infrastructure, national distribution companies were virtually nonexistent. Moving products from the south to the north or vice versa was expensive and time-consuming.

Labor Structure

In 1996, the minimum wage for laborers working in enterprises with foreign invested capital was $US 35 per month for Hanoi and HCM City and $US 30 per month for other areas of the country. Companies with more capital tended to offer higher salaries to attract the best people. In addition to wages, most enterprises with foreign invested capital were expected to provide employees a daily food allowance, transportation to and from work (if the company was located outside of Hanoi or HCM City), and work clothes.

Organized labor was increasingly making its presence known in both state-controlled and private enterprises. Workers were demanding better working conditions and higher pay and were increasingly using strikes in state and foreign enterprises to make management take their demands seriously. Most of the recent strikes had been over salary disputes and higher productivity demands by firms. In an effort to control labor unrest, the most recent draft of the labor relations bill (in thirtieth revision) passed by the National Assembly in 1996 stated that strikes could only be used as a "last resort." However, the success of recent strikes in gaining workers' demands encouraged their use of it as a "weapon of first resort."

As state-owned enterprises privatized and streamlined their workforce, national unemployment had risen from 5.8 percent in 1992 to 6.7 percent, or 2.2 million people in 1993. The government figures for 1996 put unemployment in the urban areas at 13.2 percent and about 4 percent in the rural areas. However, these figures were believed by most independent experts to understate the true unemployment rate in both the urban and rural areas.

The Vietnamese labor force was relatively young and literate. The literacy rate was about 88 percent for the working age population. The largest group in the labor force, accounting for 53 percent of the total labor force and nearly 29 percent of the total population, was between the ages of 15 and 29. While Vietnam did not face a general labor shortage, skilled workers were in short supply.

Cultural Environment

Generations of Vietnamese had lived through communism, socialism, civil war, and now a type of controlled capitalism. With the exception of farmers, most people were not used to working eight to ten-hour days, six days a week. The effect was especially pronounced in the North.

The effects of the war and socialist system also affected midday activities. At the office, many workers turned off the lights to take a nap around noon. Most shops also closed during this time and business usually picked up again by 2:00 P.M. This practice came about during the years of war when the fighting disrupted normal work schedules and activities. Sleeping also served as a coping mechanism and as a means of dealing with hunger and difficult working conditions. Although conditions had much improved, taking midday naps had remained popular.

Another interesting phenomenon was the emerging inequity gap between 'office' workers and 'factory' workers as the country moved toward industrialization. Most office workers were required to have college degrees, whereas factory workers had no educational requirements. This differential in education was beginning to show up in workers' compensation. Factory workers were increasingly uncomfortable with this rising wage gap. After all, office workers had nice air-conditioned offices to work in, while factory workers had to deal with noise, heat, cold, and humidity, as well as physically demanding and dangerous tasks.

The Vietnamese Soft Drink Industry

The Vietnamese soft drink industry dated back to the pre-1975 era when soft drinks were imported from the United States, France, and other nations. During this time, several foreign companies sold licenses to Vietnamese bottlers to produce their drinks locally. The most widely recognized brand during the 1960s and 1970s was Coca-Cola. Soft drinks were considered a luxury item during that time and were available mostly in Saigon, where the French and later Americans troops were stationed.

After the fall of Saigon, all foreign companies pulled out, and soon Vietnam was left with musty factories and rusty equipment. In the early 1980s, Vietnamese chemists began to formulate their own cola concentrates. However, these beverages were not very successful, and the soft drink market did not pick up again until the implementation of new economic reforms.

Once the Vietnamese government began to change its economic policies and governments such as the United States lifted their restrictions on doing business in the country, foreign investment and interest in Vietnam exploded. To keep themselves from being pushed out of the industry by foreign competition, most locally owned bottling companies began forming JVs with the foreign investors. They sought foreign investors to contribute capital and resources in order to upgrade the neglected facilities, equipment, and technology.

The tropical climate made the soft drink market one of the more attractive investment opportunities in Vietnam. In urban cities in 1997, the average selling price for bottled water was 2,000 dong per bottle.[1] Soft drinks cost between 900 to 2,000 dong. A bottle of beer could run between 2,000 to 5,000 dong.

In 1997, about 80 percent of the soft drinks sold in Vietnam were through large accounts—government ministries, state-owned enterprises, hotels, and restaurants. As economic conditions improved, the consumer segment of the Vietnamese soft drink market started to pick up. Both HCM Beverage Company and VBC had begun to actively target this segment. The keys to winning over consumers were branding and distribution. Despite rising consumer demand, distribution channels were not well developed. Most consumers purchased soft drinks from tiny "hawker stalls" and "mom and pop" stores. Servicing these highly fragmented vendors was difficult and expensive.

HCM BEVERAGE COMPANY'S PROBLEMS

Dinh finally returned to his office at 8:30 A.M. Johnson was impatiently waiting for him. "We had a meeting scheduled for 8:00, not 8:30," Johnson commented in a stern and disapproving voice. Dinh explained that he understood but he was too hungry to wait and did not want to have another ulcer attack. Puzzled, Johnson asked what the normal starting hours were for the marketing staff. Dinh responded in halting English,

> Well, I have been a little lenient on my staff lately because they've been overworked during the last couple of months. We've been understaffed here in this department. I need at least two more people, but I haven't heard anything from Mr. Cao. He keeps telling me that he's looking but I don't see anyone at my doorstep. You know, having the personnel department located out at the factory and reporting through Mr. Cao is a little inconvenient. So, sometimes I let my kids leave early or take longer lunches.

After an abbreviated meeting, Johnson made a mental note to himself to tell his assistant to keep an eye on Dinh and his department.

Johnson's main concern right now was to address the question of declining sales. At the last staff meeting, the sales manager, Mr. Khai, explained that there were several reasons for the sales decline. "First," he explained, "it's the rainy season. People don't drink as much when it rains. Second, it is hard for all salesmen to reach their target accounts in one day because of bad road conditions."

While there was some truth to Mr. Khai's concerns, Johnson believed that the real problem was increasing competition, not a little rain and muddy roads. The decline in sales and profits had been apparent since before he arrived. While Johnson had expected a short-term decline in profits as a result of the new focus on the consumer market segment and spending some extra money on marketing, sales, and promotional activities, the overall decline in sales revenues had been unexpected.

Johnson began to seriously question the level of loyalty among HCM Beverage Company's employees. He wondered if perhaps some were being contacted by the competition to jump ship. He also wondered why some of the larger institutional accounts were slipping in sales volume. When he asked Mr. Khai specifically about the drop in volume from large accounts, Mr. Khai simply repeated his rainy season explanation.

Privately, Johnson suspected it was more closely tied to employee motivations. He had heard rumors that some managers and salespeople were complaining that they were paid too little. Consequently, in August 1997, Johnson had put together a proposal to raise wages for supervisors, managers, senior managers, and directors (see Exhibit 4).

When he had floated the idea past Mr. Cao, he expected significant support because, as a senior manager, Mr. Cao's compensation would significantly increase with the plan. Instead, Mr. Cao gave Johnson a perplexed look and a statement that factory workers were hinting about striking to get higher wages. When Johnson pointed out that HCM Beverage Company factory workers were already being paid more than workers in other factories, Mr. Cao simply stated that now was "not a good time to unsettle the workers." The discussion was left there.

Upcoming Meeting with Patterson

While 1997 year-to-date sales were down by 15 percent, profits were down by nearly 40 percent. The fact that the JV was still profitable would be of little consolation to Kevin Patterson, with whom Johnson had a meeting in two days. Not only were sales down, but Johnson was concerned that Coca-Cola—even though it got a late start re-entering Vietnam—was on the verge of announcing major new investments in Vietnam. With Coca-Cola's much higher brand recognition, Johnson knew that Patterson would want some answers.

With JV profits down, Johnson felt there was no way he could significantly raise factory worker wages in addition to those of management. Although raising the wages for a total of about 30 supervisors, managers, senior managers and directors would also hurt profit margins in the short run, Johnson thought it was necessary to hold on to managerial talent over the long run.

As Johnson contemplated a course of action, a memo arrived from his assistant, Ms. Tracy Nguyen. Johnson had asked Nguyen, a second generation Vietnamese

EXHIBIT 4   **Monthly Wage Distribution for Vietnamese Employees**

$US	Workers	Supervisors	Managers	Senior Managers	Directors

Legend
— Proposed wage levels
✕ ✕ ✕ Current wage levels
━━━ General market levels

Total number of people	300 full-time 200 part-time	64 full-time	21 full-time	5 full-time	3 full-time

who was working for HCM Beverage as an intern from a U.S. MBA program, to make an independent assessment of the marketing and sales staffs. In her memo, she reported the following:

> Marketing and sales staff members continue to trickle in after 8:00 A.M. The day normally begins with everyone at their own desk doing their own thing. By 10 or 11 o'clock, the department is almost empty. Some will be out running personal errands. The ones left behind are either sitting behind a computer playing computer games or socializing.
>
> My lunches with them have been most useful. I found out that they feel the pay is too low at HCM Beverage Company. Also, most are not happy with how things are run. Many of the newcomers (those who have been with the company for less than one year) say that there is no room for personal growth. Of the new people hired in these two departments, three have resigned within the last three months. People say they are tired of putting in extra hours. They feel that they are overworked and underpaid.

In preparing for his meeting with Kevin Patterson in Hong Kong, Johnson had pretty much determined that the pay increase plan was necessary. However, he was not convinced that it alone would solve the sales problem—and it would only worsen the JV's profitability.

> I can't see any way to avoid a pay increase for the office staff. People like Dinh are worked too hard for what they get. It's no wonder they don't show up for meetings on time. Paying them a competitive salary can only help them take their jobs more seriously. Of course, it won't solve all our problems, but I don't think there's any way to avoid a pay increase.

Johnson was also concerned about Mr. Cao's warning to "avoid unsettling the workers." He had talked with Mr. Cao several times since that first statement without much progress as to what was really behind it. Whether the lack of progress was due to reluctance on Mr. Cao's part to talk with Johnson, Mr. Cao's limited English skills, or something else, Johnson was just not sure. Despite Mr. Cao's concern, Johnson just did not feel it was possible from a profitability perspective to significantly raise workers' wages or necessary from a competitive comparison perspective. Still Johnson worried. The company could not afford a strike. The economic and reputational effects could be devastating. If a strike happened, they might as well send out announcements to foreign firms to pick off their dissatisfied employees. Also, the company could not afford to continually spend time and money recruiting and training staff, only to lose them.

As the meeting with Patterson approached, Johnson could feel the knot in his stomach getting tighter and bigger. A marketing job back home seemed awfully appealing at the moment.

> Thinking about this meeting with Patterson has caused me to be more introspective. I realize that the longer I live here, the more frustrated I have become. When I was back home in the States, I could always find a way to make things happen. Here, it sometimes feels as though I'm trying to push water uphill. I also find myself missing things back home more. For example, every Monday night a bunch of us guys used to gather at Joe's [a sport's bar] and watch Monday Night Football. Now I get to read about the game a week later.
>
> Back home, I worked hard but I could leave my job at the office most days. Here my job has become everything. I seem to go from one problem to the next. Even my wife has commented that I seem unhappy and a bit more irritable. In some ways she is doing better than I am. She hasn't gotten over being fascinated with the place. I have.
>
> Anyway, I have to decide what to do. Patterson will want answers, not excuses.

With less than two days to finalize what he was going to present to Patterson, Johnson had little time to spare.

Endnote

1. Exchange rate as of September 1, 1997, was 12,100 VND to US$1.

Chapter Forty

Enron and the Dabhol Power Company

In September 2001, Enron Corporation (Enron) was embroiled in a long-running dispute with various levels of government in India. The dispute involved the Dabhol Power Company (DPC), a 2184-megawatt (MW) power project in the Indian state of Maharashtra. With Phase II of the multibillion dollar project 95 percent complete, Enron announced that it would sell its DPC stake because of payment disputes with its sole buyer, the Maharashtra State Electricity Board (MSEB), and the failure of the Indian central government to honor its counter-guarantee.

In response to the ongoing dispute, Enron CEO Kenneth Lay sent a strongly worded letter to India's Prime Minister Atal Behari Vajpayee questioning the government's willingness to honor its contracts and its future ability to attract foreign investment. Lay wrote:

> Our experience would indicate that contracts with governmental authorities in India really do not seem to represent anything more than a starting point for a later renegotiation and are broken by Indian governmental authorities whenever and as often as they prove inconvenient or burdensome.

ENRON CORPORATION

Houston-based Enron, formed in 1985 in a merger between InterNorth, Inc., and Houston Natural Gas Corp., was involved in various worldwide energy industries. In the 1990s, Enron coined the slogan "Creating Energy Solutions Worldwide" and

its stated vision was to become "The World's Leading Energy Company—creating innovative and efficient energy solutions for growing economies and a better environment worldwide." Enron was the largest natural gas company in the United States and operated the largest gas pipeline system in the world outside of Gazprom in Russia.

In 2001, Enron had five main businesses:[1]

- Enron Wholesale Services delivered natural gas and power and was Enron's largest and fastest-growing business. In 2000, income before interest, minority interests, and taxes (IBIT) rose 72 percent to $2.3 billion, with record physical energy volumes of 51.7 trillion British thermal units equivalent per day (TBtue/d)—a 59 percent increase over 1999.

- Enron Energy Services was the retail arm of Enron, serving business users of energy in commercial and industrial sectors. The value of its contracts in 2000 totaled more than $16 billion, increasing its cumulative contract value to more than $30 billion since late 1997.

- Enron Broadband Services was a new market for bandwidth intermediation. In 2000, Enron completed 321 transactions with 45 counterparties.

- Enron Transportation Services was responsible for U.S. interstate natural gas pipelines and provided innovative solutions to its customers.

- EnronOnline, created in 1999, was Enron's Web-based e-Commerce system used to trade more than 1200 products and streamlined Enron's back-office processes. EnronOnline allowed customers to view Enron's real-time pricing.

Enron's International Projects

Prior to 1985, Enron generated virtually all of its revenue in the United States. By 2001, Enron was involved in energy infrastructure projects across the globe. See Exhibit 1 for a summary of international projects, most of which involved natural gas (note that these projects were at varying stages of completion). The firm had a reputation as a reliable provider of turnkey natural gas projects on a timely basis, virtually all of which were project-financed and had long-term contracts with pricing agreements reached in advance. Revenues were tied to the U.S. dollar and the host government or an outside agency held responsibility for currency conversions. The development of Enron projects involved multifunctional teams that were compensated, in part, based on incentive payments tied to the NPV of the project itself. After projects were completed, operating responsibility shifted from the development team to an Enron operating group (for projects that Enron built and operated).

With reference to Enron's international business, an Enron executive stated:

> We have created a new model based on an at-risk, entrepreneurial culture; we look for opportunity in chaos. . . . we make our own rules; most people look at the world and think too small; when we went to India, the majors said we were crazy.

EXHIBIT 1
Enron International Energy Infrastructure Projects

Africa

Benin	Benin Integrated Gas and Power Project
Mozambique	Maputo Iron and Steel Project, Pande Gas Project
Nigeria	Lagos State Power Project

Middle East

Gaza Strip	Gaza Power Project
Gulf	Dolphin: Gas Supply, Distribution, and Marketing Project

Asia Pacific

Australia	Power Trading
People's Republic of China	Hainan Island Power Project, Chuanzhong Block, Chengdu Cogen Project, Gasification Utility Island for BASF/YPC Integrated, Petrochemical Project (BASF), Sichuan-Wuhan Pipeline & Power Projects & Wuhan Loop
Guam	Enron Piti Power Project
India	Dabhol Power Project, LNG Terminal at Dabhol, MetGas Pipeline Project, LNG Vessel Construction Joint Venture, Gas Authority of India (GAIL)
Japan	Industrial Power Sales and Services
Philippines	Batangas Power Project, Subic Bay Power Project, First Gas Power Corporation Fuel Supply
South Korea	Gas Distribution and Liquefied Petroleum Gas

Central America/Caribbean

Dominican Republic	Puerto Plata Power Project
Guatemala	Puerto Quetzal Power Project, PQPLLC
Jamaica	Industrial Gases Limited
Mexico	Desarollos Hidraulicos de Cancun, Industrias del Agua
Nicaragua	Corinto Power Plant
Panamá	Empresa de Generacion Electrica Bahía Las Minas
Puerto Rico	Ecoelectrica, San Juan Gas, ProCaribe, Progasco

Europe

Croatia	Natural gas combined cycle power plant at Jertovec
Italy	Sarlux Power Project
Poland	Elektrocieplownia Nowa Sarzyna Project
Spain	Arcos de la Frontera, Mora la Nova
Turkey	Trakya Power Project
United Kingdom	Teesside Power Project, TPS Black Start Project, Wilton Power Station, Wessex Water

South America

Argentina	Transportadora de Gas del Sur Pipeline, Gas Marketing, Power Marketing
Bolivia	The Bolivia-to-Brazil Pipeline, Transredes S.A.
Brazil	CEG/Cegrio, Cuiaba Integrated Energy Project, Elektro Electricidade e Serviços S.A., Gaspart
Colombia	Centragas Pipeline, Promigas E.S.P.
Venezuela	Accro III & IV Project, Venatane, Bachaquero III, CALIFE, Citadel Venezolana

MARKET REFORM IN INDIA

India's population of more than one billion inhabited the seventh largest country in the world. Issues of language and religion played a major role in Indian culture, politics, and business. Fifteen national languages were recognized by the Indian constitution and these were spoken in over 1600 dialects. India's official language, Hindi, was spoken by about 30 percent of the population. English was the official working language and, for many educated Indians, virtually their first language. Hinduism was the dominant religion, practiced by over 80 percent of the population. Besides Hindus, Muslims were the most prominent religious group, making up 14 percent of the population.

On a purchasing power parity basis, the Indian economy was the fifth largest in the world. GDP per capita was $2101 in 2001.[2] After India gained its independence from Great Britain in 1947, and until the mid-1980s, the government pursued an economic policy of self-sufficiency. This policy was often referred to as *swadeshi,* a Hindi word meaning indigenous products or made in India. The term was first used by Mahatma Gandhi during the independence movement to encourage people to buy native goods and break the British economic stranglehold on India. To many Indians, *swadeshi* evoked images of patriotism and Indian sovereignty.

After decades of socialist-oriented/statist industrial policy focused on achieving self-sufficiency, India was financially strapped and bureaucratically bloated. High tariffs kept out imports, and official government policy discouraged foreign investment. In the 1970s, Coca-Cola and IBM were among the multinational firms that left India. Efforts to reform the Indian economy began after the 1991 federal elections. The Indian government was on the verge of bankruptcy, and foreign exchange reserves were sufficient for only three months of imports. After considerable prodding by the IMF, then Prime Minister Rao introduced free market reforms in July 1991. India's economic liberalization plan moved the economy away from its traditionally protectionist policies toward actively encouraging foreign participation in the economy. As part of the plan, the Prime Minister's office set up a special "fast-track" Foreign Investment Promotion Board to provide speedy approval for foreign investment proposals. In October 1991, the Government of India opened the power industry to private sector foreign direct investment.

The economic reform program had a powerful effect. From 1994 to 1998, GDP grew at an average of almost 7 percent annually, and inflation remained under 10 percent. Foreign direct investments (FDI) reached a record high of US$2.4 billion in 1998, 20 times higher than in 1991. In January 2001, the country had a record level of $41.1 billion in foreign reserves, up from $13.5 billion in 1994 and only $1 billion 1991. Tariffs, while still high and ranging from 30–65 percent, were one-fifth the level before liberalization. By some estimates, the government's policies had produced up to $100 billion in new entrepreneurial projects in India since 1992.

Despite these efforts to encourage market reform and economic development, many hurdles remained. China attracted 10 times as much FDI. About 40 percent of the industrial economy remained government-owned. Perhaps the greatest impediment to both rapid growth and attracting foreign investment was the lack of infrastructure that met international standards. In particular, India suffered from a substantial electricity shortage.

DEMAND FOR ELECTRICITY

The Indian population was starved for electricity. It was estimated that many of India's industries were able to operate at only half their capacity because of a lack of electric power. Though India had the capacity to produce 100,000 MW, power cuts were an almost daily occurrence and parts of the country were regularly blacked out for days at a time. Analysts estimated that India urgently needed to double its capacity to maintain growth and ease poverty. The government targeted capacity increases of 111,500 MW by 2007.[3]

Virtually all of India's power was generated and managed by state-owned electricity boards (SEBs). It was widely acknowledged that these boards suffered from chronic managerial, financial, and operational problems.[4] Government-run power plants typically operated at about 50 percent capacity. In comparison, the private power plants run by Tata Steel, an Indian company, operated at around 85 percent capacity. Across India, an estimated 30 percent of power was stolen, much of it by factory owners who found that it was cheaper to pay off the SEB than to pay for electricity.

Indian power rates were among the lowest in the world. Most Indian farmers had free, or virtually free, power. Although the SEBs had been trying to raise rates, this had proved to be very difficult. In 1994 in the state of Gujarat, the opposition government encouraged farmers to blockade roads and burn government property after rural power rates were increased. The government was forced to back down and lower the amount of the increase.

Because of these problems and because all levels of government were so short of funds, the Central Government decided to turn to the private sector. The Electricity Act was amended in October 1991 to make this possible. However, the response from the private sector was poor. The act was amended again in March 1992 to provide further incentives, including a 16 percent rate of return to investors. Still, potential investors remained skeptical of the Central Government's commitment to reform and were doubtful of the SEBs' ability to pay for privately generated power. The Government took one more step. In May 1992, a delegation of Indian Central Government officials visited the United States and the United Kingdom to make a pitch for foreign investment in the power sector. The delegation included then Power Secretary S. Rajagopal, Finance Secretary K. Geethakrishan, and Cabinet Secretary Naresh Chandra. The visits were a major success. Many independent power producers (IPPs) immediately sent executives to India. By July 1995, more than 130 Memorandums of Understanding (MOUs) had been signed by the Government of India with IPPs. Twenty-three of the 41 pending electricity projects bid on by non-Indian companies were led by American firms.

THE DABHOL PROJECT

In turning to the private sector for power plant development, the Indian Government decided to give the first few private sector projects the status of pioneer projects; later these projects became known as "fast-track" projects (of which eight such projects were eventually signed). For the fast-track projects, the Central Government decided not to follow the standard public tendering process. Instead, it would negotiate with IPPs for individual projects. The rationale was that the Government was not in a strong negotiating position and, therefore, the financial risk to the IPPs had to be reduced to entice them to invest in India. At a press conference, Power Secretary S. Rajagopal said the first few projects "would not be allowed to fail."

Enron's Rebecca Mark met with the Indian delegation when it visited Houston. In June 1992, Mark and several other Enron employees, at the Indian Government's invitation, visited India to investigate power plant development opportunities. Within days, Enron had identified a potential site for a gas-fired power plant on the western coast of India in the port town of Dabhol, 180 miles south of Bombay in the state of Maharashtra. Maharashtra was India's richest state and the center of Indian industrialization. The huge port city of Bombay was the capital and the headquarters of most of India's major companies, including Air India and Tata Enterprises, the largest Indian industrial conglomerate.

Enron, acting on the Government's assurances that there would not be any tendering on the first few fast-track projects, submitted a proposal to build a 2,015 MW gas-fired power plant. The proposed project would be the largest plant Enron had ever built, the largest of its kind in the world, and, at $2.8 billion, the largest foreign investment in India. The liquefied natural gas (LNG) needed to fuel the Indian power plant would be imported from a plant Enron planned to build in Qatar. The proposal was very favorably received by both the Central Government and officials in the Maharashtra State Government. The Maharashtra State Electricity Board (MSEB) had long wanted to build a gas-fired plant to reduce its dependence on coal and oil.

Enron was the first IPP to formally submit a proposal. Later, in June 1992, Enron signed an MOU with the MSEB. A new company called Dabhol Power Company (DPC) was formed. Enron held 80 percent of the equity in DPC, and its two partners, General Electric and International Generation Co., each held 10 percent. International Generation was a joint venture between Bechtel Enterprises Inc. (Bechtel) and San Francisco-based Pacific Gas & Electric formed in early 1995 to build and operate power plants outside the United States. General Electric was contracted to supply the gas turbines, and Bechtel would be the general contractor. Exhibit 2 lists the various individuals involved with DPC, and Exhibit 3 shows the timing of the various events.

After the MOU was signed, the Maharashtra state requested that the World Bank review the project. A World Bank team found many irregularities in the agreement and noted the government had not set up an overarching framework within which to privatize power in India. The World Bank's analysis concluded that

EXHIBIT 2
**Individuals Involved
in the Dabhol Project**

Name	Title and/or Role
Lal Krishna Advani	President of the Federal BJP Party in 1996
Vinay Bansal	Chairman of MSEB
Manohar Joshi	Chief Minister of Maharashtra, deputy leader of Shiv Sena
Kenneth Lay	CEO of Enron Corporation
Rebecca Mark	Chairman and CEO of Enron
Neil McGregor	Dabhol's President
Gopinath Munde	Deputy Chief Minister of Maharashtra with direct responsibility for the state energy ministry, BJP party member.
Ajit Nimbalkar	Chairman and Managing Director of Maharashtra State Electricity Board
Sharad Pawar	Former Chief Minister of Maharashtra, voted out of office March, 1995; known as the Maratha strongman
Suresh Prabhu	Federal Power Minister in 2001
P.V. Narasimha Rao	Former Prime Minister of India (prior to 1996), and then party leader for Congress (I) Party
N.K.P. Salve	Former Federal Power Minister
Joseph Sutton	Enron Managing Director
Balashaheb "Bal" Thacker	Leader of Shiv Sena
Atal Behari Vajpayee	Prime Minister of India in 2001 and party leader for BJP

the government had not provided an overall economic justification of the project and that the agreement was one-sided in favor of Enron and encouraged the government to "verify Enron's experience" as an electricity generating company before proceeding with the project. The government of India's Central Electricity Authority experts also conducted their own analysis and concluded that the MOU was one-sided in favor of Enron and its partners. Nevertheless, the project went forward.

Following the signing of the MOU, Enron began a complex negotiation process for proposal approval, followed by more negotiations on the actual financial details. Officially, no power project could be developed without technical and economic clearance from the Central Electricity Authority. Typically, this process could take many months, or possibly years. The Foreign Investment Promotion Board (FIPB) was the Central Government's vehicle for a speedy approval process. The FIPB asked the Central Electricity Authority to give initial clearance to the Dabhol project without the detailed information normally required. However, final clearance would still be necessary at a later date.

In November 1992, Enron made a detailed presentation at a meeting chaired by the Central Government Finance Secretary and attended by various other senior government officials, including the chairman of the MSEB. (Note: The Finance Secretary was the senior civil servant in the finance department and reported directly to the Finance Minister.) From this meeting came a recommendation to the FIPB to approve the project. In turn, the Central Power Ministry, acting on the advice of the FIPB, asked the Central Electricity Authority to expedite the approval process. The Central Electricity Authority gave an in-principle (not

EXHIBIT 3
Timing of Events
Associated with
Dabhol Power
Company

October 1991	Government of India invites private sector participation in the power sector
May 1992	Indian delegation visits UK and US; Enron invited to India by government of India
June 1992	Maharashtra State Electricity Board signs MOU with Enron
February 1993	Foreign Investment Promotion Board (FIPB) grants approval
March 1993	Power Purchase Agreement negotiations start
November 1993	Central Electricity Authority clears Dabhol project
February 1994	Government of Maharashtra signs guarantee
September 1994	Government of India signs guarantee
March 1995	Dabhol financing completed
March 1995	Maharashtra State election results announced
April 1995	Construction begins; Government of Maharashtra orders a review; Munde Committee set up to investigate Dabhol Project
August 1995	Project canceled by Government of Maharashtra
January 1996	New Deal announced
December 1996	Indian High Court dismisses last of 25 lawsuits filed by workers unions and environmental groups; construction resumes
December 1996	London tribunal agrees to terminate arbitration proceedings against State Government of Maharashtra
February 1997	Police detain 1,400 trade union protesters at the construction site
May 1999	Phase 1 begins operation; Financing for Phase II secured for $1.87 billion
September 1999	Congress (I) Party wins Maharashtra state elections
August 2000	Rebecca Mark leaves Enron
December 2000	Maharashtra government official announces that the Dabhol contract should be renegotiated because the power cost is too high
January 2001	Enron no longer interested in building power plants in India; Enron assisting Indian government in redrafting Electricity Act
February 2001	Dabhol invokes Indian government guarantee to collect $17 million in overdue bills
April 2001	Enron issued a notice of arbitration to India's government to recover, at the Court of Arbitration in London, $21.9 million
April 2001	MSEB agrees to pay $28.6 million and says there are no more outstanding bills
May 2001	State government sets up a panel, the Godbole Committee set up to study PPA; MSEB rescinds contract to buy electricity from Dabhol; Enron rejects payment of $29.1 million because it came with a note saying it was submitted "under protest,"
September 2001	Letter to India PM from Ken Lay

final) clearance to proceed with the project since the Ministry of Finance had found the project satisfactory.

In March 1993, with the necessary government approvals largely in place, Enron was in a position to negotiate the financial structure of the deal. The most critical element was a Power Purchasing Agreement (PPA) with the MSEB. The PPA was the contract under which Enron, as the owner of the power plant, would supply power to the MSEB electric grid. Over the next year or so, Rebecca Mark visited India 36 times. Ajit Nimbalkar, chairman and managing director of MSEB, described the negotiations:

This is the first project of this kind that we are doing. MSEB did not have any experience in dealing with international power developers. It was a complicated exercise, for the money involved is large, and so the negotiations took a long time.[5]

MSEB turned to the World Bank for advice in the negotiations. The World Bank offered to fund a team of international consultants. The MSEB chose Freshfields, a British law firm, and the British office of the German Westdeuche Landesbank Girozentale as consultants in the PPA negotiations. The World Bank concluded that the project was "not economically viable," citing that the type of plant proposed would produce too much power at too high a price for the state.[6] Again, the World Bank's advice was not heeded and negotiations continued. In addition to negotiating the project financial structure and gaining state and central government approvals, Enron had to obtain dozens of other government approvals, some of which were based on regulations dating back to British colonial times. For example, to get permission to use explosives on the construction site, Enron had to visit the western Indian town of Nagpur, where British Imperial forces once stored munitions.[7]

In November 1993, the Central Electricity Authority officially cleared the Dabhol project. In December 1993, the MSEB signed the Dabhol PPA. The state government of Maharashtra signed a financial guarantee in February 1994 and the Central Government signed a guarantee in September 1994. These guarantees provided financial protection for Enron in the event that the MSEB was unable make its payments. The Central Government's guarantee, which was to become very controversial, was signed with Enron before the government's guarantee policy was announced publicly.

STRUCTURE OF THE DABHOL PROJECT

Although the original plans were for a 2015-MW project, the Maharashtra government decided to break the project into two phases. Phase I would be a 695-MW plant using distillate fuel instead of natural gas, and Phase II would be a 1320-MW gas-fired plant. The capital cost for Phase I would be $920 million, with an estimated turnkey construction cost of $527 million.[8] The second phase would cost about $1.9 billion.

Dabhol was broken into two phases because Enron had been unable to finalize its gas contracts and because the government had become concerned about the mounting criticism of the project. The shift from gas to distillate was done because distillate could be sourced from local refineries, helping deflect the criticism that gas imports would be a persistent drain on India's foreign exchange. Furthermore, using distillate instead of gas eliminated the need to build a port facility for Phase I.

The capital cost for Phase I included some costs for infrastructure items that would normally have been provided by the state, such as a pipeline. If these costs were deducted from the total capital cost, the cost per MW was comparable with the other fast-track power plant projects. However, Dabhol was the only project that had been finalized. The other projects were still going through planning and approval stages.

The Indian Government generally followed what was known as a fixed rate of return model. Investors were assured a 16 percent rate of return on net worth for a plant load factor of up to 68.5 percent. Beyond 68.5 percent, the rate of return on equity would increase by a maximum of 0.70 percent for each 1 percent rise in the plant load factor. Net worth was based on the total costs of building the power plant. The main objection against this model was that it provided no incentive to minimize the capital costs of investment.

The Dabhol project used a different model. An estimated tariff of Rs2.40 ($1 equaled about 36 rupees) per unit (kilowatt/hour) of electricity was established. The tariff consisted of two components: (1) a capacity charge of Rs1.20 based on the capital cost of the plant and operating and maintenance costs, and (2) an energy charge of Rs1.20 for the price of fuel. It was estimated that the plant would run at 90 percent capacity. MSEB had to make capacity payments on the established baseload capacity irrespective of the actual power purchased (a so-called take-or-pay contract). The energy charge was based on estimated fuel costs and could rise or fall. Both the capacity and energy charges had a mix of rupee and dollar components. The MSEB was required to bear the exchange risk.

With this type of tariff, the problems of a cost-plus system were eliminated and consumers would not be affected by increases in the capital cost of the project. However, the tariff was not fixed and, in particular, changes in fuel costs and exchange rates would impact the power price. For Enron and its partners, there was an incentive to become more efficient to improve shareholder returns. Based on the capital costs per MW, Dabhol was comparable to other proposed projects in India. As to the tariff of Rs2.40, other fast-track power projects had similar tariffs, as did several recently approved public sector projects. Several existing public sector plants were selling power in the Rs2.15 range (although the average tariff for state electricity boards in India was Rs1.20). Enron's projected internal rate of return on the project was 26.5 percent before tax. Dabhol was granted a five-year tax holiday and the initial purchase agreement was for 20 years. Failure to achieve electricity targets would result in substantial penalty payments by the DPC to the MSEB. In the event that MSEB and DPC could not settle disagreements, international arbitration proceedings in London would be possible as specified in the PPA.

Nevertheless, because there was no competitive bidding on the Dabhol project, critics argued that the Rs2.40 per unit was too high and that the company would be making huge profits. Kirit Parekh, director of the Indira Gandhi Institute of Development and Research, was an ardent critic:

> In the United States, power generated from gas-based plants is sold to utilities at 3–4 cents while Enron is charging 7 cents. It is a rip-off. The China Power Company, which is setting up a 2000-MW power plant in Hong Kong, and which will go on stream in 1996, is doing so at 15 percent less capital than Enron.[9]

Further criticism was directed at the company's lack of competitive bidding for its principal equipment supplier, General Electric, and its construction partner, Bechtel. Although General Electric and Enron had worked closely in the past, some critics suggested that foreign equipment suppliers were favored over Indian suppliers. Enron countered with the argument that it had awarded more than 60 contracts worth more than $100 million (Rs3.6 billion) to Indian companies.

Enron was also subject to criticism because of its plan to import gas for Phase II from its gas processing plant in Qatar. When completed, this plant would be owned by a joint venture between Enron Oil & Gas and the Qatar government. Although Enron vigorously denied it, critics suggested that Enron would make excessive profits through transfer pricing and charging arbitrary prices for the fuel. From Enron's perspective, taking responsibility for fuel supply was a means of reducing its risk, since the contract specified penalties when the plant was not able to generate electricity. Fuel supply failure would not constitute sufficient grounds for being unable to generate electricity.

The federal guarantee also came in for criticism. A World Bank report questioned the guarantee arrangement because, in its opinion, it was nothing more than a loan made by the federal government on behalf of the MSEB if it could not cover its payments to Enron. Enron's Sutton countered:

> It is only after the government of India decided as a policy to give guarantees that we also decided to ask. It would have been impossible to raise money from international bankers at competitive rates without the guarantee when others are approaching the same bankers with guarantees in their pockets.[10]

INDIAN POLITICS AT THE CENTRAL LEVEL

India's political process was based on a parliamentary system. From 1947 to 1989, some form of the Congress Party ruled India at the national, or central, level in an unbroken string of governments. Indira Gandhi, who had been Prime Minister since 1964, founded the Congress (I) Party after her defeat in the 1977 election. In 1980, Indira Gandhi and the Congress (I) Party regained power. After Indira Gandhi was assassinated in 1984, her son Rajiv became Prime Minister. In the 1989 election, Congress (I) lost and turned power over to a minority government. During the 1991 election campaign, Rajiv Gandhi was assassinated and P.V. Narasimha Rao became Congress (I) Party leader. Congress (I) regained power in a minority government Rao became Prime Minister. Rao resigned as party president in September 1996 after being charged with bribery.

In 1998, the Bharatiya Janata Party (BJP) led a 13-party coalition that defeated the Congress (I) Party. The BJP's leader, Atal Behari Vajpayee, became the Prime Minister. In English, BJP translated to the Indian People's Party. The BJP platform emphasized support for traditional Hindu goals and values, making the party less secular than the Congress (I) Party. Many of its members belonged to the urban lower middle class and distrusted free-market reforms and modern cultural values. The BJP believed it could build support among the business community that sought decentralization and deregulation but resented intervention on the part of foreign multinationals.

In the early 1990s, the BJP was openly affiliated with the Hindu fundamentalist movement known as Rashtriya Swayamsevak Sangh (RSS), which translated as

National Volunteers Core. In 1990, the RSS formed the Swadeshi Jagaran Manch, or National Awakening Forum, to promote economic nationalism. The Forum deemed the marketing of Western consumer goods frivolous and wasteful ("India needs computer chips, not potato chips"). According to the Forum's Bombay representative, "Soft drinks and instant cereals do not serve the mass of Indian people. We are not pleased with the way [Coke and Pepsi] are demolishing their rivals."[11] After elections in 1996, the BJP realized that it had been crippled by its identification as an extremist party. The central BJP government elected in 1998 took a more moderate stance, and its economic policy included free-market liberalization, except in sensitive areas where it still maintained economic nationalism.[12]

STATE POLITICS AND THE 1995 MAHARASHTRA ELECTION

The political parties of the 25 Indian states level mirrored those at the central level, although the Congress (I) historically had been less dominant. The BJP was particularly strong in the industrial, heavily populated, and largely Hindu northern states. Decision-making was decentralized in India, and many of the states had a substantial amount of power and autonomy.

On February 12, 1995, a state election was held in Maharashtra. Results were to be announced about four weeks later because the chief election commissioner in Maharashtra had a policy of delinking voting from the counting of votes. The incumbent Congress (I) Party and an alliance between the BJP and Shiv Sena parties were the primary contestants. State elections were normally held every five years. In the previous election in 1990, the Congress (I) Party had formed a majority government under Chief Minister Sharad Pawar. Pawar was confident of retaining power in the 1995 election.

The Shiv Sena was a Maharashtra-based party with the stated objective of protecting the economic interests and identity of Maharashtrians and safeguarding the interests of all Hindus. The official leader of Shiv Sena was Manohar Joshi, but he had limited power and openly admitted that the real authority was Bal Thackeray (sometimes referred to as Mr. Remote Control for his ability to control the party from an unofficial capacity). Thackeray was a newspaper cartoonist before he became a right-wing activist. A talented organizer and rousing orator, he set up the Shiv Sena Party in the mid 1960s to appeal to poor Hindus who resented the influence of foreigners and non-Maharashtrians, particularly those from South India. Thackeray was prone to provocative and somewhat threatening statements. He proposed changing the name of India to Hindustan and, during the Maharashtra election, talked about chasing non-Maharashtrians out of the state.

The Dabhol power project was a major campaign issue leading up to the 1995 election. Election Commission norms in India prohibited a state government from making decisions on vital matters in the run-up to an election. However, the BJP and Shiv Sena did not make this an issue in February. Had they done so, the Election Commission might have ordered the state government to defer the decision on Dabhol.

The BJP/Shiv Sena election campaign rhetoric left little doubt as to their sentiments—one of their slogans was "Throw Enron into the Arabian Sea." The BJP platform promoted economic nationalism and sovereignty and denounced the Dabhol project. The BJP attempted to isolate Chief Minister Pawar as the only defender of Enron. The Dabhol project was described as a typical case of bad government: the failure of the ruling party to stand up to pressure from multinationals, corruption, and compromises on economic sovereignty. The BJP had always been opposed to the project for various reasons: the social and environmental aspects, alleged bribes, the project's cost, and the lack of competitive bidding. The BJP/Shiv Sena campaign strategy painted the Congress (I) Party as anti-poor, corrupt, and partial to foreign firms. This platform evidently appealed to Maharashtrians. On March 13, the election results were announced. The BJP/Shiv Sena coalition won 138 of 288 seats in the election and, with the help of several independent members, formed the new government. The Shiv Sena's Manohar Joshi became the new Chief Minister.

Not long after the election, Enron CEO Kenneth Lay noted, "If something happens now to slow down or damage our power project, it would send extremely negative signals to other foreign investors."[13]

CONSTRUCTION BEGINS

On March 2, 1995, Enron completed the financing for Phase I of the Dabhol project. Phase I financing would come from the following sources:

- A 12-bank syndication led by the Bank of America and ABN-Amro (loans of $150 million)

- U.S. Export-Import Bank ($300 million; arranged by GE and Bechtel)

- The U.S.-based Overseas Private Investment Corp. ($298 million)

- Industrial Development Bank of India ($98 million)

Construction was soon under way. But, almost simultaneously, the new state government in Maharashtra, in keeping with its campaign promises, decided to put the project under review.

THE MUNDE COMMITTEE

One week after coming to power, Deputy Chief Minister and state BJP president Gopinath Munde ordered a review of the Dabhol project. The committee formed to carry out the review had two members from the BJP and two from the Shiv Sena. Munde, a known critic of Dabhol, was the Chairman. An open invitation to individuals to appear before the committee was followed up by letters to the MSEB and Dabhol Power Company. The committee was scheduled to submit its report by July 1.

Over the next few months, the committee held more than a dozen meetings and visited the site of the power plant. The committee was assisted by five state government departments: energy, finance, industries, planning, and law. All requests for appearances before the committee were granted. Among those making depositions were: environmental groups, energy economists, a former managing director of the Bombay Suburban Electric Supply Company, representatives of other IPPs, and representatives of the IPP Association. The Industrial Development Bank of India, a prime lender to the project, representatives from the former state government, and the Congress (I) Party did not appear before the committee.

During the committee hearings, the BJP continued its public opposition to Dabhol. The issue of irregularities—a euphemism for bribes—was raised. According to a senior BJP official:

> Though it is impossible to ascertain if kickbacks were paid to [former Maharashtra Chief Minister] Pawar, even if we can obtain circumstantial evidence, it is enough. The project has been padded up and if the review committee can establish that, it is sufficient to cancel the project.[14]

Allegations of bribery were vigorously denied by Enron. Joseph Sutton, Enron's managing director in India, had told delegates at India Power '95, a conference on the power sector held in New Delhi in March, "during the three years we have been here, we have never been asked for, nor have we paid, any bribes."[15]

On June 11, the RSS (the Hindu fundamentalist group) issued a directive to the BJP that it would like the party to honor its commitment to the *swadeshi* movement. The economic advisor to the Central BJP Party, Jay Dubashi, said:

> We think canceling this project will send the right signals. It will demonstrate that we are not chumps who can be taken for a ride. Enron probably never imagined that Sharad Pawar [former Maharashtra Chief Minister] would go out of power. They thought he would see the deal through.[16]

Pramod Mahajan, the BJP's All-India Secretary, was also fervently against Dabhol, stating that "we will go to court if necessary and decide in the long-term interest of the country."[17] Mahajan also ruled out paying penalties to Enron if the project were scrapped.

Meanwhile, Enron officials were shuttling back and forth between New Delhi and Bombay, trying to convince the press and the government of the viability of the Dabhol project. At one point, the U.S. ambassador to India, Frank Wisner, met with BJP president, L.K. Advani. Advani refused to meet Enron officials (in 1996, Advani was indicted on corruption charges). The issue was even discussed during U.S. Treasury Secretary Robert Rubin's visit to India in April. According to the Assistant Secretary of the Treasury, "we pushed for resolution of the issue."[18] In May 1995, the U.S. Department of Energy warned that failure to honor the contract would jeopardize most, if not all, other private projects proposed for international financing in India. Maharashtra had attracted more than $1 billion of U.S. investment, and more than half of all FDI projects in India were in this state. Furthermore, more than 25 percent of all FDI in India was from the United States.

In the meantime, Bechtel had not stopped construction. A spokesman for Bechtel said the company could not afford to have its 1300 workers idled during a month-long review. "We have to meet a schedule; we have to provide power according to the power purchase agreement."[19]

CANCELLATION OF THE DABHOL PROJECT

The Munde Committee report was submitted to the Maharashtra government on July 15, 1995. Prior to the release of the report, N.K.P. Salve, India's Power Minister, stressed that the "Enron contract can be canceled only if there is a legal basis for doing so, not for any arbitrary or political reason."[20] On August 2, the Indian Supreme Court dismissed a petition by a former Maharashtra legislator challenging the Dabhol project on the grounds of secrecy.

On August 3, Chief Minister Joshi (who had visited the United States in the previous month to attract investment to India) announced to the Maharashtra legislature that the cabinet unanimously agreed to suspend Phase I of the project and scrap Phase II. The following are excerpts from Chief Minister Joshi's lengthy statement in the Assembly:

> The Enron project in the form conceived and contracted for is not in the best interests of the state. . . . The sub-committee whole-heartedly recommends that the Enron-MSEB contract should be canceled forthwith. . . . Considering the grave issues involved in the matter and the disturbing facts and circumstances that have emerged pointing to extra-commercial considerations and probable corruption and illegal motives at work in the whole affair, immediate action must be initiated under the penal and anti-corruption laws by police.
>
> The wrong choice of LNG as fuel and huge inflation in capital costs, along with unprecedented favours shown to Enron in different ways, including in the fuel procurement [had all resulted in an] unreasonable fuel cost to the consumers. . . . The documentary evidence obtained by the committee shows beyond any reasonable doubt that the capital cost of Enron Plant was inflated and jacked up by a huge margin. The committee believes that the extent of the inflation may be as high as $700 million. . . . Being gas-based, this project should have been cheaper than coal-based ones but, in reality, it turns out to be the other way about.
>
> The Government should have sought some part of this for itself. . . . This contract is anti-Maharashtra. It is devoid of any self-respect; it is one that mortgages the brains of the State which, if accepted, would be a betrayal of the people. This contract is no contract at all and if, by repudiating it, there is some financial burden, the State will accept it to preserve the wellbeing of Maharashtra.[21]

Other grounds were given for cancellation: there had been no competitive bidding; Enron held secret negotiations and used unfair means to win its contract; there was potential environmental damage to a region that was relatively unpolluted; the guaranteed return was well above the norm; and concerns about the $20 million earmarked by Enron for education and project development. The BJP government charged that concessions granted to Enron would cause the state of Maharashtra to lose more than $3.3 billion in the future. The committee was also outraged that loose ends in the Dabhol project were being tied up by the Maharashtra government as late as February 25, almost two weeks after the state election. In effect, the contract had been made effective by an administration that had already been rejected by voters.

When the decision was announced, then Prime Minister Rao was on a trade and investment promotion trip to Malaysia. He indicated that the economic liberalization policies initiated by his government would not be affected by this decision. Sharad Pawar, the Chief Minister of Maharashtra at the time the original agreement was signed with Enron, criticized the BJP's decision to cancel the Dabhol power project:

> If the government of Maharashtra was serious about the industrialization of Maharashtra, and its power requirements for industrialization and agriculture, they definitely would have appointed an expert group who understands the requirement of power, about overall projection, about investment which is coming in the fields of industry and agriculture, legal sides, but this particular angle is totally missing here and that is why I am not so surprised for this type of decision which has been taken by the government of Maharashtra.[22]

On the day after the government's cancellation announcement, the *Saamna* newspaper, known as the voice of the nationalist Shiv Sena Party, published a headline that read, "Enron Finally Dumped into the Arabian Sea." Later that week, *The Economic Times* in Bombay reported that local villagers celebrated the fall of Enron.

About 2600 people were working on the Dabhol power project, and it was nearly one-third complete. More than $300 million had been invested in the project, and estimated costs per day if the project were shut down would be $200,000 to $250,000. Cancellation of Phase II was less critical because Enron had not yet secured financing commitments for this portion of the project.

A few days before the Munde Committee report was made public and anticipating a cancellation recommendation, Rebecca Mark had offered publicly to renegotiate the deal. She told the media that the company would try to meet the concerns of the MSEB. On August 3, Enron announced that while it was aware of the reported announcement in the Maharashtra Assembly on the suspension of Dabhol, the company had received no official notice to that effect. The statement issued in Houston said:

> [Enron] remains available for discussions with the government on any concerns it may have. . . . [Enron] has very strong legal defenses available to it under the project contracts and fully intends to pursue these if necessary. The DPC and the project sponsors would like to reiterate that they have acted in full compliance with Indian and U.S. laws.[23]

RENEGOTIATION

Shortly after receiving a single sentence note from the Maharashtra state government canceling the project, Enron filed for arbitration (in London), claiming $300 million in damages. The arbitration date was set for November 17, 1995. Meanwhile, DPC

EXHIBIT 4
Renegotiated Terms for the Dabhol Power Project

1. Tariff for Phase I reduced from Rs2.4/MW to Rs2.03/MW. Tariff for Phase II reduced from Rs2.4/MW to Rs1.86/MW.
2. Phase I increased in capacity from 695MW to 740MW. The overall project increased from 2015MW to 2184MW.
3. Cost savings from capital cost reductions in Phase II of the project and price reductions from GE and Bechtel.
4. Regasification project taken out of the project. Phase II to use LNG from an Enron project in Qatar. This reduced the overall capital costs by US$300 million.
5. MSEB given an option to purchase 30 percent of the equity in DPC.
6. Switch from distillate to naphtha for Phase I.

and its sponsors signed a standstill agreement with all international lenders that froze current loan agreements for DPC and extended protection to its creditors.

In September, Enron opened the doors to a negotiated settlement by publicly offering to lower the tariff to a rate similar to other Indian power projects. In January 1996, Enron announced that DPC had received a formal offer from the government of Maharashtra state to revive the project. The Maharashtra government said that it would go ahead with the project if the American partners reduced the cost of the power to be sold to the state. Enron then offered to reduce the capital cost of the project and lower the price of that power. As well, the MSEB was given the option to acquire a 30 percent equity stake in DPC. Although press reports indicated that DPC's expected rate of return dropped because of the new deal, a senior executive at Enron described the power tariff reduction as a "price reduction that was not really a price reduction. . . . Why? Because of technological advances, falling hardware costs, weakening rupee." According to Rebecca Mark:

> It's [the renegotiated deal] resulted in a good project for India and a structure that will allow us to recover our costs, including our suspension costs, and provide a very fair return to our shareholders. . . . We now have a better idea of the LNG costs, now that Enron has a more solid agreement with the government of Qatar. That's allowed us to reduce the cost of the power plant to $2 billion. Regasification will add $400 million-plus to the project. But that will be recovered through a separate gas charge.[24]

By April 1996, the new contract had been approved by the Maharashtra state cabinet, and final approval was given in July 1996. See Exhibit 4 for details on the new deal. In December 1996, 16 months after the project was suspended, construction resumed. Despite the problems with DPC, Enron continued to pursue and bid on other projects in India.

COMPLETION OF PHASE ONE

In May 1999, Phase 1 was completed and became operational. Also in May, Enron secured financing for the $1.87 billion Phase II and by the end of the year had signed long-term gas supply agreements with Oman LNG and Abu Dhabi Gas.

The second-phase financing used basically the same lenders as Phase I, with the exception of two Export-Import Banks from Japan and Belgium, which replaced the U.S. Export-Import Bank. U.S. sanctions resulting from India's nuclear testing had suspended lending by the U.S. Export-Import Bank. The financing included five loans totaling $1.414 billion, plus an equity investment of $452 million from Enron, GE, and Bechtel, based on their ownership percentage. Phase II did not have a central government counter-guarantee.

At around the same time, Enron pulled out of a $500 million LNG project in Kerala, blaming regulatory delays that had put construction two years behind. Enron was actively pursuing other nonpower projects in India. In November 1999, Enron signed an MOU with an undersea-cable operator and was in negotiations for a venture to build a fiber-optic telecommunications network in India.

NEW PROBLEMS

In a Maharashtra state election campaign in September 1999, Congress (I) Party leadership promised, if elected, to halt DPC's second phase and renegotiate the power tariff. However, Congress (I) Party leaders in New Delhi quickly distanced themselves from the anti-Enron rhetoric. A Congress official dismissed the statement as an expression of frustration by local politicians who were struggling to regain control of Maharashtra. The Congress (I) Party eventually formed a coalition government that included the Janata Dal and the Peasants and Workers Party. The Maharashtra State Electricity Board Workers' Federation also demanded renegotiation of the PPA and scrapping of the second stage of the venture.

In December 1999, Maharashtra again found itself with a power deficit. MSEB announced that certain rural areas would have uninterrupted power for only five days a week. Once Phase II of the DPC project was completed, it was expected that Maharashtra would be a power-surplus state. Also in December, Maharashtra deputy Chief Minister and Home Minister Chagan Bhujbal said at a press conference:

> We do not want to repeat the previous government's mistake of attempting to stop the [Dabhol] project. The government wants to examine how the previous government sanctioned Phase II of the project without examining the result of the first phase. Secondly, it will also review the tariff. Thirdly, it will examine whether the project was essential for a state like Maharashtra.[25]

Facing huge financial losses, the MSEB agreed in November 2000 to sell half of its 30 percent stake in DPC (acquired after the renegotiations in 1996) to Enron. This reduced the MSEB's overall stake in DPC to 15 percent and increased Enron's equity to 65 percent.

Also in November 2000, new problems arose. The MSEB's take-or-pay PPA was based on 90 percent capacity utilization. The greater the capacity utilized, the lower the per unit cost of power to MSEB. At this time, the MSEB was purchasing between 33 percent and 60 percent of the output of DPC. The government's explanation for reducing the off-take from DPC was that demand for power in the state had not grown as estimated earlier. In any event, it looked increasingly unlikely that the MSEB would be able to pay for electricity from DPC over the next few months. A declining rupee and a dollar-denominated price and increased naptha costs were contributing to higher charges for DPC power.

On February 6, 2001, Enron invoked the central government's counter-guarantee to recover $17 million that was owed by the MSEB for November 2000 power. Dabhol's president, Neil McGregor, said the government must "recognize the serious domestic and international implications of contractual agreements not being honored."[26] India's federal Power Minister, Suresh Prabhu, said that the government was "obliged to pay and [will] definitely make the payment." Enron was the first foreign company to invoke the central government's counter-guarantee.

In March 2001, MSEB imposed a claim of about $86 million on DPC for taking five hours to restart the plant after a brief shutdown, two hours longer than the contract specified. Enron disputed the claim and said that the timing suggested the MSEB was looking for ways to absolve themselves from payments that were contractually due. DPC then threatened to cut off electricity, in an effort to protect the project lenders, who had expressed concerns about difficulties getting payments. MSEB had failed to make payments since December.

On April 27, 2001, MSEB paid its March bill after Enron said it might stop selling power to the utility. In an unusual twist, DPC rejected the $29.1 million check to make a legal point (the check was then direct-deposited in a DPC bank account). DPC also delivered a sharply worded four-page letter to MSEB responding to the utility's decision to rescind its power-purchasing contract based on a claim that Dabhol misrepresented its "ramp-up" speed—the time the plant takes to go from a cold start to full power.

In May 2001, DPC turned up the heat by taking a formal step toward ending its contract with MSEB. DPC issued a preliminary termination notice, the first of several prescribed steps toward ending the contract, and said it was owed $48 million. This triggered a six-month cooling-off period. Vinay Bansal, chairman of MSEB, said it would respond to the notice. Prior to this incident, the state government had set up a panel, the Godbole Committee, to study the contract between Dabhol and MSEB. In July 2001, the MSEB was no longer buying power from DPC. In August, the Godbole Committee concluded that "the venture was always too big and too expensive for the state of Maharashtra to handle." One passage in the report described how "numerous infirmities" in the approvals process "bring into question the propriety" of such decisions.

ENRON'S RESPONSE

Enron announced that it was open to ideas, but rejected the Godbole report as a basis for discussions. Construction on Phase 2, which was 95 percent completed, was stopped and thousands of workers were laid off. In the meantime, Cogentrix of the United States, National Power of the UK, Daewoo of Korea, and Electricite de France had withdrawn from the Indian power sector over the previous two years.

In the September letter from Enron CEO Ken Lay to the Indian Prime Minister, Lay proposed selling the DPC equity for approximately $1.2 billion and the purchase of offshore lender's debt for $1.1 billion, for a total cost of $2.3 billion. He also said that "this amount strikes me as exceptionally reasonable when compared to the size of our legal claim," which Enron estimated to be between $4–5 billion. Lay concluded that if Enron were to get anything less than its full investment, it would consider this to be "an act of expropriation" by the Indian government.

Endnotes

1. Enron Annual Report, 2000.
2. Country Watch, http://www.countrywatch.com/includes/grank/gdpnumeric ppp.asp.
3. India Country Forecast, *The PRS Group, Inc.,* November 20, 2001, p. 53.
4. Michael Schuman, India Has a Voracious Need for Electricity: U.S. Companies Have a Clear Inside Track, *Forbes,* April 24, 1995.
5. Bodhisatva Ganguli & Tushar Pania, The Anatomy of a Controversial Deal, *Business India,* April 24-May 7, 1995, p. 57.
6. *The New York Times,* March 20, 2001, C1.
7. Marcus W. Brauchli, A Gandhi Legacy: Clash Over Power Plant Reflects Fight in India for Its Economic Soul, *The Wall Street Journal,* April 27, 1995, A6.
8. Ganguli & Pania, p. 59.
9. Ganguli & Pania, p. 58.
10. Ganguli & Pania, p. 56.
11. India Power Down: A Major Blow to Rao's Reform Drive, *AsiaWeek,* August 18, 1995.
12. India Country Forecast, *The PRS Group, Inc.,* December 1, 2001, p. 28.
13. Emily MacFarquhar, A Volatile Democracy, *U.S. News and World Report,* March 27, 1995, p. 37.
14. Ganguli & Pania, p. 56.
15. Ganguli & Pania, p. 55.
16. Ibid.
17. Ibid.
18. Ibid.
19. *San Francisco Business Times,* May 5, 1995 Sec. 1, p. 1.
20. Foreign Investment in India: The Enron Disease, *The Economist,* July 29, 1995, p. 48.
21. Indian State Axes $2.8 BN Dabhol Power Project, in *International Gas Report, The Financial Times,* August 4; Mahesh Vijapurkar, Enron Deal Scrapped, Ongoing Work Halted, *The Hindu,* August 4, p. 1.
22. All-India Doordarshan Television, 3 August 1995.
23. Vijapurkar, p. 1.
24. Gottschalk, Arthur, "Cabinet's OK Brings Enron Closer to Completing India Power Deal," *Journal of Commerce,* January 9, 1996.
25. State Govt Will Review Enron Project, Says Bhujbal, *The Economic Times of India,* December 7, 1999.
26. *The Wall Street Journal,* July 2, 2001, A21.

Chapter Forty-One

Crisis at Renault: The Vilvoorde Plant Closing (A)

The news took almost everyone by surprise. Late in the afternoon of February 27, 1997, Renault S.A., France's second-largest auto maker, announced that it would close its plant in Vilvoorde, Belgium, effective July 31. Vilvoorde's 3,100 employees would be out of work in just five months.

According to a Renault spokesperson, the move was necessary in order to "streamline its industrial facilities." Production at Vilvoorde would be transferred to existing plants in France and Spain, where only 1,900 workers would be needed to produce the same number of autos that had been built in Belgium. By consolidating production at fewer plants, Renault expected an annual savings of FFr850 million ($160 million) beginning in 1998.

Reaction to the Vilvoorde plant closing was swift and angry. Labor unions, politicians, and community leaders in Belgium and France expressed outrage at Renault's sudden and "brutal" decision. Vilvoorde's workers were stunned, not only because they had received no advance warning of the closure, but because by all indications their plant was profitable and running well. As recently as 1995, Renault had spent $226 million to modernize the plant—hardly an indication of impending closure.

Over the next months, repercussions of the Vilvoorde plant closure dominated European economic news. By May, initial shock had given way to deeper questions about the future of European employment in an era of intense global competition, especially in industries with substantial overcapacity. Questions were also raised about the responsibility of corporations towards their employees and other stakeholders.

RENAULT S.A.: A BRIEF COMPANY HISTORY

Renault S.A. traced its origins to 1898, when 21-year old Louis Renault assembled a motor vehicle in the Paris suburb of Billancourt. Along with his brothers, Marcel and Fernand, Louis Renault established Renault Frères and produced the world's first sedan in 1899. Over the next decades the company prospered, selling automobiles, trucks, tractors, and aircraft engines. In the 1920s and 1930s the company expanded into neighboring countries, building new plants close to local markets. One such plant was built in Vilvoorde, a few kilometers north of Brussels.

Renault grew steadily until the 1940s. During World War II, Louis Renault operated the Paris facilities for the occupying Germans. Accused of collaboration and jailed after the war, Louis Renault died in prison, and his company was nationalized by the French government in 1945. It remained nationalized until the 1990s.

In the post-war years, Renault achieved its greatest success with several popular and low-cost cars, including the 4CV in the 1950s, the Renault 4 in the 1960s and 1970s, and the Renault 5 in the 1970s and 1980s. By the mid-1980s, however, Renault's performance began to falter. Although revenues remained strong, the company was losing money due to the high costs of a bloated workforce and inefficient manufacturing operations.

Turnaround in the 1980s

Beginning under new CEO George Besse, and then under his successor, Raymond Lévy, Renault began to improve its performance. From 1985 to 1995, Renault steadily increased revenues and returned to profitability (refer to Exhibit 1). The number of automobiles produced remained steady, but the automobile workforce declined from 140,000 in 1986 to 102,000 in 1995 (refer to Exhibit 2). At the same time, Renault continued to modernize its plants, investing in new technology and emphasizing simplicity in manufacture. The result was an improvement in quality and cost.

Renault also improved its product line, offering more imaginative and attractive cars. The Twingo, introduced in 1992, was one of a new generation of mini-cars aimed at young buyers. The round-bodied car came in bright colors and featured gaily printed fabric seats. It was simple to build, requiring only 18 labor hours, about the same as small Japanese cars. Another new model, the Espace, was the first minivan in Europe. These and other new models helped boost Renault's image and improved its market position.

Leading many of these initiatives was Renault's chairman, Louis Schweitzer. The Swiss-born great-nephew of famed doctor and Nobel Prize Winner Albert Schweitzer, he had graduated from the prestigious Ecole Nationale d'Administration. During the 1970s and 1980s Schweitzer held a series of government positions, where he gained a reputation for diligence and pragmatism.[1]

EXHIBIT 1 Selected Consolidated Financial Data, 1986–1995

Financial Data in Millions of Francs	1986	1987	1988	1989	1990	1991	1992	1993	1994	1995
Revenues	122,317	147,510	161,438	174,477	163,620	171,502	184,252	169,789	178,537	**184,065**
Operating income (loss)	3,542	9,204	14,385	12,944	6,299	4,813	7,734	609	2,317	**1,259**
Pretax income (loss)	(4,916)	3,562	8,975	9,725	1,380	3,969	6,481	1,094	3,485	**1,976**
Net income (loss) excluding minority interest	(5,847)	3,256	8,834	9,289	1,210	3,078	5,680	1,071	3,636	**2,139**
Cash flow from operations	2,240	10,010	15,260	15,050	7,919	12,305	16,117	11,017	12,145	**11,669**
Investments	5,157	7,021	7,295	10,361	13,213	20,637	13,565	12,043	16,050	**15,499**
Net financial indebtedness for industrial and commercial activities	54,346	46,377	23,786	17,593	27,110	15,528	8,727	7,851	(1,458)	**3,368**
Shareholders' equity	(11,433)	(7,811)	14,012	22,466	17,014	31,331	33,965	33,877	42,784	**43,796**
Workforce	182,448	188,936	178,665	174,573	157,378	147,185	146,604	139,733	138,279	**139,950**

Source: 1995 Renault Annual Report.

EXHIBIT 2 Renault: Automobile Production and Workforce, 1986–1995

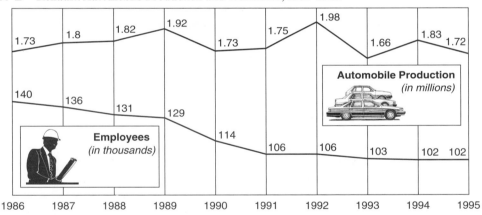

Source: *L'Express,* March 13, 1997, p. 32.

In the early 1990s, the French government began to privatize a number of state-owned companies, many of which had been nationalized under Socialist president Francois Mitterand in the early 1980s. In 1994, it sold 47 percent of Renault's shares to a variety of investors, retaining a 53 percent majority ownership. A further sale in 1996 reduced the government's holding to 46 percent (refer to Exhibit 3). Successful privatization was due in large measure to investor confidence in Renault's ability

EXHIBIT 3
Principal
Shareholders and
Voting Rights at
December 31, 1995

	%
French government[1]	52.97
AB Volvo	11.38
Templeton Group[2]	1.49
Protocol shareholders	
Lagardère Groupe	1.50
Sogepaf (Elf-Aquitaine group)[3]	1.50
Banque Nationale de Paris	1.00
Rhône-Poulenc Finance	1.00
Public including Group employees and others[4]	29.16
	100.00

[1]Includes shares reserved for distribution of bonus shares (2.87 percent).

[2]U.S. pension fund manager (exceeds the 1 percent statutory threshold).

[3]The Elf-Group, in addition to its interest as a protocol shareholder, holds 0.68 percent of Renault's equity capital.

[4]To the knowledge of the company, no other shareholder owns more than 1 percent of the equity at December 31, 1995. At that time, employees and former employees of the Group held 2.50 percent of the equity capital in the form of collectively managed and non-transferable shares. Cofiren, a 100% subsidiary of the Renault Group, holds 0.69 percent of the capital. These shares come from the stabilization funds of the market of investment certificates held by employees and former employees before the public offering of Renault capital.

Source: 1995 Renault Annual Report.

EXHIBIT 4

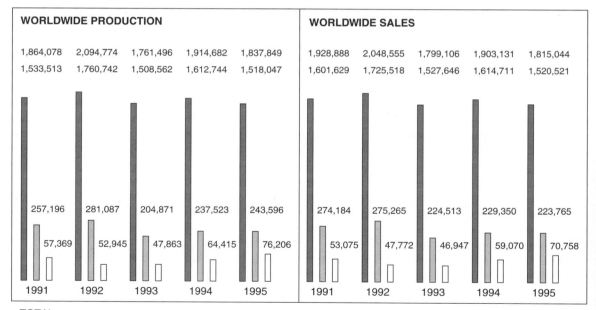

WORLDWIDE PRODUCTION	WORLDWIDE SALES

WORLDWIDE PRODUCTION

	1991	1992	1993	1994	1995
Passenger Cars	1,864,078	2,094,774	1,761,496	1,914,682	1,837,849
	1,533,513	1,760,742	1,508,562	1,612,744	1,518,047
Light Commercial Vehicles	257,196	281,087	204,871	237,523	243,596
Trucks and Buses	57,369	52,945	47,863	64,415	76,206

WORLDWIDE SALES

	1991	1992	1993	1994	1995
Passenger Cars	1,928,888	2,048,555	1,799,106	1,903,131	1,815,044
	1,601,629	1,725,518	1,527,646	1,614,711	1,520,521
Light Commercial Vehicles	274,184	275,265	224,513	229,350	223,765
Trucks and Buses	53,075	47,772	46,947	59,070	70,758

TOTAL

 Passenger Cars   Light Commercial Vehicles (less than 5 tonnes)   Trucks and Buses

Source: 1995 Renault Annual Report.

EXHIBIT 5   Geographic Distribution of Renault Revenues, 1991–1995

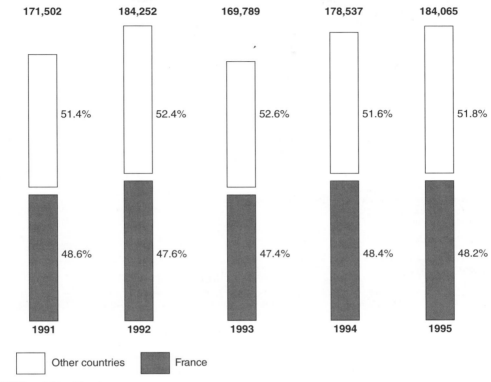

REVENUES
FRF Million

| 171,502 | 184,252 | 169,789 | 178,537 | 184,065 |

Other countries: 51.4%, 52.4%, 52.6%, 51.6%, 51.8%

France: 48.6%, 47.6%, 47.4%, 48.4%, 48.2%

1991 1992 1993 1994 1995

☐ Other countries   ■ France

Source: 1995 Renault Annual Report.

to bring its costs into line. Renault had cut about 1,500 jobs in France during each of the last five years, largely through attrition, early retirement, and part-time work plans.

Renault in 1995

By 1995, Renault was operating profitably, with sales of FFr184 billion ($33.4 billion). Passenger cars accounted for more than 80 percent of revenues (refer to Exhibit 4). In terms of geography, almost half of revenues were from Renault's home market, with the remainder largely in Western Europe (refer to Exhibit 5). In addition to its strong market position in France, where Renault held 29.2 percent of the passenger car market, it had strong positions in Spain (13.9 percent), Portugal (12.8 percent), and Belgium-Luxembourg (11.1 percent) (refer to Exhibit 6). Overall, Renault had a 10.3 percent share of the Western Europe passenger car market.

EXHIBIT 6 Renault in Western Europe—Passenger Cars

	% Change in Registrations		Renault Market Share (%)			Renault Registrations
	M.T.M.[1]	Renault	1993	1994	1995	1995
France	−2.1	−4.9	30.6	30.0	29.2	563,712
Germany	+3.3	+4.6	5.2	5.1	5.2	170,916
United Kingdom	+1.8	+6.9	5.2	5.9	6.2	120,485
Spain	−8.4	−16.9	16.3	15.3	13.9	115,906
Italy[2]	+4.1	−11.0	7.3	7.0	6.0	104,400
Belgium-Luxembourg	−7.1	−13.8	11.7	12.0	11.1	43,026
Netherlands	+2.9	−9.7	7.3	8.3	7.3	32,590
Portugal	−13.6	−25.4	14.2	14.8	12.8	25,782
Austria	+2.2	−1.1	6.4	6.7	6.5	18,264
Switzerland	−0.0	−10.2	6.4	7.4	6.7	17,856
TOTAL Western Europe[3]	**+10.8**	**−25.2**	**10.6**	**11.0**	**10.3**	**1,240,972**

[1]Total new car market.
[2]The figures have been established in accordance with the new method of counting registrations introduced in Italy in 1994.
[3]EU, Iceland, Norway, and Switzerland.
Source: 1995 Renault Annual Report.

EXHIBIT 7
Renault: Major Production Sites and Models, 1995

Source: 1995 Renault Annual Report.

Flins	Clio, Twingo
Douai	Renault 19 then Mégane
Sandouville	Safrane, Laguna, Laguna Nevada
Maubeuge	Renault 19 convertible, Express
Vilvoorde (Belgium)	Clio, Renault 21 Nevada, Mégane
Palencia (Spain)	Laguna, Renault 19 then Mégane
Valladolid (Spain)	Twingo, Clio, Express, engines
Bursa (Turkey)	Renault 9/11/12/21
Cléon	Engines, transmissions, aluminum castings
Le Mans	Front/axle assemblies, mechanical parts, iron castings
Lorient (S.B.F.M.)	Iron castings

Renault operated a large network of automobile plants, with nine large factories in France and others in Belgium, Spain, and Turkey (refer to Exhibit 7). There was considerable overlap among plants, with some models manufactured in more than one plant.

The Belgian plant, at Vilvoorde, had been operated by Renault since the 1930s. Generations of residents from Vilvoorde and surrounding communities had worked at the plant. Its workforce was thought to be among the hardest working in Renault's production network.[2] In 1995, Renault invested $226 million to install an entirely new assembly line at Vilvoorde. By 1996, the plant turned out 143,342 cars, but was operating well below its full capacity of 1,000 per day.

THE EUROPEAN AUTOMOBILE INDUSTRY IN 1996

Despite its many improvements in recent years, it was apparent in 1996 that Renault still faced major difficulties. Greater competition from a variety of rivals threatened Renault's position. New minicars, including the Opel Corsa, VW Polo, and Ford Ka, all took sales from the Twingo. The lead enjoyed by the Espace was wiped out as virtually all European automakers introduced their own minivans, including the Opel Sintra, the VW Sharan, and the Ford Galaxie. Renault's Megane sedan, introduced in 1995, found itself stacked against four new cars: Fiat Bravo and Brava, Opel Vectra, and Ford Fiesta.

Adding to Renault's challenges was a general problem facing the entire European auto industry. Until the 1990s, European automakers had been able to survive by relying on sales in their home markets. The gradual introduction of the single European market meant that cars could more easily cross borders, allowing major auto companies to compete for sales in other markets. Facing greater competition at home, companies like Fiat could no longer rely on Italian sales to survive, nor could Renault rely on French sales. The more open market, plus investments into Europe by Japanese and Korean automakers, led to a growth of productive capacity and a resulting intensification of competitive pressure. *The Wall Street Journal* summed it up simply: "The problem is overcapacity, combined with a breakdown of traditional national markets."[3]

Some companies, notably General Motors and Volkswagen, moved deliberately to reduce capacity and better match their output to demand. In early 1997, Ford Motor Company, having lost $291 million in Europe in 1996, announced the closure of its plant in Halewood, England, with the loss of 1,300 jobs. Jac Nasser, chairman of Ford Europe, said that auto companies could not merely trim prices to increase demand; they also had to reduce capacity. The present situation of overcapacity in Europe, he observed, "is not sustainable in the long run."[4] Fiat, too, made clear that it would take steps to reduce capacity.[5]

As for Renault, it was becoming clear that its output was not sufficient to justify its network of plants. One analyst estimated that Renault's plants were operating at just 78 percent of capacity.[6] Furthermore, a comparison of leading plants showed that Renault's efficiency lagged behind major rivals (refer to Exhibit 8).

RENAULT AND VILVOORDE: CHRONOLOGY OF A CRISIS

1997 began with a sense of gloom in the French auto industry. On February 14, Peugeot announced that 1996 sales had declined from 1995 levels, and indicated it would report a loss for the year. Many analysts speculated that Renault, too, would soon report weak performance for 1996.

Faced with declining performance and under pressure to reduce costs, Renault's chairman, Louis Schweitzer, and his counterpart at Peugeot, Jacques Calvet, jointly proposed a plan to the French government in which 40,000 employees

EXHIBIT 8   Major Automakers in Europe: Number of Automobiles Produced per Year per Employee at the Most Productive Factories

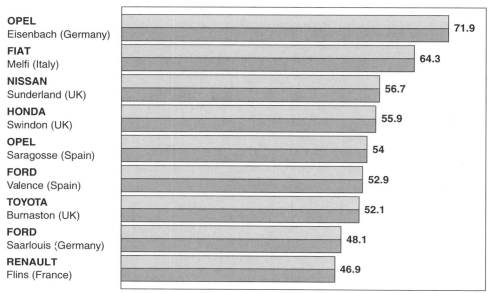

OPEL Eisenbach (Germany)	71.9
FIAT Melfi (Italy)	64.3
NISSAN Sunderland (UK)	56.7
HONDA Swindon (UK)	55.9
OPEL Saragosse (Spain)	54
FORD Valence (Spain)	52.9
TOYOTA Burnaston (UK)	52.1
FORD Saarlouis (Germany)	48.1
RENAULT Flins (France)	46.9

Source: *L'Express,* March 13, 1997, p. 30.

would receive state-funded early retirement in return for hiring 15,000 younger, cheaper workers. The government of Prime Minister Alain Juppé was wary of appearing to support the growing calls for retirement at 55, a key policy of the Socialist opposition. On February 26, after extensive consideration, the government officially rejected the plan. The very next day, Renault announced it would reduce employees in another manner—by closing the Vilvoorde plant.

Thursday, February 27   Late in the afternoon, Renault issued a brief statement that the Vilvoorde plant would close on July 31. The announcement also stated that Renault expected to report "a very significant loss" for 1996, its first loss in 10 years.

The announcement caught the town of Vilvoorde completely unaware. Some employees learned of the news on the radio as they arrived at work for the evening shift. "I heard it on TV," said one shocked worker. "I couldn't catch my breath."[7] The plant closure was especially grim news given that unemployment in Vilvoorde was already more than 12 percent. "We never expected such a brutal decision," said Vilvoorde Mayor Willy Cortois. "It's a total surprise." Cortois said that the total number of jobs lost in the Vilvoorde area could reach 6,000 because many local firms relied on the Renault factory.[8]

Friday, February 28   The news in Belgium was dominated by the plant closure. Eric Van Rompuy, a minister in the Flanders regional government, denounced the closing as "an act of terrorism against the Flemish economy." Belgian Prime Minister Jean-Luc Dehaene said his government was "concerned and stupefied" by the "brutal and unilateral decision . . . which took no account of the social repercussions." Dehaene, himself a resident of Vilvoorde, called French Prime Minister Alain Juppé in view of the French state's 46 percent ownership of Renault to register his strong protest.[9]

The Belgian response was particularly intense because of the country's heavy reliance on the automobile industry for employment and export earnings. On a per capita basis, Belgium was the biggest car producer in the world, operating plants for five companies: Ford, Volkswagen, General Motors, Volvo, and Renault. These plants employed 34,000 people and turned out 1.2 million cars a year, accounting for 15 percent of the country's export earnings. Although the Vilvoorde plant was the smallest of the five, many Belgians were fearful that other plant closures might follow.[10] With unemployment in Belgium already at 13 percent, the prospect of further job losses was of grave concern.

In Brussels, a spokesperson for the European Union Commission said Renault appeared to have broken two E.U. laws. One law, a 1975 agreement (revised in 1992) on collective redundancies, said that firms considering a reduction in employment were required to consult workers "in good time with a view to reaching an agreement." The other law, a 1994 E.U. works council directive, stipulated that company management had to "inform and consult with employees" on all important decisions. The spokesperson noted that although Renault had been among the first large companies to set up a works council, doing so in 1993, it had apparently not fulfilled its duty to consult with the council.

Meanwhile, angry Vilvoorde employees occupied the plant, shutting down all production. They also prevented the shipment of 5,000 finished cars worth BFr3 billion ($86 million), and threatened to hold "hostage" 2,000 partly assembled cars.[11]

News of the plant closure was greeted positively by shareholders. Renault shares jumped 13 percent on the Paris Bourse, reaching 146.9 Francs.

Sunday, March 2 Public opposition grew stronger and louder over the weekend. Protests spread into the streets of Brussels, where 3,500 people staged a peaceful march to denounce the plant closure. Elsewhere in Belgium, union leaders urged a boycott of Renault cars.

Responding to the public outcry, Renault chairman Louis Schweitzer met with Belgian government officials. Schweitzer explained the rationale for the closure, and reaffirmed his intention to close the Vilvoorde plant on July 31. He also indicated that Renault expected to take a FFr2.4 billion (approximately $400 million) provision in 1997 to cover severance pay and other costs associated with the plant closure.

Monday, March 3 The Belgian Employment Minister, Miet Smet, said the government would bring formal legal action against Renault for failure to inform and consult with employees. Under Belgian law, the maximum penalty for breaching such rules was BFr20 million, or about $580,000. "It's largely symbolic," a spokesman conceded. King Albert II of Belgium added his voice to the public debate, visiting the European Commission to express his concern about the plant closure.

The European Union Competition Commissioner, Karl Van Miert, stated his belief that Renault had failed to respect the E.U. directives on worker consultation. He added: "I don't understand Renault's decision because it is closing a very profitable plant in which it has invested a lot in recent years."[12]

The Belgian government asked for a meeting of the Organization for Economic Cooperation and Development to determine if a code of conduct for multinational corporations had been broken. Breaching an OECD code did not, however, carry any financial penalty.

In France, Renault's labor unions expressed concern that the closing at Vilvoorde was only the beginning of further cutbacks. "The problem will expand in France with the announcement of draconian job cuts," warned France's *Force Ouvrière* union.

Tuesday, March 4   Fears of further job cuts were well-founded. A source close to Renault said the firm intended to eliminate 2,764 French jobs, or nearly 2.8 percent of its French workforce, by the end of the year. These reductions would take place mainly through attrition, and would not involve the closing of any French plants.

Following this latest announcement, France's Industry Minister, Franck Borotra, summoned Renault's top management to new talks about their restructuring plans. He emphasized, however, that the government would not seek to intervene in exchanges between the company and Belgian authorities.

In a public statement, Renault chairman Louis Schweitzer characterized the Vilvoorde plant closing as "grave and painful," but maintained that it had been examined "attentively to make sure the need for it was incontestable on a strategic and economic level."[13] Renault also clarified the shift in jobs resulting from the closure. Production of Megane and Clio models would be shifted to plants in Spain and France. Although 3,100 jobs in Belgium would be lost, 1,900 jobs would be added at other Renault plants, primarily the Spanish plants of Palencia and Valladolid. Unemployment in Spain stood at 21 percent.

Separately, industry analysts noted that the average after-tax take-home pay of Vilvoorde workers was similar to that of French Renault workers—about $1,700 per month—but was considerably more expensive to the company because of higher social charges and tax rates in Belgium. Some estimates placed the total cost of employing a Renault worker in Belgium as 30 percent more than in France and 48 percent more than in Spain.[14]

Wednesday, March 5   In Paris, French President Jacques Chirac added his voice to the chorus of criticism, saying he was "shocked by the method" by which Renault had announced the closure at Vilvoorde. Prime Minister Alain Juppé similarly criticized the way the decision had been communicated, and summoned Louis Schweitzer to his offices at Matignon to complain about the abrupt announcement. One newspaper described the meeting as a "tongue-lashing session" with a "livid Prime Minister Alain Juppé." Schweitzer once again explained his reasons for the plant closure, adding: "I also indicated that Renault wishes to start as soon as possible talks with Vilvoorde employees on aid measures and the possibility of converting the factory for other uses."[15]

Some of Renault's Vilvoorde workers wondered openly whether Renault would have treated them differently if they were French-speaking Walloons rather than Flemish speakers. One Vilvoorde resident voiced the widely shared belief that: "Of course they closed the plant in Belgium to save jobs in France."

The leader of France's opposition Socialist Party, Lionel Jospin, called on Juppé to intervene in the closure, describing Renault's decision to close the Vilvoorde plant as "financially, industrially, and socially aberrant." He added: "Trying to play off workers from one country against those of another is not worthy of a great French and European enterprise." France's Minister of Labor and Social Affairs, Jacques Barot, took a different tack, noting that "Renault's closure is not against Belgium. Competition is raging. We realize that to be a player in this globalization of the economy we have to fight."

Industry analysts, meanwhile, took a favorable view of Renault's actions, although some claimed that the job cuts at Vilvoorde and in France represented only about 4 percent of Renault's total workforce. One analyst suggested that Renault would have to lay off as many as 10,000 employees in order to regain competitiveness, meaning another 4,000 in addition to the Vilvoorde and French cutbacks.[16]

Analysts also made clear that other automakers would have to pare their workforces, too. By one estimate, European automakers would produce 16.5 million cars and vans in 1997, but would sell only 13 million. "This looks like the beginning of a squeeze that happens periodically in the European motor industry," commented one expert.[17] An international economist in London concurred, saying that "the likelihood is that [European automakers] are going to continue pruning workforces for some time to come." These words were of scarce comfort in France, where unemployment had already reached a record level of 12.8 percent.

Friday, March 7 Renault's plan to shift production to one of its Spanish plants was dealt a blow when the European Commission blocked subsidies to Renault's Valladolid plant as long as Renault did not reverse its decision regarding Vilvoorde. In response, Renault's chairman Schweitzer repeated that the decision to shut down the Belgium plant was "irrevocable."

Thursday, March 13 Despite the public criticism levelled at Renault by French President Chirac and Prime Minister Juppé, some French press reports suggested that the French government had known of the Vilvoorde closure in advance and had given a "tacit backing" to the move. One analyst stated that the French government, still by far Renault's biggest shareholder, had "given the industry carte blanche to go ahead and restructure."[18]

Sunday, March 16 Public demonstrations in Belgium continued for the third consecutive weekend, this time involving organized labor from all over Europe. More than 50,000 European trade unionists converged on Brussels, venting their anger at job losses and what was termed "inhumane companies and uncaring governments." Delegations were present from France, Spain, Portugal, Great Britain, Germany, Luxembourg, the Netherlands, Italy, Greece, Austria, Hungary, Slovenia, and the Czech Republic. "It is a show of solidarity," said one auto worker from England. "We are all workers. We are all in the struggle."

The demonstration featured red, green, and yellow union banners, as well as noisy chants, firecrackers, and sirens. One banner read: "They follow more rules for swine fever than for us." Another said: "Renault is developing turbo-charged unemployment." French Socialist Party leader Lionel Jospin observed: "We need a better balance in the European economic and social model. It has gone too far [toward the economic]." The head of Belgium's Christian Democratic CSC trade union, Willy Pierens, exclaimed to the assembled thousands: "This is a signal of anger and indignation. A signal of solidarity against brutality. We don't want to be lied to again. We won't be cheated again."[19]

Wednesday, March 19   Renault chairman Louis Schweitzer and eleven union leaders from the Vilvoorde plant met face-to-face for the first time since the February 27 announcement. The meeting was held on neutral ground at Beauvais, north of Paris, after workers refused to travel to Renault headquarters at Boulogne-Billancourt, and Schweitzer refused to attend a meeting at Vilvoorde. In a meeting that lasted more than two hours, the union proposed a 10 percent reduction in working hours as an alternative to a full shutdown. Schweitzer rejected any such proposal, telling union leaders that the decision to close the plant was irrevocable and could not be delayed beyond July. He stated, however, his willingness to discuss the terms of the shutdown so as to reduce the impact on workers. Union leaders termed Schweitzer's position "unacceptable" and said they were very disappointed by his unwillingness to consider their proposal.[20]

Friday, March 21   After weeks of hints and speculation, Renault reported its 1996 results. It showed a loss of FFr5.25 billion ($925 million), its first loss in 10 years. Analysts were unsurprised with the figures, noting they were "pretty much bang in line" with expectations. Renault chairman Louis Schweitzer commented simply: "1996 was, as you know, a difficult year."[21]

Schweitzer also reported Renault's restructuring plan had been approved "by a very large majority" of the board of directors, and stated his expectation that with the steps it had taken, the firm would return to an operating profit by year end. With the closing of the Vilvoorde plant, said Schweitzer, "Renault has an industrial structure and plant distribution that won't require any further plant closings until 2000." He added that the Vilvoorde plant would have been closed at some point given its location, and that "the 1996 results convinced us that we could not delay the closing."[22]

Meanwhile, workers at Vilvoorde continued to occupy the plant. At Wavrin, in northern France, workers clashed with police as they occupied a Renault distribution center. Workers at Renault plants in France, however, rejected calls for a companywide strike and remained on the job.

Friday, March 28   Protests continued as 900 demonstrators clashed with police outside the headquarters of the Flemish regional government and the office of the European Union. Protesters threw cans, stones, and eggs at police.

Thursday, April 3   In the first legal ruling on the case, a Belgian court ruled that the Vilvoorde plant closure was illegal because Renault had failed to consult its workers. The Brussels labor court said Renault had breached labor consultation rules and called on it to restart discussions with its workforce. The court did not have the power to force Renault to reverse its decision, but could fine the company up to BFr20 million ($580,000) if the company did not promptly reopen talks with workers. Labor unions welcomed the court's ruling. "It is good that the judicial power in Belgium is bringing Renault back into line," said Denis de Meulemeester, a spokesperson for the Belgian metals union.[23]

Responding to the court ruling, a Renault spokesperson said: "We respect Belgian law, but economic reality being what it is" the company expected to proceed with the shutdown.[24]

Friday, April 4   One day after the Belgian ruling, a French court found that Renault had failed to consult properly with its workers and imposed a fine of FFr15,000 ($2,600) to be paid to the worker consultation body.

Legal analysts commented that neither the French nor the Belgian ruling could stop Renault from actually closing the plant. Renault chairman Schweitzer again reiterated his intention to close the plant, stating that "the ruling doesn't change the economic reality." He told one French newspaper that Vilvoorde might have to close earlier than July 31 if its workers, still on strike and occupying the factory, did not soon return to work.[25]

In a separate development, the Citroen division of Peugeot announced that it would cut 800 of its 28,400 jobs during 1997. The company added that it would present its layoff plans to employee representatives on April 15.

Friday, April 11   Nearly 69 percent of the Vilvoorde workforce voted to return to work, bringing to an end the six-week strike that began with the announced plant closure. "Work will start on Monday," said a union official, Hendrick Vermeersch. Some workers said they were still angry with Renault, but reasoned they were better off returning to work than forgoing the wages they could earn until July 31. The union warned, however, that assembly work would be difficult if almost one-third of workers wanted to continue the strike. Moreover, workers continued to occupy the factory's parking lot, where 5,000 finished cars had been blocked since the plant closure was announced.[26]

On the Paris Bourse, Renault stock closed at FFr154, reaching a 52-week high, up almost 50 percent from its 52-week low of FFr103.

Tuesday, April 15   Employees at Vilvoorde resumed work in both morning and afternoon shifts. The resumption of production had been delayed one extra day as a small number of workers had refused to start production on Monday.

Wednesday, May 7 A French appeals court reversed the lower court's ruling that Renault had been obliged to notify its unions before deciding to close the Vilvoorde plant. Renault said that the closing had been an "industrial and economic necessity," and once again confirmed it would go ahead with the closure as planned.[27]

Thursday, May 22 A wildcat strike at the Vilvoorde plant blocked production for the second day in a row. Despite the earlier vote to return to work, a small group of disgruntled workers had been able to effectively block production.[28]

Renault management, acting in compliance with the rulings of Belgian and French courts, agreed to meet with representatives of the Vilvoorde workforce on June 3 to discuss the plant shutdown. A spokesperson for Renault maintained, however, that the plant still needed to be closed as part of a vital streamlining of operations.

Sunday, May 25 In the first round of French parliamentary elections, voters repudiated the center-right government of Prime Minister Alain Juppé. The leftist coalition of Socialists, Communists, and Greens captured 42.1 percent of votes against 36.2 percent for the ruling coalition of President Chirac's Gaullists and the centrist Union for French Democracy. Several factors explained the ruling party's unpopularity, including a 12.8 percent rate of French unemployment, concerns about government support for European monetary union, and opposition to further cuts in social spending.

Thursday, May 29 Campaigning in the north of France for the second round of parliamentary voting, Socialist leader Lionel Jospin met with a delegation of workers from the Vilvoorde plant. Jospin said that if he became prime minister, he would intervene in the Renault affair and force a reconsideration of the Vilvoorde plant closure. "Representatives of the state on Renault's board will demand other measures" be taken regarding Vilvoorde, said Jospin.[29] Renault workers cheered his words, and presented him with a Renault Megane.[30]

Renault headquarters retorted that a new prime minister could not overturn the decision to close the plant. A spokesperson stated: "On March 20, the board of directors voted by a large majority to support the chairman, Louis Schweitzer. Only he can change the decision." Whether a new prime minister might be able to replace Schweitzer as chairman was open to discussion, as the French state held only 46 percent of the voting shares.[31]

Sunday, June 1 The French Socialists swept to power in parliamentary voting, taking a solid majority of more than 300 seats in the National Assembly. One news account said that French voters had "delivered a powerful rejection of the performance of the center-right governing coalition in trying to push through changes to make the economy more competitive and French society less dependent on jobs and benefits provided by the government."[32]

Monday, June 2 At 9:15 A.M., Prime Minister Alain Juppé met with President Jacques Chirac to offer his resignation. Less than two hours later, Lionel Jospin arrived at the Elysée and was asked by President Chirac to serve as France's next prime minister. Later that day, he moved into the prime minister's office at Matignon.

On the Paris Bourse, French stocks stabilized after losing more than 4 percent of their value over the previous week. Renault shares closed at FFr126.

Endnotes

1. "An aggressive driver," *Financial Times,* March 8/9, 1997.
2. "Renault's plant closing mirrors industry woes," *The Wall Street Journal,* March 6, 1997, p. B4.
3. "Renault's plant closing in Belgium reflects industry overcapacity," *The Wall Street Journal Europe,* March 4, 1997, p. 1.
4. "Europe's great cars wars: The fracas over Renault's closure of its Belgium factory is an indication of the rotten state of Europe's car industry," *The Economist,* March 8, 1997.
5. Ibid.
6. "Euro automakers catch up as Renault's downfall sparks fears for auto markets," *USA Today,* March 7, 1997.
7. "Renault's plant closing in Belgium reflects industry overcapacity," *The Wall Street Journal Europe,* March 4, 1997, p. 1.
8. "Dehaene lambastes 'brutal' decision," *Dow Jones News Service,* February 28, 1997.
9. "Renault workers protest, Belgians angered by plant closure," *USA Today,* March 4, 1997.
10. "Europe's great cars wars: The fracas over Renault's closure of its Belgian factory is an indication of the rotten state of Europe's car industry," *The Economist,* March 8, 1997.
11. "Belgium set to sue Renault over factory closure," *Financial Times,* March 4, 1997, P1.
12. Ibid.
13. "Paris calls Renault chiefs to new talks on job cuts," *Financial Times,* March 5, 1997, p. 14.
14. "Renault workers despair for Europe's job security," *Financial Times,* March 6, 1997.
15. "Euro automakers catch up: Renault's downfall sparks fear for auto markets," *USA Today,* March 7, 1997, p. 10B.
16. "The skid at Renault: Once a star, the carmaker may lose $1 billion," *Business Week,* March 17, 1997.
17. "Renault's plant closing mirrors industry woes," The *Wall Street Journal,* March 6, 1997, p. B4.
18. "The skid at Renault: Once a star, the carmaker may lose $1 billion," *Business Week,* March 17, 1997.
19. "The skid at Renault: Once a star, the carmaker may lose $1 billion," *Business Week,* March 17, 1997.
20. "Renault tells unions: Closing of Belgian plant is 'irrevocable,' " *International Herald Tribune,* March 20, 1997; *Financial Times,* March 20, 1997,

p. 2; "A Beauvais, Louis Schweitzer face a onze syndicalistes de Renault," *Le Monde,* March 20, 1997.

21. "Renault posts yearly loss as workers protest job cuts," *Wall Street Journal Europe,* March 21–22, 1997, p. 3.

22. "Renault earnings—In line with expectations," *Dow Jones News Service,* March 20, 1997.

23. "Court finds Renault's plan illegal," *International Herald Tribune,* April 4, 1997, p. 13.

24. "Renault still planning to close plant," *The New York Times,* April 4, 1997.

25. "Unions win Renault suit," *International Herald Tribune,* April 5–6, 1997, p. 9; "Renault to appeal on consultation ruling," *Financial Times,* April 5/April 6, 1997, p. 2.

26. "Renault strike in Belgium to end," *International Herald Tribune,* April 11, 1997, p. 11.

27. "Renault/Court: Vilvoorde closure costs 3,100 jobs," *Dow Jones News Service,* May 7, 1997.

28. "Renault to sell 0.9% stake in Elf back to company," *The Wall Street Journal Europe,* May 23–24, 1997, p. 8.

29. "The political lesson: forward to the past," *The International Herald Tribune,* June 2, 1997.

30. Reported on Radio France Info, May 30, 1997.

31. "M. Jospin veut faire revenir la direction de Renault sur la fermeture de Vilvoorde," *Le Monde,* June 2, 1997.

32. "Socialists recapture power in France," *International Herald Tribune,* June 2, 1997.

Chapter Forty-Two

GLOBAL Enterprises, Inc.

FEBRUARY 17, 1995

As she prepared for the next day's meeting of the Board of Directors, Jennifer Copperman-Williams, the 49 year old president and CEO of GLOBAL Enterprises, had never felt more frustrated. Despite years of work restructuring the company, GLOBAL had just reported a loss of $99 million on sales of $2.55 billion. While Copperman-Williams continued to enjoy the confidence of the Board, she knew that the next day could bring questions for which she did not have answers. In preparing for her presentation, she wondered whether to downplay the company's current problems or turn to the Board for real direction. Almost certainly the Board would push for significant changes in leadership, including the removal of several senior managers. It had become increasingly clear that key individuals stood in the way of the integration efforts that had been ongoing in the company. What was less certain to Copperman-Williams was whether the company's restructuring in fact made sense. As the architect of the company's current integration efforts, Copperman-Williams was clearly in a tough position. With the Board meeting less than 24 hours away, she had little time to spare.

The Early Years—1948 to 1970

GLOBAL traced its roots back to 1948 in Los Angeles, when Benjamin Copperman started a small company, named Precision Devices, shortly after earning a Ph.D. in Mechanical Engineering at the California Institute of Technology. During its early years, Precision focused exclusively on designing and

This fictional case was prepared as the basis for class discussion by Mr. S. M. Steele, Program Director, IBM Leadership Institute, with the assistance of Professor Allen Morrision, American Graduate School of International Management. No part of this case may be reproduced, stored in a retrieval system, used in a spreadsheet, or transmitted in any form without the express written permission of the IBM Leadership Institute, 20 Old Post Road, Armonk, NY 10504. Phone 914/765–2000.

manufacturing diagnostic and control equipment for the medical industry. As a result of several patents, sales grew rapidly, making Copperman a millionaire before he reached the age of 28.

In 1956, Precision acquired Professional Services, Inc. (PSI), for $500,000. PSI provided temporary and contract personnel to the accounting and data processing industry. Jeremy "Joco" Morris, the 26 year old owner and close personal friend of Copperman's, stayed on as President. In 1959, Precision spent $2.6 million to buy Best Brands, a Canadian automotive electronics product design and manufacturing company. Best Brands had lucrative OEM contracts with Ford and American Motors for controls, sensors, and sound systems. It also supplied a national chain of retail/wholesale automotive parts stores with after-market products. John Michaels, the owner of Best Brands, also continued as President. In 1963, Copperman paid $11.6 million for New Horizons, a Princeton, New Jersey, company that designed and manufactured flight simulators and high resolution video display devices for the aerospace industry. New Horizons also held and licensed key patents for the manufacture of solid state silicon and germanium circuits. The president of New Horizons was Carl Rose, a 34 year old with separate Ph.D.'s in physics and mathematics. Although somewhat eccentric, he was highly respected in his field and had been able to attract and retain what many regarded as a brilliant young staff.

While Copperman maintained ultimate control of each company, they continued to be managed largely as autonomous ventures. These companies, combined with Precision's core medical equipment operation, generated Group sales of $168 million in 1968.

International Expansion—1970 to 1975

In the early 1970s, the strong market and growing demand in Europe and Asia began to exceed the distribution capability of Precision's predominantly U.S.-oriented companies. Growth in these geographies seemed to require a dedicated manufacturing, marketing, and service presence. As such, Copperman began a search for international partners.

In 1975, he formed two international partnerships. One was with Nitta Nippon Electronics, a $115 million Japanese distribution company owned by Shinichi Nitta, the 53 year old founder. The other was with Rhine Mark Products, a $112 million German medical supply company owned by Friedreich Schuller, a hard driving 50 year old. The key terms of the agreements were as follows:

1. Precision Enterprises gained 50 percent ownership of both partner companies and the right to purchase the remaining 50 percent when the current owner "retired" or reached the age of 70. For Precision, the purchase price amounted to $31 million over 6 years for one-half of Nitta Nippon's equity and $24 million over 4 years for one-half of Rhine Mark's equity.

2. Nitta Nippon Electronics and Rhine Mark Products were each granted unlimited use of Precision Enterprises' patents, brand names, and technology.

EXHIBIT 1   **Organization Chart, 1975**

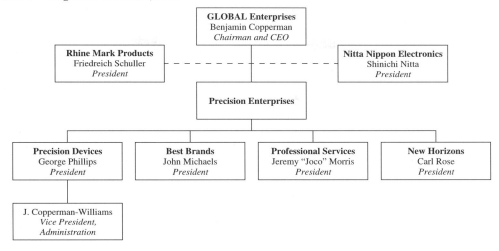

3. Each partner was given exclusive distribution and manufacturing rights for the following geographic areas:

Rhine Mark Distributors—Europe, Middle East, and Africa.

Nitta Nippon Electronics—Asia, South Pacific, and Australia.

Precision Enterprises—The Americas.

Upon ratification of the partnership agreement, GLOBAL Enterprises, Inc., a private holding company, was formed (Exhibit 1).

The Fast Growth Years—1975 to 1990

Precision Enterprises   By 1990, Precision Enterprises had become a $702 million business. Under the direction of Jennifer Copperman-Williams throughout much of the 1980s, Precision was widely regarded for providing excellent installation, maintenance, and facility operations services in the health care industry. In 1988, Precision Enterprises won the prestigious Deming Quality Award and in 1989 the U.S. Commerce Department's Baldrige Award.

Copperman-Williams was generally regarded as a hard working, no-nonsense manager. She joined the company in 1969 after receiving an MBA (with an emphasis in International Management) from U.C.L.A. and an undergraduate degree in political science from Georgetown University. She worked in a variety of marketing and finance positions and in 1975 was appointed vice president of administration for Precision Devices. Over the next nine years she also served as vice president of marketing and vice president of operation for Precision Devices. In 1984 she was named as President of Precision Enterprises.

Rhine Mark Products, Inc. By 1990, Rhine Mark had grown to $648 million in sales and $44 million in profits. With the political assistance of the European Development Council, the company opened manufacturing facilities in Germany, Italy, and France. In 1986 and again in 1988, it was honored as the "most admired" company by the European Association of Manufacturers. In 1987 Friedreich Schuller was appointed as a commissioner to the European Common Market and, in 1989, was elected to the board of directors of the European Bank of Commerce.

Schuller believed a strong centralized management system should develop strategic direction and control capital investment. He ruled with what many regarded as an iron hand, and on more than one occasion had summarily fired plant managers and vice presidents who questioned his direction or failed to produce results. Ironically, at the same time, he fiercely defended his independence from GLOBAL. He was once quoted as saying, "We have to send them half our profits, but we don't have to accept their advice or return their phone calls."

Nitta Nippon Electronics Initially, the growth in the Asia/Pacific geography outstripped GLOBAL's ability to ship product from the U.S. Over time, Nitta Nippon opened manufacturing facilities in Japan, Korea, and Singapore. In each country it was able to negotiate significant concessions on local tariffs, taxes, and administrative regulations. In return, they agreed to limit the import of components and subassemblies. By 1990, Nitta Nippon had profits of $50 million on sales of $670 million.

Shinichi Nitta was a role model for a participative management culture that valued consensus and long-term success over short-term gains. Nitta put a premium on loyalty, quality, and teamwork. He encouraged employees and suppliers to view Nitta Nippon Electronics as part of their family, and routinely sent personal notes and gifts when an employee married or had a child. In 1988 he was named as one of the "Outstanding Asian Entrepreneurs" by *Fortune* magazine. The company was also voted "the most desired place to work" by the Japanese Association of Student Engineers in 1986, 1987, and 1989.

GLOBAL Enterprises Throughout most of the 1980s, Ben Copperman devoted considerable time to helping Schuller and Nitta establish manufacturing operations in their respective geographies. Despite his best efforts, he continued to find that nationalism represented an enormous barrier to integration. To those who knew him, his biggest disappointment was his inability to effectively exploit the broad geographic scope of GLOBAL. By 1989 the relationship between the partners deteriorated to the point where they frequently would not return each other's phone calls.

Somewhat out of frustration, Copperman began to withdraw from the day to day operations of GLOBAL. He became active on several U.S. Presidential Commissions and served on the board of AMTRAK, Bankers Trust, the International Red Cross, and Brunswick.

GLOBAL Goes Public—1990 to 1991

In January 1990, Friedreich Schuller suffered a massive heart attack and died in his office on a Sunday afternoon. GLOBAL acquired the outstanding 50 percent

EXHIBIT 2
GLOBAL Common Values

> The customer is the center of everything we do.
> Performance in the marketplace is the measure of our success.
> We work together as a team to provide our customers with the most competitive products and values in the industry.
> We act with integrity.
> We value diversity and treat each other with respect.
> We provide our shareholders, partners, associates, and suppliers with a fair deal and a fair return on their investments.

ownership of Rhine Mark for $109 million and named Peter Notehelfer, the former Vice President of Manufacturing, as President.

In September 1990, Shinichi Nitta was appointed as a member of the Japanese delegation to the International Commission on Trade and Tariffs. He retired and quickly reached an agreement to sell GLOBAL the outstanding 50 percent interest in Nitta Nippon Electronics for $124 million. Hajime Takeuchi, the former Director General of Operations, was appointed President.

GLOBAL engaged Goldman-Sachs to take the company public in order to finance the buyouts. The IPO of 25 million shares at $25 was oversubscribed and on January 1, 1991, the stock was trading at $30/share. When the smoke cleared, the Copperman family had received $255 million in cash and was left with 3 million shares, or 12 percent of the outstanding stock in GLOBAL.

On March 1, 1991, Copperman addressed a special meeting of the top 95 managers where he announced his retirement from GLOBAL in order to accept an appointment as the Chairman of U.S. Presidential Commission on Productivity and Quality. In a brief statement he thanked them for their support and said,

> Your dedication to providing value to the customer, value to the stakeholders, and value to each other has been the foundation for GLOBAL's past success. The future, like the past, will require strength of character and leadership. My legacy to you is my deep faith in your ability to be guided by an unswerving commitment to the GLOBAL Common Values. (See Exhibit 2.)

Following his announcement, Jennifer Copperman-Williams was named by the board as the new President, CEO, and Chairman of GLOBAL.

The New GLOBAL—1991 to Present

Copperman-Williams' succession to the CEO job, while not unexpected, was not particularly celebrated in EMEA or Asia/Pacific. Although she was highly regarded as a capable and strong leader, she was generally perceived to have a "U.S.-centric" focus. This perception was reinforced by her announcement on April 23, 1991, that GLOBAL would reorganize into international product groups with independent geographic marketing and distribution companies (see Exhibit 3). The product groups were as follows:

Best Brands—specialized in OEM and after-market automotive sound systems, speakers, and gauges. These were manufactured in the United States, Germany, and Singapore.

EXHIBIT 3 **Organizational Chart, April 23, 1991**

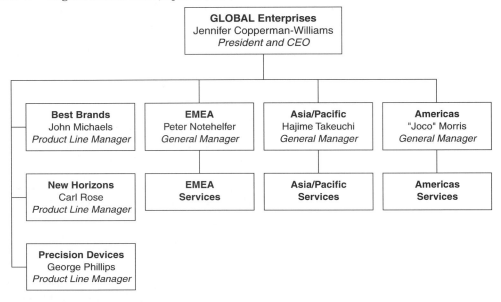

New Horizons—built its proprietary visual display and simulation technology into a leadership position in the multimedia entertainment and communications industry, with manufacturing facilities in Mexico, Italy, and Korea.

Precision Devices—specialized in "big ticket" customized medical diagnostic and process control systems with design and manufacturing facilities in the United States, Japan, and France.

Professional Services—provided consulting, programming, and facilities management services to the medical and data processing industries. This product line tended to be regionally unique and, as such, would continue to report directly to the geographies.

Under the new organization, Product Line Managers (PLMs) were paid on Market Share and Sales Operating Profit. PLMs controlled investments in R&D and all aspects of production. Country-based General Managers (GMs) were evaluated on Net Profit, Customer Satisfaction, and Employee Morale. They controlled all marketing, sales, and service activities.

Not surprisingly, many GMs were frustrated because they had lost control of product development and production. Notehelfer and Takeuchi were particularly upset at the perceived loss of power and prestige associated with the reorganization. They were also angry that their input on the restructuring had, for the most part, been ignored.

During this period, the patents on several "cash cows" and New Horizons' licenses on proprietary manufacturing processes expired. This caused intense pressure on prices and manufacturing costs and opened the door to new competition. In 1993, for the first time in history, GLOBAL lost $71 million on $2.4 billion in sales.

Key events from the perspective of the GMs and PLMs include the following:

John Michaels, PLM of Best Brands

Sales of cars and trucks and the profits of the companies that make them are hitting new highs every quarter. Unfortunately, this is happening at the expense of the independent suppliers who have had to increase productivity and cut costs just to squeeze out razor thin margins. This is particularly true in the automotive sound systems industry, which has gone through a blood bath and continues to be a basket case.

The products are all the same under the covers and the only purchase criteria are price and delivery. Brand name, while important in the after-market, is of no value in the OEM market. Hell, there are times when I could make more money buying stuff in bulk from our competitors and putting it out under our name than I could by building it in our own factories.

If we are going to succeed in this business, we must consolidate our manufacturing and cut our costs. Unfortunately, it has been almost impossible to get the geography GMs to accept this. They give it lip service until it comes time to face the music and close a plant in one of their countries. Then they cry like babies. . . . "it will kill morale, the government will go nuts, I am not going to be the GM to have the first layoff."

We need to face the facts. This is a flat commodity market where we can make some money if we are the low cost producer and pay attention to balancing demand and production. The first step was closing down our antiquated plant in Europe and doubling our production capacity in the U.S. It was painful and expensive, but we are now positioned to be much more competitive and profitable. The next step will be to close the plant in Singapore. I know it will take some time and investment capital, but if we are serious about this market we must do it. If not, we should hand out the pink slips and turn the plants into shopping malls.

Carl Rose, PLM of New Horizons

The marketplace for interactive entertainment, virtual reality, and multimedia communications is going to explode. It will dwarf the PC boom and the developing nations of Asia and eastern Europe will lead the way. The beauty of it is that we don't have to worry about the infrastructure—cable, optic, glass, cellular, satellite, laser, magnetic, digital, etc.—it doesn't matter. The value added in this market is all in the application. The winner will be the company that can integrate multiple independent complex virtual worlds in a way that brings value to the user, improves the quality of life, and helps people rediscover fun. I call it "reengineering life", the ultimate thrill in cyberspace.

We have a good start on this thing, but like any huge new market, it is crowded with deep pocket wanna-be winners. While we fight it out, the demand is going to continue to grow at a 15 percent a year with no end in sight. Anyone who misses this, or stands in the way, should be summarily executed. That includes the nay sayers in GLOBAL who just don't get it. I can't ever remember it being so hard getting funding as it is now. The future of GLOBAL is in New Horizons, and getting there faster, with more for less, is my mission.

George Phillips, PLM of Precision Devices

The aging Precision Devices product line, although approaching end of life, continues to be the most profitable for GLOBAL. Over the last four years the impact of managed health care and hospital cost constraints has slowed the industry growth rate from 12 percent per year to 5 percent. Precision has held on to 25 percent of the market by combining continued investment in R&D with highly visible, personalized, value added marketing. I could grab another 15 points of the market if we had the capital to expand production capacity and took a more aggressive pricing posture.

Unfortunately, I have not been able to convince Jennifer or the GMs to make a major investment in Precision Devices. After all, it is a cash cow and is supposed to generate the capital to invest in New Horizons, not consume it. This difference of opinion has become a source of constant frustration and frequent angry debate. I feel that Rose spends too much time in fantasy land, where the rubber meets his dreams, and never comes to grips with the fact that he has yet to show a profit. We have reached the point where continuing with New Horizons is throwing good money after bad.

Jeremy "Joco" Morris, GM, Americas

You know, at 65, I am one of the youngest senior managers in GLOBAL and although I hate to admit it, I am running out of steam. This business is beating me up. The profit margins are way down and the competition has become fierce. We are all holding our breath for Rose to ride in on his white stallion with another New Horizons blockbuster but, so far, it is not happening. Thank goodness for the services business. While it might not be the most profitable, it is surely the most fun. I really enjoy the personal relationships that have been built over the years.

Despite that, if the truth be known, I want to spend more time being a grandfather and plan to retire as soon as I have finished helping Jennifer clean up the mess that Notehelfer made when he closed his Best Brands plant. I owe her old man that much and, anyway, she has been like a daughter to me.

Peter Notehelfer, GM, Europe, Middle East, Africa

There is an old German saying, "the devil is in the details." That goes to the heart of the problem with the way GLOBAL has gutted the power and capability of the country organizations in favor of centralized U.S. control. Neither Jennifer nor her PLMs have ever had a job outside of the U.S. What do they know about our culture, about our customers, about our unique market requirements?

Case in point, look at the decision to close my Best Brands plant in favor of doubling capacity in the U.S. Michaels thought I should be a good team player and jump at the opportunity to ring up Bonn to tell them we are going to throw a bunch of Germans out of work so that we can import products from America. It sure was convenient that he wanted to double the capacity in Joco's territory and that Joco has an almost mystic ability to influence Jennifer. The whole thing was a little too cozy for me.

To top it off, we lost $58 million on the sale of the plant and paid out another $71 million in severance payments and other extraordinary charges. It was the first layoff in the history of GLOBAL, even dating back to the days of Rhine Mark. It has left me with a huge political problem and has impacted the morale of the entire European operation. It was, in my opinion, one of the dumbest business decisions you could make.

Hajime Takeuchi, GM, Asia/Pacific

We have a long and proud history of association with GLOBAL from the early days when Nitta-San formed his partnership with Copperman-San. Over the years we have seen the roots of that partnership intertwine and enrich the lives of our employees and their families. Recently, however, the pressure of being a public corporation has caused us to take the seductive road to short-term success at the expense of long-term opportunity.

Perhaps the cultural gap between Japan and the U.S. is too wide for us to understand each other. We appreciate the pressure to show profits every quarter, but we must not do so at the expense of missing the emerging opportunity in the New Horizons line. We must be patient and make personal sacrifices until we can put these hard times behind us. It is most important during these times that the young woman, who is our CEO, has the wisdom to seek guidance from Copperman-San and Nitta-San as she moves forward on the competitive battlefield.

FEBRUARY 17, 1995

Copperman-Williams met with her father over dinner to give him a personal preview of the 1994 business results (see Exhibits 4–7). With the Board meeting the next day, she had little choice but to brief her father. Although now 72 years old, Ben Copperman remained the company's biggest single shareholder and a strong supporter of his daughter. Jennifer ran through the events of the last year.

I backed Michaels' plan to consolidate the production of Best Brands to get a cost advantage which would help them grow and become profitable. The gamble worked out well and helped the Best Brands product line show a small operating profit of $30 million on sales of $628 million. In Europe, Notehelfer dragged his feet on closing his Best Brands plant and ended up paying almost $100 million

EXHIBIT 4

GLOBAL Enterprises Consolidated Income Statement—1994 (in millions)

	Americas	EMEA	Asia/Pacific	Total
Sales revenue	$858	$833	$855	$2,546
Cost of products & services	480	467	487	1,434
Depreciation & inventory charges	65	55	68	188
Gross margin	313	311	300	924
Expenses	288	288	288	864
Operation profit	25	23	12	60
Quality programs	10	10	10	30
Extraordinary charges	0	129	0	129
Net earnings before taxes	15	(116)	2	(99)
Taxes	0	0	0	0
Net earnings	15	(116)	2	(99)

EXHIBIT 5 GLOBAL Enterprises Consolidated Product Income Statement—1994 (in millions)

	Best Brands	New Horizons	Precision Devices	Services	Total
Sales revenue	$628	$528	$757	$633	$2,546
Cost of goods sold	450	349	251	384	1,434
Depreciation	23	34	108	18	183
Inventory charges	1	3	1	0	5
Gross margin	154	142	397	231	924
Marketing expense	108	198	216	161	683
Research & development	15	46	75	45	181
Operating profit	31	(102)	106	25	60
Quality programs	10	10	10	0	30
Extraordinary charges	129	0	0	0	129
Net earnings before taxes	(108)	(112)	96	25	(99)
Taxes	0	0	0	0	0
Net earnings	(108)	(112)	96	25	(99)

EXHIBIT 6
GLOBAL Enterprises
Consolidated Sources
& Uses of Cash—1994
(in millions)

	Americas	EMEA	Asia/Pacific	Total
Sources:				
Starting cash	$588	$509	$521	$1,618
Sales & receivables	895	759	812	2,466
Extraordinary cash in	0	237	0	237
Loans in	150	0	0	150
Uses:				
Production costs	458	343	449	1,250
Inventory charges	0	1	3	4
Operating expenses	288	288	288	864
Quality programs	10	10	10	30
Investment in plant	556	217	146	919
Loans out	0	150	0	150
Extraordinary cash out	0	71	0	71
Taxes	0	0	0	0
Current cash	321	425	437	1,183

dollars in separation packages and extraordinary charges. As a result, EMEA ended the year with a $115 million loss on sales of $833 million. Thank heavens for George Phillips. He milked the Precision product line to a $106 million in profit on sales of $757 million. This all went to help finance Rose, who had promised this would be the year of the big win for New Horizons. The big win turned out to be a $100 million loss on sales of $530 million. Joco squeaked in at $16 million in profit on sales of $857 million in the Americas and Takeuchi-San barely broke even in Asia/Pacific with $2 million in profit on $854 million in sales.

The PLMs have never been more at each other's throats. The restructuring was supposed to have clarified organizational responsibilities, reduced duplication of effort and cost, and leveraged our global size to make us more competitive. Yet it has only created more conflict. The PLMs and the geographies are ready for war. It's starting to show on the bottom line.

EXHIBIT 7
GLOBAL Enterprises Consolidated Balance Sheet—1994 (in millions)

	Americas	EMEA	Asia/Pacific	Total
Assets:				
Cash	$321	$425	$437	$1,183
Intercompany loans	0	150	0	150
Product inventory	5	57	134	196
Receivables	826	794	761	2,381
Plant and services fixed assets	1,695	1,075	1,285	4,055
Total assets	2,847	2,501	2,617	7,965
Liabilities:				
Bank loans	1,000	850	700	2,550
Payables	914	726	826	2,466
Intercompany loans	0	150	0	150
Stockholders' Equity:				
Common stock, par value $25.00 per share				
25 million authorized and issued	208	208	208	624
Accumulated retained earnings	725	567	883	2,175
Total liabilities	2,847	2,501	2,617	7,965

She ended the meeting by asking her father if he thought she was doing the right thing. Copperman listened quietly as his daughter finished speaking. As they stood to leave he said,

You know, I built this company by taking risks and making investments to bring new technology to the marketplace, faster and better than the competition. That is what you have been doing and it is too early to know if it will pay off. I would say you are in Act II of the opera and the fat lady is scheduled to sing next year. You know I'll support you. But I'm not sure of the other directors. You'll do what's right. Give 'em hell.

Once her father left she returned to the task at hand, which meant preparing a statement for the Board. By 8:30 p.m., alone in her office, she had penned the following remarks.

In 1994, GLOBAL generated $2.5 billion in sales and posted a loss of $97 million. I am not here to offer excuses; however, there are several items that need to be brought to your attention to help you put this record in perspective. First, we incurred a one time $130 million extraordinary charge for closing our Best Brands plant in Germany. Second, we invested an additional $100 million in our continued development of the New Horizons interactive multimedia product. If we had ducked these two tough but strategically necessary investments, we would have shown an annual profit of $130 million, or 5.5 percent net return on sales.

I want to make it very clear that I am personally responsible for our 1994 business results. While disappointing in the short term, they represent an investment in the future and are a tribute to the courage, commitment, and support of my colleagues. Despite the problems we encountered last year, GLOBAL is now well positioned in every market and has the potential to generate a 10 percent net return on sales in 1995.

I do, however, believe that our potential can best be realized by an infusion of new ideas and new leadership. As such, I have proposed an amendment to our by-laws that would require the retirement of all officers, General Managers, and Product Line Managers upon reaching age 65. In anticipation of board approval of this amendment, I have asked for, and received, the undated letters of resignation of all the GMs and PLMs. I plan to take action later today on several of them. The others, if they are over age 65, will take effect on July 1.

On a personal note, last month marked my 26th year with GLOBAL. I am thankful for the opportunity I have had to work with such a distinguished group of people. However, I too, have reached a point where it is time to move on. Therefore, I am offering my resignation to the board, to become effective on whatever date you choose. In the interim, I will continue my commitment to helping GLOBAL achieve sustained profitability and market leadership.

As Jennifer closed her note pad, she realized that a statement of this sort would provide no opportunity for turning back. Lesser action would no doubt be acceptable to the Board. Would this statement, she wondered, go too far? Or, would it not go far enough?

Chapter Forty-Three

Steve Parker and the SA-Tech Venture (A)

On September 2, 1996, SA-Tech, a joint venture between Standard Industries (Standard) of the United States and Good Fortune Enterprises (Good Fortune) of China, began operating in Huadong, a small town about 100 miles from Shanghai. The joint venture was created to manufacture various automotive heating ventilation and air conditioning (HVAC) parts. On September 13, 1996, Good Fortune's president stopped venture operations and would not allow the joint venture general manager into the plant. The general manager had been hired in China by Standard specifically for the joint venture. Good Fortune's president wrote a letter to Standard HVAC's Asia Pacific director and demanded that the general manager be replaced. After various meetings and communications between the partners, it was decided that a new general manager would be appointed and that the general manager would come from Standard. Steve Parker, a Standard manager in China working as Asia Pacific purchasing manager for Standard HVAC, was asked to be interim general manager in SA-Tech. It was now up to Parker to decide if he should accept the position and if so, what he would do to get the joint venture back on track.

STEVE PARKER'S AUTOMOTIVE CAREER

Steve Parker, 32 years old, began his automotive career with Ford Motor Company in Michigan. While attending Michigan State University, he had summer jobs at a Ford plant. After graduation with a degree in MIS in 1988, Parker worked as a

manufacturing foreman in two different Ford plants for six years. In his last position at Ford, he had about 30 unionized workers reporting to him and about $12 million of budget responsibility. In 1993 Parker left Ford and joined Standard Industries (Standard), a large automotive supplier. Standard, a tier one supplier to various automotive firms, manufactured many different types of automotive components, including HVAC parts, seat systems, steering systems, and metal pressings. Parker became a buyer at Standard with responsibility for purchasing about $75 million of components for the Standard HVAC division.

Parker viewed his manufacturing and buying experience as critical to his career because:

> I was comfortable in a factory and had worked with base level workers. The buying job gave me experience in negotiating. I negotiated several long term contracts and developed a good understanding of competitive sourcing and the value that materials and negotiating play in the business.

In 1995 Parker attended a presentation by Standard's head of business development and ventures. The presentation showed how Standard's HVAC business would go from $600 million in sales to $700 billion over the next five years as a result of foreign joint ventures. Even though Parker had never traveled outside the United States, the presentation triggered Parker's interest. After the presentation, Parker told his boss, the director of purchasing, that he would be interested in any international opportunities that might come up, especially in the area of venture negotiations. Two days later Parker's boss told him that if he was interested, there was a new purchasing position in China that had to be filled immediately. The manager selected for the position would be required to spend 50 percent of the next six months in China. The assignment was to look for suppliers in the Asia Pacific region that could support four joint ventures that were being negotiated by the HVAC division: two in China, one in Taiwan, and one in Japan. At the time, Parker was not married so moving at short notice was possible. As well, Parker's buying responsibilities had been secured with three to five year contracts, with annual cost reductions locked in, so he could easily leave his current position. Parker agreed to take the China job and within a week was in Beijing.

THE CHINESE AUTOMOBILE INDUSTRY

Standard Industries was interested in the Chinese automobile market because of the significant expected growth. Sales in 1996 were expected to increase by 20 percent to about 380,000 units, although capacity over the next few years was expected to grow to greater than 700,000 units. More than 95 percent of Chinese production was by joint ventures between Chinese firms and the major international automobile producers. In 1996 new joint venture investments were under way by General Motors, Daimler-Benz, Citroën, Honda, and other firms. In response to concerns about overcapacity, the Chinese government announced that it would not license any more automobile manufacturing joint ventures and revised its projections for future car demand from 1.2 million units in 2000 to 850,000. Adding to the competition was rampant smuggling of vehicles from Japan and South Korea, which was estimated to have reached 100,000 units.

Most of the foreign automobile firms in China were struggling. For example, in 1993 Peugeot began investing in its joint venture plant in Guangzhou to increase production to 150,000 units. In 1996 the Peugeot plant produced less than 3,000 units, down from 6,600 in 1995. Citroën would produce only 13,000 vehicles in 1996, even though its joint venture agreement permitted production of up to 300,000 units. Nevertheless, Citroën was expanding steadily. With the possible exception of Peugeot, none of the automakers appeared willing to withdraw from China, and Japanese firms, latecomers to China, were scrambling to gain a foothold.

Shanghai VW, the joint venture between Volkswagen and Shanghai Automotive Industry Corp., was unique in two respects: it was the only profitable foreign joint venture and the only one to have achieved commercially viable levels of production. Shanghai VW was formed in 1984 as the first foreign automotive venture in China. By 1996, Shanghai VW was producing more than 200,000 vehicles and had built strong supply and distribution channels. Nevertheless, until recently, Shanghai VW had minimal serious competition and, consequently, invested little in product development. The Santana model produced by Shanghai VW was more than a decade old. In addition, Volkswagen's second joint venture with First Auto Works in Changchun, formed in 1988 to produce the Jetta model, was in serious difficulty. Sales in 1996 were 25,000 units, half the target output and far less than the plant's 150,000-unit capacity. The joint venture lost an estimated $100 million in 1996.

The Chinese car market was heavily protected, with import tariffs of close to 100 percent and quotas on the number of cars imported. Foreign producers were prohibited from consolidating sales organizations of imports and joint ventures. Joint venture producers were required to have 40 percent local content in the first year of production and 60 percent and 80 percent in the second and third years. The local content rules meant that firms like General Motors actively encouraged their suppliers to invest in China. In the event that China entered the WTO, tariffs, local content rules, and other protective measures would have to be dismantled.

Despite the problems with overcapacity and profits, most industry observers expected the China automobile market to grow significantly. Discretionary incomes were rising, especially in the major cities, and with the arrival of General Motors and other OEMs, many automotive suppliers, including Standard, believed that the China market was too important to ignore. In fact, the strategic issue for most of the major auto producers and suppliers was not whether to enter the market or how to compete with Chinese companies but rather securing or consolidating profitable market share.

PARKER ARRIVES IN CHINA

Parker went to China in May 1995 as the purchasing representative to the Standard HVAC division venture negotiating team, which was headed up by Joe Ryan, a manager from Standard's business development and ventures group. Two joint venture partners in China had been identified and negotiations were underway. Because material costs for the HVAC division were always over 50 percent of total costs, it was critical to assess the supplier base during the negotiation phase. Also, because tariffs at that time were often as high as 100 percent, domestic sourcing in China was essential if the ventures were to be profitable.

Parker's job was to meet with potential suppliers and assess their potential suitability for the proposed ventures. During the venture negotiations, Joe Ryan was the only real contact with the Chinese partners and was largely on his own in terms of assessing partner competencies and designing the joint venture organization. For finance and legal issues, Ryan had to work closely with Standard's corporate legal and treasury departments. Because Ryan's personal compensation was in part dependent on successfully forming joint ventures, he was anxious to conclude the negotiations.

Almost as soon as he arrived in China, Parker began a four week trip through northeast China, an area full of crumbling state-owned manufacturing plants, often referred to as China's rust belt. For about a year, Parker traveled between China and the United States, with four weeks in China and one week in the United States. During this period he visited about 200 firms all over China as a preliminary investigation of their potential to become suppliers to Standard's joint ventures. Besides his work with the HVAC division, Parker helped support China purchasing for several other Standard divisions.

In April 1996, Parker became an expatriate based in China and was appointed Asia Pacific purchasing manager for the Standard HVAC division. In a matrix structure, he reported to both Mark Hunt, Asia Pacific director of Standard HVAC and the Standard HVAC purchasing director based in Detroit. Besides Hunt and Parker, five other American expatriates in the HVAC division were also in China. These managers were responsible for finance, sales, engineering, venture development, and marketing. Parker was based in Shanghai because most of the potential automotive suppliers were in the Shanghai region. The other Standard expatriates were based in Beijing.

Standard HVAC signed one joint venture agreement in June 1996 and the SA-Tech agreement in August 1996. After the two joint venture agreements were signed, Parker's job shifted to support for venture purchasing. He had two main tasks: train the Chinese purchasing managers in competitive sourcing and bring the ventures' purchasing departments up to QS9000 levels.

SA-TECH

The SA-Tech joint venture was negotiated over the period June 1995 to late August 1996. The Chinese partner, Good Fortune Enterprises (Good Fortune), was a large diversified Chinese company that contributed its automotive HVAC division to SA-Tech. The HVAC division, which had more than 700 employees, represented about one third of Good Fortune's total business. The other main business was tools such as pliers and screwdrivers. Good Fortune was also trying to launch a joint venture to build small cars. Good Fortune was a Chinese Township Enterprise company that was, as far as Standard and Parker knew, family controlled. At times, Good Fortune deferred to higher authorities but throughout the life of the venture, Parker and other Standard managers never truly understood who owned and controlled the partner. The venture equity split was 60 percent for Standard and 40 percent for Good Fortune. The board included three members from Standard and two from Good Fortune. The chairman of the board was from Good Fortune but this position did not have any veto rights.

Good Fortune was interested in forming the joint venture for two main reasons. One, without new technology it was only a matter of time before the company would be unable to compete against other HVAC firms that had access to Western technology. Two, in return for contributing its HVAC business to the joint venture, Good Fortune would receive a significant cash payment. The cash would come from Standard. In a worst case scenario, if SA-Tech failed, Good Fortune had managed to divest 60 percent of its HVAC division assets. The valuation of the assets was based on projected profits from SA-Tech. Standard agreed to pay Good Fortune $20 million in two installments of $10 million: one at the start of the joint venture and another 18 months later. The first payment would be due one month after the official start of the joint venture.

Standard HVAC's contribution came in two areas: technology for new products and cash. There were four different technology agreements for four different products. These agreements included a lump sum payment to Standard plus a royalty. When the joint venture was formed there was no guaranteed new business associated with the new technology.

Because the JV was not a greenfield business, joint venture startup was quite straightforward since the workforce, plant, customers, and suppliers were already in place. The most important early issue to resolve was the selection of a joint venture management team. A Chinese manager named Yin Chung Li from Dalian was hired by Joe Ryan to be SA-Tech's general manager. Mark Hunt, Standard HVAC's Asia Pacific director, believed that the best approach to joint venture management was to appoint local Chinese managers to represent Standard and then support them with the functional area expatriates based in China (like Steve Parker). Yin started work in July 1996 and was not involved in the joint venture negotiation. One of Yin's first actions was to hire 20 new employees, which included managers for engineering and manufacturing operations, quality, and sales. Standard hired a Chinese manager to be SA-Tech's chief financial officer. All of the new managers spoke English.

Good Fortune appointed the venture's HR manager, purchasing manager, and deputy general manager. The deputy general manager was Li Chu Kang, the son of Li Hong Tan, the founder and president of Good Fortune. Prior to the joint venture formation Li Chu Kang had run Good Fortune's HVAC division. None of the managers in Good Fortune or those appointed by Good Fortune to SA-Tech had a university education.

SA-Tech began operating on September 2, 1996, with a $1 million cash contribution for working capital from Standard. Ten days later, Good Fortune's president, Li Hong Tan, stopped SA-Tech from operating and would not allow Yin and his 20 hires into the plants. They were allowed only in the SA-Tech office. In reality, the business kept operating as if it was 100 percent owned by Good Fortune and not as a joint venture. At this point, the first $10 million payment had not yet been made to Good Fortune—it was due in a few weeks.

Li Hong Tan wrote a letter to Standard's Mark Hunt (Hunt was an SA-Tech board member) with 14 demands. The 14 demands were viewed by Standard as both serious, such as the request for a new general manager for SA-Tech, and frivolous, such as the general manager must have a less expensive car and the CFO must not get a car. Most issues were viewed as "face" issues by Standard. In a meeting with Mark Hunt, Yin accused the Good Fortune managers of cheating and he was unhappy about the $20 million asset agreement, even though this agreement was in place before he was hired. Yin argued that at $20 million, Standard was significantly overpaying for its 60 percent investment in Good Fortune's HVAC business.

A meeting was held on Monday, September 23 at Standard's Beijing office. Participating were Li Hong Tan, his son Li Chu Kang, Mark Hunt, and Standard's HVAC assistant director of Asian operations. It was conceded by both sides that Yin Chung Li was unsuitable as joint venture general manager and would have to be replaced. Mark Hunt had never trusted Yin (he had been hired by Joe Ryan without any consultation with Hunt) and now that Good Fortune was unhappy with Yin, he was willing to side with the partner. The Chinese side demanded that an American from Standard be appointed as general manager. It was their belief that Standard was not committed because they did not bring any expatriates to the venture. They also believed that an American manager would help them sell to other Chinese automotive OEMs.

A second meeting involving the same people was held on Wednesday. Steve Parker was called to a meeting on Friday afternoon with Mark Hunt. Hunt explained the situation to Parker:

> We would like you to be the interim general manager in SA-Tech. I am committed to doing the venture so you need to go in and establish a plan and a timeline for getting the business back on track. Originally I was not in favor of putting expatriates in our ventures because of the cost. However, I now think that we need to have our own people on the ground and be willing to pay for it. We really need to start over and do our due diligence to understand what it is going to take to bring this plant to world class level. We also need to make sure that we get this venture back on track with a process that is consistent with the way Standard runs new businesses.

Other than being told to "fix the problems and rescue the joint venture," Parker was given no specific instructions as to what should be done, mainly because within Standard, there was very little understanding of the situation. By this time, Joe Ryan, the venture development manager, had returned to the United States. His replacement was unfamiliar with the history of the joint venture. In fact, nobody in Standard knew much about the venture's operations because Ryan had worked on the project by himself and had coordinated more closely with his U.S.-based boss than the HVAC Asia Pacific director. If he accepted the position, Parker would be seconded to SA-Tech and paid by the joint venture. He would report directly to the joint venture board. He would also report informally to Mark Hunt who, in reality, was Parker's boss and responsible for decisions that would impact his career.

Chapter Forty-Four

Sicom GmbH and CD Piracy

"As far as I am concerned, it is not an issue we need to worry about," said Josef Radler in April 1997. Radler was the chief executive of the German firm Sicom GmbH (Sicom). Sicom, the leading firm in the compact disc (CD) equipment industry, produced CD replicators. CD replicators were used to produce copies of CDs from master versions. According to Radner:

> We are the world's leading manufacturer of CD replicators. When you are the biggest player, you have the biggest chance of supplying people who infringe on other people's rights. I am not going to stop selling replicators in Asia. How can I control who uses our product? What about the manufacturers of photocopiers? They must know that sometimes their machines are used to illegally copy books and other printed materials and even money. Should these companies be held responsible for illegal photocopying?

Radler had recently discussed the issue of CD piracy in China with Sicom's managing director for Asia, John Thomson. Thomson, based in Hong Kong, was adamant that CD piracy was not Sicom's concern. According to Thomson:

> I am not here to enforce the law. My job is to sell products. If I sell you a car, do I ask if you have a valid driver's license? No. It is not our responsibility to determine if our Chinese customers have licenses to import CD replicators. Sometimes we ask them and sometimes we don't. When we ask them, they just say they applied and expect to get one soon. What more are we supposed to do?

SICOM GMBH

CD replicators were used to reproduce CDs from master copies. A decade before 1997, producing CDs required large clean rooms that sealed out dust and other substances that could damage disk quality. The equipment used in these clean

rooms was very expensive, required great technical expertise to operate, and cost about $30 million. In 1987, Josef Radler developed technology that greatly simplified CD manufacturing. This technology resulted in glass-enclosed units that were much smaller than the clean rooms and could be used as self-contained assembly lines. Radler's machines were easy to use and transport, and most important, were priced at about $2.5 million. Based on the new technology, Radler had built a successful business based in Rosenheim, a small town near Munich. Sicom became the world's largest producer of CD replicators. Sales in 1996 were $120 million, 45 percent in Asia. Sicom had a reputation for high quality and timely delivery and was recognized as the industry technology leader.

Most of Sicom's replicators destined for the Asian market were air-freighted to a Hong Kong agent for shipment to final destinations. Because Hong Kong, due to become part of China in July 1997, was a free port, there were no import or export restrictions on replicators. When CD replicators arrived at a customer's premises in China, Sicom engineers were called in to set up the equipment. Sicom engineers did not attempt to determine whether the CD production line was legal or illegal.

CD PIRACY

According to one estimate, nearly 200 million pirate CDs were produced annually, with 60 percent coming from China.[1] The International Federation of the Phonographic Industry (IFPI) claimed losses of $2.2 billion due to CD piracy. Although precise data were unobtainable, the largest market for pirate CDs was thought to be Russia, mainly imported from China and Bulgaria. Despite new intellectual property laws introduced on January 1, 1997, piracy in movies, computer software, and CDs was rampant in Russia. In dollar terms, the second largest market for pirate CDs was thought to be the United States.[2] In Western Europe, Italy was considered the largest market for pirate CDs.[3] Significant declines in the sale of pirate CDs had occurred in a number of countries, including the United Kingdom, South Korea, and Thailand.

As a measure to reduce piracy, a coding system (called SID codes) was introduced in 1992 as a joint initiative by Philips Consumer Electronics, which issued licenses to use its CD manufacturing technology, and the IFPI, which oversaw the code-monitoring system. The coding system involved two code numbers applied to the silver inner part of the disc. One number identified the plant that manufactured the master CD and another number identified the plant where the disc was replicated. The latest IFPI figures estimated that 68 percent of all CD production plants worldwide were using the codes.[4] In China, the coding system became mandatory for all CD production in 1995.

CD Piracy in China

CD piracy in China began to flourish in the early 1990s when other Asian countries took steps to curb the piracy within their borders. In particular, when the government of Taiwan shut down pirate CD plants, Chinese CD piracy took off.

Despite the efforts of the Chinese government to crack down on piracy by closing CD plants and destroying illegal CDs, piracy continued to flourish. It was estimated that about 90 percent of the CDs purchased in China were counterfeit. Many of the illegal factories reportedly were joint ventures with Taiwanese businesses, which helped finance the equipment used to produce counterfeit CD product. By early 1994, China had at least 25 CD plants with a total capacity of about 75 million CDs, at a time when demand for legitimate CDs in China amounted to no more than three million units.[5]

The majority of pirate CD plants were believed to be located in the South China province of Guangdong, often operating with the cooperation and support of provincial officials. Until the development of replicators like those produced by Sicom, China-based pirate CD manufacturers struggled to deal with the environment and, in particular, the high humidity prevalent in South China. Pressing digital discs of any quality required sterile temperature- and humidity-controlled conditions that were difficult to create. The new replication equipment overcame this problem with self-contained manufacturing systems that could be operated virtually anywhere. One report suggested that with a reliable, portable power supply, pirates could produce CDs from the back of container trucks in the near future, perpetually and untraceably roving the countryside like truck-mounted Cold War Soviet missiles.[6]

Many of the pirate CDs produced in China were shipped around the world through Hong Kong. Given the huge volume of goods that passed through Hong Kong, there was little customs inspectors could do to stem the flow of illegal goods. Each day, more than 15,000 trucks and 300 container ships moved from the Chinese border to Hong Kong. Random checks were carried out only on goods destined for the Hong Kong market and on those that had to be off-loaded and stored in Hong Kong for more than 24 hours.

One of the complaints of the music industry was that Chinese restrictions against the importing of legitimate CDs contributed to the growth of the pirate industry. The situation with respect to imported music seemed to be changing. According to the IFPI, the number of titles approved for import to China had grown from 150 in 1992 to 300 in 1995 to about 450 to 600 in 1996.[7] Nevertheless, although official import quotas for recordings had been abolished, significant hurdles remained for the music companies trying to develop the Chinese market. The many steps involved in getting a license for the sale of a music recording included: identifying a Chinese record company as a business partner, showing proof of copyright ownership of the recording to be licensed, discussing trade terms, signing a letter of intent, providing a sample of the recording and translation of the lyrics for censorship review, signing a contract and registering the deal with the national copyright-administration officials, and providing a master recording once approval was obtained. Compounding the difficulties of licensing was a royalty rate as low as 10 cents per cassette or $1 per CD, long waiting periods for payment, the lack of promotion and marketing for releases, the restricted sale of products through only a single company; and the virtual impossibility of verifying sales figures.[8]

A further issue associated with the sale of legitimate CDs in China was that only about 10 percent of the population had enough disposable income to spend on consumer products such as audio recordings. Nevertheless, 10 percent of the population represented a potential market of 120 million, predominately in the country's major cities. With the growth of satellite television, Chinese consumers were becoming more aware of different forms of entertainment.

THE POLITICS OF PIRACY

The issue of piracy had become a contentious political issue. In 1994, the Recording Industry Association of America began to pressure the Chinese government to deal with the pirate CD operations. On February 26, 1995, after the threat of sanctions by the U.S. government, the Chinese government issued a 28-page agreement agreeing to the following:[9]

- to investigate all CD production lines.

- to seize and destroy all infringing products, as well as the machinery used to manufacture such products.

- to revoke business permits for factories involved in illegal production.

- to ban the export of infringing products.

- to introduce a copyright verification system that would prevent manufacture and export of CDs that had not been cleared by the Chinese government and representatives of affected copyright owners.

- to monitor CD plants for compliance and to revoke business permits of companies operating without SID codes or outside of approved verification channels.

- to abolish all quotas or other restrictions on the importation of audio products.

- to permit U.S. record companies to enter into joint ventures for the production and reproduction of audio products.

In the aftermath of the agreement, few of the provisions were implemented. CD piracy continued to grow in scale and American record companies were making only limited progress in gaining entry to China. In late 1995, the IFPI closed its branch office in Guangzhou because of reports that CD pirates had hired hit men and taken out contracts on the IFPI office staff.[10] The director-general of IFPI promised to reopen the office as soon as Chinese authorities could guarantee his staff's safety. The IFPI was also trying to stop the pirates by blocking their supplies of raw material. CDs are pressed from polycarbonate plastics. Only five companies in the world produced polycarbonate with the purity and thermal and optical characteristics necessary for CDs.

In 1996, the U.S. government once again threatened to impose trade sanctions on China if the Chinese government did not clamp down on the illegal production of U.S. films, music, and computer properties. Under an intellectual property rights agreement negotiated between the United States and China in June 1996,

China agreed that imports of CD replicators would require a license. The Chinese government promised that no new licenses would be issued. The government also agreed to the prosecution or investigation of about 70 individuals involved in the pirate trade and committed to "special enforcement" periods in which actions would be taken on illegal products already in the marketplace.

In 1997, according to Chinese government officials, no new licenses for the importation of replicators had been issued. Since signing the intellectual property rights agreement, the Chinese government had closed dozens of illegal CD operations and destroyed hundreds of thousands of pirate CDs. In December 1996, 20 illegal production lines were closed and the Chinese government indicated that new pirate plants would be shut down as they were discovered. However, the U.S. State Department estimated that at least 27 production lines with the capacity to produce 150 million CDs annually were set up in China in the second half of 1996.[11] It appeared that as the Chinese government clamped down in one region, the illegal and easily transferable factories moved to other parts of China. Within China, it was suspected that there was a market for used CD replicators. Equipment was also being moved out of China to Macau and Hong Kong.

Officials from the United States were putting pressure on their European counterparts to deal with the piracy problem at the source, which meant going after the manufacturers of CD replication equipment. Most of these firms were in Germany, Holland, and Sweden. EU officials insisted that the problem was in China and must be solved by the industry and by China. In reaction, U.S. Trade Representative Charlene Barshefsky publicly stated:

> The focus is to do whatever we can to help ensure that CD presses do not go into China. So far, in spite of our repeated efforts, the EU and member states take a see-no-evil attitude.[12]

SICOM'S SITUATION

Josef Radler recognized that his company could get caught in the middle of a battle between U.S. and EU government officials. Publicly, his position was that Sicom should not be held accountable for the actions of others:

> If CDs are being made illegally with Sicom equipment, it is up to the various countries to enforce their laws. In a free market, Sicom should be able to sell to any customer that wants the product and has the money to pay for it. We are a small company with limited resources in a highly competitive industry. If I refuse sales because I am concerned about possible illegal use of the equipment, I can assure you there are other CD equipment firms who would gladly take the orders. I have to keep my costs down and improve my technology. I cannot afford to cut my sales back. If I do, I might as well shut my business down. How am I supposed to explain that to my employees? I have worked hard to build this business and support my community. My replication equipment is the best in the industry. Why should I stop selling to certain customers just because of rumors that my customers are not using the equipment properly?

Endnotes

1. R. S. Greenberger and C. S. Smith, "Double Trouble: CD Piracy Flourishes in China and West Supplies Equipment," *The Wall Street Journal* (April 24, 1997), pp. A1, A13.
2. "Stolen melodies," *The Economist* (May 11, 1996), p. 64.
3. "One in Every 5 Music Recordings Sold in 1995 Was Pirated Copy," *Audio Week* (May 20, 1996).
4. T. Heath, "A Safer World For Replicators," *Billboard* (August 24, 1996), p. 41.
5. J. Berman, "Chinese Piracy Reform Still Murky In '96," *Billboard* (January 6, 1996).
6. B. Atwood and G. Burpee, "War On Piracy Continues In China," *Billboard* (July 20, 1996).
7. T. Duffy, "Music Imports Increasing In China," *Billboard* (June 1, 1996).
8. *Billboard,* June 1, 1996.
9. Berman, 1996.
10. B. Fox, "Chinese pirates target CD police," *New Scientist* (January 6, 1996), p. 7.
11. *The Wall Street Journal,* April 24, 1997.
12. Ibid.

Chapter Forty-Five

DSL de Mexico S.A. de C.V. (A)

In late April 1996, Lane Cook, the 28-year-old General Manager of Distribution Services Limited de Mexico (DSL), had just finished a meeting with José Hernandez, the traffic manager of SuperMart, a medium-sized Mexican retail company. DSL, a U.S.-based freight consolidator, had spent two years trying to build a business in Mexico. Despite initial successes, the collapse of the Mexican economy hit DSL's business hard. Faced with falling revenues and substantial overhead costs, Cook began an all-out effort to attract new business. SuperMart seemed like an ideal prospect.

After several weeks of negotiations, Cook believed that he had won Hernandez over and that SuperMart would soon sign a contract turning all of the company's Asian shipping business over to DSL. Prices had been agreed upon and Hernandez gave every indication of wanting to work with DSL. Cook scheduled one last meeting in ambition of finalizing all arrangements. As the meeting was drawing to a close, Hernandez brought up one last request. He insisted that he, not DSL, select DSL's trucking company subcontractor for all of SuperMart's business. Although this condition would not be included in the written contract, Hernandez made it clear that Cook's cooperation would be essential to cement the deal. Although surprised by the request, Cook asked for time to think about it. After the meeting Cook did some investigating and through a contact learned that the company Hernandez wanted to use had made arrangements to funnel payments back to Hernandez on every shipment DSL managed. Cook realized that Hernandez was waiting for a response and wondered what action to take.

THUNDERBIRD
THE AMERICAN GRADUATE SCHOOL
OF INTERNATIONAL MANAGEMENT

Copyright © 1997 Thunderbird, The American Graduate School of International Management. All rights reserved. This case was prepared by Professor Allen J. Morrison for the purpose of classroom discussion only, and not to indicate either effective or ineffective management.

COMPANY BACKGROUND

Distribution Services Limited was founded in 1978 by Philip Clarke, Sr., and Cobb Grantham. Both men served together in the Korean War and worked in Asia after the war for Sea-Land Corp., a major U.S.-based shipping company. While at Sea-Land, Clarke and Grantham recognized a potential trans-Pacific market for ocean freight consolidation. Although commonly used for shipments between North America and Europe, in the late 1970s the consolidation business had not been developed across the Pacific. Believing that the Pacific shipping market presented great opportunity, Grantham and Clarke left Sea-Land in 1978 and started DSL. Based in Hong Kong, DSL focused on consolidated orders for U.S.-based retail companies that were interested in accessing Asian markets.

Freight consolidators act as agents for either buyers or sellers interested in moving partial container loads of goods. Rather than pay for full container load volumes, customers could work with a consolidator who could pool these smaller sized orders. Consolidators could also save customers money by pre-purchasing, often at substantial discounts, large volumes of capacity with one or more shipping companies. These pre-purchases represented considerable exposure for consolidators; many lost money when anticipated demand did not materialize. However, if demand could be accurately forecast and if operations could be run smoothly, consolidators could make considerable profits. Grantham and Clarke quickly learned that the key to DSL's survival was volume. The more volume they could guarantee, the lower the rates with the shipping lines. It became clear very early on that developing and maintaining an active and healthy client base with steady transportation needs would be critical.

WORKING WITH RETAILERS

Retail shipping needs from Asia to the United States included such products as apparel, toys, shoes, electronic components and the like. The norm for U.S. retail companies was to negotiate prices that were FOB at the supplier's dock. By taking ownership of the goods overseas, retailers could handle negotiations with the freight companies themselves. For large retailers like Sears, Wal-Mart, and J.C. Penney, substantial volume discounts could be secured on massive volumes of goods being shipped. Retailers could also control shipping schedules and manage priority freight more effectively. Finally, FOB contracts enabled U.S. retailers to perform full quality inspections prior to shipping. Not only would they avoid shipping costs for inferior or damaged goods, but feedback to Asian suppliers could be immediate. This feedback minimized longer-term quality problems and increased the overall buying power of the U.S. retail companies.

To facilitate shipping and manage inspections, most large retailers established buying agents or representative offices throughout Asia. These agents or offices negotiated essentially all container load rates with shipping companies. As a result, consolidators relied on two types of retail customers: (1) small customers, including trading companies, that rarely ordered large volumes, and (2) larger retailers who, because of precise sales projections and sophisticated inventory tracking systems, ordered mixed sized lots. For example, Wal-Mart might order 8½ container loads of radios and, rather than wait to consolidate its own shipment, call in a consolidation company to expedite shipment of the half-size load.

DSL'S GROWTH

In the late 1970s and early 1980s, DSL was one of the few consolidators working the Hong Kong–Southern California route. Over its first 10 years, sales grew by an average rate between 15 percent and 20 percent. Gross margins hovered in the 15 percent range, a rate which was considered very healthy in the industry. Over time, DSL opened offices in Taiwan, Korea, China, Singapore, and many other Asian origins.

DSL benefited greatly from a close relationship with Wal-Mart. Both Cobb Grantham and Philip Clarke, Sr., had known Sam Walton since the mid-1960s when he was just establishing his first Wal-Mart stores in Arkansas, and Clarke and Walton's simple and modest personalities produced a strong friendship. Because of this relationship DSL became Wal-Mart's principal consolidator out of Southeast Asia. DSL grew as Wal-Mart grew.

DSL's work with Wal-Mart proved to be fortuitous along a number of other dimensions as well. Wal-Mart was an industry leader in inventory management. In the mid-1970s, Wal-Mart began to invest lavishly on an electronic inventory and purchasing system that would help it reduce order costs, increase its bargaining power with suppliers, and better manage inventories. In 1977, it began using electronic data transmission technologies to link its major trading partners with its order desks. The system, which became known as Electronic Data Interchange (EDI), grew to include an elaborate network that linked suppliers, shippers, warehouses, and individual stores. Wal-Mart insisted that all vendors and shippers upgrade their computer systems so they were compatible with Wal-Mart's state-of-the-art system. By following Wal-Mart's lead, DSL became entrenched in Wal-Mart technology and learned many key advantages in just-in-time (JIT) and inventory management earlier than many competitors. Skills in managing sophisticated tracking and pricing systems provided the company a source of competitive advantage. Not only would such systems raise barriers to entry in the industry, but they also made large customers like Wal-Mart more dependent on a smaller group of dedicated suppliers.

By the end of 1995, DSL had grown to a $200 million company. Of this amount, about $80 million was derived from Wal-Mart; another $50 million came from Target Stores. The balance was derived from such retailers as Edison Brothers, J.C. Penney, Fingerhut, Shopko, Hills Department Stores, the American Retail Group, as well as various U.S.-based trading houses.

As DSL grew, it began to encounter increasing competition. By the late 1980s a number of freight carriers began to move into the consolidation business. More efficient inventory management by the retailers also squeezed consolidators. One senior DSL manager commented on the evolution of the business in the 1980s and early 1990s:

> In the early days the margins were great. Business was sweet. But there are essentially no barriers to entry in the consolidation business. Logistics companies don't require a lot of capital investment. In reality, the freight business is more like a commodity business than anything else. At the drop of a hat, you could find yourself in a bidding war. Anybody could become your competitor. By the late 1980s, our gross margins before administrative costs had dropped to between 8 and 10 percent. In 1994 and 1995, they were down to about 4 percent. Our overall profits in 1995 were about 1 percent of revenue. That's still $2 million. Not bad, but not good enough.

Although Wal-Mart was DSL's largest account, the profit margin on the account was not the largest. Wal-Mart was relentless in pushing its cost down. Despite this, DSL made substantial "indirect profits" through Wal-Mart. Wal-Mart's volume covered a disproportionate amount of DSL's overhead costs. It also allowed DSL to negotiate substantial rate reductions when buying shipping space. As a result, DSL's biggest margins were actually recouped via its smaller customers. And finally, DSL charged back receiving fees to Asian manufacturers that delivered to its warehouse facility in Hong Kong. Although the margins were thin, Wal-Mart's high volume made them a very attractive account. One DSL manager explained how receiving fees worked:

> In many cases we may have a single vendor delivering 50 boxes of Wal-Mart merchandise to our dock in Hong Kong. In addition to charging Wal-Mart our consolidator fee, we charge the vendor a handling fee—in cash, right there on the spot. For 50 boxes we received, the vendor might pay us $30 in handling charges. On some days we get hundreds of vendors each paying $30. After a while it all adds up. The money is not from Wal-Mart, but it's all attributed to the Wal-Mart business.

With increasing competition across the Pacific, DSL focused on providing greater service to its customers and on developing new international markets. The emphasis on service was strongly encouraged by large retailers who were increasingly outsourcing noncore activities. In its early days, DSL would simply inform customers that their shipments had arrived in Long Beach and give directions for pick-up. Over time, retailers demanded a wider range of U.S.-based services including full logistics support in shipping goods to final destinations throughout the United States. DSL soon began breaking up orders at its Long Beach warehouse and shipping directly to retail distribution centers around the country. By the mid-1980s, DSL had set up support offices in several large U.S. cities, including Dallas, San Francisco, New York, Chicago, and Miami.

EXPANSION TO MEXICO

In 1988, DSL's regional director in San Francisco made contact with a large Bay-area trading company that did considerable business with a major Mexican retailer. The trading company, which was buying goods in Asia and selling them to the Mexican retailer, asked DSL to assist in shipping, customs clearances, and the like. In response, DSL in 1990 formed a joint venture with a Mexico City-based shipping agent to assist in managing the new business. DSL viewed the joint venture as a stand alone entity and initially provided little attention or investment.

Throughout the early 1990s trade between the United States and Mexico flourished in part because of the establishment of maquiladora industries. In August 1992, the Prime Minister of Canada and Presidents of Mexico and the United States announced the North American Free Trade Agreement (NAFTA) which would come into effect on January 1, 1994. The passage of NAFTA clearly caught DSL's attention as it promised a dramatic increase in trade between the United States and Mexico.

In 1992, Troy Ryley, a recent graduate from The American Graduate School of International Management–Thunderbird, was hired by DSL to examine the company's joint venture in Mexico. Ryley recommended that DSL break off the relationship with its partner and establish a wholly owned affiliate in Mexico that would pursue more aggressive growth objectives. A small office was set up in Mexico City and Ryley began the DSL effort. Initial discussions with the largest retailers in Mexico—Gigante, Comercial Mexicana, and Grupo Cifra—appeared promising. Gigante had the largest number of grocery and merchandise stores (over 100) in Mexico; Cifra had approximately 80 grocery and merchandising stores but also owned restaurants and a variety of smaller specialty retail chains. Cifra's total retail revenues of over \$U.S.1.2 billion placed it as the largest overall retailer in Mexico. Cifra was also regarded as the best run and most financially sound retailer in the country.

DSL DE MEXICO S.A. DE C.V.

In October 1993, Wal-Mart opened its first store in Mexico as a 50-50 joint venture with Cifra. Within the month, DSL became incorporated in Mexico and began handling not only Wal-Mart's consolidated freight from Asia, but also its domestic consolidation of Mexican suppliers for delivery to its new Mexico Supercenters. In November 1993, DSL subcontracted the use of a small warehouse in Mexico City. DSL placed two employees in the facility to do administrative work but relied on subcontractors for equipment and manual labor. DSL's main accounts were Gigante, Comercial Mexicana, and the newly arrived Wal-Mart. For each of these accounts, DSL acted as the sole consolidator of shipments from Asia to Mexico. To assist, DSL established a small operation in Laredo, Texas, that would help process trans-shipments through the United States and coordinate customs crossings to and from Mexico. In addition, DSL acted as Wal-Mart's sole consolidator within Mexico, a role that included working with Wal-Mart's Mexican vendors by consolidating their small orders and sending full truck loads to the Mexican stores.

In the summer of 1994, Wal-Mart announced an aggressive expansion plan that called for the opening of 100 stores in Mexico by late 1996. Shortly thereafter, DSL rented a larger, 15,000-square-foot warehouse facility in Mexico City.

In November 1994, Lane Cook was appointed General Manager of DSL de Mexico. Cook, 28, was hired by DSL in 1994 when he graduated with a master's degree from The American Graduate School of International Management–Thunderbird. DSL had been impressed with Cook's experience in Latin America, his Spanish skills, and his ability to work independently under difficult conditions. A native of Phoenix, Arizona, Cook had worked for several years in Argentina and had done consulting work in Mexico prior to going back to school. Cook's first position with DSL was in operations in Mexico. When Troy Ryley returned to the United States in November 1994, Cook was asked to take over as DSL de Mexico's General Manager.

By early 1995, Wal-Mart had 33 stores in Mexico, including 22 Sam's Clubs and 11 Wal-Mart Supercenters. In March 1995 DSL moved into a 75,000-square-foot, two-year-old warehouse facility located in the northern outskirts of Mexico City. The new facility was near the main north-south highway connecting Mexico City with Laredo, Texas, and could effectively handle the loading and unloading of 25 trucks. It was leased with the intention of enabling DSL to grow with Wal-Mart demand. Cook commented on the choice of the facility:

> Here it was early December of 1994, and our year-end results were looking very good. It was Christmas time, and our warehouse was overloaded with cargo, and Wal-Mart was demanding that if we were going to continue, we needed a better facility. We were also very positive on the outlook for Mexico and our ability to generate new customers through premium service. When I went to the ownership and gave them my proposal, the Wal-Mart business clinched it. They saw that we were shipping 240 truckloads a month out of a 15,000-square-foot warehouse. Our people were putting in 18 and 20 hour days, week after week because the old warehouse couldn't handle the volume. It was time to move.

HARD TIMES FOR DSL DE MEXICO: THE DEVALUATION

Two days after DSL signed a contract on the new warehouse, Mexico moved to devalue the peso. Between December 20, 1994, and February 1, 1995, the peso's value fell close to 40 percent against the U.S. dollar, and caused what most Mexican experts call the worst economic crisis in Mexico's history. (See Exhibit 1 for a review of the devaluation of the Mexican peso.) Given that the lease was denominated in pesos, the devaluation substantially lowered DSL's warehouse cost in U.S. dollar terms. However, the devaluation also paralyzed the Mexican economy. Imports went into a tailspin, drying up DSL's Asian consolidation business. Purely domestic business also suffered. Cook reflected back on the impact of the devaluation:

> Imports died. So did disposable income. DSL's business was general, non-food merchandise, and after the devaluation all people were buying was food. That's all they could afford. January through June are typically our off months. We would normally expect to move about 180 truckloads a month. In January 1995,

EXHIBIT 1   The Devaluation of the Mexican Peso

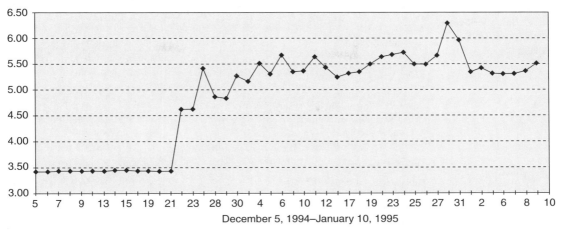

December 5, 1994–January 10, 1995

we handled 80 truckloads. After that it went up to 125 truckloads per month and it hasn't really changed. The devaluation cost us between 20 percent and 30 percent of our domestic volume, and over 50 percent of our import volume. The only positive effect was that our exports are on the rise. It has been a challenge to get senior management in the U.S. to understand the extent of our problems because they are so busy, and they have other priorities at present. Also, DSL de Mexico is still comparatively small—pocket change in comparison to Asian business.

COOK RESPONDS

Cook had considerable latitude in responding to the crisis in Mexico. As General Manager, Cook reported to C.J. Charlton, DSL's regional director of Texas, Arkansas, and Mexico. Charlton, 58, was based in Bentonville, Arkansas, and had been an active supporter of DSL's Mexican investments. Charlton in turn, reported to Executive Vice President Darse Crandall, who was based at Corporate Headquarters in Long Beach, California. DSL's management philosophy was founded strongly on the importance of delegation. Cook saw Charlton three or four times per year—either in Mexico or in the United States. Cook commented on their organizational ties:

> In general, he knows a lot that's going on. I give him a weekly activity report via our e-mail system. Even more importantly is the fact that most of the truckloads coming into or out of Mexico go through one of DSL's sister companies—a truck brokerage firm called ETA. Charlton is the president of ETA. This means we are in continuous contact over mutual clients and operations. We also end up talking on the phone about twice a week. But his hands-off approach has helped me develop skills and experience a lot faster than any other way.

EXHIBIT 2
DSL de Mèxico S.A.
de C.V., Balance Sheet
December 31, 1995
(N$ Pesos)

Current Assets	
Cash	112,390
Investments	1,138,744
Accounts Receivable	4,705,728
	5,956,862
Fixed Assets	
Transportation Equipment	127,272
Warehouse Equipment	305,852
Office Equipment & Furniture	410,976
Accrued Depreciation	(188,044)
	656,056
Deferred Assets	
Guarantee Deposits	243,200
Advance Payments	57,654
Installation Expenses	483,482
Amortization-Installation	(19,780)
	764,556
Total Assets	7,377,474
Current Liabilities	
Suppliers	1,500,716
Allowance for Profit Sharing	22,234
Allowance for Income Tax	62,774
Taxes Payable	365,746
Accounts Payable-DSL*	5,585,606
Other Creditors	160,260
Total Liabilities	7,697,336
Capital	
Capital Stock	100,00
1994 Loss	(557,188)
Current Profit	137,326
Total Capital	(319,862)
Total Liabilities and Capital	7,377,474

*Dollar denominated

With business hurting, Cook moved quickly to cut costs. In May 1995, the only other American manager (running operations) at DSL de Mexico was transferred back to the United States. By summer 1995, DSL de Mexico's staff had been drastically reduced. The office staff shrunk from nine to seven people: an accountant and an assistant who managed billings, three people who ran import/export traffic and customer service, a messenger, and Cook. Cook described his job as a cross between being operations manager, financial officer, sales director, and warehouse manual laborer. The DSL de Mexico warehouse staff went from 48 people on two shifts to a single shift of 14. The company also contracted external firms to provide security. DSL de Mexico's financial statements are found in Exhibits 2 and 3.

EXHIBIT 3
DSL de Mexico S.A. de C.V., Income Statement January 1– December 31, 1995 (N$ Pesos)

	Amount	Percentage
Net Sales	21,479,002	100%
Sales Cost	0	
Gross Income	**21,479,002**	**100%**
Minus		
General Office Expenses	3,947,252	18.38%
General Warehouse Expenses	16,082,538	74.88%
Financial Income	(423,926)	(1.96)%
Foreign Exchange Losses	1,712,536	7.97%
Other Revenues and Expenses	(61,730)	(0.29)%
Operating Earnings	**222,332**	**1.00%**
Minus		
Allowance for Profit Sharing	22,234	0.10%
Allowance for Income Tax	62,772	0.29%
Net Profit	137,326	0.64%

WAL-MART GOES IT ALONE

By late summer of 1995, the Mexican economy was beginning to show signs of stability. Many at DSL believed that the worst was over. These hopes were shattered when, in July 1995, Wal-Mart broke ground on its own distribution and warehouse facility only 1.5 miles from DSL's building. In establishing an in-house distribution system, Wal-Mart turned to its wholly owned affiliate, McLane. Based in Temple, Texas, McLane, a national distribution and food processing company, was purchased by Wal-Mart in 1990. With 1995 sales approaching $8 billion, McLane owned a nationwide trucking operation, four food processing plants and two food storage warehouses. McLane had little international experience and none at all in Latin America.

As Wal-Mart grew in Mexico, it first invited McLane to assist with grocery distribution. McLane did a surprisingly good job with groceries and soon pushed for the entire Wal-Mart distribution account. The decision to turn the entire distribution operation over to McLane clearly caught DSL by surprise. Another surprise came in late 1995 when Wal-Mart and Cifra agreed to merge their distribution systems in Mexico. The new joint venture distribution company, DCW, would be managed entirely by McLane. Some observers predicted that Wal-Mart would eventually purchase all of Cifra's grocery and merchandise stores.

By the summer of 1996, DCW was managing all of Wal-Mart's and Cifra's grocery and general merchandise distribution in Mexico. DSL continued to act as a consolidator for Asian goods purchased by both companies but lost its domestic consolidation business. Lane Cook reflected on the loss of business:

> The Wal-Mart domestic consolidation account was a huge percentage of our business in Mexico, as we hadn't had much time to diversify. We put a lot of

investment in our new warehouse facility for the account. We put $100,000 into capital improvement—office space, telephone lines (which are very expensive in Mexico), computers, furniture, and so on. We modified some of the facilities as well to better handle their freight. We also signed a two-year lease on the new facility—equivalent to U.S. $210,000 per year in rent. As long as you're just coordinating movements you have no fixed costs or no big capital frontage. Getting into a warehouse you've got fixed costs . . . So all of a sudden, we have a huge fixed cost that we could do five times as many international movements and we still couldn't pay the rent because coordinating movements is a tiny portion of revenues; the real earnings come from warehouse handling—inventory. With the loss of Wal-Mart, we are down from about 80 percent capacity to about 35 percent capacity in our facility.

PRESSURE TO RAISE REVENUES

With so much unused capacity and costs cut to the bone, Cook was under enormous pressure to raise revenues. DSL's U.S. offices helped considerably here. By the summer of 1996, DSL had 20 offices in the United States and many of these had large accounts that did business in Mexico. The collapse of the peso brought about a significant increase in U.S. imports from Mexico. DSL de Mexico regularly received requests for transport price quotes from DSL U.S. offices.

Despite this ongoing interest, Cook believed that the key to growth lay within developing local business, including warehouse accounts. Here, the company faced steep competition.

Service is essentially a misunderstood concept in Mexico. We have trucking companies in Mexico that are slow, often late, and prone to lose some of the boxes on the way. This is actually a common occurrence here and this is what many customers are used to. If most customers can find a shipper who can move $100,000 of cargo for 300 pesos cheaper (under $40 U.S.), they'll switch. They don't view quality service as a tangible value. Part of the reason is that many Mexican companies only look at direct costs—they throw all the rest in administration and overhead. They don't quantify what good service could actually do for them. So, if we are ever going to be successful, we have to educate and convince our customers that time, accuracy and information can save them money. Probably our biggest challenge is that we sell a very ambiguous service. We are not the cheapest. We use a lot of computers and special tracking systems. We have systems that our competitors and many customers don't have. The market in Mexico is probably 10 years behind the U.S. in terms of service technology, so this is new to them.

THE SUPERMARKET ISSUE

With business off and significant overheads to cover, Cook began working overtime to build sales. In May 1996, Cook approached SuperMart, a medium-sized, Mexico City-based general merchandise retailer. SuperMart had a 60-year history in Mexico and revenues in excess of $U.S. 150 million. Initially Cook proposed that DSL engage in a broad array of services with SuperMart. After several meetings with José Hernandez, SuperMart's 58-year-old traffic manager, Cook switched the proposal to the management of SuperMart's import shipments from Asia. Cook estimated that this would be a $U.S.60,000–70,000 business for DSL.

Under normal practices, SuperMart would take possession of the goods in Asia and contract with DSL for shipping to Mexico via the United States. DSL would in turn buy freight space across the Pacific to Long Beach, California, and then arrange ground transportation for the shipments through Laredo, Texas, and on to Mexico City. As a result, DSL's Hong Kong, Long Beach, and Laredo offices would all be involved in managing the shipments. Cook's office in Mexico City would select the transportation company that would bring the freight from the Laredo border to Mexico City and track the shipment for SuperMart.

Hernandez seemed convinced of DSL's capabilities and he and Cook spent considerable time negotiating fees and other arrangements. Cook explained what happened next.

> After about three weeks of meetings and several late night dinners, Hernandez promised us the contract at an agreed upon price but only on the condition that he select the trucking company in Mexico. I later found out through a mutual contact that Hernandez had a bank account here in Mexico City as well as a bank account in Laredo and that the trucking company he selected promised to make a payment to his American bank account whenever a shipment was made. The Laredo bank would then wire the money to Hernandez's Mexico City account. I am sure he didn't want this in the contract because he was worried his boss would find out.
>
> I have thought long and hard about this. On the one hand, the Mexican trucking company he suggested quoted me competitive rates. I am not sure we could do much better. As a result, part of me says, who cares? It's his problem. On the other hand, I am thinking that if they can spare kickback payments to Hernandez, they should be able to lower their prices by that amount to make DSL that much more competitive.
>
> If I don't respond favorably, I am pretty sure that SuperMart will take its business elsewhere. Unfortunately, this is the type of account that we need to see DSL through the tough times here in Mexico. Although there definitely are a lot worse things we could be involved with, I am still troubled by it and wonder what exactly to do. Maybe we should abide by the norms of business here in Mexico. What Hernandez asked for is not that unusual.

Chapter Forty-Six

Staffing Foreign Expansion: Rentsch Enters Poland

In the months after the Berlin Wall fell, Dr. Rudolf Rentsch, CEO of the Rentsch Group, decided his company would need to set up a manufacturing plant in Central and Eastern Europe (CEE). The Rentsch Group manufactured cigarette packaging and counted among its customers many multinational tobacco companies. These customers would very likely invest in the newly opened region, and if Rentsch wanted to supply their packaging, it would need a local presence.

In 1991, Dr. Rentsch asked Horst Hochrein to assess opportunities for expansion to CEE. Hochrein had 23 years' experience at Rentsch in positions ranging from engineering to key account sales. After an extensive study, Hochrein recommended that Rentsch set up a manufacturing plant in Poland.

Rentsch's board of directors approved the proposal to establish a plant in Poland, and Hochrein was appointed as project manager. By December 1993, Rentsch had purchased a bankrupt printing company, called Polgraf, in the city of Łódź.

But acquiring a company was only the first step. To begin operation by the target date of May 1994, Polgraf's manufacturing plant would have to be entirely rebuilt and new equipment installed.

Perhaps even more challenging was staffing the new venture. Polgraf had 60 employees, some of high quality but many lacking in skills, and none experienced in manufacturing cigarette packaging.

Research Associate Janet Shaner prepared this case under the supervision of Professor Philip Rosenzweig as a basis for class discussion rather than to illustrate either effective or ineffective handling of a business situation.

How, Hochrein wondered, could he create a capable workforce in such a short amount of time?

BACKGROUND ON THE RENTSCH GROUP

Rentsch's Origins

The Rentsch Group traced its origins to a small company founded in 1848 in Rickenbach, Switzerland. George and Eugen Rentsch purchased the company in 1901, and for the next 93 years the company was family owned and managed.[1]

By the 1990s, Rentsch specialized in the manufacture of cigarette packaging. Customers included multinational tobacco companies, among them British American Tobacco (BAT), Philip Morris, Reemtsma, R.J. Reynolds, Rothmans, and SEITA (the state-owned French cigarette company). These large customers accounted for most of Rentsch's revenues, but it also sold to a variety of other local or state cigarette companies.

Manufacturing Process and Technology

Rentsch designed and manufactured cigarette boxes. The packing of cigarettes into boxes was handled by the cigarette companies.

The manufacture of cigarette boxes called for specialized capital equipment and raw materials. Printing rollers, engraved for each unique cigarette package, were the most important capital equipment. Each of Rentsch's plants used the same rotogravure machines, costing about SFr 8 million each, supplied by the Swiss company Bobst. Raw materials included paperboard and ink. High quality paperboard was sourced from companies in Sweden, Finland, and Germany. Printing inks could be sourced locally, but each supplier's products had to pass customer quality assurance tests.

Rentsch prided itself on its leadership in manufacturing process innovation. In 1969 it was the first company in Europe to install a rotogravure printing machine with in-line cutting and creasing capabilities. With this new technology, Rentsch developed a unique process for manufacturing cigarette packages called "hinge lids." This machine manufactured the complete product by printing, varnishing, creasing, embossing and cutting high quality paperboard into a cigarette package, with a capacity of 600 million to 700 million packages per year.

Rentsch's International Growth

Until the 1970s, Rentsch had operated entirely in Switzerland. Over the next two decades it expanded internationally at a gradual rate, mainly to provide local production for major customers that were expanding globally.

Rentsch took its first step abroad in 1975 with a greenfield plant in France, thereby gaining entry to the EEC. Located in Ungersheim, in France's Alsace region, the new plant was one hour's drive from Rickenbach. The plant's first managing director (MD) was Swiss, and he commuted to France each day. The

EXHIBIT 1   Rentsch Manufacturing Locations

Source: Company records.

second MD was also Swiss but moved to Ungersheim. The third and all subsequent MDs were French.

Rentsch next expanded to Germany, where it acquired a packaging plant in 1979. In 1991, it bought a plant on the Spanish island of Tenerife. The following year, Rentsch formed a joint venture with the Portuguese state tobacco monopoly and subsequently acquired 100 percent ownership of a plant in Lisbon.

In each instance, Rentsch acquired plants with a good workforce, including skilled employees, capable management and expertise in cigarette packaging. As a consequence, it had not needed to send expatriates for long-term assignments. Rather, it could train employees in Rentsch production methods by sending a few technicians from Switzerland for short-term assignments, or by bringing a select number of employees to Switzerland for training.

Organization Structure

By 1993, Rentsch had manufacturing operations in five countries: Switzerland (260 production employees); Ungersheim, France (200 employees); Berlin, Germany (100 employees); Lisbon, Portugal (100 employees); and Santa Cruz on Tenerife (150 employees) (*refer to* Exhibit 1 *for a map of the manufacturing locations*). It continued to manage its activities from central headquarters in Rickenbach, where 100 employees handled the major staff functions: engineering/technical support, research and development, sales and marketing, and finance (*refer to* Exhibit 2 *for an organization chart*).

EXHIBIT 2   Rentsch Organization Structure

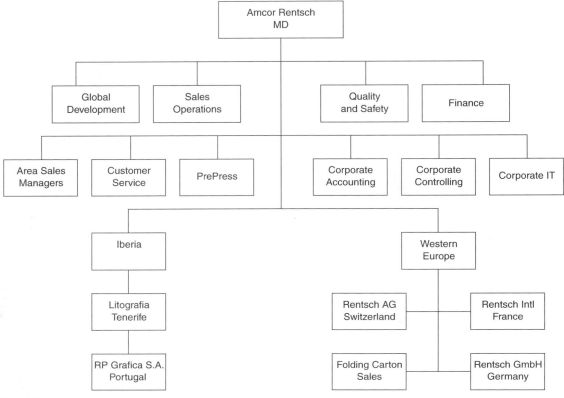

Source: Company records.

RENTSCH POLSKA

While Rentsch was expanding into Spain and Portugal in the early 1990s, it also kept its eye on Eastern Europe. Horst Hochrein's study had identified Poland as the best place for Rentsch to invest. As Hochrein recalled:

> Poland was the right country for Rentsch. In 1993 Poles smoked close to 90 billion cigarettes—that's more than 2,300 cigarettes per person—along with Hungary, the highest in the region [*refer to* Exhibit 3]. That demand could support five modern high-tech packaging machines, and the country had none. It was a pioneer country. For our business, I could see money lying on the streets.

Yet many factors about Poland were troubling. After 40 years of communism, Poland remained in deep economic crisis. Inflation rates were 40 percent to 50 percent, interest rates stood at 30 percent to 35 percent, and GDP/capita was relatively low at $1,900. Most manufactured technology was old, and many buildings were poorly maintained.

EXHIBIT 3A **Cigarettes Consumed per Year (1993)**

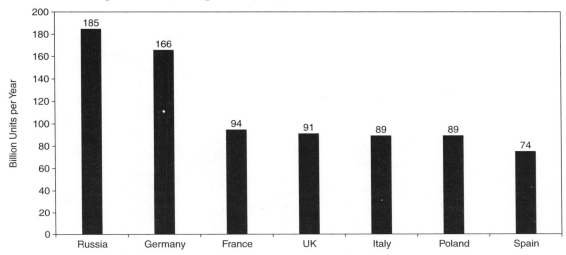

EXHIBIT 3B **Cigarettes Consumed per Capita (1993)**

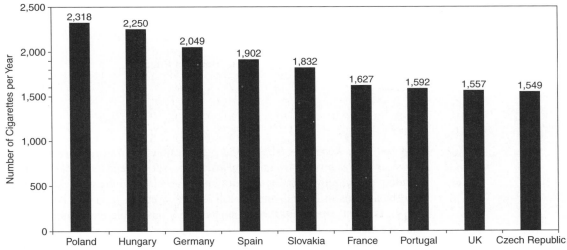

Source: Euromonitor.

By 1993 Rentsch was ready to move forward, and Hochrein searched for a plant location. He focused on the center of the country to facilitate efficient distribution to the six state-owned cigarette companies (*refer to* Exhibit 4). For six months, Rentsch discussed a joint venture with a Warsaw company, but the deal fell through. Searching for an alternative, Hochrein sent letters to the city council of Łódź, the country's third largest city with approximately one million people. More

EXHIBIT 4 Polish Cigarette Packaging Locations

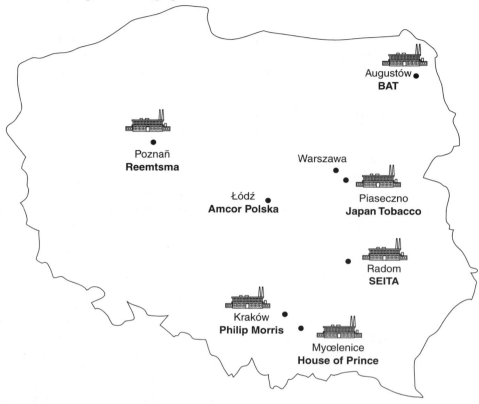

Source: Company records.

importantly for Rentsch, Łódź had the greatest number of printing companies in Poland, as well as seven universities in art, music, science and technical disciplines including polygraphy (printing and design). Łódź also had the greatest number of small businesses in Poland, and several leading Western firms, including Coca-Cola and Gillette, had plants there, suggesting a hospitable environment for foreign investment.

Łódź's business development councillor invited Hochrein to visit the city and set up a meeting at which the managing directors of the town's 13 printing companies presented the capabilities of their respective firms. Hochrein decided that none of these companies was suitable as a candidate for acquisition, but he was impressed by the supportive attitude of the city council.

One month later, the business development councillor told Rentsch about another printing company, called Polgraf. Hochrein recalled:

> We bought the company because it was the best we found. It had a decrepit building, but a good location, land for expansion and 60 employees.

In December 1993, Rentsch bought the company, including its manufacturing plant, for SFr 10 million. The new subsidiary was called Rentsch Polska.

Starting Up: Technical and Supply Challenges

To help get the new organization moving, Hochrein accepted Rentsch Polska's first order from a state-owned cigarette factory in the city of Poznan. Delivery was set for May 1994. In Hochrein's view, it was not only important to meet the deadline but also to exceed quality standards. He believed that Polish customers would be skeptical about a local plant's ability to produce high quality products—according to one manager, they were twice as critical about Polish production as they were about production from existing western plants.

Before the order could be met, Rentsch Polska would need to rebuild entirely the manufacturing plant. Rentsch Polska planned first to install a used offset press transferred from another European plant, then to install a rotogravure press. Paperboard, rollers, inks, and other raw materials could be sourced from Western Europe until local suppliers had been identified and developed.

Human Resource Challenges

Perhaps more critical than the installation of equipment were the human resource challenges. Rentsch had acquired plants before, most recently in Spain and Portugal, and the new Polish plant would be organized in a similar way.

However, the people in Spain and Portugal were already skilled in printing high quality cigarette packaging—only modest training was required for them to master Rentsch's specific technical needs. In contrast, none of Polgraf's 60 employees was experienced in printing cigarette packaging. The employees at Rentsch Polska not only needed to be trained from scratch in printing cigarette packaging but also required coaching in business skills such as purchasing, managing people and teamwork. Hochrein would have to approach staffing and training Rentsch Polska in a different way from what had been done in previous internationalization experiences.

Hochrein planned for Rentsch Polska to grow initially to 90 employees, as shown in Exhibit 5. Hochrein wanted Rentsch Polska to be "self-sufficient" because Poland was relatively far from its Swiss headquarters, and he believed that the customers, employees, financial systems, and government relations were different from those in other European countries. However, Rentsch Polska would still have to rely on headquarters for product development and technical support and for the coaching ability of experienced Rentsch employees.

Hochrein had to consider staffing and training at three levels: managing director, middle management, and production workers.

Managing Director

Polgraf's MD was not considered suitable as the new head of Rentsch Polska, and Hochrein's first major decision was naming a new top manager. One option was to place an experienced Rentsch manager on site as the MD. Hochrein,

EXHIBIT 5
Proposed Rentsch
Polska Organization

Source: Company records.

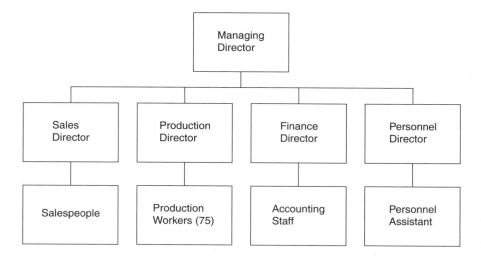

currently the project manager for Rentsch Polska, was a logical candidate to serve as its first MD.

A second option was to look for a local manager to serve as MD. Since no suitable candidates were found among the existing managers, Hochrein looked elsewhere. One candidate came to mind: Jerzy (George) Czubak, a member of the supervisory board appointed by the owner-insurance company to sell Polgraf. He was 34, lived in Łódź, had studied theater at university and led the student anti-Communist movement. Czubak spoke English and Russian and had good relationships with the local authorities. Although he had no printing experience, Czubak had started his first business in 1984, having to get his business permit in another region and then open a Łódź branch because of his anti-Communist activities. Czubak had impressed Hochrein as being decent and honest.

Hochrein debated whether it was better to serve as MD himself or to appoint George Czubak. He was tempted to appoint the local man, but wondered how to assess Czubak's capabilities, and how to ensure appropriate supervision.

Middle Management: Sales, Production, Finance, Personnel

Polgraf's existing middle management team included a production manager and a finance manager. Their capabilities were not well known. Furthermore, there was no sales manager or personnel manager.

Hochrein considered a few options. Should he keep the existing management team and try to bring it up to standard? Should he hire a new team with Polish managers? Or should he look to managers elsewhere in Rentsch's European operations to serve as expatriates? Rentsch had avoided sending long-term expatriates to other countries, but perhaps in Poland it would be necessary.

Production Employees

Most of Polgraf's 60 employees were production workers. Some were reliable and competent, although none was experienced in cigarette packaging. Others were known to drink on the job. There was a large gap between their present skill level and the skills of workers in other Rentsch plants, where new employees spent a full year in training—three months as a helper, then a roller and reel changer, then an ink mixer and, finally, an assistant second printer—and a second full year to become a good printer.

Hochrein's plan called for 75 production employees. With 13 printing companies in Łódź, Rentsch Polska could find new printers, but they still would not be skilled in printing cigarette packaging. Perhaps it was better to hire younger employees with no printing experience. Hochrein wondered how he should go about building a competent production workforce.

Rentsch had no central training group, which made Hochrein's decision more difficult. In each previous acquisition, employees had been trained by their counterparts who traveled from the head office in Switzerland or one of the existing plants. In other instances, select employees were sent to Rentsch plants, such as when Spanish workers from Tenerife, already skilled in printing, went to learn the "Rentsch way" in Rentsch's French, Swiss and German plants. In Poland, however, the situation was different: Rentsch employees seemed less interested in traveling to Poland than to Spain or Portugal, and the number of Polish employees requiring training made it very costly to send them all to plants around Europe.

Despite the immediate challenges he faced, Hochrein remained optimistic about Rentsch Polska. He observed:

> I can see a wonderful company, with 200 employees in the next four years, producing top quality products with a large export business.

But exactly how Hochrein should go about staffing Rentsch Polska was not clear.

Endnote

1. In December 1994, Rentsch was purchased by Amcor, an Australian multinational paper and packaging company with annual sales of A$6 billion (SFr 6.24 billion). The company then became known as Amcor-Rentsch.

Chapter Forty-Seven

Mabuchi Motor Co., Ltd.

In September 1995, a full year had elapsed since Mabuchi Motor Co., Ltd., the world's most successful producer of small electric motors, had implemented a new management training program at one of its foreign operations in China. The program, called New Integrated Headquarters and Overseas Operations (NIHAO), was intended to improve the management skills of local managers in Mabuchi's foreign operations to enable the corporation to maintain its strategy of cost minimization and to allow continued aggressive production expansion. The Manager of Mabuchi's Internal Affairs Department, Nobukatsu Hirano, was responsible for the development and implementation of NIHAO.

A BRIEF HISTORY OF MABUCHI MOTOR CO., LTD.

(See Exhibit 1 for an overview.)

After founding Kansai Rika Kenkyusho, a scientific research institute, in 1946, Kenichi Mabuchi invented the world's first high performance horseshoe-shaped magnetic motor, a significant improvement over prior technology. In the coming years, this product was refined and experiments were undertaken to develop the process of mass production of these small motors.

IVEY

Richard Ivey School of Business
The University of Western Ontario

Anthony Goerzen prepared this case under the supervision of Professor Paul W. Beamish solely to provide material for class discussion. The authors do not intend to illustrate either effective or ineffective handling of a managerial situation. The authors may have disguised certain names and other identifying information to protect confidentiality.

EXHIBIT 1
Summary of
Important Events in
Mabuchi's History

1946	K. Mabuchi designed the world's first horseshoe-shaped magnetic motor
1954	Tokyo Science Industrial Co. is established to begin production
1957	Mabuchi Shoji Co. Ltd. is established to undertake export operations
1958	Mabuchi Industrial Co. is established
1964	Factory is constructed in Kowloon, Hong Kong
1965	Sales office is established in the United States
1966	Sales office is established in Germany
1969	Factory is constructed in Taipei, Taiwan
1978	Factory is constructed in Hukou, Hsinchu, Taiwan
1979	Factory is constructed in Kaohsiung, Taiwan
1984	Mabuchi stock is listed for public sale via the over-the-counter market
	Technical Center is established in Japan to centralize R&D activity
1986	Mabuchi becomes a member of the Tokyo Stock Exchange second section
	Factory is constructed in Dongguang, Guangdong, China
1987	A representative office is established in Singapore
	Factory is constructed in Dalian, China
1988	Mabuchi becomes a member of the Tokyo Stock Exchange first section
1989	Factory is constructed in Chemor, Perak, Malaysia
1992	New Technical Center is completed
	Sales office is established in China
1993	Factory is constructed in Wu Jiang, Jiangsu, China
1994	Factory is constructed in Wangfandian, Liaoning, China

In 1954, Kenichi and his brother, Takaichi Mabuchi, set up a workshop within a toy company to begin production of small electric motors under the name of Tokyo Science Industrial Co. for the Japanese toy industry. In an effort to diversify from the toy business and into emerging markets for small motors, the Mabuchi brothers established their own trading company in 1957 under the name of Mabuchi Shoji Co., Ltd.

Their modest business continued to grow when, in 1964, Mabuchi established a production facility in Hong Kong despite the fact that the yen was very weak, trading at the time at ¥360:US$1. Subsequently, in 1969, a second offshore facility was constructed in Taiwan. These early investments in foreign production were rather unusual for a Japanese company; already by that time, most buyers considered goods produced in Asia outside of Japan to be of inferior quality. Nonetheless, by the end of the 1960s, Mabuchi had established sales offices in both Germany and the United States to manage its developing markets.

In the following decade, the markets for small motors grew significantly in Europe, the United States, and Japan. Mabuchi was encouraged to continue its strategy of production expansion, establishing new plants in Taiwan in 1978 and 1979. By this time, many of the firms that had previously manufactured small motors had fallen away, leaving Mabuchi as the dominant world force commanding about 60 percent of total international demand. Although Mabuchi's main customers were the Japanese manufacturers of audio and visual equipment (i.e., CD players, camcorders, VCRs, etc.), the company also had strong sales positions in Europe and in North America. As Japan's producers became dominant in the expanding world market for consumer electronic products, Mabuchi also enjoyed significant growth in sales and profitability. Throughout the period of 1970 to 1980, in fact, sales multiplied more than six-fold.

Throughout the 1980s, Mabuchi continued to expand production with a focus on China in order to take advantage of the low cost of Chinese labor. In 1986, Mabuchi constructed a firm in the southern Chinese city of Dongguang. It also expanded its production base by subcontracting its requirements on a commission basis to a collection of firms in the free trade zone near Shenzhen, Guangdong, just over the border from Hong Kong. In 1987, Mabuchi made headlines in the popular press by establishing in Dalian, Liaoning, the first Japanese wholly owned subsidiary in China. By 1988, Mabuchi relied on Chinese operations to supply over 40 percent of its total output of small motors. Therefore, in an attempt to diversify from this reliance on China, Mabuchi added a fifth wholly owned production unit in 1989, this time in Malaysia. During this period, Mabuchi's main market remained the audio and visual equipment manufacturers but it was also enjoying strong growth in the automotive and precision tool markets. Just as the Malaysian plant reached full capacity in 1990, Mabuchi's consolidated sales totalled over ¥60 billion and net income reached a new high of nearly ¥7 billion.

From record highs in 1991 of net income (almost ¥10 billion) and earnings per share (¥230 per share), these indicators dropped in 1992 and 1993 due to the depreciating Japanese currency and high capital depreciation costs. In 1993, net income and EPS were 64 percent and 57 percent, respectively, of what they had been two years prior. Nonetheless, Mabuchi continued along its path of expansion, constructing a plant in 1993 in Wu Jiang, Jiangsu, China and following with another Chinese plant in the next year in Wangfandian, Liaoning. At this point, the share of Mabuchi's production that came from China exceeded 70 percent. To diminish its reliance on Chinese output, Mabuchi began actively seeking another production base outside China as established markets continued to grow and new markets were being developed. By 1995, producing over one billion motors a year, Mabuchi's forecast for all markets was bullish and its overall demand figure was projected at double-digit growth. In the view of senior management, there was still a lot of potential to be developed in the small motor business.

THE ELECTRIC MOTOR INDUSTRY

In the 1950s and 1960s, the main markets for small electric motors were toys and games including racing cars and model airplanes although, toward the end of this period, the audio and timepiece markets were beginning to emerge. In the 1970s, new applications for small electric motors were being found in household electronics such as blenders and shavers as well as other applications such as hand-held power tools including circular saws, hedge trimmers, and drills. Throughout the 1980s, the audio and visual markets for motors were very strong as consumer electronic goods firms successfully developed new markets for VCRs, cameras, and camcorders. At the same time, the market for small motors in the automotive industry began to expand rapidly when options such as power windows, power locks, and cruise control became standard features on new cars. By this time, the average car contained between 15 to 20 micro motors while many luxury cars contained three times that number. In the 1990s, with toys becoming more sophisticated (and, hence, requiring more motors), household electronics, audio, and visual equipment becoming increasingly common possessions of the average consumer, and automobiles becoming more automated, demand for motors continued to be great. At the same time, new markets for small motors emerged in such areas as personal computers, computer peripherals, and communication technology including pagers and cellular phones. The market for small electric motors had been very strong for many years and expectations were bullish for the foreseeable future.

Despite its strong worldwide position, Mabuchi was still not free to pick and choose its markets. Johnson Electric, also a well-established and successful family-owned business, was an aggressive competitor absorbing the 35 percent to 40 percent balance of market share not occupied by Mabuchi. A Hong Kong company established in 1959, Johnson Electric had accumulated over HK$1.5 billion in sales and profits of HK$350 million. With over 90 percent of its production capacity in technically sophisticated but low cost operations in southern China, Johnson Electric tried to take away any developing or established markets over which Mabuchi did not have firm control.

MABUCHI MANAGEMENT STYLE AND ORGANIZATIONAL STRUCTURE

Mabuchi's management philosophy was based on the assumption that all people are essentially the same, having similar needs and wants. Whether in an affluent developed country or faced with the struggles that are part of every day life in less developed economies, people have a common longing for security, peace, ease of living, and freedom from want. In Mabuchi's view, the small electric motor had the capacity to contribute to the fulfillment of these desires by freeing people from the demands and dangers that come with physical labor. It was also believed that the motor had the capacity to increase productivity to the point where these common goals were easier to achieve. This attempt to lift the activities of the firm out of the everyday and onto a higher plane was common for Japanese firms. Traditionally, Japanese firms had placed a greater emphasis than many of their western counterparts on finding ways to encourage employees to take on the organization's goals as their own.

In certain ways, Mabuchi was not a typical Japanese organization. Partial evidence of this can be found in the firm's early willingness to develop offshore production capability. However, Mabuchi's management style was, nonetheless, more or less characteristic of Japanese companies. There was a great respect for hierarchy and the lines of authority were very clear (see Exhibit 2). Throughout its history, Mabuchi's head office had always firmly controlled the activities of its subsidiaries, setting standards for both product quality and work practices.

EXHIBIT 2   Mabuchi Motor Co., Ltd. Organizational Structure

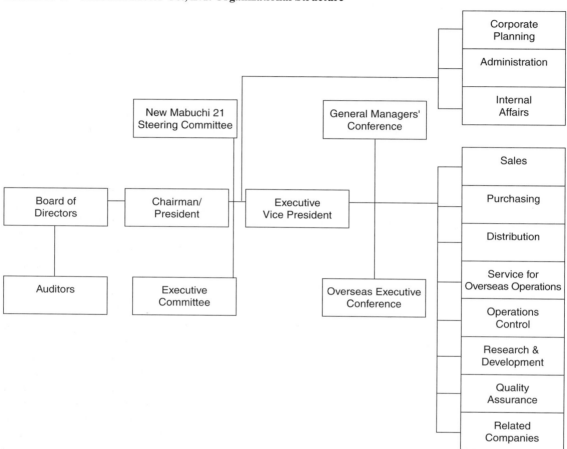

MABUCHI CORPORATE STRATEGY

The cornerstones of Mabuchi's strategy were the diversification of both production bases and markets, the maintenance of high quality standards, and the minimization of production costs. Since small motors had become a low technology item that could be easily reproduced by new or established competitors, Mabuchi also believed that, tactically, it was very important to move quickly once an opportunity emerged. In other words, quick response time to market opportunities could enhance competitive advantage by simply occupying the maximum amount of competitive space.

Diversification

Although a single product company, Mabuchi had always been concerned with diversification of both markets and production locations. In its earliest days, the company moved away from excessive dependence on the toy industry, stretching instead for other markets. By 1995, Mabuchi divided its markets for small motors into four basic segments: audio and visual equipment, automotive products, information and communication equipment, and home and industrial equipment. One of the significant benefits of its diversified market position was that, since the demand cycles of these market segments were not closely related, when one market slowed, others tended to pick up, thus smoothing the demand. The fact was, however, that in many years the demand from all segments was up at the same time.

Similarly, Mabuchi's ongoing effort was to maintain a diverse base of production facilities. While it might have been easier to locate all plants in China, where costs of labor were among the lowest in the Asian Pacific region, Mabuchi attempted to reduce its dependence on a single country by maintaining facilities in other locations such as Taiwan, Hong Kong, Malaysia; in addition, it was searching for another non-Chinese location in 1995. While this aspect of its market strategy may have been more difficult to implement, the company believed it added a measure of security to its long-term plans.

Quality

In the view of top management, one of the responsibilities of running a worldwide production network was to guarantee an identical level of high quality product no matter where that particular product came from. The primary method of maintaining quality control was to ensure that all operations adhered to the standards set by the head office Technical Center. As early as 1984, Mabuchi had established the Technical Center, relocated and refurbished in 1992, where new technologies were tested and new products were developed. In general, technical service and the management of the international network of subsidiaries were centrally located and, once a new product or work practice was devised, it was then introduced to Mabuchi affiliates as quickly as possible by head office personnel. The various plants were expected to attempt to implement as closely as possible the patterns and processes devised in corporate headquarters.

Cost Minimization

Mabuchi endeavoured to maximize its competitiveness by minimizing its costs of labor, making its work practices more efficient, reducing the variety of products offered, and streamlining its administration.

Cost of Labor Since small electric motors were a labor-intensive product, one of the key competitive considerations was, of course, the relative cost of labor. It was this factor that led to the establishment of Mabuchi's first offshore production facility in Hong Kong in 1964 where, at the time, labor rates were low. By 1995, all of Mabuchi's production capability had been shifted outside of Japan to take advantage of the low cost labor available elsewhere. In fact, since labor rates in the 1990s in

Taiwan and Hong Kong had become expensive relative to those available in other East Asian countries, Mabuchi was forced to begin realigning its production distribution away from these locations in order to stay cost competitive. Rather than abandoning these high cost facilities, however, the sites that were experiencing escalating costs of labor were made to change their focus, concentrating instead on higher value-added operations such as the fabrication and maintenance of production equipment for other plants.

Efficient Work Practices   Mabuchi's top management clearly believed that there was one best way to build small motors. These methods were developed over years of experience with new methods being tested in the Technical Center. One of the many roles of expatriate managers was to ensure that the methods of production designed in Japan were mirrored in their foreign locations.

Reduction of the Variety of Products Offered   While many organizations worldwide had attempted to satisfy their increasingly demanding customers by offering tailor-made products, Mabuchi steadfastly resisted this trend. Senior management believed, instead, that customers cared more about price than selection. Although selling about four million motors a day, at least 70 percent of total sales were made up of no more than 20 models. Further, about 55 percent of total sales consisted of 10 models. In general, Mabuchi concentrated on producing as few models as possible in order to achieve greater speed of production and, hence, lower average costs.

Streamlining of Administration   In 1971, Mabuchi reorganized its administration of marketing and production to concentrate responsibility for these functions in the head office. Since then, Japanese personnel had always been in firm control over the activities of all subsidiaries. This initiative was originally an effort to reduce duplication of effort and inefficiency in management control. However, beginning in the early 1990s, the firm began to try to shift many of these responsibilities back to the individual subsidiaries. Given the rapid growth in production over the 1970s and 1980s, Mabuchi's centralized, multilingual organization had become cumbersome and difficult to manage for the head office administrative staff. Mabuchi management felt that their organization resembled a train where the head office was the locomotive, the only source of power, pulling the totally dependent subsidiaries behind. As a result, Mabuchi began to encourage subsidiary managers to communicate directly with their counterparts in other subsidiaries in an effort to attain greater corporate-wide administrative effectiveness and operational efficiency.

STRATEGIC INITIATIVES AT MABUCHI

In 1992, in the spirit of Kaizen (continuous improvement), Takaichi Mabuchi announced the formulation of the New Mabuchi 21 Steering Committee made up of a select group of 20 young (under 35 years) Mabuchi managers under the leadership of Executive Vice President Akira Ohnishi. This committee was charged with the task of examining and making recommendations on three key aspects of Mabuchi's business:

1. product quality

2. delivery lead time

3. costs of production

To address the product quality issue, the New Mabuchi 21 Steering Committee recommended implementing ISO 9000 standards at all plants. To reduce delivery lead-time, the Committee introduced the Coordinated Mabuchi Production and Sales System (COMPASS) program, a computer-based management information system designed to improve and quicken the transfer of information between departments and between subsidiaries. Finally, the Steering Committee determined that in order to decrease costs of production, the number of Japanese managers posted to foreign subsidiaries must be reduced.

THE PLAN TO DEVELOP A TRAINING PROGRAM FOR FOREIGN MANAGERS

In many East Asian countries, the cost of maintaining a Japanese expatriate (salary, travel allowances, accommodation, etc.) was 10 to 20 times that of a local manager. According to a major U.S.-based institution that focused on international human resource management, the all-inclusive cost of maintaining a senior-level Japanese manager in China was no less than US$400,000 annually and approximately US$325,000 for a mid-level Japanese manager. Even a lower level technician from Japan would cost at least US$175,000 annually including salary, bonus, and travel allowances. In 1995, Mabuchi had 84 expatriates in various locations abroad (see Exhibit 3). Notwithstanding the cost, there did not exist a large pool of local management talent that Mabuchi could draw on in its foreign locations; therefore, a program had to be implemented to train local personnel to enable them to achieve Mabuchi's standards of production efficiency and product quality.

Mabuchi's corporate strategy included aggressive plans to continue expansion of production to reduce the possibility of the emergence of new competition or, for that matter, the loss of developing markets to current competitors. Further, since Mabuchi's market position was based on a reputation for supplying high quality products on a timely basis, all established plants were required to continue to run at a steady state and new plants had to be brought on stream without major difficulties.

Therefore, in late 1992 it became the responsibility of Nobukatsu Hirano, Manager of Internal Affairs, to oversee the establishment of detailed plans to fulfill these important and related goals. Since Mabuchi had limited previous experience in developing corporate training programs for foreign personnel, Andersen Consulting was retained to assist in elaborating a detailed plan. Under the direction of Mr. Hirano, a team of five Mabuchi employees and two Andersen Consulting people worked out a plan they named the New Integrated Headquarters And Overseas Operations (NIHAO). It was decided that the Dalian plant would be the first to go through the NIHAO program.

EXHIBIT 3   Mabuchi Motor Co., Ltd. Local Management/Expatriates Levels (as of December 1995)

Plant Location	Workers	Group Leaders	Foremen	Section Chiefs	Factory Managers	Managing Directors	Total Employed
Wangfandian	214	12/0	2/0	6/0	1/0	0/1	236
Guang Dong 1	5,407	288/0	58/0	5/5	0/1	0/1	5,765
Guang Dong 2	6,378	340/0	68/0	5/9	0/1	0/1	6,802
Guang Dong 3	4,877	260/0	52/0	14/4	0/1	0/1	5,209
Guang Dong 4	1,405	75/0	15/0	11/0	0/1	0/1	1,508
Guang Dong 5	6,947	370/0	74/0	5/9	0/1	0/1	7,407
Taipei	1,889	101/0	20/0	15/4	0/1	0/1	2,031
Hukou	1,716	92/0	18/0	9/10	0/1	0/1	1,847
Dalian	7,605	405/0	81/0	5/18	1/0	0/1	8,116
Chemor	3,848	205/0	41/0	9/3	0/1	0/1	4,108
Wu Jiang	1,942	104/0	21/0	11/2	0/1	0/1	2,082
Total	42,228	2,252/0	450/0	95/64	2/9	0/11	45,111

A REVIEW OF NIHAO

Fundamentally, the training program was intended to reinforce the hierarchical notion of management control where each management level was expected to play a specified role. The standardization of management practice was emphasized where tasks were to be divided between management levels so that there was no overlap or omission of duties. Further, it was clearly spelled out that there should be no individual differences in tasks or procedures when comparing personnel in similar positions; in other words, Mabuchi saw little room for individual interests or capabilities when it came to the fulfillment of managerial tasks. Overall, management was seen as a generalist task that was suited to some people and not to others and, if an individual could not complete the tasks as per company policy, he or she should be reassigned to a more suitable, perhaps more specialized, task.

A second major element of the training program was the requirement for regular performance evaluation of all employees. The belief at Mabuchi was that, if an individual was not evaluated and challenged to improve, then morale would inevitably decline. All managers were, therefore, required to formally evaluate their subordinates twice a year. In actual practice, the subordinate was required to evaluate himself/herself and the manager was then required to review this self-criticism and formalize the process with a signature. Repeated unsatisfactory performance evaluations were expected to lead to demotion, whereas satisfactory evaluations usually resulted in significant bonuses. Regular workers and group leaders were often awarded bonuses of as much as 150 percent of salary and higher level managers (i.e., factory and section managers) were commonly given bonuses of up to 300 percent of regular salary.

While it was a common experience for foreign-owned companies to lose valuable employees once improved management skills made the individual more marketable, Mabuchi did not expect to encounter this problem. First of all, to reduce the attractiveness of other employers, the corporate policy was to pay at levels higher than the local average as well as to provide all benefits required by Chinese labor regulations. Further, Mabuchi believed it could offer the sort of upward mobility necessary to retain capable young managers. In fact, Mabuchi could point to the fact that the President of its Taiwanese subsidiary, a local manager from Taiwan, had even been appointed to the corporate board of directors in 1993. An explicit goal of the NIHAO training program was to allow local managers to take over key positions as their skills developed to sufficient levels.

THE IMPLEMENTATION OF NIHAO

With five different training manuals designed to address the concerns of each level of management (see Exhibit 4), a delegation of Mabuchi staff traveled to Dalian to commence the training program. In a series of seminars that were given in Japanese and then translated into Chinese, the sessions began with the upper levels of the hierarchy and then proceeded to include lower echelons on a level-by-level basis. After each session, a short test was administered to determine whether the main points were being grasped. In cases where test results were not satisfactory, remedial sessions were offered. Subsequent batteries of seminars were held to enhance and reinforce the understanding of the management trainees regarding the basic concepts of the division of labor and the responsibilities of management. These later sessions, however, were led by a Mandarin-speaking Mabuchi employee and a Chinese Andersen Consulting employee to improve the level of comprehension.

In order to determine to what extent Mabuchi's management training program had an impact, Andersen Consulting was asked to conduct periodic follow-up tests. It was soon realized that the trainees in Dalian were having great difficulty in internalizing some of the essential aspects of Mabuchi's requirements of management, personnel management in particular. It seemed that the Chinese managers, regardless of prior experience, were either not capable of, or perhaps simply not accustomed to, controlling their subordinates. The clear division between subordinate and superior was not being manifested in actual practice. Mabuchi was convinced that it had hired the best managerial talent that Dalian had to offer—yet perhaps the prior exposure of these people to the methods of management in Chinese state-owned enterprises made them poorly suited to the demands of a capitalist enterprise.

Similarly, the performance evaluations were not being completed with the rigor required by Mabuchi where less than satisfactory performance was not being met with remedial action or demotion. Evaluations were a central component of Mabuchi's management incentive system; however, the Chinese were more sensitive to personal networks and were also accustomed to a more collective approach to compensation. For example, after a particular foreman had been awarded a performance bonus, the foreman's subordinates demanded a similar bonus in keeping with what had become a Chinese custom—when one person in a work group receives a reward, the entire group shares the benefit. However, this was not Mabuchi corporate policy and, in fact, went counter to the concept of isolating

EXHIBIT 4
**Mabuchi Motor
Dalian Ltd.
Organizational
Structure**
Title (number of
positions)

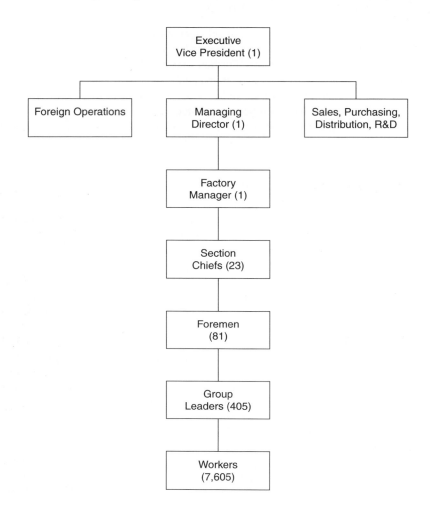

people for individual reward in order to encourage everyone to attempt to achieve
their personal best. The discontented employees were eventually pacified when a
subsidiary-wide raise was given, although the situation was not formally resolved.

The corporation's future plans for expansion hinged on its ability to move quickly
into new markets, producing high quality micro motors efficiently. NIHAO was expected to play a central role in Mabuchi's process of organizational development.

Name Index

Subject Index

Note: Company names are bold.

ACRONYM	PROPER NAME
ADB	Asian Development Bank
AfDB	African Development Bank
AFIC	Asian Finance and Investment Corporation
AFTA	Asian Free Trade Agreement
ASEAN	Association of Southeast Asian Nations
ATPA	Andean Trade Preference Act
BIS	Bank for International Settlements
BOP	Balance of Payments
CIM	Computer-Integrated Manufacturing
CIS	Commonwealth of Independent States
CISG	UN Convention on Contracts for the International Sale of Goods
CEMA	Council for Mutual Economic Assistance
CRA	Country Risk Assessment
DB	Development Bank
DC	Developed Country
DFIs	Development Finance Institutions
DISC	Domestic International Sales Corporation
EBRD	European Bank for Reconstruction and Development
ECOWAS	Economic Community of West African States
EMU	Economic and Monetary Union
EEA	European Economic Area
EFTA	European Free Trade Association
EMCs	Export Management Companies
EMCF	European Monetary Cooperation Fund
EMS	European Monetary System
EPO	European Patent Organization
ETC	Export Trading Company
ETUC	European Trade Union Confederation
EU	European Union
FCPA	Foreign Corrupt Practices Act
FDI	Foreign Direct Investment
FSC	Foreign Sales Corporation
FTAA	Free Trade Agreement of the Americas
FTZ	Foreign Trade Zone
Fx	Foreign Exchange
G7	Group of Seven
GATT	General Agreement on Tariffs and Trade
GC	Global Company
GDP	Gross Domestic Product
GNP	Gross National Product
GSP	Generalized System of Preferences
IAC	International Anti-counterfeiting Coalition
IC	International Company
IDA	International Development Association

ACRONYM	PROPER NAME
IDB	Inter-American Development Bank
IEC	International Electrotechnical Commission
IFC	International Finance Corporation
IMF	International Monetary Fund
IPLC	International Product Life Cycle
IRC	International Revenue Code
ISA	International Seabed Authority
ISO	International Organization for Standardization
ITA	International Trade Administration
JIT	Just-in-Time
JV	Joint Venture
LAIA	Latin American Integration Association (formerly LAFTA)
LDC	Less Developed Country
LIBOR	London Interbank Offer Rate
LOST	Law of the Sea Treaty
MERCOSUR	Free Trade Agreement between Argentina, Brazil, Paraguay, and Uruguay
MNC	Multinational Company
MNE	Multinational Enterprise
NAFTA	North American Free Trade Agreement
NATO	North Atlantic Treaty Organization
NIC	Newly Industrializing Country
NTBs	Nontariff Barriers
OECD	Organization for Economic Cooperation and Development
OPEC	Organization of Petroleum Exporting Countries
PPP	Purchasing Power Parity
PRC	People's Republic of China
PTA	Preferential Trade Area for Eastern and Southern Africa
SACC	Southern African Development Coordination Conference
SBA	Small Business Administration
SBC	Strategic Business Center
SBU	Small Business Unit
SDR	Special Drawing Rights
SEZ	Special Economic Zone
TQM	Total Quality Management
UN	United Nations
UNCTAD	UN Conference on Trade and Development
VAT	Value Added Tax
VER	Voluntary Export Restraint
VRAs	Voluntary Restraints Agreements
WEC	World Energy Council
WIPO	World Intellectual Property Organization
WTO	World Trade Organization

COUNTRY	CAPITAL
Afghanistan	Kabul
Albania	Tirana
Algeria	Algiers
Andorra	Andorra la Vella
Angola	Luanda
Antigua and Barbuda	St. John's
Argentina	Buenos Aires
Armenia	Yerevan
Australia	Canberra
Austria	Vienna
Azerbaijan	Baku
Bahamas	Nassau
Bahrain	Manama
Bangladesh	Dhaka
Barbados	Bridgetown
Belarus	Minsk
Belgium	Brussels
Belize	Belmopan
Benin	Porto-Novo
Bhutan	Thimphu
Bolivia	La Paz
Bosnia and Herzegovina	Sarajevo
Botswana	Gaborone
Brazil	Brasilia
Brunei	Bandar Seri Begawan
Bulgaria	Sofia
Burkina Faso	Ouagadougou
Burundi	Bujumbura
Cambodia	Phnom Penh
Cameroon	Yaounde
Canada	Ottawa
Cape Verde	Praia
Central African Republic	Bangui
Chad	N'Djamena
Chile	Santiago
China	Beijing
Colombia	Bogotá
Comoros	Moroni
Congo	Brazzaville
Congo (formerly Zaire)	Kinshasa
Costa Rica	San José
Cote d'Ivoire	Yamoussoukro
Croatia	Zagreb
Cuba	Havana
Cyprus	Nicosia
Czech Republic	Prague
Denmark	Copenhagen
Djibouti	Djibouti
Dominica	Roseau
Dominican Republic	Santo Domingo
Ecuador	Quito
Egypt	Cairo
El Salvador	San Salvador
Equatorial Guinea	Malabo
Eritrea	Asmara
Estonia	Tallinn
Ethiopia	Addis Ababa
Fiji	Suva
Finland	Helsinki
France	Paris
Gabon	Libreville
The Gambia	Banjul
Georgia	Tbilisi
Germany	Berlin
Ghana	Accra
Greece	Athens
Grenada	St. George's
Guatemala	Guatemala City
Guinea	Conakry
Guinea-Bissau	Bissau
Guyana	Georgetown
Haiti	Port-au-Prince
Honduras	Tegucigalpa
Hungary	Budapest
Iceland	Reykjavik
India	New Delhi
Indonisia	Jakarta
Iran	Tehran
Iraq	Baghdad
Ireland	Dublin

COUNTRY	CAPITAL
Israel	Jerusalem
Italy	Rome
Jamaica	Kingston
Japan	Tokyo
Jordan	Amman
Kazakhstan	Astana
Kenya	Nairobi
Kiribati	Tarawa
Korea, North	Pyongyang
Korea, South	Seoul
Kuwait	Kuwait City
Kyrgyzstan	Bishkek
Laos	Vientiane
Latvia	Riga
Lebanon	Beirut
Lesotho	Maseru
Liberia	Monrovia
Libya	Tripoli
Liechtenstein	Vaduz
Lithuania	Vilnius
Luxembourg	Luxembourg
Macedonia	Skopje
Madagascar	Antananarivo
Malawi	Lilongwe
Malaysia	Kuala Lumpur
Maldives	Male
Mali	Bamako
Malta	Valletta
Marshall Islands	Majuro
Mauritania	Nouakchott
Mauritius	Port Louis
Mexico	Mexico City
Micronesia	Palikir
Moldova	Chisinau
Monaco	Monaco
Mongolia	Ulaanbaatar
Morocco	Rabat
Mozambique	Maputo
Myanmar	Rangoon
Namibia	Windhoek
Nauru	Yaren
Nepal	Kathmandu
The Netherlands	Amsterdam
New Zealand	Wellington
Nicaragua	Managua
Niger	Niamey
Nigeria	Abuja
Norway	Oslo
Oman	Muscat
Pakistan	Islamabad
Palau	Koror
Panama	Panama City
Papua New Guinea	Port Moresby
Paraguay	Asunción
Peru	Lima
Philippines	Manila
Poland	Warsaw
Portugal	Lisbon
Qatar	Doha
Romania	Bucharest
Russia	Moscow
Rwanda	Kigali
Saint Kitts and Nevis	Basseterre
Saint Lucia	Castries
Saint Vincent and the Grenadines	Kingstown
San Marino	San Marino
Sao Tome and Principe	Sao Tome
Saudi Arabia	Riyadh
Senegal	Dakar
Seychelles	Victoria
Sierra Leone	Freetown
Singapore	Singapore
Slovakia	Bratislava
Slovenia	Ljubljana
Solomon Islands	Honiara
Somalia	Mogadishu
South Africa	Pretoria
Spain	Madrid
Sri Lanka	Colombo
Sudan	Khartoum
Suriname	Paramaribo
Swaziland	Mbabane

COUNTRY	CAPITAL
Sweden	Stockholm
Switzerland	Bern
Syria	Damascus
Taiwan	Taipei
Tajikistan	Dushanbe
Tanzania	Dar es Salaam
Thailand	Bangkok
Togo	Lome
Tonga	Nuku'alofa
Trinidad and Tobago	Port-of-Spain
Tunisia	Tunis
Turkey	Ankara
Turkmenistan	Ashgabat
Tuvalu	Funafuti
Uganda	Kampala
Ukraine	Kiev
United Arab Emirates	Abu Dhabi
United Kingdom	London
United States of America	Washington, DC
Uruguay	Montevideo
Uzbekistan	Tashkent
Vanuatu	Vila
Vatican City	
Venezuela	Caracas
Vietnam	Hanoi
Western Samoa	Apia
Yemen	Sanaa
Yugoslavia	Belgrade
Zambia	Lusaka
Zimbabwe	Harare

ALPHABETICAL LISTING OF CASES

Coventry University